OCS Study
MMS 2002-046

Boating Uses, Economic Significance, and Information Inventory for North Carolina's Offshore Area, "The Point"

I0423766

Volume III: Data Inventory Related to the Hatteras Middle Slope Area Bibliography

MMS
U.S. Department of the Interior
Minerals Management Service
Gulf of Mexico OCS Region

OCS Study
MMS 2002-046

Boating Uses, Economic Significance, and Information Inventory for North Carolina's Offshore Area, "The Point"

Volume III: Data Inventory Related to the Hatteras Middle Slope Area Bibliography

Compilers

Steve W. Ross
Ernst F. Aschenbach III
Jacquie Ott

Prepared under MMS Contract
1435-01-98-CA-30949
by
North Carolina National Estuarine Research Reserve
North Carolina Division of Coastal Management
One Marvin Moss Lane
Wilmington, North Carolina 28409

Published by

U.S. Department of the Interior
Minerals Management Service
Gulf of Mexico OCS Region

New Orleans
August 2002

DISCLAIMER

This report was prepared under contract between the Minerals Management Service (MMS) and the North Carolina Division of Coastal Management. This report has been technically reviewed by the MMS, and it has been approved for publication. Approval does not signify that the contents necessarily reflect the views and policies of the MMS, nor does mention of trade names or commercial products constitute endorsement or recommendation for use. It is, however, exempt from review and compliance with the MMS editorial standards.

REPORT AVAILABILITY

Extra copies of this model and user guide may be obtained from the Public Information Office (Mail Stop 5034) at the following address:

U.S. Department of the Interior
Minerals Management Service
Gulf of Mexico OCS Region
Public Information Unit (MS 5034)
1201 Elmwood Park Boulevard
New Orleans, Louisiana 70123-2394
Telephone: (504) 736-2519 or
1-800-200-GULF

CITATION

Suggested citation:

Ross, S., E. F. Aschenbach III, and J. Ott. 2002. Boating Uses, Economic Significance, and Information Inventory for North Carolina's Offshore Area, "The Point"; Volume III: Data Inventory Related to the Hatteras Middle Slope Area Bibliography. U.S. Dept. of the Interior, Minerals Management Service, Gulf of Mexico OCS Region, New Orleans, LA. OCS Study MMS 2002-046. 350 pp.

ABOUT THE COVER

Cover photo courtesy of Dr. William Lang, Minerals Management Service.

TABLE OF CONTENTS

LIST OF FIGURES

LIST OF TABLES

ABSTRACT

The U.S. East Coast continental slope from Norfolk Canyon to Cape Lookout, North Carolina represents a dramatic transition between the Middle Atlantic Bight (MAB) province of major submarine canyons and the South Atlantic Bight province of the Blake Plateau. The central portion of this region, just north of Cape Hatteras, is unique hydrographically: 1) as the zone where the northward flowing Gulf Stream meets the southward flowing Virginia current, and 2) as the zone where the Gulf Stream crosses the underlying southward flowing Western Boundary Undercurrent. Recent investigations revealed that the Hatteras Slope (in the area of undetermined geographic extent) is characterized by anomalous biological and physical attributes, including extremely high densities of benthic infauna, unusual communities of benthic fishers and megafaunal invertebrates, a relatively high rate of particulate sedimentation, and sedimentary evidence for an exceptionally high flux of labile organic carbon to the bottom. A portion of this area has long been known as "The Point."

In addition to the unique physical and biological attributes of "The Point" region, portions of the area have been targets for potential hydrocarbon exploration, particularly in Minerals Management Services blocks 467 and 510 in the Manteo Unit. Such exploration has been considered problematic because of a lack of appropriate environmental data that would allow evaluation of potential exploration impacts. A number of workshops and meetings have occurred over the last decade and a special panel was appointed to review the state of knowledge needed to review the state of knowledge needed to evaluate impacts around "The Point" area. One very important discovery learned during this process is that "The Point" is a productive and important fishing area, with physical conditions that concentrate biota (birds, marine mammals, turtles, fishes) in a relatively small part of the ocean. Gradually various types of data have accumulated for "The Point" area, improving our understanding of many issues, but the studies were not coordinated.

Although the quantity of data has increased for the Hatteras slope area around "The Point", a complete catalogue of all past and ongoing studies was not previously available. The absence of a centralized data management tool has hindered attempts to discuss and evaluate the impacts of proposed hydrocarbon exploration. This project was funded to gather information on all past and current studies conducted in all scientific disciplines related to this area, generate an annotated, computerized bibliography of these studies and reference them to a Geographic Information System (GIS). The project study area was identified as a region 40 km north and south of the proposed Mobile Oil wildcat well with depth boundaries of 20-2000 m. We identified a total of 414 references to published, unpublished, and ongoing studies relevant to the study area. These references were annotated, entered into a ProCite digital database, and sorted into the following chapters: Fishery, Invertebrate, Marine Bird, Marine Mammal, Marine Reptile, Biological Oceanography, Chemical Oceanography, Geological Oceanography, Physical Oceanography, Sargassum, Socioeconomic. To the extent possible, the locations of data collection effors in these studies were determined and imported into the ArcView GIS system from which example maps were generated to geographically illustrate the bibliography. This task was not funded as a data synthesis nor an interactive digital product. However, we believe it is an important foundation for future Environmental Impact Statements or Environmental Assessment efforts in this area off of North Carolina. We hope that it will serve as a model for other such efforts.

INTRODUCTION

The U.S. East Coast continental slope from Norfolk Canyon south to Cape Lookout, North Carolina represents a dramatic physiographic and sedimentological transition between the Middle Atlantic Bight (MAB) province of major submarine canyons and the South Atlantic Bight province of the Blake Plateau (BP) (Pratt and Heezen 1964; Uchupi and Emery 1967; Rowe and Menzies 1968; Rhoads 1993). The northern portion of the transition region, beginning just south of Norfolk Canyon, approximates physiographic, sedimentary and faunistic conditions characteristic of the overall MAB (Blake et al. 1987). The central portion of this region, just north of Cape Hatteras, is unique hydrographically: 1) as the zone where the northward flowing Gulf Stream meets the southward flowing Virginia current (Ford et al. 1952; Bumpus and Lauzier 1965; Heezen 1968; Norcross and Stanley 1967; Csanady and Hamilton 1988), and 2) as the zone where the Gulf Stream crosses the underlying southward flowing Western Boundary Undercurrent (Barrett 1965; Heezen 1968; Richardson and Knauss 1971).

Recent investigations revealed that the Hatteras slope (in an area of undetermined geographic extent) is characterized by anomalous biological and physical attributes. These include the highest densities of benthic infauna anywhere along the U.S. East Coast continental slope (Blake et al. 1987; Brown 1991; Schaff et al. 1992), unusual communities of benthic fishes and megafaunal invertebrates (Rowe 1971; Blake et al. 1987; Hecker 1993; Sulak and Ross 1996; S. Stancyk, pers. comm.), a particulate sedimentation rate much higher than that of adjacent regions (Schaff et al. 1992), and sedimentary evidence for an exceptionally high flux of labile organic carbon to the bottom (Schaff et al. 1992). Unusually high levels of suspended matter with atypically high percentages of combustible organic matter have been reported (Heezen 1968; Manheim et al. 1970) in overlying surface waters of the area.

In addition to the unique physical and biological attributes of this region, the area has been a target for potential hydrocarbon exploration for over a decade, particularly in Minerals Management Service blocks 467 and 510 in the Manteo Unit (Figures 1 and 2). Although no wells have been drilled and only two plans of exploration (POE) were filed (Chevron Oil in 1982 and Mobil Oil in 1990), this area remains of great interest to oil companies. Generally, these POEs (as well as other proposals) have been considered problematic because of a lack of appropriate environmental data needed to evaluate potential impacts. In fact, the concerns over potential biological effects to the area from hydrocarbon exploration and the lack of scientific data prompted many of the above cited (and other) recent studies. A number of workshops and information exchange meetings have occurred over the last decade and a special panel was appointed to review the state of knowledge needed to evaluate impacts around "The Point" area (Costlow et al. 1992). Gradually various types of data have accumulated for "the Point" area, greatly improving our understanding of many issues, but the studies were not coordinated. One very important thing learned in this process of data accumulation is that "The Point" (see Currin and Ross 1999) is a productive and important fishing area, with physical conditions that concentrate biota (birds, marine mammals, turtles, fishes) in a relatively small part of the ocean.

Although the quantity of data has increased for the Hatteras slope area around "The Point", a complete catalogue of all past and ongoing studies was not previously available. The absence of a centralized data management tool has hindered attempts to discuss and evaluate the impacts of proposed hydrocarbon exploration. A centralized compilation of studies for this area was considered critical; therefore, a high priority, "short-term", task to conduct a data or research inventory of the region surrounding "The Point" was identified in the February 1998 state-federal Information Transfer Meeting (Raleigh, NC, Vigil 1998). It was suggested that this effort be tied to a Geographic Information System (GIS). To fulfill this recommendation the US Dept. of the Interior Minerals Management Service funded this project. Our objectives were to gather information on all past and current studies conducted in all scientific disciplines related to an area surrounding "The Point", generate an annotated, computerized bibliography of these studies and reference them to a Geographic Information System. While this task is not a data synthesis, it should be an important foundation of future Environmental Impact Statement or Environmental Assessment efforts. We hope that it will serve as a model for other such efforts.

METHODS

Study Area Definition

First, we defined boundaries for the data search area encompassing the proposed oil exploration sites or blocks and relevant biological and physical characteristics in the region known as "The Point." We selected a study area surrounding the proposed Mobil oil exploratory well site in block 467 (35° 29' 23.6" N; 74° 46' 12.7" W) which was roughly a rectangle bordered east and west by the 20 m and 2000 m depth contours, respectively. The north and south borders extended 40 kilometers (21.6 nautical miles) in either direction from the proposed drill site (Figure 2). For many purposes any area delineated in the open ocean is a compromise between being too small or too large; however, we feel the area selected for this data inventory includes adequate information that can be related to impact and environmental assessment for "The Point" region.

Data Acquisition

Information and research (published, unpublished, and ongoing) within, overlapping, or directly related to the defined study area were identified using our in-house library resources, electronic literature searches, library literature searches, and interviews with researchers. All potential candidates for inclusion in the bibliography were reviewed for relevance to the study area, often by comparing reference location data to the study area base map. Unpublished and/or unanalyzed (e.g., R/V *Dan Moore*, National Marine Fisheries Service, etc.) data were the most difficult to locate and define. Most of these were included based on previous research and experience of the senior author (S.W. Ross). We attempted to acquire copies of all references included in the data base. We grouped the references or studies into major categories (see below) which became the individual bibliographic chapters for this report.

Development of a Computer-Based Relational Database

A keyword-searchable electronic database was constructed using bibliographic software (ProCite version 4.03). The ProCite database allowed for an electronic archive that could be searched in a variety of ways (e.g., by keywords, authors, dates). Metadata (descriptive components of the bibliographic entry) were entered into the ProCite database for each citation (Table 1). The abstract of each published or otherwise written report was duplicated in the database. For citations lacking an abstract (e.g., some reports, unpublished data or programs), we generated a descriptive abstract for the entry, noted by an asterisk (*) within the bibliography.

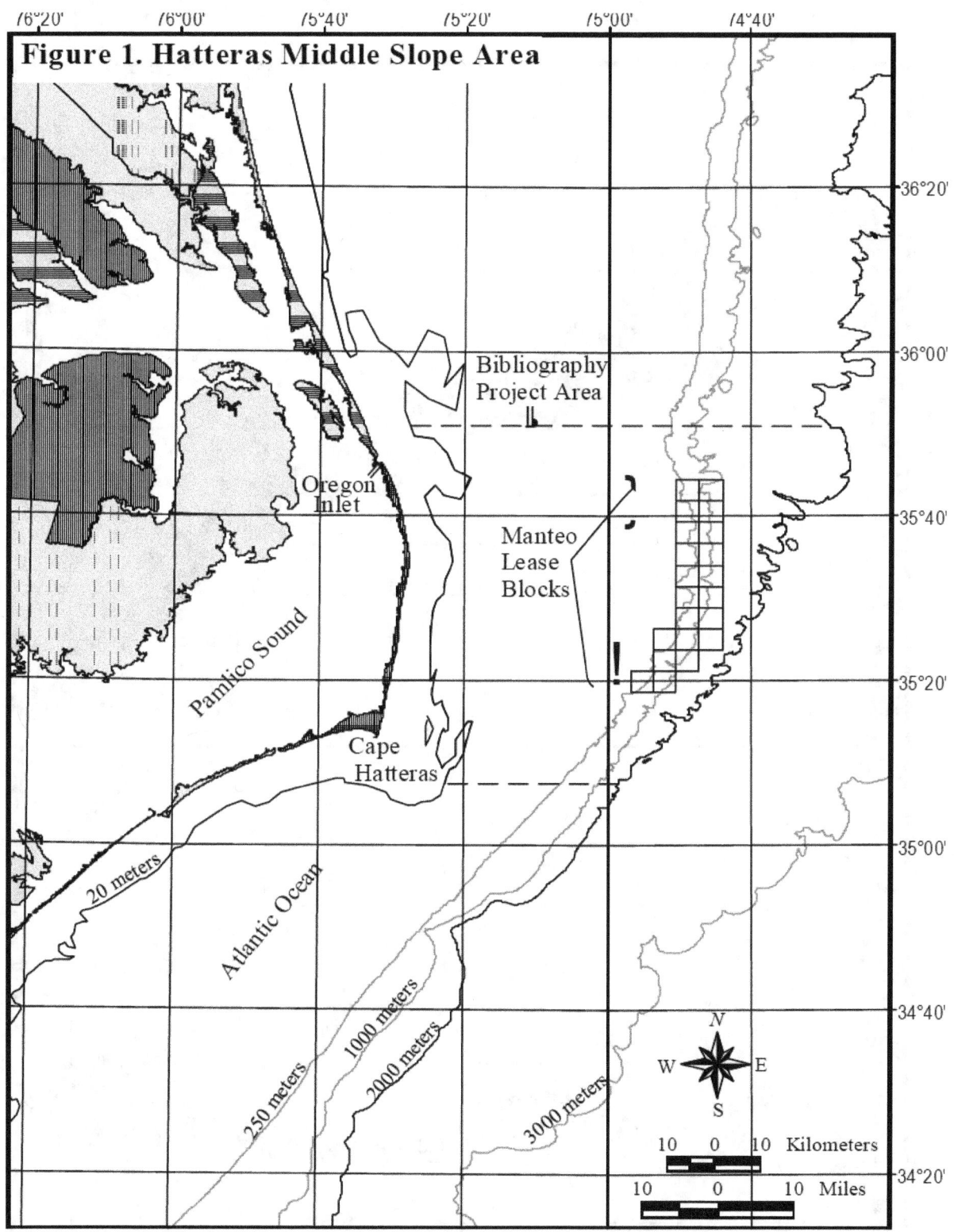

Figure 1. Hatteras Middle Slope Area

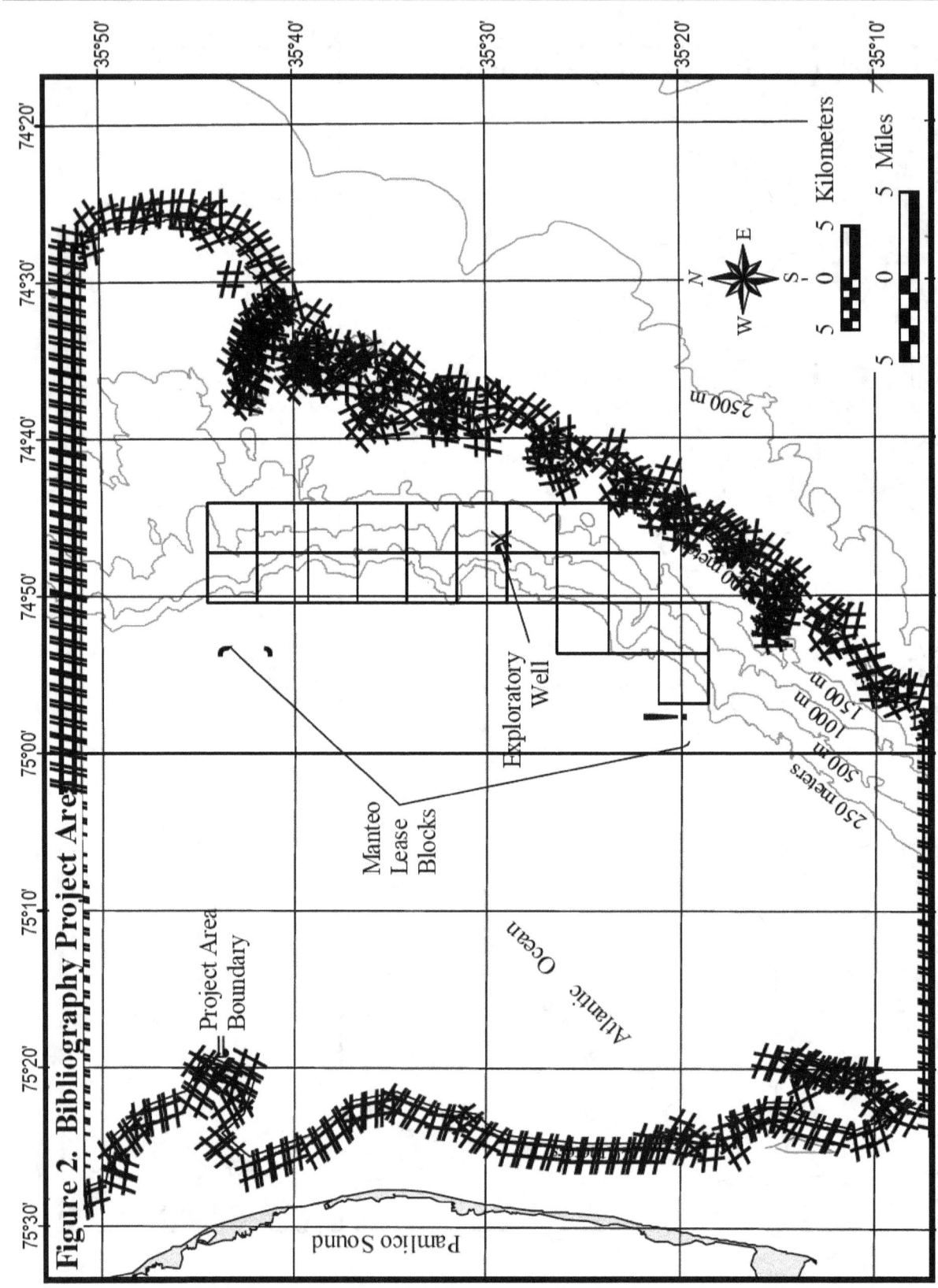

Figure 2. Bibliography Project Area

Two levels of keywords were developed and applied to each citation in the ProCite database. First, we classified each citation into one or more general groupings (Table 2) that became the report chapters. These general keywords defined the broad scientific disciplines represented by the studies and allowed the references to be sorted into chapters. While many of the keywords below can be considered biological oceanography, this particular keyword usually referred to biological topics not represented by the other keywords (e.g., plankton, productivity). A multidisciplinary citation was assigned multiple general keywords and thus may be cited in multiple report chapters (see Appendix I). Second (and in addition to the above general keywords), if keywords were provided by the publication, these were entered. If descriptive keywords were not provided, we assigned several descriptive words or phrases that characterized the work. Keywords were not printed in the following bibliography chapters.

Geographic Locations for Study Sites and Database Used for GIS

Georeferencing each citation (the general study area or all the stations in a citation) was the most time consuming task of the project. As the bibliography was developed, we created a spreadsheet database (using Microsoft Excel, Office 97 version) that summarized the major information for each citation. Initially this database included the author or principal investigator, reference title, date, and general keywords (Table 2). To this was added a variety of information needed to manipulate the data (e.g., information about the type of data, reference to figures, sorting information, and location data). The main purpose of this database was to create a computer framework for entry of the location data and subsequent GIS applications. Since it was a working tool and was also quite large, it was not reproduced in this report.

Station or study area location data provided within citations varied in geographic resolution, from specific geographic coordinates to broad area coverages. Consequently, our first step was to determine a general location class for each citation, based on the available information. The location classes include: 1) Mappable, 2) Focused on the Manteo Lease Blocks, 3) Covering the Hatteras Middle Slope Area, 4) Broad Regional Study, and 5) Based on a Fisheries Survey Database.

For the citations assigned to location class 1, "Mappable", three different methods were used to develop the location information required for GIS analysis.

First, when explicit geographic coordinates (including depths) were presented for stations or study areas in a citation, these coordinates were entered into the Excel spreadsheet. These were the simplest data to process.

Second, some citations described a study area as a range of geographic locations (e.g., from 35° to 35.5° N and 74.8° to 75° W). Polygons for these study areas were constructed using ArcView GIS by assigning latitudes and longitudes to the four corners surrounding the locations. The study area was delineated by digitizing a polygon connecting the four corners.

Third, some citations provided a hardcopy map of the study area, but not specific geographic coordinates. For these studies, a best approximation was created by digitally reproducing (drawing) the study area boundary on a detailed computer display of the bibliography base map. If only part of the citation's study area entered our target area, we digitized just this portion.

Location classes two through four include citations that are general in nature or provide verbal descriptions of the study area coverage, but no explicit geographic coordinates. Studies that are "Focused on the Manteo Lease Blocks" (class 2) present information directly related to the exploratory well site and surrounding lease blocks. Those in location class 3 are studies of the conditions specific to the Hatteras Middle Slope, but have a wider areal converge than those in class 2. Finally, citations that are broad in nature (e.g., related to the entire Atlantic Ocean) or present general discussions are included in location class 4 (Broad Regional Studies).

Table 1. Metadata entered into ProCite for each citation.

ProCite template information
Author(s)
Editor [1]
Title of work
Date of meeting [1]
Publication date
Publisher [1]
Journal or Book Title
Volume [1]
Edition [1]
Extent of work (number of pages)
Note (Study site location, reference to a research cruise/s or another study)
Abstract
Keywords

[1] if applicable

Table 2. General keywords used to group citations into report chapters. One or more of these was associated with each citation.

Fishery
Invertebrate
Marine birdbird
Marine mammal
Marine reptilereptile
Biological Oceanography
Chemical Oceanography
Geological Oceanography
Physical Oceanography
Sargassum
Socioeconomic

Some citations used information from large fisheries survey databases and were assigned to location class 5. The data were collected during one or a series of research cruises conducted by agencies (e.g., National Marine Fisheries Service) often as long-term surveys and often for purposes different than those of the citation. These studies did not report the original station numbers nor the exact station locations and at best only presented a large scale map of stations sampled (e.g., Berrien and Sibunka 1999). From these citations we could only determine that sampling did or did not occur within the study area. In order to relate some geospatial framework to these citations, the original digitized cruise data were obtained from the parent agencies (when possible) and put in dBase files separate from the file derived from the bibliography (described above). Since it was impossible to determine from such references which stations were used, the locations of all sample stations within the study area for all time periods from these agency databases were plotted using their geographic coordinates (converted by us to decimal degrees). For example, many citations used the National Marine Fisheries Survey, Northeast Fisheries Center Woods Hole Laboratory survey database. We documented this database as a separate citation entry and plotted all the stations from this survey (up to a certain cut off date) within the study area. All other references that used all or a portion of this database were then referred to the whole group of potential stations plotted. While this has inherent inaccuracies for individual citations, it was the only practical way to tie such references to geographic locations.

The Geographic Information System

The NC National Estuarine Research Reserve Geographic Information System (GIS) was used to facilitate screening of references and to generate maps of the georeferenced citations. We used the ArcView (version 3.1) GIS software. The initial step was to develop a digital base map of the area covered (see above) in this bibliography. Digital files were obtained for the shoreline, basic bathymetry (20 meter plus 250 meter depth contours), oil lease blocks, and the proposed exploratory well site related to the study area defined above (Figure 2).

Geographic coordinates as available for each citation were entered into the Excel spreadsheet and converted to latitude and longitude in decimal degrees. The Excel file was then converted to dBase format (required by ArcView) and imported into ArcView as a table. Because a variety of information was furnished for each citation record, the citations could be sorted and displayed within ArcView in many different ways. For example, sample stations for the different projects may be plotted using unique map symbols or colors for each investigator or author.

The GIS maps that resulted from the citations may have explicit point samples, general survey stations used by many citations, and polygons of various types. Many maps, especially those in the Fisheries section, could have multiple levels of complexity depending on how the data are sorted or displayed. Agency data, for example, could be plotted by cruise type, gear, individual project, individual cruise, and many other characteristics (e.g., Figures 5 and 6). Maps that depict the study areas and sites for the relevant citations are provided at the end of each bibliography chapter. The map keys include the symbols for the mapped studies, as well as a listing of the unmappable citations by general location class (i.e., "Focused on the Manteo Lease Blocks").

RECOMMENDATIONS

This report represents a compilation of the references to the data that have been collected in a small area bounding the Manteo Exploration units. However, the scope of the project did not allow taking full advantage of existing technology to give the data base maximum utility. Also, now that the references, their locations, and their data have been identified, some actual manipulations of the data are feasible (assuming the data themselves can be assembled in one place). The following recommendations for future work expand upon this project and would greatly improve our abilities to assess this ocean region around "The Point."

I. Expand/improve the location data base. Some station locations could not be determined from published material, and it was beyond the scope of this project to search out the original raw data. However, this is feasible, given sufficient time, and would greatly expand the project utility, especially the GIS component of the project.

II. Repackage the project into an interactive, electronic product on CD-ROM. Since the bibliography is electronic (ProCite), as are the data (dbase and Excel) and the maps (ArcView), all of these could be tied together and used on computer. As various maps are viewed on screen the locations could be queried to deliver the literature sources and full citations. Data could be sorted in many ways and presented (and printed) as maps. The CD could include the appropriate software to allow it to be used as a stand alone product.

III. Acquire data from the cited projects/studies and digitize them (if not already done). This is the most ambitious and time consuming recommendation and could complement numbers I and II (above). The data to obtain would include (but not be limited to) station specific species lists, environmental data, and overall catch summaries by station. A variety of GIS and biodiversity applications could then be developed for the project area. In this format this could serve as a real time, interactive Environmental Assessment tool.

ACKNOWLEDGMENTS

This project was funded by a grant from the Minerals Management Service (New Orleans office, US Dept. of Interior), and we thank Dr. Ann Scarbourough-Bull, Greg Boland, and William Lang of MMS for facilitating our work. We thank the following for assistance in locating literature and/or helping with reviews: Dr. Thomas Bailey (Harbor Branch Oceanographic Inst.), Dr. Annette C. Broderick (Marine Turtle Research Group, Univ. of Wales, Swansea, UK), Michael Coyne (Marine Turtle News-Online), Dr. Karen L. Eckert, (Executive Director, Wider Caribbean Sea Turtle Network, San Diego, CA), Dr. B.J. Godley (Marine Turtle Research Group, Univ. of Wales, Swansea, UK), Johnny Lancaster (NC State Univ. and NCNERR), David Lee (NC State Museum of Natural Sciences), Angela Mast (Noticiero de Tortugas Marinas-Online), Dr. Charles Paull (Monterey Bay Aquarium Research Inst.), Andrew Shepherd, (NURC, UNC-W, Wilmington, NC), Dr. Stephen E. Stancyk (Univ. South Carolina, Columbia, SC), and Diane Walker (Public Services Librarian, Virginia Institute of Marine Science, Gloucester Point, VA). In addition, J. Lancaster assisted with the ProCite software.

FISHERY CHAPTER

FISHERY CHAPTER

Abernathy, S.A., M.T. Baer, C.S. Benner, M.S. Brody, D.K. Francois, J.K. Gilliam, L.K. Good, C.J. Ohara, and J.V. Martin. 1989. Atlantic Outer Continental Shelf: Description of the Mid-Atlantic Environment. Abernathy, S.A. (ed.). U.S. Department of the Interior, Minerals Management Service, Atlantic OCS Region, Environmental Assessment Section. Herndon, VA. 167 p.

*This document discusses the major issues and areas of concern for the mid-Atlantic environment that are considered in the planning process for oil and gas leasing and operations on the Outer Continental Shelf. The issues are addressed with respect to the potential environmental consequences of mid-Atlantic oil and gas exploration, development and production. Sections discussing the Physical Environment (e.g., geology, non-petroleum minerals, physical oceanography, chemical oceanography and water quality, ocean dumping, meteorology, air quality), Biological Resources (e.g., plankton, benthos, fishery resources, marine reptiles, marine mammals, marine and coastal birds, estuaries, wetlands, sensitive coastal habitats, canyon areas), Socioeconomic Environment, and other issues (e.g., archaeological resources, marine vessel traffic, National Aeronautics and Space Administration/ Department of Defense activities, oil and gas infrastructure, marine sanctuaries, and estuarine research reserves) are included. Most figures showing fisheries resource distributions are from fisheries data compiled for bottom-trawl and shellfish surveys of the National Marine Fisheries Service, Northeast Fisheries Center, Woods Hole, MA.

Able, K.W., and M.P. Fahay. 1998. The First Year in the Life of Estuarine Fishes in the Middle Atlantic Bight. Rutgers University Press, New Brunswick, NJ. 342 p.

*An unprecedented research effort has been directed at the early life-history stages of fishes during the last three decades. This period has seen the first two Larval Fish Conferences, a workshop on eggs, larvae, and juveniles in Atlantic coast estuaries, the CalCOFI ichthyoplankton program (1951-1994), the Ahlstrom Symposium on ontogeny and systematics of fishes, several regional ichthyoplankton guides, and, in the Middle Atlantic Bight the R/V Dolphin 1965 -1966 ichthyoplankton surveys followed by the MARMAP 1977-1987 surveys. These efforts have ranged from extensive surveys of oceanic waters to behavioral studies of juvenile fishes in estuaries. The incorporation of otolith studies to back-calculate aspects of the early life history and laboratory studies of factors influencing survival of these early stages have also increased steadily. Few efforts, however, have bridged the morphological, physiological, ecological, and behavioral transition between pelagic larva and settled juvenile. We therefore decided to focus on this transition within the estuarine fish fauna of the Middle Atlantic Bight, hoping in the process that our summaries might have applications to young-of-the-year fishes in other ecosystems as well. We felt confident we could accomplish this focused approach because we each had had experience in various aspects of' early life-history studies, either in cooperative efforts with each other or with many of our colleagues.

Able, K.W., M.P. Fahay, and G.R. Shepherd. 1995. Early life history of black sea bass, *Centropristis striata,* in the mid-Atlantic Bight and a New Jersey estuary. Fishery Bulletin 93: 429-445.

This study focuses on composite field collections and in situ observations from the mid-Atlantic Bight continental shelf and a New Jersey estuary in order to elucidate aspects of the early life history of age 0+ black sea bass, *Centropristis striata*. Spawning in the mid-Atlantic Bight is prolonged (April through November, with a peak between June and September) and is most intense in the southern portion of this range. Between 1977 and 1987, larvae were collected between Cape Hatteras, North Carolina, and Long Island, New York. In New Jersey coastal waters larvae first appear in July but can occur into November. Recently settled individuals (15-24 mm total length [TL]) were collected at an inner continental shelf site and an adjacent estuary from July through October. By fall, fishes from these areas were 18-91 mm TL, and many had moved offshore from New Jersey estuarine waters and other estuaries to inner continental shelf waters between southern Massachusetts and Cape Hatteras. Subsequently, they continued to move offshore and during their first winter, they were concentrated near the shelf or slope break in the southern portion of the mid-Atlantic Bight. Some age 0+ individuals moved back into New Jersey estuaries in early spring, at sizes approximating those of the previous fall (50-96 mm TL). Thus, black sea bass reach relatively small sizes after 12 months of growth partly because little or no growth occurs during their first winter. This year class reached sizes of 78-175 mm TL by midsummer and 134-225 mm TL by the following fall.

During summer, benthic juveniles were collected or observed primarily in a variety of structured habitats. On the inner continental shelf they were found among accumulations of surfclam *Spisula solidissima* valves or among smaller pieces of shell, and occasionally in burrows in exposed clay. While in the estuary, they were collected from areas with a variety of structured habitats, such as shell accumulations in marsh creeks and peat banks. The data suggest that during their first summer, black sea bass have similar densities and growth rates in estuarine and inner continental shelf habitats, and thus both areas serve as nurseries.

Able, K.W. and S.C. Kaiser. 1994. Synthesis of summer flounder habitat parameters. NOAA Coastal Ocean Program, Coastal Ocean Office, Decision Analysis Series No. 1. Silver Spring, MD. 68 p. + appendices.

*(Modified from their Executive Summary) The summer flounder, Paralichthys dentatus, is overexploited and is currently at very low levels of abundance. This is reflected in the compressed age structure of the population and the low catches in both commercial and recreational fisheries. Declining habitat quantity and quality may be contributing to these declines, however we lack a thorough understanding of the role of habitats in the population dynamics of this species. Stock structure is unresolved and current interpretations, depending on the technique and study area, suggest that there may be two or three spawning populations. If so, these stocks may have differing habitat requirements. In response to this lack of knowledge, this document summarizes and synthesizes the available information on summer flounder habitat in all life history stages (eggs, larvae, juveniles and adults) and identifies areas where further research is needed.

Several levels of investigation were conducted in order to produce this document. First, an extensive search for summer flounder habitat information was made, which included both the primary and gray literature as well as unanalyzed data. Second, state and federal fisheries biologists and resource managers in all states within the primary range of summer flounder (Massachusetts to Florida) were interviewed along with a number of fish ecologists and summer flounder experts from the academic and private sectors. Finally, information from all sources was analyzed and synthesized to form a coherent overview.

A comprehensive bibliography on all aspects of the distribution, biology, and ecology of summer flounder is provided with both an author index and a subject index for easy reference. This bibliography also serves as the primary reference for literature cited in the text. Finally, a list of researchers who are considered experts on summer flounder and a list of potential user groups of this document are included.

Able, K.W., R.E. Matheson, W.W. Morse, M.P. Fahay, and G. Shepherd. 1989. Patterns of Summer Flounder, *Paralichthys dentatus,* Early Life History in the Mid-Atlantic Bight and New Jersey Estuaries. Fishery Bulletin 88: 1-12.

The summer flounder *Paralichthys dentatus* spawned throughout the Mid-Atlantic Bight and Georges Bank during 1977-85. Spawning peaked in fall but extended from September through January. Planktonic larvae (2-13 mm) were most abundant in the Mid-Atlantic Bight September-May. At approximately 11-14 mm, some larvae entered New Jersey estuaries; but their occurrence, especially during winter and early spring, was sporadic. Young-of-the-year were more frequently collected after May. During the first summer inshore they grew rapidly and reached 160-320 mm TL. Young-of-the-year emigrated from the estuaries in fall and were most abundant on the shallow portions of the adjacent continental shelf. Some evidence suggests that young-of-the-year in the northern Mid-Atlantic Bight reach a larger size than those from the southern portion. An hypothesis to explain the observed rarity of small juveniles in northern estuaries in some years is that some juveniles utilize the continental shelf as a nursery and enter estuaries at a larger size. This hypothesis requires testing.

Ahrenholz, D.W., W.R. Nelson, and S.P. Epperly. 1987. Population and Fishery Characteristics of Atlantic Menhaden, *Brevoortia Tyrannus*. Fishery Bulletin 85 (3): 569-600.

A stock assessment analysis of the Atlantic menhaden, *Brevoortia tyrannus*, fishery was conducted with purse seine landings data from 1940 to 1981 and port sampling data from 1955 to 1981. Virtual population (cohort) analysis was used to estimate historical stock sizes, rates of fishing, and numbers of recruits. The population exploitation rate (age 1 and older) ranged from 0.29 to 0.51 and averaged about 0.38 for the 1955-79 period. Recruitment at age 0.5 during the 1955-79 period ranged from 1.5 to 18.6 billion fish, with a mean of 5.1 billion. Classical spawner-recruitment relationships describe the data poorly. Growth and mortality data were used to examine yield per recruit for temporal and geographic fishing areas and for the entire fishery. Size at age data, while supporting an earlier hypothesis of density dependent growth, show a trend toward slower apparent growth in the 1970's than is explained by this hypothesis alone. Yield per recruit of Atlantic menhaden dropped from 107 g for the 1970-72 period to 57 g for the 1976-78 period. A Graham-Schaefer production model estimate of maximum sustainable yield (MSY) for the 1955-79 period was 414,000 metric tons. A modified Pella-Tomlinson production model provided a MSY estimate of 557,000 metric tons. The latter estimate is probably unattainable given current temporal and geographic fishing patterns. Results of these analyses indicate that the Atlantic menhaden fishery suffers from growth overfishing.

Almeida, F.P., T.R. Azarovitz, L. O'Brien, and E.W. Pritchard. 1984. The distribution of major finfish and shellfish species collected during NEFC Bottom trawl surveys, 1965-1978. Woods Hole Laboratory Reference Document No. 84-21. Northeast Fisheries Center, Woods Hole Laboratory. Woods Hole, MA. 101 p.

*This report describes synoptic bottom trawl surveys of the offshore fishery resources of the Northwest Atlantic continental shelf have been conducted by the North east Fisheries Center since the autumn of 1963. These surveys provided the data for examining the temporal and spatial distribution of 46 finfish and shellfish species occurring on the shelf.

Anderson, E.D. 1979. Assessment of the northwest Atlantic mackerel, Scomber scombrus, stock. NOAA Technical Report SSRF-732. 13 p.

The status of the Atlantic mackerel, Scomber scombrus, stock in the International Commission for the Northwest Atlantic Fisheries (ICNAF) convention area is analyzed in this paper. Total catch declined from a high of 431,606 t in 1972 to an estimated 92,000 t in 1977. The U.S. spring bottom trawl survey has shown a continuous decrease in Atlantic mackerel abundance since 1968. Fishing mortality (F) in 1977 was estimated at 0.39, nearly one-half of the 1976 level and the lowest since 1972. The 1974 year class appears to be the strongest since 1969, whereas the 1975 and 1976 year classes appear to be very weak. Spawning stock biomass decreased from 1.8 million t in 1970-72 to an estimated 402,500 t at the beginning of 1978, which is slightly below the 1962-67 level when catches averaged only about 25,000 t. A zero catch in 1978 would increase the 1979 spawning stock by 6%; a catch of 23,500 t (F = 0.07) would maintain the spawning stock at the 1978 level.

Anderson, E.D. 1985. Analysis of Various Sources of Pelagic Shark Catches in the Northwest and Western Central Atlantic Ocean and Gulf of Mexico with Comments on Catches of Other Large Pelagics. pp. 1-14. *In:* National Oceanic and Atmospheric Administration. Shark Catches from Selected Fisheries Off The U.S. East Coast. NOAA Technical Report NMFS 31. National Oceanic and Atmospheric Administration, National Marine Fisheries Service Scientific Publications Office. Seattle, WA.

Various sources of catch of pelagic sharks during 1960-81 in the Northwest and Western Central Atlantic Ocean and Gulf of Mexico, particularly within the United States Fishery Conservation Zone (FCZ), were identified and quantified. These sources included reported statistics, but principally unreported bycatch in fisheries directed towards other species. Total catch estimates during 1965-80 averaged 9,800 t (metric tons) per year and peaked at 17,300 t in 1977 in the Atlantic FCZ and averaged 6,800 t per year and peaked at 10,200 t in 1980 in the Gulf FCZ. The major source of catch in the Atlantic FCZ was the U.S. recreational fishery, followed by the United States and Canadian swordfish longline fisheries and the Japanese tuna longline fisheries. The major sources of catch in the Gulf FCZ were the recreational fishery and the U.S. shrimp, groundfish, and snapper- grouper fisheries. A comparison between long-term average catches and recent levels in both areas suggests that pelagic sharks may be excessively exploited at the present time.

Anderson, W.W. and J.W. Gehringer. 1959a. Physical oceanographic, biological, and chemical data, South Atlantic coast of the United States, M/V Theodore N. Gill cruise 7. US Department of the Interior, US Fish and Wildlife Service, Special Scientific Report — Fisheries No. 278. 277 p.

*This report documents stations sampled throughout the South Atlantic Bight during June-July 1954. Weather, water chemistry, and sea state data were collected. Plankton samples were collected and fish were sampled by dip net and trolling. A few stations were near or within the southern border of our study area.

—. 1959b. Physical oceanographic, biological, and chemical data, South Atlantic coast of the United States, M/V Theodore N. Gill cruise 8. US Department of the Interior, US Fish and Wildlife Service, Special Scientific Report — Fisheries No. 303. 227 p.

*This report documents stations sampled throughout the South Atlantic Bight during August — September 1954. Weather, water chemistry, and sea state data were collected. Plankton samples were collected and fish were sampled by dip net and trolling. A few stations were near or within the southern border of our study area.

Anderson, W.W., J.W. Gehringer, and E. Cohen. 1956. Physical oceanographic, biological, and chemical data, South Atlantic coast of the United States, Theodore N. Gill cruise 2. US Department of the Interior, US Fish and Wildlife Service, Special Scientific Report — Fisheries No. 198. 270 p.

*This report documents stations sampled throughout the South Atlantic Bight during May 1953. Weather, water chemistry, and sea state data were collected. Plankton samples were collected and fish were sampled by dip net and trolling. A few stations were near or within the southern border of our study area.

Azarovitz, T. Unpublished database. Groundfish Surveys 1967-1994. NOAA/NMFS, Northeast Fisheries Center. Woods Hole, MA.

*This is an unpublished fisheries database. Data were collected from 1967 to 1994 by the NOAA/NMFS, Northeast Fisheries Center. The Principal Investigator is listed as Tom Azarovitz. Select sample locations and related data were computerized as part of the North Carolina SEAMAP Hardbottom data project by Moser et al. (1995). SEAMAP Hardbottom data (sample locations) within the defined project area for The Point were sorted and mapped using ArcView GIS (J. Ott, pers. comm., 15 Nov 99).

Bailey, T., M. Youngbluth, and G. Owen. 1991. Metabolic Rates of Zooplankton and Micronekton from Deep-water Pelagic Environments at Cape Hatteras. p. 5. *In:* Shepard, A. (ed.). NURC/UNCW 1991 Undersea Research: Informational Meeting. National Undersea Research Center, University of North Carolina at Wilmington. Wilmington, NC.

Our submersible-based observations in August 1990 indicated that "The Point" east of Cape Hatteras was a highly structured environment dominated by one species of myctophid fish and several species of crustaceans and gelatinous zooplankton. In fact, in our ca. 25 years of combined submersible experience, we have not encountered such high population densities of gelatinous zooplankton or myctophid fishes at any other location. These high standing stocks provide the unique opportunity to study major faunal components (i.e., fishes, crustaceans, and gelatinous zooplankton) of the midwater community, simultaneously.

Our research plan for 1991 will determine the distribution, abundance, and metabolic rates of numerically dominant species of midwater zooplankton and micronekton. These data will allow us to define the energetic and trophic relationships of zooplankton and micronekton in deep-water communities.

Barbieri, L.R., M.E. Chittenden Jr, and S.K. Lowerre-Barbieri. 1994. Maturity, spawning, and ovarian cycle of Atlantic croaker, Micropogonias undulatus, in the Chesapeake Bay and adjacent coastal waters. Fishery Bulletin 92: 671-685.

The reproductive biology of Atlantic croaker, *Micropogonias undulates*, collected during 1990-91 from commercial catches in Chesapeake Bay and in Virginia and North Carolina coastal waters (n=3,091), was studied by using macroscopic and microscopic gonad staging, the gonadosomatic index, oocyte diameter distributions, and histological analysis. Atlantic croaker are multiple spawners with asynchronous oocyte development and indeterminate fecundity. Mean length at first maturity for males and females was 182 and 173 mm TL, respectively. More than 85% of both sexes were mature by the end of their first year and all were mature by age 2. Spawning extends over a protracted period (July-December), but individual fish apparently spawn over a shorter interval. Eleven gravid and runningripe females were collected within the Chesapeake Bay suggesting some spawning occurs in estuarine waters. Monthly sex ratios indicated a strong predominance of females during the main period of spawning. A high incidence of atretic, advanced yolked oocytes in spawning females collected throughout the spawning season suggests that a surplus production of yolked oocytes may be part of the reproductive strategy of Atlantic croaker.

Bedsole, L.H., Jr., B.F. Holland Jr., and J.W. Gillikin Jr. 1980. RV Dan Moore Cruise Report No. 38: Part I: December 1979 February 1980 Mesh Selectivity Study for Summer Flounder *(Paralichthys dentatus)*; Part II: February — March 1980 Offshore Anadromous Fish Investigations from Cape Lookout to Chesapeake Bay Entrance. North Carolina Division of Marine Fisheries, Department of Natural Resources and Community Development. Morehead City, NC.

*During December 1979 February 1980, the RV Dan Moore conducted three cruises in the Atlantic Ocean between Cape Lookout, NC and Chesapeake Bay entrance, VA. The objectives of these cruises were: 1) To obtain mesh size selectivity data from North Carolina's winter trawl fishery, with emphasis on mesh selectivity for summer flounder, 2) To examine the effect of gilling various species, particularly spiny dogfish, on the selectivity of the different mesh sizes tested, and to determine the optimum mesh size(s) to minimize the gilling effect, 3) To provide a basis for evaluating the effect on summer flounder landings which could result from a change in cod-end mesh size under actual fishing conditions.

Berrien, P.L. 1978. Eggs and larvae of Scomber scombrus and Scomber japonicus in continental shelf waters between Massachusetts and Florida. Fishery Bulletin 76(1): 95-115.

Larval *Scomber scombrus* and *Scomber japonicus* from the western North Atlantic Ocean are compared. At 4 to 11 mm *S. japonicus* are deeper bodied, and at 3 to 15 mm have greater preanus lengths than *S. scombrus* of comparable sizes. *Scomber scombrus* larvae are more heavily pigmented than *S. japonicus*, particularly on the dorsal trunk surface and at the cleithral sympysis.

In continental shelf waters between Martha's Vineyard, Mass., and Palm Beach, Fla., 1966-68, *S. scombrus* eggs occurred north of Cape Hatteras, N.C., mostly in the shoreward half of shelf waters, during spring and summer. Surface temperatures associated with egg occurrences varied from 6.3° to 16.9° C. *Scomber japonicus* eggs were taken south of Cape Hatteras, in the outer half of shelf waters, during winter and spring cruises. Surface temperatures associated with egg occurrences ranged from 20.4° to 25.4° C.

Larval *S. scombrus* occurred north of Cape Hatteras during spring and summer with concurrent surface temperatures ranging from 12.3° to 20.7° C. With the exception of three specimens, *S. japonicus* larvae occurred south of Cape Hatteras and were taken where the surface temperature ranged from 16.0° to 29.4° C.

Berrien, P.L., M.P. Fahay Jr., A.W. Kendall, and W.G. Smith. 1978. Ichthyoplankton from the RV Dolphin Survey of the Continental Shelf Waters Between Martha's Vineyard, MA and Cape Lookout, NC, 1965-1966. National Marine Fisheries Service, Northeast Fisheries Center. Sandy Hook, NJ. 152 p.

*These are cruise data for: Ichthyoplankton from the R/V Dolphin Survey of the Continental Shelf Waters Between Martha's Vineyard, MA and Cape Lookout, NC 1965-66. Digital files containing sample location data were entered directly into ArcView 3.1 GIS.

Berrien, P., and J. Sibunka. 1999. Distribution Patterns of Fish Eggs in the U.S. Northeast Continental Shelf Ecosystem, 1977-1987. NOAA Technical Report NMFS 145. Northeast Fisheries Sciences Center, National Marine Fisheries Service. Highlands, NJ. 310 p.

This atlas presents information on fish eggs and temperature data collected from broadscale ichthyoplankton surveys conducted off the U.S. northeast coast from 1977 to 1987. Distribution and abundance information is provided for 33 taxa in the form of graphs and contoured egg-density maps by month and survey. Comments are included on interannual and interseasonal trends in spawning intensity. Data on 14 additional but less numerous taxa are provided in a tabular form.

Blair, N., L. Levin, and D. DeMaster. 1991. Biology and Carbon Cycling on the Carolina Slope. p. 9. Shepard, A. (ed.). NURC/UNCW 1991 Undersea Research: Informational Meeting. National Undersea Research Center, University of North Carolina at Wilmington. Wilmington, NC.

Resources as diverse as fisheries, some minerals and fossil fuels, as well as the atmosphere and climate have been linked to the cycling of carbon and the associated biogenic nutrients along continental margins. The continental slope is an area which has been poorly studied even though it is the site of intense biogeochemical activity. An interdisciplinary program which focuses on the biogeochemistry of the Carolina slope environment is currently underway to investigate the relationship of carbon cycling with the sediment-dwelling ecosystem. Three sites, all at 850 meters water depth, have been studied. Sites I and II, which are off Charleston, South Carolina, and Cape Lookout, North Carolina, respectively, are representative of typical slope environments in terms of animal populations, sediment geochemistry and sediment accumulation. Site III, which is off of Cape Hatteras and near "The Point," has significantly higher populations of bottom-dwelling animals, different animal species and higher rates of organic matter degradation. Biogenic methane formation occurs at Site III but not at the other sites. These differences are thought to be related to the delivery rate of organic matter (food) to the seafloor. The convergence of boundary currents in this region may prove to be an important controlling factor by transporting organic matter into the area or by stimulating localized surface production via the delivery of nutrients. In contrast to the other sites, the sea floor at Site III is an area of high-relief and is more prone to episodic sedimentation and mass wasting. The combination of the high-relief bottom with the relatively large delivery rate of organic carbon to the seafloor may have resulted in a uniquely adapted ecosystem.

Future directions in research include identifying the sources of the sedimentary organic matter and the relationship between the ocean physics and the carbon delivery rate. The rates of organic matter delivery, decomposition and burial need to be measured as they represent important controls on the benthic ecosystems. Specific relationships between the benthic communities, the carbon cycle and sediment dynamics are to be investigated. Descriptions of the cliff-face communities are needed as they represent an important component of the overall ecosystems at Site III.

Boreman, J. 1983. Status of bluefish along the Atlantic coast, 1982. Laboratory Reference Document No. 83-28. National Marine Fisheries Service, Northeast Fisheries Center, Woods Hole Lab. Woods Hole, MA.

(Modified from the Executive Summary) Spawning of bluefish occurs ln two major areas along the Atlantic coast: south of Cape Hatteras and in the Middle Atlantic Bight. Juveniles move inshore to bays and estuaries from Florida to Cape Cod. Most bluefish are mature by age 2, and the sex ratio remains 1:1 (males:females) úor all age groups. Growth is rapid, especially during the first growing season.

Existing regulations on bluefish catch focus on minimum size limits imposed by many states along the Atlantic coast, and limits on foreign catch in the FCZ. A bluefish fishery management plan currently being prepared by the Mid-Atlantic Fishery Management Council proposes unrestricted harvest for US recreational anglers, an allowance for limited expansion of the conventional commercial fishery, and restrictions on the use of "non-conventional commercial gear (e.g., purse seines and otter trawls).

NEFC inshore and offshore trawl surveys have also had increasing catch rates of bluefish during the 1970's. Most of the bluefish caught in the inshore surveys have been less than 30 cm (12 in) in length (presumed age 0). The offshore survey catches have included equal numbers of fish less than and fish greater than 30 cm (12 in). Older bluefish (> 55 cm or 21.7 in) appear to be more vulnerable to capture in the offshore surveys than younger age groups, probably because of their distribution habits.

Catch per tow of bluefish in the fall inshore survey north of Cape May appears to be an adequate index of recruitment, since it is correlated with commercial and recreational harvests 2-4 years later. This index shows that recruitment has been relatively high in recent years and projections for commercial and recreational harvest in 1983 and 1984 are favorable.

Brown, S.K., R. Mahon, K.G.T. Zwanenburg, K.R. Buja, L.W. Claflin, R.N. O'Boyle, B. Atkinson, M. Sinclair, G. Howell, and M.E. Monaco. 1996. East Coast of North America groundfish: Initial explorations of biogeography and species assemblages. National Oceanic and Atmospheric Administration. Silver Spring, MD. 111 p.

This report contains the initial analysis of research demersal trawl survey data for the east coast of North America from Cape Hatteras, North Carolina, USA in the south, to Cape Chidley, Labrador, Canada in the north, using individual trawl sets. The analyses were conducted as part of the process of defining and mapping demersal fish assemblages. The underlying goal is to describe and map species assemblages, and to evaluate evidence for ecological regime and assemblage distribution shifts on a decadal time scale. A related goal is to evaluate the extent to which the Atlantic cod decline along the east coast of North America can be explained by changes in the environment, as evidenced by changes in the ecosystem (Doubleday 1995). Because work is continuing on the project, recommendations are provided for future analyses, and implications of the results to data for fishery management are briefly discussed.

Bullis, H.R., Jr., and R.C. Cummins Jr. 1974. North Carolina Summary Atlas of Exploratory Fishing by National Marine Fisheries Service, 1956-1974. MARMAP Contribution Number 6. National Marine Fisheries Service, Southeast Fisheries Center. Miami, FL.

*This atlas has been prepared for the NC Marine Fisheries Resources Conference to be held September 18-19, 1974, at New Bern, NC. The first Federal exploratory fishing survey of North Carolina waters was conducted in 1950 by the RV Albatross III and the results of this cruise were given by Donald Powell (1951). However, it was not until 1956 that a formal program was established for exploring the latent fishery potential of the Southeastern Atlantic coast of the United States. This program, initially based in Jacksonville, Florida, was conducted with chartered commercial fishing vessels. A permanent station was established in Brunswick, Georgia, in 1959, and was affiliated with the Service's Exploratory fishing Base at Pascagoula, MI. Exploratory fishing cruises were planned and coordinated with the Pascagoula-based operations and all exploratory fishing information that accrued from this work was routinely added to the database maintained at Pascagoula. This report summarizes these data for the activities conducted off North Carolina during the period of 1956 to the present (1974).

Butler, J.N., B.F. Morris, J. Cadwallader, and A.W. Stoner. 1983. Studies of Sargassum and the Sargassum Community. Special Publication No. 22. Bermuda Biological Station for Research.

*Chapter 1, The Quantity of Sargassum in the Sargasso Sea, and Chapter 2, The Sargassum Community, include the defined study area for The Point.

The quantity and distribution of *Sargassum* in the Sargasso Sea, as estimated by various investigators, is reviewed. There has apparently been no significant change in the biomass of *Sargassum* from 1933 to 1981, except for an area northeast of the Antilles (20-25° N, 62-68° W) where measurements made in November 1977 and November 1980 were about 0.1% of values measured in February and March 1933. Because of the lack of change in the Bermuda region, the Bahamas region, or the Gulf Stream region, this effect does not appear to be due to pollution or broad climatic changes; it is most likely due to a seasonal or long-term shift of the currents defining the southwestern boundary of the Sargasso Sea.

Motile macrofauna on *Sargassum* were identified and counted for 244 samples taken at Station 'S' near Bermuda, and for 155 samples taken from other parts of the western North Atlantic and Caribbean. The nature of this community and its seasonal variations are discussed. Preliminary studies of the food web, as well as of the microfauna (copepods) and sessile fauna are reported. Although petroleum hydrocarbon residues are found in all samples of *Sargassum* and its larger associated fauna, the variability of individual samples is so extreme that no correlation of community structure with hydrocarbon pollution could be demonstrated.

Checkley, D.M., Jr., S. Raman, L. Maillet, and K.M. Mason. 1988. Winter Storm Effects on the Spawning and Larval Drift of a Pelagic Fish. Nature 335 (6188): 346-348.

Recruitment for many marine organisms depends on survival and transport of eggs and larvae from spawning grounds to nursery areas. We investigated the effects of winter storms and the Gulf Stream on the spawning, development and drift of the Atlantic menhaden, *Brevoortia tyrannus,* which spawns offshore and metamorphoses in estuaries. Spawning was maximal during storms in water upwelled near the western edge of the Gulf Stream. Eggs and larvae drifted shoreward with abundant food in the warm surface stratum of a density-driven circulation maintained by the large sea-air heat flux. We suggest that the Atlantic menhaden and other species have evolved to reproduce in winter near warm boundary currents, including the Gulf Stream and Kuroshio, as a result of physical conditions that permit the rapid development and shoreward drift of their eggs and larvae, with consequent high recruitment and fitness.

—. 1989. Winter Storm Effects on the Spawning and Larval Drift of a Pelagic Fish. pp. 45-46. *In*: Crawford, K. (ed.). Proceedings: 1989 Marine Expo: The Natural Resources Associated with Mobil's Proposed Drill Site. NC Outer Continental Shelf Office, NC Department of Administration. Raleigh, NC.

Recruitment for many marine organisms depends on survival and transport of eggs and larvae from spawning grounds to nursery areas. We investigated the effects of winter storms and the Gulf Stream on the spawning, development and drift of the Atlantic menhaden, *Brevoortia tyrannus,* which spawns offshore and metamorphoses in estuaries. Spawning was maximal during storms in water upwelled near the western edge of the Gulf Stream. Eggs and larvae drifted shoreward with abundant food in the warm surface stratum of a density-driven circulation maintained by the large sea-air heat flux. We suggest that the Atlantic menhaden and other species have evolved to reproduce in winter near warm boundary currents, including the Gulf Stream and Kuroshio, as a result of physical conditions that permit the rapid development and shoreward drift of their eggs and larvae, with consequent high recruitment and fitness.

Clark, J., W.G. Smith, A.W. Kendall Jr, and M.P. Fahay. 1969. Studies of Estuarine Dependance of Atlantic coastal fishes. US Fish and Wildlife Service, Technical Papers of the Bureau of Sport Fisheries and Wildlife 28. 132 p.

*This is Data Report I covering surveys (eight cruises: Dec 1965-Dec 1966) from Cape Cod, MA to Cape Lookout, NC by the R/V Dolphin. These cruises were directed toward larval fishes. Temperatures, salinities, and lists of catches from plankton and midwater nets are reported in tables and maps. Station transects L and M overlap our study area.

Colvocoresses, J.A., and J.A. Musick. 1984. Species associations and community composition of middle Atlantic bight continental shelf demersal fishes. Fishery Bulletin 82 (2): 295-313.

Cluster analyses of seasonal NMFS Groundfish Survey bottom trawl catches on the Middle Atlantic Bight continental shelf revealed consistent species associations and faunal zones over a 9-year period. Boundaries between faunal zones tended to follow isotherms and isobaths. During the late winter-early spring, the following zones were found: Northern inner shelf, northern mid-shelf, southern inner- and mid-shelf, and outer shelf-shelf break. Five species groups were identified: A small cryophilic group restricted to the first zone, a cold-water boreal group found in the first two zones, a ubiquitous boreal/resident group containing the major dominants, a warm-temperature group confined to the warmer southern and outer shelf waters, and a group of slope residents confined to the deepest zone. During the fall, five faunal zones were found: Southern inner/mid-shelf, northern inner shelf, northern mid-shelf, outer shelf, and shelf break. Five species associations were largely analogous to those in the spring, with the following exceptions: The cryophilic group was absent, the ubiquitous group contained mixed boreal and warm-temperature elements, and a second outer shelf group was recognized. The most notable change in the distribution of groups from the spring was a general northward shift and a sharply defined inshore movement of the temperate group.

Continental Shelf Associates, Inc. 1983. North Carolina Fisheries and Environmental Data Search and Synthesis Study: Final Report. Continental Shelf Associates, Inc. Jupiter, FL.

Available information on the living marine resources and habitats of the North Carolina OCS, from shore to a depth of 200 m (656 ft), was collected, annotated, and synthesized. Over 1,450 published and unpublished data sources were reviewed. Written synthesis chapters summarized the geology, oceanography, biological communities, commercial and sport fisheries, endangered and threatened species, and sensitive biological areas and unique habitats. Data gaps were identified, implications to OCS development were discussed, and suggestions for additional research were provided. In addition, a computer program was designed to catalog and sort all of the pertinent annotated information sources. The purpose of this computer program is to provide the MMS with a useful and viable method of maintaining, updating, and expanding the data base.

The North Carolina OCS is a transition zone between the South and Middle Atlantic Bight. The climate, proximity and behavior of the Gulf Stream, and the presence of cuspate projecting shoals and capes influence unique oceanographic and biological features. Extensive hard/live bottom areas are present within Onslow Bay and along the North Carolina continental shelf edge. Upwelling along the North Carolina continental shelf edge and the intrusion of nutrient rich eddies into middle- and inner-shelf waters occur frequently along this coast. The upwelling-eddy, formation-intrusion phenomenon is not well understood and its ecological implications are just beginning to be studied. The present lack of knowledge in this area makes risk assessment for OCS development activities difficult. Additional studies of the coupling of physical and biological processes along the North Carolina continental shelf are needed in order to formulate effective OCS management policies for that area.

—. 1989. CSA Live Bottom Survey. Continental Shelf Associates, Inc. Jupiter, FL. 45 p.

This report describes the results of a Live-Bottom Survey (LBS) conducted from 9 to 24 July 1989. The purpose of this video/still camera photodocumentation survey was to document the topographical features, substrate types, and associated biota at the sites around the proposed well location and proposed anchor locations. As shown in Figure 1.2, the survey area extends into Manteo Area Blocks 466, 510, and 511. Proposed anchor locations were chosen to be placed in relatively low-relief areas based on bathymetric and high-resolution geophysical data. Water depths within the sites surveyed ranged from 305 to 1,355 m (1,001 to 4,446 ft). Due to the water depth and the highly irregular topography within the survey area, a state-of-the-art deepwater remotely operated vehicle (ROV) was needed to obtain the survey data. Other less sophisticated options, such as towed video/still camera systems or lesser ROV systems, would not have performed satisfactorily.

—. 1991. Ichthyoplankton in the Vicinity of Manteo Area Block 467 from June to November 1990. Continental Shelf Associates, Inc. Jupiter, FL.

*Ichthyoplankton survey of Manteo Area block 467 of the Mid-Atlantic Bight, off the North Carolina coast. Five cruises aboard FV Brothers Pride, from June-November 1990. Ichthyoplankton assemblage at the proposed wellsite was similar to assemblages at most other sampling sites in terms of overall taxonomic composition and abundance of taxa. Results indicated the assemblages at the wellsite were not unique. The ichthyoplankton assemblages observed at the proposed wellsite and adjacent waters were more similar to assemblages previously described from larval fish surveys in the eastern Gulf of Mexico and South Atlantic Bight than those described from collections in the Mid-Atlantic Bight.

Costlow, J., K. Brink, M. Orbach, C. Peterson, J. Teal, and A. Robertson. 1992. North Carolina Environmental Sciences Review Panel. Report to the Secretary of the Interior from the North Carolina Environmental Sciences Review Panel as mandated by the Oil Pollution Act of 1990. 83 p.

The Oil Pollution Act of 1990, in a section cited as the Outer Banks Protection Act, prohibits the Secretary of the Interior from proceeding with a number of actions relative to development of oil and gas resources offshore North Carolina for which he is responsible under the Outer Continental Shelf Lands Act (OCLSA). Actions prohibited include: (1) conducting a lease sale; (2) issuing any new lease; (3) approving any exploration plan; (4) approving any development and production plan; (5) approving any application for permit to drill; and (6) permitting any drilling. The prohibition on these actions is mandated to remain in effect until the latter of: (1) October 1, 1991 or (2) 45 days of contiguous session of the Congress following the submission of a written report from the Secretary certifying that the information available to him is sufficient to carry out his responsibilities under the OCSLA.

In his report, the Secretary is required to take into consideration findings and recommendations of a panel established by the Outer Banks Protection Act, the North Carolina Environmental Sciences Review Panel, and to include a detailed explanation of any differences between his certification if sufficient information and the findings and recommendations of this group. The panel is charged by the Act with: (1) assessing the adequacy of the available physical oceanographic, ecological, and socioeconomic information to enable the Secretary to fulfill his responsibilities under the OCSLA and (2) identifying any additional information deemed essential to enable the Secretary to carry out these responsibilities. The Panel's response to this charge is the subject of this document.

As provided in the Outer Banks Protection Act, the North Carolina Environmental Sciences Review Panel is composed of five members, a marine scientist selected by the Secretary of the Interior, a marine scientist selected by the Governor of North Carolina, and three scientists, one each from the disciplines of physical oceanography, ecology, and social sciences, selected jointly by the Secretary and the Governor from a list developed by the National Academy of Sciences. Unless specifically indicated in the text, the conclusions and recommendations presented in the report represent the unanimous decision of the Panel members. A summary of findings including Physical Oceanography, Ecology, Socioeconomics, Sources of Information, Adequacy of Information, and Panel's Recommended Studies is included. Appendix A: Literature Review, and Appendix B: Factors Influencing the Definition if Adequacy of Information are also included.

Coston-Clements, L., L.R. Settle, D.E. Hoss, and F.A. Cross. 1991. Utilization of the *Sargassum* Habitat by Marine Invertebrates and Vertebrates — A Review. National Marine Fisheries Service, NOAA, Southeast Fisheries Science Center, Beaufort Lab. Beaufort, NC. 32 p.

Numerous species of brown algae (Class Cyclosporeae: Order Fucales: Family Fucaceae) of the genus *Sargassum* occur throughout the world's tropical and temperate oceans. The pelagic complex in the western North Atlantic is comprised primarily of *Sargassum natans* and *S. fluitans*. Both species are hyponeustonic and fully adapted to a pelagic existence (Parr, 1939). Known commonly as gulf-weed, sea holly, or sargassum, they are characterized by a brushy, highly branched thallus (stem) with numerous leaf-like blades and berry-like pneumatocysts (floats). These floating plants may be up to several meters in length-but are typically much smaller. There is a well known assemblage of small fishes associated with sargassum rafts, many of which serve as forage for commercially or recreationally exploited species (Table 2). Dooley (1972) described 54 species from 23 families in the sargassum community of the Florida Current. Only 14 species from 11 families are known from the Sargasso Sea (Fedoryako, 1980; 1989). During the pelagic stage, hatchling loggerhead, *Caretta caretta*, green, *Chelonia mydas*, Kemp's ridley, *Lepidochelys kempi*, and hawksbill, *Eretmochelys imbricata*, sea turtles have been observed in sargassum off Florida, Georgia, North Carolina, and Texas (Smith, 1968; Fletemeyer, 1978; Carr and Meylan, 1980; Carr, 1986; 1987a; Schwartz, 1988; 1989; Manzella and Williams, 1991; Schwartz, pers. comm.). Schwartz (1988) reported numerous loggerhead hatchlings captured during commercial trawling for sargassum. This observation constitutes the largest known aggregation of loggerhead hatchlings encountered off the North Carolina coast.

Crawford, K. (ed.). 1989. Proceedings: 1989 Marine Expo: The Natural Resources Associated with Mobil's Proposed Drill Site. NC Outer Continental Shelf Office, NC Department of Administration. Raleigh, NC. 64 p.

*This report contains abstracts from each presenter. Chapter topics include: Mobil's Proposal, Geologic Overview — Introduction and Potential for Oil and Gas Discovery, Oceanographic Conditions, Comments on Last MMS Modeling, Biological Production Near the Bottom (invertebrates), Fisheries Resources, Commercial and Recreational Marine Fisheries, Winter Storm Effects on Spawning and Larval Drift of Pelagic Fish, Marine Birds, Sea Turtles in North Carolina, Marine Mammals, Plenary Session, Summary. Each chapter also cited individually when appropriate.

Currin, M., and S.W. Ross. 1999. Characterization of Recreational and Commercial Fisheries at "The Point" — Offshore North Carolina. Contractor's Report to NC Division of Coastal Management. Prepared under MMS Contract 1435-01-98-CA-30949 to Mac Currin. 24 p.

*This report describes the commercial and recreational fishery at "The Point." The report attempts to draw geographic boundaries around "The Point" based on fishery data gathered from a survey.

Desfosse, J.C., J.A. Musick, A.D. Estes, and P. Lyons. 1990. Stock identification of summer flounder (Paralichthys dentatus) in the southern Mid-Atlantic Bight. Virginia Inst. of Marine Science, Final Report to Virginia Marine Resources Commission (F-61-R, WB-86-01-04). Gloucester Point, VA. 55 p.

A total of 12,339 summer flounder were tagged from Virginia waters during 1987-89. A total of 874 were recaptured for an overall return rate of 7.1%. Most of the returns (48.5%) were from Virginia waters, or areas to the south. A smaller number (21.6%) were from areas north and offshore of Virginia. Another 29.9% were recaptured and returned with inadequate location data. Examining only the returns with adequate location data, yielded a separation of 69.2% and 30.8% between the groups. No differences were noted in the sizes at tagging between these groups. Tagged flounder held at VIMS exhibited no behavioral differences from untagged fish. No differences in growth and mortality were noted in these fish. The sex ratio of males to females was 1:1.16. Male summer flounder reached 50% maturity at approximately 280 mm, while females reached 50% maturity at about 330 mm. A total of 1040 flounder were successfully aged. The population was dominated by young fish (0-2 years old). The compression of age structure is indicative of a population being heavily overfished.

Diaz, R.J., J.A. Blake, and D.P. Lohse. 1993a. Volume II Final Report: Benthic Study of the Continental Slope off Cape Hatteras, North Carolina. Virginia Inst. of Marine Science, School of Marine Science, College of William and Mary, Gloucester Pt., VA. Science Applications International Corporation, Woods Hole, MA. 135 p.

*This is a study of the nature and spatial extent of continental slope benthic communities off Cape Hatteras, NC, with emphasis on the Manteo Area lease block 467. Macrofaunal abundance and biomass in this area is higher than anywhere else along the entire South Atlantic continental slope and rise. Species composition of the infauna off Cape Hatteras is also different from other slope habitats. Species richness and diversity are lower with a high degree of dominance by species that are cosmopolitan in distribution. Trends in abundance of invertebrate megafauna on the continental slope off Cape Hatteras appear to be similar to the macrofauna. Demersal fish fauna in this area is distinctive in composition and population density. Overall, abundance of benthic fish off Cape Hatteras is four to seven times higher than the adjacent area. Site sediment characteristics (e.g., source, texture, and physico-chemistry) and potential impact to benthic community by sediment discharge during drilling are described. Volume III contains Appendices A-E.

Much of the data in this report were used in the Special Deep Sea Research issue (1994. 41 (4-6)).

Diaz, R.J., J. Blake, B. Hecker, and D.C. Rhoads. 1993b. A Highly Productive Area of the Continental Slope Off Cape Hatteras. Benthic Ecology Meeting, 1-4 April, 1993, Mobile, AL. 57 p.

The continental slope off Cape Hatteras is atypical for the U.S. Atlantic coast. Unusually high numbers of infauna, megafauna, and demersal fish were found over a broad area. Benthic organisms appear to be well adapted to physical processes that converge on the Cape Hatteras continental slope. These physical processes impart a high degree of instability to the bottom and also supply large amounts of organic matter which sustain the elevated densities and biomass. The nature of these communities and mechanisms which regulate them will be discussed.

Diaz, R.J., G.R. Cutter, and J.A. Blake. 1998. Appendix F: A Review: Findings of the Benthic Study of the Continental Slope Off Cape Hatteras, North Carolina. pp. 121-136. *In*: Vigil, D.L. (ed.). North Carolina/Minerals Management Service Technical Workshop on Manteo Unit Exploration: February 4-5, 1998. U.S. Dept. of the Interior, Minerals Management Service, Gulf of Mexico OCS Region. New Orleans, LA.

*These are the proceedings from a workshop/meeting (February 4-5, 1998) between the North Carolina Department of Environment and Natural Resources, the U.S. Dept. of the Interior's Minerals Management Service (MMS), and others. The geographic area discussed is approximately 45 miles east-northeast of Cape Hatteras, NC, referred to as the Manteo Unit. This workshop reviewed environmental and socioeconomic information known and needed on the Manteo Unit. The MMS's Gulf of Mexico OCS Regional Director gave an MMS perspective on history and status of the area. Chevron gave a presentation on how an exploratory well would be drilled. The scientific characterization was presented in greater detail by scientific experts who spoke on the following disciplines: physical environment, habitat and living resources, seabirds, marine mammals, sea turtles, and social and economic issues. Specific chapters are cited individually, when appropriate.

Because of the potential environmental impacts associated with development and production activities, the Oil Pollution Act of 1990 mandated that a panel of experts be convened. This panel, North Carolina Environmental Sciences Review Panel (Costlow et al. 1992), was to consider whether the available scientific information was adequate for making decisions about oil and gas leasing, exploration, and development off North Carolina. The Costlow et al. (1992) report to the Secretary of the Interior made several recommendations on the information needed to understand the basic ecology of the leased areas. Among them was the recommendation that the spatial extent of the benthic community found within some of the lease blocks should be determined before any exploration or development activity occurred off Cape Hatteras. The present study was developed by the Minerals Management Service to determine the aerial extent of the community found by Blake et al. (1985, 1987). Results are published as a special issue of Deep-Sea Research Part II (Diaz et al. 1994a), which included a CD-ROM with data and selected bottom images (Cutter et al. 1994a).

Sediments and Sedimentation Rates, Biological Communities (invertebrates and fish), Physical Habitat (geomorphology), Benthic Community Characterization and Distribution are discussed.

Dryfoos, R.L., R.P. Cheek, and R.L. Kroger. 1973. Preliminary analyses of Atlantic Menhaden, *Brevoortia tyrannus*, migrations, population structure, survival and exploitation rates, and availability as indicated from tag returns. Fishery Bulletin 71 (3): 719-734.

Over 1 million adult Atlantic menhaden, *Brevoortia tyrannus*, were tagged from Long Island to Florida between 1966 and 1969. Tag recoveries indicate these fish migrated northward in spring and early summer and southward in fall. As the fish grew older and larger, they also migrate farther northward each spring. Calculation of rates of interchange between fishing areas indicated that 21% of the recoveries from fish released in Chesapeake Bay in 1967 and 1968 accounted for 72% of the catch of tagged fish 1 year later in New York and New Jersey.

Preliminary estimates of population parameters were made from tag-recovery and catch data. Survival rates determined yearly from ratio of recoveries, however, varied due to fluctuations in availability. Annual survival rates averaging 0.23 were calculated with Robson-Chapman catch curve analysis and age composition of catch methods. From tag recoveries exploitation rate was estimated to be 50%, instantaneous fishing mortality rate (F) was 0.95, and instantaneous natural mortality (M) was 0.52. tag returns also indicated that significant fluctuations in availability of Atlantic menhaden occurred in Chesapeake Bay.

Edwards, R.L., R.L. Livingstone Jr. and P.E. Hamer. 1962. Winter water temperatures and an annotated list of fishes Nantucket Shoals to Cape Hatteras: Albatross Cruise no. 126. Special Scientific Report Fisheries No. 397. U.S. Department of the Interior, Fish and Wildlife Service. Washington, DC.

Cruise no. 126 of the Albatross III was planned and conducted to gather information about the distribution of fishes across the Continental Shelf from Nantucket Shoals to Cape Hatteras during the late winter period when water temperatures generally are at their minimum. The shelf here has a general hydrographic similarity from north to south, well described by Bigelow (1933), that makes it a particularly worthwhile area in which to study the relation of fish distribution to water temperature, depth, and other factors of the environment. Since the fish of this portion of the shelf support several different, relatively important food and industrial fisheries, as well as an intensive marine sport fishery, Cruise no. 126 served to provide data valuable to several research programs. This area has a distinctive fauna attributed in part to the thermal barrier present across the shelf at Cape Hatteras, as well as another such barrier, less marked, separating the waters of southern New England and the Gulf of Maine.

Epperly, S.P., J. Braun, A.J. Chester, F.A. Cross, J.V. Merriner, and P.A. Tester. 1995. Winter distribution of sea turtles in the vicinity of Cape Hatteras and their interactions with the summer flounder trawl fishery. Bulletin of Marine Science 56(2): 547-568.

Aerial surveys of North Carolina offshore waters between Cape Lookout and the North Carolina/Virginia state line were conducted November 1991-March 1992 to determine the abundance of sea turtles in the area where a trawl fishery for summer flounder was active, and to relate the distribution of turtles to physical oceanographic processes. Turtles were sighted throughout the winter as far north as Oregon Inlet. Individual surveys yielded surface density estimates greater than 12 turtles / 100 km^2, depending on the method of analysis. The distribution of turtles appeared to be related to water temperature, with turtles being mostly in waters >11?C. Favorable temperature and depth regimes for sea turtles occur throughout the winter along the western edge of the Gulf Stream from the vicinity of Cape Hatteras southward. The nearshore waters of Raleigh Bay, more than any other nearshore area of the South Atlantic Bight, are affected in the winter by the warm, fast-moving Gulf Stream and its frontal eddies that impinge upon and override the narrow continental shelf. Characteristically the waters in the vicinity of Cape Hatteras are warmer in the winter than nearshore areas to the south. The narrowness of the continental shelf and the influence of the Gulf Stream on these nearshore regions serve to concentrate sea turtles emigrating from nearshore waters in the Middle Atlantic Bight and Pamlico and Core Sounds in the late fall and early winter. Thus, sea turtles can be at greater risk for interaction with fishing activity on the continental shelf near Cape Hatteras, during the winter, than in any other area in the South Atlantic Bight. The summer flounder fishery, operating between Cape May, New Jersey and Cape Lookout, North Carolina during November 1991-February 1992, was monitored for interactions with sea turtles. Observers were aboard nearly 6% of the reported trips landed in Virginia and North Carolina. The sea turtle catch comprised loggerheads (60%), Kemp's ridleys (36%), greens (2%), and a hawksbill (1%). The catch of Kemp's ridleys during November-December 1991 south of Cape Hatteras was high (N = 26). Overall turtle catch rates were similar to those reported for the Atlantic shrimp fishery, but catch rates south of Cape Hatteras were 6-8 times higher than catch rates north of the Cape. A total of 1,063 turtles was estimated to have been caught November 1991-February 1992, and 89-181 were estimated to have died as a result of the trawl fishery. None of the turtles tagged during this study was recaptured during the study period, but three were recaptured subsequently; one had been resuscitated. Trawl activity was aggregated, and a number of turtles required resuscitation after 60 min tows. Sea turtle conservation regulations are needed for this fishery because the turtle/fishery interaction is great (> 1,000 turtles estimated caught), the proportion caught that is Kemp's ridleys is high (35%), and the physical processes that concentrate the sea turtles on the fishing grounds are operable every winter.

Fedoryako, B.I. 1989. A Comparative Characteristic of Oceanic Fish Assemblages Associated with Floating Debris. Journal of Ichthyology 29: 128-137.

A comparative characteristic of fish assemblages associated with oceanic debris (drifting macrophytes, terrestrial material and epipelagic invertebrates) of tropical ocean zones was made. In the floating debris of the oceanic pelagial 110 species of 35 families were found. About 30% of all fish species were found only in some assemblages. The highest species diversity was associated with macrophytes (75% of all species), and terrestrial material (78% of all species). Representatives of the majority of common species, up to a certain size, occurred in the macrophytes. Fishes associated with drifting macrophytes formed more abundant assemblages than those associated with terrestrial material. Over 50% of species associated with oceanic flotsam occurred commonly in the neritic zone. With the increasing distance of the flotsam from the coast the species diversity decreases and the dominant species change.

Flescher, D.D. 1980. Guide to Some Trawl-Caught Marine Fishes From Maine to Cape Hatteras, North Carolina. NOAA Technical Report NMFS Circular 431. U.S. Department of Commerce, National Oceanic and Atmospheric Administration, National Marine Fisheries Service. 34 p.

Fishes covered are those regularly caught during trawl operations. Similar shaped fishes are grouped together. On each page the written keys are connected by lines to the fish illustrations: consequently, technical terms in the keys are illustrated as they are used. Notes on the size and range of each fish are included.

Flores-Coto, C., and S. M. Warlen. 1993. Spawning time, growth, and recruitment of larval spot, *Leiostomus xanthurus,* into a North Carolina estuary. Fishery Bulletin 91: 8-22.

Larval spot *Leiostomus xanthurus* were sampled weekly as they recruited to the Newport River estuary near Beaufort Inlet, North Carolina to determine their density, and age and size composition. Density data and otolith age distributions were used to calculate the relative contribution of birth-week cohorts to the seasonal recruitment of spot larvae. The protracted 1987-88 spawning season extended from mid-October to mid-March, with 90% in a 2-month period beginning mid-November. Larvae were recruited to the estuary over 5 months at a mean age of 82 d and mean standard length of 17.2 mm. Smaller, younger larvae generally immigrated to the estuary early (December-January) and late (late April), while larger, older larvae immigrated during the interim peak recruitment period (February to mid-April). In any recruitment week, larvae were from 2-10 birthweek cohorts, but recruitment was strongly influenced by the number of larvae of the dominant cohorts.

Larval spot were also sampled in the ocean between Cape Fear and Oregon Inlet off North Carolina to determine their distribution, abundance, and size and age composition. Age and size of larvae were inversely related to distance from shore. Highest densities of larvae were generally found outside the 30 m isobath. Distribution data supported the hypothesis that spot spawned south of Cape Hatteras on the outer continental shelf contribute to recruitment in Chesapeake Bay. A Kolmogorov-Smirnov test did not demonstrate a significant difference between birthdate distributions for ocean and estuarine larvae. This implied that mortality was not age- specific for larvae collected at different times. A Laird-Gompertz growth equation fit to age and size data for larvae collected in the ocean and estuary predicted that they grew from 1.2 mm at hatching to 16.1 mm in 80 d.

Fogt, J. 1992. Yellowfin and bigeye: the ups and downs of Mid-Atlantic fishing. Sport Fishing. June/July: 68-75.

*This article describes sport fishing for yellowfin and bigeye tunas in the mid Atlantic area from off Maryland to middle North Carolina. Information on distributions in relation to temperatures and seasons is provided. Most of the article is about fishing techniques. "The Point" is specifically mentioned as a productive fishing area off NC.

George, R.Y., and A.W. Hulbert (eds.). 1989. North Carolina Coastal Symposium. National Undersea Research Program, NOAA. Rockville, MD. 582 p.

*This is a multidisciplinary marine scientific proceedings, with frequent reference to the North Carolina coastal oceanography. Two studies (also cited individually) include maps with study plots (p. 283; reef site) or migratory movements (p. 309; sea turtles) in the project study area. Zoogeography and ecology of fishes inhabiting North Carolina's marine waters to depths of 600 meters are included. The transcript from a speaker representing Outer Continental Shelf (p. 549) mentions off-shore oil drilling off North Carolina coast and mid-Atlantic region but does not refer to a specific site.

Gettleson, D.A. 1992. Results of a Benthic Visual Survey Within the Manteo Block 467. pp. 159-168. *In*: U.S. Department of the Interior, Minerals Management Service. Proceedings of the Fourth Atlantic OCS Region Information Transfer Meeting, September 1991. U.S. Department of the Interior, Minerals Management Service. Herndon, VA.

The Fourth Atlantic Outer Continental Shelf (OCS) Regional Information Transfer Meeting (ITM) was held on 24-25 September 1991, in Wilmington, NC. The focus of the meeting was on the OCS off North Carolina, specifically on activities related to a proposed exploratory well for oil and gas by Mobil on Block 467 a site 40 miles off the coast of North Carolina. The area of industry interest is known as the Manteo Prospect, while the activities surrounding the proposed drilling are referred to collectively as the Manteo Project. The wildcat wellsite is in 2,690 ft. (857 m) of water near the edge of the Gulf Stream. It is also near a fishing ground known locally as "The Point." The area is believed

to be gas prone rather than oil prone. The estimated size of the resource could be as high as 5 trillion cubic feet of gas.

The purpose of the meeting was to exchange information on the leasing background, legislative activities, scientific results, and socioeconomic studies. Legislative-related reports include descriptions of the Oil Pollution Act of 1990, the Outer Banks Protection Act, the Environmental Studies Review Panel, and the North Carolina Physical Oceanography Panel. Reports of studies on marine life include benthic diatoms, benthic fauna, pelagic seabirds, sea turtles, and right whales. One report describes the use of airships (blimps) for ocean research a capability relevant to North Carolina because of the east coast airship facility is located in the state. Local marine science facilities described include NOAA's National Undersea Research Center at the University of North Carolina at Wilmington (NURC/UNCW) and the national marine Fisheries Service laboratory in Beaufort.

Developments in oil spill cleanup technology and capabilities are described by both the Coast Guard and the industry. A socioeconomic report describes the effects of the oil and gas activities on the tourist industry. Lastly, research on the restoration of salt marshes indicates that rehabilitation of an area is possible when development or an accident has occurred. While the emphasis of the meeting was on oil and gas, two reports described the results of projects related to offshore sand mining. The appendix lists the names and addresses of speakers. Individual chapters are cited individually when appropriate.

*This summary describes the results of a video- and still-camera photodocumentation survey conducted from 9-24 July 1989 in the Manteo Area Block 467 (Figure 37). Block 467 is located along a steep, highly irregular portion of the continental slope on the northern fringe of the Hatteras canyon system. The purpose of this survey was to document topographical features, substrate types, and associated biota around a proposed well and anchor locations in block 467 (figure 38). Water depths within the sites surveyed ranged from 299 to 1,393 m (980-4,570 ft). Because of the water depth and the highly irregular topography within the survey area, a deepwater remotely operated vehicle (ROV) was used to obtain the survey data. Live bottom site characterization (invertebrates and fish present) is described.

Gillikin, J.W., Jr., L.H. Bedsole Jr., and B.F. Holland Jr. 1980a. RV Dan Moore Cruise Report No. 39: Offshore Anadromous Fish Investigations from Cape Lookout to Chesapeake Bay Entrance. North Carolina Division of Marine Fisheries, Department of Natural Resources and Community Development. Morehead City, NC.

*From 17-26 March 1980 the RV Dan Moore reassumed its investigation of offshore stocks of anadromous fishes (river herring, shad, striped bass, and sturgeon) east of Cape Lookout shoals to the Chesapeake Bay entrance. This was the first segment of a federally funded anadromous study. Depths ranged from 15 to 20 fathoms.

Gillikin, J.W., Jr., J.V. Guthrie, and B.F. Holland Jr. 1980b. RV Dan Moore Cruise Report No. 45: A summary of three cruises for summer flounder (*Paralichthys dentatus*) and other finfinsh from Ocracoke Inlet, NC to Chincoteague Inlet, VA. North Carolina Division of Marine Fisheries, Department of Natural Resources and Community Development. Morehead City, NC.

*The objectives of the RV Dan Moore October, November, and December 1980 cruises were to investigate oceanic concentrations of summer flounder (*Paralichthys dentatus*) and to obtain catch data on other commercially important species occurring in the study area. In addition, information regarding size composition, ovary maturation of females, and distribution of flounder by month, geographic area, and temperature regimes was gathered at a total of 69 stations. Depths ranged from 7 to 30 fathoms.

—. 1981. RV Dan Moore Cruise Report No. 49: Offshore Anadromous Fish Survey from Ocracoke Inlet to Oregon Inlet, NC. North Carolina Division of Marine Fisheries, Department of Natural Resources and Community Development. Morehead City, NC.

*This report describes anadromous fishery investigation conducted offshore North Carolina from 27 April 1 May, 1981. Target species include river herring, shad, striped bass, and sturgeon. Depths ranged from 5 to 18 fathoms.

Gillikin, J.W., Jr., D.L. Taylor, and B.F. Holland Jr. 1978. RV Dan Moore Cruise Report No. 24: Cape Lookout, NC to Little Machipongo Inlet, VA. North Carolina Division of Marine Fisheries, Department of Natural Resources and Community Development. Morehead City, NC.

*During April 1978 (two cruise segments), the RV Dan Moore completed investigations of anadromous fish stocks (river herring, shad, striped bass and sturgeon) offshore North Carolina and Virginia for the 1978 season. The first segment extended from Cape Hatteras, NC to Little Machipongo Inlet, VA during 11-20 April. The second segment was conducted from Cape Lookout to Cape Hatteras during 24-28 April. Sample stations were along the beach in the vicinity of 15 to 20 fathoms.

—. 1979. RV Dan Moore Cruise Report No. 33: Cape Lookout, NC to Little Machipongo Inlet, VA. North Carolina Division of Marine Fisheries, Department of Natural Resources and Community Development. Morehead City, NC.

*During February and March 1979 the RV Dan Moore continued its investigations of offshore stocks of anadromous fishes (river herring, shad, striped bass and sturgeon) between Cape Lookout, NC and Little Machipongo Inlet, VA. In response to local fishermen and dealers, reports of calico scallop catches were investigated offshore Ocracoke Inlet. Depths were 12 to 14 fathoms.

Goldstein, B. 1986. Bluewater Giants: a fisherman's biology of the largest tuna, the bluefin. Sport Fishing. May: 50-57.

*This is a popular article on bluefin tuna that emphasizes biology and life history. Taxonomy and identification of the tunas are discussed. Areas off Oregon Inlet and Cape Hatteras, NC are mentioned in a description of migrations and distributions. Status of the fishery is reviewed.

Grosslein, M.D., and T.R. Azarovitz. 1982. Fish Distribution: MESA New York Bight Atlas Monograph 15. New York Sea Grant Institute. Albany, NY. 182 p.

The Middle Atlantic Bight is a complex ecosystem characterized by rapid latitudinal change in water temperature s and associated fauna. Subtropical and boreal fish fauna overlap in the region from Cape Hatteras to Georges Bank, resulting in a highly diverse fish community with large seasonal fluctuations in distribution. The general ecology of 43 important species of fish and shellfish in the Middle Atlantic Bight is summarized in terms of 1) distribution and seasonal movements, 2) populations size and fisheries, 3) reproduction-growth-life span, 4) feeding interrelationships, and 50 environmental sensitivity to pollutants and natural environmental factors. Most species found in the Bight also spawn there; thus environmental conditions and water quality in the Bight control the reproductive success of the populations occurring there. The geographic and seasonal distribution of spawning in the Bight is described for major species through the distribution of their larvae, the life stage believed to be most vulnerable to natural environmental changes and pollution.

The monograph concludes with an examination of the relative importance of natural environmental factors versus man's impacts in controlling fish abundance. Population declines and reduced productivity due to pollution have been demonstrated for both shellfish and fishes although chiefly in inshore-waters; as yet there is no clear evidence of major impact of pollution on populations in offshore waters but there is concern about possible undetected impacts and potential future effects because of growing pressure for substantially increased ocean dumping. Declines in biomass of many populations clearly have been related to excessive fishing pressure in recent years, and there will be a continuing need for some control over fishing mortality rates if we are to achieve optimum yields from our fishery resources. However, so far it appears that natural mortality factors operating in the first year of life exert the greatest control over annual fluctuations in fish populations.

Gudger, E.W. 1932. The abundance of the dolphin, Coryphaena hippurus, on the North Carolina coast. Journal of the Mitchell Scientific Society. May: 237-244.

*The paper reviews the abundance and distribution of dolphin off NC, especially around the Cape Hatteras area. Because dolphin eat flying fishes, the relationship between dolphin occurrence and flying fish distribution is discussed.

Guthrie, J.V., B.F. Holland Jr., and J.W. Gillikin Jr. 1980. RV Dan Moore Cruise Report No. 44: An offshore reconnaissance of summer flounder *(Paralichthys dentatus)* and other finfish from Ocracoke Inlet, NC to Chincoteague Inlet, VA. North Carolina Division of Marine Fisheries, Department of Natural Resources and Community Development. Morehead City, NC.

*The objectives of the RV Dan Moore October 1980 cruise were to investigate oceanic concentrations of summer flounder (*Paralichthys dentatus*) and to obtain catch data on other commercially important species occurring in the study area. In addition, information regarding size composition, ovary maturation of females, and distribution of flounder by geographical area, and temperature regimes was gathered at a total of 23 randomly selected stations.

—. 1981. RV Dan Moore Cruise Report No. 47: Segment I: Offshore Anadromous Fish Survey from Cape Lookout to Chesapeake Bay; Segment II: Reconnaissance of Calico Scallops, *Argopecten gibbus,* on the Traditional Scallop Grounds East of Cape Lookout Shoals. North Carolina Division of Marine Fisheries, Department of Natural Resources and Community Development. Morehead City, NC.

*Segment I of this report describes anadromous fishery investigation conducted offshore North Carolina and Virginia from 16 25 March, 1981. Target species include river herring, shad, striped bass, and sturgeon. Segment II of this report is a reconnaissance of Calico Scallops, *Argopecten gibbus*, during February 1981. Depths ranged from 5 to 19 fathoms.

Hamm, D.C. and B.M. Slater. 1979. Survey of the recreational billfish and shark fisheries, May 1, 1977 to April 30, 1978. NOAA, National Marine Fisheries Service, Southeast Fisheries Center. NOAA Technical Memorandum NMFS-SEFC-5. Miami, FL. 168 p.

*(Modified from the Executive Summary) The Technical and Information Management Services (TIMS) of the Southeast Fisheries Center, National Marine Fisheries Service (NMFS) designed and conducted a survey to estimate the number of billfish caught by the recreational fishery in the western North Atlantic Ocean during the 1 year period, May 1, 1977 to April 30, 1978. The survey assumed that all fishing done in these waters by recreational fishermen would be done from boats 20-65 feet long (except Florida where 18 and 19 foot boats were included) and registered in an Atlantic or Gulf of Mexico coastal state, Puerto Rico, the U.S. Virgin Islands, or with the Coast Guard as a documented vessel. Whenever possible, boats were eliminated from the population based on propulsion and use codes as reported in the boat registration files. A sample of 56,241 boats was selected by systematic random sampling from a stratified population of 389,930 boats.

Questionnaires requesting billfish and shark catch and effort information were sent to the selected 56,241 registered boat owners on June 8, 1978. Approximately 3 weeks after the first mailing, a second mailing of about 33,200 questionnaires was sent to those people not responding to the first mailing. In August, telephone interviews were conducted with a subsample of the nonrespondents to the mail questionnaire.

Hare, J.A. and R.K. Cowen. 1996. Transport mechanisms of larval and pelagic juvenile bluefish (*Pomatomus saltatrix*) from South Atlantic Bight spawning grounds to Middle Atlantic Bight nursery habitats. Limnology and Oceanography 41(6): 1264-1280.

In this study we examined the mechanisms by which *Pomatomus saltatrix* (Pisces: Pomatomidae) larvae and pelagic juveniles are transported from South Atlantic Bight spawning grounds to Middle Atlantic Bight estuarine nursery habitats. Data on larval and pelagic juvenile distributions, estuarine juvenile recruitment, hydrography, wind speed and direction and satellite-derived, sea surface temperature were used to examine potential larval transport mechanisms. On the basis of these analyses, a scenario for northward transport of *P. saltatrix* was developed. Gulf Stream-associated flow moves *P. saltatrix* larvae northeastward from their South Atlantic Bight spawning grounds. Larval transport from the Gulf Stream to the Middle Atlantic Bight shelf edge occurs in warm-core ring streamers, but some more developed individuals may swim across. Finally, *P. saltatrix* pelagic juveniles actively swim across the Middle Atlantic Bight shelf, a behavior initiated when the surface shelf-slope temperature front dissipates in late spring. This scenario predicts that the number of South Atlantic Bight-spawned P. saltatrix juveniles entering estuaries (i.e. recruitment) is determined in part by warm-core ring streamer activity. The timing of recruitment, however, is determined almost entirely by the timing of the dissipation of the surface shelf-slope temperature front.

Hogans, W.E., and K.J. Sulak. 1992. *Diocus lycenchelus*, New Species (Copepoda: Chodracanthidae) Parasitic on the Eelpout, *Lycenchelys verrillii* (Zoarcidae), from the Hatteras Slope of the Northwest Atlantic Ocean. Bulletin of Marine Science 51(3): 301-308.

A new species of parasitic copepod, *Diocus lycenchelus,* is described from the demersal zoarcid fish *Lycenchelys verrillii* caught off Cape Hatteras, U.S.A. The new species differs from its congeners in the shape of the cephalothorax, trunk (ventrolateral processes), fine structure of appendages (mandible, second maxilla, first thoracic leg) and site of infection (the nares). A comparison of the morphology of *D. lycenchelus* n. sp. is made with that of the other four recognized species of *Diocus* (*D. frigidus, D. gobinus, D. semilunaris, and D. sadoensis*).

Holland, B.F., and A.B. Powell. 1975. Section II: Anadromous Fisheries Research Program, Northern Coastal Region — Offshore North Carolina. Project AFCS-8, Job 3. North Carolina Division of Marine Fisheries, Department of Natural Resources and Community Development. Morehead City, NC. 62 p.

*During the period 1 November 1972 through 30 June 1973 sampling for anadromous fishes was conducted aboard the RV Dan Moore from Cape Lookout, NC to Chesapeake Bay entrance, VA. Unsuccessful capture of alosids (*Alosa aestivalis, A. mediocris, A. pseudoharengus, and A. sapidissima*) by traditional gear (Yankee No. 36 and 41 nets, midwater trawl) resulted in the design of an efficient modified wing trawl.

All anadromous fishes were found in depths ≤ 36.6 m. Yearly differences in the depth distribution of blueback herring (*A. aestivalis*), alewife (*A. pseudoharengus*), and American shad (*A. sapidissima*) were observed; however, no correlation with water temperature was evident. Anadromous fishes were captured from November through May. Maximum concentrations were found between Cape Hatteras and Chesapeake Bay. River herring (*A. aestivalis* and *A. pseudoharengus)* were found in maximum concentration from February through April. Striped bass (*Morone saxatilis*) were captured from November through April; Atlantic sturgeon (*Acipenser oxyrhincus*) from November through May. A notable decrease in catches of river herring and American shad from the years 1972-73 to 1973-74 was apparent. When years were combined, 11,233 blueback herring, 2,244 alewife, 40 American shad, 4 hickory shad, 49 sturgeon were tagged and released. Negative tagging results suggested that, at least, the tagging of river herring may not be feasible.

Recruitment of striped bass to the offshore stock appeared to occur during their sixth year. Age groups 6-9 appeared dominant. Male striped bass were rarely captured. Notably, absent from alewife populations were age groups 3 and 4; however, 2-year old alewife were common. The modal age group was represented by 5-year olds. No significant differences between alewife sex ratios were observed. Five and 6-year old blueback herring were the predominant modal age group. Yearlings and 3-year old fish were abundant during the years 1973-74; whereas, 2-year and 3-year olds were the dominant younger fish encountered during 1972-73. Males were found at a significantly higher ratio than females.

Alewife appeared to initiate gonad development earlier in the season than blueback herring. Both species had more advanced ovaries during the 1973-74 season; a time when relatively warmer water temperatures were observed. Size at sexual maturation for female alewife and blueback herring was about 210 mm (FL) and 200 mm (FL), respectively. Analysis of spawning marks on river herring scales showed that the majority of male blueback herring commenced spawning at age IV; whereas, the majority of females did not begin spawning until age V. Most alewife (males and females) spawned at age IV.

Foreign fishing activity during this period appeared to be negligible off North Carolina.

Holland, B.F., A. Powell, and J. Gillikin. 1975a. RV Dan Moore Cruise Report No. 1: Cape Hatteras, NC to SC State Line. North Carolina Division of Marine Fisheries, Department of Natural Resources and Community Development. Morehead City, NC.

*The following RV Dan Moore monthly cruise report presents catch data which may be of use to commercial fishermen and marine fishery scientists. This represents the first cruise report of this nature. The purpose of this October 1974 cruise was to investigate oceanic concentrations of the southern flounder (*Paralichthys lethostigma*). This flounder does not occur in the traditional winter-trawl-fishery (the summer flounder or fluke, *P. dentatus*, is the sole contributor to that fishery). Surveys both along the beach and the 10 fathom curve (where bottom allowed) from Cape Hatteras Bight to South Carolina failed to locate this species. The majority of flounder captured were summer flounder.

Holland, B.F., and G.F. Yelverton. 1973. Distribution and Biological Studies of Anadromous Fishes Offshore North Carolina. Special Scientific Report No. 24. In conjunction with NOAA, National Marine Fisheries Service, Under Federal Aid Project No. AFC-5-3. Division of Commercial and Sports Fisheries; North Carolina Department of Natural and Economic Resources. Morehead City, NC.

During the period 1 February 1968 to 1 July 1971, the R/V Dan Moore occupied 1,038 trawl stations from Cape Romain, South Carolina, to Cape Charles, Virginia, in depths of 3 to 300 fathoms. A total of 9,734 anadromous fishes was collected. Striped bass, (*Morone saxatilis*), blueback herring (*Alosa aestivalis*), and a few hickory shad (*Alosa mediocris*) were found between Cape Lookout and the North Carolina/Virginia border. American shad (*Alosa sapidissima*) and alewife (*Alosa pseudoharengus*) were taken from Hatteras Inlet and from Wimble Shoals, North Carolina, to Cape Charles, Virginia. Two species of sturgeon, *Acipenser oxyrhyncus* and *Acipenser brevirostrum*, were collected mainly between Cape Lookout and North Carolina/Virginia border. Definite seasonal differences in abundance were noted in the ocean off North Carolina. Anadromous fishes were most abundant from December through March. Few anadromous fishes were collected in depths of more than 20 fathoms. Scale analyses of 290 striped bass, 134 American shad, 76 blueback herring and 50 alewife indicated these fish ranged from 2 to 15, 2 to 11, 2 to 8, and 4 to 8 years old respectively. Growth and size relationships were also determined. The peak annulus formation for striped bass, probably occurs in early December. A total of 3,174 anadromous fishes was tagged. As of November 1971, no tags had been returned from any of the 1,204 clupeids tagged. Tag returns from the 187 tagged Atlantic sturgeon indicated a seasonal migration southward during November-January and northward after January. A total of 1,752 striped bass was tagged. As of 1 November 1971, 197 tags had been returned. Tag returns indicated that striped bass overwintering off the North Carolina coast enter Pamlico and Albemarle Sounds, and move northward along the Atlantic coast to Maine during the spring and summer. An annual fishing mortality rate of 35 percent for striped class was projected from the 3.6 percent mean monthly rate. Stomach analysis indicated that striped bass remain active and opportunistic feeders during the winter. Adult American shad eat fish, sometimes to the extent they can be considered a major food item. Juvenile American shad feed occasionally on anchovies. The mean fecundity of 35 striped bass was 2,462,372. The mean fecundity of 43 American shad was 281,137. Examination of the gonads of striped bass, American shad, blueback herring, alewife revealed a predominance of striped bass, American shad, alewife and male blueback herring in the ocean off North Carolina. Sampling among foreign fishing vessels revealed that the east Germans and others were taking anadromous fishes off the North Carolina coast. Offshore and Chowan River samples of blueback herring and alewife were compared, and similarities and differences were noted utilizing age class composition and length-weight relationships.

Holland, B.F., Jr., J.W. Gillikin Jr., and L.H. Bedsole Jr. 1980a. RV Dan Moore Cruise Report No. 40: Offshore Anadromous Fish Investigations from Cape Lookout to Chesapeake Bay Entrance. Division of Commercial and Sports Fisheries; North Carolina Department of Natural and Economic Resources. Morehead City, NC.

*From 21-30 April 1980 the RV Dan Moore reassumed its investigation of offshore stocks of anadromous fishes (river herring, shad, striped bass, and sturgeon) east of Cape Lookout shoals to the Chesapeake Bay entrance. This was the second leg of a federally funded anadromous project. Depths were 4 to 20 fathoms.

—. 1980b. RV Dan Moore Cruise Report No. 41: Offshore Anadromous Fish Investigations from Cape Lookout to Chesapeake Bay Entrance. Division of Commercial and Sports Fisheries; North Carolina Department of Natural and Economic Resources. Morehead City, NC.

*From 12-21 May 1980 the RV Dan Moore reassumed its investigation of offshore stocks of anadromous fishes (river herring, shad, striped bass, and sturgeon) east of Cape Lookout shoals to the Chesapeake Bay entrance. This was the final cruise of the first year of a three-year federally funded anadromous project. Depths were 4 to 19 fathoms.

Holland, B.F., Jr., J.W. Gillikin Jr., and J.V. Guthrie. 1981a. RV Dan Moore Cruise Report No. 51: Segment I: Calico Scallop Reconnaissance from Ocracoke to New River Inlet, NC (October November 1981); Segment II: Flounder Mesh Selectivity Study (November December 1981). North Carolina Division of Marine Fisheries, Department of Natural Resources and Community Development. Morehead City, NC.

*Segment I of this report describes Calico Scallop Reconnaissance from Ocracoke to New River Inlet, NC (October-November 1981). Segment II of this report describes Flounder Mesh Selectivity Study (November-December 1981) off North Carolina's coast. Depths ranged from 11 to 14 fathoms.

—. 1981b. RV Dan Moore Cruise Report No. 46: Segment I: Offshore Anadromous Fish Survey from Cape Lookout to Chesapeake Bay; Segment II: Reconnaissance of Calico Scallops, *Argopecten gibbus*, on the Traditional Scallop Grounds East of Cape Lookout Shoals. North Carolina Division of Marine Fisheries, Department of Natural Resources and Community Development. Morehead City, NC.

*Segment I of this report describes anadromous fishery investigation conducted offshore North Carolina and Virginia from January-April 1981. Target species include river herring, shad, striped bass, and sturgeon. Segment II of this report is a reconnaissance of Calico Scallops, *Argopecten gibbus*, during August 1980. Depths were 5 to 20 fathoms.

—. 1981c. RV Dan Moore Cruise Report No. 48: Offshore Anadromous Fish Survey from Cape Lookout to Chesapeake Bay Entrance. North Carolina Division of Marine Fisheries, Department of Natural Resources and Community Development. Morehead City, NC.

*This report describes anadromous fishery investigation conducted offshore North Carolina and Virginia from 16-25 March 1981. Target species include river herring, shad, striped bass, and sturgeon. Depths ranged from 5 to 17 fathoms.

Holland, B.F., Jr., J.W. Gillikin Jr., and D.L. Taylor. 1978a. RV Dan Moore Cruise Report No. 23: Cape Lookout, NC to Little Machipongo Inlet, VA. North Carolina Division of Marine Fisheries, Department of Natural Resources and Community Development. Morehead City, NC.

*The RV Dan Moore investigated anadromous fish stocks (river herring, shad, striped bass and sturgeon) from Cape Lookout, NC to Little Machipongo Inlet, VA. During the March 1978 cruise, sample stations were along the beach in the vicinity of 15 to 20 fathoms.

—. 1978b. RV Dan Moore Cruise Report No. 29: Initiation of Raleigh Bay Trawl Survey. North Carolina Division of Marine Fisheries, Department of Natural Resources and Community Development. Morehead City, NC.

*The RV Dan Moore initiated a preliminary trawl survey of Raleigh Bay, NC in October. This survey is a direct extension of the Onslow Bay trawl survey which began in October 1977 and was completed this past August (see cruise report nos. 18, 20. 25, and 27). The RV Dan Moore had previously trawled extensively in Raleigh Bay during the anadromous fish (river herring, shad, striped bass and sturgeon) and summer flounder projects. Previous efforts were mainly concentrated from the beach to the 20 fathom contour. The main objectives of the current survey were: 1) To define and designate areas of trawlable bottom, 2) To define and designate areas where pots and/or traps should be used rather than trawls, 3) To define and designate those areas where hook and line may be the only feasible method of fishing.

—. 1979a. RV Dan Moore Cruise Report No. 32: Cape Lookout, NC to Little Machipongo Inlet, VA. North Carolina Division of Marine Fisheries, Department of Natural Resources and Community Development. Morehead City, NC.

*From January-April 1979, the emphasis of the RV Dan Moore cruises will be on investigations of offshore stocks of anadromous fishes (river herring, shad, striped bass and sturgeon) offshore North Carolina and Virginia. Depths ranged from 5 to 15 fathoms.

—. 1979b. RV Dan Moore Cruise Report No. 37: Rock Shrimp (*Sicyonia brevirostris*) Investigations in Long, Onslow and Raleigh Bay, NC. North Carolina Division of Marine Fisheries, Department of Natural Resources and Community Development. Morehead City, NC.

*From 15-24 October and from 29 October to 1 November 1979, the RV Dan Moore conducted trawling operations in Long, Onslow and Raleigh bays, NC in search of Rock Shrimp (*Sicyonia brevirostris*). The primary objectives of this cruise were to: 1) Investigate the relative abundance, distribution and size composition of rock shrimp, 2) To determine if rock shrimp occur in sufficient quantities in Long, Onslow and Raleigh bays (offshore NC) to support a potential commercial fishery. Depths on the first segment (20-55 miles south of Southport, NC and from 10-35 miles south of Cape Lookout) were 12-31 fathoms. Depths sampled on the second segment (east of Cape Lookout and to 10-15 miles south of Cape Hatteras) were 17-30 fathoms.

Holland, B.F., Jr., S.G. Keefe, and J.A. Vaughn. 1975b. RV Dan Moore Cruise Report No. 9: Cape Hatteras, NC to Shallotte Inlet, NC. North Carolina Division of Marine Fisheries, Department of Natural Resources and Community Development. Morehead City, NC.

*The purpose of the RV Dan Moore November 1975 cruise was to investigate oceanic concentrations of the southern flounder (*Paralichthys lethostigma*) and to obtain catch data which may be of use to commercial fishermen and marine fishery scientists. Southern flounder does not occur in the traditional winter trawl-fishery (comprised solely by summer flounder, *Paralichthys dentatus*), but is present during October. This suggests this flounder was in the process of making a spawning and overwintering run to oceanic waters. This was based on knowledge of the summer flounder. A wing trawl was used in the vicinity of the 10 fathom contour.

—. 1976. RV Dan Moore Cruise Report No. 12: Cape Lookout, NC to Little Machipongo Inlet, VA. North Carolina Division of Marine Fisheries, Department of Natural Resources and Community Development. Morehead City, NC.

*During January 1976 to June 1976 the emphasis of the RV Dan Moore will be on investigations of the offshore stocks of anadromous fishes (river herring, shad, striped bass and sturgeon) in North Carolina and Virginia. A wing trawl, selective for pelagic fishes such as herring, trout and mackerel was used in the vicinity of 10-15 fathom contours.

Hoss, D.E. 1992. Research at the Beaufort Laboratory. pp. 51-54. *In*: Department of the Interior, Minerals Management Service. Proceedings of the Fourth Atlantic OCS Region Information Transfer Meeting, September 1991. U.S. Department of the Interior, Minerals Management Service. Herndon, VA.

The Fourth Atlantic Outer Continental Shelf (OCS) Regional Information Transfer Meeting (ITM) was held on 24-25 September 1991 in Wilmington, NC. The focus of the meeting was on the OCS off North Carolina, specifically on activities related to a proposed exploratory well for oil and gas by Mobil on Block 467 a site 40 miles off the coast of North Carolina. The area of industry interest is known as the Manteo Prospect, while the activities surrounding the proposed drilling are referred to collectively as the Manteo Project. The wildcat wellsite is in 2,690 ft. (857 m) of water near the edge of the Gulf Stream. It is also near a fishing ground known locally as "The Point." The area is believed to be gas prone rather than oil prone. The estimated size of the resource could be as high as 5 trillion cubic feet of gas.

The purpose of the meeting was to exchange information on the leasing background, legislative activities, scientific results, and socioeconomic studies. Legislative-related reports include descriptions of the Oil Pollution Act of 1990, the Outer Banks Protection Act, the Environmental Studies Review Panel, and the North Carolina Physical Oceanography Panel. Reports of studies on marine life include benthic diatoms, benthic fauna, pelagic seabirds, sea turtles, and right whales. One report describes the use of airships (blimps) for ocean research a capability relevant to North Carolina because of the east coast airship facility is located in the state. Local marine science facilities described include NOAA's National Undersea Research Center at the University of North Carolina at Wilmington (NURC/UNCW) and the National Marine Fisheries Service laboratory in Beaufort.

Developments in oil spill cleanup technology and capabilities are described by both the Coast Guard and the industry. A socioeconomic report describes the effects of the oil and gas activities on the tourist industry. Lastly, research on the restoration of salt marshes indicates that rehabilitation of an area is possible when development or an accident has occurred. While the emphasis of the meeting was on oil and gas, two reports described the results of projects related to offshore sand mining. The appendix lists the names and addresses of speakers. Individual chapters are cited individually when appropriate.

*This section describes the ongoing research at the National Marine Fisheries Laboratory in Beaufort, NC. A description of North Carolina marine reptile, marine mammal, coastal, and fishery research is included.

Johnson, H.B., D.W. Crocker, B.F. Holland, J.W. Gilliken, D.L. Taylor, M.W. Street, J.G. Loesch Jr., W.H. Kriete, and J.G. Travelstead. 1978. Biology and Management of Mid-Atlantic Anadromous Fishes Under Extended Jurisdiction: Annual Report, Anadromous Fish Project 1978. North Carolina — Virginia AFCS 9-2. NC Department of Natural Resources and Community Development, Division of Marine Fisheries. Morehead City, NC. Virginia Institute of Marine Science. Gloucester Point, VA. 175 p.

*This is a joint presentation by North Carolina Division of Marine Fisheries (Part I) and the Virginia Institute of Marine Science, Department of Ichthyology (Part II). It is for the period of 1 October 1976 to 30 September 1979 and is the completion report for the P.L. 89-304 project "Biology and Management of Mid-Atlantic Anadromous Fishes Under Extended Jurisdiction." Species of concern are: alewife (*Alosa pseudoharengus*), blueback herring (*Alosa aestivalis*), hickory shad (*Alosa mediocris*), American shad (*Alosa sapidissima*), striped bass (*Morone saxatilis*), Atlantic sturgeon (*Acipenser oxyrhyncus*), shortnose sturgeon (*Acipenser brevirostrum).*

Johnson, H.B., S.E. Winslow, D.W. Crocker Jr., B.F. Holland, J.W. Gillikin, D.L. Taylor, J.G. Loesch Jr., W.H. Kriete, J.G. Travelstead, E.J. Foell, and M.A. Hennigar. 1981. Biology and Management of Mid-Atlantic Anadromous Fishes Under Extended Jurisdiction: Completion Report, Anadromous Fish Project 1977-1979. Special Scientific Report No. 36. NC Department of Natural Resources and Community Development, Division of Marine Fisheries. Morehead City, NC. Virginia Institute of Marine Science. Gloucester Point, VA. 204 p.

*This is a cooperative study (between Virginia Institute of Marine Science and NC Division of Marine Fisheries) of life history characteristics of anadromous fishes of North Carolina and Virginia. Mentioned are: striped bass (*Morone saxatilis*), blueback herring (*Alosa aestivalis*), hickory shad (*Alosa mediocris*), American shad (*Alosa sapidissima*), alewife (*Alosa pseudoharengus*), sturgeon (*Acipenser oxyrhyncus),* shortnose sturgeon (*Acipenser brevirostrum).* Kepone concentration in tissues is also mentioned. Estimates of total landings by gear type are obtained from catch-per-unit-of effort (c/f) and the total units of gear fished. The c/f and the estimated landings can also be used as a relative indicator (index) of stock abundance by a simple comparison with such estimates in prior years.

Johnson, A.G., W.A. Fable Jr., M.L. Williams, and L.E. Barger. 1983. Age, growth, and mortality of king mackerel, Scomberomorus cavalla, from the southeastern United States. Fishery Bulletin 81(1): 97-106.

Age, growth, and mortality of king mackerel, Scomberomorus cavalla, from the southeastern United States were studied. Otoliths from 1,449 fish were used to estimate age composition, growth rates, and mortality rates of this species.

Age composition varied between locations (Texas, Louisiana, Florida, South Carolina, and North Carolina). The majority of older fish were found in Louisiana waters. The oldest females were 14+ years old and the oldest males were 9+ years old. Compensatory growth was found in both sexes. The von Bertalanffy growth equations were as follows: Males (all areas) $l_t = 965(1-e^{-0.28(t+1.17)})$; females from Louisiana $l_t = 1,529(1 — e^{-0.14(t+2.08)})$; and females (excluding Louisiana) $l_t = 1,067(1 — e^{-0.29(t+0.97)})$ where l = fork length (mm) and t = years. The mean annual mortality rate determined by six methods of analysis ranged from 0.32 to 0.42. The length-weight relations of king mackerel were for males: $W = 0.8064 \times 10^{-5}L^{2.9928}$; for females: $W = 0.8801 \times 10^{-5}L^{2.9827}$, where W = weight in grams and L = fork length in millimeters.

Keefe, S.G., B.F. Holland Jr., and J.W. Gillikin Jr. 1977. RV Dan Moore Cruise Report No. 16: Cape Lookout, NC to Little Machipongo Inlet, VA. North Carolina Division of Marine Fisheries, Department of Natural Resources and Community Development. Morehead City, NC.

*From 11 April to 2 June 1977 sampling to monitor the stocks of anadromous fishes (river herring, shad, striped bass and sturgeon) was conducted offshore North Carolina and Virginia during three cruise segments (Segment 1: 11-18 April; Segment 2: 25-30 April; and Segment 3: 16-31 May). A wing trawl, selective for herring, bluefish, and mackerel was used.

—. 1978. RV Dan Moore Cruise Report No. 22: Cape Lookout, NC to Little Machipongo Inlet, VA. North Carolina Division of Marine Fisheries, Department of Natural Resources and Community Development. Morehead City, NC.

*From February-April 1978, the emphasis of the RV Dan Moore cruises was on investigations of anadromous fishes (river herring, shad, striped bass and sturgeon) from Cape Lookout, NC to Little Machipongo Inlet, VA. Sample stations were along the beach in the vicinity of 15-20 fathoms. Sampling was extended off the Chesapeake Bay entrance to 21 fathoms.

Keefe, S.G., J.A. Vaughn, and B.F. Holland Jr. 1975. RV Dan Moore Cruise Report No. 10: Cape Lookout, NC to Little Machipongo Inlet, VA. North Carolina Division of Marine Fisheries, Department of Natural Resources and Community Development. Morehead City, NC.

*The purpose of the RV Dan Moore November 1975 cruise was to investigate oceanic concentrations of flounder (*Paralichthys* spp.) and to obtain catch data which may be of use to commercial fishermen and marine fishery scientists. In addition, information regarding size composition, ovary maturation of females, and distribution of the flounder stock by geographical area and temperature regimes was gathered. A wing trawl was used in the vicinity of 10-15 fathom contours.

—. 1976. RV Dan Moore Cruise Report No. 13: Cape Lookout, NC to Little Machipongo Inlet, VA. North Carolina Division of Marine Fisheries, Department of Natural Resources and Community Development. Morehead City, NC.

*The primary objective of the February 1976 cruise was to continue monitoring the offshore stocks of anadromous fishes (alewife, blueback herring, American and hickory shad, striped bass and sturgeon) in North Carolina and Virginia. A wing trawl, selective for pelagic fishes such as herring, trout and mackerel was used in the vicinity of 10-15 fathom contours.

Kendall, A.W., Jr. 1972. Description of black sea bass, *Centropristis striata* (Linneaus), larvae and their occurrences north of Cape Lookout, NC, in 1966. Fishery Bulletin 70(4): 1243-1259.

Larvae of black sea bass collected during RV Dolphin ichthyoplankton surveys of the Middle Atlantic continental shelf are described. Development of most meristic characters occurs between 6 and 10 mm standard length. The larvae are identified by characteristic ventral pigment patterns, body shape, meristic counts, and lack of extensive armature. The 147 larvae were taken during cruises from June to November 1966, from 4 to 82 km from shore. They were found in tows from the surface to 33 m in water varying in surface temperature from 14.3 to 28.0° C and surface salinity from 30.3 to 34.6 $^0/_{00}$.

Kendall, A.W., Jr., and J.W. Reintjes. 1975. Geographic and hydrographic distribution of Atlantic menhaden eggs and larvae along the middle Atlantic Coast from RV Dolphin Cruises: 1965-66. Fishery Bulletin 73(2): 317-335.

Atlantic menhaden, *Brevoortia tyrannus*, eggs and larvae were collected during eight ichthyoplankton cruises of the RV Dolphin from December 1965 to December 1966. On each cruise tows were made with a Gulf V plankton net at stations along 14 transects from the coast to the edge of the continental shelf of Martha's Vineyard, MA, to Cape Lookout, NC. Larvae resulting from a protracted spawning season were taken throughout the year. Eggs were taken over the middle of the shelf in fall. Seasonal shifts in geographic pattern of larvae indicated spawning started in summer off New Jersey and New York, became widespread in the Middle Atlantic Bight in fall, and continued into winter off North Carolina. Larvae were equally distributed in shallow (0-15m) and deep (18-33m) tows during night and day. Larvae occurred over a water temperature range from 0 to 25° C and a salinity range of 29 to 36 $^0/_{00}$. Seasonal distribution of larvae suggests some of the annual variation in year classes may be due to cold-related mortality of larvae entering the middle Atlantic estuaries in the fall.

Kennelly, S.J. 1999. Areas, depths, and times of high discard rates of scup, *Stenotomus chrysops*, during demersal fish trawling off the Northeastern United States. Fishery Bulletin 97: 185-191.

*In the waters of the northeastern United States, many stocks of commercial and recreational species have declined in recent years. Although much of the blame for these declines is ascribed to sustained overfishing, there also has been substantial concern over bycatch and discarding practices in key fisheries of the region, especially those involving demersal trawling. This study describes both commercial and recreational scup (or porgy, *Stenotomus chrysops*) fishery. The impact of overfishing, exploitation of 0-2 year class, incidental bycatch and subsequent discarding from demersal trawlers is discussed.

Kirby-Smith, W.W. 1989a. Biological Production Near the Bottom. p. 25. *In*: Crawford, K. (ed.). Proceedings: 1989 Marine Expo: The Natural Resources Associated with Mobil's Proposed Drill Site. NC Outer Continental Shelf Office, NC Department of Administration. Raleigh, NC.

Satellite photographs show that North Carolina has an incredibly diverse oceanographic setting which, in turn, produces highly diverse communities of fishes and invertebrates. The three bottom types found off the continental shelf of North Carolina include; 1) sand, 2) shell, and 3) rock outcrops. Across the continental shelf, the primary producers that support fisheries include microalgae and macroalgae. The bottom-dwelling microalgae (small microscopic plants) grow, rapidly and are very important to the total productivity of the whole water column. As much as half of the primary productivity on the shelf may be due to this benthic component. The secondary producers on rock outcrops, which include sponges, corals, worms and small arthropods, are a major food source for small fish. From a scientific perspective, the proposed drill site is an exciting area with a high biomass and low diversity. In my opinion, the exploration well itself would have little or no impact on the resources in the area; however, a major find of oil or gas could lead to a tremendous amount of industrial development, which could compete economically with other coastal industries, such as tourism and fisheries.

—. 1989b. The Community of Small Macroinvertebrates Associated with Rock Outcrops in the Continental Shelf of North Carolina. pp. 279-305. *In*: George, R.Y., and A.W. Hulbert (eds.). North Carolina Coastal Symposium. National Undersea Research Program, NOAA. Rockville, MD.

Communities of small benthic organisms associated with rock outcrops on the continental shelf of North Carolina were examined for patterns in community structure related to season and depth. The communities were dominated by polychaetes, amphipods and mollusks. The number of species per 0.5m² ranged from 40 to 214 and the number of individuals from 180 to 1657. Diversity was high with H' values of 4 to 6. Diversity was slightly greater at the middle shelf stations as compared to inner and outer shelf. The number of species and individuals was greatest at all three locations in the spring and fall and least in the winter and summer: a pattern similar to that of temperate coastal plankton. An index of community similarity indicated the presence of cold (winter/spring) and warm (summer/fall) communities at each of the three locations. Moreover at the middle and inner shelf the communities were more related to season (cold and warm) than to location (inner and middle). Outer shelf communities also had a strong seasonal component but were very different when compared with the middle and inner shelf communities. Different sampling gear (grabs versus diver suction) may explain some of the outer shelf uniqueness.

*The site ISO4 location data cited by Kirby-Smith are incorrect. Data cited by Kirby-Smith for site ISO4 resulted from unpublished data collected during a SCUBA dive by S.W. Ross on 18 August 1980. The correct location for this site [SWR -SCUBA-80-20] is 35° 20.7'N; 75° 21.2'W; depth 70-80 feet. Selected fish, invertebrate, and bottom habitat data were collected. These data are unpublished and the site was not visited again (S.W. Ross, pers. comm., 19 November 1999).

Kohler, N.E., J.G. Casey, and P.A. Turner. 1998. NMFS Cooperative shark tagging program, 1962-93: an atlas of shark tag and recapture data. Marine Fisheries Review 60(2): 1-87.

*(Modified from the Introduction) The National Marine Fisheries Service Cooperative Shark Tagging Program (CSTP) is part of continuing research directed to the study of the biology of large Atlantic sharks. The CSTP was initiated in 1962 at the Sandy Hook Laboratory, NJ under the Dept. of Interior's U.S. Fish and Wildlife Service. During the late 1950's and early 1960's, sharks were considered a liability to the economy of resort communities, of little or no commercial value, and a detriment to fishermen in areas where sharks might damage expensive fishing gear or reduce catches of more commercially valuable species.

Several shark attacks along the New Jersey coast at that time gave rise to public concern about a perceived shark menace. In response to that concern, a shark longline survey was conducted in 1961 from Jones Inlet, NY, to Cape Henlopen, DE. When the details of the survey were made public, hundreds of recreational fishermen interested in fishing for sharks as "big game" in the rapidly expanding offshore recreational fisheries offered to assist biologists in their research on sharks. This was the genesis of the CSTP.

This paper broadly summarizes the tagging and recapture (T/R) information from the CSTP for 1962 through 1993. T/R data are presented in an atlas format to provide an overview of the 32 year database and show the extent of the tagging effort, areas of release and recapture, sources of recaptures, and movements of tagged sharks with respect to state boundaries, the 200-mile U.S. Exclusive Economic Zone and waters of other countries.

Langfelder, J., T.B. Curtin, D.N. Hyman, G. Janowitz, J. Maiolo, W. Queen, F.Y. Sorrell, M. Amien, V. Bellis, M. Brinson, G. Davis, C.Y. Lee, C. O'Rear, L. Pearce, C.Y. Peng, S. Riggs, B. Smith, M. Sobsey, and P. Tschetter. 1979. Final Report: Ocean Outfall Wastewater Disposal Feasibility and Planning, Report No. 79-1. Dept. of Marine Science and Engineering, NCSU; Report No. 5, Institute for Coastal and Marine Resources, ECU. 482 p.

*This report follows an EIS format and is cited as a single document. Individual chapters are not stand-alone documents. Major findings of the study were: 1) Construction and operation of a well designed and operated sewage treatment plant that utilizes an ocean outfall and secondary treatment should not adversely affect the water column on fishery resources. Some build up of effluent constituents may occur in the bottom sediments in the immediate vicinity of the diffuser and could result in bottom community changes. 2) Effluent discharge should have essentially no adverse affect on recreational swimming in the areas of the diffuser. Areas now closed to shellfishing in the estuaries could be reopened as a result of reduced pathogen loadings: these pathogens are presently coming from septic tanks and treatment plants that discharge into these waters. 3) Centralized sewer systems will increase land values, allow reduced lot size and stimulate growth. This will lead to change in the population composition and demands for expanded goods and services.

Lee, D.S. 1986b. Seasonal, Thermal, and Zonal Distribution of Ocean Sunfish, *Mola mola* (Linnaeus), off the North Carolina Coast. Brimleyana 12: 75-83.

Most previous information on the ocean sunfish, *Mola mola*, has been derived from beached specimens and contributed little to our understanding of typical distributional patterns or the species. More than 60 encounters with *Mola mola* in North Carolina's offshore waters reveal that this fish is an epipelagic migrant, occurring in shallow water (0 to 40 fathoms in depth) commonly in the spring between mid-march and mid-June. In the fall it has been seen less frequently (mid-October through November), and the species is essentially absent in the winter.

Loesch, J.G., Jr., W.H. Kriete, H.B. Johnson, B.F. Holland, S.G. Keefe, and M.W. Street. 1977. Biology and Management of Mid-Atlantic Anadromous Fishes Under Extended Jurisdiction: Annual Report, Anadromous Fish Project 1977. North Carolina — Virginia AFCS 9-1. Virginia Institute of Marine Science. Gloucester Point, VA. NC Department of Natural Resources and Community Development, Division if Marine Fisheries. Morehead City, NC. 183 p.

*This is a cooperative study (between Virginia Institute of Marine Science and NC Division of Marine Fisheries, Morehead City, NC) of life history characteristics of anadromous fishes of North Carolina and Virginia. Mentioned are: striped bass (*Morone saxatilis*), blueback herring (*Alosa aestivalis*), hickory shad (*Alosa mediocris*), American shad (*Alosa sapidissima*), alewife (*Alosa pseudoharengus*), sturgeon (*Acipenser oxyrhyncus*), sturgeon (*Acipenser brevirostrum*). Kepone concentration in tissues is also mentioned. Estimates of total landings by gear type are obtained from catch-per-unit-of effort (c/f) and the total units of gear fished. The c/f and the estimated landings can also be used as a relative indicator (index) of stock abundance by a simple comparison with such estimates in prior years.

Magnuson, J.J., C.L. Harrington, D.J. Stewart, and G.N. Herbst. 1981. Responses of macrofauna to short-term dynamics of a Gulf Stream front on the continental shelf. pp. 441-448. *In*: Richards, F.R. (ed.). Coastal Upwelling. American Geophysical Union.

Benthic and near-bottom fishes, decapod crustaceans, and echinoderms were sampled in two areas through which a Gulf Stream front moved just north of Cape Hatteras along 75°13′ W longitude in October 1977. We tested the hypothesis that the frontal aggregations resulted from the response of organisms to the front itself rather than to a geographically fixed feature of the region. The front, 8.5° C and 3.5 °/oo wide, was characterized by horizontal gradients of at least 0.5 °C/km and speeds of 30 cm/s. Bottom trawling was conducted day and night in each area (northern and southern) when the front was present and when it was absent. Both areas contained more species and individuals of fish when the front was present. Atlantic croaker, weakfish, and spot left when the front left. Decapods exhibited some response to the front, especially at night. During the day, fewer echinoderms were caught when the front was present — perhaps because the sudden changes in temperature induced burrowing. During the day all three groups were more abundant in the northern than in the southern area in terms of species and individuals. The front itself and more geographically fixed features both influenced distributions.

Marshall, N. 1951. Hydrography of North Carolina waters. pp. 1-76. *In*: Taylor, H.F. (ed.). Survey of Marine Fisheries of North Carolina. University of North Carolina Press. Chapel Hill, NC.

*This paper synthesizes hydrographic data for all of NC's marine waters, including the major estuaries. Offshore bathymetry is provided. Offshore temperature data are provided and the Gulf Stream circulation is discussed. The relationship between hydrography and offshore fisheries is discussed, particularly in the Cape Hatteras area.

McGowan, M.F. and W.J. Richards. 1989. Bluefin tuna, Thunnus thynnus, larvae in the Gulf Stream off the southeastern United States: satellite and shipboard observations of their environment. Fishery Bulletin 87: 615-631.

The primary spawning area of the western Atlantic stock of bluefin tuna is presumed to be in the Gulf of Mexico. However, bluefin tuna larvae were collected in April and May 1985 along the shelf edge from Palm Beach, Florida to Cape Fear, North Carolina and offshore as far as 260 km east of Jacksonville, Florida over the Blake Plateau. Satellite and shipboard sea-temperature data indicate that the larvae over the shelf edge were advected there in meanders of the Gulf Stream. Bluefin larvae previously reported in the Straits of Florida and off Cape Hatteras were also in the Gulf Stream according to retrospective analyses of temperature and salinity data. Based on age-length relationships and current velocity, one small larva was probably spawned north of Miami, Florida while others could have been advected into the Gulf Stream from the eastern Gulf. Spawning by a few unspent migrating adults could also account for some bluefin larvae in this region. The estimated total larvae off the southeastern United States in 1985 could have been produced by 5% of the spawning stock. Bluefin larvae were found within a narrow range of sea surface temperatures and salinities at offshore stations. Preliminary assessment of larval habitat indicates that waters off the southeastern United States are unfavorable for growth and survival of bluefin larvae relative to hypothesized larval retention areas in the Gulf of Mexico.

Minerals Management Service. 1982a. South Atlantic OCS Area Living Marine Resources Study Year II: Final Report Executive Summary. Minerals Management Service contract AA551-CT1-18. Minerals Management Service, Washington, DC.

Live bottom areas are known to be important to commercial and recreational fisheries in the South Atlantic Bight, but biological studies of these areas have been limited. As a result, very little data exists on the structure of invertebrate and fish communities present in these hard-bottom habitats, and information is lacking on what effects offshore oil and gas exploration might have on live-bottom communities. Because more information was needed for recent and upcoming Outer Continental

Shelf (OCS) Lease Sales, the Bureau of Land Management initiated the "South Atlantic OCS Area Living Marine Resources Study." The primary objectives of this study during the first year were to: 1) Characterize the invertebrate and nektonic communities associated with several representative live-bottom areas from Cape Hatteras, NC to Northern Florida and elevate factors which might influence community structure such as depth, latitude, and season (summer vs. winter), 2) Characterize the food habits of selected fish species of commercial and recreational importance, 3) Conduct a limited assessment of bottom topography and substrate type, 4) Evaluate the potential effects of oil- and gas-related activities on live-bottom communities.

Results obtained from the first year sampling program were presented in a 1981 report available through the National Technical Information Service. Objectives of the second-year study were the same as those listed above; however, seasonal sampling was increased to include all seasons. In addition, some study areas were changed to include portions of the shelf not previously studied, while others were sampled during both years to allow assessment of persistence in the distribution patterns observed during the first year. This report summarizes the results and conclusions obtained from the second year (1981) sampling program.

—. 1982b. South Atlantic OCS Area Living Marine Resources Study Year II: Final Report Volume I. Minerals Management Service contract AA551-CT1-18. Minerals Management Service, Washington, DC.

Live bottom areas are known to be important to commercial and recreational fisheries in the South Atlantic Bight, but biological studies of these areas have been limited. As a result, very little data exists on the structure of invertebrate and fish communities present in these hard-bottom habitats, and information is lacking on what effects offshore oil and gas exploration might have on live-bottom communities. Because more information was needed for recent and upcoming Outer Continental Shelf (OCS) Lease Sales, the Bureau of Land Management initiated the "South Atlantic OCS Area Living Marine Resources Study." The primary objectives of this study during the first year were to: 1) Characterize the invertebrate and nektonic communities associated with several representative live-bottom areas from Cape Hatteras, NC to Northern Florida and elevate factors which might influence community structure such as depth, latitude, and season (summer vs. winter), 2) Characterize the food habits of selected fish species of commercial and recreational importance, 3) Conduct a limited assessment of bottom topography and substrate type, 4) Evaluate the potential effects of oil- and gas-related activities on live-bottom communities.

Results obtained from the first year sampling program were presented in a 1981 report available through the National Technical Information Service. Objectives of the second-year study were the same as those listed above; however, seasonal sampling was increased to include all seasons. In addition, some study areas were changed to include portions of the shelf not previously studied, while others were sampled during both years to allow assessment of persistence in the distribution patterns observed during the first year. This report summarizes the results and conclusions obtained from the second year (1981) sampling program.

—. 1982c. South Atlantic OCS Area Living Marine Resources Study Year II: Final Report Volume II. Minerals Management Service contract AA551-CT1-18. Minerals Management Service, Washington, DC.

Live bottom areas are known to be important to commercial and recreational fisheries in the South Atlantic Bight, but biological studies of these areas have been limited. As a result, very little data exists on the structure of invertebrate and fish communities present in these hard-bottom habitats, and information is lacking on what effects offshore oil and gas exploration might have on live-bottom communities. Because more information was needed for recent and upcoming Outer Continental

Shelf (OCS) Lease Sales, the Bureau of Land Management initiated the "South Atlantic OCS Area Living Marine Resources Study." The primary objectives of this study during the first year were to: 1) Characterize the invertebrate and nektonic communities associated with several representative live-bottom areas from Cape Hatteras, NC to Northern Florida and elevate factors which might influence community structure such as depth, latitude, and season (summer vs. winter), 2) Characterize the food habits of selected fish species of commercial and recreational importance, 3) Conduct a limited assessment of bottom topography and substrate type, 4) Evaluate the potential effects of oil- and gas-related activities on live-bottom communities.

Results obtained from the first year sampling program were presented in a 1981 report available through the National Technical Information Service. Objectives of the second-year study were the same as those listed above; however, seasonal sampling was increased to include all seasons. In addition, some study areas were changed to include portions of the shelf not previously studied, while others were sampled during both years to allow assessment of persistence in the distribution patterns observed during the first year. This report summarizes the results and conclusions obtained from the second year (1981) sampling program.

Minkler, R. Unpublished database. Bottom Trawl Surveys 1957-1984. NOAA/NMFS, Southeast Fisheries Center. Pascagoula, FL.

*This is an unpublished fisheries database. Data were collected from 1957 to 1984 by the NOAA/NMFS, Southeast Fisheries Center. The Principal Investigator is listed as Rick Minkler. Select sample locations and related data were computerized as part of the North Carolina SEAMAP Hardbottom data project by Moser et al. (1995). SEAMAP Hardbottom data (sample locations) within the defined project area for The Point were sorted and mapped using ArcView GIS (J. Ott, pers. comm., 15 Nov 99).

Morse, W.W. 1980. Maturity, spawning, and fecundity of Atlantic Croaker, *Micropogonias undulatus*, occurring North of Cape Hatteras, North Carolina. Fishery Bulletin 78 (1): 190-195.

*This is a note describing life history of Atlantic Croaker, *Micropogonias undulatus*, in the Cape Hatteras, NC area.

Moser, M.L., P.J. Austin, and J.B. Bichy. 1997. Effects of mat morphology on large *Sargassum*-associated fishes: observations from a remotely operated vehicle (ROV) and free-floating video camcorders. Attachment 10. *In*: South Atlantic Fishery Management Council. Essential Fish Habitat Workshop # 9: October 7 — 8, 1997 Pelagic Habitat Sargassum and Water Column. South Atlantic Fishery Management Council. Charleston, SC.

Attachment 10: Vagile larger juvenile and adult fishes are often under-represented in traditional sampling of *Sargassum*-associated fishes in the open ocean. We used underwater video recordings from free-floating camcorders and a remotely operated vehicle (ROV) to assess the relative abundance of large mobile fishes under large *Sargas*sum mats (> 10 m diameter), under dispersed clumps of *Sargassum* (< 1 m diameter), and in open water without *Sargassum* as a reference. In addition, we conducted dipnet sampling in each *Sargassum* treatment for a comparison to traditional methods. All samples were obtained in September 1992 along the western wall of the Gulf Stream off Cape Hatteras, North Carolina. A total of 31 fish taxa were identified from both video and dipnet collections. Only 8 taxa were identified in both video and dipnet collections, while 11 taxa were seen only in video and 10 were only found in dipnet collections. Dipnet collections were dominated by juvenile balistids and other small, cryptic fishes, while the video observations were mainly of larger, rapidly-moving carangids. Fish diversity increased with the amount of continuous *Sargassum* habitat: four taxa were observed when no *Sargassum* was present, 12 under clumps, and 19 under mats. Our results indicated that mat morphology significantly affects the *Sargassum*-associated fishes, and that both video and traditional capture methods are complementary and should be used together to accurately census this community.

*This is the same abstract from Moser et al. (1998)

—. 1998. Effects of mat morphology on large *Sargassum*-associated fishes: observations from a remotely operated vehicle (ROV) and free-floating video camcorders. Environmental Biology of Fishes 51: 391-398.

Vagile larger juvenile and adult fishes are often under-represented in traditional sampling of *Sargassum*-associated fishes in the open ocean. We used underwater video recordings from free-floating camcorders and a remotely operated vehicle (ROV) to assess the relative abundance of large mobile ashes under large *Sargassum* mats (> 10 m diameter), under dispersed clumps of *Sargassum* (< 1 m diameter), and in open water without *Sargassum* as a reference. In addition, we conducted dipnet sampling in each *Sargassum* treatment for a comparison to traditional methods. All samples were obtained in September 1992 along the western wall of the Gulf Stream off Cape Hatteras, North Carolina. A total of 31 fish taxa were identified from both video and dipnet collections. Only 8 taxa were identified in both video and dipnet collections, while 11 taxa were seen only in video and 10 were only found in dipnet collections. Dipnet collections were dominated by juvenile balistids and other small, cryptic fishes, while the video observations were mainly of larger, rapidly-moving carangids. Fish diversity increased with the amount of continuous *Sargassum* habitat: four taxa were observed when no *Sargassum* was present, 12 under clumps, and 19 under mats. Our results indicated that mat morphology significantly affects the *Sargassum*-associated fishes, and that both video and traditional capture methods are complementary and should be used together to accurately census this community.

Moser, M.L., S.W. Ross, S.W. Snyder, and R.C. Dentzman. 1995. Distribution of Bottom Habitats on the Continental Shelf off North Carolina. Final Report to Marine Resources Research Institute, South Carolina Department of Marine Resources for the Southeast Area Monitoring and Assessment Program — Bottom Mapping Workgroup. Wilmington, NC. 80 p.

*This report documents the compilation and evaluation of the North Carolina SEAMAP Hardbottom data. In situ observations of hard bottom type and relief were made using submersibles or SCUBA. These data are in video and/or 35 mm still photographs. Black and white, 35 mm still photographs from RV Eastward research cruises (1964-1973) also provided evidence of bottom type and relief. USACOE drilling logs (1983) characterized sub-surface stability. Fish trawl and trap data from NMFS-Woods Hole (groundfish surveys 1964-1994), NMFS- Pascagoula (archive data 1954-1984), SEAMAP data (since 1984) and NCDMF (RV Dan Moore, and reef data) were evaluated for the presence of obligate (primary) reef fishes as evidence for the location of hard or non-hard bottoms. This report is part of a CD-ROM for the whole S. Atlantic Bight, published by the Florida DNR (S.W. Ross, pers. comm. 31 Dec 99).

Moser, M.L., S.W. Ross, and K.J. Sulak. 1996. Metabolic responses to hypoxia of *Lycenchelys verrillii* (wolf eelpout) and *Glyptocephalus cynoglossus* (witch flounder); sedentary bottom fishes of the Hatteras/Virginia Middle Slope. Marine Ecology Progress Series 144: 57-61.

We collected wolf eelpouts *Lycenchelys verrillii* and witch flounder *Glyptocephalus cynoglossus* from Hatteras (North Carolina, USA) and Virginia (USA) Middle Slope sites using a submersible, and made shipboard measurements of their respiration rates and survival in hypoxic (<10% O2 saturation) and anoxic conditions. Both species from the Hatteras site reduced their respiration rates as ambient oxygen decreased, but eelpouts from the Virginia site maintained a constant respiration rate until oxygen saturation dropped below 20 %. Moreover, eelpouts from the Hatteras site were significantly more tolerant of hypoxic conditions than fish from the Virginia site and survived anoxia for short periods. These results and our submersible observations of fish behavior support the hypothesis that the Hatteras Middle Slope fauna is exposed to short-term hypoxia events.

Musick, J.A. 1979. Community Structure of Fishes on the Continental Slope and Rise Off the Middle Atlantic Coast of the United States. Virginia Institute of Marine Science School of Marine Science, College of William and Mary. Gloucester Point, VA. 124 p.

Otter trawl cruises were conducted off the middle Atlantic coast of the U. S. from 1971 to 1975. More than 50,000 specimens of demersal fishes were captured during this program at depths of 75 m to 3000 m. Species assemblages were distributed along a coenocline with bathymetric areas of rapid faunal change (anantoclines) and of more gradual faunal change (aganoclines). Between 75 m and 3000 m anantoclines were found at 150 to 200 m, 400 to 600 m, 900 to 1000 m, 1350 to 1500 m, and 1900 to 2100 m. Species diversity (H1) increased between the continental shelf and slope, remained constant to about 1800 m, then declined rapidly. This pattern was primarily related to species richness, not evenness. Numerical abundance increased between the shelf and slope, then declined exponentially. Biomass increased between the continental shelf and slope and then remained fairly constant out to a depth of about 1800 m beyond which there was an exponential decline (but not as steep as that for numerical abundance). The average size of fishes was about the same on the shelf and upper- slope out to a depth of about-1800 m beyond which size increased by threefold. This size increase is contrary to that found for the meiofauna and macrofauna. The difference in strategies lies in the mobility of fishes which allows them to maintain viable sexually reproducing populations at relatively small population size. Biomass of fishes was of the same order of magnitude as that reported by other workers for the infauna at similar depths. This apparent contradiction of classic trophic pyramid structure is resolved because the mobility of fishes allows them to utilize pelagic as well as benthic food sources. The declines in diversity and biomass and the increase in average size of fishes, all occurred at around 1800 m near the slope-rise border beyond which regular food sources of continental origin are absent.

Musick, J.A. and L.P. Mercer. 1977. Seasonal distribution of black sea bass, Centropristis striata, in the Mid-Atlantic Bight with comments on the ecology and fisheries of the species. Transactions of the American Fisheries Society 106(1): 12-25.

Black sea bass in the Middle Atlantic Bight spawn in the summer, at depths of 18 to 45 m, primarily from Virginia to Montauk, Long Island. Young of the year become demersal at 13-24 mm total length and enter estuarine nursery grounds. In fall black sea bass migrate south and offshore to the Chesapeake Bight where the entire population spends the winter. Larger and older fish move offshore sooner than do young of the year and winter in deeper water (73-165 m). Black sea bass may tolerate temperatures as low as 6 C but are captured in larger numbers and more frequently in waters 9 C and above. In the spring sea bass migrate inshore and to the north; adults to their coastal spawning areas, juveniles to estuarine nursery areas (including lower Chesapeake Bay).

In recent years, the commercial catch per effort of sea bass has dropped and the fishery lands fewer large and medium size fish. Concurrently domestic trawling effort has decreased somewhat whereas effort by the recreational, foreign trawl, and pot fisheries has increased. Black sea bass appear to be overharvested.

Because sea bass are incompletely metagonous, protogynous hermaphrodites, heavy fishing pressure may cause the sex ratio of the population to so favor females that the number of remaining males may not be sufficient to sustain adequate reproduction. Conversely, behavioral interactions among individuals in the population may act homeostatically to initiate sex reversal, thus maintaining a relatively constant (though skewed) sex ratio in the population. It is necessary to understand the mechanisms controlling sex reversal in black sea bass before the effects of fishing pressure on the population can be evaluated.

National Marine Fisheries Service, Southeast Fisheries Center. 1974. Cruise Reports — North Carolina 1956 — 1974. National Marine Fisheries Service, Southeast Fisheries Center. Miami, FL. 164 p.

*This is a compilation of Cruise Reports in North Carolina between 1956 — 1974, arranged by date. Vessels in this report included:

R/V George M. Bowers Cruise Number 7A; December 6, 1956.
R/V George M. Bowers Cruise Number 112; October 13, 1972.
R/V George M. Bowers Cruise Number 115; April 27, 1973.
R/V George M. Bowers Cruise Number 122; May 29, 1974.
M/V Silver Bay Cruise Number 18, October 7, 1959.
M/V Silver Bay Cruise Number 20; December 18, 1959.
M/V Silver Bay Cruise Number 22; March 24, 1960.
M/V Silver Bay Cruise Number 25; August 5, 1960.
M/V Silver Bay Cruise Number 29; March 28, 1961.
M/V Silver Bay Cruise Number 32; August 30, 1961.
M/V Silver Bay Cruise Number 35; December 22, 1961.
M/V Silver Bay Cruise Number 39; June 19, 1962.
M/V Silver Bay Cruise Number 40; August 27, 1962.
M/V Silver Bay Cruise Number 43; no date provided.
M/V Silver Bay Cruise Number 45; no date provided.
M/V Silver Bay Cruise Number 56; April 29, 1964.
R/V Oregon Cruise Number 93, August 24, 1964.
R/V Oregon Cruise Number 93; September 3, 1964.
R/V Oregon Cruise Number 100; April 23, 1965.
R/V Oregon Cruise Number 116; April 7, 1967.
R/V Oregon Cruise Number 125; January 29, 1968.
R/V Oregon Cruise Number 127; March 29, 1968.
R/V Oregon Cruise Number 129; May 28, 1968.
R/V Oregon Cruise Number 131; August 5, 1968.
R/V Oregon Cruise Number 133; September 24, 1968.
R/V Oregon Cruise Number 135; December 3, 1968.
R/V Oregon II Cruise Number 10, September 3, 1969.
R/V Oregon II Cruise Number 17; June 15, 1970.
R/V Oregon II Cruise Number 25; June 10, 1970.
R/V Oregon II Cruise Number 33; March 22, 1972.

National Oceanic and Atmospheric Administration, National Marine Fisheries Service, and Northeast Fisheries Center. 1977. Fishermen's Report Catch of Delaware II During Summer Groundfish Survey 77-09, July 27 to August 5, 1977 (covering southern New England and middle Atlantic shelf). U. S. Department of Commerce, National Oceanic and Atmospheric Administration, National Marine Fisheries Service, Northeast Fisheries Center, Sandy Hook Laboratory. Highlands, NJ. 18 p.

The included charts and station data are designed to show where important species were found in some quantity during the newly initiated summer groundfish survey. In addition, a section of each species chart includes information pertinent to the biology of that species. All tows were made with a #36 otter trawl equipped with rollers, 9-meter (5 fathom) legs, and 544-kg (1200 lb.) BMV oval doors. The cod end and upper belly of the trawl were lined with ½-inch mesh netting to retain smaller fish. Because of the short tow time (one-half hour), the catches listed are low when compared to standard commercial tows. The bias caused by the day-night catchability of some fish, depth limitations of vessels, and the fact that randomly selected stations will not necessarily fall on fish concentrations will have to be appreciated. Time of year and area of coverage should also be considered because of the movement of migrating and spawning fish. The metric system is used for all lengths, weights, and depths in this report. An English-metric conversion chart is attached. For, further information, please call or write to the National Marine Fisheries Service.

Nesbit, R.A, and W.C. Neville. 1935. Conditions Affecting the Southern Winter Trawl Fishery. U.S. Department of Commerce, Bureau of Fisheries, Fisheries Circular. Fishery Circular No. 18: 12 p.

*With the opening of another season of the winter-trawl fishery off the Virginia capes, questions have been raised as to what might be expected during the coming winter (Jan.-Mar. 1935). It is the present intention to answer these questions as completely as is permitted by the results of the Bureau's studies of the winter and summer fishery for scup, sea bass, and fluke, these being the three most important fishes in the southern winter-trawl fishery. The discussion will be more complete as to scup for there is more information on that fish than on sea bass or fluke. However, much of what is said about scup in the winter fishery generally applies to sea bass and fluke since all three fishes were subject to the same conditions and were affected in about the same general way, though to differing degrees. This paper also discusses Changes in the Summer Fishery, Changes in the Winter Fishery, Changes in Temperature, Scup Scatter in Warm Winters, Sea Bass in Warmer Water Than Scup, Fluke in More Northerly Part of Ground, Outlook for the Winter of 1935 (January- March), and Conservation Problems.

Nickerson, S.R., and D.G. Mountain. 1983. Surface and Bottom Temperature and Salinity Distributions on the Continental Shelf, Cape Hatteras to Cape Sable from MARMAP Cruises, 1977-1982. Northeast Fisheries Center, Woods Hole Laboratory. Woods Hole, MA. 83 p.

*This report presents surface and bottom temperature and salinity distributions observed on twenty-five cruises between 1977 and 1982. These cruises were part of the Marine Resources Monitoring and Assessment Program (MARMAP) conducted by the Northeast Fisheries Center, National Marine Fisheries Service. The area observations extended over the continental shelf from Cape Hatteras to Nova Scotia, although complete coverage was not made on all cruises due to time and weather limitations. Generally, the area was covered from south to north over a period of approximately six weeks. Vessels included are:

1977: Argus cruise 77-10; 15 Oct-11 Nov
       Mt. Mitchell-Kelez cruise 77-11; 12 Nov-04 Dec
1978: Delaware II cruise 78-02; 14 Feb-13 Mar
       Argus cruise 78-04; 13 Apr-24 May
       Albatross IV cruise 78-07; 22 Jun-01 Jul
       Belogosrk cruise 78-01; 09 Aug-05 Sep
       Belogosrk cruise 78-03; 05-20 Oct
       Belogosrk cruise 78-04; 16-29 Nov
1979: Delaware II cruise 79-03; 23 Feb-15 Mar
       Delaware II cruise 79-05; 06 29 May
       Albatross IV cruise 79-06; 17 Jun-12 Jul
       Belogosrk cruise 79-01; 11 Aug-02 Sep
       Albatross IV cruise 79-11; 03 Sep-29 Oct
       Albatross IV cruise 79-13; 15 Nov-20 Dec

1980: Albatross IV cruise 80-02; 27 Feb-04 Apr
      Delaware II cruise 80-03; 23 May-12 Jun
      Erika cruise 80-04; 25-29 Jun
      Albatross IV cruise 80-10; 24 Sep-30 Oct
      Albatross IV cruise 80-12; 19 Nov-21 Dec
1981: Albatross IV cruise 81-01; 17 Feb-24 Mar
      Kelez cruise 81-03, 04; 18 Mar-09 Apr
      Delaware II cruise 81-03; 20 May-18 Jun
      Albatross IV cruise 81-14; 16 Nov-22 Dec
1982: Albatross IV cruise 82-02; 16 Feb-25 Mar
      Delaware II cruise 82-03; 17 May-11 Jun
      Albatross IV cruise 82-09; 15 Nov-22 Dec.

Nixon, S.W., and Jones C.W. 1997. Age and growth of larval and juvenile Atlantic croaker, *Micropogonias undulatus,* from the Middle Atlantic Bight Atlantic and estuarine waters of Virginia. Fishery Bulletin 95: 773-784.

Sagittal otoliths were used to determine age and growth of 605 larval and juvenile Atlantic croaker, *Micropogonias undulatus*, collected in the Middle Atlantic Bight and estuarine waters of Virginia. This study is the first to use age-based analysis for young Atlantic croaker collected in this region. A Laird-Gompertz model ($r^2=0.95$) was used to describe the growth of Atlantic croaker up to 65 mm standard length (SL) and 142 days (t): $SL_{(t)} = 2.657 \exp \{4.656 [1-\exp (-0.0081t)]\}$; where $SL_{(t)} =$ standard length at day t. Spatial and temporal patterns in the size and age of Atlantic croaker showed a pattern of inshore immigration from offshore spawning grounds, and faster early-season growth compared with late-season growth. Back-calculated hatching dates of Atlantic croaker collected in Virginia estuaries indicated a protracted spawning period over 8 months, from early July 1987 to early February 1988, with at least 82% of spawning occurring from August to October. Regression analysis indicated that early-spawned larvae (July through August) grew more than 39% faster than late-spawned larvae (September through February). Lapillar and sagittal otoliths were compared with light microscopy; ages were underestimated with lapillar otoliths, which were particularly inadequate in determining the age of older juveniles. The relation between SL and sagittal otolith maximum diameter was best described by a fourth order polynomial ($r^2=0.99$) and faster-growing Atlantic croaker had larger otoliths (12%) than the same size slower-growing fish.

Norcross, B.L. 1983. Climate scale environmental factors affecting year-class fluctuations of Atlantic Croaker, *Micropogonias undulatus,* in the Chesapeake Bay. Ph.D. Dissertation. School of Marine Science, College of William and Mary. Gloucester Point, VA. 387 p.

A conceptual life history of the Atlantic croaker (*Micropogonias undulatus*) identifies the effects of the environment on juvenile recruitment. In a multi-disciplinary approach to modeling, the major effects are investigated, quantified and presented in a flow chart.

The model is divided into three sub models, each representing a major component which affects juvenile recruitment.

North/south spawning location in the Mid-Atlantic Bight is affected by the bottom water temperature as influenced by the cessation of the summer winds in relation to timing of croaker migration. The pelagic phase is the most critical time in the life history of a larval croaker as they are subjected to wind-induced transport which may cause direct loss off the shelf and entrainment in the Gulf Stream, or indirect loss by prolonging time in transit to the nursery area. The magnitude of this wind-included effect is a function of the direction, strength, duration and time relative to spawning and is incorporated in an equation to predict year-class strength of croaker.

The juvenile croaker overwinter in the Chesapeake Bay system. Winter temperature is shown to be the predominant variable affecting year-class survival to the following summer in very cold years. However, in very warm years, the predictive capabilities of the model are improved when a measure of fall recruitment, i.e. wind-induced transport, is incorporated.

Croaker is basically a density-independent stock as, juvenile recruitment is erratic and dependent upon these environmental parameters. The effect of spawning stock size is only apparent after accounting for density-independent effects, and slightly improves the explained variance of the statistical relationship. Year-class strength and fishing pressure cause interannual variability in commercial catch. Overfishing a weak year class reduce spawning potential, and several poor year classes in a row magnify this. The model, tested for the 1982-82 data, predicts a strong year class.

Norcross, B.L. and H.M. Austin. 1988. Middle Atlantic Bight meridional wind component effect on bottom water temperatures and spawning distribution of Atlantic croaker. Continental Shelf Research. 8(1): 69-88.

Predominantly southerly winds over the Middle Atlantic Bight result in offshore flow in surface waters and corresponding onshore flow in a bottom Ekman layer. Seasonal heating results in maximum surface temperatures in August while the bottom onshore Ekman flow results in cold summer bottom water temperatures. Bottom temperatures do not peak until autumn after the seasonal wind shift resulting in a cessation of the southerly winds and overturning of the surface waters. Strong episodes of this onshore bottom flow of cold water (upwelling) have been previously reported as unusually cold surf zone temperatures.

Fifteen-day moving averages of meridional components of winds from Norfolk International Airport, Virginia revealed few of the 15 years examined in which there was an abrupt seasonal shift in wind patterns from summer to winter regimes. Twenty-six collections of bottom water temperature data were reviewed for the Middle Atlantic Bight during the years 1967-1981. The average time of cessation of the strong southerly (summer) meridional wind component during those years was the end of August/beginning of September. A correlation of 0.74 exists between the time of cessation and the extent (km^2) of warm nearshore bottom waters, as indicated by the 16° C isotherm. The transition from a southerly to a northerly wind pattern occurs over a period of time ranging from 10 days to 3 months, while the response of ocean bottom isotherms to the cessation of the southerly component can typically be seen in 10-20 days.

Migration and spawning behavior of many fish is cued by water temperatures. The autumn areal distribution of the Atlantic croaker (Micropogonias undulates) is strongly correlated ($r^2 = 0.78$) with the areal distribution of bottom waters warmer than 16° C on the shelf. Furthermore, there is a correlation ($r^2 = 0.64$) between the time of cessation of the summer southerly wind and the areal extent of croaker. Therefore, we propose that if the wind relaxation occurs prior to the autumn migration of croaker out of the estuaries, spawning would occur in northern and middle sections of the Middle Atlantic Bight. Prolonged summer winds would keep the nearshore waters cool, and force croaker to migrate further southward to spawn, potentially shifting the distribution of juvenile recruitment to Pamlico Sound with entrance through Oregon Inlet in the Middle Atlantic Bight or through inlets south of Cape Hatteras.

Olney, J.E. and G.R. Sedberry. 1983. Dragonet larvae (Teleostei, Callionymidae) in continental shelf waters off the Eastern United States. Biological Oceanography 3(1): 103-122.

The seasonal distribution and abundance of larvae of the fish family Callionymidae are reported from plankton collections in continental shelf waters off the eastern United States. Larvae of Callionymus pauciradiatus and C. bairdi were distinguished by meristic variations and pigment patterns.

Callionymid larvae occurred in collections during all months sampled and peak densities were observed during summer and fall. Larvae of C. pauciradiatus dominated collections, constituting 90% of all larvae captured. Greatest densities of C. pauciradiatus were observed during late summer and early fall in mid-shelf regions of the South Atlantic Bight. Larvae of C. bairdi were most abundant along outer shelf stations. Abundance and size data indicate that previously unknown spawning populations of C. pauciradiatus inhabit mid-shelf regions as far north as Cape Hatteras, North Carolina. Larvae of C. bairdi in eastern U.S. shelf waters likely originate from tropical adult populations having extended spawning seasons.

Orbach, M. 1989. Plenary Session: How Could These Resources be Affected By the Proposed Drilling and What Mitigation Measures Might be Used to Prevent Irreversible Damage. pp. 63-64. *In*: Crawford, K. (ed.). Proceedings: 1989 Marine Expo: The Natural Resources Associated with Mobil's Proposed Drill Site. NC Outer Continental Shelf Office, NC Department of Administration. Raleigh, NC.

*The following is a summary of the plenary session.

There appears to be a good deal of baseline information available about Mobil's proposed drill site area. However, there was a general consensus that there are serious gaps in our understanding of the relationships and functions of the many communities found in and around the exploration area known as the "Manteo Prospect." Some major areas of concern include protection of area benthos, impacts on community ecology, and effects of drilling discharges .

There was almost unanimous support for a monitoring program of the drilling operations and their impacts. Programs should be devised to examine: 1) The fate of drilling discharges, including dispersion (range and extent) and accumulation along fronts and the ocean bottom; and 2) The effects (both chemical and mechanical) of drilling discharges on the benthos, the indigenous fisheries (including eggs/larvae), prey species, forage strategies, and the sargassum communities.

Concerns were also raised regarding the effects the ship and anchor system might have on the biota as a result of displacement, noise, or collisions, and the impacts of exploration activities on the commercial and recreational fisheries found at "The Point."

Because of previous scientific work done at or near the proposed drill site, this area may be well suited to such monitoring programs. Not only would information from these programs be vital for developing mitigation measures, but it could also serve as a critical database on which to build a management framework for future development. In addition, data already collected on local fish resources, marine birds, the benthos and bottom conditions, and physical oceanography could provide an excellent base for further research.

This text also mentions marine mammals and Threatened and Endangered species (marine reptiles).

Orbach, M.K. 1998a. Habitat and Living Resources Review: Social and Economic Issues. pp. 64-67. *In:* Vigil, D.L. (ed.). North Carolina/Minerals Management Service Technical Workshop on Manteo Unit Exploration: February 4-5, 1998. U.S. Dept. of the Interior, Minerals Management Service, Gulf of Mexico OCS Region. New Orleans, LA.

*These are the proceedings from a workshop/meeting (conducted on February 4-5, 1998) between the North Carolina Department of Environment and Natural Resources, and the U.S. Department of the Interior's Minerals Management Service (MMS). The geographic area being discussed is approximately 45 miles east-northeast of Cape Hatteras, NC, referred to as the Manteo Unit. This workshop reviewed environmental and socioeconomic information known and needed on the Manteo Unit. The MMS's Gulf of Mexico OCS Regional Director gave an MMS perspective on history and status of the area. Chevron gave a presentation on how the exploratory well would be drilled. The scientific characterization was presented in greater detail by a number of scientific experts who spoke on the following disciplines physical environment, habitat and living resources, seabirds, marine mammals, sea turtles, and social and economic issues. Specific chapters are cited individually, when appropriate.

As a result of the recommendations of the North Carolina Environmental Science review Panel mandated by the Outer Banks Protection Act (Costlow et al. 1992), the North Carolina Socioeconomic Study (NCSS) was commissioned by the Atlantic OCS region of the Minerals Management Service (MMS). This study, which was completed in 1993, had five objectives: 1) a characterization of base case socioeconomic conditions in the five most potentially affected North Carolina counties, including standard aggregate variables, the structure of related industries, and relationships among private and public sector entities in the subject areas; 20 detailed community studies on representative communities potentially affected by OCS development, including sociocultural variables necessary to establish the context of the role and effect of potential OCS activities; 3) an aesthetic and perceptual issues study of representative components of the potentially affected populations in the region; 4) infrastructure studies performed in the potentially affected communities, focusing on the potential for changes in local and regional fiscal relationships derived from future OCS activity; and 5) the design of a longitudinal socioeconomic monitoring program that employs the key variables identified in the base case, community, infrastructure, and risk perception studies. This five-volume study was submitted to MMS in 1993 (NCSS 1993).

—. 1998b. Social and Economic Issues Work Session Results: Socioeconomic Issues Associated With Human Uses of "The Point." pp. 87-89. *In:* Vigil, D.L. (ed.). North Carolina/Minerals Management Service Technical Workshop on Manteo Unit Exploration: February 4-5, 1998. U.S. Dept. of the Interior, Minerals Management Service, Gulf of Mexico OCS Region. New Orleans, LA.

*These are the proceedings from a workshop/meeting (conducted on February 4-5, 1998) between the North Carolina Department of Environment and Natural Resources, and the U.S. Department of the Interior's Minerals Management Service (MMS). The geographic area being discussed is approximately 45 miles east-northeast of Cape Hatteras, NC, referred to as the Manteo Unit. This workshop reviewed environmental and socioeconomic information known and needed on the Manteo Unit. The MMS's Gulf of Mexico OCS Regional Director gave an MMS perspective on history and status of the area. Chevron gave a presentation on how the exploratory well would be drilled. The scientific characterization was presented in greater detail by a number of scientific experts who spoke on the following disciplines physical environment, habitat and living resources, seabirds, marine mammals, sea turtles, and social and economic issues. Specific chapters are cited individually, when appropriate.

The group addressed the question, "What socioeconomic information is needed for North Carolina and MMS to adequately judge a POE/EA regarding an exploratory well in the Manteo Prospect"? The following informational needs were discussed: (1) An update to the ECU study data. The information collected is now more than 10 years old. This information should include 1990 census data as well as document changes to the fishing industry and the continued increase in the tourism and retirement industry. (2) Establishment of a monitoring program. (3) Detailed assessment of uses and users of "The Point." This might include some kind of cost/benefit analysis of The Point uses. (4) Economic modeling (demand curves, cost/benefit analysis).

Pacheco, A.L. 1973. Proceedings of a Workshop on Egg, Larval, and Juvenile Stages of Fish in Atlantic Coastal Estuaries. National Marine Fisheries Center, Middle Atlantic Coastal Fisheries Center. Highlands, NJ.

*The purpose of the Charleston workshop was to assess the role of Atlantic estuaries as nursery grounds for economically important fishes and to encourage further work on estuaries. This was to be accomplished through a joint review and discussion of data by participants from each of the coastal states. This workshop is being held to provide an opportunity for joint review and discussion of information on the occurrence of fish eggs, larvae, and juveniles in Atlantic estuaries. Specific objectives are to present appropriate scientific papers, with publication of a volume of collected contributions; to provide a forum for informal discussions among biologists active in estuarine fish research; to encourage and assist in dissemination of unpublished data on estuarine fish nurseries; and to assess the present state of knowledge and recommend future lines of research.

Note: The General Discussion section located on pp. 325 — 330 mentions RV Dolphin (1963-1964; 1965-1966); RV Dan Moore (no specific dates); and RV Dolphin (December 1965-December 1966) in reference to studies "...within the Carolina sounds, " and "...off the coast of New Jersey."

Palmquist, R.B., P.W. Schuhmann, and J.A. Michael. 2000. Economic Analysis of "The Point" and Adjacent Counties: Baseline Information, Valuation, and Potential Impacts. Final Report to the North Carolina Division of Coastal Management and the U.S. Minerals Management Service under a grant from the North Carolina Department of Environment and Natural Resources, Agency Reference No. 5-9081. 46 p.

*The purpose of this study is to generate baseline economic information for the counties that might be affected by off-shore oil and gas exploration, explore the potential impacts of an oil spill off the Outer banks, provide information on the value of recreational fishing at "The Point," and estimate the potential losses to recreational fishing at "The Point" if there were an oil spill. This study also presents information on the effects of coastal oil releases elsewhere to guide the scenarios used here. First, the report describes the economies of affected coastal counties and the role of tourism and commercial fishing in these areas. Next, the report describes the impacts of several significant oil spill cases in the U.S. that will be used to develop possible spill scenarios for North Carolina. Following that, the appropriateness of economic base and input-output analysis to this case is discussed, and the techniques are used to describe the baseline economies and to analyze the potential impacts on the coastal economy of an oil spill.

Pearson, J.C. 1932. Winter Trawl Fishery Off the Virginia and North Carolina Coasts. U.S. Department of Commerce, Bureau of Fisheries, Fisheries Circular. Investigative Report No. 10 (I): 31 p.

*A winter trawl fishery has been established recently off the Virginia and North Carolina coasts and has expanded greatly during the past two years. This has been brought about by a considerable number of northern fishing vessels from Boston, Gloucester, New York, New Bedford, Bridgeport, Providence, Camden, and Wildwood, equipped with otter trawls, which are operating mainly out of Hampton Roads (VA) ports. Most of these vessels are engaged during the spring and summer months in purse seining for mackerel off the New England, New York and New Jersey coasts, often working in early spring as far south as North Carolina. Others are regularly engaged in flounder dragging off the southern New England or New Jersey coasts during the summer season. These vessels have found little to do during the winter months in northern waters, and with the development of this new fishery are turning to south waters. During the in winter of 1930-31 an increasing number of these vessels endeavored to open up the vast supply of summer shore fishes which winter in the deeper and warmer oceanic water in the general vicinity of Cape Hatteras NC. In view of the promising future of this fishery it was thought desirable for the Bureau of Fisheries to undertake a study of the fish in all its various aspects. This paper discusses History of the fishery, Location of the Fishery, Methods of the Fishery, Method of Investigation, Composition of Catch (e.g., quantity, species, size). Characteristics of scup, porgy fishery; croaker fishery, summer flounder or fluke fishery, sea bass fishery, gray sea trout and weakfish fishery, total catch data, and the socioeconomic impact of these fisheries are also discussed.

Phalen, P. Unpublished database (a). North Carolina Artificial Fishing Reef Construction Through January 1994. North Carolina Division of Marine Fisheries. Morehead City, NC.

*This is an unpublished database. Data were collected through January 1994 by the NC Division of Marine Fisheries. The Principal Investigator is listed as Steve Murphy. Select sample locations and related data were computerized as part of the North Carolina SEAMAP Hardbottom data project by Moser et al. (1995). SEAMAP Hardbottom data (sample locations) within the defined project area for The Point were sorted and mapped using ArcView GIS (J. Ott, pers. comm. 15 Nov 99).

—. Unpublished database (b). RV Dan Moore Studies, Anadromous Fish Survey 1968-1981. North Carolina Division of Marine Fisheries. Morehead City, NC.

*This is an unpublished fisheries database. Data were collected from 1968 to 1981 by the NC Division of Marine Fisheries. The Principal Investigator is listed as Paul Phalen. Select sample locations and related data were computerized as part of the North Carolina SEAMAP Hardbottom data project by Moser et al. (1995). SEAMAP Hardbottom data (sample locations) within the defined project area for The Point were sorted and mapped using ArcView GIS (J. Ott, pers. comm. 15 Nov 99).

—. Unpublished database (c). RV Dan Moore Studies, Exploratory Fish/General Survey 1968-1969, 1971-1981. North Carolina Division of Marine Fisheries. Morehead City, NC.

*This is an unpublished fisheries database. Data were collected from 1968-1969, and 1971-1981 by the NC Division of Marine Fisheries. The Principal Investigator is listed as Paul Phalen. Select sample locations and related data were computerized as part of the North Carolina SEAMAP Hardbottom data project by Moser et al. (1995). SEAMAP Hardbottom data (sample locations) within the defined project area for The Point were sorted and mapped using ArcView GIS (J. Ott, pers. comm. 15 Nov 99).

—. Unpublished database (d). RV Dan Moore Studies, Flounder Survey 1973-1976. North Carolina Division of Marine Fisheries. Morehead City, NC.

*This is an unpublished fisheries database. Data were collected from 1973 to 1976 by the NC Division of Marine Fisheries. The Principal Investigator is listed as Paul Phalen. Select sample locations and related data were computerized as part of the North Carolina SEAMAP Hardbottom data project by Moser et al. (1995). SEAMAP Hardbottom data (sample locations) within the defined project area for The Point were sorted and mapped using ArcView GIS (J. Ott, pers. comm. 15 Nov 99).

—. Unpublished database (e). RV Dan Moore Studies, Lobster Survey 1968-1973. North Carolina Division of Marine Fisheries. Morehead City, NC.

*This is an unpublished fisheries database. Data were collected from 1968 to 1973 by the NC Division of Marine Fisheries. The Principal Investigator is listed as Paul Phalen. Select sample locations and related data were computerized as part of the North Carolina SEAMAP Hardbottom data project by Moser et al. (1995). SEAMAP Hardbottom data (sample locations) within the defined project area for The Point were sorted and mapped using ArcView GIS (J. Ott, pers. comm., 15 Nov 99).

—. Unpublished database (f). RV Dan Moore Studies, Net Selectivity Testing 1979-1981. North Carolina Division of Marine Fisheries. Morehead City, NC.

*This is an unpublished fisheries database. Data were collected from 1979-1981 by the NC Division of Marine Fisheries. The Principal Investigator is listed as Paul Phalen. Select sample locations and related data were computerized as part of the North Carolina SEAMAP Hardbottom data project by Moser et al. (1995). SEAMAP Hardbottom data (sample locations) within the defined project area for The Point were sorted and mapped using ArcView GIS (J. Ott, pers. comm. 15 Nov 99).

—. Unpublished database (g). RV Dan Moore Studies, Squid Project 1974. North Carolina Division of Marine Fisheries. Morehead City, NC.

*This is an unpublished fisheries database. Data were collected in 1974 by the NC Division of Marine Fisheries. The Principal Investigator is listed as Paul Phalen. Select sample locations and related data were computerized as part of the North Carolina SEAMAP Hardbottom data project by Moser et al. (1995). SEAMAP Hardbottom data (sample locations) within the defined project area for The Point were sorted and mapped using ArcView GIS (J. Ott, pers. comm. 15 Nov 99).

Phalen, P. S. 1980. Computerization of RV Dan Moore Data Relevant to OCS Phosphates Area on the North Carolina's Continental Shelf. North Carolina Division of Marine Fisheries, Department of Natural Resources and Community Development. Morehead City, NC.

The RV Dan Moore, an 85 foot steel stern trawler, collected over 4,400 samples during service with the North Carolina Division of Marine Fisheries (DMF), 1968-1981. The vessel's purpose was to conduct applied research to enable the Division to manage and develop coastal fisheries resources for the benefit of all North Carolinians. Objectives of individual cruises included gear tests, fish tagging, relative abundance and distribution surveys, biological investigations (i.e., age and growth), bottom type surveys, etc. Information collected consisted of location, environmental, and catch data. In many instances, these RV Dan Moore data are the only biological data for certain areas of the Continental Shelf. Results of cruises were summarized in bulletins from 1968-1974. Complete cruise reports describing methods and results were filed for the remaining cruises.

The RV Dan Moore data that were found necessary to the contractor to complete an economic feasibility study of OCS Phosphates-Environmental Impact Statement have been coded, key entered, and summarized. The following completion report identifies the amount and type of data entered and summarizes the objectives, methods, and result of cruises that sampled within the specified OCS phosphates areas.

Powell, A., B.F. Holland, and J. Gillikin. 1975a. RV Dan Moore Cruise Report No. 2: Currituck Beach to Cape Lookout Bight, NC. North Carolina Division of Marine Fisheries, Department of Natural Resources and Community Development. Morehead City, NC.

*The following RV Dan Moore monthly cruise report presents catch data which may be of use to commercial fishermen and marine fishery scientists. The purpose of the November 1974 cruise was to tag summer flounder (*Paralichthys dentatus*) in order to obtain information on seasonal movements and migration. In addition, information regarding the size composition and distribution of the flounder stock by geographical area and temperature regimes was gathered.

—. 1975b. RV Dan Moore Cruise Report No. 3: Currituck Beach to Bogue Inlet, NC. North Carolina Division of Marine Fisheries, Department of Natural Resources and Community Development. Morehead City, NC.

*The purpose of the December 1974 cruise was to continue tagging summer flounder (*Paralichthys dentatus*) and obtain information as outlined in Cruise Report No. 2. A preliminary account of summer flounder migration was also included in that report. Efforts from Currituck Beach to Bogue Inlet, NC resulted in the tagging of 1,462 summer flounder. From November 1973 to the present, a total of 7,300 flounder have been tagged.

—. 1975c. RV Dan Moore Cruise Report No. 5: Onslow Bay, NC to Virginia Beach, VA; Anadromous Fish Survey, Calico Scallop Explorations. North Carolina Division of Marine Fisheries, Department of Natural Resources and Community Development. Morehead City, NC.

*Two separate cruises were accomplished during February 1975. A state supported calico scallop investigation was undertaken to determine if calico scallops were present in areas which previously supported a scallop fishery. A modified 8-foot tumbler dredge was utilized. The majority of sea time was used to obtain data for the federal-aid anadromous fish project outlined in the January 1975 cruise report.

—. 1975d. RV Dan Moore Cruise Report No. 4: Ocracoke Inlet, NC to Chesapeake Bay, VA. North Carolina Division of Marine Fisheries, Department of Natural Resources and Community Development. Morehead City, NC.

*The purpose of the March 1975 cruise was to investigate the offshore populations of anadromous fishes as outlined in Cruise Report No. 4 (January 1975).

—. 1975e. RV Dan Moore Cruise Report No. 6: Cape Hatteras, NC to Cape Henry, VA. North Carolina Division of Marine Fisheries, Department of Natural Resources and Community Development. Morehead City, NC.

*The purpose of the March 1975 cruise was to investigate the offshore populations of anadromous fishes as outlined in Cruise Report No. 4 (January 1975).

—. 1975f. RV Dan Moore Cruise Report No. 7: Cape Hatteras, NC to Cape Henry, VA. North Carolina Division of Marine Fisheries, Department of Natural Resources and Community Development. Morehead City, NC.

*Three days were utilized during April 1975 to investigate areas for calico scallop populations. Major effort was expended in an area 20-nautical miles off Bogue Inlet, NC. A modified tumbler dredge was used.

—. 1975g. RV Dan Moore Cruise Report No. 8: Cape Hatteras, NC to Cape Henry, VA. North Carolina Division of Marine Fisheries, Department of Natural Resources and Community Development. Morehead City, NC.

*The purpose of the RV Dan Moore May 1975 cruise was to obtain information on anadromous fishes as outlined in Cruise Report No. 4 (January 1975).

Renaud, M., G. Gitschlag, E. Klima, A. Shah, D. Koi, and J. Nance. 1993. Loss of shrimp by turtle excluder devices (TEDS) in coastal waters of the United States, North Carolina to Texas: March 1988-August 1990. Fishery Bulletin 91: 129-137.

Observers from the National Marine Fisheries Service collected information on catch rates of shrimp aboard commercial shrimp vessels during March 1988-August 1990. Comparisons were made between nets equipped with Turtle Excluder Devices (TEDS) and standard shrimp nets. Three types of TEDs were tested: Georgia TEDs with and without accelerator funnels, and Super Shooter TEDs with funnels.

Fishing areas, time of day, and duration of tows were controlled by the captain of each vessel to simulate commercial conditions. A statistically-significant (P<0.05) mean loss in shrimp catch-per-unit-effort (CPUE) of 0.24 lb/h (3.6%) and 0.93 lb/h (13.6%) was exhibited by nets equipped with Georgia TEDs (with and without funnels, respectively) compared with standard nets. There was no significant difference in shrimp CPUE between standard nets and nets equipped with Super Shooter TEDs with a funnel.

Richards, S.W., and A.W. Kendall Jr. 1973. Distribution of sand lance, *Ammodytes* sp., larvae on the continental shelf from Cape Cod to Cape Hatteras from RV Dolphin Surveys in 1966. Fishery Bulletin 71 (2): 371-386.

Post larvae of one species of sand lance, which resembled *Ammodytes marinus* exactly, were collected along the east coast of the United states between Martha's Vineyard, MA and Cape Hatteras, NC (lat. 41 to 35 N), in January-February, April, May and December 1966. They were more abundant in tows taken at night than in tows taken during the day. Recently hatched specimens (4-8 mm) were more abundant in shallow water. Diurnal migrations are probably related to feeding in all larger size groups.

The greatest abundance of sand lance larvae occurred in winter off the mouths of the principal estuaries (southern New England, Delaware, and Chesapeake bays). Dispersing rapidly offshore, they were taken all the way to the edge of the continental shelf. As they grew, abundance appeared to be directly related to that of plankton organisms, which in turn were somewhat affected by the presence of estuaries along the coast. By mid-may, larvae were not available to us in this region, probably moving to coastal beaches, up into the estuaries, or onto the bottom.

Ross, J. 1989. Commercial and Recreational Marine Fisheries off North Carolina's Outer Banks. pp. 40-44. *In*: Crawford, K. (ed.). Proceedings: 1989 Marine Expo: The Natural Resources Associated with Mobil's Proposed Drill Site. NC Outer Continental Shelf Office, NC Department of Administration. Raleigh, NC.

*This section provides an overview of year round, recreational fishing, commercial fishing, and fisheries harvests in the study area. The potential project-related-impacts to fisheries-based socioeconomics, and the impact of project-related pollution are discussed. Sargassum is mentioned.

Ross, J.L. 1991. Assessment of the North Carolina Winter Trawl Fishery: September 1985 — April 1988. Special Scientific Report No. 54. NC Department of the Environment, Health and Natural Resources, Division of Marine Fisheries. Morehead City, NC.

The North Carolina winter trawl fishery is conducted during mid-September through April from offshore Long Island, New York to west of Cape Lookout, North Carolina. The fishery is partitioned into three components: the nearshore flounder, deepwater, and flynet fisheries. Species specific CPUEs, size-age composition of the catches and landings were assessed for 1985-88 and compared with 1982-85 catches and landings.

Summer flounder (*Paralichthys dentatus*) dominated nearshore flounder and deepwater trawl catches. During the 1985-88 seasons, nearshore flounder trip CPUEs averaged 59% less than during the 1982-85 seasons. The relative abundance of large summer flounder was lowest in 1987-88; concurrently, low CPUEs suggested growth overfishing may be occurring. Weakfish (*Cynoscion regalis*) was the dominant species in flynet catches. The CPUEs fluctuated with no well-defined trend. The annual age and size frequency distributions were compressed towards smaller, younger fish; age 1 fish dominated catches, and age 2-10 fish became less abundant. Atlantic croaker (*Micropogonias undulatus*) was a dominant component of the flynet catches. The CPUEs declined 67% from 1985-86 to 1987-88, but were still higher than occurring 1982-85. Size and age composition of the catches were consistent since 1983-84 and catches were dominated by age 1 and 2 fish (86-95%). Bluefish (*Pomatomus saltatrix*) occurred in catches of all gears, but were targeted only occasionally with flynets. The CPUEs were lower during the last five seasons than during 1982-83, but improved in 1987-88.

Winter trawls took a broad size (153-840 mm FL) and age (0-9) range of bluefish. Spot (*Leiostomus xanthurus*) were occasionally abundant in the flynet fishery, but most were small and marketed as scrapfish; age 0 and 1 fish accounted for greater than 88% of the catches annually. Scup (*Stenotomus chrysops*) were a significant component of the deepwater catches and fishery; however, catches and landings have steadily declined. Growth overfishing may be occurring, as the relative abundance of large fish has declined since 1982-83. Black sea bass (*Centropristis striata*) was a dominant species in deepwater catches. The CPUEs fluctuated with no persistent trend. Black sea bass recruited at the size of first maturity of females, and the relative abundance of large fish declined.

Overall biomass caught by winter trawlers declined. During 1987-88, total biomass/trip was 17% lower and total biomass/day was 21 % lower than the six-season (1982-88) mean. Landings of marketable finfish during 1985-88 were less than in previously monitored seasons. The trend in the scrap fish:marketable fish ratio has tended to increase in recent sampling seasons.

The harvest of unmarketable-size fish was excessive for sciaenids, and signs of growth overfishing were noted for virtually all target species. The size of fish caught during 1987-88 was in all cases, except for bluefish and spot, smaller than at the project's inception in 1982. Management plans should initially focus trawlers towards the harvest of larger, mature fish.

*This citation includes invertebrate data (squid and crabs).

Ross, J.L., J.B. Sullivan and D.A. DeVries. 1985. Assessment of North Carolina Commercial Finfisheries: 1 July 1983 to 30 June 1984. Annual Progress Report for Project 2-386-R. NC Department of Natural Resources and Community Development, Division of Marine Fisheries. Morehead City, NC. 161 p.

Adult finfish were sampled for relative abundance, species composition and size distribution from the 1983 long haul seine and pound net fisheries in Pamlico Sound, N.C. and the 1983-84 winter trawl fishery in the Atlantic Ocean off North Carolina. Pound net and long haul seine samples were dominated by Atlantic croaker, Atlantic menhaden, weakfish, spot, and bluefish. Dominant species in the winter trawl fishery were weakfish, scup, bluefish, Atlantic croaker and summer flounder. Protein systems of Atlantic croaker and bluefish were examined electrophoretically to determine if stocks could be differentiated by this technique. No consistent patterns were found. A total of 31,604 young-of-year Atlantic croaker were tagged and released, mostly in Pamlico Sound and its tributaries during Fall, 1983. In addition, 92 fish were tagged and released near the mouth of York River, VA. As of 31 August 1984, 1,395 fish were recaptured. Initial movement appeared to be southward within Pamlico Sound and into the ocean. Fish greater than 149 mm TL had a higher return rate than smaller fish. Principal recapture methods were shrimp trawls, gill nets, and book and line.

*This citation includes invertebrate data (squid and crabs).

Ross, J.L., D.A. DeVries, III, J.H. Hawkins, and J.B. Sullivan. 1986. Assessment of North Carolina Commercial Finfisheries 1 April, 1982 to 30 June 1985 Fishing Seasons. Project 2-386-R. North Carolina Department of Natural Resources and Community Development, Division of Marine Fisheries. Morehead City, NC. 418 p.

This is a Comprehensive Assessment of North Carolina finfisheries for 1982 — 1985 fishing seasons. The winter trawl fishery produced 32.1-35.9% of all finfish (excluding menhaden) landed in North Carolina. From fall 1982 to spring 1985, 43, 67 and 84 catches were sampled during the respective seasons. Catches were partitioned by gear (flynet, nearshore flounder trawl, deepwater trawls) and area (north of Cape Hatteras, Cape Hatteras to Cape Lookout, west of Cape Lookout) to facilitate analyzes of seasonal fishing patterns and catches. The relationships between average catch/species from samples and commercial landings are presented herein.

The nearshore flounder fishery occurred from late November through January and accounted for 18.6 — 37.3 % of the catches sampled. Summer flounder (*Paralichthys dentatus*), dominated these catches, although their relative abundance declined from 93.7 to 88.6% during the study. The CPUE (mean weight/trip) was highest in 1983-84 (9,687 kg) and lowest in 1982-83 (5,584 kg). Fish <300 mm TL accounted for 9.8 -14.6% and fish >400 mm TL for 21.4 — 26.0% of the catches with no significant changes noted during the period.

Deepwater trawling occurred from December through April, accounting for 18.6 — 31.3% of the samples. This fishery was dominated (94.0 — 98.0%) each season by scup (*Stenotomus chrysops*), (*Paralichthys dentatus*), black sea bass (*Centropristis striata*), and squids. The CPUE of *S. chrysops* declined from 9,708 kg in 1982-83 to 2,003 kg in 1984-85 as did the percent of fish >200 mm FL, from 58.5 to 18.8%. The CPUE of *C. striata* increased from 1,314 to 3,449 kg and the proportion of large fish increased during the study. The CPUE of *P. dentatus* increased from 1,377 — 4,431 kg from 1982-83 to 1984-85; their size composition did not change significantly during the study; smaller fish were captured in deepwater than in the nearshore fishery.

Flynet fishing occurred from September through April and comprised 31.3 — 62.8 % of the samples. Catches were dominated by weakfish (*Cynoscion regalis*) in 1982-83 (52.8%) and 1983-84 (61.9%) and by Atlantic croaker (*Micropogonias undulatus*) (38.6%) and *C. regalis* (35.6%) in 1984-85. Bluefish (*Pomatomus saltatrix*), spot (*Leiostomus xanthurus*), and butterfish (*Peprilus traicanthus*) were also regularly captured. The CPUE of *C. regalis* was highest in 1983-84 (7,598 kg) and lowest in 1984-85 (4,780 kg). Fish of age 0-XII were landed; age 0 and I individuals composed 90% of the catches. The CPUE of *M. undulatus* increased from 2,344 kg in 1982-83 to 5, 190 kg/catch in 1984-85; age 0-V fish were landed. Age I-III fish constituted 98.9-99.9% of the catches. A declining trend in CPUE and landings of *P. saltatrix* was indicated; age 0-XI individuals were sampled; age 0-I fish composed 87.7-88.8% of the catches in 1982-84 and 57.9% in 1984-85. Flynets produced the greatest relative percentage of scrapfish and inshore flounder trawls the lowest.

*This citation includes invertebrate data (squid and crabs).

Ross, J.L., and D.W. Moye. 1989. Assessment of North Carolina Commercial Finfisheries 1985-1987 Fishing Seasons. Project 2-419-R. North Carolina Department of Natural Resources and Community Development, Division of Marine Fisheries. Morehead City, NC. 293 p.

This is a Comprehensive Assessment of North Carolina finfisheries for 1985 — 1987 fishing seasons. The North Carolina winter trawl fishery was active from mid-September through April and fished grounds from off New York to west of Cape Lookout. The fishery was partitioned into three components: the nearshore flounder, deepwater, and flynet fisheries. Species specific CPUEs, size-age composition of the catches and landings were assessed for 1985-88 and compared with 1982-1985 catches and landings. Summer flounder (*Paralichthys dentatus*) dominated nearshore flounder and deepwater trawl catches. During the 1985-88 seasons, nearshore flounder trip CPUEs averaged 59% less than during the 1982-85 seasons. The relative abundance of summer flounder was lowest for the six season period in 1987-88 and concurrent with low CPUEs suggested growth overfishing may be occurring. Weakfish (*Cynoscion regalis*) were the dominant species in flynet catches. CPUEs during the last six seasons fluctuated with no well defined trend. The annual age and size frequency distributions were compressed towards smaller, younger fish; age 1 fish dominated catches, and age 2-10 fish have become much less abundant. Atlantic Croaker (*Micropogonias undulatus*) were a dominant component of the flynet catches. CPUEs declined 67% from 1985-86 to 1987-88, but were still higher for the period than during 1982-85. The size and age composition of the catches has been consistent since 1983-84, and catches since were dominated by age 1 and 2 fish (86-95%). Bluefish (*Pomatomus saltatrix*) occurred in catches by all trawl gears but were targeted only occasionally with flynets. CPUEs were lower during the last 5 seasons than during 1982-83, but were improved in 1987-88. Bluefish caught by winter trawlers included a broad size (153-840 mm FL) and age (0-9) distribution. Spot (*Leiostomus xanthurus*) were occasionally an abundant component of the flynet fishery, but most were undersized and marketed as scrapfish. Age 0 and 1 fish accounted for greater than 88% of the catches annually. Scup (*Stenotomus chrysops*) were a significant component of the deepwater fishery, however catches and lading s have steadily declined. Growth overfishing was indicated with the relative abundance of large fish having declined since 1982-83. Black sea bass (*Centropristis striatus*) were a dominant species in deepwater catches. CPUEs have fluctuated with no persistent trend. They were recruited at the size of first maturity in females and the relative abundance of large fish has declined. Overall biomass caught by winter trawlers has generally declined. Overall biomass caught by winter trawlers has generally declined. Total biomass/trip was 17% lower and total biomass/day was 21% lower during 1987-88 than the six season 1982-85 mean. Seasonal marketable finfish landings were each less than any season from 1982-85. The proportion of scrapfish to marketable finfish has generally increased over the six season period.

*This citation includes invertebrate data (squid and crabs).

Ross, J.L., J.B. Sullivan, and D. A. DeVries. 1984. Assessment of North Carolina Commercial Finfisheries: 1 April 1982 to 30 June 1983. Annual Progress report for project 2-386-R. NC Department of Natural Resources and Community Development, Division of Marine Fisheries. Morehead City, NC. 108 p.

Adult finfish were sampled for relative abundance, species composition and size distribution from the 1982 long haul seine and pound net fisheries in Pamlico Sound, N.C. and the 1982-83 winter trawl fishery in the Atlantic Ocean off North Carolina. Pound net and long haul seine samples were dominated by Atlantic croaker, Atlantic menhaden, weakfish, spot, and bluefish. Dominant species in the winter trawl fishery were weakfish, scup, bluefish, Atlantic croaker and summer flounder. Protein systems of Atlantic croaker were examined electrophoretically to determine if stocks could be differentiated by this technique. No consistent patterns were found. A total of 29,325 young-of-year and 598 adult Atlantic croaker were tagged and released, mostly in Pamlico Sound and its tributaries during Fall, 1982. Similar numbers of T-bar and cinch-up tags were used. The latter tag provided much better long-term retention. Initial movement appeared to be southward within Pamlico Sound and into the ocean. During Spring and Summer, 1983, tags were returned from the mouth of Chesapeake Bay to southern North Carolina, although most came from Pamlico Sound and its tributaries.

The principal recapture methods were shrimp trawl, long haul seine, hook and line, and gill net.

*This citation includes invertebrate data (squid and crabs).

Ross, S.W. 1985a. A Summary of Biological Processes in the Proposed VACAPES EMPRESS II Area Off North Carolina Relating to Plankton Communities, Pelagic Macroinvertebrates, Ichthyofauna, Sea turtles, Marine Mammals, and Sea Birds. Appendix B. *In:* U.S. Department of the Navy. EMPRESS II: Supplemental Draft Environmental Impact Statement for the Proposed Operation of the Navy Electromagnetic Pulse Radiation Environment Simulator for Ships (Empress II) in the

Chesapeake Bay and Atlantic Ocean. United States Navy. Environmental/ Intergovernmental Section. Atlantic Division. Naval Facilities Engineering and Command. Norfolk, VA.

*This technical report appears as Appendix B within the "EMPRESS II: Supplemental Draft Environmental Impact Statement for the Proposed Operation of the Navy Electromagnetic Pulse Radiation Environment Simulator for Ships (Empress II) in the Chesapeake Bay and Atlantic Ocean" report. This technical report is a Summary of Biological Processes in the Proposed VACAPES EMPRESS II area off North Carolina Relating to Planktonic Communities, Pelagic Macroinvertebrates, Ichthyofauna, Sea turtles, Marine Mammals, and Sea Birds. Technical reports supporting this summary have been written by authorities in each discipline and are included in Appendices. These supporting technical reports are cited individually. The southern portion of VACAPES EMPRESS II Area of North Carolina overlaps with the northern portion of the defined study area for the Data Inventory Related to the Hatteras Middle Slope (The Point) Area.

—. 1985b. An Assessment of the Distribution and Composition of the Ichthyofauna in the Proposed VACAPES EMPRESS II Area of North Carolina. Appendix E. *In:* U.S. Department of the Navy. EMPRESS II: Supplemental Draft Environmental Impact Statement for the Proposed Operation of the Navy Electromagnetic Pulse Radiation Environment Simulator for Ships (Empress II) in the Chesapeake Bay and Atlantic Ocean. United States Navy. Environmental/ Intergovernmental Section. Atlantic Division. Naval Facilities Engineering and Command. Norfolk, VA.

The Department of the Navy has proposed to periodically operate an electromagnetic pulse simulator in the Chesapeake Bight off North Carolina ($36°$ 28'N, $75°$ 32.5'W). The site, called VACAPES, occurs in a shallow temperate zone characterized by a large seasonal flux of fishes. Although maximum fish species richness is attained during the late summer-fall, peak numbers and biomass generally occur during the cool weather periods of extensive fish migrations. Most of the fishes move offshore and south during fall-winter and inshore and north as water temperatures increase during spring summer. Many of the commercially/ recreationally important species spawn in or near the area during cool weather and their larvae are transported into nearshore or estuarine nursery areas. Major commercial exploitation occurs during this time; however, recreational fishing in the area is restricted to summer-fall months.

At least 134 fishes were recorded from trawl sampling in the VACAPES area. Although as many as 300 fishes could occur there, the 134 represent the dominant forms. The most numerous species were Atlantic Croaker, Atlantic menhaden, spot, blueback herring, butterfish, weakfish, Atlantic mackerel, alewife, summer flounder, and spiny dogfish. Some pelagic fishes which are difficult to collect but that may be very important to this area are bluefish, American sand lance (not always pelagic), anchovies, and tunas.

—. 1988. Age, Growth, and Mortality of Atlantic Croaker in North Carolina, with Comments on Population Dynamics. Transactions of the American Fisheries Society 117: 461-473.

Atlantic croakers *Micropogonias undulatus* collected during 1979-1981 in North Carolina were aged $(N = 2,369)$ with scales and length frequencies. Eight age-classes were observed, but fish more than 3-4 years old were uncommon. Mean observed total lengths (TL) for ages 1-7 were 192, 271, 320, 371, 430, 473, and 514 mm, respectively. The largest Atlantic croaker aged was 521 mm TL (age 7). Sizes-at-age from scale data agreed well with length frequencies. Scales may be used to age Atlantic croaker up to age 5, but beyond this, annual marks are difficult to validate. Growth was rapid until age 1. The von Bertalanffy growth coefficient (K = 0.20) indicated that maximum size was attained slowly. The total annual mortality rate calculated from a catch curve of age-1-5 fish in a long-haul seine fishery was 73%. The relationship between weight (W, g) and total length (mm) was W = 3.21 x $10^{-9}(TL)^{3.23}$; $N = 1.947$. Two groups of Atlantic croaker may overlap in North Carolina; the group that occurs mainly offshore and north of Cape Lookout exhibits greater size-at-age and greater longevity than the more southerly, inshore group.

—. 1989. Fisheries Resources Potentially Impacted by Proposed Drilling on the U.S. Atlantic Continental Slope and Rise off Cape Hatteras, North Carolina. pp. 26-39. *In*: Crawford, K. (ed.). Proceedings: 1989 Marine Expo: The Natural Resources Associated with Mobil's Proposed Drill Site. NC Outer Continental Shelf Office, NC Department of Administration. Raleigh, NC.

The offshore waters of North Carolina contain a tremendous diversity of fishes and other biota. In fact, there are more marine fish species in our coastal waters than off any other East or Gulf coast state except Florida. Many of these species support extensive commercial and recreational fisheries. One reason for such a diverse fauna is that several distinct water masses come together in North Carolina, usually around Cape Hatteras. Tropical, warm temperate, and cold temperate animals occur here in relation to changing seasons. Many different kinds of habitats also occur here, allowing fishes to expand into a variety of niches. The following exhibits will provide a general, brief overview of the types of fishes inhabiting the Mobil drill site and will cover some important aspects of the upper water column, continental shelf, and estuaries that are relevant to both exploration and production of offshore mineral resources.

—. 1991. Fisheries Resources Potentially Impacted by Proposed Drilling On the US Atlantic Continental Slope and Rise Off Cape Hatteras, North Carolina. p. 6. *In*: Shepard, A. (ed.). NURC/UNCW 1991 Undersea Research: Informational Meeting. National Undersea Research Center, University of North Carolina at Wilmington. Wilmington, NC.

An area known colloquially as "The Point" by fishermen, lies within the Manteo oil and gas lease blocks, just north of block 467, site of the proposed exploratory drill hole. 'The Point" is characterized by a productive pelagic fishery and complex submarine topography. Although a small, canyon-like feature underlies the area, "The Point" is not a spot on the bottom, but rather a shifting location that may coincide with the confluence of water masses.

In 1991, we will use a research submersible to describe the pelagic and benthic fish populations near Manteo Block 467. Specific objectives are to determine the distribution of: (1) pelagic fish with respect to depth and hydrographic features throughout the water column; and (2) benthic fish with respect to depth and topographic features.

—. 1998. Habitat and Living Resource Review: Scientific Data for Fisheries and *Sargassum* at the Hatteras Middle Slope (Including "The Point" and Manteo Exploration Unit). pp. 37-42. *In*: Vigil, D.L. (ed.). North Carolina/Minerals Management Service Technical Workshop on Manteo Unit Exploration: February 4-5, 1998. U.S. Dept. of the Interior, Minerals Management Service, Gulf of Mexico OCS Region. New Orleans, LA.

*These are the proceedings from a workshop/meeting (conducted on February 4-5, 1998) between the North Carolina Department of Environment and Natural Resources, and the U.S. Department of the Interior's Minerals Management Service (MMS). The geographic area being discussed is approximately 45 miles east-northeast of Cape Hatteras, NC, referred to as the Manteo Unit. This workshop reviewed environmental and socioeconomic information known and needed on the Manteo Unit. The MMS's Gulf of Mexico OCS Regional Director gave an MMS perspective on history and status of the area. Chevron gave a presentation on how the exploratory well would be drilled. The scientific characterization was presented in greater detail by a number of scientific experts who spoke on the following disciplines physical environment, habitat and living resources, seabirds, marine mammals, sea turtles, and social and economic issues. Specific chapters are cited individually, when appropriate.

The purpose of this review is to provide a brief summary of the state of fisheries and *Sargassum* knowledge in and near to the geographic region proposed for oil exploration activities off of North Carolina (referred to here as the Hatters Middle Slope, HMS). This will result in a basic listing of what we know about the subjects and what we still need to know. This treatment is restricted to the HMS area and thus is not to be a complete description of the North Carolina ichthyofauna. Time and space constraints imposed by the North Carolina/Minerals Management Service Technical Workshop do not allow a full treatment of this subject nor a detailed presentation of the data that support various conclusions. Prioritized and expanding the list of data needs will require additional discussions, some completed at this meeting, with input from a variety of scientist, managers, and the public. Since the last such summaries (1989 and 1991), considerable data have been collected (much of it published) related to the HMS. Ironically, the major impetus (upper water column fishery concerns around "The Point") for research here resulted in most studies being conducted on or near the bottom close to the proposed drill site rather than studies about the processes driving fisheries at "The Point." This section discusses Benthic Slope, Mid-Water Mesopelagic, Surface-Upper Water Column, Sargassum Community, Commercial/Recreational Fisheries, Oil Exploration/Development Concerns, and a Summary of Data/Study Needs including: Trophodynamic/Energetic Pathways (Plus Other Life History Data); Fisheries at "The Point;" Data Inventory Around HMS and "The Point;" Larval Fish Data; Lighting Effects; Mechanisms Structuring Benthic and Mid-water Fish Communities of the HMS; and Physical Oceanography.

—. Unpublished (a). Selected fish, invertebrate and bottom habitat data.

*These are unpublished data, collected by S.W. Ross during a SCUBA dive on 18 August 1980. The location for this site [SWR -SCUBA-80-20] is 35° 20.7'N; 75° 21.2'W; depth 70-80 feet. Selected fish, invertebrate, and bottom habitat data were collected. These data are unpublished and the site was not visited again. This site (no date presented) is listed as ISO4 by Kirby-Smith (1989). The location data assigned for site ISO4 by Kirby-Smith (1989) were incorrect and these data were collected by S.W. Ross [SWR -SCUBA-80-20] (S.W. Ross, pers. comm. 19 November 1999).

—. Unpublished database (b). SCUBA and Submersible Surveys.

*This is an unpublished SCUBA and Submersible Survey database. Data were collected S.W. Ross. Part of this unpublished database is cited in Parker & Ross (1986). Select sample locations and related data were computerized as part of the North Carolina SEAMAP Hardbottom data project by Moser et al. (1995). SEAMAP Hardbottom data (sample locations) within the defined project area for The Point were sorted and mapped using ArcView GIS (J. Ott. pers., comm. 15 Nov 99).

Ross, S.W., and A. Scarborough-Bull. 1998. Biological Environment Work Session Results: Fisheries. pp. 76-79. *In*: Vigil, D.L. (ed.). North Carolina/Minerals Management Service Technical Workshop on Manteo Unit Exploration: February 4-5, 1998. U.S. Dept. of the Interior, Minerals Management Service, Gulf of Mexico OCS Region. New Orleans, LA.

*These are the proceedings from a workshop/meeting (conducted on February 4-5, 1998) between the North Carolina Department of Environment and Natural Resources, and the U.S. Department of the Interior's Minerals Management Service (MMS). The geographic area being discussed is approximately 45 miles east-northeast of Cape Hatteras, NC, referred to as the Manteo Unit. This workshop reviewed environmental and socioeconomic information known and needed on the Manteo Unit. The MMS's Gulf of Mexico OCS Regional Director gave an MMS perspective on history and status of the area. Chevron gave a presentation on how the exploratory well would be drilled. The scientific characterization was presented in greater detail by a number of scientific experts who spoke on the following disciplines physical environment, habitat and living resources, seabirds, marine mammals, sea turtles, and social and economic issues. Specific chapters are cited individually, when appropriate.

The goal of this session was to raise scientific concerns/issues regarding the potential impacts of OCS drilling on fisheries. The session specifically recommended information needs on a short-term and long-term basis. The short-term was defined as the time period before exploratory drilling would take place in the Manteo Unit offshore North Carolina. The long-term was defined as the time period before development activities took place in the same location. Due to time constraints, the session spent more time in short-term information needs.

Two major short-term issues were raised concerning fisheries and oil and gas exploration. (1) There is a need to define and describe usage of the area known as The Point. (2) There is a need to synthesize and inventory existing data. Three long-term issues were raised for discussion. Three major long-term issues were raised concerning fisheries and oil and gas exploration. (1) There is a need to better understand the trophodynamics/energetic pathways at The Point. (2) There is a need to understand ichthyoplankton and its ecological role at The Point. (3) There is a need to understand structuring mechanisms. Four additional issues were raised concerning fisheries and oil and gas exploration on a long-term basis. Due to time constraints these concerns were not discussed in detail. (1) Concerns related to discharges from both drilling and production. (2) Concerns related to the presence of either temporary or permanent structures. (3) Concerns related to the effects of noise. (4) Concerns related to the presence of lights. Any endeavors on this project should be tied to the study of the effects of light on the seabirds that feed and/or roost at The Point.

Ross, S.W., K.J. Sulak, and T.A. Munroe. 2001. Association of *Syscenus infelix* (Crustacea:

Isopoda: Aegidae) with benthopelagic rattail fishes, *Nezumia* spp. (Macrouridae), along the western North Atlantic continental slope. Mar. Biol. 138(3): 595-601.

During submersible surveys along the continental slope (summers of 1991 and 1992, 184-847 m) between False Cape, Virginia and Cape Hatteras, North Carolina, USA we observed the aegid isopod, *Syscenus infelix* Harger, attached to the macrourid *Nezumia bairdii* (Goode and Bean). This is the first report of *S. infelix* attached to fishes in the western North Atlantic. The association of this blind isopod with its host appears species-specific. The large, conspicuous isopod always attached to a fish in the same location, the dorsal midline, immediately behind the first dorsal fin. Attachment appears to be long-term, with the isopod forming a characteristic scar consisting of a distinct discolored oval depression with seven small, dark impressions that coalesce as the fish grows. Only one *S. infelix* was found on each host fish. The isopod occurred on 23.7% of *N. bairdii* observed from submersible on the middle continental slope off Virginia and North Carolina, compared with 16.6% of 1,236 museum specimens of the same species (based on inspection for scars) collected at latitudes 26° -64° N. Prevalence of the fish-isopod association was not correlated with depth or latitude. We also found identical scars on preserved specimens of *N. aequalis* (2.6% of 660 specimens), *N. sclerorhynchus* (1.2% of 86 specimens), and *N. suilla* (14.3% of 7 specimens), mostly from areas outside the range of *N. bairdii*. No scars were found on museum specimens of *N. atlantica* (n=27), *N . cyrano* (n=57), or *N. longebarbata* (n=7). The low incidence of isopod attachment on these species suggests that *N. bairdii* is the preferred host. Infestation by the isopod appears to result in erosion of host fish scales and tissue. We propose that *S. infelix* is an obligate associate of its host fish and should be considered parasitic.

Ross, S.W., K.J. Sulak, J. Gartner, and D.S. Lee. Unpublished data. Ongoing project: Definition of Ecological/Trophic Linkages Among Fishes and Other Nekton in the Area Known as The Point — North Carolina Continental Shelf Slope.

*This is an on-going study of fishes, invertebrates, sargassum and marine birds at the area known as The Point. The emphasis is on trophic linkages throughout the water column. The summer 1999 and 2000 stations were mapped (Fig. 7).

Rotunno, T., and R.K. Cowen. 1997. Temporal and spatial spawning patterns of the Atlantic butterfish, *Peprilus triacanthits,* in the South and Middle Atlantic Bights. Fishery Bulletin 95: 785-799.

Three species of the stromateoid genus *Peprilus* have been found to occur in the northwest Atlantic: *P. triacanthus* (butterfish), *P. burti* (gulf butterfish), and *P. alepidotus* (harvestfish). *Peprilus triacanthus* and *P. alepidotus* reportedly spawn from May through August and June through July, respectively. *Peprilus burti* spawns twice yearly: February through May and September through November. Collections of larvae and juveniles of *Peprilus spp.* from the northern South Atlantic (SAB) and Mid-Atlantic (MAB) Bights during both the spring and summer of 1988 and 1989 suggest that either a combination of species was spawning or that reported spawning dates were suspect. Species identification of *Peprilus* in these collections was determined with morphometric, meristic, and pigment character analyses. Specimens sampled had counts for caudal vertebrae (18-19) and ventral midline melanophores (11-16) consistent with those found for *P. triacanthus* in previous studies. By analyzing otoliths, we estimated larval and juvenile growth rates to be approximately 0.23 mm/day. Backcalculation of hatch dates suggests either two spawning events for *P. triacanthus,* February through mid-April and mid-May through late July, or one extended spawning period beginning in late February and ending in late July. This study reveals that *P. triacanthus* spawns for a much longer period than previously thought, it is possible that *P. triacanthus* spawns during the spring in the SAB and summer in the MAB as a strategy to extend the duration of its spawning period. This strategy is one used by other north-south migrating species and warrants further study.

Schwartz, F.J. 1989. Zoogeography and Ecology of Fishes Inhabiting North Carolina's Marine Waters to Depths of 600 m. pp. 335-374. *In*: George, R.Y., and A.W. Hulbert (eds.). North Carolina Coastal Symposium. National Undersea Research Program, NOAA. Rockville, MD.

More than 650 species of fishes within 149 families are known to occur in waters that extend from the inshore high tide mark seaward to offshore depths of 600 m off North Carolina. These waters include estuarine, coastal, continental shelf, and slope habitats. The fishes are treated by province, depth distribution, habitat, type of fish, type of migrant, seasonality, and where known. Comments are presented on a species' biology and interaction with a specific community or environment located in the Middle and South Atlantic bights. The interplay and influence or control of their abundance by geological and environmental features such as Hatteras barrier, Charleston Bump, eddies, water temperatures, salinities, rivers, and the Gulf Stream area also noted.

Settle, L.R. 1993. Spatial and Temporal Variability in the Distribution and Abundance of Larval and Juvenile Fishes Associated with Pelagic *Sargassum*. M.S. Thesis. University of North Carolina at Wilmington. 65 p.

A survey of the larval and juvenile fishes associated with the pelagic Sargassum habitat in the South Atlantic Bight and adjacent western Atlantic Ocean was conducted from July 1991 through March 1993. Fishes representing 104 taxonomic categories were identified, including reef fishes, coastal demersal, coastal pelagic, epipelagic and mesopelagic species. The most important families were Balistidae and Carangidae, each represented by 15 species. Species composition, species diversity and abundance varied both seasonally and regionally. Diversity was highest during spring through fall over the outer continental shelf and in the Gulf Stream. Abundance decreased from spring through winter and from the continental shelf into offshore waters. The numbers of fishes and fish biomass were found to be positively correlated with the wet weight of algae in most cases examined. The results of this study will be useful to fisheries managers assessing the potential impacts of commercial *Sargassum* harvesting in the region.

—. 1997. Commercial harvest of pelagic Sargassum: A summary of landings since June 1995. Attachment 11. *In*: South Atlantic Fishery Management Council. Essential Fish Habitat Workshop # 9: October 7 — 8, 1997 Pelagic Habitat Sargassum and Water Column. South Atlantic Fishery Management Council. Charleston, SC.

Attachment 11: The commercial harvest of pelagic *Sargassum* resumed in June 1995. To date the fishery is prosecuted by a single firm, Aqua-10 Corporation of Beaufort, North Carolina. Aqua-10 processes the raw algae into a variety of agricultural fertilizers and dietary supplements used in the swine and poultry industries. The firm purchases algae harvested by local fishing vessels. Two vessels, the FV Outer Banks (16.5 m snapper boat) and the FV Rising Sun (15 m long-liner) have been equipped with Sargassum nets by Aqua- 10. The gear consists of a 1.2 in x 0.9 n frame trawl rigged with 7.6 am mesh trawl webbing. The vessels harvest algae ancillary to their normal fishing activities. When algae are landed, Aqua-10 notifies the NMFS, Beaufort Laboratory. The algae are examined for by-catch at dockside and at the processing plant. Vessel captains are interviewed to obtain data on the date and location of harvests, effort, and by-catch.

All algae have been harvested from off the North Carolina coast from northern Onslow Bay to northeast of Cape Hatteras (Fig. 2). Although Sargassum has been harvested on the continental shelf, most was obtained in the Gulf Stream (Fig. 3). The observed by-catch has been minimal in terms of numbers of individuals. No sea turtles and few fishes have been noted. Most fish have been young juveniles and are generally in advanced stages of decomposition. Identifiable taxa include filefish (*Monacanthus hispidus*), amberjacks (*Seriola* spp.), blue runner (*Caranx crysos*), jacks (*Caranx* spp.), flyingfish (Exocoetidae), sergeant major (*Abudefduf saxatilis*), gray triggerfish (*Balistes capriscus*), sargassum fish (*Histrio histrio*), and pipefish (*Syngnathus* spp.). The most commonly observed macrofaunal by-catch have been crustaceans including several shrimp (genera *Hippolyte*, *Latreutes*, and *Leander*) and crabs (genera *Planes* and *Portunus*).

Shepard, A. (ed.). 1991. Undersea Research at The Point. NURC/UNCW 1991 Undersea Research: Informational Meeting. National Undersea Research Center, University of North Carolina at Wilmington. Wilmington, NC. 9 p.

*This 9 page handout provides a summary of research being conducted at "The Point" area (Manteo Lease Block 467).

The National Undersea Research Center at the University of North Carolina at Wilmington (NURC/UNCW), funded by a grant from the National Oceanic and Atmospheric Administration's Office of Undersea Research, was established in 1980 to promote, facilitate, and conduct research in the Southeastern United States utilizing undersea techniques, including advanced wet diving and manned and unmanned submersibles. A main Center goal is to provide information to NOAA that will assist the agency in fulfilling its charter to explore, understand, conserve and manage the U.S. marine environment and associated resources. To help meet this goal, the Center supports and conducts interdisciplinary oceanographic research projects studying continental margin processes, particularly the interactions and linkages between estuarine, continental shelf, and slope (including submarine canyon) environments.

Shepard, A., and A.H. Hulbert (eds.). 1994. Workshop Report: Present and Future Research Initiatives on the Upper Hatteras Slope off North Carolina. National Undersea Research Center at the University of North Carolina at Wilmington. Wilmington, NC. 30p.

*This report is the result of the May 1993 workshop held in Raleigh, NC. The topics of discussion were research (present and planned) at the Upper Hatteras Slope and potential funding sources. The workshop was sponsored by National Undersea Research Center at the University of North Carolina at Wilmington. The report provides a brief description of invertebrates, biological oceanography, chemical oceanography, geological oceanography (bathymetry, oil and gas exploration), physical oceanography, fisheries, and *Sargassum*. Appendix A is a workshop agenda and list of speakers. No abstracts for speakers are provided. Appendix B is a list of potential funding sources. Appendix C contains a list of relevant publications.

Shepherd, G.R. 1982. Growth, Reproduction, and mortality of weakfish, *Cynoscion regalis,* and size/age structure of the fisheries in the middle Atlantic region. Masters Thesis. Rutgers, The State University of New Jersey. New Brunswick, NJ. 69 p.

This thesis describes life history characteristics of weakfish, *Cynoscion regalis*, of the middle Atlantic region of the United States. Fish were collected by the National Marine Fisheries Service (NMFS) groundfish survey (1979-1981), between Cape Fear, North Carolina and Cape Cod, MA in depths less than 200 m (Grosslein, 1969). Additional samples from commercial fishing operations (May 1980 — June 1981) in Gardener's Bay, Long Island, Sandy Hook Bay, New Jersey and Delaware Bay, New Jersey. Virginia commercial catch was used for December sample.

Shepherd, G. and C.B. Grimes. 1983. Geographic and historic variations in growth of weakfish, Cynoscion regalis, in the Middle Atlantic Bight. Fishery Bulletin 81(4): 803-813.

The growth of weakfish, Cynoscion regalis, throughout the Middle Atlantic Bight was examined. Six geographic subdivisions were initially established for growth comparisons. Covariate analysis of the total length-scale size relationship revealed three distinct regions. Back-calculated lengths at age were compared using analysis of variance and showed significant differences between regions ($P < 0.001$) and between sexes ($P < 0.05$). Mean lengths at age of northern weakfish were greater than southern fish and females were larger than males after age 6. Maximum mean lengths at age were also greater in the north, 81 cm at age 11, and became progressively smaller towards the south, declining to 42 cm at age 4 in the southernmost region. The growth variations may result from varying allocations of energy to somatic growth according to environmental and migratory requirements. Growth differences resulting from the availability of food items in each habitat are also examined.

Mean and maximum lengths at age have charged over the past 50 years, with current growth greater than in 1929 or 1952. A possible relationship exists between fluctuating population sizes and historic growth variations. The current age/size structure of weakfish fisheries in Delaware Bay is discussed.

Shepherd, G.R., and M. Terceiro. 1994. The Summer Flounder, Scup, and Black Sea Bass Fishery of the Middle Atlantic Bight and Southern New England Waters. NOAA Technical Report NMFS 122. Woods Hole Laboratory, Northeast Fisheries Science Center, National Marine Fisheries Service. Woods Hole, MA. 13 p.

Summer flounder, *Paralichthys dentatus*, scup, *Stenotomus chrysops*, and black sea bass, *Centropristis striata*, co-occur within the Middle Atlantic Bight and off southern New England and are important components of commercial and recreational fisheries. The commercial otter trawl fishery for these species is primarily a winter fishery, whereas the recreational fishery takes place between late spring and autumn. The otter trawl fishery generally targets summer flounder, and less frequently scup, while black sea bass occurs as bycatch. Trips in which all three species were present yielded highest aggregate landings per unit of effort (LPUE) levels and occurred more often than trips landing only one or two species. More than 50% of the trips in the trawl fishery landed at least two of the three species. In contrast, greater than 75% of the recreational landings of each species occurred as a result of trips landing only one species. Differences in the fisheries resulted from the interactions of seasonal changes in species distributions and gear selectivity.

Smith, W.G. 1973. The distribution of summer flounder *Paralichthys dentatus*, eggs and larvae on the continental shelf between Cape Cod and Cape Lookout, 1965-66. Fishery Bulletin 71(2): 527-535.

Eggs and larvae of summer flounder, *Paralichthys dentatus*, were collected with Gulf V plankton nets between Cape Cod, MA, and Cape Lookout, NC, during a 1-year survey of Continental Shelf Waters. The most productive spawning grounds were located off New York and New Jersey. Spawning began in northern parts of the survey area, progressed southward with the season, and ended off Cape Lookout. We collected eggs north of Chesapeake Bay from September to December and south of the Bay from November to February, and larvae north of Chesapeake Bay from September to February and south of the Bay from November to May. Most spawning occurred at temperatures between 12 and 19° C, but the pelagic eggs were caught at mean temperatures from 9.1 to 22.9° C, and larvae from 0 to 23.1° C.

Smith, W.G., J.D. Sibunka, and A. Wells. 1975. Seasonal Distributions of Larval Flatfishes (Plueuronectiformes) on the Continental Shelf Between Cape Cod, Massachusetts, and Cape Lookout, North Carolina, 1965-66. National Oceanographic and Atmospheric Administration (NOAA), National Marine Fisheries (NMFS). Seattle, WA. 68 p.

Larval flatfishes, representing 4 families, 17 genera, and 15 species, were identified from collections taken during a 1-yr. survey designated to locate spawning grounds and trace dispersion of fish eggs and larvae on the Continental shelf. Most flatfishes began spawning in the spring, a time of marked seasonal temperature change. The seasonal distribution of larvae indicated that: 1.) bothids had longer spawning seasons than pleuronectids; 2.) pleuronectids spawned largely in the northern half of the survey area during the spring; 3.) most bothids spawned in the southern half, beginning in spring and continuing through early fall; 4.) although cynoglossids spawned incidentally off North Carolina, most of their larvae were transported into the survey area from spawning grounds south of Cape Lookout; 5.) the few representatives of the family Solenidae originated south of Cape Lookout; 6.) spawning that began in the spring proceeded from the south to north as the season progressed, but spawning that began in the fall proceeded from north to south, suggesting that the onset of spawning is triggered by spring warming and fall cooling; 7.) most species spawned within a relatively narrow range of temperature; 8.) salinity had no apparent influence on spawning.

Sogard, S.M., K.W. Able, and M.P. Fahay. 1992. Early life history of the tautog, *Tautoga onitis,* in the Mid-Atlantic Bight. Fishery Bulletin 90: 529-539.

Spawning patterns, larval distribution, and juvenile growth characteristics were examined for tautog *Tautoga onitis* in New Jersey and the Mid-Atlantic Bight. We analyzed data from plankton surveys (1972-1990) over the continental shelf and in the Great Bay-Mullica River estuarine system. Data on size and abundance of juveniles were derived from throw trap and trawl collections in New Jersey estuaries (1988-89). In addition, we validated the daily deposition of otolith increments and used increment counts to estimate juvenile age and growth patterns. Extensive egg and larval collections indicated that spawning occurs from April through September, with a peak in June and July. Spawning over the continental shelf is concentrated off Long Island and Rhode Island. Based on validated daily increments in sagittal otoliths and the formation of a well-defined settlement mark, tautog larvae spend about 3 weeks in the plankton. Both spawning and settlement occur over a prolonged period, based on otolith back-calculations. Three methods of estimating young-of-the-year growth rates, including length-frequency progressions, otolith age/fish-size comparisons, and direct measurement of growth in caging experiments, indicated an average growth rate of about 0.5 mm/day during the peak midsummer growing season. Length-frequency distributions suggested tautog reach a rnodal size of about 75 mm SL after their first summer, and 155 mm by the end of their second summer.

South Atlantic Fishery Management Council. 1998. FINAL Habitat Plan for the South Atlantic Region: Essential Fish Habitat Requirements for Fishery Management Plans of the South Atlantic Fishery Management Council: The Shrimp Fishery Management Plan; The Red Drum Fishery Management Plan; The Snapper Group Fishery Plan; The Coastal Migratory Pelagics Fishery Management Plan; The Golden Crab Fishery Management Plan; The Spiny Lobster Fishery Management Plan; The Coral, Coral Reefs, and Live/Hard Bottom Fishery Management Plan; The Sargassum Habitat Fishery Management Plan; and The Calico Scallop Fishery Management Plan. South Atlantic Fishery Management Council. Charleston, SC. 457 p.

*This report emphasizes South Atlantic Coast nearshore habitat (shore to 200m isobath). On pages 125-133 Sargassum habitat is described. Page 134-135 mentions "The Point" within Section 3.2.3.2.1 Description of Water Column Habitats. Figure A Water Masses off Cape Hatteras, is located on p. 135 and shows a schematic diagram of "The Point," relative to the Gulf Steam, Virginia (longshore) Current and Sargasso Sea. Table 18b taxonomic list of larval and early-juvenile fishes from offshore of Cape Lookout to Cape Hatteras including the region known as "The Point" is located on pp. 139-145. Oil and gas exploration, development and transposition are mentioned in section 4.1.2.4 on page 323 (Off shore Cape Hatteras, NC is mentioned, but no specific reference to "The Point" is made).

Stancyk, S.E. (In press). Predation behavior in echinoderms. *In*: Candia Carnevali, M.D. (ed.). Proceedings of the Fifth European Conference on Echinoderms, Milan Italy, 7-12 September 1998. A. A. Balkema, Rotterdam.

This study describes predation behavior on swimming organisms by *Ophiura sarsi*. Aluminum Frame, vexar mesh cages with yellow polypropylene rope on the bottom were used during this study. Each cage contained 5 brittlestars with 2 arms removed. Other cages, which had been left out a year, there was heavy epifaunal growth, including recently metamorphosed crinoids. Although there was lots of particulate material in the water, these cages did not get buried, and often had burrowing fish associated with them (S. Stancyk, pers. comm. 15 July 1999).

Stancyk, S.E., C. Muir, and T. Fujita. 1998. Predation Behavior on swimming organisms by *Ophiura sarsi*. pp. 425-429. *In*: R. Mooi, and M. Telford (eds.). Echinoderms: San Francisco Proceedings of the Ninth International Echinoderm Conference. A. A. Balkema, Rotterdam.

This study describes predation behavior on swimming organisms by *Ophiura sarsi*. Aluminum Frame, vexar mesh cages with yellow polypropylene rope on the bottom were used during this study. Each cage contained 5 brittlestars with 2 arms removed. Other cages, which had been left out a year, there was heavy epifaunal growth, including recently metamorphosed crinoids. Although there was lots of particulate material in the water, these cages did not get buried, and often had burrowing fish associated with (S. Stancyk, pers. comm. 15 July 1999).

Stillwell, C.E., and N.E. Kohler. 1993. Food habits of the sandbar shark, *Carcharhinus plumbeus,* off the U.S. northeast coast, with estimates of daily ration. Fishery Bulletin 91: 138-150.

Food habits data from 415 sandbar sharks collected in the area between Cape Hatteras and Georges Bank (Great South Channel) were examined. Mean fork length (FL) and body weight (BW) were 55.0 cm and 1.72 kg for pups, 123.0 cm and 23.0 kg for juveniles, and 166.0 cm and 52.3 kg for adults. Of all juvenile and adult stomachs, 49% contained prey, primarily fish (teleosts and skates). Of stomachs from pups, 80% held food remains consisting almost exclusively of soft blue crabs. The mean percentage of stomach content volume to BW is 1.16 for pups, and 0.42 for juveniles and adults. Daily ration estimates as percentage of mean BW are 1.43 for pups, and 0.86 for juveniles and adults. Annual food consumption is estimated to be 5.1 times the mean BW for pups, and 3.1 times for juveniles and adults.

Sulak, K.J. 1992. Demersal Fish Fauna on the Continental Slope in the Vicinity of The Point. pp. 135-138. *In*: Department of the Interior, Minerals Management Service. Proceedings of the Fourth Atlantic OCS Region Information Transfer Meeting, September 1991. U.S. Department of the Interior, Minerals Management Service. Herndon, VA.

The Fourth Atlantic Outer Continental Shelf (OCS) Regional Information Transfer Meeting was held on 24-25 September 1991, in Wilmington, NC. The focus of the meeting was on the OCS off North Carolina, specifically on activities related to a proposed exploratory well for oil and gas by Mobil on Block 467 a site 40 miles off the coast of North Carolina. The area of industry interest is known as the Manteo Prospect, while the activities surrounding the proposed drilling are referred to collectively as the Manteo Project. The wildcat wellsite is in 2,690 ft. (857 m) of water near the edge of the Gulf Stream. It is also near a fishing ground known locally as "The Point." The area is believed to be gas prone rather than oil prone. The estimated size of the resource could be as high as 5 trillion cubic feet of gas.

The purpose of the meeting was to exchange information on the leasing background, legislative activities, scientific results, and socioeconomic studies. Legislative-related reports include descriptions of the Oil Pollution Act of 1990, the Outer Banks Protection Act, the Environmental Studies Review Panel, and the North Carolina Physical Oceanography Panel. Reports of studies on marine life include benthic diatoms, benthic fauna, pelagic seabirds, sea turtles, and right whales. One report describes the use of airships (blimps) for ocean research a capability relevant to North Carolina because of the east coast airship facility is located in the state. Local marine science facilities described include NOAA's National Undersea Research Center at the University of North Carolina at Wilmington (NURC/UNCW) and the National Marine Fisheries Service laboratory in Beaufort.

Developments in oil spill cleanup technology and capabilities are described by both the Coast Guard and the industry. A socioeconomic report describes the effects of the oil and gas activities on the tourist industry. Lastly, research on the restoration of salt marshes indicates that rehabilitation of an area is possible when development or an accident has occurred. While the emphasis of the meeting was on oil and gas, two reports described the results of projects related to offshore sand mining. The appendix lists the names and addresses of speakers. Individual chapters are cited individually when appropriate.

*This section provides a brief overview of Demersal Fish Fauna on the Continental Slope in the Vicinity of "The Point," based on five *Johnson Sea Link* submersible dives made in July 1991. The purpose was to identify, quantify, and characterize the demersal (bottom living) fish fauna of this region. Future studies are suggested.

Sulak, K.J., and S.W. Ross. 1993. Analysis of Submersible Videotapes for Demersal Fish Faunas from the Continental Slope in The Point Region. Appendix B. *In*: Diaz, R.J., J.A. Blake, and D.P. Lohse (eds.). Volume III Appendices: Benthic Study of the Continental Slope Off Cape Hatteras, North Carolina. Virginia Institute of Marine Science. School of Marine Science. College of William and Mary. Gloucester Pt., VA. Science Applications International Corporation. Woods Hole, MA.

*Evidence from ongoing research suggests that the benthic fauna, including demersal fish, in the region of "The Point" (see Appendix A for description and location) on the continental slope is unique. The goal of this project was to use videotapes, obtained using submersibles, to evaluate and compare the demersal deep-sea fish fauna from three adjacent regions of the continental slope. Videotapes provided by the National Undersea Research Center, University of North Carolina — Wilmington of dives made by the submersibles "JSL" and "Pisces III" between False Cape, VA and Cape Lookout, NC were screened to identify segments acceptable as transects. Acceptable segments were those where the submersible was at an appropriate altitude and speed (0.2 — 0.3 knots) and where there was sufficient light and clarity (water column and video system) to identify and count individuals. Some tapes unsuitable for analysis nonetheless contained good close-up segments of individual species and habitat types. A list of the tapes, which were analyzed, is presented in Appendix B-1. The tapes selected for review came from three regions. Tapes from the northern area came from a single series of dives between 36° 45' — 36° 46' N. The tapes from the southern area came from the area between 32° 53' — 34° 15' N.

—. 1996. Lilliputian bottom fish fauna of the Hatteras upper middle continental slope. Journal of Fish Biology 49 (Suppl. A): 91-113.

Submersible data from two areas along the Carolina-Virginia continental slope reveal a Hatteras upper middle slope (HMS) (35°30'N, 74°50'W) demersal fish fauna remarkable for diminutive size of individuals within and across species, a fauna which is accordingly termed 'Lilliputian'. Contrast of HMS submersible data with Virginia trawl and submersible data support this finding. The four top-ranking HMS fishes, *Lycenchelys verrillii, Glyptocephalus cynoglossus, Myxine glutinosa* and *Nezumia bairdii,* are all significantly smaller than on the Virginia upper middle slope. Also peculiar to the HMS is the dominance of sedentary benthic species, rarity of active benthopelagic foragers, and markedly elevated fish population density. Species composition of the HMS fauna differs from that of the general Middle Atlantic Bight fauna; notably absent are species of otherwise continuous distribution along the U.S. East Coast (e.g. *Synaphobranchus affinis, Nezumia aequalis).* Since HMS megafaunal and macrofaunal invertebrate communities are also anomalous, the Lilliputian phenomenon among HMS bottom fishes provides a characteristic biotic signature of a pervasively restructured benthic boundary layer community. The authors hypothesize that the HMS faunal anomaly reflects a limiting factor, episodic sediment surface hypoxia, peculiar to this region of high particulate organic carbon flux from surface waters. Results indicate that substantial changes in fish faunal composition and structure can occur on a small geographic scale on the open soft-substrate continental slope.

Taylor, D.L., B.F. Holland Jr., and J.W. Gillikin Jr. 1978. RV Dan Moore Cruise Report No. 31. North Carolina Division of Marine Fisheries, Department of Natural Resources and Community Development. Morehead City, NC.

*During December 1978, the RV Dan Moore completed preliminary trawl survey of Raleigh Bay, NC that began in October (cruise report 29). Extensive trawling of Raleigh Bay, NC from beach to the 20 fathom contour has already been conducted during the anadromous fish (river herring, shad, striped bass and sturgeon) and summer flounder projects. Effort this month, as well as in October, was concentrated in the offshore area from 20 fathoms to 100 fathom contour. The main objectives of the survey were: 1) To define and designate areas of trawlable bottom, 2) To define and designate areas where pots and/or traps should be used rather than trawls, 3) To define and designate those areas where hook and line may be the only feasible method of fishing.

—. 1979. RV Dan Moore Cruise Report No. 34: Cape Lookout, NC to Little Machipongo Inlet, VA. North Carolina Division of Marine Fisheries, Department of Natural Resources and Community Development. Morehead City, NC.

*From 2-11 April, the RV Dan Moore completed its investigations of offshore stocks of anadromous fishes (river herring, shad, striped bass and sturgeon) between Cape Lookout, NC and Little Machipongo Inlet, VA. Depths were 15 to 20 fathoms.

Trent, L., R.O. Williams, R.G. Taylor, C.H. Saloman, and C.H. Manooch, III. 1983. Size, sex ratio, and recruitment in various fisheries of king mackerel, Scomberomorus cavalla, in the southeastern United States. Fishery Bulletin 81(4): 709-721.

Data from over 54,000 king mackerel, Scomberomorus cavalla, were analyzed to evaluate spatial and temporal variations in size and sex composition in seven areas of the southeastern United States. Data were obtained from the recreational hook-and-line fishery of coastal states from Texas to North Carolina and from commercial hook-and-line and gill net fisheries of south Florida. Of the three types of gear, recreational hook and line appeared to be the least selective and gill net the most selective for particular sizes of king mackerel.

Size composition in each area varied considerably among months; patterns of size change were discernible in some areas. Sizes of king mackerel varied significantly among areas and years. Catches from south and northwest Florida contained high proportions of small fish (<700 mm FL); those from Texas and North Carolina contained mostly medium-sized fish (700-900 mm FL). Mean lengths of king mackerel were larger in 1978 than in 1977 in all areas except northwest Florida. In northwest Florida, modal fork lengths were 749 mm in 1968-69,649 mm in 1977, and 549 mm in 1978. The majority of the smallest fish (400-600 mm FL) were recruited to the fisheries in Florida, but the range and areas of abundance of king mackerel smaller than this are not known. For purposes of evaluating effects of minimum size regulations, the king mackerel population was divided into groups (the Florida winter, immature, spawning, and Louisiana groups).

Females dominated catches in all size groups and in all areas and years, except for south Florida in 1978. Annual, or ranges of annual, estimates of percentage female by area were as follows: Texas, 60.8-62.2%; Louisiana, 91.9-92.2%; northwest Florida, 57.1-75.1%; south Florida, 40.2-75.4%; and North Carolina, 75.8%. Females predominated in 31 of 38 sample groups at lengths <900 mm FL, and in all sample groups at lengths >899 mm FL.

U. S. Department of Commerce, National Oceanic and Atmospheric Administration, National Marine Fisheries Service. 1985. Shark Catches from Selected Fisheries Off The U.S. East Coast. NOAA Technical Report NMFS 31. U. S. Department of Commerce, National Oceanic and Atmospheric Administration, National Marine Fisheries Service, Scientific Publications Office. Seattle, WA. 22 p.

Various sources of catch of pelagic sharks during 1960-81 in the Northwest and Western Central Atlantic Ocean and Gulf of Mexico, particularly within the United States Fishery Conservation Zone (FCZ), were identified and quantified. These sources included reported statistics, but principally unreported bycatch in fisheries directed towards other species. Total catch estimates during 1965-80 averaged 9,800 t (metric tons) per year and peaked at 17,300 t in 1977 in the Atlantic FCZ and averaged 6,800 t per year and peaked at 10,200 t in 1980 in the Gulf FCZ. The major source of catch in the Atlantic FCZ was the U.S. recreational Fishery, followed by the United States and Canadian swordfish longline Fisheries and the Japanese tuna longline fisheries. The major sources of catch in the Gulf FCZ were the recreational Fishery and the U.S. shrimp, groundfish, and snapper- grouper fisheries. A comparison between long-term average catches and recent levels in both areas suggests that pelagic sharks may be excessively exploited at the present time.

U.S. Department of the Interior, Minerals Management Service. 1990. Atlantic Outer Continental Shelf: Final Environmental Report on Proposed Exploratory Drilling Offshore North Carolina. U.S.

Department of the Interior, Minerals Management Service, Atlantic OCS Region, Environmental Assessment Section. Herndon, VA.

*Topics include: fisheries, birds, marine mammals, physical oceanography, chemical oceanography, geology, gas and oil production. The proposed action is to drill a single exploratory well approximately 72 km (45 mi.) east-northeast of Cape Hatteras, NC in 820 m (2,690 ft) of water. Total depth for the proposed well is 4,267 m (14,000 ft) and the location is on Block 467 on the Minerals Management Service Protraction diagram NI 18-2. The proposal has been submitted by Mobil for itself and 7 partners to drill the well on the approved 21-block exploration unit.

U.S. Department of the Interior, Minerals Management Service. 1992. Proceedings of the Fourth Atlantic OCS Region Information Transfer Meeting, September 1991. U.S. Department of the Interior, Minerals Management Service. Herndon, VA. 198 p.

The Fourth Atlantic Outer Continental Shelf (OCS) Regional Information Transfer Meeting (ITM) was held on 24-25 September 1991, in Wilmington, NC. The focus of the meeting was on the OCS off North Carolina, specifically on activities related to a proposed exploratory well for oil and gas by Mobil on Block 467 a site 40 miles off the coast of North Carolina. The area of industry interest is known as the Manteo Prospect, while the activities surrounding the proposed drilling are referred to collectively as the Manteo Project. The wildcat wellsite is in 2,690 ft. (857 m) of water near the edge of the Gulf Stream. It is also near a fishing ground known locally as "The Point." The area is believed to be gas prone rather than oil prone. The estimated size of the resource could be as high as 5 trillion cubic feet of gas.

The purpose of the meeting was to exchange information on the leasing background, legislative activities, scientific results, and socioeconomic studies. Legislative-related reports include descriptions of the Oil Pollution Act of 1990, the Outer Banks Protection Act, the Environmental Studies Review Panel, and the North Carolina Physical Oceanography Panel. Reports of studies on marine life include benthic diatoms, benthic fauna, pelagic seabirds, sea turtles, and right whales. One report describes the use of airships (blimps) for ocean research a capability relevant to North Carolina because of the east coast airship facility is located in the state. Local marine science facilities described include NOAA's National Undersea Research Center at the University of North Carolina at Wilmington (NURC/UNCW) and the National Marine Fisheries Service laboratory in Beaufort.

Developments in oil spill cleanup technology and capabilities are described by both the Coast Guard and the industry. A socioeconomic report describes the effects of the oil and gas activities on the tourist industry. Lastly, research on the restoration of salt marshes indicates that rehabilitation of an area is possible when development or an accident has occurred. While the emphasis of the meeting was on oil and gas, two reports described the results of projects related to offshore sand mining. The appendix lists the names and addresses of speakers. Individual chapters are cited individually when appropriate.

U.S. Department of the Navy. 1985. EMPRESS II: Supplemental Draft Environmental Impact Statement for the Proposed Operation of the Navy Electromagnetic Pulse Radiation Environment Simulator for Ships (Empress II) in the Chesapeake Bay and Atlantic Ocean. United States Navy. Environmental/ Intergovernmental Section. Atlantic Division. Naval Facilities Engineering and Command. Norfolk, VA.

*This is a National Environmental Policy Act document characterizing the proposed EMPRESS II project. Appendix B contains a Summary of Biological Processes in the Proposed VACAPES EMPRESS II area off North Carolina Relating to Planktonic Communities, Pelagic Macroinvertebrates, Ichthyofauna, Sea turtles, Marine Mammals, and Sea Birds. Technical reports supporting this summary have been written by authorities in each discipline and are included in Appendices. The technical reports are cited individually. The southern portion of VACAPES EMPRESS II Area of North Carolina overlaps with the northern portion of the defined study area for the Data Inventory Related to the Hatteras Middle Slope (The Point) Area.

Ustach, J. Unpublished database. RV Eastward Studies, Underwater Camera Data 1965-1973. Duke University Marine Laboratory. Beaufort, NC.

*This is an unpublished database. Data were collected from 1965 to 1973 by the Duke University Marine Laboratory. The contact person is Joseph Ustach. Select sample locations and related data were computerized as part of the North Carolina SEAMAP Hardbottom data project by Moser et al. (1995). SEAMAP Hardbottom data (sample locations) within the defined project area for The Point were sorted and mapped using ArcView GIS (J. Ott, pers. comm. 15 Nov 99).

Vaughn, J.A., B.F. Holland Jr., and S.G. Keefe. 1976. RV Dan Moore Cruise Report No. 14: Cape Lookout, NC to Little Machipongo Inlet, VA. North Carolina Division of Marine Fisheries, Department of Natural Resources and Community Development. Morehead City, NC.

*The primary objective of the March 1976 cruise was to continue monitoring the offshore stocks of anadromous fishes (alewife, blueback herring, American and hickory shad, striped bass and sturgeon) in North Carolina and Virginia. A wing trawl, selective for pelagic fishes such as herring, trout and mackerel was used in the vicinity of 10-15 fathom contours.

Vigil, D.L. (ed.). 1998. North Carolina/Minerals Management Service Technical Workshop on Manteo Unit Exploration: February 4-5, 1998. U.S. Dept. of the Interior, Minerals Management Service. Gulf of Mexico OCS Region. New Orleans, LA. 168 p.

*These are the proceedings from a workshop/meeting (conducted on February 4-5, 1998) between the North Carolina Department of Environment and Natural Resources, and the U.S. Department of the Interior's Minerals Management Service (MMS). The geographic area being discussed is approximately 45 miles east-northeast of Cape Hatteras, NC, referred to as the Manteo Unit. This workshop reviewed environmental and socioeconomic information known and needed on the Manteo Unit. The MMS's Gulf of Mexico OCS Regional Director gave an MMS perspective on history and status of the area. Chevron gave a presentation on how the exploratory well would be drilled. The scientific characterization was presented in greater detail by a number of scientific experts who spoke on the following disciplines physical environment, habitat and living resources (invertebrates and fish), seabirds, marine mammals, sea turtles, and social and economic issues. Specific chapters are cited individually, when appropriate.

Wilk, S.J. and M.J. Silverman. 1976. Fish and hydrographic collections made by the research vessels Dolphin and Delaware II during 1968-72 from New York to Florida. NOAA Technical Report NMFS SSRF-697. 159 p.

Information is given in tabular form for fish and hydrographic observations collected during 18 cruises made by the research vessels Dolphin and Delaware II from New York to Florida during 1968-72. Tables include station locations with related hydrographic observations and number, weight, and size range of fish species caught.

Wilk, S.J., W.G. Smith, D.E. Ralph, and J. Sibunka. 1980. Population structure of summer flounder between New York and Florida based on linear discriminant analysis. Transactions of the American Fisheries Society. 109(3): 265-271.

We used a stepwise linear discriminant analysis to investigate the population structure of summer flounder, Paralichthys dentatus (Linnaeus). Analysis was based on 18 morphometric and meristic variables taken from 1,214 specimens collected in coastal waters between Montauk Point, New York and Cape Canaveral, Florida. Two populations were identified: one in the Middle Atlantic Bight, or between New York and Cape Hatteras, North Carolina; the other in the South Atlantic Bight, or between Cape Hatteras and Florida. Discriminant analysis coefficients, based on five morphometric variables taken from specimens collected at geographic extremes of the survey area, provide a mathematical means for classifying summer flounder into either the northern or southern population with an accuracy of 93%.

Witzell, W.N. 1999. Distribution and relative abundance of sea turtles caught incidentally by the U.S. pelagic longline fleet in the western North Atlantic Ocean, 1992-1995. Fisheries Bulletin 97: 200-211.

*This paper examines the seasonal distribution and relative abundance of threatened and endangered sea turtles (e.g., loggerhead sea turtle, *Caretta caretta*; and leatherback sea turtle, *Dermochelys coriacea*) caught incidentally by the U.S. Atlantic pelagic longline fishery for tuna, *Thunnus* spp., and swordfish, *Xiphias gladius* from 1992 through 1995. Sargassum is mentioned.

Wollam, M.B. 1970. Description and distribution of larvae and early juveniles of king mackerel, *Scomberomorus cavalla* (Cuvier), and Spanish mackerel, *Scomberomorus maculatus* (Mitchill); (Pisces: Scombridae); in the Western North Atlantic. Technical Series No. 61. Florida Department of Natural Resources, Division of Marine Resources. St. Petersburg, FL. 35 p.

Larvae and juveniles of both king and Spanish mackerel collected by the Florida Department of Natural Resources Marine Research Laboratory are described and figured. Nine additional king mackerel juveniles were loaned by the Bureau of Sport Fisheries' Sandy Hook Marine Laboratory. This report constitutes the first description of the developmental stages of king mackerel and a redescription of some larval stages of Spanish mackerel.

Initial identifications are based on the number of vertebral and/or myomere elements with pigmentation patterns and morphometrics providing corroborative evidence. King mackerel have 42 to 43 vertebrae and/or myomeres; larval stages have a large melanophore on the medial surface of the dentary about one third of the distance from the mandibular symphysis; juveniles stages have a saddle-shaped patch of pigmentation on the flank under the second dorsal finlets, and only the anterior five interracial membranes of the first dorsal fin are pigmented. Spanish mackerel have 52 to 53 vertebrae and/or myomeres; larval stages may have a small chromatophore between the lower jaw rami about one half the distance from the mandibular symphysis; juvenile stages have a lateral band of pigmentation extending the length of the trunk, and all of the interracial membranes of the first dorsal fin are pigmented. A conspicuous spiny projection of the supraoccipital crest present in the larvae of both species is thought to be a generic character.

Meristic data falls within the range of the adults, except for the presence of one or two additional first dorsal fin spines in some juvenile Spanish mackerel.

Distribution and seasonality of the larvae and juveniles indicate that these mackerels spawn in the summer while in the northern portion of their ranges. This implies that mackerels in the eastern Gulf of Mexico may be reproductively isolated from those along the Atlantic coast.

A previous description of larval stages of Spanish mackerel from 3.0 to 5.75 mm SL is shown to be incorrect.

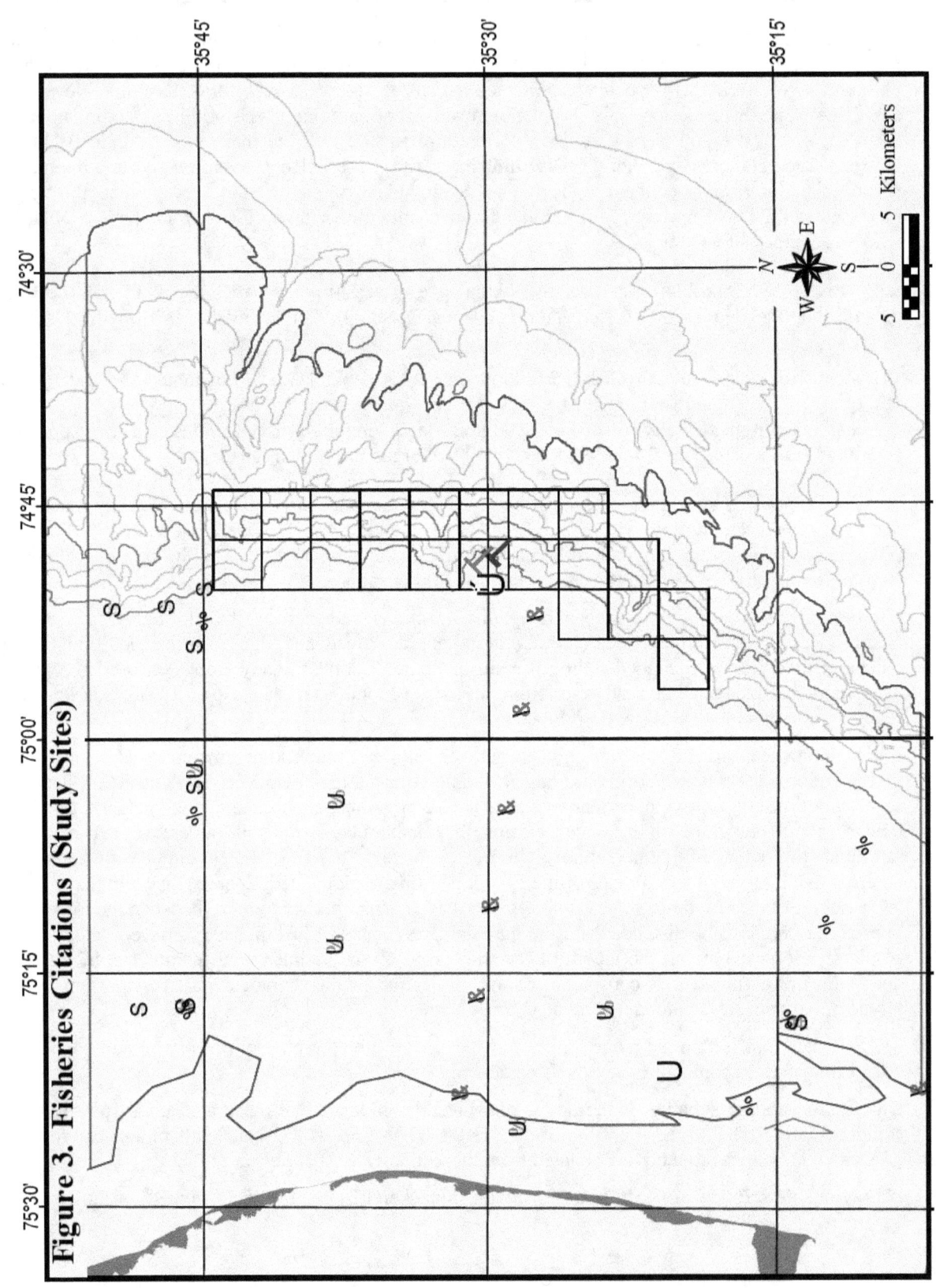

Figure 3. Fisheries Citations (Study Sites)

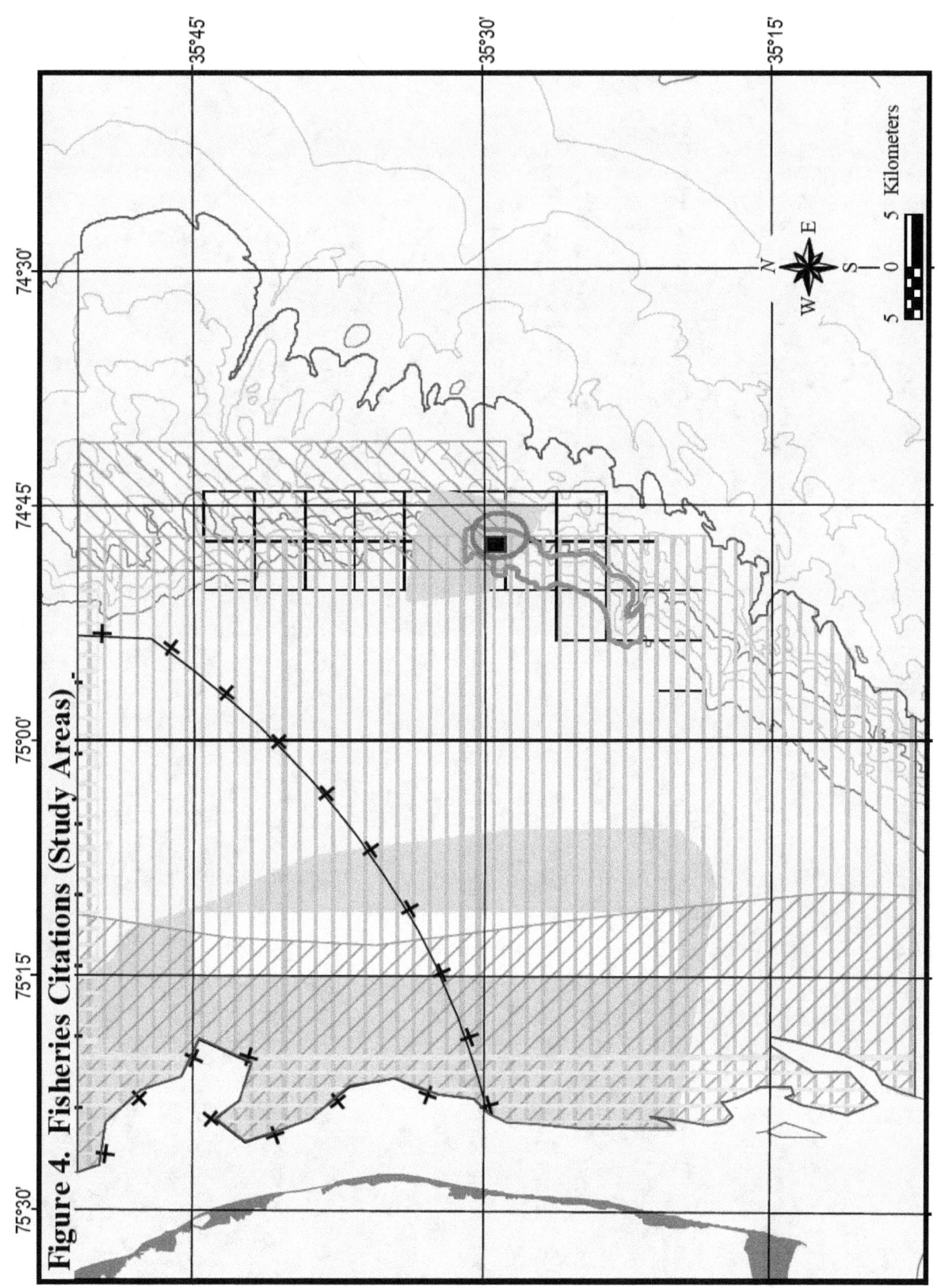

Figure 4. Fisheries Citations (Study Areas)

Key to Fisheries Citations (Figures 3 and 4).

Study Area Boundary

Lease Blocks

Mapped Citations

Barbieri et al. (1994)

Berrien (1978); Clark et al. (1969)

Continental Shelf Assts. (1983)

Continental Shelf Assts. (1989)

Currin & Ross (1999)

Langfelder et al. (1979)

Edwards et al. (1962)

Hogans & Sulak (1992)

Kirby-Smith (1989b); Ross, S. (unpub.a)

Magnuson et al. (1981)

Moser et al. (1996)

Moser et al. (1997, 1998)

NOAA-Natl. Mar. Fish. Serv.- NE Fish. Center (1977)

Ross, S. (1985a, 1985b); U.S. Dept. Navy (1985)

Ross, J. (1991); Ross, S. (1988)

Ross et al. (1984)

Ross et al. (2001); Sulak & Ross (1996)

Stancyk (in press); Stancyk et al. (1998)

Sulak & Ross (1993)

Wollam (1970)

Studies that Focus on the Manteo Lease Blocks

Crawford (1989)

Diaz et al. (1993a, 1998)

Gettleson (1992)

Ross & Scarborough-Bull (1998)

Shepard & Hulbert (1994)

U.S.D.O.I.-Minerals Mgmt. Service (1990, 1992)

Vigil (1998)

Studies that Cover the Hatteras Middle Slope Area ("The Point")

Bailey et al. (1991)

Continental Shelf Assts. (1991)

Diaz et al. (1993b)

Fogt (1992)

Gudger (1932)

Kirby-Smith (1989a)

Orbach (1989, 1998a, 1998b)

Ross, J. (1989)

Ross, S. (1989, 1991, 1998)

Shepard (1991)

Sulak (1992)

Key to Fisheries Citations (Figures 3 and 4) (con't.).

Broad Regional Studies

Abernathy et al. (1989)
Able & Kaiser (1994)
Able et al. (1989)
Ahrenholz et al. (1987)
Anderson (1985)
Blair et al. (1991)
Boreman (1983)
Brown et al. (1996)
Butler et al. (1983)
Checkley et al. (1988, 1989)
Costlow et al. (1992)
Coston-Clements et al. (1991)
Desfosse et al. (1990)
Dryfoos et al. (1973)
Epperly et al. (1995)
Fedoryako (1989)
Flescher (1980)
Flores-Coto & Warlen (1993)
George & Hulbert (1989)
Goldstein (1986)
Hamm & Slater (1979)
Hare & Cowen (1996)
Hoss (1992)
Johnson et al. (1983)
Kendall & Reintjes (1975)
Kennelly (1999)
Kohler et al. (1998)
Lee (1986b)

Marshall (1951)
McGowen & Richards (1989)
Minerals Mgmt. Service (1982a-c)
Morse (1980)
Musick (1979)
Nesbit & Neville (1935)
Nickerson & Mountain (1983)
Nixon & Jones (1997)
Norcross (1983)
Palmquist et al. (2000)
Pearson (1932)
Renaud et al. (1993)
Ross & Moye (1989)
Ross et al. (1985, 1986)
Rotunno & Cowen (1997)
Schwartz (1989)
S. Atlantic Fishery Mgmt. Council (1998)
Settle (1993, 1997)
Shepherd & Terceiro (1994)
Smith (1973)
Smith et al. (1975)
Stillwell & Kohler (1993)
Trent et al. (1983)
U.S. Dept. Of Commerce-NOAA (1985)
Witzell (1999)

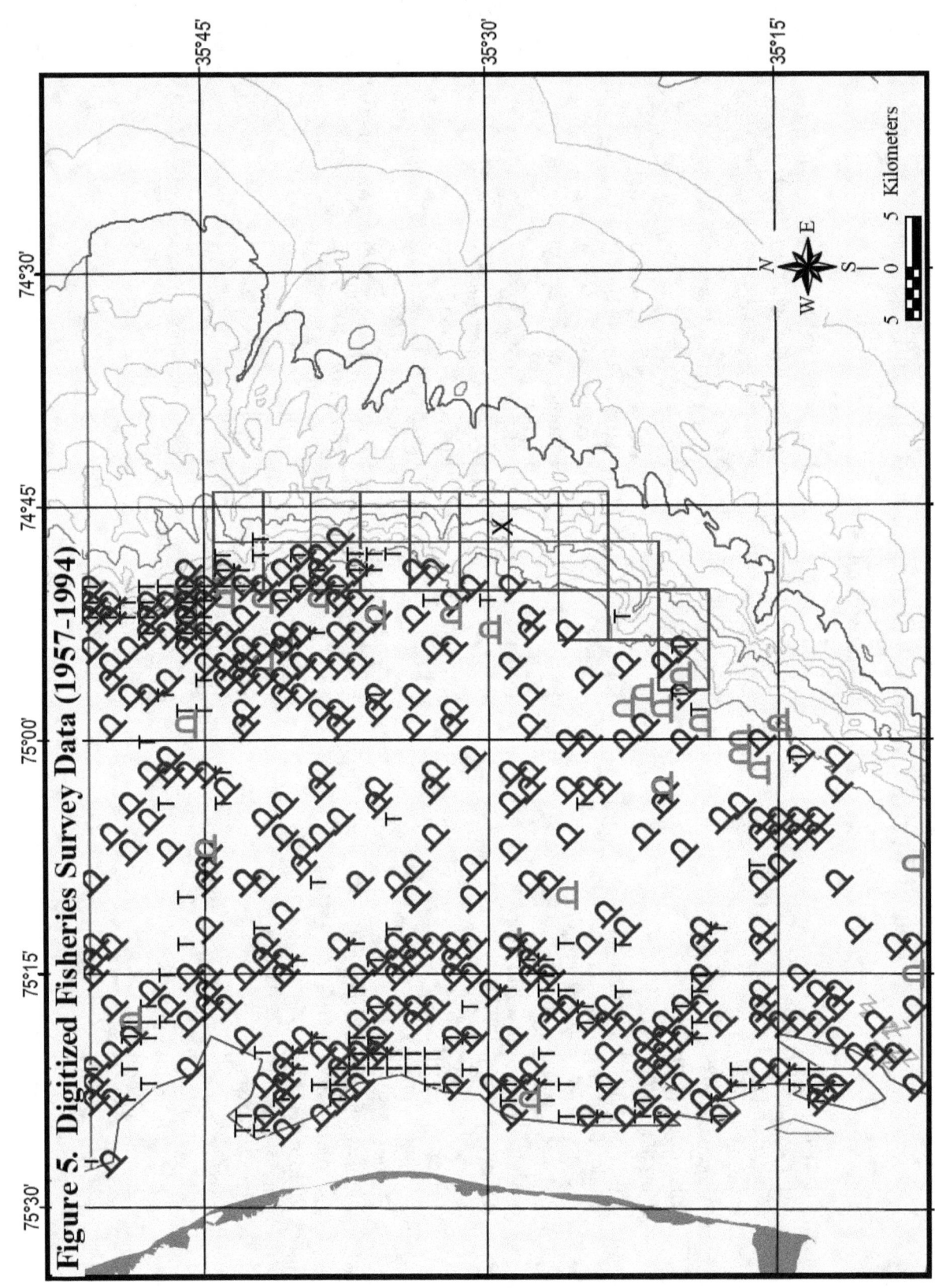

Figure 5. Digitized Fisheries Survey Data (1957-1994)

Key to Figure 5. Digitized Fisheries Survey Data (1957-1994)

Study Area Boundary

Exploratory Well

Lease Blocks

NCDMF Fisheries Surveys:
R/V Dan Moore Trawls (1968-1981)

NMFS Southeast Fisheries Center:
Bottom Trawls (1957-1984)

NMFS Northeast Fisheries Center:
Bottom Trawls (1967-1994)

Duke Marine Lab:
Underwater Camera Surveys (1965-1973)

SCUBA and Submersible Surveys:
Ross (unpub. a, unpub. b)

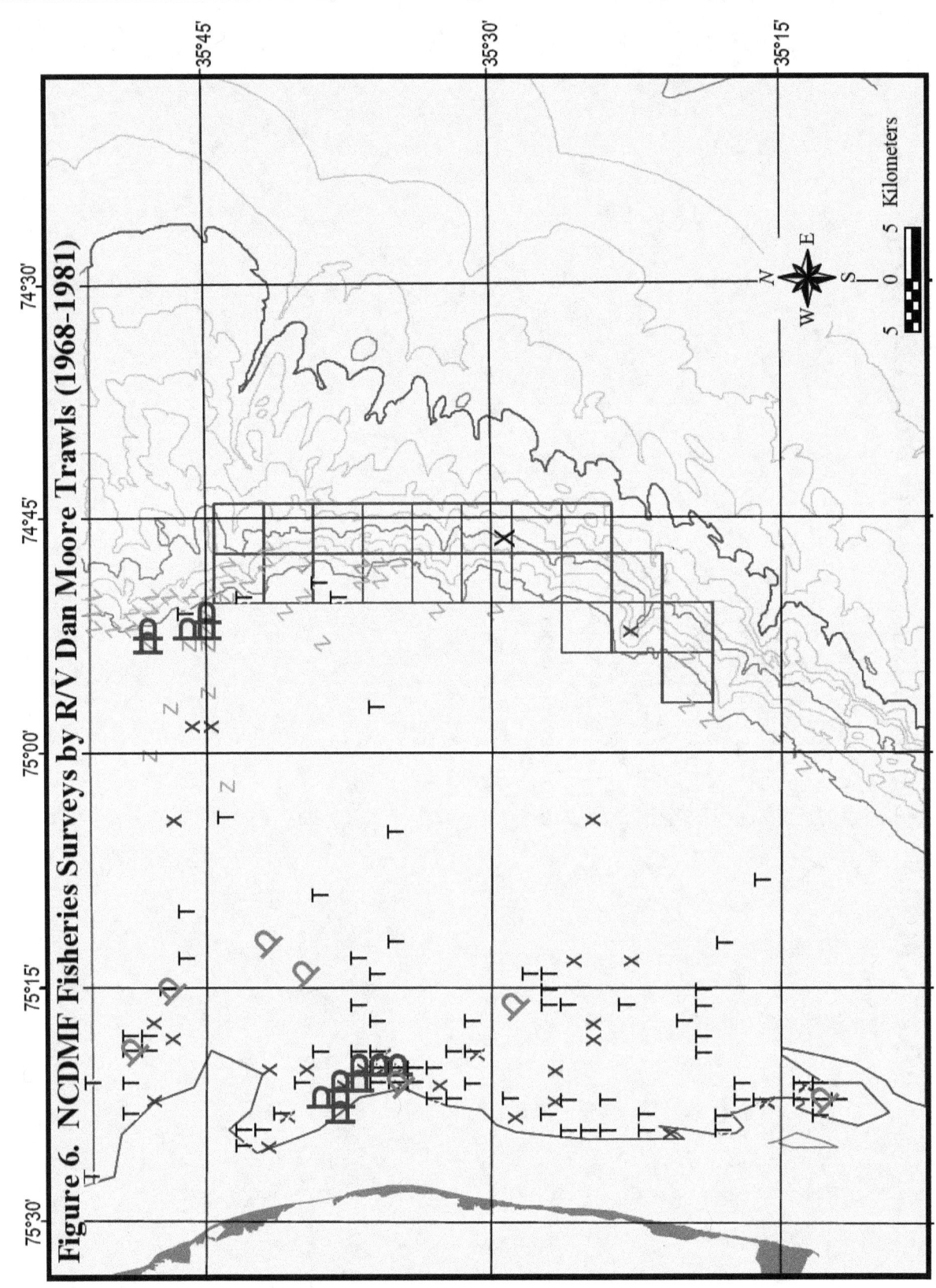

Figure 6. NCDMF Fisheries Surveys by R/V Dan Moore Trawls (1968-1981)

Key to Figure 6. NCDMF Fisheries Surveys by R/V Dan Moore Trawls (1968-1981)

Study Area Boundary
x Exploratory Well
Lease Blocks
x Flounder Survey (1973-1976)
Lobster Survey (1968-1973)
z Squid Survey (1974)
T Anadromous Fish Survey (1968-1981)
Exploratory and General Surveys (1968-1969; 1977-1981)
Net Selectivity Study (1979-1981)

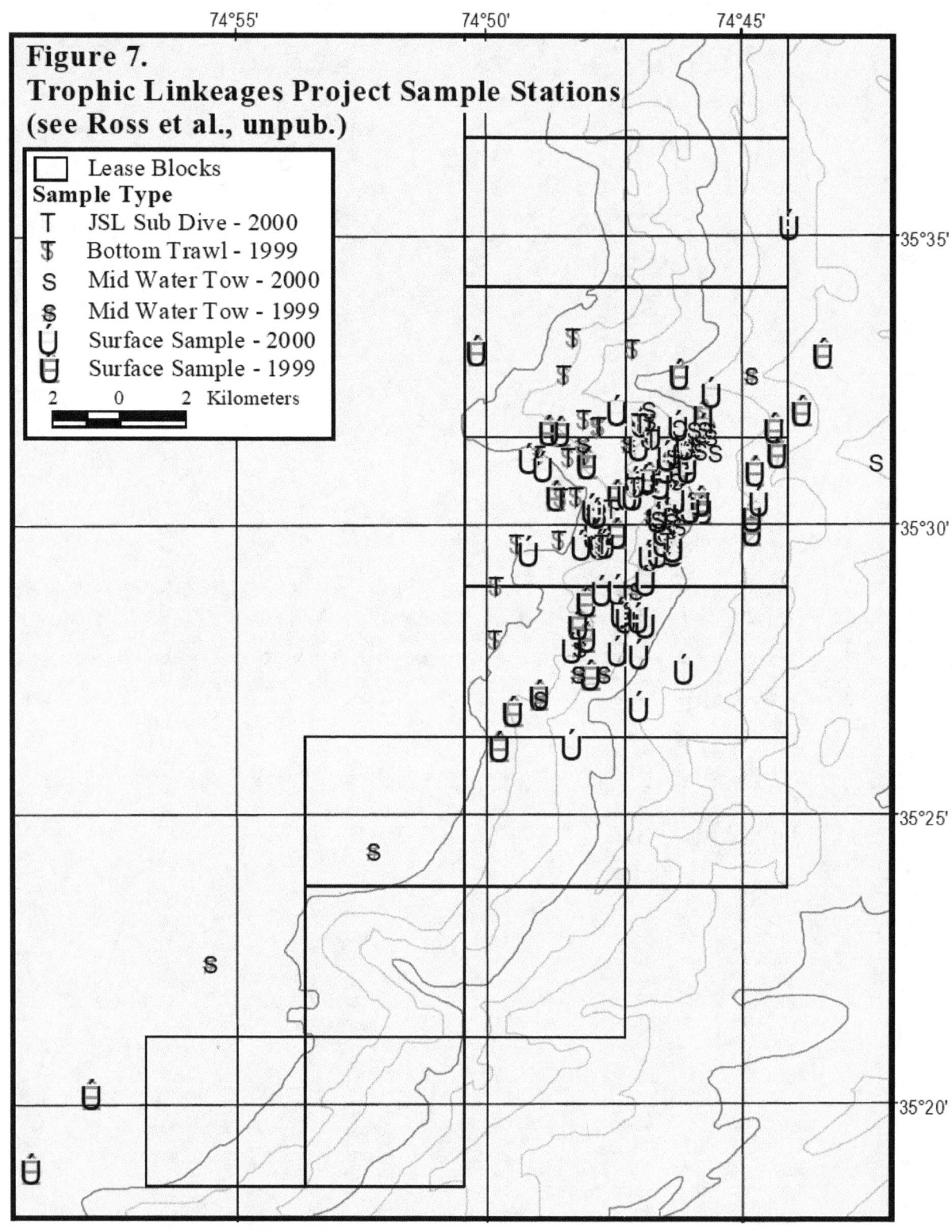

Figure 7.
Trophic Linkeages Project Sample Stations
(see Ross et al., unpub.)

INVERTEBRATE CHAPTER

INVERTEBRATE CHAPTER

Abernathy, S.A., M.T. Baer, C.S. Benner, M.S. Brody, D.K. Francois, J.K. Gilliam, L.K. Good, C.J. Ohara, and J.V. Martin. 1989. Atlantic Outer Continental Shelf: Description of the Mid-Atlantic Environment. Abernathy, S.A. (ed.). U.S. Department of the Interior, Minerals Management Service, Atlantic OCS Region, Environmental Assessment Section. Herndon, VA. 167 p.

*This document discusses the major issues and areas of concern for the mid-Atlantic environment that are considered in the planning process for oil and gas leasing and operations on the Outer Continental Shelf (OCS). The issues are addressed with respect to the potential environmental consequences of mid Atlantic oil and gas exploration, development and production. A section discussing The Physical Environment (e.g., geology, non-petroleum minerals, physical oceanography, chemical oceanography and water quality, ocean dumping, meteorology, air quality), Biological resources (e.g., plankton, benthos, fishery resources, marine reptiles, marine mammals, marine and coastal birds, estuaries, wetlands, sensitive coastal habitats, canyon areas), Socioeconomic Environment, and other issues (e.g., archaeological resources, marine vessel traffic, National Aeronautics and Space Administration/ Department of Defense activities, oil and gas infrastructure, marine sanctuaries, and estuarine research reserves) is included. Most of the figures showing fisheries resource distribution are taken from fisheries data compiled for bottom-trawl and shellfish surveys of the National Marine Fisheries Service, Northeast Fisheries Center, Woods Hole, MA.

Able, K.W., M.P. Fahay, and G.R. Shepherd. 1995. Early life history of black sea bass, *Centropristis striata,* in the mid-Atlantic Bight and a New Jersey estuary. Fishery Bulletin 93: 429-445.

This study focuses on composite field collections and in situ observations from the mid-Atlantic Bight continental shelf and a New Jersey estuary in order to elucidate aspects of the early life history of age 0+ black sea bass, *Centropristis striata*. Spawning in the mid-Atlantic Bight is prolonged (April through November, with a peak between June and September) and is most intense in the southern portion of this range. Between 1977 and 1987, larvae were collected between Cape Hatteras, North Carolina, and Long Island, New York. In New Jersey coastal waters larvae first appear in July but can occur into November. Recently settled individuals (15-24 mm total length [TL]) were collected at an inner continental shelf site and an adjacent estuary from July through October. By fall, fishes from these areas were 18-91 mm TL, and many had moved offshore from New Jersey estuarine waters and other estuaries to inner continental shelf waters between southern Massachusetts and Cape Hatteras. Subsequently, they continued to move offshore and during their first winter, they were concentrated near the shelf or slope break in the southern portion of the mid-Atlantic Bight. Some age 0+ individuals moved back into New Jersey estuaries in early spring, at sizes approximating those of the previous fall (50-96 mm TL). Thus, black sea bass reach relatively small sizes after 12 months of growth partly because little or no growth occurs during their first winter. This year class reached sizes of 78-175 mm TL by midsummer and 134-225 mm TL by the following fall.

During summer, benthic juveniles were collected or observed primarily in a variety of structured habitats. On the inner continental shelf they were found among accumulations of surfclam *Spisula solidissima* valves or among smaller pieces of shell, and occasionally in burrows in exposed clay. While in the estuary, they were collected from areas with a variety of structured habitats, such as shell accumulations in marsh creeks and peat banks. The data suggest that during their first summer, black sea bass have similar densities and growth rates in estuarine and inner continental shelf habitats, and thus both areas serve as nurseries.

Almeida, F.P., T.R. Azarovitz, L. O'Brien, and E.W. Pritchard. 1984. The distribution of major finfish and shellfish species collected during NEFC Bottom trawl surveys, 1965-1978. Woods Hole Laboratory Reference Document Number 84-21. Northeast Fisheries Center, Woods Hole Laboratory. Woods Hole, MA. 101 p.

*This report describes synoptic bottom trawl surveys of the offshore fishery resources of the Northwest Atlantic continental shelf have been conducted by the North east Fisheries Center since the autumn of 1963. These surveys provided the data for examining the temporal and spatial distribution of 46 finfish and shellfish species occurring on the shelf.

Ashjian, C.J., S.L. Smith, C.N. Flagg, A.J. Mariano, W.J. Behrens, and P.V.Z. Lane. 1994. The influence of a Gulf Stream meander on the distribution of zooplankton biomass in the Slope Water, and the Gulf Stream, and the Sargasso Sea, described using a shipboard acoustic Doppler current profiler. Deep-Sea Research I 41(1): 23-50.

The influence of a Gulf Stream meander on the distribution of zooplankton biomass in the Slope Water, the Gulf Stream, and the Sargasso Sea, described using a shipboard acoustic Doppler current profiler Patterns in zooplankton biomass distribution in a Gulf Stream meander were documented wing a ship-mounted acoustic Doppler current profiler (ADCP) in fall 1988 as part of the BIOSYNOP program. The dominant signal in biomass was the regional variation between water masses, with greatest biomass recorded in the Slope Water, intermediate biomass at the Slope Water-Gulf Stream front, and lowest biomass in the Gulf Stream/Sargasso Sea. Biomass was more variable in the Slope Water than in the Sargasso Sea. Diel variation, a consequence of diel vertical migration, was also observed. Comprehensive maps of the surveyed region documented meander associated enhancement of zooplankton biomass. Elevated biomass was documented in the region downstream of the meander crest, where entrainment of Slope Water and convergence of flow are hypothesized to occur. The ADCP was demonstrated to be an effective means of documenting patterns in zooplankton biomass, including estimates of the variability (patchiness).

Atkinson, L.P., D.W. Menzel, and K.A. Bush. 1985. Oceanography of the Southeastern U.S. Continental Shelf. American Geophysical Union. Washington, DC. 156 p.

*This book contains 12 chapters: an introduction; four chapters on physical oceanography; a chapter on hydrography and nutrients; four biological chapters (covering phytoplankton, zooplankton, bacteria, and macroinfauna); a chemical chapter on trace metals; and a summary chapter describing future research plans. Research included was conducted between 1975 and the early 1980's and was largely funded by the Department of Energy and the Minerals Management Service (formerly Bureau of Land Management). The South Atlantic Bight (SAB) extends from the temperate waters of Cape Hatteras, NC to subtropical waters of West Palm Beach, FL. The ocean region is influenced by Gulf Stream dynamics on the eastern boundary, synoptic winds and weather events, river and estuarine inputs.

Azarovitz, T. Unpublished database. Groundfish Surveys 1967-1994. NOAA/NMFS, Northeast Fisheries Center. Woods Hole, MA.

*This is an unpublished fisheries database. Data were collected from 1967 to 1994 by the NOAA/NMFS, Northeast Fisheries Center. The Principal Investigator is listed as Tom Azarovitz. Select sample locations and related data were computerized as part of the North Carolina SEAMAP Hardbottom data project by Moser et al. (1995). SEAMAP Hardbottom data (sample locations) within the defined project area for The Point were sorted and mapped using ArcView GIS (J. Ott, pers. comm. 15 Nov 99).

Bailey, T.G., M.J. Youngbluth, and G.P. Owen. 1995. Chemical composition and metabolic rates of gelatinous zooplankton from midwater and benthic boundary layer environments off Cape Hatteras, North Carolina, USA. Marine Ecology Progress Series 122: 121-34.

Quantitative determinations of chemical composition and oxygen consumption rates were made for 7 species of gelatinous zooplankton (ctenophores and medusae) from midwater and benthic boundary layer habitats off Cape Hatteras, NC, USA. Although there were no apparent trends in chemical composition with depth of occurrence, midwater species were generally less robust, in terms of protein and lipid content, than those from benthopelagic depths. These differences in chemical compositions between midwater and benthopelagic species are probably related to factors associated with swimming behaviors required for prey capture and predator avoidance. Measurements of carbon specific metabolic rates (0.59 to 17.9 ul O mg^{-1} C h^{-1}) indicated that minimum daily rations required by mesopelagic gelatinous zooplankton can impact carbon cycling and energy transfer in deep-water ecosystems. These data are consistent with a growing inventory of metabolic measurements undertaken with submersible platforms and strongly implicate gelatinous zooplankton as ecologically important components of pelagic communities.

Bailey, T., M. Youngbluth, and G. Owen. 1991. Metabolic Rates of Zooplankton and Micronekton from Deep-water Pelagic Environments at Cape Hatteras. p. 5. *In:* Shepard, A. (ed.). NURC/UNCW 1991 Undersea Research: Informational Meeting. National Undersea Research Center, University of North Carolina at Wilmington. Wilmington, NC.

Our submersible-based observations in August 1990 indicated that "The Point" east of Cape Hatteras was a highly structured environment dominated by one species of myctophid fish and several species of crustaceans and gelatinous zooplankton. In fact, in our ca. 25 years of combined submersible experience, we have not encountered such high population densities of gelatinous zooplankton or myctophid fishes at any other location. These high standing stocks provide the unique opportunity to study major faunal components (i.e., fishes, crustaceans, and gelatinous zooplankton) of the midwater community, simultaneously.

Our research plan for 1991 will determine the distribution, abundance, and metabolic rates of numerically dominant species of midwater zooplankton and micronekton. These data will allow us to define the energetic and trophic relationships of zooplankton and micronekton in deep-water communities.

Blair, N.E., L.A. Levin, D.J. DeMaster, and G. Plaia. 1996. The short-term fate of fresh algal carbon in continental slope sediments. Limnol. Oceanogr. 41(6): 1208-1219.

Emplacement of tracer mixture containing ^{13}C-labeled green algae on the sea floor of the continental slope offshore Cape Hatteras, North Carolina, elicited a rapid responses over 1.5 d from the dense benthic community. Certain deposit-feeding annelids (e.g. *Scalibregma inflatum* and *Aricidea quadrilobata*) became heavily labeled with ^{13}C-labeled organic matter was transported to a depth of at least 4-5 cm into the seabed during the 1.5 d period, presumably as a consequence of feeding-associated activity. Nonlocal transport produced subsurface peaks in organic ^{13}C at 2-3 cm. Dissolved inorganic ^{13}C, produced by the oxidation of the labeled algae, penetrated to 10-cm depth. The transport of highly reactive organic matter from the sediment surface at initial velocities $\geq$ 3 cm d^{-1} is expected to be an important control of subsurface benthic processes in slope environments characterized by abundant macrofaunal populations. Anaerobic processes, which are enhanced on the Cape Hatteras slope relative to adjacent areas, may be promoted by the rapid injection of reactive material into subsurface sediments. The transport, in turn, is a consequence of the dense infaunal populations that are supported by the rapid depositions of organic carbon in this region.

Blake, J.A. 1993. Life History Analysis of Five Dominant Infaunal Polychaete Species from the Continental Slope off North Carolina. J. Mar. Biol. Assoc. U.K. 73: 123-141.

Observations were made on the reproduction and life history of five species of polychaetes collected from the continental slope off North Carolina, USA. Three species were studied at a 2000-m lower slope station off Cape Lookout (*Aurospio dibranchiata, Microrbinia linea,* and *Pholoe anoculata*) and the other two at a 600-m upper slope station off Cape Hatteras (*Cossura longocirrata* and *Scalibregma inflatum*). *Aurospio dibranchiata,* a surface feeding spionid, exhibited seasonality in egg diameter and size-frequency data, with the larger sizes occurring in late summer months. *Pholoe anoculata,* a small carnivorous scale worm, did not exhibit any evidence of seasonality in size-frequency data at the 2000-m station. Sexually mature specimens were absent from this population, but were present at shallower slope depths, indicating year-round recruitment into the lower slope from middle and upper slope populations. *Microrbinia linea,* a small subsurface deposit feeding orbiniid, exhibited year-round reproduction and recruitment. *Cossura longocirrata,* a deposit-feeding cossurid, exhibited patterns of spring recruitment that were similar to previously studied populations on the continental shelf. *Scalibregma inflatum,* a deposit-feeding scalibregmatid, did not exhibit any evidence of seasonality, and is presumed to have a year-round reproduction. It is postulated that benthic infaunal organisms that feed at the water-sediment interface are more likely to utilize immediately seasonal pulses of sedimentation by phytoplankton to the bottom than deeper burrowing subsurface deposit feeders. In this regard, surface deposit feeders would be more likely to exhibit seasonality in their reproduction and recruitment than subsurface deposit feeders.

—. 1994. Vertical distribution of benthic infauna in continental slope sediments off Cape Lookout, North Carolina. Deep-Sea Research II Vol. 41(4-6): 919-927.

The vertical distribution of 30 species of benthic infauna from continental slope (583-3000 m) sediments off Cape Lookout, North Carolina was closely correlated with feeding types. Carnivores, omnivores, filter feeders, and surface deposit feeders were mostly concentrated in the upper 0-2 cm of the cores. The depth distribution of subsurface deposit feeders was more variable, even among related taxa.

Blake, J.A., and R. Avent. 1998. Biological Environment Work Session Results: Benthic Ecology. pp. 80-83. *In*: Vigil, D.L. (ed.). North Carolina/Minerals Management Service Technical Workshop on Manteo Unit Exploration: February 4-5, 1998. U.S. Dept. of the Interior, Minerals Management Service, Gulf of Mexico OCS Region. New Orleans, LA.

*These are the proceedings from a workshop/meeting (conducted on February 4-5, 1998) between the North Carolina Department of Environment and Natural Resources, and the U.S. Department of the Interior's Minerals Management Service (MMS). The geographic area being discussed is approximately 45 miles east-northeast of Cape Hatteras, NC, referred to as the Manteo Unit. This workshop reviewed environmental and socioeconomic information known and needed on the Manteo Unit. The MMS's Gulf of Mexico OCS Regional Director gave an MMS perspective on history and status of the area. Chevron gave a presentation on how the exploratory well would be drilled. The scientific characterization was presented in greater detail by a number of scientific experts who spoke on the following disciplines physical environment, habitat and living resources, seabirds, marine mammals, sea turtles, and social and economic issues. Specific chapters are cited individually, when appropriate.

Numerous isolated studies have been pursued for several decades on the benthic ecology, community structure, and density of the benthic communities of the middle Atlantic continental shelf and slope. Earlier Woods Hole Oceanographic Institution, Virginia Institute of Marine Science, Duke University Marine Laboratory, and others' investigation in the 1960's and 1970's resulted in the development of many of the recent concept in deep sea ecology, distribution, and diversity. Some of these investigations were conducted off the Cape Hatteras region of North Carolina. The MMS sponsored the U.S. South Atlantic Slope and Rise Program (ACSAR; 1983-1986) which resulted in two large reports (Blake et al. 1985; 1987) and presentations at the 1984 and 1985 MMS Information Transfer Meetings. The first phase of the "Study of the Biological Processes on the U.S. South Atlantic Slope ad Rise" was conducted from a large area from the Georgia Bight northward to the region around Cape Hatteras. The second phase was conducted in a much smaller area off the Carolinas. This effort identified some unique biological conditions and processes off Cape Hatteras including the upper slope in the Manteo leasing area. This section also discussed Data Gaps and Future Investigations, Considerations for an Industry Exploration Plan, and Post Discharge Monitoring.

Blake, J.A., and R.J. Diaz. 1998. Habitat and Living Resources Review: Benthic Ecology of the Cape Hatteras Continental Slope. pp. 43-51. *In*: Vigil, D.L. (ed.). North Carolina/Minerals Management Service Technical Workshop on Manteo Unit Exploration: February 4-5, 1998. U.S. Dept. of the Interior, Minerals Management Service, Gulf of Mexico OCS Region. New Orleans, LA .

*These are the proceedings from a workshop/meeting (conducted on February 4-5, 1998) between the North Carolina Department of Environment and Natural Resources, and the U.S. Department of the Interior's Minerals Management Service (MMS). The geographic area being discussed is approximately 45 miles east-northeast of Cape Hatteras, NC, referred to as the Manteo Unit. This workshop reviewed environmental and socioeconomic information known and needed on the Manteo Unit. The MMS's Gulf of Mexico OCS Regional Director gave an MMS perspective on history and status of the area. Chevron gave a presentation on how the exploratory well would be drilled. The scientific characterization was presented in greater detail by a number of scientific experts who spoke on the following disciplines physical environment, habitat and living resources, seabirds, marine mammals, sea turtles, and social and economic issues. Specific chapters are cited individually, when appropriate.

The benthic communities of the continental slope off the Carolinas has been described as part of extensive surveys conducted by the Minerals Management Service to assess potential impacts due to exploratory drilling for oil and gas. The initial effort was the Atlantic Continental Slope Rise (ACSAR) Program, which included transects across the Carolina slope from Cape Hatteras in the north to off the Charleston Bump in the south (Blake et al. 1985, 1987; Blake and Grassle 1994). Out of 15 stations sampled for benthic infauna, the most unusual were found off Cape Hatteras in Manteo Lease Block 510 at a depth of 550 m. The benthic fauna at this site included unusually high densities of infauna, epifaunal invertebrates, and fish (Blake and Grassle 1994; Hecker 1994). Much of the surface was seen to be carpeted with white tubes that later proved to be a giant foraminiferan, *Bathysiphon filiformis*. A control site at 2000 m down slope from the 550 m station also exhibited unusually high densities of infauna for a depth range. Overall, the abundance and biomass of the benthos was found to be about 6 and 10 times higher than other areas of the Carolina slope. This section discusses MMS Field Surveys and Methods, Results and Discussion, Sedimentology, and Benthic Communities. Figure 4; Location of Benthic Stations and Camera Transects on the Cape Hatteras Slope in 1992, indicating sampling occurred in designated study area, is located on page 45.

Blake, J.A., and J.F. Grassle. 1994. Benthic community structure on the U.S. South Atlantic slope off the Carolinas: Spatial heterogeneity in a current-dominated system. Deep-Sea Research II Vol. 41(4-6): 835-874.

*Faunal communities of the continental slope and rise seaward of North and South Carolina (U.S.A.) are strongly influenced by the Gulf Stream, the Western Boundary Undercurrent, and an increasingly steep declination of the slope toward Cape Hatteras. Sixteen stations in depths of 600-3500 m were sampled to characterize the sediment and benthic macrofauna. Box cores were taken along four transects Cape Hatteras, Cape Lookout, Cape Fear, and Charleston. On the Cape Hatteras transect infaunal densities at the 600-m station were as high as those typical of shallower waters, and the dominant organisms were species that are more characteristic of continental shelf depths. There is high, nearly continuous sedimentation of terrigenous fine sandy sediments that are funneled over the Cape Hatteras slope by southerly-flowing, long-shelf currents. We postulate that organic material is transported rapidly over the site and that the high depositional rates are enhanced by scavenging activities of filter-feeding organisms. Large, deep-burrowing deposit feeders serve to carry organic material deep into the sediments. The shallow stations on the Charleston transects were dominated by sand waves generated by the Gulf Stream, while deeper stations were enriched by microalgae transported downslope. Transects off Cape Lookout and Cape Fear were more typical of those found elsewhere in the western North Atlantic.

Blake, J.A., B. Hecker, J.F. Grassle, B. Brown, M. Wade, P.D. Boehm, E. Baptiste, B. Hilbig, N. Maciolek, R. Petrecca, R.E. Ruff, V. Starczak, and L. Watling. 1987. Study of Biological Processes on the U.S. South Atlantic Slope and Rise: Phase 2. U.S. Department of the Interior, Minerals Management Service, Atlantic OCS Region, Environmental Assessment Section. Herndon, VA.

A total of 16 stations were sampled during a 2 year field program designed to characterize the biological, chemical, and sedimentary processes on the slope and rise off North and South Carolina. Box cores were taken along a 4 transects at depths of 600 to 3500 m. The infauna yielded a total of 1202 species, 520 of which were new to science. Annelids were dominant taxa in terms of density and numbers of species. Species diversity was highest at an 800 m site off Charleston. Infaunal densities were highest on the upper slope (600 m) and lowest on the rise (3000 m). Life history analysis yielded evidence of seasonality for two polychaete species. Two stations off Cape Hatteras in depths of 600 m and 2000 m had higher infaunal density, lower species diversity, and higher biomass than elsewhere on the Atlantic slope and rise. Higher than normal lead and carbon inventories suggest enhanced scavenging processes in this area. Faunal patterns on the Cape Lookout transect were generally typical for other localities on the Atlantic Slope and Rise. Faunal changes were detected off Cape Fear and Charleston that may be related to the influence of the Gulf Stream and associated sediment changes. Epifauna were most unusual on the Charleston Bump, where a hard bottom fauna dominated by filter feeding corals and sponges thrives in an area strongly swept by the Gulf Stream. Consistent faunal differences were found between the upstream and downstream sides of the bump. Data generated in the infaunal and epifaunal surveys supported the view that a partial zoogeographic barrier exists on the slope off North Carolina. This break was most evident between Cape Lookout and Cape Fear.

Blake, J.A., and B. Hilbig. 1994. Dense infaunal assemblages on the continental slope off Cape Hatteras, North Carolina. Deep-Sea Research II Vol. 41(4-6): 875-899.

*Unusually dense assemblages of benthic infaunal invertebrates have been discovered in continental slope sediments off Cape Hatteras, North Carolina. Densities were highest on the upper slope, ranging from 24,055 to 61,244 (mean = 46,255) individuals m^2 in nine samples taken at a 600-m site in 1984 and 1985, and from 15,522 to 89,566 (mean = 37,282) individuals m^2 in single samples at 15 stations over a wider depth range of 530 to 1535 m in 1992. A lower slope station at 2000 m sampled six times in 1984-1985 and again in 1992, had densities consistently higher than 8500 individuals m^2. Species richness and diversity are consistently lower on the Cape Hatteras slope than at other locations off North Carolina and elsewhere in the western North Atlantic.

Brodziak, J., and L. Hendrickson. 1999. An analysis of environmental effects on survey catches of squids *Loligo pealei* and *Illex illecebrosus* in the northwest Atlantic. Fishery Bulletin 97(1): 9-24.

An analysis of environmental effects on autumn survey catches of two commercially exploited squid species, *Loligo pealei* and *Illex illecebrosus*, was conducted. Research survey data collected during 1967-94 were used to determine the significance and relative importance of average depth tow, time of day bottom temperature on bottom trawl catches of *L. pealei*, a neritic species, and *I. illecebrosus*, an oceanic species. We examined habitat associations of both species by using randomization methods and found that *L. pealei* was consistently associated with all of the environmental factors examined. In comparison with *L. pealei*, catches of *I. illecebrosus* were much lower and associations with environmental factors were inconsistent. We also examined whether environmental conditions affected catches of juveniles and adult squid differentially. Depth had an important effect on the magnitude of juvenile and adult *L. pealei* catches, with the ratio of juvenile to adult catches decreasing with depth. Depth had a similar, but less pronounced, effect on. *I. illecebrosus* catches. Time of day also affected *L. pealei* and *I. illecebrosus* catches. Catches of both species were lowest at night and diel effects were more pronounced for juveniles than for adults. Bottom and surface temperatures had substantial effect on catches of juvenile and adult *L. pealei* and *I. illecebrosus* catches. The joint effects of depth stratification time of day and annual squid abundance on survey catches were also analyzed to determine correction factors for diel differences in catchability of juvenile and adult squid. Significant diel differences in catchability were detected for juvenile and adult *L. pealei* and for juvenile *I. illecebrosus* and diel correction factors were determined for survey catches of these size categories. In contrast, significant diel differences in catchability of adult *I. illecebrosus* were not detected.

Brown, B. 1991. Biomass of Deep-Sea Benthic Communities: Polychaetes and other Invertebrates. Bulletin of Marine Science 48(2): 401-411.

Biomass measurements were made for benthic samples from the U.S. Atlantic continental slope and rise as part of a program on benthic processes in the deep sea. Box-core samples were collected from off Georges Bank near Massachusetts south to off Georgia, primarily along the 2000-m depth contour. Ash-free dry weight (AFDW) measurements were made on replicates from six stations. Samples were sieved through nested 0.3 mm and 2.0 mm screens. AFDW biomass ranged between 0.1665 and 2.1439 g m^{-2}. Polychaetes dominated biomass in the 0.3-mm fractions and in the 2.0-mm fraction except whenever large organisms, such as echinoderms, were present. Wet weight biomass was measured on samples taken from off Cape Hatteras in depths varying between 583 and 3500 m. A sharp decrease (five- to ten-fold) in biomass was observed between 2000 and 3000 m depth.

Butler, J.N., B.F. Morris, J. Cadwallader, and A.W. Stoner. 1983. Studies of *Sargassum* and the *Sargassum* Community. Special Publication No. 22. Bermuda Biological Station for Research.

*Chapter 1 The Quantity of *Sargassum* in the Sargasso Sea, and Chapter 2 The *Sargassum* Community include the defined study area for The Point.

The quantity and distribution of *Sargassum* in the Sargasso Sea, as estimated by various investigators, is reviewed. There has apparently been no significant change in the biomass of *Sargassum* from 1933 to 1981, except for an area northeast of the Antilles (20-25° N, 62-68° W) where measurements made in November 1977 and November 1980 were about 0.1% of values measured in February and March 1933. Because of the lack of change in the Bermuda region, the Bahamas region, or the Gulf Stream region, this effect does not appear to be due to pollution or broad climatic changes; it is most likely due to a seasonal or long-term shift of the currents defining the southwestern boundary of the Sargasso Sea.

Motile macrofauna on *Sargassum* were identified and counted for 244 samples taken at Station 'S' near Bermuda, and for 155 samples taken from other parts of the western North Atlantic and Caribbean. The nature of this community and its seasonal variations are discussed. Preliminary studies of the food web, as well as of the microfauna (copepods) and sessile fauna are reported. Although petroleum hydrocarbon residues are found in all samples of *Sargassum* and its larger associated fauna, the variability of individual samples is so extreme that no correlation of community structure with hydrocarbon pollution could be demonstrated.

Chen, Chin, and N.S. Hillman. 1970. Shell-bearing Pteropods as Indicators of Water Masses off Cape Hatteras, North Carolina. Bulletin of Marine Science 20(2): 350-367.

Three water masses occur within a radius of 120 nautical miles off Cape Hatteras, North Carolina. Several species of shell-bearing pteropods characterize these water masses: subarctic *Limacina retroversa* in the slope water, subtropical *Limacina inflata* in the Sargasso Sea, and tropical *Limacina trochiformis* and *Creseis virgula* in the Gulf Stream.

The pattern of vertical distribution of pteropod species is compatible with the seasonal structure of the water. In summer, a thin, warm surface layer bearing tropical species of pteropods overlies thick, cold, slope water carrying subarctic species in the region of 35°30′N to 37°10′N. In winter, the slope water surfaces at about 36N. The sharp gradient exhibited by the vertical slope of isotherms acts as a temperature barrier separating subarctic from tropical species of pteropods.

Pteropod shells are found in sediments beneath the Gulf Stream at depth of about 400-2150 m. *Creseis virgula conica* is the dominant species in the sediments.

Coston-Clements, L., L.R. Settle, D.E. Hoss, and F.A. Cross. 1991. Utilization of the *Sargassum* Habitat by Marine Invertebrates and Vertebrates — A Review. National Marine Fisheries Service, NOAA, Southeast Fisheries Science Center, Beaufort Laboratory. Beaufort, NC. 32 p.

Numerous species of brown algae (Class Cyclosporeae: Order Fucales: Family Fucaceae) of the genus *Sargassum* occur throughout the world's tropical and temperate oceans. The pelagic complex in the western North Atlantic is comprised primarily of *Sargassum natans* and *S. fluitans*. Both species are hyponeustonic and fully adapted to a pelagic existence (Parr, 1939). Known commonly as gulf-weed, sea holly, or sargassum, they are characterized by a brushy, highly branched thallus (stem) with numerous leaf-like blades and berry-like pneumatocysts (floats). These floating plants may be up to several meters in length-but are typically much smaller. There is a well known assemblage of small fishes associated with sargassum rafts, many of which serve as forage for commercially or recreationally exploited species (Table 2). Dooley (1972) described 54 species from 23 families in the sargassum community of the Florida Current. Only 14 species from 11 families are known from the Sargasso Sea (Fedoryako, 1980; 1989). During the pelagic stage, hatchling loggerhead, *Caretta caretta*, green, *Chelonia mydas*, Kemp's ridley, *Lepidochelys kempi*, and hawksbill, *Eretmochelys imbricata*, sea turtles have been observed in sargassum off Florida, Georgia, North Carolina, and Texas (Smith, 1968; Fletemeyer, 1978; Carr and Meylan, 1980; Carr, 1986; 1987a; Schwartz, 1988; 1989; Manzella and Williams, 1991; Schwartz, pers. comm.). Schwartz (1988) reported numerous loggerhead hatchlings captured during commercial trawling for sargassum. This observation constitutes the largest known aggregation of loggerhead hatchlings encountered off the North Carolina coast.

Crawford, K. (ed.). 1989. Proceedings: 1989 Marine Expo: The Natural Resources Associated with Mobil's Proposed Drill Site. NC Outer Continental Shelf Office, NC Department of Administration. Raleigh, NC. 64 p.

*This report contains abstracts from each presenter. Chapter topics include: Mobil's Proposal, Geologic Overview — Introduction and Potential for Oil and Gas Discovery, Oceanographic Conditions, Comments on Last MMS Modeling, Biological Production Near the Bottom (invertebrates), Fisheries Resources, Commercial and Recreational Marine Fisheries, Winter Storm Effects on Spawning and Larval Drift of Pelagic Fish, Marine Birds, Sea Turtles in North Carolina, Marine Mammals, Plenary Session, Summary. Each chapter also cited individually when appropriate.

Curtin, T.B. 1979a. Ocean Outfall Wastewater Disposal Feasibility and Planning: Oceanographic Field Observations off North Carolina Spring Survey 12 — 22 May 1978, Report No. 79-4. Dept. of Marine Science and Engineering, NCSU. 242 p.

The objectives of the oceanographic field observations within the overall Ocean Outfall Feasibility and Planning Study (Langfelder et al. 1979) were both to provide input data for boundary condition initialization and to provide reference data for diagnostic testing of a series of coastal numerical circulation models under development. The data acquisition program was designed to parallel the model development in that a series of successive scales of variability were addressed. These scales have been defined as the shelf-scale, the nearshore scale, and the diffusive scale, and were characterized for the purposes of the study by temporal and spatial resolutions. Of particular overall interest in this project, with its ultimate focus on the nearshore coastal environment, was the interaction of the larger regional scale processes with those on smaller or local scale.

*Shellfish closure is discussed.

—. 1979b. Ocean Outfall Wastewater Disposal Feasibility and Planning: Oceanographic Field Observations off North Carolina Winter Survey 2-12 February 1978, Report No. 79-3. Dept. of Marine Science and Engineering, NCSU. 149 p.

The objectives of the oceanographic field observations within the overall Ocean Outfall Feasibility and Planning Study (Langfelder et al. 1979) were both to provide input data for boundary condition initialization and to provide reference data for diagnostic testing of a series of coastal numerical circulation models under development. The data acquisition program was designed to parallel the model development in that a series of successive scales of variability were addressed. These scales have been defined as the shelf-scale, the nearshore scale, and the diffusive scale, and were characterized for the purposes of the study by temporal and spatial resolutions. Of particular overall interest in this project, with its ultimate focus on the nearshore coastal environment, was the interaction of the larger regional scale processes with those on smaller or local scale.

*Shellfish closure is discussed.

—. 1979c. Ocean Outfall Wastewater Disposal Feasibility and Planning: Oceanographic Field Observations off North Carolina Fall Survey 1-11 November 1977, Report No. 79-5. Dept. of Marine Science and Engineering, NCSU. 248 p.

The objectives of the oceanographic field observations within the overall Ocean Outfall Feasibility and Planning Study (Langfelder et al. 1979) were both to provide input data for boundary condition initialization and to provide reference data for diagnostic testing of a series of coastal numerical circulation models under development. The data acquisition program was designed to parallel the model development in that a series of successive scales of variability were addressed. These scales have been defined as the shelf-scale, the nearshore scale, and the diffusive scale, and were characterized for the purposes of the study by temporal and spatial resolutions. Of particular overall interest in this project, with its ultimate focus on the nearshore coastal environment, was the interaction of the larger regional scale processes with those on smaller or local scale.

*Shellfish closure is discussed.

—. 1979d. Ocean Outfall Wastewater Disposal Feasibility and Planning: Oceanographic Field Observations Off North Carolina Summer Survey 2-12 August 1977, Report No. 79-2. Dept. of Marine Science and Engineering, NCSU. 303 p.

The objectives of the oceanographic field observations within the overall Ocean Outfall Feasibility and Planning Study (Langfelder et al. 1979) were both to provide input data for boundary condition initialization and to provide reference data for diagnostic testing of a series of coastal numerical circulation models under development. The data acquisition program was designed to parallel the model development in that a series of successive scales of variability were addressed. These scales have been defined as the shelf-scale, the nearshore scale, and the diffusive scale, and were characterized for the purposes of the study by temporal and spatial resolutions. Of particular overall interest in this project, with its ultimate focus on the nearshore coastal environment, was the interaction of the larger regional scale processes with those on smaller or local scale.

*Shellfish closure is discussed.

Cutler, E.B. 1975. Zoogeographical barrier on the continental slope off Cape Lookout, North Carolina. Deep-Sea Research 22: 893-901.

The distribution of Sipuncula and Pogonophora on the continental slope off North and South Carolina suggests a zoogeographical barrier southeast of Cape Lookout, North Carolina around 34 N between 150 and 2500 m for 14 of 27 species found. Similarity coefficients and a group average cluster analysis support the conclusions. This barrier may result from the effects of bottom currents on larval dispersion.

*The area from 31° N to 36° N was sampled.

Cutler, E.B., and K. Doble. 1979. North Carolina continental slope zoogeographical barrier. Deep-Sea Research 26(A): 851-853.

Collections of sipunculans and pogonophorans from depths between 150 and 2000 m around latitude 35°30'N were analyzed and used to supplement earlier information from this region. The addition of eight pogonophoran species from this area and minor revisions of earlier data reaffirm and strengthen the hypothesis that a zoogeographical barrier for slope dwelling infauna exists around 34° N off Cape Lookout, North Carolina.

Cutter, G.R., R.J. Diaz, and J.A. Blake. 1994a. Deep-Sea Research II: CD-ROM APPENDIX. Deep-Sea Research II Vol. 41(4-6): 981-982.

The contents of the CD-ROM Appendix are data and images of the bottom from five of the articles in this issue. The CD-ROM was mastered in a format that can be read by both Macintosh and PC computers. It is organized in an hierarchical structure by folders, with data in one and images in another. To access a particular file, sequentially open folders until the file of interest appears. Data and figure captions are provided as: (.txt) ASCII text with no line breaks; (.tlb) ASCII text with line breaks; (.wor) Microsoft Word; and (.wp) Word Perfect 5.1 files. Images are in TIFF format (.tif). Data (ACSAR, Hatteras), Images and Captions (ACSAR, Profile, 3Dbathy, Sled, Surface, x-ray) are included.

Cutter, G.R., R. Diaz, and J. Lee. 1994b. Foraminifera from the continental slope off Cape Hatteras, North Carolina. Deep-Sea Research II 41(4-6): 951-963.

The recent benthic meiofaunal foraminiferal assemblage from the continental slope (590-2003 m) off Cape Hatteras, North Carolina exhibits high species richness and evenness, moderate diversity values, and lacks numerically dominant species. The preserved planktic assemblage has relatively low species richness, high evenness, low diversity, and a few numerically dominant species. Approximately 9% of the benthic species are those that typically live within continental shelf depth ranges. The benthic assemblage abundances and diversities do not follow depth patterns or geophysical characteristics. No biogeographic boundary can be described within the study area for meiofaunal foraminifers. Oxygen limitation does not appear to be a factor affecting the benthos of the North Carolina continental slope based upon the community structure of the benthic foraminifers, if total assemblage is assumed to reflect the recently living community. The high carbonate content of sediments in the area may be explained by foraminiferal tests. Within the study area, the foraminiferal assemblages are uniform, and probably reflect relative consistency of primary environmental variables as well as dynamic downslope transport and high influx of material from the water column in the vicinity where the Gulf Stream and the Western Boundary Undercurrent cross.

Diaz, R.J., J.A. Blake, and D.P. Lohse. 1993a. Volume II Final Report: Benthic Study of the Continental Slope off Cape Hatteras, North Carolina. Virginia Institute of Marine Science, School of Marine Science, College of William and Mary, Gloucester Pt., VA. Science Applications International Corporation, Woods Hole, MA. 135 p.

*This is a study of the nature and spatial extent of continental slope benthic communities off Cape Hatteras, NC, with emphasis on the Manteo Area lease block 467. Macrofaunal abundance and biomass in this area higher than anywhere else along the entire South Atlantic continental slope and rise. Species composition of the infauna off Cape Hatteras is also different from other slope habitats. Species richness and diversity are lower with a high degree of dominance by species that are cosmopolitan in distribution. Trends in abundance of invertebrate megafauna on the continental slope off Cape Hatteras appear to be similar to the macrofauna. Demersal fish fauna off Cape Hatteras is distinctive in terms of composition and population density. Overall, abundance of benthic fish off Cape Hatteras is four to seven times higher than adjacent area. Site sediment characteristics (e.g., source, texture, and physico-chemistry) and potential impact to benthic community by sediment discharge during drilling are described. Volume III contains Appendices A-E.

Much of the data in this report were used in the Special Deep Research issue (1994. 41 (4-6)).

Diaz, R.J., J. Blake, B. Hecker, and D.C. Rhoads. 1993b. A Highly Productive Area of the Continental Slope Off Cape Hatteras. Benthic Ecology Meeting, 1-4 April 1993, Mobile, AL. 57 p.

The continental slope off Cape Hatteras is atypical for the U.S. Atlantic coast. Unusually high numbers of infauna, megafauna, and demersal fish were found over a broad area. Benthic organisms appear to be well adapted to physical processes that converge on the Cape Hatteras continental slope. These physical processes impart a high degree of instability to the bottom and also supply large amounts of organic matter which sustain the elevated densities and biomass. The nature of these communities and mechanisms which regulate them will be discussed.

Diaz, R.J., G.R. Cutter, and J.A. Blake. 1998. Appendix F: A Review: Findings of the Benthic Study of the Continental Slope Off Cape Hatteras, North Carolina. pp. 121-136. *In*: Vigil, D.L. (ed.). North Carolina/Minerals Management Service Technical Workshop on Manteo Unit Exploration: February 4-5, 1998. U.S. Dept. of the Interior, Minerals Management Service, Gulf of Mexico OCS Region. New Orleans, LA.

*These are the proceedings from a workshop/meeting (conducted on February 4-5, 1998) between the North Carolina Department of Environment and Natural Resources, and the U.S. Department of the Interior's Minerals Management Service (MMS). The geographic area being discussed is approximately 45 miles east-northeast of Cape Hatteras, NC, referred to as the Manteo Unit. This workshop reviewed environmental and socioeconomic information known and needed on the Manteo

Unit. The MMS's Gulf of Mexico OCS Regional Director gave an MMS perspective on history and status of the area. Chevron gave a presentation on how the exploratory well would be drilled. The scientific characterization was presented in greater detail by a number of scientific experts who spoke on the following disciplines physical environment, habitat and living resources, seabirds, marine mammals, sea turtles, and social and economic issues. Specific chapters are cited individually, when appropriate.

Because of the potential environmental impacts associated with development and production activities, the Oil Pollution Act of 1990 mandated that a panel of experts be convened. This panel, North Carolina Environmental Sciences Review Panel (Costlow et al. 1992), was to consider whether the available scientific information was adequate for making decisions about oil and gas leasing, exploration, and development off North Carolina. The Costlow et al. (1992) report to the Secretary of the Interior made several recommendations on the information needed to understand the basic ecology of the leased areas. Among them was the recommendation that the spatial extent of the benthic community found within some of the lease blocks should be determined before any exploration or development activity occurred off Cape Hatteras. The present study was developed by the Minerals Management Service to determine the aerial extent of the community found by Blake et al. (1985, 1987). Results are published as a special issue of Deep-Sea Research Part II (Diaz et al. 1994a), which included a CD-ROM with data and selected bottom images (Cutter et al. 1994a).

Sediments and Sedimentation Rates, Biological Communities (invertebrates and fish), Physical Habitat (geomorphology), Benthic Community Characterization and Distribution are discussed.

Diaz, R.J., G.R. Cutter, and D.C. Rhoads. 1994. The importance of bioturbation to continental slope sediment structure and benthic processes off Cape Hatteras, North Carolina. Deep-Sea Research II 41(4-6): 719-734.

Even though the continental slope off Cape Hatteras has sediment accumulation rates on the order of 1 cm/year, large areas of soft sediment are intensively reworked by infaunal organisms. Primary sedimentary structures are dominated by the bioturbation activities of a deep burrowing infauna (to at least 30 cm). The layer actively mixed by the benthos, as evidenced by sediment profile and X-ray images, is estimated to range from 5 to 20 cm, with the residence time for particles within the surface mixed layer ranging from about 4.5 to 18 years. The biological mixing parameter (G) ranges from 0.4 to 5.5, which indicates moderate to strong biological mixing relative to accumulation and strata formation. Bioturbation contributes to the dynamic forces affecting the surface sediments by decreasing compaction of sediment layers and dilating sediment fabrics by sediment mixing, and introducing large water-filled burrows and voids to subsurface sediments. The sediment profile images captured numerous subsurface feeding voids, and worms in the process of making deep burrows, many of which extended below the 5 to 10 cm average depth of the apparent color redox potential discontinuity layer. High rates of accumulation of organic-rich sediment lead to high standing stocks of benthos and intensive feeding/burrowing activity that result in organic rich stratagraphic sequences that are thoroughly mixed. Cape Hatteras is an apparent focusing point for the transport of shallow water sediments to the deep sea. Sediments across other areas of the continental slope just 100's of kilometers south of Cape Hatteras are not as thoroughly mixed or biologically active.

Fedoryako, B.I. 1989. A Comparative Characteristic of Oceanic Fish Assemblages Associated with Floating Debris. Journal of Ichthyology 29: 128-137.

A comparative characteristic of fish assemblages associated with oceanic debris (drifting macrophytes, terrestrial material and epipelagic invertebrates) of tropical ocean zones was made. In the floating debris of the oceanic pelagial 110 species of 35 families were found. About 30% of all fish species were found only in some assemblages. The highest species diversity was associated with macrophytes (75% of all species), and terrestrial material (78% of all species). Representatives of the majority of common species, up to a certain size, occurred in the macrophytes. Fishes associated with drifting macrophytes formed more abundant assemblages than those associated with terrestrial material. Over 50% of species associated with oceanic flotsam occurred commonly in the neritic zone. With the increasing distance of the flotsam from the coast the species diversity decreases and the dominant species change.

George, R.Y., and A.W. Hulbert (eds.). 1989. North Carolina Coastal Symposium. National Undersea Research Program, NOAA. Rockville, MD. 582 p.

*This is a multidisciplinary Marine Scientific Proceedings, with frequent reference to the North Carolina Coastal Oceanography. Two studies (also cited individually) include maps with study plots (p. 283; reef site) or migratory movements (p. 309; sea turtles) in the project study area. Zoogeography and ecology of fishes inhabiting North Carolina's Marine Waters to depths of 600 meters is included. The transcript from speaker representing Outer Continental Shelf (p. 549) mentions off-shore oil drilling off North Carolina Coast and mid-Atlantic region. The speaker does not refer to a specific site.

Gettleson, D.A. 1992. Results of a Benthic Visual Survey within the Manteo Block 467. pp. 159-168. *In*: U.S. Department of the Interior, Minerals Management Service. Proceedings of the Fourth Atlantic OCS Region Information Transfer Meeting, September 1991. U.S. Department of the Interior, Minerals Management Service. Herndon, VA.

The Fourth Atlantic Outer Continental Shelf (OCS) Regional Information Transfer Meeting (ITM) was held on 24-25 September 1991 in Wilmington, NC. The focus of the meeting was on the OCS off North Carolina, specifically on activities related to a proposed exploratory well for oil and gas by Mobil on Block 467 a site 40 miles off the coast of North Carolina. The area of industry interest is known as the Manteo Prospect, while the activities surrounding the proposed drilling are referred to collectively as the Manteo Project. The wildcat wellsite is in 2,690 ft. (857 m) of water near the edge of the Gulf Stream. It is also near a fishing ground known locally as "The Point." The area is believed to be gas prone rather than oil prone. The estimated size of the resource could be as high as 5 trillion cubic feet of gas.

The purpose of the meeting was to exchange information on the leasing background, legislative activities, scientific results, and socioeconomic studies. Legislative-related reports include descriptions of the Oil Pollution Act of 1990, the Outer Banks Protection Act, the Environmental Studies Review Panel, and the North Carolina Physical Oceanography Panel. Reports of studies on marine life include benthic diatoms, benthic fauna, pelagic seabirds, sea turtles, and right whales. One report describes the use of airships (blimps) for ocean research a capability relevant to North Carolina because of the east coast airship facility is located in the state. Local marine science facilities described include NOAA's National Undersea Research Center at the University of North Carolina at Wilmington (NURC/UNCW) and the national marine Fisheries Service laboratory in Beaufort.

Developments in oil spill cleanup technology and capabilities are described by both the Coast Guard and the industry. A socioeconomic report describes the effects of the oil and gas activities on the tourist industry. Lastly, research on the restoration of salt marshes indicates that rehabilitation of an area is possible when development or an accident has occurred. While the emphasis of the meeting was on oil and gas, two reports described the results of projects related to offshore sand mining. The appendix lists the names and addresses of speakers. Individual chapters are cited individually when appropriate.

*This summary describes the results of a video- and still-camera photodocumentation survey conducted from July 9 to 24, 1989 in the Manteo Area Block 467 (Figure 37). Block 467 is located along a steep, highly irregular portion of the continental slope on the northern fringe of the Hatteras canyon system. The purpose of this photodocumentation survey was to document the topographical features, substrate types, and associated biota around a proposed well and anchor locations in block 467 (figure 38). Water depths within the sites surveyed ranged from 299 to 1,393 meters (980 to 4,570 feet). Because of the water depth and the highly irregular topography within the survey area, a state-of the-art deepwater remotely operated vehicle was used to obtain the survey data. Live bottom site characterization (invertebrates and fish present) are described.

Gillikin, J.W., Jr., D.L. Taylor, and B.F. Holland Jr. 1979. RV Dan Moore Cruise Report No. 33: Cape Lookout, NC to Little Machipongo Inlet, VA. North Carolina Division of Marine Fisheries, Department of Natural Resources and Community Development. Morehead City, NC.

*During February and March 1979 the RV Dan Moore continued its investigations of offshore stocks of anadromous fishes (river herring, shad, striped bass and sturgeon) between Cape Lookout, NC and Little Machipongo Inlet, VA. In response to local fishermen and dealers, reports of calico scallop catches were investigated offshore Ocracoke Inlet. Depths were 12 to 14 fathoms.

Gooday, A.J., L.A. Levin, C.L. Thomas, and B. Hecker. 1992. The Distribution and Ecology of *Bathysiphon filiformis* Sars and *B. major* De Folin (Protista, Foraminiferida) on the Continental Slope Off North Carolina. Journal of Foraminiferal Research 22(2): 129-146.

Two large species of the agglutinated foraminiferal genus *Bathysiphon* are common in samples and photographs from bathyal depths on the North Carolina continental slope: *B. filiformis* off Cape Hatteras (588-930 m bathymetric depth) and *B. major* off Cape Lookout (850-1950 m depth). The sampling area, and particularly the 850 m station where *B. filiformis* is abundant (mean densities of 59-154 per m^2), is believed to receive large inputs of organic material from various sources. This is consistent with the previously observed occurrence of large *Bathysiphon* species in regions of high food supply. Ten camera sled transects across the eastern U.S. continental slope between 32°N and 41°N emphasize the abundance of *B. filiformis* in the Cape Hatteras area compared with its rarity or absence elsewhere along the continental slope.

Box cores, bottom photographs, and direct submersible observations indicate that *B. filiformis* tubes project above the sediment in an arcuate curve with only the lower 1 cm or so buried. Bathysiphon major adopts a similar orientation but has a greater proportion (50- 80%) of the tube buried. The voluminous, dense, granular protoplasm of both species contains biogenic particles (including diatoms, in *B. filiformis only*), dinoflagellate cysts, fungal remains, pollen grains, tintinnid loricae, polychaete jaws and setae, benthic foraminiferal tests, and fish tooth fragments), suggesting that they feed mainly on material derived from the sediment surface. Submersible observations indicate that *B. filiformis* is patchily distributed at 100 m scales. Smaller scale dispersion patterns (analyzed from photographs) are generally random but with a tendency to be aggregated at lower densities and uniform at higher densities.

A variety of metazoans and foraminifers live epifaunally on the outer surfaces of *B. filiformis* tubes. The most frequently occurring metazoans were larvae and juveniles of an unidentified gastropod and a tubiculous terebellid polychaete *Nicolea* sp. The most common epifaunal foraminifers were *Tritaxis conica* and *Trochammina* sp. Tubes of *B. major*, however, are virtually devoid of epifauna. Our results support the view that large, agglutinated rhizopod tests may influence the structure of deep-water benthic communities. However, in the case of *Bathysiphon* on the North Carolina continental slope, the effect appears limited to taxa directly associated with the foraminiferal tubes.

Gray, I.E., M.E. Downey, and M.J. Cerame-Vivas. 1968. Sea-Stars of North Carolina. Fishery Bulletin 67(1): 127-163.

Descriptions, keys to identification, and photographs are given for the 22 genera and 33 species of North Carolina asteroids. The starfish fauna is predominantly "southern." Eighteen species are distributed from North Carolina southward, nine range from North Carolina northward, and six occur both north and south of North Carolina. The affinities of the various species to the principal marine biotic provinces discussed. Thirteen tropical and subtropical species occur only in an extension of the Caribbean Province along the outer shelf. Only four of the 33 species on the Continental Shelf can be considered abundant: *Astropecten articulatus*, *Luidia clathrata*, *Astropecten americanus*, and *Asterias forbesii*.

Grosslein, M.D., and T.R. Azarovitz. 1982. Fish Distribution: MESA New York Bight Atlas Monograph 15, New York Sea Grant Institute. Albany, NY. 182 p.

The Middle Atlantic Bight is a complex ecosystem characterized by rapid latitudinal change in water temperature s and associated fauna. Subtropical and boreal fish fauna overlap in the region from Cape Hatteras to Georges Bank, resulting in a highly diverse fish community with large seasonal fluctuations in distribution. The general ecology of 43 important species of fish and shellfish in the Middle Atlantic Bight is summarized in terms of 1) distribution and seasonal movements, 2) populations size and fisheries, 3) reproduction-growth-life span, 4) feeding interrelationships, and 50 environmental sensitivity to pollutants and natural environmental factors. Most species found in the Bight also spawn there; thus environmental conditions and water quality in the Bight control the reproductive success of the populations occurring there. The geographic and seasonal distribution of spawning in the Bight is described for major species through the distribution of their larvae, the life stage believed to be most vulnerable to natural environmental changes and pollution.

The monograph concludes with an examination of the relative importance of natural environmental factors versus man's impacts in controlling fish abundance. Population declines and reduced productivity due to pollution have been demonstrated for both shellfish and fishes although chiefly in inshore-waters; as yet there is no clear evidence of major impact of pollution on populations in offshore waters but there is concern about possible undetected impacts and potential future effects because of growing pressure for substantially increased ocean dumping. Declines in biomass of many populations clearly have been related to excessive fishing pressure in recent years, and there will be a continuing need for some control over fishing mortality rates if we are to achieve optimum yields from our fishery resources. However, so far it appears that natural mortality factors operating in the first year of life exert the greatest control over annual fluctuations in fish populations.

Guthrie, J.V., B.F. Holland Jr., and J.W. Gillikin Jr. 1981. RV Dan Moore Cruise Report No. 47: Segment I: Offshore Anadromous Fish Survey from Cape Lookout to Chesapeake Bay; Segment II: Reconnaissance of Calico Scallops, *Argopecten gibbus,* on the Traditional Scallop Grounds East of Cape Lookout Shoals. North Carolina Division of Marine Fisheries, Department of Natural Resources and Community Development. Morehead City, NC.

*Segment I of this report describes anadromous fishery investigation conducted offshore North Carolina and Virginia from 16-25 March 1981. Target species include river herring, shad, striped bass, and sturgeon. Segment II of this report is a reconnaissance of Calico Scallops, *Argopecten gibbus*, during February 1981. Depths ranged from 5 to 19 fathoms.

Hastie, L.C. 1995. Deep-Water Geryonid Crabs: A Continental Slope Resource. Oceanography and Marine Biology: An Annual Review 1995 33: 561-584.

The potentially exploitable deep-water crabs of the family Geryonidae are widely distribution on the continental slopes of the world, at depths of 200-1200m. Presently, only two species are of commercial importance: *Chaceon maritae* in South West African waters, and *C. quinquedens* off the northeastern coast of North America. Interest in these fisheries, which have operated since the 1970s, has resulted in exploratory surveys for the other marketable species of the genera *Chaceon* and *Geryon*. Given the deep-water distribution at low temperatures, slow growth and maturation rates, and possibly infrequent recruitment of geryonid crabs, it is doubtful if high yields are sustainable. Hence, the choice facing geryonid fishery managers may be between a large open "boom and bust" short-term fishery, or a much smaller restricted long-term fishery that hopefully could be sustained. However, more knowledge or geryonid biology and population dynamics is required before any effective management measures can be implemented.

Hecker, B. 1994. Unusual megafaunal assemblages on the continental slope off Cape Hatteras. Deep-Sea Research II 41(4-6): 809-834.

Megafaunal assemblages were studied in August September 1992 using a towed camera sled along seven cross-isobath transects on the continental slope off Cape Hatteras. A total of 20,722 megafaunal organisms were observed on 10,918 m^2 of the sea floor between depths of 157 and 1924 m. These data were compared with data previously collected off Cape Hatteras in 1985 and at other locations along the eastern U.S. coast between 1981 and 1987. Megafaunal populations on the upper and lower slopes off Cape Hatteras were found to be similar, in terms of density and species composition, to those observed at the other locations.

In contrast, megafaual abundances were found to be elevated (0.88 and 2.65 individuals per m^2 during 1985 and 1992, respectively) on the middle slope off Cape Hatteras when compared to most other slope locations (<0.5 individuals per m^2). These elevated abundances mainly reflect dense populations of three demersal fish, two eelpouts (*Lysenchelys verillii* and *Lycodes atlanticus*) and the witch flounder *Glyptocephalus cynoglossus*, and a large anemone (*Actinauge verrilli*). These four species dominated the megafauna off Cape Hatteras, whereas they represented only a minor component of megafaunal populations found at other slope locations. Additionally, numerous tubes of the foraminiferan Bathysiphon filiformis were observed off Cape Hatteras, but not elsewhere. The high density of demersal fish found off Cape Hatteras appears to be related to the high densities of infaunal prey reported from this area. The high densities of *A. verrilli* and *B. filiformis* may be related to the same factors responsible for the high infaunal densities, namely enhanced nutrient inputs in the form of fine particles. Extreme patchiness also was observed in the distributions of the middle slope taxa off Cape Hatteras. This patchiness may reflect the habitat heterogeneity of this exceptionally rugged slope and the sedentary nature of the organisms inhabiting it.

Hilbig, B. 1994. Faunistic and zoogeographical characterization of the benthic infauna on the Carolina continental slope. Deep-Sea Research II 41(4-6): 929-950.

The species composition of the benthic infauna on the Carolina continental slope is described, based on the analysis of 146 quantitative boxcore samples taken between 1983 and 1986 and in 1992. The samples were collected between Cape Hatteras and the Charleston Bump in depths ranging from 600 to 3500 m. From these samples, nearly 1300 species were identified, more than one-third of them being new to science. Almost half of all species were polychaetes, the largest family being the Spionids with 63 species. Arthropods accounted for about 22% of all species, about one-third of which belonged to the tanaidaceans. Among the mollusks (16% of all species), the largest group was thyasirid bivalves. Pogonophorans were represented by 15 species. Distributional patterns of some of the major taxa are discussed, and the existence of a zoogeographical barrier off Cape Hatteras and/or Cape Lookout is revisited. The most striking difference between the slope off Cape Hatteras and comparable depths further south (e.g. Cape Lookout) is the greatly reduced number of polychaetes off Cape Hatteras. The zoogeographical barrier reported by Cutler [(1975) 22, 893-901] exists for most cumaceans, some aplacophorans, and many polychaetes identified from the present data set, but it appears to be virtually nonexistent for bivalves.

Hogans, W.E., and K.J. Sulak. 1992. *Diocus lycenchelus,* New Species (Copepoda: Chodracanthidae) Parasitic on the Eelpout, *Lycenchelys verrillii* (Zoarcidae), from the Hatteras Slope of the Northwest Atlantic Ocean. Bulletin of Marine Science 51(3): 301-308.

A new species of parasitic copepod, *Diocus lycenchelus,* is described from the demersal zoarcid fish *Lycenchelys verrillii* caught off Cape Hatteras, U.S.A. The new species differs from its congeners in the shape of the cephalothorax, trunk (ventrolateral processes), fine structure of appendages (mandible, second maxilla, first thoracic leg) and site of infection (the nares). A comparison of the morphology of *D. lycenchelus* n. sp. is made with that of the other four recognized species of *Diocus* (*D. frigidus, D. gobinus, D. semilunaris, and D. sadoensis*).

Holland, B.F., Jr., J.W. Gillikin Jr., and J.V. Guthrie. 1981a. RV Dan Moore Cruise Report No. 51: Segment I: Calico Scallop Reconnaissance from Ocracoke to New River Inlet, NC (October-November 1981); Segment II: Flounder Mesh Selectivity Study (November-December 1981). North Carolina Division of Marine Fisheries, Department of Natural Resources and Community Development. Morehead City, NC.

*Segment I of this report describes Calico Scallop Reconnaissance from Ocracoke to New River Inlet, NC (October-November 1981). Segment II of this report describes Flounder Mesh Selectivity Study (November-December 1981) off North Carolina's coast. Depths ranged from 11 to 14 fathoms.

—. 1981b. RV Dan Moore Cruise Report No. 46: Segment I: Offshore Anadromous Fish Survey from Cape Lookout to Chesapeake Bay; Segment II: Reconnaissance of Calico Scallops, Argopecten gibbus, on the Traditional Scallop Grounds East of Cape Lookout Shoals. North Carolina Division of Marine Fisheries, Department of Natural Resources and Community Development. Morehead City, NC.

*Segment I of this report describes anadromous fishery investigation conducted offshore North Carolina and Virginia from January-April 1981. Target species include river herring, shad, striped bass, and sturgeon. Segment II of this report is a reconnaissance of Calico Scallops, *Argopecten gibbus*, during August 1980. Depths were 5 to 20 fathoms.

Holland, B.F., Jr., J.W. Gillikin Jr., and D.L. Taylor. 1979b. RV Dan Moore Cruise Report No. 37: Rock Shrimp (*Sicyonia brevirostris*) Investigations in Long, Onslow and Raleigh Bay, NC. North Carolina Division of Marine Fisheries, Department of Natural Resources and Community Development. Morehead City, NC.

*From 15-24 October, and from 29 October-1 November 1979, the RV Dan Moore conducted trawling operations in Long, Onslow and Raleigh Bay, NC in search of Rock Shrimp (*Sicyonia brevirostris*). The primary objectives of this cruise were to: 1) Investigate the relative abundance, distribution and size composition of rock shrimp, 2) To determine if rock shrimp occur in sufficient quantities in Long, Onslow and Raleigh bays (offshore NC) to support a potential commercial fishery.

Depths on the first segment (20-55 miles south of Southport, NC and from 10-35 miles south of Cape Lookout) were 12 to 31 fathoms. Depths sampled on the second segment (east of Cape Lookout and to 10-15 miles south of Cape Hatteras) were 17 to 30 fathoms.

Kirby-Smith, W.W. 1985. Invertebrate Zooplankton and Pelagic Macroinvertebrates in the Proposed EMPRESS II VAVAPES Area off North Carolina . Appendix D. *In:* U.S. Department of the Navy. EMPRESS II: Supplemental Draft Environmental Impact Statement for the Proposed Operation of the Navy Electromagnetic Pulse Radiation Environment Simulator for Ships (Empress II) in the Chesapeake Bay and Atlantic Ocean. United States Navy. Environmental/ Intergovernmental Section. Atlantic Division. Naval Facilities Engineering and Command. Norfolk, VA.

The VACAPES area where EMPRESS will operate is located off the northeastern coast of North Carolina within an area known as the Virginian Sea. A mixing of Chesapeake Bay and middle Atlantic coastal water (the Virginian Current) define the physical and chemical environment and in large part determine the distribution of invertebrate zooplankton and pelagic macroinvertebrates in the VACAPES area. Invertebrate zooplankton include large numbers of species from many phyla. Holoplankton dominate over meroplankton although the latter may be extremely important to commercial fisheries (e.g. larval blue crabs). Copepods dominate the holoplankton. Species expected to commonly occur in the VACAPES area are listed. Pelagic macroinvertebrates of the area include mollusca (squid) and crustacea (shrimp and crabs). The life history and distribution of commercially important species are discussed, particularly as they might interact with EMPRESS. There are no species of special concern (endangered or threatened) among the invertebrate zooplankton or pelagic invertebrates.

Sources of information and sources for primary literature concerning these groups come from a number of publications: Marine Ecosystem Analysis (MESA) Program, Volumes 13 and 15, New York Sea Grant Institute (Grosslein and Azarovitz 1982); North Carolina Fisheries and Environmental Data Search and Synthesis Study (Continental Shelf Associates, Inc 1983); A Summary and Analysis of Environmental Information on the Continental Shelf and Blake Plateau from Cape Hatteras to Cape Canaveral (1977), Volume 1, Book 1, (Center for Natural Areas 1977); A Checklist of Biota of the Lower Chesapeake Bay (Wass 1972). These publications are used as sources for primary literature which specifically includes the VACAPES area or which includes organisms expected to occur in the area. Recent literature is presented based upon references obtained by library search of marine journals.

—. 1989a. Biological Production Near the Bottom. p. 25. *In*: Crawford, K. (ed.). Proceedings: 1989 Marine Expo: The Natural Resources Associated with Mobil's Proposed Drill Site. NC Outer Continental Shelf Office, NC Department of Administration. Raleigh, NC.

Satellite photographs show that North Carolina has an incredibly diverse oceanographic setting which, in turn, produces highly diverse communities of fishes and invertebrates. The three bottom types found off the continental shelf of North Carolina include; 1) sand, 2) shell, and 3) rock outcrops. Across the continental shelf, the primary producers that support fisheries include microalgae and macroalgae. The bottom-dwelling microalgae (small microscopic plants) grow, rapidly and are very important to the total productivity of the whole water column. As much as half of the primary productivity on the shelf may be due to this benthic component. The secondary producers on rock outcrops, which include sponges, corals, worms and small arthropods, are a major food source for small fish. From a scientific perspective, the proposed drill site is an exciting area with a high biomass and low diversity. In my opinion, the exploration well itself would have little or no impact on the resources in the area; however, a major find of oil or gas could lead to a tremendous amount of industrial development, which could compete economically with other coastal industries, such as tourism and fisheries.

—. 1989b. The Community of Small Macroinvertebrates Associated with Rock Outcrops in the Continental Shelf of North Carolina. pp. 279-305. *In*: George, R.Y., and A.W. Hulbert (eds.). North Carolina Coastal Symposium. National Undersea Research Program, NOAA. Rockville, MD.

Communities of small benthic organisms associated with rock outcrops on the continental shelf of North Carolina were examined for patterns in community structure related to season and depth. The communities were dominated by polychaetes, amphipods and mollusks. The number of species per 0.5m² ranged from 40 to 214 and the number of individuals from 180 to 1657. Diversity was high with H' values of 4 to 6. Diversity was slightly greater at the middle shelf stations as compared to inner and outer shelf. The number of species and individuals was greatest at all three locations in the spring and fall and least in the winter and summer: a pattern similar to that of temperate coastal plankton. An index of community similarity indicated the presence of cold (winter/spring) and warm (summer/fall) communities at each of the three locations. Moreover at the middle and inner shelf the communities were more related to season (cold and warm) than to location (inner and middle). Outer shelf communities also had a strong seasonal component but were very different when compared with the middle and inner shelf communities. Different sampling gear (grabs versus diver suction) may explain some of the outer shelf uniqueness.

*The site ISO4 location data cited by Kirby-Smith are incorrect. Data cited by Kirby-Smith for site ISO4 resulted from unpublished data collected during a SCUBA dive by S.W. Ross on 18 August 1980. The correct location for this site [SWR -SCUBA-80-20] is 35° 20.7'N; 75° 21.2'W; depth 70-80 feet. Selected fish, invertebrate, and bottom habitat data were collected. These data are unpublished and the site was not visited again (S.W. Ross, pers. comm., 19 November 1999).

Langfelder, J., T.B. Curtin, D.N. Hyman, G. Janowitz, J. Maiolo, W. Queen, F.Y. Sorrell, M. Amien, V. Bellis, M. Brinson, G. Davis, C.Y. Lee, C. O'Rear, L. Pearce, C.Y. Peng, S. Riggs, B. Smith, M. Sobsey, and P. Tschetter. 1979. Final Report: Ocean Outfall Wastewater Disposal Feasibility and Planning, Report No. 79-1. Dept. of Marine Science and Engineering, NCSU; Report No. 5, Institute for Coastal and Marine Resources, ECU. 482 p.

*This report follows an EIS format and is cited as a single document. Individual chapters are not stand-alone documents. Major findings of the study were: 1) Construction and operation of a well designed and operated sewage treatment plant that utilizes an ocean outfall and secondary treatment should not adversely affect the water column on fishery resources. Some build up of effluent constituents may occur in the bottom sediments in the immediate vicinity of the diffuser and could result in bottom community changes. 2) Effluent discharge should have essentially no adverse affect on recreational swimming in the areas of the diffuser. Areas now closed to shellfishing in the estuaries could be reopened as a result of reduced pathogen loadings: these pathogens are presently coming from septic tanks and treatment plants that discharge into these waters. 3) Centralized sewer systems will increase land values, allow reduced lot size and stimulate growth. This will lead to change in the population composition and demands for expanded goods and services.

Levin, L.A. 1991. Interactions Between Metazoans and Large, Agglutinating Protozoans: Implications for the Community Structure of Deep-Sea Benthos. American Zoologist 31: 886-900.

Large agglutinating protozoans belonging to the Foraminiferida (suborder Astrorhizina) and the Xenophyophorea are conspicuous, often dominant faunal elements in the deep sea. A review of known and suspected interactions between these forms and metazoans reveals a potentially significant role for the protozoans in structuring deep-sea metazoan assemblages. Direct interactions include provision to metazoans of (a) hard or stable substratum, (b) refuge from predators or physical disturbance, and (c) access to enhanced dietary resources. In some instances, rhizopod tests may provide a nursery function. Xenophyophore modification of flow regimes, particle flux, bottom skin friction and sediment characteristics appear likely and we believed to account for altered composition and abundance of meiofauna and macrofauna in the vicinity of rhizopod tests. Some analogous interactions are observed between metazoans and biogenic sediment structures in shallow water. However, metazoan-rhizopod associations are hypothesized to be more highly developed and complex in the deep sea than are comparable shallow-water associations, due to rhizopod abilities to enhance scarce food resources and to low rates of disturbance in much of the deep sea. Agglutinating rhizopods appear to be a significant source of heterogeneity on the deep-sea floor and large tests often represent 'hotspots' of metazoan activity. As such, they are hypothesized to have contributed to the origin and maintenance of metazoan diversity in the deep sea by providing distinct microenvironments in which species can specialize.

Levin, L., N. Blair, D. DeMaster, G. Plaia, W. Fornes, C. Martin, and C. Thomas. 1997. Rapid subduction of organic matter by maldanid polychaetes on the North Carolina slope. Journal of Marine Research 55: 595-611.

In situ tracer experiments conducted on the North Carolina continental slope reveal that tube-building worms (Polychaeta: Maldanidae) can, without ingestion, rapidly subduct freshly deposited, algal carbon (^{13}C-labeled diatoms) and inorganic materials (slope sediment and glass beads) to depths of 10 cm or more in the sediment column. Transport over 1.5 days appears to be nonselective but spatially patchy, creating localized, deep hotspots. As a result of this transport, relatively fresh organic matter becomes available soon after deposition to deep-dwelling microbes and other infauna, and both aerobic and anaerobic processes may be enhanced. Comparison of tracer subduction with estimates from a diffusive mixing model using ^{234}Th-based coefficients, suggests that maldanid subduction activities, within 1.5 d of particle deposition, could account for 25-100% of the mixing below 5 cm that occurs on 100-day time scales. Comparison of community data from the North Carolina slope for different places and times indicate a correlation between the abundance of deep-welling maldanids and the abundance and the dwelling depth in the sediment column of other infauna. Pulsed inputs of organic matter occur frequently in margin environments and maldanid polychaetes are a common component of continental slope macrobenthos. Thus, the activities we observe are likely to be widespread and significant for chemical cycling (natural and anthropogenic materials) on the slope. We propose that species like maldanids, that rapidly redistribute labile organic matter within the seabed, probably function as keystone resource modifiers. They may exert a disproportionately strong influence (relative to their abundance) on the structure of infaunal communities and on the timing, location and nature of organic matter diagenesis and burial in continental margin sediments.

Magnuson, J.J., C.L. Harrington, D.J. Stewart, and G.N. Herbst. 1981. Responses of macrofauna to short-term dynamics of a Gulf Stream front on the continental shelf. pp. 441-448. *In*: Richards, F.R. (ed.). Coastal Upwelling. American Geophysical Union.

Benthic and near-bottom fishes, decapod crustaceans, and echinoderms were sampled in two areas through which a Gulf Stream front moved just north of Cape Hatteras along 75°13′ W longitude in October 1977. We tested the hypothesis that the frontal aggregations resulted from the response of organisms to the front itself rather than to a geographically fixed feature of the region. The front, 8.5° C and 3.5 °/oo wide, was characterized by horizontal gradients of at least 0.5 °C/km and speeds of 30 ^{cm}/s. Bottom trawling was conducted day and night in each area (northern and southern) when the front was present and when it was absent. Both areas contained more species and individuals of fish when the front was present. Atlantic croaker, weakfish, and spot left when the front left. Decapods exhibited some response to the front, especially at night. During the day, fewer echinoderms were caught when the front was present — perhaps because the sudden changes in temperature induced burrowing. During the day all three groups were more abundant in the northern than in the southern area in terms of species and individuals. The front itself and more geographically fixed features both influenced distributions.

Milliman, J. D., R. J. Diaz, J. A. Blake, and G. R. Cutter Jr. (eds.). 1994. Topical Studies in Oceanography: Input, Accumulation and Cycling of Materials on the Continental Slope Off Cape Hatteras. Deep-Sea Research Part II 41. 982 p.

*This is a compilation of studies on Input, Accumulation and Cycling of Materials on the Continental Slope Off Cape Hatteras. Geology, sediments, organics, and benthic fauna are discussed. A CD-ROM is included. Each chapter (study) is cited independently, when appropriate. Some papers in this issue were derived from Diaz et al. (1993).

Minerals Management Service. 1982a. South Atlantic OCS Area Living Marine Resources Study Year II: Final Report Executive Summary. Minerals Management Service contract AA551-CT1-18. Minerals Management Service, Washington, DC.

Live bottom areas area known to be important to commercial and recreational fisheries in the South Atlantic Bight, but biological studies of these areas have been limited. As a result, very little data exists on the structure of invertebrate and fish communities present in these hard-bottom habitats, and information is lacking on what effects offshore oil and gas exploration might have on live-bottom communities. Because more information was needed for recent and upcoming Outer Continental Shelf (OCS) Lease Sales, the Bureau of Land Management initiated the "South Atlantic OCS Area Living Marine Resources Study." The primary objectives of this study during the first year were to: 1) Characterize the invertebrate and nektonic communities associated with several representative live-bottom areas from Cape Hatteras, NC to Northern Florida and elevate factors which might influence community structure such as depth, latitude, and season (summer vs. winter), 2) Characterize the food habits of selected fish species of commercial and recreational importance, 3) Conduct a limited assessment of bottom topography and substrate type, 4) Evaluate the potential effects of oil- and gas-related activities on live-bottom communities.

Results obtained from the first year sampling program were presented in a 1981 report available through the National Technical Information Service. Objectives of the second-year study were the same as those listed above; however, seasonal sampling was increased to include all seasons. In addition, some study areas were changed to include portions of the shelf not previously studied, while others were sampled during both years to allow assessment of persistence in the distribution patterns observed during the first year. This report summarizes the results and conclusions obtained from the second year (1981) sampling program.

—. 1982b. South Atlantic OCS Area Living Marine Resources Study Year II: Final Report Volume I. Minerals Management Service contract AA551-CT1-18. Minerals Management Service, Washington, DC.

Live bottom areas area known to be important to commercial and recreational fisheries in the South Atlantic Bight, but biological studies of these areas have been limited. As a result, very little data exists on the structure of invertebrate and fish communities present in these hard-bottom habitats, and information is lacking on what effects offshore oil and gas exploration might have on live-bottom communities. Because more information was needed for recent and upcoming Outer Continental Shelf (OCS) Lease Sales, the Bureau of Land Management initiated the "South Atlantic OCS Area Living Marine Resources Study." The primary objectives of this study during the first year were to: 1) Characterize the invertebrate and nektonic communities associated with several representative live-bottom areas from Cape Hatteras, NC to Northern Florida and elevate factors which might influence community structure such as depth, latitude, and season (summer vs. winter), 2) Characterize the food habits of selected fish species of commercial and recreational importance, 3) Conduct a limited assessment of bottom topography and substrate type, 4) Evaluate the potential effects of oil- and gas-related activities on live-bottom communities.

Results obtained from the first year sampling program were presented in a 1981 report available through the National Technical Information Service (NTIS). Objectives of the second-year study were the same as those listed above; however, seasonal sampling was increased to include all seasons. In addition, some study areas were changed to include portions of the shelf not previously studied, while others were sampled during both years to allow assessment of persistence in the distribution patterns observed during the first year. This report summarizes the results and conclusions obtained from the second year (1981) sampling program.

—. 1982c. South Atlantic OCS Area Living Marine Resources Study Year II: Final Report Volume II. Minerals Management Service contract AA551-CT1-18. Minerals Management Service, Washington, DC.

Live bottom areas area known to be important to commercial and recreational fisheries in the South Atlantic Bight, but biological studies of these areas have been limited. As a result, very little data exists on the structure of invertebrate and fish communities present in these hard-bottom habitats, and information is lacking on what effects offshore oil and gas exploration might have on live-bottom communities. Because more information was needed for recent and upcoming Outer Continental Shelf (OCS) Lease Sales, the Bureau of Land Management initiated the "South Atlantic OCS Area Living Marine Resources Study." The primary objectives of this study during the first year were to: 1) Characterize the invertebrate and nektonic communities associated with several representative live-bottom areas from Cape Hatteras, NC to Northern Florida and elevate factors which might influence community structure such as depth, latitude, and season (summer vs. winter), 2) Characterize the food habits of selected fish species of commercial and recreational importance, 3) Conduct a limited assessment of bottom topography and substrate type, 4) Evaluate the potential effects of oil- and gas-related activities on live-bottom communities.

Results obtained from the first year sampling program were presented in a 1981 report available through the National Technical Information Service. Objectives of the second-year study were the same as those listed above; however, seasonal sampling was increased to include all seasons. In addition, some study areas were changed to include portions of the shelf not previously studied, while others were sampled during both years to allow assessment of persistence in the distribution patterns observed during the first year. This report summarizes the results and conclusions obtained from the second year (1981) sampling program.

Moser, M.L., S.W. Ross, S.W. Snyder, and R.C. Dentzman. 1995. Distribution of Bottom Habitats on the Continental Shelf off North Carolina. Final Report to Marine Resources Research Institute, South Carolina Department of Marine Resources for the Southeast Area Monitoring and Assessment Program — Bottom Mapping Workgroup. Wilmington, NC. 80 p.

*This report documents the compilation and evaluation of the North Carolina SEAMAP Hardbottom data. In situ observations of hard bottom type and relief were made using submersibles. These data are in video and/or 35 mm still photographs. Black and white, 35 mm still photographs from RV Eastward research cruises (1964-1973) also provided evidence of bottom type and relief. USACOE drilling logs (1983) characterized sub-surface stability. Fish trawl and trap data from NMFS-Woods Hole (groundfish surveys 1964-1994), NMFS- Pascagoula (archive data 1954-1984), SEAMAP data (since 1984) and NCDMF (RV Dan Moore, and reef data) were evaluated for the presence of obligate (primary) reef fishes as evidence for the location of hard or non-hard bottoms. This report is part of a

CD-ROM for the whole S. Atlantic Bight, published by the Florida DNR (S.W. Ross, pers. comm. 31 Dec 99).

Myers, T.D. 1968. Horizontal and Vertical Distribution of Thecosomatous Pteropods off Cape Hatteras. Ph.D. Dissertation. Department of Zoology, Duke University. 223 p.

Cape Hatteras, North Carolina lies at the confluence of the warms northerly flowing Gulf Stream and a cool, southerly flowing Virginian Coastal Current. Previous workers have demonstrated marked north-south changes in the species composition of benthic marine invertebrates at Cape Hatteras and have noted that this change is associated with the different types of water present in the area.

This investigation attempts to determine whether a similar change in faunal composition can be found in a holoplanktonic group of animals in the waters off Cape Hatteras. The Thecosomata, or shelled pteropods were chosen for study.

A total of 26 species of Thecosomata within 9 genera have been found in six water types sampled in the Cape Hatteras area. The greatest number of thecosomes was found in the upper 60 meters of the water column with a concentration maximum of 10,000-20,000 animals/1,000 m^3 water filtered being present as a persistent feature of the 15-30 meter depth range in the Gulf Stream and Sargasso Sea. The number of species present in the water column is 5-8 In Carolinian Coastal Water, 12-17 in Gulf Stream and Sargasso Sea, one in winter Virginian Coastal Water and Slope Water, and 1-5 in seminar Virginian Coastal Water and Slope Water.

Phalen, P. Unpublished database (e). RV Dan Moore Studies, Lobster Survey 1968-1973. North Carolina Division of Marine Fisheries. Morehead City, NC.

*This is an unpublished fisheries database. Data were collected from 1968 to 1973 by the North Carolina Division of Marine Fisheries. The Principal Investigator is listed as Paul Phalen. Select sample locations and related data were computerized as part of the North Carolina SEAMAP Hardbottom data project by Moser et al. (1995). SEAMAP Hardbottom data (sample locations) within the defined project area for The Point were sorted and mapped using ArcView GIS (J. Ott, pers. comm. 15 Nov 99).

—. Unpublished database (g). RV Dan Moore Studies, Squid Project 1974. North Carolina Division of Marine Fisheries. Morehead City , NC.

*This is an unpublished fisheries database. Data were collected in 1974 by the North Carolina Division of Marine Fisheries. The Principal Investigator is listed as Paul Phalen. Select sample locations and related data were computerized as part of the North Carolina SEAMAP Hardbottom data project by Moser et al. (1995). SEAMAP Hardbottom data (sample locations) within the defined project area for The Point were sorted and mapped using ArcView GIS (J. Ott, pers. comm. 15 Nov 99).

Powell, A., B.F. Holland, and J. Gillikin. 1975c. RV Dan Moore Cruise Report No. 5: Onslow Bay, NC to Virginia Beach, VA; Anadromous Fish Survey, Calico Scallop Explorations, North Carolina Division of Marine Fisheries, Department of Natural Resources and Community Development. Morehead City, NC.

*Two separate cruises were accomplished during February 1975. A state supported calico scallop investigation was undertaken to determine if calico scallops were present in areas which previously supported a scallop fishery. A modified 8-foot tumbler dredge was utilized. The majority of sea time was used to obtain data for the federal-aid anadromous fish project outlined in the January 1975 cruise report.

—. 1975f. RV Dan Moore Cruise Report No. 7: Cape Hatteras, NC to Cape Henry, VA, North Carolina Division of Marine Fisheries, Department of Natural Resources and Community Development. Morehead City, NC.

*Three days were utilized during April 1975 to investigate areas for calico scallop populations. Major effort was expended in an area 20-nautical miles off Bogue Inlet, NC. A modified tumbler dredge was used.

Renaud, M., G. Gitschlag, E. Klima, A. Shah, D. Koi, and J. Nance. 1993. Loss of shrimp by turtle excluder devices (TEDS) in coastal waters of the United States, North Carolina to Texas: March 1988-August 1990. Fishery Bulletin 91: 129-137.

Observers from the National Marine Fisheries Service collected information on catch rates of shrimp aboard commercial shrimp vessels during March 1988-August 1990. Comparisons were made between nets equipped with Turtle Excluder Devices (TEDS) and standard shrimp nets. Three types of TEDs were tested: Georgia TEDs with and without accelerator funnels, and Super Shooter TEDs with funnels.

Fishing areas, time of day, and duration of tows were controlled by the captain of each vessel to simulate commercial conditions. A statistically-significant ($P<0.05$) mean loss in shrimp catch-per-unit-effort (CPUE) of 0.24 lb/h (3.6%) and 0.93 lb/h (13.6%) was exhibited by nets equipped with Georgia TEDs (with and without funnels, respectively) compared with standard nets. There was no significant difference in shrimp CPUE between standard nets and nets equipped with Super Shooter TEDs with a funnel.

Rhoads, D.C., and B. Hecker. 1994. Processes on the continental slope off North Carolina with special reference to the Cape Hatteras region. Deep-Sea Research II 41(4-6): 965-980.

Historical data from the slope off Cape Hatteras show this environment to be atypical of the rest of the Atlantic slope in terms of high rates of sedimentation and high benthic/demersal standing stocks. This paper focuses on identifying potential sources for sediments and nutrients on the Hatteras slope and on likely transport mechanisms.

Sediments consist mainly of subequal mixtures of sand, silt, and clay and contain an average of 1% carbon. This pool of carbon represents weathered organic matter containing polyunsaturated fatty acids (PUFA) and sterols typical of relatively refractory shelf/estuarine sediments. The labile organic fraction is derived from phytoplankton and zooplankton as reflected in short chain fatty acids ($<$ C22), planktic sterols, and chlorophyll a that are found in higher concentrations than observed elsewhere on the eastern U.S. continental slope. The inventory of organic nitrogen is much higher on the mid-slope (800-1000 m) than shallower or deeper bottom areas as predicted from plots of organic nitrogen versus grain-size for the U.S. Atlantic continental margin. The mid- slope region is the major focusing area for sedimentation. Bioturbation is an important diagenetic process that has profound influence on sediment profiles of sulphate, methane, fatty acids, sterols, chlorophyll a, viable diatoms, and metals. The low inventory of relatively refractory carbon (1%) stands in contrast to high measured rates of organic carbon sedimentation (28-121 g organic C m-2 year- 1). This paradox is probably related to high remineralization rates in the water column and on the bottom. The refractory nature of the small residual pool of deposited organic matter may define the trophic niche filled by those benthos found on this slope that are more typically encountered on the shelf (e.g. oligochaetes and opportunistic polychaetes).

A likely mechanism for high input rates of both organic and inorganic particulates to the Hatteras slope may be attributed to the position of Cape Hatteras relative to the adjacent narrow shelf. The Cape extends outward almost to the shelf edge topographically diverting sediment and primary production seaward that is moving southward along the outer shelf (the 'funnel' hypothesis). Transport of outer shelf sands to the slope may take place by the impingement of Gulf Stream eddies on the outer shelf and upper slope as well as by storm-generated waves. Once shelf sediment is deposited on the upper slope, it is apparently redistributed, as no strong on-shore to off-shore or depth-related gradients are observed in any of the measured sedimentary parameters.

The Hatteras slope apparently represents an estuarine type of sedimentary/nutrient regime that is displaced to an otherwise oceanic deep-sea environment by outwelling and funneling of nutrients and sediments from the shelf to the slope.

Ross, J.L. 1991. Assessment of the North Carolina Winter Trawl Fishery: September 1985 — April 1988. Special Scientific Report No. 54. NC Department of the Environment, Health and Natural Resources, Division of Marine Fisheries. Morehead City, NC.

The North Carolina winter trawl fishery is conducted during mid-September through April from offshore Long Island, New York to west of Cape Lookout, North Carolina. The fishery is partitioned into three components: the nearshore flounder, deepwater, and flynet fisheries. Species specific CPUEs, size-age composition of the catches and landings were assessed for 1985-88 and compared with 1982-85 catches and landings.

Summer flounder (*Paralichthys dentatus*) dominated nearshore flounder and deepwater trawl catches. During the 1985-88 seasons, nearshore flounder trip CPUEs averaged 59% less than during the 1982-85 seasons. The relative abundance of large summer flounder was lowest in 1987-88; concurrently, low CPUEs suggested growth overfishing may be occurring. Weakfish (*Cynoscion regalis*) was the dominant species in flynet catches. The CPUEs fluctuated with no well-defined trend. The annual age and size frequency distributions were compressed towards smaller, younger fish; age 1 fish dominated catches, and age 2-10 fish became less abundant. Atlantic croaker (*Micropogonias undulatus*) was a dominant component of the flynet catches. The CPUEs declined 67% from 1985-86 to 1987-88, but were still higher than occurring 1982-85. Size and age composition of the catches were consistent since 1983-84 and catches were dominated by age 1 and 2 fish (86-95%). Bluefish (*Pomatomus saltatrix*) occurred in catches of all gears, but were targeted only occasionally with flynets. The CPUEs were lower during the last five seasons than during 1982-83, but improved in 1987-88.

Winter trawls took a broad size (153-840 mm FL) and age (0-9) range of bluefish. Spot (*Leiostomus xanthurus*) were occasionally abundant in the flynet fishery, but most were small and marketed as scrapfish; age 0 and 1 fish accounted for greater than 88% of the catches annually. Scup (*Stenotomus chrysops*) were a significant component of the deepwater catches and fishery; however, catches and landings have steadily declined. Growth overfishing may be occurring, as the relative abundance of large fish has declined since 1982-83. Black sea bass (*Centropristis striata*) was a dominant species in deepwater catches. The CPUEs fluctuated with no persistent trend. Black sea bass recruited at the size of first maturity of females, and the relative abundance of large fish declined.

Overall biomass caught by winter trawlers declined. During 1987-88, total biomass/trip was 17% lower and total biomass/day was 21 % lower than the six-season (1982-88) mean. Landings of marketable finfish during 1985-88 were less than in previously monitored seasons. The trend in the scrap fish: marketable fish ratio has tended to increase in recent sampling seasons.

*This citation includes invertebrate data (squid and crabs).

Ross, J.L., J.B. Sullivan and D.A. DeVries. 1985. Assessment of North Carolina Commercial Finfisheries: 1 July 1983 to 30 June 1984. Annual Progress Report for Project 2-386-R. NC

Department of Natural Resources and Community Development, Division of Marine Fisheries. Morehead City, NC. 161 p.

Adult finfish were sampled for relative abundance, species composition and size distribution from the 1983 long haul seine and pound net fisheries in Pamlico Sound, N.C. and the 1983-84 winter trawl fishery in the Atlantic Ocean off North Carolina. Pound net and long haul seine samples were dominated by Atlantic croaker, Atlantic menhaden, weakfish, spot, and bluefish. Dominant species in the winter trawl fishery were weakfish, scup, bluefish, Atlantic croaker and summer flounder. Protein systems of Atlantic croaker and bluefish were examined electrophoretically to determine if stocks could be differentiated by this technique. No consistent patterns were found. A total of 31,604 young-of-year Atlantic croaker were tagged and released, mostly in Pamlico Sound and its tributaries during Fall, 1983. In addition, 92 fish were tagged and released near the mouth of York River, VA. As of 31 August 1984, 1,395 fish were recaptured. Initial movement appeared to be southward within Pamlico Sound and into the ocean. Fish greater than 149 mm TL had a higher return rate than smaller fish. Principal recapture methods were shrimp trawls, gill nets, and book and line.

*This citation includes invertebrate data (squid and crabs).

Ross, J.L., D.A. DeVries, III, J.H. Hawkins, and J.B. Sullivan. 1986. Assessment of North Carolina Commercial Finfisheries 1 April, 1982 to 30 June 1985 Fishing Seasons. Project 2-386-R. North Carolina Department of Natural Resources and Community Development, Division of Marine Fisheries. Morehead City, NC. 418 p.

This is a Comprehensive Assessment of North Carolina finfisheries for 1982 — 1985 fishing seasons. The winter trawl fishery produced 32.1-35.9% of all finfish (excluding menhaden) landed in North Carolina. From fall 1982 to spring 1985, 43, 67 and 84 catches were sampled during the respective seasons. Catches were partitioned by gear (flynet, nearshore flounder trawl, deepwater trawls) and area (north of Cape Hatteras, Cape Hatteras to Cape Lookout, west of Cape Lookout) to facilitate analyzes of seasonal fishing patterns and catches. The relationships between average catch/species from samples and commercial landings are presented herein.

The nearshore flounder fishery occurred from late November through January and accounted for 18.6 — 37.3 % of the catches sampled. Summer flounder (*Paralichthys dentatus*), dominated these catches, although their relative abundance declined from 93.7 to 88.6% during the study. The CPUE (mean weight/trip) was highest in 1983-84 (9,687 kg) and lowest in 1982-83 (5,584 kg). Fish <300 mm TL accounted for 9.8 -14.6% and fish >400 mm TL for 21.4 — 26.0% of the catches with no significant changes noted during the period.

Deepwater trawling occurred from December through April, accounting for 18.6 — 31.3% of the samples. This fishery was dominated (94.0 — 98.0%) each season by scup (*Stenotomus chrysops*), (*Paralichthys dentatus*), black sea bass (*Centropristis striata*), and squids. The CPUE of *S. chrysops* declined from 9,708 kg in 1982-83 to 2,003 kg in 1984-85 as did the percent of fish >200 mm FL, from 58.5 to 18.8%. The CPUE of *C. striata* increased from 1,314 to 3,449 kg and the proportion of large fish increased during the study. The CPUE of *P. dentatus* increased from 1,377 — 4,431 kg from 1982-83 to 1984-85; their size composition did not change significantly during the study; smaller fish were captured in deepwater than in the nearshore fishery.

Flynet fishing occurred from September through April and comprised 31.3 — 62.8 % of the samples. Catches were dominated by weakfish (*Cynoscion regalis*) in 1982-83 (52.8%) and 1983-84 (61.9%) and by Atlantic croaker (*Micropogonias undulatus*) (38.6%) and *C. regalis* (35.6%) in 1984-85. Bluefish (*Pomatomus saltatrix*), spot (*Leiostomus xanthurus*), and butterfish (*Peprilus traicanthus*) were also regularly captured. The CPUE of *C. regalis* was highest in 1983-84 (7,598 kg) and lowest in 1984-85 (4,780 kg). Fish of age 0-XII were landed; age 0 and I individuals composed 90% of the catches. The CPUE of *M. undulatus* increased from 2,344 kg in 1982-83 to 5, 190 kg/catch in 1984-85; age 0-V fish were landed. Age I-III fish constituted 98.9-99.9% of the catches. A declining trend in CPUE and landings of *P. saltatrix* was indicated; age 0-XI individuals were sampled; age 0-I fish composed 87.7-88.8% of the catches in 1982-84 and 57.9% in 1984-85. Flynets produced the greatest relative percentage of scrapfish and inshore flounder trawls the lowest.

*This citation includes invertebrate data (squid and crabs).

Ross, J.L., and D.W. Moye. 1989. Assessment of North Carolina Commercial Finfisheries 1985-1987 Fishing Seasons. Project 2-419-R. North Carolina Department of Natural Resources and Community Development, Division of Marine Fisheries. Morehead City, NC. 293 p.

This is a Comprehensive Assessment of North Carolina finfisheries for 1985 — 1987 fishing seasons. The North Carolina winter trawl fishery was active from mid-September through April and fished grounds from off New York to west of Cape Lookout. The fishery was partitioned into three components: the nearshore flounder, deepwater, and flynet fisheries. Species specific CPUEs, size-age composition of the catches and landings were assessed for 1985-88 and compared with 1982-1985 catches and landings. Summer flounder (*Paralichthys dentatus*) dominated nearshore flounder and deepwater trawl catches. During the 1985-88 seasons, nearshore flounder trip CPUEs averaged 59% less than during the 1982-85 seasons. The relative abundance of summer flounder was lowest for the six season period in 1987-88 and concurrent with low CPUEs suggested growth overfishing may be occurring. Weakfish (*Cynoscion regalis*) were the dominant species in flynet catches. CPUEs during the last six seasons fluctuated with no well defined trend. The annual age and size frequency distributions were compressed towards smaller, younger fish; age 1 fish dominated catches, and age 2-10 fish have become much less abundant. Atlantic Croaker (*Micropogonias undulatus*) were a dominant component of the flynet catches. CPUEs declined 67% from 1985-86 to 1987-88, but were still higher for the period than during 1982-85. The size and age composition of the catches has been consistent since 1983-84, and catches since were dominated by age 1 and 2 fish (86-95%). Bluefish (*Pomatomus saltatrix*) occurred in catches by all trawl gears but were targeted only occasionally with flynets. CPUEs were lower during the last 5 seasons than during 1982-83, but were improved in 1987-88. Bluefish caught by winter trawlers included a broad size (153-840 mm FL) and age (0-9) distribution. Spot (*Leiostomus xanthurus*) were occasionally an abundant component of the flynet fishery, but most were undersized and marketed as scrapfish. Age 0 and 1 fish accounted for greater than 88% of the catches annually. Scup (*Stenotomus chrysops*) were a significant component of the deepwater fishery, however catches and lading s have steadily declined. Growth overfishing was indicated with the relative abundance of large fish having declined since 1982-83. Black sea bass (*Centropristis striatus*) were a dominant species in deepwater catches. CPUEs have fluctuated with no persistent trend. They were recruited at the size of first maturity in females and the relative abundance of large fish has declined. Overall biomass caught by winter trawlers has generally declined. Overall biomass caught by winter trawlers has generally declined. Total biomass/trip was 17% lower and total biomass/day was 21% lower during 1987-88 than the six season 1982-85 mean. Seasonal marketable finfish landings were each less than any season from 1982-85. The proportion of scrapfish to marketable finfish has generally increased over the six season period.

*This citation includes invertebrate data (squid and crabs).

Ross, J.L., J.B. Sullivan, and D.A. DeVries. 1984. Assessment of North Carolina Commercial Finfisheries: 1 April 1982 to 30 June 1983. Annual Progress report for project 2-386-R. NC Department of Natural Resources and Community Development, Division of Marine Fisheries. Morehead City, NC. 108 p.

Adult finfish were sampled for relative abundance, species composition and size distribution from the 1982 long haul seine and pound net fisheries in Pamlico Sound, N.C. and the 1982-83 winter trawl fishery in the Atlantic Ocean off North Carolina. Pound net and long haul seine samples were dominated by Atlantic croaker, Atlantic menhaden, weakfish, spot, and bluefish. Dominant species in the winter trawl fishery were weakfish, scup, bluefish, Atlantic croaker and summer flounder. Protein systems of Atlantic croaker were examined electrophoretically to determine if stocks could be differentiated by this technique. No consistent patterns were found. A total of 29,325 young-of-year and 598 adult Atlantic croaker were tagged and released, mostly in Pamlico Sound and its tributaries during Fall, 1982. Similar numbers of T-bar and cinch-up tags were used. The latter tag provided much better long-term retention. Initial movement appeared to be southward within Pamlico Sound and into the ocean. During Spring and Summer, 1983, tags were returned from the mouth of Chesapeake Bay to southern North Carolina, although most came from Pamlico Sound and its tributaries. The principal recapture methods were shrimp trawl, long haul seine, hook and line, and gill net.

*This citation includes invertebrate data (squid and crabs).

Ross, S.W. 1985a. A Summary of Biological Processes in the Proposed VACAPES EMPRESS II Area Off North Carolina Relating to Plankton Communities, Pelagic Macroinvertebrates, Ichthyofauna, Sea turtles, Marine Mammals, and Sea Birds. Appendix B. *In:* U.S. Department of the Navy. EMPRESS II: Supplemental Draft Environmental Impact Statement for the Proposed Operation of the Navy Electromagnetic Pulse Radiation Environment Simulator for Ships (Empress II) in the Chesapeake Bay and Atlantic Ocean. United States Navy. Environmental/Intergovernmental Section. Atlantic Division. Naval Facilities Engineering and Command. Norfolk, VA.

*This technical report is Appendix B within the "EMPRESS II: Supplemental Draft Environmental Impact Statement for the Proposed Operation of the Navy Electromagnetic Pulse Radiation Environment Simulator for Ships (Empress II) in the Chesapeake Bay and Atlantic Ocean" report. This technical report is a Summary of Biological Processes in the Proposed VACAPES EMPRESS II area off North Carolina Relating to Planktonic Communities, Pelagic Macroinvertebrates, Ichthyofauna, Sea turtles, Marine Mammals, and Sea Birds. Technical reports supporting this summary have been written by authorities in each discipline and are included in Appendices. These supporting technical reports are cited individually. The southern portion of VACAPES EMPRESS II Area of North Carolina overlaps with the northern portion of the defined study area for the Data Inventory Related to the Hatteras Middle Slope (The Point) Area.

Ross, S.W. Unpublished (a). Selected fish, invertebrate and bottom habitat data.

*These are unpublished data, collected by S.W. Ross during a SCUBA dive on 18 August 1980. The location for this site [SWR -SCUBA-80-20] is 35° 20.7'N; 75° 21.2'W; depth 70-80 feet. Selected fish, invertebrate, and bottom habitat data were collected. These data are unpublished and the site was not visited again. This cite (no date presented) is listed as ISO4 by Kirby-Smith (1989). The location data assigned for site ISO4 by Kirby-Smith (1989) were incorrect and these data were collected by S.W. Ross [SWR -SCUBA-80-20] (S.W. Ross, pers. comm. 19 November 1999).

Ross, S.W., K.J. Sulak, and T.A. Munroe. 2001. Association of *Syscenus infelix* (Crustacea: Isopoda: Aegidae) with benthopelagic rattail fishes, *Nezumia* spp. (Macrouridae), along the western North Atlantic continental slope. Mar. Biol. 138(3): 595-601.

During submersible surveys along the continental slope (summers of 1991 and 1992, 184-847 m) between False Cape, Virginia and Cape Hatteras, North Carolina, USA we observed the aegid isopod, *Syscenus infelix* Harger, attached to the macrourid *Nezumia bairdii* (Goode and Bean). This is the first report of *S. infelix* attached to fishes in the western North Atlantic. The association of this blind isopod with its host appears species-specific. The large, conspicuous isopod always attached to a fish in the same location, the dorsal midline, immediately behind the first dorsal fin. Attachment appears to be long-term, with the isopod forming a characteristic scar consisting of a distinct discolored oval depression with seven small, dark impressions that coalesce as the fish grows. Only one *S. infelix* was found on each host fish. The isopod occurred on 23.7% of *N. bairdii* observed from submersible on the middle continental slope off Virginia and North Carolina, compared with 16.6% of 1,236 museum specimens of the same species (based on inspection for scars) collected at latitudes 26° -64° N. Prevalence of the fish-isopod association was not correlated with depth or latitude. We also found identical scars on preserved specimens of *N. aequalis* (2.6% of 660 specimens), *N. sclerorhynchus* (1.2% of 86 specimens), and *N. suilla* (14.3% of 7 specimens), mostly from areas outside the range of *N. bairdii*. No scars were found on museum specimens of *N. atlantica* (n=27), *N. cyrano* (n=57), or *N. longebarbata* (n=7). The low incidence of isopod attachment on these species suggests that *N. bairdii* is the preferred host. Infestation by the isopod appears to result in erosion of host fish scales and tissue. We propose that *S. infelix* is an obligate associate of its host fish and should be considered parasitic.

Ross, S.W., K.J. Sulak, J. Gartner, and D.S. Lee. Unpublished data. Ongoing project: Definition of Ecological/Trophic Linkages Among Fishes and Other Nekton in the Area Known as The Point — North Carolina Continental Shelf Slope.

*This is an on-going study of fishes, invertebrates, sargassum and marine birds at the area known as The Point. The emphasis is on trophic linkages throughout the water column. The summer 1999 and 2000 stations were mapped (Fig 7).

Rowe, G.T. 1971. Observations on bottom currents and epibenthic populations in Hatteras Submarine Canyon. Deep-Sea Research 18: 569-581.

Bottom currents and populations of large epifauna were surveyed using bottom photography in the Pamlico axis of the Hatteras Submarine Canyon system. Most species known to be numerically dominant along the continental slope north and south of the canyon were absent or found in reduced densities, whereas other species were found only near or in the canyon and can be considered canyon indicator species. The implication of previous studies (Rowe and Menzies 1969; Sanders and Hessler 1969) that narrow faunal zonation is continuous along the margins of ocean basins must be modified to acknowledge the exceptional zonations found in canyons.

The photographs and current meter data indicated that the bottom current to the southwest along the lower continental rise, but turned to the west and northwest, or up the canyon, at lesser depths. Indurated sedimentary outcrops common to the canyon were probably a result of intermittent slumping and turbidity current flows.

Schaff, T. 1991. Spatial Heterogeneity of Continental Slope Benthos Off the Carolinas. Ph.D. Dissertation. NC State University, Department of Marine, Earth and Atmospheric Sciences. 111 p.

Spatial heterogeneity in macrofaunal and microbial communities was examined at three continental slope sites (160 km apart) off Charleston, SC (35° 52'N, 76° 27'W), Cape Lookout, NC (34° 15'N, 75° 44'W) and Cape Hatteras, NC (35° 24'N, 74° 48'W), all at 850m water depth, on large (100-km) and small (10cm-100m) scales. Significant variation was found on 100-km scales, among sites, in both microbial and macrofaunal community structure. One site (off Cape Hatteras) was found to have macrofaunal abundances (>55,000/m^2) higher than any previously recorded from this depth. The Cape Hatteras site exhibited higher polychaete diversity, and profoundly different macrofaunal species composition than the other two sites. Sites off Cape Lookout, NC and Charleston, SC had significantly different macrofaunal abundances (21, 319 individuals/m^2 and 9,438 ind/m^2 respectively) but similar polychaete species composition, taxonomic representation, and polychaete diversity patterns.

Small-scale heterogeneity was examined at two sites off Cape Lookout and Cape Hatteras, NC. Off Cape Lookout, macrofaunal and microbial communities were examined on a 10-100 cm scale, in comparison of sediment mounds, pits and level areas. NO significant differences were found in sediment microbial counts or total macrofaunal distributions. Differences related to biogenic structures were observed in the abundances of one polychaete species (Paraonidae, *Levesenia gracilis*) and infaunal anemones.

Off Cape Hatteras, infaunal heterogeneity was examined on a 100 m scale by comparing an area of high foraminiferan (*Bathysiphon filiformis*) tube densities with an area lacking these tubes. No significant differences were found in the distribution and abundance of bacteria between the two areas. The only significant difference found in macrofaunal densities was in the 5-10 cm vertical fraction, and was due to the presence of high numbers of reproductive oligochaetes. The only other taxa to show a response to the presence of the tubes was *Nicolea* sp. 1, which lives epifaunally on the tube exterior.

From these investigations, I conclude that the Carolina slope fauna at 850 m is fairly homogenous on small (10-100m scales), but that significant variation in faunal abundance and composition occurs on 100-200 km scales. This heterogeneity is probably related to variable influence from the Gulf Stream, varying angle of the slope floor, and influence from other currents and oceanographic processes (e.g., upwelling) that occur off Cape Hatteras.

Schaff, T.R., and L.A. Levin. 1994. Spatial heterogeneity of benthos associated with biogenic structures on the North Carolina continental slope. Deep-Sea Research II 41(4-6): 901-918.

The objective of this study was to determine if biogenic features such as mounds, pits and tubes produce small-scale (0.1 — 100 m) spatial heterogeneity in macrofaunal community structure on the continental slope off North Carolina at 850 m. Macrofaunal and microbial communities associated with sediment mounds, pits and level areas were compared off Cape Lookout, North Carolina. No significant differences were found in sediment microbial counts or total macrofaunal distributions. One paraonid polychaete (*Levensenia gracilis*) was more abundant in pits than in other samples, and infaunal anemones exhibited depressed densities in sediment mounds.

At a second site, off Cape Hatteras, North Carolina, infaunal heterogeneity associated with the tube-building foraminiferan *Bathysiphon filiformis* was examined by comparing an area with high tube densities (93.8 m-2) with an area 100 m away without tubes. No significant differences were found in the distribution and abundances of bacteria between the two areas. The only significant difference found in infaunal densities was the presence of high numbers of reproductive oligochaetes in the 5-10 cm fraction beneath the tube beds. One terebellid polychaete species (*Nicolea* sp.), which lives exclusively on *B. filiformis* tubes, was absent in the non-tube area.

With a few exceptions, the biogenic or microbial structures examined at these two sites appeared to exert only minor influence on macrofaunal or microbial community structure. Within each site, slope assemblages examined in this study appeared to be homogeneous on the small scales examined.

Schaff, T., L. Levin, N. Blair, D. DeMaster, R. Pope, and S. Boehme. 1992. Spatial heterogeneity of benthos on the Carolina continental slope: large (100 km)-scale variation. Marine Ecology Progress Series 88: 143-160.

Large-scale spatial heterogeneity of macrofaunal and microbial communities was examined on the continental slope off North and South Carolina, USA, by comparing 3 sites, separated by 130 to 150 km and all at 850 m water depth. Significant variation was found among macrofaunal assemblages at all 3 sites, and between microbial counts at 2 sites. We investigated the hypothesis that 100 km scale heterogeneity was driven by variation in organic C flux to the sea floor. The northernmost site (Site III, off Cape Hatteras, NC) was found to have macrofaunal abundances (>55000 m^{-2}) higher than any previous recorded from this depth, and significantly higher than those at Site II (off Cape Lookout, North Carolina) (21319 m^{-2}) or Site I (off Charleston, SC) (9438 m^{-2}). Trends in macrofaunal abundance did not follow those sediment TOC (total organic carbon), but agreed well with estimates of total carbon flux for the three sites. Mixing coefficients determined from profiles of naturally occurring ^{234} Th (half life 24 d) indicate that the sediments at Site III are mixed 2 to 6 times faster than at the other 2 sites, which is consistent with the trends in macrofaunal abundance and biomass. Using ^{14} C-based sedimentation rates and sediment carbon content, we estimated carbon flux to be 0.6, 20 and > 70 g C m ^{2} yr $^{-1}$ at sites I, II and III, respectively. Inventories of ^{234} Th and downcore concentration profiles of dissolved $SO_4^=$, CO_2 and CH_4 within the sediment provided evidence that the flux of metabolized carbon was greater at Site III than at the other sites. Polychaetes, which comprised 43, 74 and 65 % of the fauna at Sites I, II and III, respectively, exhibited lower diversity, higher dominance, and a completely different species composition at Site III than at the other 2 sites. *Scalibregma inflatum* and *Aricidea quadrilobata* comprised 33 % of total macrofauna at Site III, but were absent at Sites I and II. The species composition, high dominance, and prevalence of juveniles among polychaetes at Site III is suggestive of a response to organic enrichment. Enrichment of the Site III benthos is attributed to physical oceanographic and geophysical causes, including Gulf Stream-induced upwelling, a confluence of currents focused by bottom topography, and lateral inputs resulting from mass wasting processes. Despite significant differences in macrofaunal abundance, Sites I and II exhibited considerable overlap in microbial counts, polychaete species composition, dominance and diversity patterns.

Settle, L.R. 1997. Commercial harvest of pelagic Sargassum: A summary of landings since June 1995. *In*: South Atlantic Fishery Management Council. Essential Fish Habitat Workshop # 9: October 7 — 8, 1997 Pelagic Habitat Sargassum and Water Column. South Atlantic Fishery Management Council. Charleston, SC. May 1997. 66 p.

Attachment 11: The commercial harvest of pelagic *Sargassum* resumed in June 1995. To date the fishery is prosecuted by a single firm, Aqua-10 Corporation of Beaufort, North Carolina. Aqua-10 processes the raw algae into a variety of agricultural fertilizers and dietary supplements used in the swine and poultry industries. The firm purchases algae harvested by local fishing vessels. Two vessels, the FV Outer Banks (16.5 m snapper boat) and the FV Rising Sun (15 m long-liner) have been equipped with Sargassum nets by Aqua-10. The gear consists of a 1.2 in x 0.9 n frame trawl rigged with 7.6 am mesh trawl webbing. The vessels harvest algae ancillary to their normal fishing activities. When algae are landed, Aqua-10 notifies the NMFS, Beaufort Laboratory. The algae are examined for by-catch at dockside and at the processing plant. Vessel captains are interviewed to obtain data on the date and location of harvests, effort, and by-catch.

All algae have been harvested from off the North Carolina coast from northern Onslow Bay to northeast of Cape Hatteras (Fig. 2). Although Sargassum has been harvested on the continental shelf, most was obtained in the Gulf Stream (Fig. 3). The observed by-catch has been minimal in terms of numbers of individuals. No sea turtles and few fishes have been noted. Most fish have been young juveniles and are generally in advanced stages of decomposition. Identifiable taxa include filefish (*Monacanthus hispidus*), amberjacks (*Seriola* spp.), blue runner (*Caranx crysos*), jacks (*Caranx* spp.), flyingfish (Exocoetidae), sergeant major (*Abudefduf saxatilis*), gray triggerfish (*Balistes capriscus*), sargassum fish (*Histrio histrio*), and pipefish (*Syngnathus* spp.). The most commonly observed macrofaunal by-catch have been crustaceans including several shrimp (genera *Hippolyte*, *Latreutes*, and *Leander*) and crabs (genera *Planes* and *Portunus*).

Shepard, A. (ed.). 1991. Undersea Research at the Point. NURC/UNCW 1991 Undersea Research: Informational Meeting. National Undersea Research Center, University of North Carolina at Wilmington. Wilmington, NC. 9 p.

*This 9 page handout provides a summary of research being conducted at "The Point" area (Manteo Lease Block 467).

The National Undersea Research Center at the University of North Carolina at Wilmington (NURC/UNCW), funded by a grant from the National Oceanic and Atmospheric Administration's Office of Undersea Research (OUR), was established in 1980 to promote, facilitate, and conduct research in the Southeastern United States utilizing undersea techniques, including advanced wet diving and manned and unmanned submersibles. A main Center goal is to provide information to NOAA that will assist the agency in fulfilling its charter to explore, understand, conserve and manage the U.S. marine environment and associated resources. To help meet this goal, the Center supports and conducts interdisciplinary oceanographic research projects studying continental margin processes, particularly the interactions and linkages between estuarine, continental shelf, and slope (including submarine canyon) environments.

Shepard, A., and A.H. Hulbert (eds.). 1994. Workshop Report: Present and Future Research Initiatives on the Upper Hatteras Slope off North Carolina. National Undersea Research Center at the University of North Carolina at Wilmington. Wilmington, NC. 30p.

*This report is the result of the May 1993 workshop held in Raleigh, NC. The topics of discussion were research (present and planned) at the Upper Hatteras Slope (UHS) and potential funding sources. The workshop was sponsored by National Undersea Research Center at the University of North Carolina at Wilmington. The report provides a brief description of the UHS invertebrates, biological oceanography, chemical oceanography, geological oceanography (bathymetry, oil and gas exploration), physical oceanography, fisheries, and *Sargassum*. Appendix A is a workshop agenda and list of speakers. No abstracts for speakers are provided. Appendix B is a list of potential funding sources. Appendix C contains a list of publications pertaining to the UHS.

Shepard, A., C. Jensen, and A. Hulbert. 1992. Epibenthic, Megafaunal Invertebrates on the Continental Slope off the Carolinas. Appendix A. *In:* Diaz, R.J., J.A. Blake, and D.P. Lohse. Volume III Appendices: Benthic Study of the Continental Slope Off Cape Hatteras, North Carolina, Virginia Institute of Marine Science, School of Marine Science, College of William and Mary. Gloucester Pt., VA; Science Applications International Corporation. Woods Hole, MA.

*From 1989-1991, NURC/UNCW funded submersible research near and in the Manteo Lease Blocks, by Drs. Lisa Levin, Neal Blair and David DeMaster of North Carolina State University. Their data, taken by submersible at depths of 800 m, revealed that the density of megafauna and infuana at Cape Hatteras were significantly higher than at two other slope sites more than 60 nm south of the proposed well site (Schaff 1991). Furthermore, their densities were comparable to those reported by Blake et al. (1987) from a 600 m site upslope from the proposed well site.

Shephard, A.N., T. Schaff, N. Mountford, and A.W. Hulbert. 1993. Relationship of Benthic Infauna and Slope Angle on the Continental Slope Off Cape Hatteras, NC. Benthic Ecology Meeting, 1-4 April 1993, Mobile, AL. 57 p.

Minerals Management Service was recently charged, by legislative mandate, with describing the nature and extent of the benthic community inhabiting oil and gas lease blocks on the Continental

Slope off Cape Hatteras, NC. Once the benthic community is described, the assumption is that the potential impacts of oil and gas exploration and development activities can be assessed. A significant difficulty with this assumption is that the area of the lease blocks is extremely rugged. The primary techniques used to sample infauna on MMS funded research have been surface deployed box cores. Such box cores generally sample on relatively flat bottom. NOAA's National Undersea Research Center at the University of North Carolina at Wilmington (NURC/UNCW) funded a manned submersible cruise in 1992, in part, to sample steep areas that are inaccessible to surface deployed box cores. Preliminary results suggest that substrate angle significantly affects infaunal abundance and species composition. In rugged, non-indurated areas, substrate angle must be considered when describing benthic communities.

South Atlantic Fishery Management Council. 1998. FINAL Habitat Plan for the South Atlantic Region: Essential Fish Habitat Requirements for Fishery Management Plans of the South Atlantic Fishery Managment Council: The Shrimp Fishery Management Plan; The Red Drum Fishery Management Plan; The Snapper Group Fishery Plan; The Coastal Mirgratory Pelagics Fishery Management Plan; The Golden Crab Fishery Management Plan; The Spiny Lobster Fishery Management Plan; The Coral, Coral Reefs, and Live/Hard Bottom Fishery Management Plan; The Sargassum Habitat Fishery Management Plan; and The Calico Scallop Fishery Management Plan. South Atlantic Fishery Management Council. Charleston, SC. 457 p.

*This report emphasizes South Atlantic Coast, nearshore habitat (shore to 200m isobath). Page 134-135 mentions "The Point" within Section 3.2.3.2.1 Description of Water Column Habitats. Figure A Water Masses off Cape Hatteras, is located on p. 135 and shows a schematic diagram of "The Point," relative to the Gulf Steam, Virginia (longshore) Current and Sargasso Sea. Table 18b taxonomic list of larval and early-juvenile fishes from offshore of Cape Lookout to Cape Hatteras including the region known as "The Point" is located on pp. 139-145. Oil and gas exploration, development and transposition are mentioned in section 4.1.2.4 on page 323 (Offshore Cape Hatteras, NC is mentioned, but no specific reference to "The Point" is made).

Stancyk, S.E. (In press). Predation behavior in echinoderms. *In*: Candia Carnevali, M. D. (ed.). Proceedings of the Fifth European Conference on Echinoderms, Milan Italy, 7-12 September 1998. A. A. Balkema, Rotterdam.

This study describes predation behavior on swimming organisms by *Ophiura sarsi.* Aluminum Frame, vexar mesh cages with yellow polypropylene rope on the bottom were used during this study. Each cage contained 5 brittlestars with 2 arms removed. Other cages, which had been left out a year, there was heavy epifaunal growth, including recently metamorphosed crinoids. Although there was lots of particulate material in the water, these cages did not get buried, and often had burrowing fish associated with them (S. Stancyk, pers. comm. 15 July 1999).

Stancyk, S.E., C. Muir, and T. Fujita. 1998. Predation Behavior on swimming organisms by *Ophiura sarsi.* pp. 425-429. *In*: R. Mooi, and M. Telford (eds.). Echinoderms: San Francisco Proceedings of the Ninth International Echinoderm Conference. A. A. Balkema, Rotterdam.

This study describes predation behavior on swimming organisms by *Ophiura sarsi.* Aluminum Frame, vexar mesh cages with yellow polypropylene rope on the bottom were used during this study. Each cage contained 5 brittlestars with 2 arms removed. Other cages, which had been left out a year, there was heavy epifaunal growth, including recently metamorphosed crinoids. Although there was lots of particulate material in the water, these cages did not get buried, and often had burrowing fish associated with (S. Stancyk, pers. comm. 15 July 1999).

Stancyk, S., W. Dodson, and R. Aronson. 1991. Food Chain Dynamics Involving Brittlestars on the Carolina Slope. p. 4. *In*: Shepard, A. (ed.), NURC/UNCW 1991 Undersea Research: Informational Meeting. National Undersea Research Center, University of North Carolina at Wilmington. Wilmington, NC.

Brittlestars are common bottom-dwelling organisms whose role in energy flow in marine ecosystems is poorly known. In shallow waters, burrowing brittlestars occur in extremely dense beds and suffer heavy sublethal predation. Dense aggregations of surface-dwelling brittlestars are relatively rare, probably because of predation. In the deeper waters of the continental slope, however, dense beds of the brittlestar *Ophiura sarsii* occur, both off North Carolina and in other places in the world. Previous information implied that predation on these animals was low, but dives off North Carolina revealed a substantial amount of sublethal predation, as evidenced by regenerating arms. An investigation is currently underway to elucidate the population biology and trophic linkages of *Ophiura sarsii* at sites of about 500m depth at 'The Point," where dense concentrations of large animals occur. Eight dives during the summer of 1991 are planned to: 1) survey populations and quantify densities, distribution, size of patches, and sediment/water characteristics; 2) make representative collections of animals to determine reproductive state, population size structure, growth band numbers, and sublethal predation frequency; 3) carry out short-term experiments with cages and tethered animals to learn about predation frequency; and 4) carry out short-term cage experiments to determine rates of regeneration.

Sulak, K.J., and S.W. Ross. 1996. Lilliputian bottom fish fauna of the Hatteras upper middle continental slope. Journal of Fish Biology 49, suppl. A: 91-113.

Submersible data from two areas along the Carolina-Virginia continental slope reveal a Hatteras upper middle slope (HMS) (35°30′N, 74°50′W) demersal fish fauna remarkable for diminutive size of individuals within and across species, a fauna which is accordingly termed 'Lilliputian'. Contrast of HMS submersible data with Virginia trawl and submersible data support this finding. The four top-ranking HMS fishes, *Lycenchelys verrillii, Glyptocephalus cynoglossus, Myxine glutinosa* and *Nezumia bairdii,* are all significantly smaller than on the Virginia upper middle slope. Also peculiar to the HMS is the dominance of sedentary benthic species, rarity of active benthopelagic foragers, and markedly elevated fish population density. Species composition of the HMS fauna differs from that of the general Middle Atlantic Bight fauna; notably absent are species of otherwise continuous distribution along the U.S. East Coast (e.g., *Synaphobranchus affinis, Nezumia aequalis)*. Since HMS megafaunal and macrofaunal invertebrate communities are also anomalous, the Lilliputian phenomenon among HMS bottom fishes provides a characteristic biotic signature of a pervasively restructured benthic boundary layer community. The authors hypothesize that the HMS faunal anomaly reflects a limiting factor, episodic sediment surface hypoxia, peculiar to this region of high particulate organic carbon flux from surface waters. Results indicate that substantial changes in fish faunal composition and structure can occur on a small geographic scale on the open soft-substrate continental slope.

U.S. Department of the Interior, Minerals Management Service. 1992. Proceedings of the Fourth Atlantic OCS Region Information Transfer Meeting, September 1991. U.S. Department of the Interior, Minerals Management Service. Herndon, VA. 198 p.

The Fourth Atlantic Outer Continental Shelf (OCS) Regional Information Transfer Meeting (ITM) was held on 24-25 September, 1991, in Wilmington, NC. The focus of the meeting was on the OCS off North Carolina, specifically on activities related to a proposed exploratory well for oil and gas by Mobil on Block 467 a site 40 miles off the coast of North Carolina. The area of industry interest is known as the Manteo Prospect, while the activities surrounding the proposed drilling are referred to collectively as the Manteo Project. The wildcat wellsite is in 2,690 ft. (857 m) of water near the edge of the Gulf Stream. It is also near a fishing ground known locally as "The Point." The area is believed to be gas prone rather than oil prone. The estimated size of the resource could be as high as 5 trillion cubic feet of gas.

The purpose of the meeting was to exchange information on the leasing background, legislative activities, scientific results, and socioeconomic studies. Legislative-related reports include descriptions of the Oil Pollution Act of 1990, the Outer Banks Protection Act, the Environmental Studies Review Panel, and the North Carolina Physical Oceanography Panel. Reports of studies on marine life include benthic diatoms, benthic fauna, pelagic seabirds, sea turtles, and right whales. One report describes the use of airships (blimps) for ocean research a capability relevant to North Carolina because of the east coast airship facility is located in the state. Local marine science facilities described include NOAA's National Undersea Research Center at the University of North Carolina at Wilmington and the National Marine Fisheries Service laboratory in Beaufort.

Developments in oil spill cleanup technology and capabilities are described by both the Coast Guard and the industry. A socioeconomic report describes the effects of the oil and gas activities on the tourist industry. Lastly, research on the restoration of salt marshes indicates that rehabilitation of an area is possible when development or an accident has occurred. While the emphasis of the meeting was on oil and gas, two reports described the results of projects related to offshore sand mining. The appendix lists the names and addresses of speakers. Individual chapters are cited individually when appropriate.

U.S. Department of the Navy. 1985. EMPRESS II: Supplemental Draft Environmental Impact Statement for the Proposed Operation of the Navy Electromagnetic Pulse Radiation Environment Simulator for Ships (Empress II) in the Chesapeake Bay and Atlantic Ocean. United States Navy. Environmental/ Intergovernmental Section. Atlantic Division. Naval Facilities Engineering and Command. Norfolk, VA.

*This is a National Environmental Policy Act document characterizing the proposed EMPRESS II project. Appendix B contains a Summary of Biological Processes in the Proposed VACAPES EMPRESS II area off North Carolina Relating to Planktonic Communities, Pelagic Macroinvertebrates, Ichthyofauna, Sea turtles, Marine Mammals, and Sea Birds. Technical reports supporting this summary have been written by authorities in each discipline and are included in Appendices. The technical reports are cited individually. The southern portion of VACAPES EMPRESS II Area of North Carolina overlaps with the northern portion of the defined study area for the Data Inventory Related to the Hatteras Middle Slope (The Point) Area.

Vigil, D.L. (ed.). 1998. North Carolina/Minerals Management Service Technical Workshop on Manteo Unit Exploration: February 4-5, 1998. U.S. Dept. of the Interior, Minerals Management Service. Gulf of Mexico OCS Region. New Orleans, LA. 168 p.

*These are the proceedings from a workshop/meeting (conducted on February 4-5, 1998) between the North Carolina Department of Environment and Natural Resources (DENR), and the U.S. Department of the Interior's Minerals Management Service (MMS). The geographic area being discussed is approximately 45 miles east-northeast of Cape Hatteras, North Carolina, referred to as the Manteo Unit. This workshop reviewed environmental and socioeconomic information known and needed, on the Manteo Unit. The MMS's Gulf of Mexico OCS Regional Director gave an MMS perspective on history and status of the area. Chevron gave a presentation on how the exploratory well would be drilled. The scientific characterization was presented in greater detail by a number of scientific experts who spoke on the following disciplines physical environment, habitat and living resources (invertebrates and fish), seabirds, marine mammals, sea turtles, and social and economic issues. Specific chapters are cited individually, when appropriate.

Weston, D.P. 1988. Macrobenthos-sediment relationships on the continental shelf off Cape Hatteras, North Carolina. Continental Shelf Res. 8(3): 267-286.

The complex current regime associated with Cape Hatteras, North Carolina results in an unusually broad range of sediment textures for open shelf areas of comparable spatial extent. The median grain size ranged from coarse to very fine sand, while the percentage of silt and clay ranged from O to 27%. Four assemblages of macrobenthic species were recognized, separable on the basis of sediment characteristics: (1) a muddy, very fine sand assemblage dominated by the polychaetous annelid *Lumbrineris impatiens;* *(2)* a fine to medium sand assemblage dominated by the archiannelid *Polygordius sp.;* (3) a well-sorted, fine sand assemblage dominated by the amphipod *Protohaustorius* cf. *deichmannae;* and (4) a medium to coarse sand assemblage characterized by the polychaetes *Hemipodus roseus* and *Hesionura elongate.* Multiple discriminant analysis and detrended correspondence analysis, a linear ordination technique, were used to identify which of eight sediment parameters were most useful in interpreting faunal patterns. Sediment sorting, as reflective of sediment mobility, was important in determining the dominance of fossorial species. The percentage of very fine sand and the combined percentage of silt and clay were found to be of greatest value in differentiating biotic assemblages. This conclusion is supported by similar results from previous estuarine studies, and is probably a result of surface area-related control of the type and quantity of food resources for deposit feeders.

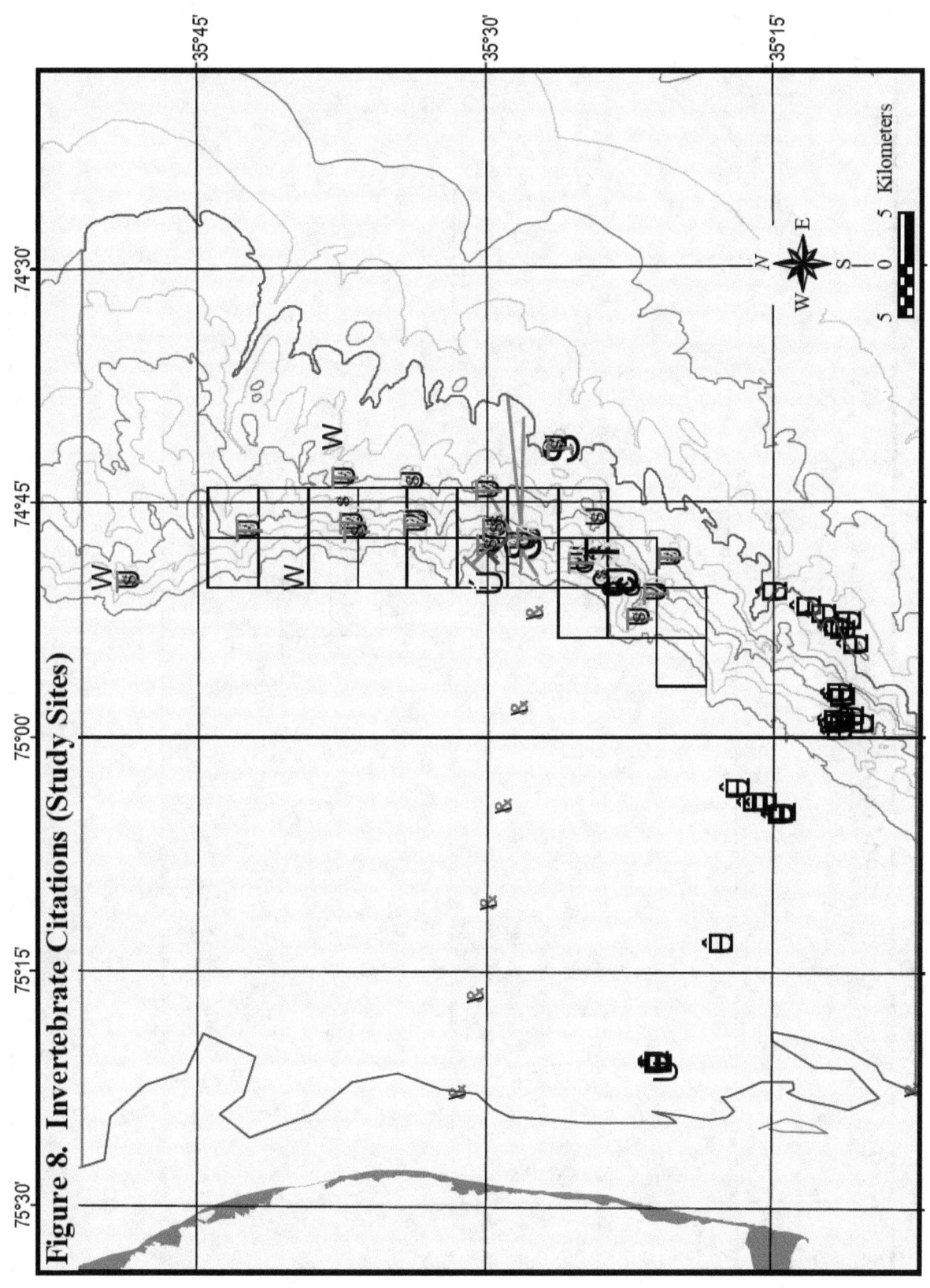

Figure 8. Invertebrate Citations (Study Sites)

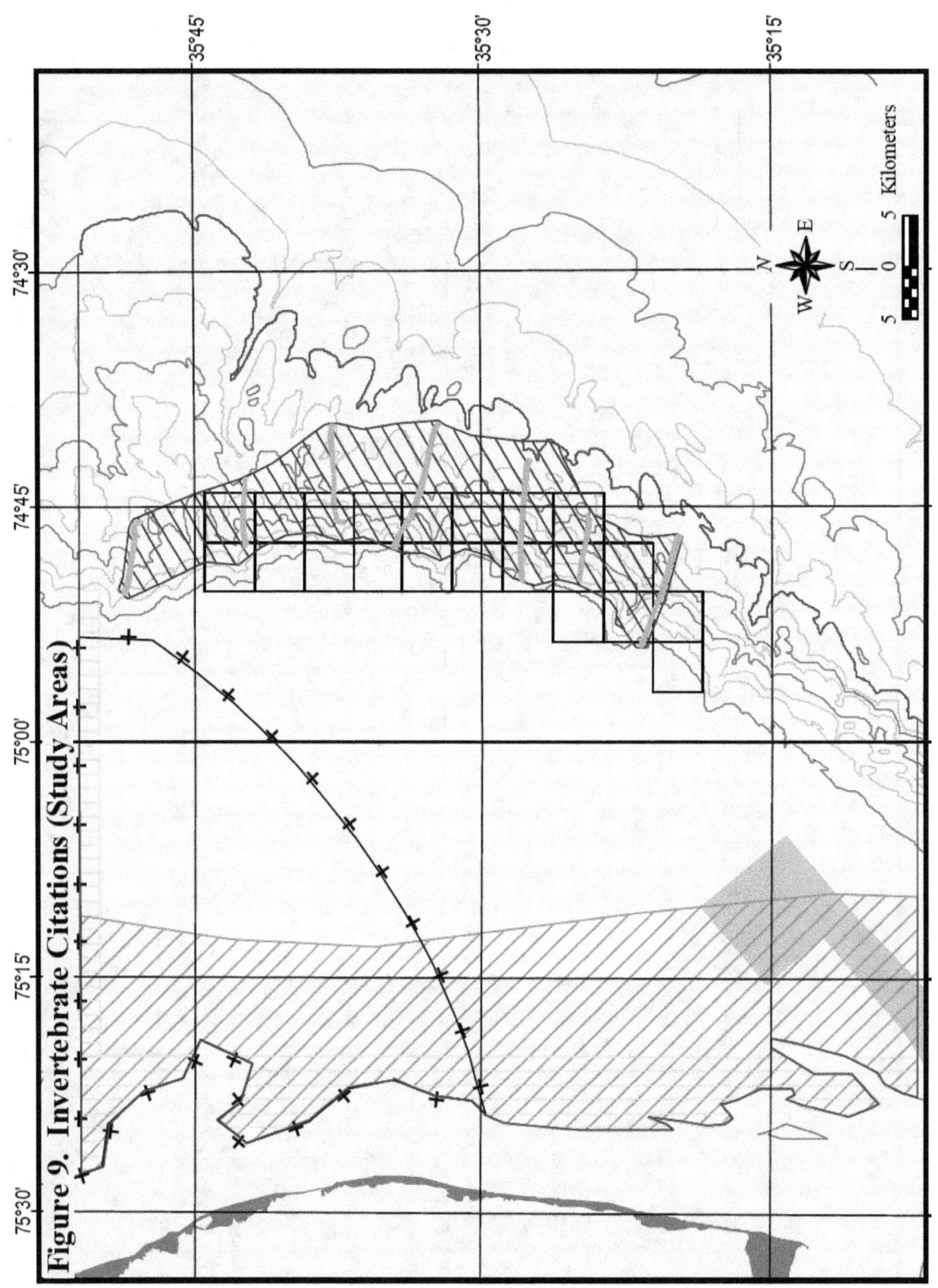

Figure 9. Invertebrate Citations (Study Areas)

Key to Invertebrate Citations (Figures 8 and 9).

/\/ Study Area Boundary

☐ Lease Blocks

Mapped Citations

U Blair et al. (1996); Levin (1991); Levin et al. (1997)

S Blake (1993; 1994; Blake & Grassle (1994)

T Blake & Diaz (1998); Cutter et al. (1994b)

U Blake & Hilbig (1994); Hilbig (1994)

/\/ Blake et al. (1987)

W Chen & Hillman (1970)

& Curtain (1979 a-d); Langfelder et al. (1979)

▨ Cutter et al. (1994a); Milliman et al. (1994); Rhoads & Hecker (1994)

§ Diaz et al. (1994); Schaff (1991); Schaff & Levin (1994)

c Gooday et al. (1992)

▦ Hecker (1994)

↗↗ Hogans & Sulak (1992)

X✝ Kirby-Smith (1985); Ross, S. (1985a); U.S. Dept. Navy (1985)

U Kirby-Smith (1989b); Ross, S. (unpub.a) Magnuson et al. (1981)

Ê Myers (1968)

▭ Ross, J. (1991)

▨ Ross et al. (1984)

Ú Ross et al. (2001); Sulak & Ross (1996)

Mapped Citations (con't)

T Schaff et al. (1992)

↗ Stancyk (in press); Stancyk et al. (1998)

▨ Weston (1988)

Studies that Focus on the Manteo Lease Blocks

Blake & Advent (1998)
Crawford (1989)
Diaz et al. (1993a, 1998)
Gettleson (1992)
Shepard & Hulbert (1994)
Shepard et al. (1992)
Shephard et al. (1993)
U.S.D.O.I.-Minerals Mgmt. Service (1992)
Vigil (1998)

Studies that Cover the Hatteras Middle Slope Area ("The Point")

Bailey et al. (1991, 1995)
Diaz et al. (1993b)
Kirby-Smith (1989a)
Shepard (1991)
Stancyk et al. (1991)

Key to Invertebrate Citations (Figures 8 and 9) (con't).

Broad Regional Studies

Abernathy et al. (1989)
Ashjian et al. (1994)
Atkinson et al. (1985)
Brown (1991)
Butler et al. (1983)
Coston-Clements et al. (1991)
Cutler (1975)
Cutler & Doble (1979)
Fedoryako (1989)
George & Hulbert (1989)
Hastie (1995)
Minerals Mgmt. Service (1982a-c)
Renaud et al. (1993)
Ross & Moye (1989)
Ross et al. (1985, 1986)
Rowe (1971)
Settle (1997)
S. Atlantic Fishery Mgmt. Council (1998)

Studies Based on Large Digitized Databases

Able et al. (1995)
Almeida et al. (1984)
Azarovitz (unpub.)
Brodziak & Hendrickson (1999)
Gillikin et al. (1979)
Gray et al. (1968)
Grosslein & Azarovitz (1982)
Guthrie et al. (1981)
Holland et al. (1979b, 1981a, 1981b)
Moser et al. (1995)
Phalen (unpub. e, unpub. g)
Powell et al. (1975c, 1975f)
Ross et al. (unpub.)

MARINE BIRD CHAPTER

MARINE BIRD CHAPTER

Abernathy, S.A., M.T. Baer, C.S. Benner, M.S. Brody, D.K. Francois, J.K. Gilliam, L.K. Good, C.J. Ohara, and J.V. Martin. 1989. Atlantic Outer Continental Shelf: Description of the Mid-Atlantic Environment. Abernathy, S. A. (ed.). U.S. Department of the Interior, Minerals Management Service, Atlantic OCS Region, Environmental Assessment Section. Herndon, VA. 167 p.

*This document discusses the major issues and areas of concern for the mid-Atlantic environment that are considered in the planning process for oil and gas leasing and operations on the Outer Continental Shelf (OCS). The issues are addressed with respect to the potential environmental consequences of mid Atlantic oil and gas exploration, development and production. A section discussing The Physical Environment (e.g., geology, non-petroleum minerals, physical oceanography, chemical oceanography and water quality, ocean dumping, meteorology, air quality), Biological resources (e.g., plankton, benthos, fishery resources, marine reptiles, marine mammals, marine and coastal birds, estuaries, wetlands, sensitive coastal habitats, canyon areas), Socioeconomic Environment, and other issues (e.g., archaeological resources, marine vessel traffic, National Aeronautics and Space Administration/ Department of Defense activities, oil and gas infrastructure, marine sanctuaries, and estuarine research reserves) is included. Most of the figures showing fisheries resource distribution are taken from fisheries data compiled for bottom-trawl and shellfish surveys of the National Marine Fisheries Service, Northeast Fisheries Center, Woods Hole, MA.

Blair, N. 1998. A Scientific Overview of the Region Surrounding Lease Blocks 467 and 510. pp. 14-17. *In*: Vigil, D.L. (ed.). North Carolina/Minerals Management Service Technical Workshop on Manteo Unit Exploration: February 4-5, 1998. U.S. Dept. of the Interior, Minerals Management Service, Gulf of Mexico OCS Region. New Orleans, LA.

*These are the proceedings from a workshop/meeting (conducted on February 4-5, 1998) between the North Carolina Department of Environment and Natural Resources, and the U.S. Department of the Interior's Minerals Management Service (MMS). The geographic area being discussed is approximately 45 miles east-northeast of Cape Hatteras, NC, referred to as the Manteo Unit. This workshop reviewed environmental and socioeconomic information known and needed on the Manteo Unit. The MMS's Gulf of Mexico OCS Regional Director gave an MMS perspective on history and status of the area. Chevron gave a presentation on how the exploratory well would be drilled. The scientific characterization was presented in greater detail by a number of scientific experts who spoke on the following disciplines physical environment, habitat and living resources, seabirds, marine mammals, sea turtles, and social and economic issues. Specific chapters are cited individually, when appropriate.

The continental margin offshore Cape Hatteras, NC has been the focus of numerous oceanographic studies. The objective of this report is to provide an overview of physical, biological, geological, and chemical processes that operate in the region so that the results from individual disciplinary studies can be placed in a system-wide context. This section discusses hydrocarbon potential, water column observations and processes, benthic observations and processes, summary and the future.

Brinkley, E.S. 1994a. Spring Migration of Seabirds off Central North Carolina: 22 May 1992, with Notes on two Skua (*Catharacta*) Taxa. The Chat 58: 94-101.

*The concentration of pelagic seabirds and other marine biota along frontal eddies of the western edge of the Gulf Stream in the northern summer is a well-documented phenomenon (Haney and McGillivary 1985, Haney 1986a-c) and is well-known to sports fishermen in the Southern Atlantic

Bight. Less material has been published, however, on the concentration of migrants along this front in the northern spring. The timing of the spring migration varies over the three- week period extending from the second week in May through about the first week in June at these latitudes, with significant but lesser movement of terns, jaegers, scuas, shearwaters, and storm-petrels on either side of this period. An excursion of 22 May 1992 yielded a diversity and density of species that advances our assessment of spring migration off North Carolina.

—. 1994b. Evasive Maneuvers of Black-capped Petrel (*Pterodroma hasitata*). The Chat 58: 18-21.

*On 30 August 1992, H. Fenton Day III and I observed a group of 25 distant birds soaring at heights 50-80 meters over "The Point" (35°33' N, 74°53' W), east-southeast of Oregon Inlet, North Carolina. From a distance of roughly a half-kilometer, the birds seemed to be gulls soaring together in a tight, ascending column. The time of initial observation was 1245 EDT; it was a hot day with moderate winds (5-10 knots), with good conditions for the formation of thermals over the Gulf Stream, and soaring gulls, if a little out of place, seemed plausible.

Browne, M.M. 1980. External Parasites (Mallophaga and Acarina) of Wilson's Storm Petrel, *Oceanites oceanicus* Kuhl, off the North Carolina Coast. Ph.D. Dissertation. North Carolina State University, Department of Entomology. 84 p.

The ectoparasitic species (Mallophaga and Acarina) were examined from Wilson's storm petrels (Oceanites oceanicus) collected off the North Carolina coast — April to September, 1976-1978. Four species of Mallophaga from two suborders and two families were found: Amblycera, Menoponidae-*Ancistrona vagelli*; Ischnocera, Philopteridae-*Halipeurus pelagicus*, *Philoceanus robertsi*, and *Saemundssonia marina*. Three species in three families of feather mites (Analgoidea) were found: Proctophyllodidae, *Brephosceles* sp. Xolagidae, *Ingrassia* sp. and Avenzoariidae *Zachvatkinia hydrobatidii*. Birds were examined for location of ectoparasites, frequency of occurrence, age, and sex of adult ectoparasites. The age, sex, date of collection, and wing-molt of the petrels were recorded in relation to the ectoparasite load.

Buckley, P.A. 1973. A massive spring movement, including three species new to North Carolina, at Cape Hatteras National Seashore. American Birds 27(1): 8-10.

Much remains to be learned about the distribution and abundance of seabirds off the Atlantic Coast of North America, where — unlike the Pacific Coast — observations have been few (although increasing, especially off the Maritime Provinces, New England and Long Island) or practically lacking (New Jersey south to Florida). The area of the Outer Banks of North Carolina in particular (marine waters of Cape Hatteras and Cape Lookout National Seashores) has almost never been surveyed for pelagic, by means of offshore boat trips, particularly surprising in view of the proximity of the Gulf Stream to Cape Hatteras (sometimes as close as 9-10 miles). Recently, in the summer and fall of 1972, trips out of Hatteras Village and Morehead City, NC into and beyond the Gulf Stream have given an indication of the wealth and diversity of seabirds there, recording, for example, hundreds of Audubon's Shearwaters (*Puffinus, lherminieri*), several Black-capped Petrels (*Pterodroma hasitata*) at least two Black-browed Albatrosses (*Diomedea melanophris*) White-tailed Tropicbird (*Phaethon lepturus*), Bridled Tern (*Sterna anaethetus*), and slightly further north a White-faced Storm Petrel (*Palagodroma marina*) — in addition to the pair of the latter species seen at Oregon Inlet, N.C. after a hurricane in 1971.

This paper reports a seabird movement seen, from shore at Cape Hatteras National Seashore in late May 1970, of a magnitude possibly never before recorded on the Atlantic Coast of North America. Among the commoner species were three others never before recorded from the Carolinas, and in fact almost unknown south of New England waters. Observations were all by the writer and F. G.

Buckley, and both observers were previously familiar with all species see, from much pelagic bird work, especially ocean crossings.

Carter, J.H., III, and J.F. Parnell. 1974. Little Gulls at Cape Hatteras, N.C. The Chat 38: 40.

*On 10 March 1973, the authors observed three Little Gulls (*Larus minutus*) at the tip of Cape Hatteras, near Buxton, NC. The birds were feeding over the ocean with a large flock of Bonaparte's Gulls (*Larus philadelphia*). The Little Gulls appeared slightly smaller than the Bonaparte's Gulls in flight. Two of the Little Gulls were immatures, and the third was an adult in winter plumage. The distinctive field marks of the immatures (dark crown patch, tail band, and dark wing-stripe) were repeatedly noted at close range by both authors. The adult was easily distinguished in flight by the very dark underwing. Although the weather was foggy, Parnell obtained recognizable photographs of an immature Little Gull.

Clapp, R.B., D. Morgan-Jacobs, and R.C. Banks. 1982a. Marine birds of the Southeastern United States and Gulf of Mexico. Part II: Anseriformes. FWS/OBS-82/20. U.S. Fish and Wildlife Service, Office of Biological Services. Washington, DC. 492 p.

Information on the seasonal distribution and abundance of 41 species of waterfowl of the order Anseriformes that occur in the coastal southeastern United States has been compiled and mapped from the literature. In many instances this provides the first synthesis of knowledge about a species for this region. For the species we consider most important in coastal areas we also provide information on worldwide distribution, habitat, food, and various aspects of life history. This information was gathered in an attempt to assess the possible effects of offshore oil development on populations of marine birds in the southeast.

The susceptibility of birds to oil depends not only on their juxtaposition in time and space, but also on currents and climatic factors and on the stage of the life or annual cycle and the behavior of the species. Contamination by oil may result in matting of the feathers with death following from chilling, starvation, and the ingestion of oil during preening. Among the birds covered by this report, the sea ducks and diving ducks are considered the most susceptible to oil pollution in the southeast. Most of the other ducks, geese, and swans covered in the report are relatively insusceptible to oil pollution because they are seldom found in areas where oiling is likely to occur.

One of the conclusions reached by this report is that we know very little about the status and populations of some of the anatids that occur in the southeast. Some of these species (e.g., the scoters) are among those that may be expected to be most detrimentally affected by development of oil resources. In general, most species that are widely hunted are relatively well studied, but much is unknown of those that are not game birds.

Clapp, R.B., D. Morgan-Jacobs, and R.C. Banks. 1983. Marine Birds of the Southeastern United States and Gulf of Mexico. Part III: Charadriiformes. FWS/OBS-83/30. U.S. Fish and Wildlife Service, Division of Biological Services. Washington, DC. 853p.

Information on the seasonal distribution and abundance of 22 species of marine birds of the order Charadriiformes that occur in the coastal southeastern United States has been compiled and mapped from the literature. In many instances this provides the first synthesis of knowledge about a species for this region. We also provide information on global distribution, habitat and food for all species, and include information on various aspects of life history for the 16 species that we consider most important in coastal areas. This information was gathered in an attempt to assess the possible effects of offshore oil development on populations of marine birds in the southeast.

The susceptibility of birds to oil depends not only on their juxtaposition in time and space, but also on currents, climatic factors, the stage of the life or annual cycle, and the behavior of the species. Contamination by oil may result in matted feathers with death following from chilling, starvation, and ingestion of oil during preening. Few of the species covered in this report are at great hazard from the direct effects of oiling, but populations of most of these species are highly susceptible to environmental change. Large concentrations of wintering, breeding, and migrant gulls and terns occur in the southeast and in some instances make up a large proportion of the global or North American population. Consequently, this report includes most of the marine birds that we believe most likely to be detrimentally affected by the development of oil resources.

One of the conclusions reached by this report is that we still know very little about the status and populations of some of the charadriiforms that occur in the southeast. Additional surveys of colonial marine birds in the southeast and nearby waters are badly needed to ensure that we know enough about then, to prevent their untimely loss from our coastal areas.

Clapp, R. B., R.C. Banks, D. Morgan-Jacobs, and W.A. Hoffman. 1982b. Marine birds of the Southeastern United States and Gulf of Mexico. Part I: Gaviiformes through Pelecaniformes. FWS/OBS-82/01. U.S. Fish and Wildlife Service. Office of Biological Services, Washington, D.C. 637p.

Information on the seasonal distribution and abundance of 39 species of marine birds of the Orders Gaviiformes, Podicipediformes, Procellariiformes, and Pelecaniformes that occur off the southeastern shores of the United States and in the Gulf of Mexico has been compiled and mapped from thousands of literature citations; in many instances this provides the first synthesis of knowledge about a species for this area. Information on worldwide distribution, habitat, food, and various aspects of life history is also summarized. This information was gathered to assess the possible effects of offshore oil development on populations of marine birds.

Susceptibility of birds to oil depends not only on their juxtaposition in time and space, but also on currents, climatic factors, the stage in the life or annual cycle, and the behavior of the species. Contamination by oil may result in matted feathers; death may soon follow from chilling or starvation, or from the toxic effects of oil ingested when the birds attempt to preen themselves. Oil from feathers may be transferred to eggs by incubating birds and may greatly reduce reproductive success.

Among the birds covered by this volume, loons and grebes are considered the most susceptible to oil pollution. Cormorants, pelicans, and boobies are moderately susceptible and the truly pelagic birds, including most of the Procellariiformes, are the least susceptible.

Little is known about the occurrence of seabirds off our shores, but our knowledge is increasing. Recent ornithological studies offshore have revealed concentrations of species previously thought to occur rarely, if at all. More than 63% of the Manx Shearwaters ever seen off the southeastern coast were sighted in the last 5 years (1975-1979) and 37% were seen during the last 2 years (1978-1979) covered by this report. Comparable figures for Wilson's Storm-petrel are 40% and 26%. Nonetheless, observations are limited. Future trips to locate or count birds should be scheduled when birds are expected to be present at periods when little previous information was obtained.

Additional research should be conducted on the distribution and status of birds that use the marine environment. More attention should be directed toward investigating the status and distribution of pelagic birds, toward learning the abundance and distribution of marine birds that nest in the southeastern states, and toward discovering the distribution and status of birds that are transients or winter visitors in the southeast. Research is also needed to determine the numbers and proportion of each species that are being oiled in the southeast so that the effects of oil pollution can be assessed more adequately.

Crawford, K. (ed.). 1989. Proceedings: 1989 Marine Expo: The Natural Resources Associated with Mobil's Proposed Drill Site. NC Outer Continental Shelf Office, NC Department of Administration. Raleigh, NC. 64 p.

*This report contains abstracts from each presenter. Chapter topics include: Mobil's Proposal, Geologic Overview — Introduction and Potential for Oil and Gas Discovery, Oceanographic Conditions, Comments on Last MMS Modeling, Biological Production Near the Bottom (invertebrates), Fisheries Resources, Commercial and Recreational Marine Fisheries, Winter Storm Effects on Spawning and Larval Drift of Pelagic Fish, Marine Birds, Sea Turtles in North Carolina, Marine Mammals, Plenary Session, Summary. Each chapter also cited individually when appropriate.

Dittmann, D.L., R.M. Zink, and J.A. Gerwin. 1989. Evolutionary Genetics of Phalaropes. Auk 106: 326-331.

*The three species of phalaropes- Wilson's (*Phalaropus tricolor*), Red-necked (*P. lobatus*), and Red (*P. fulicaria*) have long been considered a natural group (Cramp, 1983), often equated with a monophyly; and they have been classified at the familial, subfamilial, or tribal rank. An early diagnosis (Ridgeway 1991) of the group read "Toes with a conspicuous lateral membrane, sometimes developed into broad scalloped lobes; tarsus excessively compressed, plumage of underparts very dense, gull-like." Several other characteristics, such as the distinctive whirling foraging behavior (Hayman et al. 1986), pronounced reverse sexual dimorphism in plumage coloration, and the lobed toes (and basal webbing) are characteristics often cited as support for naturalness (monophyly) of the group (Cramp 1983). It is unclear which of these traits qualify as synapomorphies (i.e. uniquely derived for phalaropes). For example, although each species possesses webbing on the toes, each has a distinctive pattern (illustrated in Coues [1972]). The distinctive whirling foraging behavior also differs in detail among species (Cramp 1983). Strauch (1978) analyzed 70 skeletal characteristics and found only one synapomorphy, namely a particular condition of the bill, which is apparently identical in each species of phalarope. Thus, the monophyly of the phalaropes, although widely assumed, is not based on many traits that are shared by all species. The question of phalarope monophyly aside, based on plumage pattern, behavioral and vocal similarities, distribution, and habitat, most authors consider the Red and red-necked phalaropes to be sister taxa and the Wilson's most primitive (Cramp 1983, Jehl 1968). For example, although each phalarope species was once placed in a monotypic genus (e.g., Ridgeway 1919, Hellmayr and Conover 1948), the Wilson's Phalarope was retained in a monotyptic genus long after the other two were made congeneric.

Haney, C., D.S. Lee, K.M. Fristrup, and M. Socci. 1991. Seabird attraction to ephemeral food sources: geometry of recruitment distance in experimentally-induced foraging flocks (abstract). Pacific Seabird Group Meeting. Victoria, BC.

*This citation includes research conducted within the defined study area for The Point (D. Lee, pers. comm. 24 February 2000). Mr. Lee did not have a copy of this document and we could not otherwise find the document.

Haney, C., D.S. Lee, and M. Socci. 1993. Air-sea heat flux, ocean wind fields, and offshore dispersal by gulls during winter (abstract). Pacific Seabird Group Annual Meeting. Seattle, WA.

*This citation includes research conducted within the defined study area for The Point (D. Lee, pers. comm. 24 February 2000). Mr. Lee did not have a copy of this document and we could not otherwise find the document.

Haney, J.C., and D.S. Lee. 1994. Air-sea Heat flux, Ocean Wind Fields, and Offshore Dispersal of Gulls. The Auk 111(2): 427-440.

Gull numbers in pelagic habitats off the southeastern United States were weakly associated with seasonal variability in mean wind speeds, but strongly associated with accumulated air-sea heat flux (a surrogate for temperature inversions; i.e. pre-thermal condition) and wind-speed variance (an energy source for flight, as well as a thermal inducement). Single meteorological variables accounted for as much as 59 to 93% of seasonal changes in gull abundance. Gulls (including nonbreeders) delayed dispersal to oceanic waters until onset of winter meteorological conditions, several months after cessation of breeding. Our findings support Woodcock's convective-soaring hypothesis, which ascribed gull dispersal in winter to boundary layering along eastern continental margins. We extend this model by linking gull morphology and flight to energy-efficient reliance on air-sea interactions and spatial patterns in seasonal wind fields. Summer meteorological conditions in much of the western North Atlantic Ocean facilitate coastal foraging by gulls, but act to preclude efficient foraging to and in offshore habitats. The presence or absence of coherence (meteorological consistency) in the aerial environment may have acted to select and maintain divergent life history strategies in gulls and certain other inshore feeders.

Haney, J.C., D.S. Lee, and R.D. Morris. 1999. Bridled Tern (*Sterna anaethetus*). The Birds of North America 468: 1-24.

*A discussion of distinguishing characteristics, distribution, systematics, migration, habitat, food habits, behavior, breeding and migratory distribution for the Bridled Tern (*Sterna anaethetus*) including the defined study area for The Point.

Hass, T. 1997. Distributions of pelagic seabirds in relation to dynamic features of the Gulf Stream. Ph.D. Dissertation. University of North Carolina, Chapel Hill. 181p.

While the boundaries that delimit terrestrial habitats are often clear, distinctions between habitats of the open ocean are usually subtle, and few examples of habitat selection by pelagic seabirds have been documented. Several long-term studies have demonstrated that pelagic seabirds associate with particular water masses, but none has examined whether the distributions of seabirds consistently shift in synchrony with real-time changes in the positions of oceanographic features. Furthermore, in most studies the processes that underlie the associations between seabirds and water masses have been unclear.

I studied seabirds off the coast of North Carolina during May-September of 1992-1995. Black-capped Petrels (*Pterodroma hasitata*) and Band-rumped Storm-Petrels (*Oceanodroma castro*) were most abundant in interior waters of the Gulf Stream and appeared to track these waters as the Gulf Stream shifted toward and away from the coast. In multivariate analyses both species showed significant associations with variables indicating interior waters of the Gulf Stream. In addition, Black-capped Petrels were almost twice as abundant on days in which the Gulf Stream moved offshore as on days in which its position remained stable or moved onshore.

Offshore movements of the Gulf Stream occurs when troughs of Gulf Stream meanders (100-km concave bends in the current) pass through a region. Near Cape Hatteras, where the continental slope is exceptionally steep, this process induces upwelling of deep water along the edge of the Gulf Stream, thereby concentrating prey for seabirds near the surface. Elevations in the abundance of Black-capped Petrels thus coincided with indications of upwelling. By focusing on movements of an oceanographic boundary current, this investigation has revealed an important pattern in the distribution of seabirds.

—. (in press). An additional record of Bulwer's Petrel, *Bulweria bulwerii,* of the southeastern United States of America. Marine Ornithology.

*This citation includes research conducted within the defined study area for The Point (D. Lee, pers. comm. 24 February 2000). Mr. Lee did not have a copy of this document and we could not otherwise find the document.

Helmuth, W.T. 1920. Extracts from notes made while in the Naval Service. The Auk 37(2): 255-261.

*In the fall of 1917 the ship on which I served as seaman was assigned to inspection duty on the Atlantic and Gulf coasts of the United States, under Rear-admiral C. McR. Winslow's flag. We left the navy yard at Brooklyn on October 20,1917, and proceeded up the New England coast as far as Machiasport, Maine, which we reached on November first. We then journeyed south, close inshore, up the Delaware River to Philadelphia, thence to Norfolk, Va., arriving on Thanksgiving day. We left Norfolk on February 23, 1918, proceeding south to Key West, Fla. From here we went directly to Pensacola, Fla.; from Pensacola to New Orleans, up the south pass of the Mississippi; from New Orleans to Galveston, Texas; thence to Port Arthur, Texas, and across the Gulf of Mexico to Tampa, Fla., arriving on April 1, 1918. From Tampa our course took us again to Key West, up the east coast of Florida to Jacksonville, and thence north to Charleston, S.C., stopping at Brunswick and Savannah, Ga.

During this time I had excellent opportunities to study the birds met with offshore, and a few chances to watch land birds on our all too infrequent "liberties" in various places. Some of these notes may be of interest to readers of 'The Auk,' and I append them herewith.

Jones, H.L. 1967. Status of the Razorbill in the Carolinas. The Chat 31: 55-57.

*On the morning of 16 February 1964, Julian Meadows and I found a dead Razorbill (*Alca torda*) near the north end of Wrightsville Beach, North Carolina. The bird was slightly oiled on the head, but otherwise was in excellent condition. The specimen was prepared by James Parnell and placed in the bird collection at North Carolina State University.

The remainder of this note describes the status of this species in the Carolinas.

Lee, D.S. 1977. Occurrence of the Black-capped Petrel in North Carolina Waters. The Chat 41: 1-2.

*The Black-capped Petrel (*Pterodroma hasitata*) is the only species of gadfly petrel known to occur in the northwestern Atlantic with any regularity. Robbins et al. (1966) describe it as a casual summer visitor to eastern North America during storms. The AQU Checklist (1975) lists it as rare and occurring north of Florida only accidentally. Therefore, it is interesting to report that this species appears to be a regular, though uncommon, offshore summer and early fall resident of North Carolina.

The remainder of this note describes the status of this species offshore North Carolina.

—. 1979. Second Record of the South Trinidad Petrel (*Pterodroma arminjoniana*) for North America. American Birds 33: 138-139.

*On August 20, 1978 a field party from the North Carolina State Museum of Natural History collected a single dark phase South Trinidad Petrel (*Pterodroma arminjoniana*) 74 km ESE of Oregon Inlet, Dare County, NC. The only previous North American record is of a hurricane-driven specimen taken near Ithaca, New York, although there is another reported occurrence in the Northern Hemisphere an individual struck the rigging of a yacht December 31, 1905, in the mid-Atlantic, at 21°51'N, 43°35' W).

The remainder of this note describes the status of this species offshore North Carolina.

—. 1984. Petrels and storm-petrels in North Carolina's offshore waters: including species previously unrecorded for North America. American Birds 38(2): 151-163.

Although there may have been various reported instances of the occurrence of Band-rumped Storm-Petrels (synonymous with Harcourt's and Madeiran Storm-Petrel) in the United States, particularly in the Southeast, all are associated with storms and the species has been assumed to be an accidental. Peterson (1980) lists it as accidental in Florida, North Carolina, Montana, Indiana, Delaware, Pennsylvania and the District of Columbia, Ontario, and Quebec. It is also known from South Carolina (Shuler 1973), Tennessee (USNM 526349), and Texas (Oberholser 1974); there are single records for Brazil and Cuba. The northern and inland records certainly result from storm-blown casualties, In fact, Murphy (1936) cites several of the above-mentioned records as classic examples of long-range transport of birds trapped in eyes of hurricanes. The species is recognized as being highly pelagic, staying well out at sea, generally rather solitary, and an inhabitant of tropical and subtropical seas, The eleven coastal records for the Southeast are summarized by Clapp et al. (1982), and all appear to be storm-related. In order to present these records in perspective, a review of all the species of petrels found off the North Carolina coast is also provided.

—. 1985c. Results of a Ten-year Study of Marine Birds South of the Virginia Cape Region: Their Potential Impact with EMPRESS II. Appendix H. *In:* U.S. Department of the Navy. EMPRESS II: Supplemental Draft Environmental Impact Statement for the Proposed Operation of the Navy Electromagnetic Pulse Radiation Environment Simulator for Ships (Empress II) in the Chesapeake Bay and Atlantic Ocean. United States Navy. Environmental/ Intergovernmental Section. Atlantic Division. Naval Facilities Engineering and Command. Norfolk, VA.

*This report describes a 10-year survey of marine birds of North Carolina's offshore waters. The southern portion of the VACAPES EMPRESS II Area of North Carolina overlaps with the northern portion of the defined study area for the Data Inventory Related to the Hatteras Middle Slope (The Point) Area.

—. 1986a. Seasonal distribution of marine birds in North Carolina waters, 1975-1986. American Birds 40 (3): 409-412.

*In 1979, Lee and Booth (American Birds 33: 715-721) summarized information on the seasonal occurrence of pelagic birds off the North Carolina coast. Since that time a fair amount of additional information has become available, outdating that study. Major changes include the documentation of additional bird species, the extension of known seasonal occurrences for many, if not most species, changes in our knowledge about the relative abundance or recognized status of several species, and nomenclature.

The remainder of this note describes the status of pelagic bird species offshore North Carolina.

—. 1986c. Second Record of the Cape Petrel in the Western North Atlantic. The Chat 50: 118-119.

*On 26 July 1985 Captain Allen Foreman and his mate John Gallup saw a bird they identified as a Cape Petrel (*Daption capense*). It was flying 42 miles ENE of Oregon Inlet, Dare County, NC, and was over water 200 fathoms in depth. The bird was watched for a minute or more while near a Black Tern (*Chilodonias niger*). The captain and mate each independently described the size, plumage, and behavior of the bird to me in late July of 1985 and again in June of 1986. Although neither was aware of the significance of the record, on both occasions they were able to recognize the species from illustrations in standard field and seabird guides. Because of the distinctive plumage of the species in question and their familiarity with local marine birds (Captain Foreman has been accompanying me during my seabird studies for the past 9 years), I have confidence in the authenticity of this record. For example, Foreman and his mate Dick Harris provided sight descriptions of Masked Boobies (*Sula dactylatra*) from off the North Carolina coast (Lee and Platania 1979) several years prior to the "official" recognition of their occurrence presented by bird watchers (Davis and Needham 1983). Likewise, they alerted me to the presence of two types of tropicbirds off the North Carolina coast prior to confirmation that Red-billed Tropicbirds (*Phaethon aethereus*) were in the North Atlantic off the Carolina coast. While there is always some question of the validity of records not documented by specimens or photographs, in this particular case, the fact that this sight record is not corroborated by someone with formal background in bird study has little, if any, bearing on judging the validity of the identification.

The remainder of this note describes the sight records of Cape Petrel (*Daption capense)* offshore North America and worldwide.

—. 1987a. Common Loons wintering in Offshore Waters. The Chat 51(2): 40-42.

*Between 1975 and 1986 I have had the opportunity to observe Common Loons (*Gavia immer*) far at sea off the North Carolina coast. Many of my records are of spring migrants (N=98), but some additional individuals (N=35) found during the winter months were assumed to be winter residents. Although individuals were encountered regularly, at no time did the species appear to be common far offshore, except perhaps during spring migration. No Red-throated Loons (*G. stellata*) were seen offshore at any season during the 11-year study period. My sightings were made mostly at distances between 20 and 35 miles (32-56 km) from shore and in waters of 20 to 500 fathoms in depth. Regular occurrence far at sea was not expected. Cramp and Simmons (1977), for example, state that Common Loons remain within a few kilometers of shore throughout most of their winter range. Clapp et al. (1982) noted: "Common Loons in winter are normally marine but remain within a few kilometers of shore. They regularly use enclosed harbors and inlets. Bent (1919) referred to groups of wintering loons sometimes far out at sea; but this does not seem to agree with most recent observations." Most researchers studying offshore faunas in the southeastern United States to date have not discussed loons. Rowlett (1980), however, does indicate 0.1 to 1.0 Common Loons per hour in deep waters (40-500 fathoms) of the Northern Chesapeake Bight in February, April, and May. Studies on wintering Common Loons are few (e.g. McIntyre 1978) and were conducted in sounds along beach fronts.

The remainder of this note describes the status of this species offshore North Carolina.

—. 1987b. December records of seabirds off North Carolina. Wilson Bulletin 99(l): 116-121.

*Little published information is available concerning offshore winter seabird fauna of the southeastern United States. The only overview of the local seasonal variation in seabirds is that by Lee and Booth (1979). Their summaries were based mostly on North Carolina field studies done from late spring through early fall, and provide little new information on the winter distribution of marine birds. Clapp et al. (1982, 1983) compiled records of all marine birds for the southeastern States, but offshore information was generally unavailable for the winter. During the last few winters I conducted 11 offshore survey trips into shelf and shelf-edge waters off North Carolina during December. All trips departed from Oregon Inlet, North Carolina (29 December 1977; 5 and 30 December 1978; 3 and 28 December 1982; 12, 20, 28, and 29 December 1984; 5 and 22 December 1985). Survey routes typically extended 35 to 55 miles offshore, transecting inshore, shelf, shelf-edge, and Gulf Stream waters.

—. 1988a. Biases in age and sex ratios of seabirds off the North Carolina Coast. Progr. Meeting Colonial Waterbird Soci. and Pacific Seabird Gr. p. 28.

*This citation includes research conducted within the defined study area for The Point (D. Lee, pers. comm. 24 February 2000). Mr. Lee did not have a copy of this document and we could not otherwise find the document.

—. 1988b. First record of Wilson's Storm-Petrels on a Christmas Bird Count. American Birds 41(4): 1331-1333.

*On December 20, 1986, The Continental Shelf North Carolina Count Participants recorded a minimum of 351 Wilson's Storm Petrels. The Wilson's Storm-Petrels. The Wilson's Storm-Petrel (*Oceanites oceanicus*) is such an abundant species in the North Atlantic Ocean during the warmer months, the significance of its occurrence in late December can easily be overlooked. Furthermore, the number of birds encountered is striking when one considers that nearly all new Christmas Bird Count records are of single vagrant birds.

The remainder of this note describes the status of this species offshore North Carolina.

—. 1988c. The Little Shearwater (Puffinus assimilis) in the western North Atlantic. American Birds 42(2): 213-216.

*A summary of the reported occurrence for the past century and an examination of at-sea identification of the cryptic black-and-white shearwaters found in North Atlantic waters.

—. 1989a. Marine Birds. Proceedings: 1989 Marine Expo: The Natural Resources Associated with Mobil's Proposed Drill Site. pp. 47-48. *In*: Crawford, K. (ed.). NC Outer Continental Shelf Office, NC Department of Administration. Raleigh, NC.

Although the current information on the biology, distribution, and season of occurrence of seabirds, marine mammals, and marine turtles in North Carolina is still incomplete, it is better than what is available for most other areas of the world. The 14-year extensive study conducted by the N.C. State Museum is perhaps the longest and most intensive ocean study conducted of seabirds and marine mammals conducted anywhere. North Carolina has the largest documented marine bird and marine mammal fauna of any geographic unit in the North Atlantic. It is primarily the location of the state in relation to tropical and subtropical areas, migration routes, and oceanic currents that accounts for the diversity of species.

Many of the species normally observed represent small populations that could be threatened by local oil spills and the follow-up use of dispersants. Large portions of the total populations of many of these species assemble regularly or seasonally in deep waters off the Outer Banks of North Carolina. At least eleven species could be heavily damaged by oil spills in North Carolina's offshore waters. Moreover, although many of the organisms, particularly birds, have not been regarded as endangered by the U.S. Fish and Wildlife Service, present data suggest possible oversights. Most birds have relatively protracted periods of occurrence off the state's shores. There are several factors that account for this, the more obvious of which include: (1) local oceanic currents and upwellings that provide important foraging areas for both low and high latitude species, (2) extended migratory periods for particular species because of the staggered schedules of various age groups, and (3) a typically long adolescence in some species during which sub-adults may linger in local waters for extended periods before returning to nesting areas.

—. 1989b. Jaegers and skuas in the Western North Atlantic: some historical misconceptions. American Birds 43(1): 18-20.

*For many decades long-tailed Jaegers (*Stercorarius longicaudus*) were considered very rare spring and fall transients over the western North Atlantic. This paper discusses sightings and distribution offshore North Carolina, USA.

—. 1991a. Offshore Research of NC State Museum in Area of the Point. pp. 2-3. *In:* Shepard, A. (ed.). NURC — UNCW 1991 Undersea Research: Informational Meeting. National Undersea Research Center, University of North Carolina at Wilmington. Wilmington, NC.

Although the current information on the biology, distribution, and season of occurrence of seabirds, marine mammals, and marine turtles in North Carolina is still incomplete, it is better than what is available for most other areas of the world. A 15- year extensive study conducted by the NC State Museum (NCSM) is perhaps the longest and most intensive ocean study of seabirds and marine mammals conducted anywhere. The Hatteras area has long been regarded as a biological "Mason-Dixon Line" between boreal and tropical maritime elements. North Carolina is at a latitude usually associated with temperate seas; however, boreal, temperate, and tropical species are transported, or follow prey items transported by converging oceanic currents to the outer continental shelf area at Hatteras. This, in part, explains the diversity. North Carolina has the largest documented marine bird (over 50 species) and marine mammal (28 species) fauna of any geographic unit in the North Atlantic. Much of what has been added to fauna of the state is the result of studies in the area known as "The Point." It is primarily the location of the state in general, and "The Point" in particular, in relation to tropical and subtropical areas, migration routes and oceanic currents that account for the diversity of species. The relatively rich diversity is offset by comparatively low densities, but many of the species found here are tropical ones with small populations, so densities are naturally low. For a tropical — subtropical environment the densities are really quite high. The *Sargassum* community is also discussed.

—. 1991b. Pelagic seabirds off the North Carolina coast: An overview of 16 years of surveys. pp. 77-86. *In*: Proceedings of Fourth Atlantic Outer Continental Shelf Region Informational Transfer Meetings. MMS/OCS Study 92-0001.

*This citation includes research conducted within the defined study area for The Point (D. Lee, pers. comm. 24 February 2000). Mr. Lee did not have a copy of this document and we could not otherwise find the document.

—. 1992a. Manx Shearwaters off the Southeastern U.S. Coast. Wilson Ornithological Society Meeting 1992. p. 14.

*This citation includes research conducted within the defined study area for The Point (D. Lee, pers. comm. 24 February 2000). Mr. Lee did not have a copy of this document and we could not otherwise find the document.

—. 1992b. Pelagic Seabirds off the North Carolina Coast: An Overview of 16 Years of Surveys. pp. 78-86. *In*: Department of the Interior, Minerals Management Service. Proceedings of the Fourth Atlantic OCS Region Information Transfer Meeting, September 1991. U.S. Department of the Interior, Minerals Management Service. Herndon, VA.

The Fourth Atlantic Outer Continental Shelf (OCS) Regional Information Transfer Meeting (ITM) was held on 24-25 September, 1991, in Wilmington, NC. The focus of the meeting was on the OCS off North Carolina, specifically on activities related to a proposed exploratory well for oil and gas by Mobil on Block 467 a site 40 miles off the coast of North Carolina. The area of industry interest is known as the Manteo Prospect, while the activities surrounding the proposed drilling are referred to collectively as the Manteo Project. It is also near a fishing ground known locally as "The Point." The area is believed to be gas prone rather than oil prone. The estimated size of the resource could be as high as 5 trillion cubic feet of gas.

The purpose of the meeting was to exchange information on the leasing background, legislative activities, scientific results, and socioeconomic studies. Legislative-related reports include descriptions of the Oil Pollution Act of 1990, the Outer Banks Protection Act, the Environmental Studies Review Panel, and the North Carolina Physical Oceanography Panel. Reports of studies on marine life include benthic diatoms, benthic fauna, pelagic seabirds, sea turtles, and right whales. One report describes the use of airships (blimps) for ocean research a capability relevant to North Carolina because of the east coast airship facility is located in the state. Local marine science facilities described include NOAA's National Undersea Research Center at the University of North Carolina at Wilmington (NURC/UNCW) and the National Marine Fisheries Service laboratory in Beaufort.

Developments in oil spill cleanup technology and capabilities are described by both the Coast Guard and the industry. A socioeconomic report describes the effects of the oil and gas activities on the tourist industry. Lastly, research on the restoration of salt marshes indicates that rehabilitation of an area is possible when development or an accident has occurred. While the emphasis of the meeting was on oil and gas, two reports described the results of projects related to offshore sand mining. The appendix lists the names and addresses of speakers. Individual chapters are cited individually when appropriate.

*This section provides a brief overview of pelagic seabirds off the North Carolina coast with an overview of 16 years of surveys. Figure 14, An Example of Seabird Sightings Compiled by the North Carolina State Museum, is on page 78. The role of sargassum patches as bird habitat is described.

—. 1995a. Marine Birds off the Coast of North Carolina. The Chat 59(4): 113-188.

Records of 71 species of sea birds occurring along and off the North Carolina coast are summarized from published literature sources and from fifteen years (1975-1989) of offshore observations. At least 15 species of birds not previously established as occurring off North Carolina were documented with specimens or photographs during this study, and an additional 7 have been reported based on sightings.

The relatively rich foraging grounds off the Outer Banks of North Carolina account for such a diversity of species of marine birds that assigning the status of accidental or vagrant to even the rarer species might not be appropriate. The local marine micro-environments, are highly variable and account for the area's ability to provide a large species diversity. Seabirds are often simultaneously represented by temperate, boreal, and subtropical species all within a small geographical area. During the spring and fall, migrant species also contribute to the diversity. Although the Hatteras offshore area does not have the predictable large biomass of the Grand Banks during the summer months, it has the largest documented species diversity of pelagic seabirds (Lee 1986) and marine mammals (see Lee et al. 1982) in the western North Atlantic.

The distribution of seabirds in North Carolina's offshore waters is neither even nor random. Clear preferences for certain zones and seasons exist and are discussed in the individual species accounts.

—. 1995b. The Pelagic Ecology of Manx Shearwaters *Puffinus puffinus* off the Southeastern United States of America. Marine Ornithology 23: 107-119.

Knowledge of the biology of Manx Shearwaters *Puffinus puffinus* is largely based on data obtained in and around breeding colonies. In this paper I provide information on various aspects of the marine ecology of this shearwater. The information presented here on age and sex ratios, masses, moult sequence and food habits is the first recorded away from the species' breeding grounds. Whereas not common, Manx Shearwaters occur regularly in pelagic zones off the southeastern United States of America and the number of birds appears to be increasing. As expected, most occurrences are from migration periods and 38% of the total records and reports (n=121) are from the northern spring (March-May). The timing of migration is masked by the presence of birds throughout the northern winter and a small number of summer records. The local occurrence of moulting adults and immatures indicates that at least some segment of the population does not undergo transequatorial migration. Based on banding records and other information it appears that summer birds are largely, and perhaps exclusively, immatures that need not return to their nesting areas in northern latitudes.

—. 1999a. A closer look: Manx Shearwater. Birding 31(6): 522-531.

*This citation includes research conducted within the defined study area for The Point (D. Lee, pers. comm. 24 February 2000). Mr. Lee did not have a copy of this document and we could not otherwise find the document.

—. 1999b. Pelagic Seabirds and the Proposed Exploration for Fossil Fuels off North Carolina: A Test for Conservation Efforts of a Vulnerable International Resource. The Journal of the Elisha Mitchell Scientific Society 115(4): 294-315.

Exploratory drilling is an issue of importance to international conservation because of the regular occurrence of a number of species of rare and globally endangered seabirds occurring in the immediate vicinity of a proposed oil/gas drill site on the Outer Continental Shelf of North Carolina. Species of primary concern include: Black-capped Petrel (*Pterodroma hasitata*), Bermuda Petrel (*P. cahow*), Herald Petrel (*P. arminjoniana*), Fea's Petrel (*P. feae*), and Roseate Tem (*Sterna dougallii*). The area also supports a high diversity of seabirds (49 species) and has been nominated as a globally Important Bird Area. Various factors attract birds to the site making them vulnerable to potential man-made catastrophic events. Lighting associated with the drilling operation is expected to have a major negative impact on several rare species. A secondary concern of disrupting the local marine system and the further depletion of existing stocks of rare seabirds is economic. A growing recreational seabird watching industry has developed on North Carolina's Outer Banks. Educational aspects alone of this industry are an important resource for the understanding of international conservation ethics. Offshore gas/oil exploration potentially jeopardizes both the fauna and the existing educational/ecotourism dependent on the Outer Continental Shelf. Despite these concerns, current conservation strategies and existing regulations do not appear to address the situation, and an internationally important faunal assemblage is in danger.

—. 2000. Color morph bias and conservation concerns for a tropical Pterodroma. Chat 64(1): 15-20.

*This citation includes research conducted within the defined study area for The Point (D. Lee, pers. comm. 24 February 2000). Mr. Lee did not have a copy of this document when requested. The document was not available from University of North Carolina — Wilmington library or via their interlibrary services (J. Ott, pers. comm. 7 March 2000).

Lee, D.S., D.B. Wingate, and H.W. Kale. 1981. Records of Tropicbirds in the North Atlantic and upper Gulf of Mexico, with comments on field identification. American Birds 35(6): 887-890.

*Despite its seemingly accidental occurrence, recent records of the Red-billed Tropicbird, *Phaethon aethereus*, in the North Atlantic suggest that it may occur more frequently than is generally believed.

On October 9,1975, an individual was found sick on a beach near Jacksonville, Florida. On May 16, 1979, Lee collected two specimens *ca.* 40 miles east of Oregon Inlet, Dare County, North Carolina, and on September 1, 1979, a sick Red-billed Tropicbird was found beached near Stuart, Martin County, Florida. These birds represent the third through sixth documented records of the species for eastern North America. Additionally a photo record at the North Carolina State Museum of Natural History is available for May 1981.

Lee, D. S., and E.W. Irvin. 1983. Tropicbirds in the Carolinas: Status and Period of Occurrence of Two Tropical Pelagic Species. The Chat 47(1): 1-13.

*The recent documentation of a second species of tropicbird in the northwest Atlantic Ocean makes it desirable to summarize and evaluate the current knowledge of the status and the season of occurrence for the two tropicbirds in the offshore waters of the Carolinas. The records presented here provide a needed base against which future records can be tallied. They come from a widely diverse body of published sight reports, unpublished records maintained at the North Carolina State Museum, and personal field experience. Few specimens, photographic records, or literature reports provide enough details to separate the two species of Atlantic tropicbirds. This is understandable because prior to 1964 there was little reason to suspect that any tropicbird seen off the coast of North America was anything other than a White-tailed (*Phaethon lepturus*). The reported occurrence of the Red-billed Tropicbird (*P. aethereus*) off the southeastern coast makes the specific identification of previous sight reports suspect. It is our purpose to alert readers to this problem as well as to evaluate the status of these two species based on the fragmentary information presently available.

Lee, D.S., and J. Booth Jr. 1979. Seasonal distribution of offshore and pelagic birds in North Carolina waters. American Birds 33(5): 715-721.

Until recently the geographical and seasonal distribution of offshore and pelagic birds has constituted one of the weakest areas in our knowledge of North American avifauna. While the distribution of seabirds on the West Coast is now relatively well known (eg. Sanger 1970, Ainley 1977), along the eastern seaboard only the North Atlantic region has been surveyed (Wynne- Edwards 1951, Murphy 1967, Finch et al. 1978), although Richard Rowlett is currently surveying Maryland's offshore waters. There is little need to elaborate on the problems of observing, identifying, photographing, or collecting birds at sea. Much of the published information available on seabirds of the central Atlantic states is based on storm casualties, which do not necessarily reflect normal patterns of distribution, and on widely scattered reports from oceanic trips. Special mention of Paul DuMont's and Robert Ake's offshore excursions should be made since observations from their trips have not only allowed a large number of bird students the opportunity to see unusual pelagic species, but also have contributed significantly to our knowledge of seasonal occurrence. Compiling of these reports, literature records, museum specimens and data obtained from our observations provides a fairly complete summary of the fragmentary knowledge of these birds in local offshore waters.

Lee, D.S., and J.C. Haney. 1984. The Genus *Sula* in the Carolinas: An Overview of the Phenology and Distribution of Gannets and Boobies in the South Atlantic Bight. The Chat 48(2): 29-45.

*Five of the eight recognized species of the genus *Sula* are known from the southeastern United States. Of these only the Northern Gannet (*Sula bassana*) occurs regularly in the Carolinas, but both the Masked Booby (*S. dactylatra*), formerly Blue-faced, and the Brown Booby (*S. leucogaster*) have been reported from North and South Carolina. Of the two remaining species, the Red-footed Booby (*S. sula*) is generally restricted to the Caribbean and disperses northward into the Florida Keys and Gulf of Mexico, whereas the Blue-footed Booby (*S. nebouxii*) is an eastern Pacific species with one accidental and astonishing record from south Padre Island, Texas (5 October 1976, photograph Amer. Birds 31: 349-351).

—. 1996. Manx Shearwater (*Puffinus puffinus*). The Birds of North America 257: 1-28.

*A discussion of distinguishing characteristics, distribution, systematics, migration, habitat, food habits, behavior, breeding and migratory distribution for the Manx Shearwater (*Puffinus puffinus*) including the defined study area for The Point.

Lee, D.S., and K.O. Horner. 1989. Movements of Land-based Birds off the Carolina Coast. Brimleyana 15: 111-121.

Although the occurrence of land-based birds at sea during migration periods is well known, relatively little information is available on the species composition of the flocks detected by radar. This paper lists 96 species documented from the offshore waters of North and South Carolina, offer evidence for offshore movements by groups of birds other than nocturnal migrants, and suggest temporal changes in flock composition.

Lee, D. S., and M.C. Socci . 1989. Potential Effects of Oil Spills on Seabirds and Selected Other Oceanic Vertebrates Off the North Carolina Coast. North Carolina Biological Survey and the North Carolina State Museum of Natural Sciences. Occasional Papers of the NC Biological Survey. 1989-1. Raleigh, NC. 64p.

*The primary purpose of this report is to delineate the possible detrimental effects of an offshore oil spill' on the marine fauna of North Carolina. Understandably, there is much concern about oil reaching North Carolina's beaches and coastal fauna. Unfortunately, the effects of oil on the offshore ecosystem may be even more devastating and less obvious. Many of the offshore fauna, particularly birds, either exist at low populations or have such low reproductive output that population recovery in the event of a kill would be difficult. As will be pointed out, large portions of the total populations of many of these species assemble regularly or seasonally in deep waters off the Outer Banks of North Carolina. Therefore, these species would be particularly vulnerable to oil pollution, and adequate strategies must be developed to protect them if a spill should occur.

Since 1975, the North Carolina State Museum (NCSM) has been studying the marine birds, mammals, and, to a lesser extent, turtles off the coast of North Carolina (Lee 1984, 1986; Lee and Palmer 1981). By chance, the principal study site has been in the general oil-lease area and centered near "The Point," a well-known deep-sea area for sport and commercial fishing southeast of Oregon Inlet. Much of what is presented in this report has been compiled from unpublished information collected during the studies and is on file in the North Carolina State Museum. (Figure 1 illustrates the current oil-lease sites, and Figures 2 through 13 show various monthly observation points recorded during the 14 years of study. Collectively, these figures illustrate the general area of the surveys. Table I provides the total number of field days per month devoted to offshore surveys.)

Any group interested in oil exploration or oil drilling off the North Carolina coast must consider the state's unique position in the Atlantic ecosystem. North Carolina has the largest documented marine bird and mammal fauna of any geographic unit in the North Atlantic. In part, the documented diversity is a result of intensive field research. Studies by the NCSM staff have provided some of the most extensive long-term surveys available for any oceanic area. More than one- third of the birds known from the state's offshore waters were first documented by these studies. However, it is primarily the location of the state in relation to tropical and subtropical areas, migration routes, and oceanic currents that accounts for the diversity of species. For example, the winter avifauna is composed essentially of boreal species that winter in or migrate through North Carolina waters. The summer avifauna consists mainly of foraging tropical and subtropical birds or vagrants of species that normally migrate in the eastern Atlantic. Many of these birds, and others discussed in this report, appear to reach either the northern or southern limits of their known or expected ranges in North Carolina waters (Lee and Booth 1979).

Another reason that oil companies must give special consideration to North Carolina's marine avifauna is that most birds have relatively protracted periods of occurrence off the state's shores. There are several factors that account for this, the more obvious of which include (1) local oceanic currents and upwellings that provide important foraging areas for both low- and high-latitude species, (2) extended migratory periods for particular species because of the staggered schedules of various age groups, and (3) a typically long adolescence in some species during which subadults may linger in local waters for extended periods before returning to nesting areas. Therefore, an oil spill in any season could affect a large number of birds.

Several endangered species occur off the North Carolina coast. In addition, many species in the area represent populations of special concern, i.e., they are species whose global populations could be damaged by an oil spill. Although many of the organisms, particularly birds, have not been regarded as endangered by the United States Fish and Wildlife Service, present data suggest possible oversights. Before the NCSM studies, it was not known that significant portions of certain populations concentrate off the Outer Banks, making them particularly vulnerable to kills occurring there. Furthermore, before the threat of oil spills, nothing in their marine environment could be considered immediately harmful.

Appendix I and Appendix II provide complete lists of the marine birds, mammals, and turtles presently known from North Carolina.

Lee, D.S., and M.L. Moser. 1998. Importance des S*argasses* pelagiques pour la recherché alimentaire des oiseaux marins. El Pitirre 11(3): 111-112.

Based on gut contents of 16 genera and 38 seabird species (n = 1033) and 240 days of at sea observations we document importance and species specific variation in use of *Sargassum* 'reefs'. Over half the seabird species studied forage in this tropical pelagic community. We classify these birds as *Sargassum* specialists (> 25% occurrence of associated prey), users (up to 25% of prey), and incidentals (evidence of use but no associated prey identified).

Sargassum association was documented in most Procellariiforms (9 of 10 species) and less frequently in Charadriiforms (12 of 25). Five seabirds had > 25 % documented use (Audubon's Shearwaters, 59%; Masked Boobies, 100%; Red-necked Phalaropes, 62%; Royal Terns, 40%; and Bridled Terns, 58%). These birds target *Sargassum* for feeding, and the presence or absence of this alga drives local occurrence and abundance. Selected prey tends to be small (15-40 mm) fishes, but each avian species used the resource in specific ways.

It is assumed that birds use this community throughout the tropical and sub-tropical North Atlantic. In view of the low productivity of nutrient poor surface waters in the tropics, the importance of *Sargassum* to seabird abundance and seasonal distribution is assumed to be high. Estimates in the Sargasso Sea (an area larger than the United States) suggest a standing crop of 2.0 — 5.5 metric tons/sq. nautical mile. In the Gulf Stream off the Carolina coast an additional standing crop of 57,290 tons occurs, where *Sargassum* productivity is estimated at 27,074 tons/year. The number of fishes/ton is about 2,400 individuals and the total fish biomass is usually > 1% of the *Sargassum*.

Lee, D.S., and M. Walsh-McGehee. 1998. The White-tailed Tropicbird *Phaethon lepturus*. The Birds of North America 353: 1-24.

*A discussion of distinguishing characteristics, distribution, systematics, migration, habitat, food habits, behavior, breeding and migratory distribution for the White-tailed Tropicbird *Phaethon lepturus* including the defined study area for The Point.

Lee, D.S., W.A. McLellan, R. Boettcher, and W.H. Lang. 1998. Habitat and Living Resources Review: Recent Information on Pelagic Seabirds, Marine Mammals, and Sea Turtles of the North Carolina Outer Continental Shelf and an Evaluation of Effects of Proposed Offshore Oil and Gas Exploration. pp. 53-63. *In*: Vigil, D.L. (ed.). North Carolina/Minerals Management Service Technical Workshop on Manteo Unit Exploration: February 4-5, 1998. U.S. Dept. of the Interior, Minerals Management Service, Gulf of Mexico OCS Region. New Orleans, LA.

*These are the proceedings from a workshop/meeting (conducted on February 4-5, 1998) between the North Carolina Department of Environment and Natural Resources, and the U.S. Department of the Interior's Minerals Management Service (MMS). The geographic area being discussed is approximately 45 miles east-northeast of Cape Hatteras, NC, referred to as the Manteo Unit. This workshop reviewed environmental and socioeconomic information known and needed on the Manteo Unit. The MMS's Gulf of Mexico OCS Regional Director gave an MMS perspective on history and status of the area. Chevron gave a presentation on how the exploratory well would be drilled. The scientific characterization was presented in greater detail by a number of scientific experts who spoke on the following disciplines physical environment, habitat and living resources, seabirds, marine mammals, sea turtles, and social and economic issues. Specific chapters are cited individually, when appropriate.

During the late 1980's, the state of North Carolina responded to a proposal by the Mobil Oil Corporation to undertake exploratory gas/oil operations in Federal lease blocks on the Outer Continental Shelf (OCS) known as the Manteo Unit. One of the products resulting form the permit request was a report that addressed potential biological effects from offshore drilling activities as the related to sea birds and other fauna of the region (Lee and Socci 1989). Chevron USA now proposes an exploratory well on one of the same Manteo blocks originally leased to various oil companies by the Minerals Management Service (MMS). Since 1989, additional information concerning the seabirds, marine mammals, and sea turtles on the North Carolina OCS has been obtained, and new research is planned or underway. This paper is intended to highlight recent development and briefly mention some concerns associated with offshore oil and gas activities that may affect these animals (e.g., Pelagic Seabirds: Globally Endangered Species, Seabirds of Concern; Marine Mammals; Sea Turtles; Potential Effects From Drillship Operations).

Lee, D.S., and W.H. Lang. 1998. Biological Environment: Surface Biota. pp. 84-86. *In*: Vigil, D.L. (ed.). North Carolina/Minerals Management Service Technical Workshop on Manteo Unit Exploration: February 4-5, 1998. U.S. Dept. of the Interior, Minerals Management Service, Gulf of Mexico OCS Region. New Orleans, LA.

*These are the proceedings from a workshop/meeting (conducted on February 4-5, 1998) between the North Carolina Department of Environment and Natural Resources (DENR), and the U.S. Department of the Interior's Minerals Management Service (MMS). The geographic area being discussed is approximately 45 miles east-northeast of Cape Hatteras, North Carolina, referred to as the Manteo Unit. This workshop reviewed environmental and socioeconomic information known and needed, on the Manteo Unit. The MMS's Gulf of Mexico OCS Regional Director gave an MMS perspective on history and status of the area. Chevron gave a presentation on how the exploratory well would be drilled. The scientific characterization was presented in greater detail by a number of scientific experts who spoke on the following disciplines physical environment, habitat and living resources, seabirds, marine mammals, sea turtles, and social and economic issues. Specific chapters are cited individually, when appropriate.

Surface biota during this session was defined as a catch-word phrase to refer to a combination of seabirds, cetaceans, (whales and dolphins), and sea turtles. The group was tasked to discuss immediate concerns that could result from one exploratory drillship's activities on the surface biota in the Manteo Unit. Once potential effects of the exploration well were discussed, remaining time was spent on additional concerns, assuming further development and production were to occur.

Lee, D.S., and N. Vina. 1993. A Re-evaluation of the Status of the Endangered Black-Capped Petrel, *Pterodroma hasitata*, in Cuba. Ornithological Neotropical 4: 99-101.

*The Black-capped Petrel, *Pterodroma hasitata*, is the only extant gadfly petrel known to breed in the West Indies region. Now seriously threatened or endangered, breeding populations are known on only one of the five historically documented breeding islands (the extinct *Pterodroma* of Jamaica is considered a separate species; Mike Imber, pers. comm.). The extant breeding populations on the island of Hispaniola (Dominican Republic and Haiti) are small, fragmented, and currently believed to be declining, although the exact sizes, locations, and detailed chronologies of the breeding colonies remain poorly-studied. Nesting sites are now limited to open-canopy highland forest on inaccessible cliff faces. In addition to direct exploitation by colonists in previous centuries and recent declines in breeding habitat due to deforestation, introduced predators may have played a role in the species' decline. In the late 1970's the reported discovery of a nesting population in a remote area in Cuba (see below) suggested that the species had at least one additional nesting area and that this one was relatively stable.

Lee has heard these Petrels vocalizing at sea off the North Carolina coast in December.

Lee, D.S., and R.A. Rowlett. 1979. Additions to the Seabird Fauna of North Carolina. The Chat 43(1): 1-9.

During the last several years the knowledge of North Carolina's pelagic and offshore avifauna has been greatly enhanced. Not only is information available concerning expected seasonal occurrence of the known fauna (Lee and Booth, in prep.), but documented seabird diversity has significantly increased. Although some information has been obtained accidentally from storm casualties, most of the recent data are a direct result of numerous planned offshore trips for the express purpose of observing and identifying birds at sea. These trips have contributed significantly to the understanding of the seasonal and geographic distribution of seabirds in the western North Atlantic. This paper provides documentation of seven species not previously recognized as occurring in North Carolina's offshore waters, and additional records for the Black-capped Petrel.

The records presented here are mostly incidental observations from a long-range study by Lee on the natural history of seabirds in North Carolina's offshore waters. Information on measurements, geographical and seasonal distribution, food items, and resource partitioning will be presented elsewhere. Studies on external parasites (M.M. Browne, N.C. State University), internal parasites (Ron Mobley, N.C. State University), heavy metal concentrations (Joseph Bonaventura. Duke University Marine Laboratory), and the oil glands (David W. Johnston, University of Florida) of these birds are in progress. Specimens have been deposited in the systematics collection of the North Carolina State Museum (NCSM) and the United States National Museum (USNM), and measurements of those cited in this paper are summarized in Table 1.

Lee, D.S., and S.P. Platania. 1979. Unverified Sight Records of Seabirds in North Carolina Waters. The Chat 43: 79-81.

*Five seabirds not officially recognized as occurring in North Carolina's offshore waters have been sighted off Oregon Inlet between June 1977 and the present. These observations are, for the most part, probably inadequate for admission of the species to the state list. Our intent here is to inform bird students of these unverifiable occurrences so they will be aware of the possibility of encountering these species during those brief observation periods typical of offshore field trips. Although some of this information was available when the paper concerning additions to North Carolina's seabirds (Lee and Rowlett 1979) was submitted for publication, these birds were intentionally not included with those documented by specimens.

Lee, D.S., and S.W. Cardiff. 1993. Status of the Arctic Tern in the Coastal and Offshore Waters of the Southeastern United States. Journal of Field Ornithology 64(2): 158-168.

Sixty-one records of the Arctic Tern (*Sterna paradisaea*) in the coastal southeastern United States (Maryland-Texas, through spring 1991) that were mostly subsequent to a compilation of records by Clapp et at. (1983) are summarized, and a re-analysis of the 81 total regional records (excluding eight questionable reports) is presented. Data are provided on 11 specimen records. There are still no acceptable records for Alabama, Mississippi or Texas, and only sight records for Maryland and South Carolina. This summary supports the findings of Clapp et al. (1983) in that the majority (88%) of records are from spring, and that fall migration through the region is very limited (12%; no fall specimens or photographs). Spring migration is generally later and more protracted than previously indicated. The scarcity of Arctic Terns in fall is attributed to the clockwise Atlantic migration route. The species' relative rarity in spring may result from migration routes that are well-offshore and largely bypass the recessed coast of the southeastern U.S.; June and July birds found along the northern Gulf Coast probably strayed and became "trapped" in the Gulf of Mexico. Caution in the identification of Arctic Terns, and in the evaluation of all (especially early spring) records of this species from the southeastern U.S., is advocated.

Moser, M.L. and D.S. Lee. 1992. A Fourteen-Year Survey of Plastic Ingestion by Western North Atlantic Seabirds. Colonial Waterbirds 15(1): 83-94.

To evaluate the incidence of ocean-borne plastic particle ingestion by western North Atlantic seabirds, we analyzed the gut contents of 1033 birds collected off the coast of North Carolina from 1975-1989. Twenty-one of 38 seabird species (55%) contained plastic particles. Procellariiform birds contained the most plastic and the presence of plastic was clearly correlated with feeding mode and diet. Plastic ingestion by procellariiforms increased over the 14 year study period, probably as a result of increasing plastic particle availability. Some seabirds showed a tendency to select specific plastic shapes and colors, indicating that they may be mistaking plastics for potential prey items. We found no evidence that seabird health was affected by the presence of plastic, even in species containing the largest quantities: Northern Fulmars (*Fulmarus glacialis*), Red Phalaropes (*Phalaropus fulicaria*) and Greater Shearwaters (*Puffinus gravis*).

Orbach, M. 1989. Plenary Session: How Could These Resources be Affected By the Proposed Drilling and What Mitigation Measures Might be Used to Prevent Irreversible Damage. pp. 63-64. *In*: Crawford, K. (ed.). Proceedings: 1989 Marine Expo: The Natural Resources Associated with Mobil's Proposed Drill Site. NC Outer Continental Shelf Office, NC Department of Administration. Raleigh, NC.

*The following is a summary of the plenary session.

There appears to be a good deal of baseline information available about Mobil's proposed drill site area. However, there was a general consensus that there are serious gaps in our understanding of the relationships and functions of the many communities found in and around the exploration area known as the "Manteo Prospect." Some major areas of concern include protection of area benthos, impacts on community ecology, and effects of drilling discharges .

There was almost unanimous support for a monitoring program of the drilling operations and their impacts. Programs should be devised to examine: 1) The fate of drilling discharges, including dispersion (range and extent) and accumulation along fronts and the ocean bottom; and 2) The effects (both chemical and mechanical) of drilling discharges on the benthos, the indigenous fisheries (including eggs/larvae), prey species, forage strategies, and the sargassum communities.

Concerns were also raised regarding the effects the ship and anchor system might have on the biota as a result of displacement, noise, or collisions, and the impacts of exploration activities on the commercial and recreational fisheries found at "The Point."

Because of previous scientific work done at or near the proposed drill site, this area may be well suited to such monitoring programs. Not only would information from these programs be vital for developing mitigation measures, but it could also serve as a critical database on which to build a management framework for future development. In addition, data already collected on local fish resources, marine birds, the benthos and bottom conditions, and physical oceanography could provide an excellent base for further research.

Platania, S.F., G.S. Grant, and D.S. Lee. 1986. Core Temperatures of Non-nesting Western Atlantic Seabirds. Brimleyana 12: 13-18.

Core body temperatures of 23 species of birds collected off the North Carolina coast did not differ with sex, weight, time of day, or season. Within the orders Procellariiformes and Charadriiformes, there seems to be no correlation of temperature with mass. Temperature data on injured birds are similar to those of ones recently killed. Results of this study compared favorably with those obtained by other researchers and indicate no significant differences between body temperatures of foraging and non-incubating procellariiform birds at the nesting colonies. Temperature differences between birds taken at sea and those studied at nesting sites amount to about 1 °C and are best attributed to the activity state of the birds.

Ross, S.W. 1985a. A Summary of Biological Processes in the Proposed VACAPES EMPRESS II Area Off North Carolina Relating to Plankton Communities, Pelagic Macroinvertebrates, Ichthyofauna, Sea turtles, Marine Mammals, and Sea Birds. Appendix B. *In:* U.S. Department of the Navy. EMPRESS II: Supplemental Draft Environmental Impact Statement for the Proposed Operation of the Navy Electromagnetic Pulse Radiation Environment Simulator for Ships (Empress II) in the Chesapeake Bay and Atlantic Ocean. United States Navy. Environmental/ Intergovernmental Section. Atlantic Division. Naval Facilities Engineering and Command. Norfolk, VA.

*This technical report is Appendix B within the "EMPRESS II: Supplemental Draft Environmental Impact Statement for the Proposed Operation of the Navy Electromagnetic Pulse Radiation Environment Simulator for Ships (Empress II) in the Chesapeake Bay and Atlantic Ocean" report. This technical report is a Summary of Biological Processes in the Proposed VACAPES EMPRESS II area off North Carolina Relating to Planktonic Communities, Pelagic Macroinvertebrates, Ichthyofauna, Sea turtles, Marine Mammals, and Sea Birds. Technical reports supporting this summary have been written by authorities in each discipline and are included in Appendices. These supporting technical reports are cited individually. The southern portion of VACAPES EMPRESS II Area of North Carolina overlaps with the northern portion of the defined study area for the Data Inventory Related to the Hatteras Middle Slope (The Point) Area.

Ross, S.W., and A. Scarborough-Bull. 1998. Biological Environment Work Session Results: Fisheries. pp. 76-79. *In*: Vigil, D.L. (ed.). North Carolina/Minerals Management Service Technical Workshop on Manteo Unit Exploration: February 4-5, 1998. U.S. Dept. of the Interior, Minerals Management Service, Gulf of Mexico OCS Region. New Orleans, LA.

*These are the proceedings from a workshop/meeting (conducted on February 4-5, 1998) between the North Carolina Department of Environment and Natural Resources, and the U.S. Department of the

Interior's Minerals Management Service (MMS). The geographic area being discussed is approximately 45 miles east-northeast of Cape Hatteras, NC, referred to as the Manteo Unit. This workshop reviewed environmental and socioeconomic information known and needed on the Manteo Unit. The MMS's Gulf of Mexico OCS Regional Director gave an MMS perspective on history and status of the area. Chevron gave a presentation on how the exploratory well would be drilled. The scientific characterization was presented in greater detail by a number of scientific experts who spoke on the following disciplines physical environment, habitat and living resources, seabirds, marine mammals, sea turtles, and social and economic issues. Specific chapters are cited individuallí, when appropriate.

The goal of this session was to raise scientific concerns/issues regarding the potential impacts of OCS drilling on fisheries. The session specifically recommended information needs on a short-term and long-term basis. The short-term was defined as the time period before exploratory drilling would take place in the Manteo Unit offshore North Carolina. The long-term was defined as the time period before development activities took place in the same location. Due to time constraints, the session spent more time in short-term information needs.

Two major short-term issues were raised concerning fisheries and oil and gas exploration. (1) There is a need to define and describe usage of the area known as The Point. (2) There is a need to synthesize and inventory existing data. Three long-term issues were raised for discussion. Three major long-term issues were raised concerning fisheries and oil and gas exploration. (1) There is a need to better understand the trophodynamics/energetic pathways at The Point. (2) There is a need to understand ichthyoplankton and its ecological role at The Point. (3) There is a need to understand structuring mechanisms. Four additional issues were raised concerning fisheries and oil and gas exploration on a long-term basis. Due to time constraints these concerns were not discussed in detail. (1) Concerns related to discharges from both drilling and production. (2) Concerns related to the presence of either temporary or permanent structures. (3) Concerns related to the effects of noise. (4) Concerns related to the presence of lights. Any endeavors on this project should be tied to the study of the effects of light on the seabirds that feed and/or roost at The Point.

Ross, S.W., K.J. Sulak, J. Gartner, and D.S. Lee. Unpublished data. Ongoing project: Definition of Ecological/Trophic Linkages Among Fishes and Other Nekton in the Area Known as The Point — North Carolina Continental Shelf Slope.

*This is an on-going study of fishes, invertebrates, sargassum and marine birds at the area known as The Point. The emphasis is on trophic linkages. The summer 1999 and 2000 stations were mapped (Fig. 7). Seabird data were collected throughout the cruise.

Rowlett, R.A. 1978. A Massive Flight of Cory's Shearwaters at Cape Hatteras. The Chat 42: 45-46.

*A massive migration of Cory's Shearwaters (*Puffinas diomedea*) was observed from the beach at Cape Point, Cape Hatteras, Dare County, NC., on 28 October 1974. A total of more than 8850 Cory's were counted during 4 hours of continuous observation in the morning and 3 hours late in the afternoon. In addition, Greater Shearwaters (*P. gravis*), Sooty Shearwaters (*P. griseus*), Northern Gannets (*Morus bassanus*), Pomarine Jaegers (*Stercorarius pomarinus*), Parasitic jaegers (*S. parasiticus*), Black-legged Kittiwakes (*Rissa tridactyla*), and Roseate Terns (*Sterna dougallii*) were seen. Table I summarizes our observations. The Point is mentioned.

Shepard, A. (ed.). 1991. Undersea Research at The Point. NURC/UNCW 1991 Undersea Research: Informational Meeting. National Undersea Research Center, University of North Carolina at Wilmington. Wilmington, NC. 9 p.

*This handout provides a summary of research being conducted at "The Point" area (Manteo Lease Block 467).

The National Undersea Research Center at the University of North Carolina at Wilmington, funded by a grant from the National Oceanic and Atmospheric Administration's (NOAA) Office of Undersea Research (OUR), was established in 1980 to promote, facilitate, and conduct research in the Southeastern United States utilizing undersea techniques, including advanced wet diving and manned and unmanned submersibles. A main Center goal is to provide information to NOAA that will assist the agency in fulfilling its charter to explore, understand, conserve and manage the U.S. marine environment and associated resources. To help meet this goal, the Center supports and conducts interdisciplinary oceanographic research projects studying continental margin processes, particularly the interactions and linkages between estuarine, continental shelf, and slope (including submarine canyon) environments.

Tove, M.H. 1997a. Fea's Petrel in North America. Birding 29(3): 207-214.

One of the world's more controversial seabird groups in regard to taxonomy and identification is the soft-plumaged petrel complex. Most authorities currently recognize three species in the complex: Soft-plumaged Petrel (*Pterodroma mollis*), which is widespread throughout the Southern Hemisphere; Fea's Petrel (*P. feae*); and Zino's Petrel (*P. madeira*), which is nearly extinct. Fea's and Zino's Petrels breed only in the eastern Atlantic. Until recently, no member of this complex was thought to occur in the ABA Area. Then, one of them began to be seen regularly off North Carolina, as will be described in Part 11 of this two-part article. Conventional wisdom held that the three species were almost indistinguishable from each other in the field and nearly so in the hand. But, after a thorough re-examination of distribution, breeding cycles, and field identification of the three species, it has been determined that Fea's is the species being seen in the ABA Area.

—. 1997b. Fea's Petrel in North America. Birding 29(4): 309-315.

Part I of this article, which appeared in the June 1997 Birding, summarized the taxonomy, distribution, and identification of the soft-plumaged petrel complex: Soft-plumaged Petrel, Fea's Petrel, and Zino's Petrel. Since 1981, members of this complex have been seen in the ABA Area-primarily off North Carolina and regularly since 1991 -with 17 records documented here in Part II as involving Fea's Petrels or probable Fea's Petrels.

U.S. Department of the Interior, Minerals Management Service. 1989. Environmental Report Visual II: Study Area for Coastal North Carolina. U.S. Department of the Interior, MMS Minerals Management Service, Atlantic OCS Region.

*This map was developed using base mapping from Espey, Houston and Associates, Inc. Draft (base) map is included. This map (Environmental Report Visual II: Study Area for Coastal North Carolina) includes the project area and specifically shows lease blocks, including Manteo Lease Block 467. Features include: Habitat types, Bird Nesting Habitat (described by species), National Wildlife Refuge Boundaries, National Seashore Boundaries, Endangered/Threatened Species (e.g., birds, plants, sea turtles).

U.S. Department of the Interior, Minerals Management Service. 1990. Atlantic Outer Continental Shelf: Final Environmental Report on Proposed Exploratory Drilling Offshore North Carolina, U.S. Department of the Interior, Minerals Management Service, Atlantic OCS Region, Environmental Assessment Section. Herndon, VA.

*Topics include: fisheries, birds, marine mammals, physical oceanography, chemical oceanography, geology, gas and oil production. The proposed action is to drill a single exploratory well approximately 72 km (45 mi) east-northeast of Cape Hatteras, NC in 820 m (2,690 ft) of water. Total depth for the proposed well is 4,267 m (14,000 ft) and the location is on Block 467 on the Minerals Management Service Protraction diagram NI 18-2. The proposal has been submitted by Mobil for itself and 7 partners to drill the well on the approved 21-block exploration unit.

U.S. Department of the Interior, Minerals Management Service. 1992. Proceedings of the Fourth Atlantic OCS Region Information Transfer Meeting, September 1991. U.S. Department of the Interior, Minerals Management Service. Herndon, VA. 198 p.

The Fourth Atlantic Outer Continental Shelf (OCS) Regional Information Transfer Meeting (ITM) was held on 24-25 September, 1991, in Wilmington, NC. The focus of the meeting was on the OCS off North Carolina, specifically on activities related to a proposed exploratory well for oil and gas by Mobil on Block 467 a site 40 miles off the coast of North Carolina. The area of industry interest is known as the Manteo Prospect, while the activities surrounding the proposed drilling are referred to collectively as the Manteo Project. The wildcat wellsite is in 2,690 ft. (857 m) of water near the edge of the Gulf Stream. It is also near a fishing ground known locally as "The Point." The area is believed to be gas prone rather than oil prone. The estimated size of the resource could be as high as 5 trillion cubic feet of gas.

The purpose of the meeting was to exchange information on the leasing background, legislative activities, scientific results, and socioeconomic studies. Legislative-related reports include descriptions of the Oil Pollution Act of 1990, the Outer Banks Protection Act, the Environmental Studies Review Panel, and the North Carolina Physical Oceanography Panel. Reports of studies on marine life include benthic diatoms, benthic fauna, pelagic seabirds, sea turtles, and right whales. One report describes the use of airships (blimps) for ocean research a capability relevant to North Carolina because of the east coast airship facility is located in the state. Local marine science facilities described include NOAA's National Undersea Research Center at the University of North Carolina at Wilmington (NURC/UNCW) and the National Marine Fisheries Service laboratory in Beaufort.

Developments in oil spill cleanup technology and capabilities are described by both the Coast Guard and the industry. A socioeconomic report describes the effects of the oil and gas activities on the tourist industry. Lastly, research on the restoration of salt marshes indicates that rehabilitation of an area is possible when development or an accident has occurred. While the emphasis of the meeting was on oil and gas, two reports described the results of projects related to offshore sand mining. The appendix lists the names and addresses of speakers. Individual chapters are cited individually when appropriate.

U.S. Department of the Navy. 1985. EMPRESS II: Supplemental Draft Environmental Impact Statement for the Proposed Operation of the Navy Electromagnetic Pulse Radiation Environment Simulator for Ships (Empress II) in the Chesapeake Bay and Atlantic Ocean. United States Navy. Environmental/Intergovernmental Section. Atlantic Division. Naval Facilities Engineering and Command. Norfolk, VA.

*This is a National Environmental Policy Act (NEPA) document characterizing the proposed EMPRESS II project. Appendix B contains a Summary of Biological Processes in the Proposed VACAPES EMPRESS II area off North Carolina Relating to Planktonic Communities, Pelagic Macroinvertebrates, Ichthyofauna, Sea turtles, Marine Mammals, and Sea Birds. Technical reports supporting this summary have been written by authorities in each discipline and are included in Appendices. The technical reports are cited individually. The southern portion of VACAPES EMPRESS II Area of North Carolina overlaps with the northern portion of the defined study area for the Data Inventory Related to the Hatteras Middle Slope (The Point) Area.

Vigil, D.L. (ed.). 1998. North Carolina/Minerals Management Service Technical Workshop on Manteo Unit Exploration: February 4-5, 1998. U.S. Dept. of the Interior, Minerals Management Service. Gulf of Mexico OCS Region. New Orleans, LA. 168 p.

*These are the proceedings from a workshop/meeting (conducted on February 4-5, 1998) between the North Carolina Department of Environment and Natural Resources, and the U.S. Department of the Interior's Minerals Management Service (MMS). The geographic area being discussed is approximately 45 miles east-northeast of Cape Hatteras, NC, referred to as the Manteo Unit. This workshop reviewed environmental and socioeconomic information known and needed on the Manteo Unit. The MMS's Gulf of Mexico OCS Regional Director gave an MMS perspective on history and status of the area. Chevron gave a presentation on how the exploratory well would be drilled. The scientific characterization was presented in greater detail by a number of scientific experts who spoke on the following disciplines physical environment, habitat and living resources (invertebrates and fish), seabirds, marine mammals, sea turtles, and social and economic issues. Specific chapters are cited individually, when appropriate.

Watson, G.E., D.S. Lee, and E.S. Backus. 1986. Status and subspecific identity of White-faced Storm-Petrels in the western North Atlantic Ocean. American Birds 40(3): 401-407.

Since 1885, there have been at least 47 records of White-faced Storm-Petrels (*Pelagodroma marina*) in the western North Atlantic Ocean (Table 1). Some of the earliest records are of pelagic sightings from vessels crossing the Atlantic Ocean. Others, particularly in recent years, have been recorded on day trips or short cruises within 100 miles of the coast from Cape Hatteras, North Carolina, North to waters off southern New England. Twelve were collected as specimens; ten of these have been preserved and photographs exist of an eleventh permitting identification of the subspecies that reaches North American waters.

Whaling, P., D.S. Lee, J. Bonaventura, and M. Rentzepis. 1980. The body burden approach of looking at natural mercury accumulation in pelagic seabirds (abstract). Annual Meeting of American Ornithologist's Union.

*This citation includes research conducted within the defined study area for The Point (D. Lee, pers. comm. 24 February 2000). Mr. Lee did not have a copy of this document and we could not otherwise find the document.

Whaling, P. and P.E. Olsen. 1981. Substantial levels of natural mercury found in three species of pelagic seabird (abstract). Southeastern Coastal and Estuarine Birds: A Conference. Baruch Institute, Univ. of SC.

*This citation includes research conducted within the defined study area for The Point (D. Lee, pers. comm. 24 February 2000). Mr. Lee did not have a copy of this document and we could not otherwise find the document.

Wiley, H., and D.S. Lee. 1998. Long-tailed Jeager *Stercorarius longicaudus*. The Birds of North America 365.

*A discussion of distinguishing characteristics, distribution, systematics, migration, habitat, food habits, behavior, breeding and migratory distribution for the Long-tailed Jeager *Stercorarius longicaudus* including the defined study area for The Point. This citation includes research conducted within the defined study area for The Point (D. Lee, pers. comm. 24 February 2000). Mr. Lee did not have a copy of this document and we could not otherwise find the document.

Wiley, R.H., and D.S. Lee. 1999. Parasitic Jeager *Stercorarius parasiticus*. The Birds of North America 445: 1-28.

*A discussion of distinguishing characteristics, distribution, systematics, migration, habitat, food habits, behavior, breeding and migratory distribution for the Parasitic Jeager *Stercorarius parasiticus* including the defined study area for The Point.

—. 2000. Pomarine Jeager *Stercorarius pomarinus*. The Birds of North America 483.

*A discussion of distinguishing characteristics, distribution, systematics, migration, habitat, food habits, behavior, breeding and migratory distribution for the Pomarine Jeager *Stercorarius pomarinus* including the defined study area for The Point. This citation includes research conducted within the defined study area for The Point (D. Lee, pers. comm. 24 February 2000). Mr. Lee did not have a copy of this document and we could not otherwise find the document.

Wingate, D.B., T. Haas, E.S. Brinkley, and J.B. Patteson. 1998. Identification of Bermuda Petrel. Birding 30: 18-36.

Though there have been several probable sight records of Bermuda Petrel in the ABA Area over the last three decades, the species has been documented with photographs within the ABA Area only once, on 26 May 1996 off Hatteras, North Carolina; these photographs are reproduced in the following article. Since its rediscovery in 1951, when only 17 pairs were found, the species has made a slow but steady comeback from the brink of extinction, with 52 nesting pairs at Bermuda and a world population of about 180 birds as of 1996. Past sight records have been clouded by confusion over the identification of this rare seabird, especially its differences from its presumed close relative, the Black-capped Petrel. Increases in both numbers of Bermuda Petrels and in Gulf Stream pelagic trips off the coast of North Carolina might result in more records of the "Cahow" in the ABA Area. In order to distinguish Bermuda Petrel at sea from a small Black-capped Petrel, the following features (in decreasing order of importance) should be observed or evident in photographs:
— A dark eye-patch with deep gray plumage surrounding it, merging with a gray crown and nape, rather than a well-defined dark cap.
— A very limited, amount of white in a narrow fringe bordering the black rump, with the rest of the uppertail area uniformly gray or dark gray — or an uppertail area entirely dark.
— A diffuse area of pale gray, or gray-brown extending down the side of the neck and breast, giving the bird a hooded or cowled appearance overall, rather than a narrow, dark, elongate mark at the side of the breast, as in Black-capped Petrel.
— A relatively small head and especially a smaller bill with less overall arch in the nail of the maxilla, than Black-capped Petrel.
— Underwing pattern similar to that of Black-capped Petrel but with more dark plumage relative to the white internal areas of the underwing.
— Overall size at sea noticeably smaller than, and flight behavior distinctly different from, Black-capped Petrel: the Bermuda Petrel is more buoyant, with wings held slightly bowed and oriented closer to the horizontal than to the vertical during dynamic flight.

For all of these features to he considerable, it is helpful to have numbers of Black-capped Petrels in the vicinity for comparison, and to have a prolonged study of the suspected Bermuda Petrel at close range. On most pelagic trips conducted off North Carolina, fortunately, Black-capped Petrels are observed in good numbers, so that such a comparison would likely be possible.

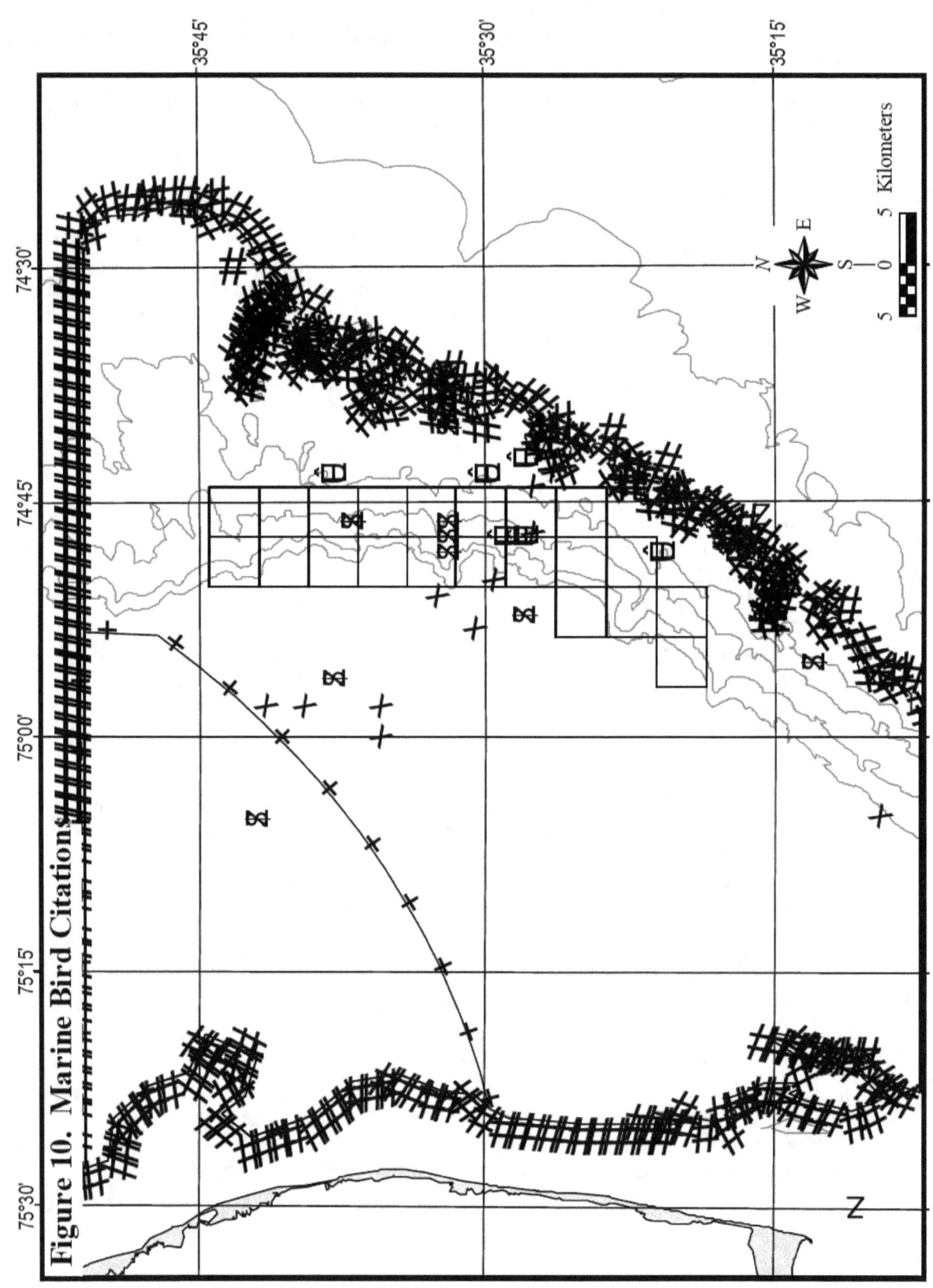

Figure 10. Marine Bird Citations.

Key to Marine Bird Citations (Figure 10).

 Study Area Boundary

☐ Lease Blocks

Mapped Citations

✖ Lee (1988b)

N Lee (1988c)

✚ Lee & Rowlett (1979)

✖ Ross, S. (1985a); U.S. Dept. Navy (1985)

⊟ Tove (1997b)

Studies that Focus on the Manteo Lease Blocks

Blair (1998)
Crawford (1989)
Lee & Lang (1998)
Ross & Scarborough-Bull (1998)
U.S.D.O.I.-Minerals Mgmt. Service (1990, 1992)
Vigil (1998)

Studies that Cover the Hatteras
Middle Slope Area ("The Point")

Browne (1980)
Buckley (1973)
Lee (1989a, 1991a, 1992b, 1999b)
Lee et al. (1998)
Orbach (1989)
Shepard (1991)
U.S.D.O.I.-Minerals Mgmt. Service (1989)

Studies Based on Large
Digitized Databases

Ross et al. (unpub.)

Broad Regional Studies

Abernathy et al. (1989)
Brinkley (1994a, 1994b)
Carter & Parnell (1974)
Clapp et al. (1982a, 1982b, 1983)
Dittmann et al. (1989)
Haney & Lee (1994)
Haney et al. (1991, 1993, 1999)
Hass (1997, in press)
Helmuth (1920)
Jones (1967)
Lee & Booth (1979)
Lee & Cardiff (1993)
Lee & Haney (1984, 1996)
Lee & Horner (1989)
Lee & Irvin (1983)
Lee & Moser (1998)
Lee & Platania (1979)
Lee & Socci (1989)
Lee & Vina (1993)
Lee & Walsh-McGehee (1998)
Lee (1977, 1979, 1984, 1985c, 1986a, 1986c)
Lee (1987a, 1987b, 1988a, 1989b,1991b, 1992a)
Lee (1995a, 1995b, 1999a, 2000)
Lee et al. (1981)
Moser & Lee (1992)
Platania et al. (1986)
Rowlett (1978)
Tove (1997a)

Watson et al. (1986)
Whaling & Olsen (1981)
Whaling et al. (1980)
Wiley & Lee (1998, 1999, 2000)
Wingate et al (1998)

MARINE MAMMAL CHAPTER

MARINE MAMMAL CHAPTER

Abernathy, S.A., M.T. Baer, C.S. Benner, M.S. Brody, D.K. Francois, J.K. Gilliam, L.K. Good, C.J. Ohara, and J.V. Martin. 1989. Atlantic Outer Continental Shelf: Description of the Mid-Atlantic Environment. Abernathy, S. A. (ed.). U.S. Department of the Interior, Minerals Management Service, Atlantic OCS Region, Environmental Assessment Section. Herndon, VA. 167 p.

*This document discusses the major issues and areas of concern for the mid-Atlantic environment that are considered in the planning process for oil and gas leasing and operations on the Outer Continental Shelf (OCS). The issues are addressed with respect to the potential environmental consequences of mid Atlantic oil and gas exploration, development and production. A section discussing The Physical Environment (e.g., geology, non-petroleum minerals, physical oceanography, chemical oceanography and water quality, ocean dumping, meteorology, air quality), Biological resources (e.g., plankton, benthos, fishery resources, marine reptiles, marine mammals, marine and coastal birds, estuaries, wetlands, sensitive coastal habitats, canyon areas), Socioeconomic Environment, and other issues (e.g., archaeological resources, marine vessel traffic, National Aeronautics and Space Administration/ Department of Defense activities, oil and gas infrastructure, marine sanctuaries, and estuarine research reserves) is included. Most of the figures showing fisheries resource distribution are taken from fisheries data compiled for bottom-trawl and shellfish surveys of the National Marine Fisheries Service, Northeast Fisheries Center, Woods Hole, MA.

Bowen, W.B., III. 1989. Marine Mammals and Drilling. p. 62. *In*: Crawford, K. (ed.). Proceedings: 1989 Marine Expo: The Natural Resources Associated with Mobil's Proposed Drill Site. NC Outer Continental Shelf Office, NC Department of Administration. Raleigh, NC.

There are approximately seven species of whales and dolphins that frequent the North Carolina coastal waters from the 100 fathom mark to the inner bays and sounds. Of these seven, three are baleen whales and four are toothed whales and dolphins. The Right Whale (*Eubalaena glacialis*), Atlantic Bottlenose Dolphin (*Tursiops truncatus*) and the Pigmy Sperm Whale are the most dominant. Of these, the Right Whale is the most endangered. Right Whales utilize southern migration routes in the fall to Florida and South Carolina, with many of them remaining along the South Carolina coast where calving and females with calves feed. Then they proceed north in the spring utilizing routes from as near as 500 yards of the shoreline past to the Gulf Stream. There is little known about their habits in vicinity of drilling sites or how they react to heavy boat traffic. Dolphins in the Gulf of Mexico are known to leave drilling sites for weeks to months. The reason may be due to disturbance of the site causing changes to the food source or from sound disturbance. Much can be learned from this type of operation, before, during, and after the fact. By so doing, this will allow all parties to correct or eliminate future problems.

CETAP: Cetacean and Turtle Assessment Program. 1979. A Characterization of Marine Mammals and Turtles in the Mid- and North- Atlantic Areas of the U.S. Outer Continental Shelf: Annual Report for 1979, Cetacean and Turtle Assessment Program, University of Rhode Island. 68 p.

Published reports of sea turtles in the region from Cape Hatteras to Nova Scotia are limited primarily to records of strandings of dead or dying individuals (Bleakney, 1965, Brongersma, 1972). Schwartz (1967) reported the occurrence of sea turtles in near-shore and bay waters of Maryland and Lazell (1976) reported records around Cape Cod, Massachusetts, with added comments and questions about sea turtle in the area. Babcock (1919) summarized information on sea turtles in the Northeast, including locality data, but his work did not include Kemp's ridley turtle, which may have been mistakenly identified at the time as the hawks- bill. While sea turtles have long been known from the region, no comprehensive studies of the temporal distributions and relative numbers were made prior to this study. This chapter addresses data generated in the first year of a study on marine turtles in United States waters up to 200 n.mi. offshore from Cape Hatteras, North Carolina to Nova Scotia as part of the CETAP (Cetacean and Turtle Assessment Program) funded by the Bureau of Land Management. This chapter includes all 1978 and 1979 data collected on Turtle Watch Group (TWG) field efforts, all other CETAP field efforts, and analyses of the data generated by these groups. Additional information contributed by other observers is included as well.

All sea turtles in the area are classified as endangered or threatened. The purpose of this ongoing project is to provide basic information on sea turtles for resource management. Completion of the entire project may change certain data interpretations, ideas, or suppositions presented herein.

Crawford, K. (ed.). 1989. Proceedings: 1989 Marine Expo: The Natural Resources Associated with Mobil's Proposed Drill Site. NC Outer Continental Shelf Office, NC Department of Administration. Raleigh, NC. 64 p.

*This report contains abstracts from each presenter. Chapter topics include: Mobil's Proposal, Geologic Overview — Introduction and Potential for Oil and Gas Discovery, Oceanographic Conditions, Comments on Last MMS Modeling, Biological Production Near the Bottom (invertebrates), Fisheries Resources, Commercial and Recreational Marine Fisheries, Winter Storm Effects on Spawning and Larval Drift of Pelagic Fish, Marine Birds, Sea Turtles in North Carolina, Marine Mammals, Plenary Session, Summary. Each chapter also cited individually when appropriate.

Hoss, D.E. 1992. Research at the Beaufort Laboratory. pp. 51-54. *In*: Department of the Interior, Minerals Management Service. Proceedings of the Fourth Atlantic OCS Region Information Transfer Meeting, September 1991. U.S. Department of the Interior, Minerals Management Service. Herndon, VA.

The Fourth Atlantic Outer Continental Shelf (OCS) Regional Information Transfer Meeting (ITM) was held on 24-25 September, 1991, in Wilmington, NC. The focus of the meeting was on the OCS off North Carolina, specifically on activities related to a proposed exploratory well for oil and gas by Mobil on Block 467 a site 40 miles off the coast of North Carolina. The area of industry interest is known as the Manteo Prospect, while the activities surrounding the proposed drilling are referred to collectively as the Manteo Project. The wildcat wellsite is in 2,690 ft. (857 m) of water near the edge of the Gulf Stream. It is also near a fishing ground known locally as "The Point." The area is believed to be gas prone rather than oil prone. The estimated size of the resource could be as high as 5 trillion cubic feet of gas.

The purpose of the meeting was to exchange information on the leasing background, legislative activities, scientific results, and socioeconomic studies. Legislative-related reports include descriptions of the Oil Pollution Act of 1990, the Outer Banks Protection Act, the Environmental Studies Review Panel, and the North Carolina Physical Oceanography Panel. Reports of studies on marine life include benthic diatoms, benthic fauna, pelagic seabirds, sea turtles, and right whales. One report describes the use of airships (blimps) for ocean research a capability relevant to North Carolina because of the east coast airship facility is located in the state. Local marine science facilities described include NOAA's National Undersea Research Center at the University of North Carolina at Wilmington (NURC/UNCW) and the National Marine Fisheries Service laboratory in Beaufort.

Developments in oil spill cleanup technology and capabilities are described by both the Coast Guard and the industry. A socioeconomic report describes the effects of the oil and gas activities on the tourist industry. Lastly, research on the restoration of salt marshes indicates that rehabilitation of an area is possible when development or an accident has occurred. While the emphasis of the meeting was on oil and gas, two reports described the results of projects related to offshore sand mining. The appendix lists the names and addresses of speakers. Individual chapters are cited individually when appropriate.

*This section describes the ongoing research at the National Marine Fisheries Laboratory in Beaufort, NC. A description of North Carolina marine reptile, marine mammal, coastal, and fishery research is included.

Kraus, S.D. 1992. Right Whales Along the Southeastern United States. pp. 119-25. *In*: Department of the Interior, Minerals Management Service. Proceedings of the Fourth Atlantic OCS Region Information Transfer Meeting, September 1991. U.S. Department of the Interior, Minerals Management Service. Herndon, VA.

The Fourth Atlantic Outer Continental Shelf (OCS) Regional Information Transfer Meeting (ITM) was held on 24-25 September, 1991, in Wilmington, NC. The focus of the meeting was on the OCS off North Carolina, specifically on activities related to a proposed exploratory well for oil and gas by Mobil on Block 467 a site 40 miles off the coast of North Carolina. The area of industry interest is known as the Manteo Prospect, while the activities surrounding the proposed drilling are referred to collectively as the Manteo Project. The wildcat wellsite is in 2,690 ft. (857 m) of water near the edge of the Gulf Stream. It is also near a fishing ground known locally as "The Point." The area is believed to be gas prone rather than oil prone. The estimated size of the resource could be as high as 5 trillion cubic feet of gas.

The purpose of the meeting was to exchange information on the leasing background, legislative activities, scientific results, and socioeconomic studies. Legislative-related reports include descriptions of the Oil Pollution Act of 1990, the Outer Banks Protection Act, the Environmental Studies Review Panel, and the North Carolina Physical Oceanography Panel. Reports of studies on marine life include benthic diatoms, benthic fauna, pelagic seabirds, sea turtles, and right whales. One report describes the use of airships (blimps) for ocean research a capability relevant to North Carolina because of the east coast airship facility is located in the state. Local marine science facilities described include NOAA's National Undersea Research Center at the University of North Carolina at Wilmington and the National Marine Fisheries Service laboratory in Beaufort.

Developments in oil spill cleanup technology and capabilities are described by both the Coast Guard and the industry. A socioeconomic report describes the effects of the oil and gas activities on the tourist industry. Lastly, research on the restoration of salt marshes indicates that rehabilitation of an area is possible when development or an accident has occurred. While the emphasis of the meeting was on oil and gas, two reports described the results of projects related to offshore sand mining. The appendix lists the names and addresses of speakers. Individual chapters are cited individually when appropriate.

*This section describes the importance of coastal North Carolina (and the entire Southeastern United States) as a migratory corridor for right whales (*Eubalaena glacialis*).

Lee, D.S. 1985a. Marine Mammals off the North Carolina Coast with Particular Reference to Possible Impact of Proposed EMPRESS II. Appendix G. *In:* U.S. Department of the Navy. EMPRESS II: Supplemental Draft Environmental Impact Statement for the Proposed Operation of the Navy Electromagnetic Pulse Radiation Environment Simulator for Ships (Empress II) in the Chesapeake Bay and Atlantic Ocean. United States Navy. Environmental/Intergovernmental Section. Atlantic Division. Naval Facilities Engineering and Command. Norfolk, VA.

*This report documents the marine mammals known to occur in North Carolina's offshore waters. The southern portion of the VACAPES EMPRESS II Area of North Carolina overlaps with the northern portion of the defined study area for the Data Inventory Related to the Hatteras Middle Slope (The Point) Area.

—. 1991a. Offshore Research of NC State Museum in Area of the Point. pp. 2-3. *In*: Shepard, A. (ed.). NURC — UNCW 1991 Undersea Research: Informational Meeting. National Undersea Research Center, University of North Carolina at Wilmington. Wilmington, NC.

Although the current information on the biology, distribution, and season of occurrence of seabirds, marine mammals, and marine turtles in North Carolina is still incomplete, it is better than what is available for most other areas of the world. A 15- year extensive study conducted by the NC State Museum (NCSM) is perhaps the longest and most intensive ocean study of seabirds and marine mammals conducted anywhere. The Hatteras area has long been regarded as a biological "Mason-Dixon Line" between boreal and tropical maritime elements. North Carolina is at a latitude usually associated with temperate seas; however, boreal, temperate, and tropical species are transported, or follow prey items transported by converging oceanic currents to the outer continental shelf area at Hatteras. This, in part, explains the diversity. North Carolina has the largest documented marine bird (over 50 species) and marine mammal (28 species) fauna of any geographic unit in the North Atlantic. Much of what has been added to fauna of the state is the result of studies in the area known as "The Point." It is primarily the location of the state in general, and "The Point" in particular, in relation to tropical and subtropical areas, migration routes and oceanic currents that account for the diversity of species. The relatively rich diversity is offset by comparatively low densities, but many of the species found here are tropical ones with small populations, so densities are naturally low. For a tropical — subtropical environment the densities are really quite high. The *Sargassum* community is also discussed.

Lee, D.S., and M.C. Socci . 1989. Potential Effects of Oil Spills on Seabirds and Selected Other Oceanic Vertebrates Off the North Carolina Coast. North Carolina Biological Survey and the North Carolina State Museum of Natural Sciences. Occasional Papers of the NC Biological Survey. 1989-1. Raleigh, NC. 64p.

*The main purpose of this report is to delineate the possible detrimental effects of an offshore oil spill on the marine fauna of North Carolina. Understandably, there is concern about oil reaching North Carolina's beaches and coastal fauna. Unfortunately, the effects of oil on the offshore ecosystem may be even more devastating and less obvious. Many of the offshore fauna, particularly birds, exist at low populations or have such low reproductive output that population recovery in the event of a spill would be difficult. Large portions of the total populations of many of these species assemble regularly or seasonally in deep waters off the Outer Banks of North Carolina. These species would be particularly vulnerable to oil pollution, and adequate strategies must be developed to protect them if a spill should occur.

Since 1975, the North Carolina State Museum (NCSM) has been studying the marine birds, mammals, and, to a lesser extent, turtles off the coast of North Carolina. By chance, the principal study site has been in the general oil-lease area and centered near "The Point", a well-known deep-sea area for sport and commercial fishing southeast of Oregon Inlet. Much of what is presented in this report has been compiled from unpublished information collected during the studies and is on file in the NCSM. (Figure 1 illustrates the current oil-lease sites, and Figures 2-13 show various monthly observation points recorded during the 14 years of study. Collectively, these figures illustrate the general area of the surveys. Table I provides the total number of field days per month devoted to offshore surveys.)

Anyone interested in oil exploration or drilling off North Carolina must consider the state's unique position in the Atlantic ecosystem. North Carolina has the largest documented marine bird and mammal fauna of any geographic unit in the North Atlantic. In part, the documented diversity is a result of intensive field research. Studies by the NCSM have provided extensive long-term surveys available for any oceanic area. More than one-third of the birds known from the state's offshore waters were first documented by these studies. However, it is primarily the location of the state in relation to tropical and subtropical areas, migration routes, and oceanic currents that accounts for the diversity of species. For example, the winter avifauna is composed essentially of boreal species that winter in or migrate through North Carolina waters. The summer avifauna consists mainly of foraging tropical and subtropical birds or vagrants of species that normally migrate in the eastern Atlantic. Many of these birds, and others, appear to reach either the northern or southern limits of their known or expected ranges in NC waters.

Another reason that oil companies must give special consideration to North Carolina's marine avifauna is that most birds have relatively protracted periods of occurrence here. There are several factors that account for this, the more obvious of which include: (1) local oceanic currents and upwellings that provide important foraging areas for both low and high latitude species, (2) extended migratory periods for particular species, and (3) a typically long adolescence in some species during which subadults may linger in local waters for extended periods before returning to nesting areas. Therefore, an oil spill in any season could affect a large number of birds.

Several endangered species occur off the North Carolina coast. In addition, many species in the area represent populations of special concern, i.e., they are species whose global populations could be damaged by an oil spill. Although many of the organisms, particularly birds, have not been regarded as endangered by the US Fish and Wildlife Service, present data suggest possible oversights. Before the NCSM studies, it was not known that significant portions of certain populations concentrate off the Outer Banks, making them particularly vulnerable to spills occurring there. Furthermore, before the threat of oil spills, nothing in their marine environment could be considered immediately harmful.

Appendix I and Appendix II provide complete lists of the marine birds, mammals, and turtles presently known from North Carolina.

Lee, D.S., W.A. McLellan, R. Boettcher, and W.H. Lang. 1998. Habitat and Living Resources Review: Recent Information on Pelagic Seabirds, Marine Mammals, and Sea Turtles of the North Carolina Outer Continental Shelf and an Evaluation of Effects of Proposed Offshore Oil and Gas Exploration. pp. 53-63. *In*: Vigil, D.L. (ed.). North Carolina/Minerals Management Service Technical Workshop on Manteo Unit Exploration: February 4-5, 1998. U.S. Dept. of the Interior, Minerals Management Service, Gulf of Mexico OCS Region. New Orleans, LA.

*These are the proceedings from a workshop/meeting (conducted on February 4-5, 1998) between the North Carolina Department of Environment and Natural Resources, and the U.S. Department of the Interior's Minerals Management Service (MMS). The geographic area being discussed is approximately 45 miles east-northeast of Cape Hatteras, NC, referred to as the Manteo Unit. This workshop reviewed environmental and socioeconomic information known and needed on the Manteo Unit. The MMS's Gulf of Mexico OCS Regional Director gave an MMS perspective on history and status of the area. Chevron gave a presentation on how the exploratory well would be drilled. The scientific characterization was presented in greater detail by a number of scientific experts who spoke on the following disciplines physical environment, habitat and living resources, seabirds, marine mammals, sea turtles, and social and economic issues. Specific chapters are cited individually, when appropriate.

During the late 1980's, the state of North Carolina responded to a proposal by the Mobil Oil Corporation to undertake exploratory gas/oil operations in Federal lease blocks on the Outer Continental Shelf (OCS) known as the Manteo Unit. One of the products resulting form the permit request was a report that addressed potential biological effects from offshore drilling activities as the related to sea birds and other fauna of the region (Lee and Socci 1989). Chevron USA now proposes an exploratory well on one of the same Manteo blocks originally leased to various oil companies by the Minerals Management Service (MMS). Since 1989, additional information concerning the seabirds, marine mammals, and sea turtles on the North Carolina OCS has been obtained, and new research is planned or underway. This paper is intended to highlight recent development and briefly mention some concerns associated with offshore oil and gas activities that may affect these animals (e.g., Pelagic Seabirds: Globally Endangered Species, Seabirds of Concern; Marine Mammals; Sea Turtles; Potential Effects From Drillship Operations).

Lee, D.S., and W.H. Lang. 1998. Biological Environment: Surface Biota. pp. 84-86. *In*: Vigil, D.L. (ed.). North Carolina/Minerals Management Service Technical Workshop on Manteo Unit Exploration: February 4-5, 1998. U.S. Dept. of the Interior, Minerals Management Service, Gulf of Mexico OCS Region. New Orleans, LA .

*These are the proceedings from a workshop/meeting (conducted on February 4-5, 1998) between the North Carolina Department of Environment and Natural Resources, and the U.S. Department of the Interior's Minerals Management Service (MMS). The geographic area being discussed is approximately 45 miles east-northeast of Cape Hatteras, NC, referred to as the Manteo Unit. This workshop reviewed environmental and socioeconomic information known and needed on the Manteo Unit. The MMS's Gulf of Mexico OCS Regional Director gave an MMS perspective on history and status of the area. Chevron gave a presentation on how the exploratory well would be drilled. The scientific characterization was presented in greater detail by a number of scientific experts who spoke on the following disciplines physical environment, habitat and living resources, seabirds, marine mammals, sea turtles, and social and economic issues. Specific chapters are cited individually, when appropriate.

Surface biota during this session was defined as a catch-word phrase to refer to a combination of seabirds, cetaceans, (whales and dolphins), and sea turtles. The group was tasked to discuss immediate concerns that could result from one exploratory drillship's activities on the surface biota in the Manteo Unit. Once potential effects of the exploration well were discussed, remaining time was spent on additional concerns, assuming further development and production were to occur.

Orbach, M. 1989. Plenary Session: How Could These Resources be Affected By the Proposed Drilling and What Mitigation Measures Might be Used to Prevent Irreversible Damage. pp. 63-64. *In*: Crawford, K. (ed.). Proceedings: 1989 Marine Expo: The Natural Resources Associated with Mobil's Proposed Drill Site. NC Outer Continental Shelf Office, NC Department of Administration. Raleigh, NC.

*The following is a summary of the plenary session.

There appears to be a good deal of baseline information available about Mobil's proposed drill site area. However, there was a general consensus that there are serious gaps in our understanding of the relationships and functions of the many communities found in and around the exploration area known as the "Manteo Prospect." Some major areas of concern include protection of area benthos, impacts on community ecology, and effects of drilling discharges.

There was almost unanimous support for a monitoring program of the drilling operations and their impacts. Programs should be devised to examine: 1) The fate of drilling discharges, including dispersion (range and extent) and accumulation along fronts and the ocean bottom; and 2) The effects (both chemical and mechanical) of drilling discharges on the benthos, the indigenous fisheries (including eggs/larvae), prey species, forage strategies, and the sargassum communities.

Concerns were also raised regarding the effects the ship and anchor system might have on the biota as a result of displacement, noise, or collisions, and the impacts of exploration activities on the commercial and recreational fisheries found at "The Point."

Because of previous scientific work done at or near the proposed drill site, this area may be well suited to such monitoring programs. Not only would information from these programs be vital for developing mitigation measures, but it could also serve as a critical database on which to build a management framework for future development. In addition, data already collected on local fish resources, marine birds, the benthos and bottom conditions, and physical oceanography could provide an excellent base for further research.

*This text also mentions marine mammals and Threatened and Endangered species (marine reptiles).

Ross, S.W. 1985a. A Summary of Biological Processes in the Proposed VACAPES EMPRESS II Area Off North Carolina Relating to Plankton Communities, Pelagic Macroinvertebrates, Ichthyofauna, Sea turtles, Marine Mammals, and Sea Birds. Appendix B. *In:* U.S. Department of the Navy. EMPRESS II: Supplemental Draft Environmental Impact Statement for the Proposed Operation of the Navy Electromagnetic Pulse Radiation Environment Simulator for Ships (Empress II) in the Chesapeake Bay and Atlantic Ocean. United States Navy. Environmental/ Intergovernmental Section. Atlantic Division. Naval Facilities Engineering and Command. Norfolk, VA.

*This technical report is Appendix B in the "EMPRESS II: Supplemental Draft Environmental Impact Statement for the Proposed Operation of the Navy Electromagnetic Pulse Radiation Environment Simulator for Ships (Empress II) in the Chesapeake Bay and Atlantic Ocean" report. The report is a Summary of Biological Processes in the Proposed VACAPES EMPRESS II area off North Carolina Relating to Planktonic Communities, Pelagic Macroinvertebrates, Ichthyofauna, Sea turtles, Marine Mammals, and Sea Birds. Technical reports supporting this summary were written by authorities in each discipline and are included in Appendices. These supporting technical reports are cited individually. The southern portion of VACAPES EMPRESS II Area of North Carolina overlaps with the northern portion of the defined study area for the Data Inventory Related to the Hatteras Middle Slope (The Point) Area.

Shepard, A. (ed.). 1991. Undersea Research at The Point. NURC/UNCW 1991 Undersea Research: Informational Meeting. National Undersea Research Center, University of North Carolina at Wilmington. Wilmington, NC. 9 p.

*This handout provides a summary of research being conducted at "The Point" area (Manteo Lease Block 467).

The National Undersea Research Center at the University of North Carolina at Wilmington, funded by a grant from the National Oceanic and Atmospheric Administration's (NOAA) Office of Undersea Research, was established in 1980 to promote, facilitate, and conduct research in the Southeastern United States utilizing undersea techniques, including advanced wet diving and manned and unmanned submersibles. A main Center goal is to provide information to NOAA that will assist the agency in fulfilling its charter to explore, understand, conserve and manage the U.S. marine environment and associated resources. To help meet this goal, the Center supports and conducts interdisciplinary oceanographic research projects studying continental margin processes, particularly the interactions and linkages between estuarine, continental shelf, and slope (including submarine canyon) environments.

U.S. Department of the Interior, Minerals Management Service. 1990. Atlantic Outer Continental Shelf: Final Environmental Report on Proposed Exploratory Drilling Offshore North Carolina, U.S.

Department of the Interior, Minerals Management Service, Atlantic OCS Region, Environmental Assessment Section. Herndon, VA.

*Topics include: fisheries, birds, marine mammals, physical oceanography, chemical oceanography, geology, gas and oil production. The proposed action is to drill a single exploratory well approximately 72 km (45 mi) east-northeast of Cape Hatteras, NC in 820 m (2,690 ft) of water. Total depth for the proposed well is 4,267 m (14,000 ft) and the location is on Block 467 on the Minerals Management Service Protraction diagram NI 18-2. The proposal has been submitted by Mobil for itself and 7 partners to drill the well on the approved 21-block exploration unit.

U.S. Department of the Interior, Minerals Management Service. 1992. Proceedings of the Fourth Atlantic OCS Region Information Transfer Meeting, September 1991. U.S. Department of the Interior, Minerals Management Service. Herndon, VA. 198 p.

The Fourth Atlantic Outer Continental Shelf (OCS) Regional Information Transfer Meeting (ITM) was held on 24-25 September, 1991, in Wilmington, NC. The focus of the meeting was on the OCS off North Carolina, specifically on activities related to a proposed exploratory well for oil and gas by Mobil on Block 467 a site 40 miles off the coast of North Carolina. The area of industry interest is known as the Manteo Prospect, while the activities surrounding the proposed drilling are referred to collectively as the Manteo Project. The wildcat wellsite is in 2,690 ft. (857 m) of water near the edge of the Gulf Stream. It is also near a fishing ground known locally as "The Point." The area is believed to be gas prone rather than oil prone. The estimated size of the resource could be as high as 5 trillion cubic feet of gas.

The purpose of the meeting was to exchange information on the leasing background, legislative activities, scientific results, and socioeconomic studies. Legislative-related reports include descriptions of the Oil Pollution Act of 1990, the Outer Banks Protection Act, the Environmental Studies Review Panel, and the North Carolina Physical Oceanography Panel. Reports of studies on marine life include benthic diatoms, benthic fauna, pelagic seabirds, sea turtles, and right whales. One report describes the use of airships (blimps) for ocean research a capability relevant to North Carolina because of the east coast airship facility is located in the state. Local marine science facilities described include NOAA's National Undersea Research Center at the University of North Carolina at Wilmington and the National Marine Fisheries Service laboratory in Beaufort.

Developments in oil spill cleanup technology and capabilities are described by both the Coast Guard and the industry. A socioeconomic report describes the effects of the oil and gas activities on the tourist industry. Lastly, research on the restoration of salt marshes indicates that rehabilitation of an area is possible when development or an accident has occurred. While the emphasis of the meeting was on oil and gas, two reports described the results of projects related to offshore sand mining. The appendix lists the names and addresses of speakers. Individual chapters are cited individually when appropriate.

U.S. Department of the Navy. 1985. EMPRESS II: Supplemental Draft Environmental Impact Statement for the Proposed Operation of the Navy Electromagnetic Pulse Radiation Environment Simulator for Ships (Empress II) in the Chesapeake Bay and Atlantic Ocean. United States Navy. Environmental/ Intergovernmental Section. Atlantic Division. Naval Facilities Engineering and Command. Norfolk, VA.

*This is a National Environmental Policy Act document characterizing the proposed EMPRESS II project. Appendix B contains a Summary of Biological Processes in the Proposed VACAPES EMPRESS II area off North Carolina Relating to Planktonic Communities, Pelagic Macroinvertebrates, Ichthyofauna, Sea turtles, Marine Mammals, and Sea Birds. Technical reports supporting this summary have been written by authorities in each discipline and are included in Appendices. The technical reports are cited individually. The southern portion of VACAPES EMPRESS II Area of North Carolina overlaps with the northern portion of the defined study area for the Data Inventory Related to the Hatteras Middle Slope (The Point) Area.

Vigil, D.L. (ed.). 1998. North Carolina/Minerals Management Service Technical Workshop on Manteo Unit Exploration: February 4-5, 1998. U.S. Dept. of the Interior, Minerals Management Service. Gulf of Mexico OCS Region. New Orleans, LA. 168 p.

*These are the proceedings from a workshop/meeting (February 4-5, 1998) between the North Carolina Department of Environment and Natural Resources and the U.S. Department of the Interior's Minerals Management Service (MMS). The geographic area being discussed is approximately 45 miles east-northeast of Cape Hatteras, NC, referred to as the Manteo Unit. This workshop reviewed environmental and socioeconomic information known and needed on the Manteo Unit. The MMS's Gulf of Mexico OCS Regional Director gave an MMS perspective on history and status of the area. Chevron gave a presentation on how the exploratory well would be drilled. The scientific characterization was presented in greater detail by a number of scientific experts who spoke on the following disciplines physical environment, habitat and living resources (invertebrates and fish), seabirds, marine mammals, sea turtles, and social and economic issues. Specific chapters are cited individually, when appropriate.

Wiley, D.N., R.A. Asmutis, T.D. Pitchford, and D.P. Gannon. 1994. Stranding and mortality of humpback whales, *Megaptera novaeangliae*, in the mid-Atlantic and southeast United States, 1985-1992. Fishery Bulletin 93: 196-205.

Marine mammal strandings are a result of, or result in, mortality that may be attributed to natural or anthropogenic factors. As such, stranding data can provide insight on spatial distribution, seasonal movements, and mortality factors pertaining to marine mammal populations (Woodhouse, 1991; Mead).

The general distribution and migratory movements of humpback whales, *Megaptera novaeangliae*, in the western North Atlantic are well known from numerous studies based on the identification of individual animals and on other techniques. Humpbacks feed in high latitude areas during the summer months, including waters of the Gulf of Maine, eastern Canada, West Greenland, and Iceland (Hain et al., 1982; Martin et al., 1984; Perkins et al., 1984; Katona and Beard 1990). In the winter, whales from all populations migrate to breeding grounds in the West Indies (Balcomb and Nichols, 1982; Mattila and Clapham, 1989; Mattila et al., 1989; Katona and Beard 1990). Between these migratory end points, little is known of the distribution of the species. In recent years, however, there has been an apparent increase in the frequency of sightings of humpback whales off the mid-Atlantic coast of the United States (Swingle et al., 1993). Furthermore, a considerable number of strandings have been documented along the mid-Atlantic and southeast coasts, many in midwinter, a time when the majority of humpbacks are thought to be located in tropical waters. In this paper, we analyze data from these strandings, discuss implication regarding distribution and possible spatial segregation by age class and examine apparent causes of mortality.

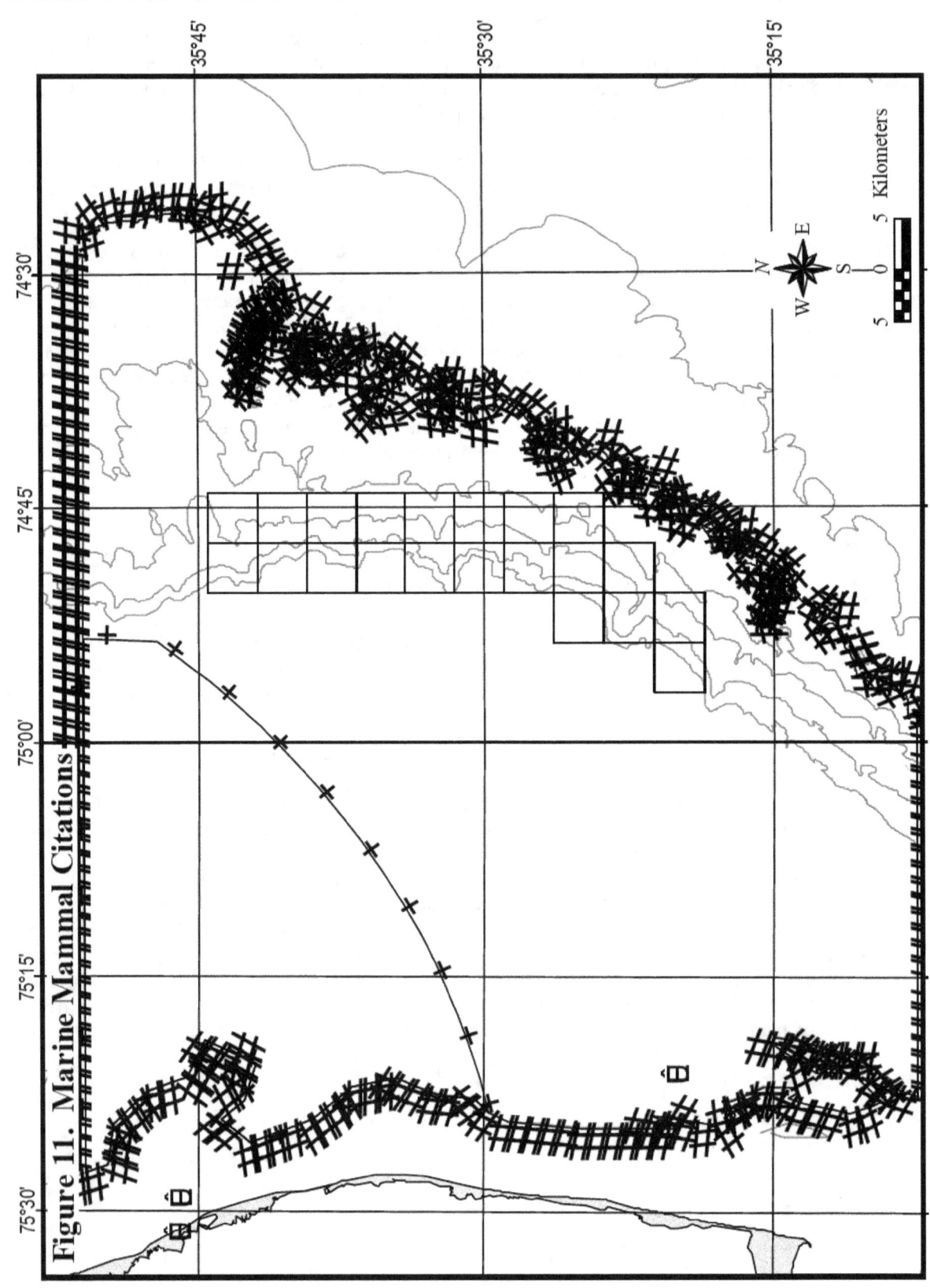

Figure 11. Marine Mammal Citations

Key to Marine Mammal Citations (Figure 11).

Study Area Boundary

Lease Blocks

Mapped Citations

Ross, S. (1985a); U.S. Dept. Navy (1985)

Wiley et al. (1994)

Studies that Cover the Hatteras Middle Slope Area ("The Point")

Lee (1991)
Lee et al. (1998)
Orbach (1989)
Shepard (1991)

Broad Regional Studies

Abernathy et al. (1989)
CETAP (1979)
Hoss (1992)
Kraus (1992)
Lee (1985a)
Lee & Socci (1989)

Studies that Focus on the Manteo Lease Blocks

Bowen (1989)
Crawford (1989)
Lee & Lang (1998)
U.S.D.O.I.-Minerals Mgmt. Service (1990, 1992)
Vigil (1998)

MARINE REPTILE CHAPTER

MARINE REPTILE CHAPTER

Abernathy, S.A., M.T. Baer, C.S. Benner, M.S. Brody, D.K. Francois, J.K. Gilliam, L.K. Good, C.J. Ohara, and J.V. Martin. 1989. Atlantic Outer Continental Shelf: Description of the Mid-Atlantic Environment. Abernathy, S.A. (ed.). U.S. Department of the Interior, Minerals Management Service, Atlantic OCS Region, Environmental Assessment Section. Herndon, VA. 167 p.

*This document discusses the major issues and areas of concern for the mid-Atlantic environment that are considered in the planning process for oil and gas leasing and operations on the Outer Continental Shelf. The issues are addressed with respect to the potential environmental consequences of mid Atlantic oil and gas exploration, development and production. A section discussing The Physical Environment (e.g., geology, non-petroleum minerals, physical oceanography, chemical oceanography and water quality, ocean dumping, meteorology, air quality), Biological resources (e.g., plankton, benthos, fishery resources, marine reptiles, marine mammals, marine and coastal birds, estuaries, wetlands, sensitive coastal habitats, canyon areas), Socioeconomic Environment, and other issues (e.g., archaeological resources, marine vessel traffic, National Aeronautics and Space Administration/ Department of Defense activities, oil and gas infrastructure, marine sanctuaries, and estuarine research reserves) is included. Most of the figures showing fisheries resources are taken from bottom-trawl and shellfish surveys of the National Marine Fisheries Service, Northeast Fisheries Center, Woods Hole, MA.

CETAP: Cetacean and Turtle Assessment Program. 1979. A Characterization of Marine Mammals and Turtles in the Mid- and North- Atlantic Areas of the U.S. Outer Continental Shelf: Annual Report for 1979, Cetacean and Turtle Assessment Program, University of Rhode Island. 68 p.

Published reports of sea turtles in the region from Cape Hatteras to Nova Scotia are limited primarily to records of strandings of dead or dying individuals (Bleakney, 1965, Brongersma, 1972). Schwartz (1967) reported the occurrence of sea turtles in near-shore and bay waters of Maryland and Lazell (1976) reported records around Cape Cod, Massachusetts, with added comments and questions about sea turtle in the area. Babcock (1919) summarized information on sea turtles in the Northeast, including locality data, but his work did not include Kemp's ridley turtle, which may have been mistakenly identified at the time as the hawks- bill. While sea turtles have long been known from the region, no comprehensive studies of the temporal distributions and relative numbers were made prior to this study. This chapter addresses data generated in the first year of a study on marine turtles in United States waters up to 200 n.mi. offshore from Cape Hatteras, North Carolina to Nova Scotia as part of the CETAP (Cetacean and Turtle Assessment Program) funded by the Bureau of Land Management. This chapter includes all 1978 and 1979 data collected on Turtle Watch Group (TWG) field efforts, all other CETAP field efforts, and analyses of the data generated by these groups. Additional information contributed by other observers is included as well.

All sea turtles in the area are classified as endangered or threatened. The purpose of this ongoing project is to provide basic information on sea turtles for resource management. Completion of the entire project may change certain data interpretations, ideas, or suppositions presented herein.

Coles, W.C., and J.A. Musick. 2000. Satellite sea surface temperature analysis and correlation with sea turtle distribution off North Carolina. Copeia 2000(2): 551-554.

We used satellite sea surface temperature data and aerial survey data to identify an upper (28 C) and lower (13.3 C) thermal limit to preferred loggerhead sea turtle temperatures. The available temperature range for the turtles to occupy, during this study (May 1991 to Sept. 1992), was 4.9 C to

32.2 C. These thermal limits fall within the ranges previously identified in the laboratory. This study suggests that sea turtles are not geographically randomly distributed but stay within preferred temperature ranges which are seasonally variable.

Coston-Clements, L., L.R. Settle, D.E. Hoss, and F.A. Cross. 1991. Utilization of the Sargassum Habitat by Marine Invertebrates and Vertebrates — A Review. National Marine Fisheries Service. NOAA. Southeast Fisheries Science Center, Beaufort Laboratory. Beaufort, NC. 32 p.

Numerous species of brown algae (Class Cyclosporeae: Order Fucales: Family Fucaceae) of the genus *Sargassum* occur throughout the world's tropical and temperate oceans. The pelagic complex in the western North Atlantic is comprised primarily of *Sargassum natans* and *S. fluitans*. Both species are hyponeustonic and fully adapted to a pelagic existence (Parr, 1939). Known commonly as gulf-weed, sea holly, or sargassum, they are characterized by a brushy, highly branched thallus (stem) with numerous leaf-like blades and berry-like pneumatocysts (floats). These floating plants may be up to several meters in length-but are typically much smaller. There is a well known assemblage of small fishes associated with sargassum rafts, many of which serve as forage for commercially or recreationally exploited species (Table 2). Dooley (1972) described 54 species from 23 families in the sargassum community of the Florida Current. Only 14 species from 11 families are known from the Sargasso Sea (Fedoryako, 1980; 1989). During the pelagic stage, hatchling loggerhead, *Caretta caretta*, green, *Chelonia mydas*, Kemp's ridley, *Lepidochelys kempi*, and hawksbill, *Eretmochelys imbricata*, sea turtles have been observed in sargassum off Florida, Georgia, North Carolina, and Texas (Smith, 1968; Fletemeyer, 1978; Carr and Meylan, 1980; Carr, 1986; 1987a; Schwartz, 1988; 1989; Manzella and Williams, 1991; Schwartz, pers. comm.). Schwartz (1988) reported numerous loggerhead hatchlings captured during commercial trawling for sargassum. This observation constitutes the largest known aggregation of loggerhead hatchlings encountered off the North Carolina coast.

Crawford, K. (ed.). 1989. Proceedings: 1989 Marine Expo: The Natural Resources Associated with Mobil's Proposed Drill Site. NC Outer Continental Shelf Office, NC Department of Administration. Raleigh, NC. 64 p.

*This report contains abstracts from each presenter. Chapter topics include: Mobil's Proposal, Geologic Overview — Introduction and Potential for Oil and Gas Discovery, Oceanographic Conditions, Comments on Last MMS Modeling, Biological Production Near the Bottom (invertebrates), Fisheries Resources, Commercial and Recreational Marine Fisheries, Winter Storm Effects on Spawning and Larval Drift of Pelagic Fish, Marine Birds, Sea Turtles in North Carolina, Marine Mammals, Plenary Session, Summary. Each chapter also cited individually when appropriate.

Epperly, S.P., J. Braun, A.J. Chester, F.A. Cross, J.V. Merriner, and P.A. Tester. 1995. Winter distribution of sea turtles in the vicinity of Cape Hatteras and their interactions with the summer flounder trawl fishery. Bulletin of Marine Science 56(2): 547-568.

Aerial surveys of North Carolina offshore waters between Cape Lookout and the North Carolina/Virginia state line were conducted November 1991-March 1992 to determine the abundance of sea turtles in the area where a trawl fishery for summer flounder was active, and to relate the distribution of turtles to physical oceanographic processes. Turtles were sighted throughout the winter as far north as Oregon Inlet. Individual surveys yielded surface density estimates greater than 12 turtles / 100 km^2, depending on the method of analysis. The distribution of turtles appeared to be related to water temperature, with turtles being mostly in waters >11° C. Favorable temperature and depth regimes for sea turtles occur throughout the winter along the western edge of the Gulf Stream from the vicinity of Cape Hatteras southward. The nearshore waters of Raleigh Bay, more than any other nearshore area of the South Atlantic Bight, are affected in the winter by the warm, fast-moving Gulf Stream and its frontal eddies that impinge upon and override the narrow continental shelf. Characteristically the waters in the vicinity of Cape Hatteras are warmer in the winter than nearshore areas to the south. The narrowness of the continental shelf and the influence of the Gulf Stream on these nearshore regions serve to concentrate sea turtles emigrating from nearshore waters in the Middle Atlantic Bight and Pamlico and Core Sounds in the late fall and early winter. Thus, sea turtles can be at greater risk for interaction with fishing activity on the continental shelf near Cape Hatteras, during the winter, than in any other area in the South Atlantic Bight. The summer flounder fishery, operating between Cape May, New Jersey and Cape Lookout, North Carolina during November 1991-February 1992, was monitored for interactions with sea turtles. Observers were aboard nearly 6% of the reported trips landed in Virginia and North Carolina. The sea turtle catch comprised loggerheads (60%), Kemp's ridleys (36%), greens (2%), and a hawksbill (1%). The catch of Kemp's ridleys during November-December 1991 south of Cape Hatteras was high (N = 26). Overall turtle catch rates were similar to those reported for the Atlantic shrimp fishery, but catch rates south of Cape Hatteras were 6-8 times higher than catch rates north of the Cape. A total of 1,063 turtles was estimated to have been caught November 1991-February 1992, and 89-181 were estimated to have died as a result of the trawl fishery. None of the turtles tagged during this study was recaptured during the study period, but three were recaptured subsequently; one had been resuscitated. Trawl activity was aggregated, and a number of turtles required resuscitation after 60 min tows. Sea turtle conservation regulations are needed for this fishery because the turtle/fishery interaction is great (> 1,000 turtles estimated caught), the proportion caught that is Kemp's ridleys is high (35%), and the physical processes that concentrate the sea turtles on the fishing grounds are operable every winter.

Epperly, S.P., N.B. Thompson, J.A. Keinath, J.A. Musick, and D.T. Crouse. 1989. Sea Turtles in North Carolina. pp. 49-61. *In*: Crawford, K. (ed.). Proceedings: 1989 Marine Expo: The Natural Resources Associated with Mobil's Proposed Drill Site. NC Outer Continental Shelf Office. NC Department of Administration. Raleigh, NC.

In 1973 Congress enacted the Endangered Species Act (PL93-205) immediately listing the leatherback (*Dermochelys coriacea*), hawksbill (*Eretmochelys imbricata*), and Kemp's ridley (*Lepidochelys kempi*) as endangered sea turtles. In 1978 the loggerhead (*Caretta caretta*), green (*Chelonia mydas*), and olive ridley (*L. olivacea*) were listed as threatened species except that the Florida and Mexican Pacific coast breeding populations of green sea turtles, and the Mexican Pacific coast breeding population of olive ridleys were listed as endangered (U.S. Dept. Commerce 1978). Only the flatback sea turtle of Australia (*C. depressa*) has not been listed. Of the six species of sea turtles in the Atlantic Ocean, all but one of them, the olive ridley, has been reported off the coast of North America.

In summary, the offshore waters of North Carolina regularly harbor all North American species of sea turtles except the hawksbill, which is infrequently reported. Inshore waters of the Pamlico-Albemarle Estuarine Complex and of the Chesapeake Bay seasonally contain numbers of loggerhead and Kemp's ridley sea turtles, and in Pamlico and Core Sounds, the green sea turtle is also present. The turtles' seasonal abundance in the area is probably a function of water temperature — as the waters warm they immigrate or migrate through, and as the waters cool, they emigrate. Sea turtles are capable of hibernating and sometimes overwinter in cool waters by burying in the substrate (Ogren and McVea 1982). Although there have been a couple of reports of turtles overwintering in North Carolina (T. Henson, N.C. Wildlife Resources Commission, pers. commun.), there are no data to indicate the extent to which turtles hibernate in the state's waters.

George, R.Y., and A.W. Hulbert (eds.). 1989. North Carolina Coastal Symposium. National Undersea Research Program, NOAA. Rockville, MD. 582 p.

*This is a multidisciplinary Marine Scientific Proceedings, with frequent reference to the North Carolina Coastal Oceanography. Two studies (also cited individually) include maps with study plots (p. 283; reef site) or migratory movements (p. 309; sea turtles) in the project study area. Zoogeography and ecology of fishes inhabiting North Carolina's Marine Waters to depths of 600 meters are included. The transcript from speaker representing Outer Continental Shelf (p. 549) mentions offshore oil drilling off North Carolina Coast and mid-Atlantic region. The speaker does not refer to a specific site.

Hoss, D.E. 1992. Research at the Beaufort Laboratory. pp. 51-54. *In*: Department of the Interior, Minerals Management Service. Proceedings of the Fourth Atlantic OCS Region Information Transfer Meeting, September 1991. U.S. Department of the Interior, Minerals Management Service. Herndon, VA.

The Fourth Atlantic Outer Continental Shelf (OCS) Regional Information Transfer Meeting (ITM) was held on 24-25 September, 1991, in Wilmington, NC. The focus of the meeting was on the OCS off North Carolina, specifically on activities related to a proposed exploratory well for oil and gas by Mobil on Block 467 a site 40 miles off the coast of North Carolina. The area of industry interest is known as the Manteo Prospect, while the activities surrounding the proposed drilling are referred to collectively as the Manteo Project. The wildcat wellsite is in 2,690 ft. (857 m) of water near the edge of the Gulf Stream. It is also near a fishing ground known locally as "The Point." The area is believed to be gas prone rather than oil prone. The estimated size of the resource could be as high as 5 trillion cubic feet of gas.

The purpose of the meeting was to exchange information on the leasing background, legislative activities, scientific results, and socioeconomic studies. Legislative-related reports include descriptions of the Oil Pollution Act of 1990, the Outer Banks Protection Act, the Environmental Studies Review Panel, and the North Carolina Physical Oceanography Panel. Reports of studies on marine life include benthic diatoms, benthic fauna, pelagic seabirds, sea turtles, and right whales. One report describes the use of airships (blimps) for ocean research a capability relevant to North Carolina because of the east coast airship facility is located in the state. Local marine science facilities described include NOAA's National Undersea Research Center at the University of North Carolina at Wilmington (NURC/UNCW) and the National Marine Fisheries Service laboratory in Beaufort.

Developments in oil spill cleanup technology and capabilities are described by both the Coast Guard and the industry. A socioeconomic report describes the effects of the oil and gas activities on the tourist industry. Lastly, research on the restoration of salt marshes indicates that rehabilitation of an area is possible when development or an accident has occurred. While the emphasis of the meeting was on oil and gas, two reports described the results of projects related to offshore sand mining. The appendix lists the names and addresses of speakers. Individual chapters are cited individually when appropriate.

*Ongoing research at the National Marine Fisheries Laboratory in Beaufort, NC is described. A description of North Carolina marine reptile, marine mammal, coastal, and fishery research is included.

Keinath, J.A. 1992. Sea Turtles Off the North Carolina Coast. pp. 111-117. *In*: Department of the Interior, Minerals Management Service. Proceedings of the Fourth Atlantic OCS Region Information Transfer Meeting, September 1991. U.S. Department of the Interior, Minerals Management Service. Herndon, VA.

The Fourth Atlantic Outer Continental Shelf (OCS) Regional Information Transfer Meeting was held on 24-25 September, 1991, in Wilmington, NC. The focus of the meeting was on the OCS off North Carolina, specifically on activities related to a proposed exploratory well for oil and gas by Mobil on

Block 467 a site 40 miles off the coast of North Carolina. The area of industry interest is known as the Manteo Prospect, while the activities surrounding the proposed drilling are referred to collectively as the Manteo Project. The wildcat wellsite is in 2,690 ft. (857 m) of water near the edge of the Gulf Stream. It is also near a fishing ground known locally as "The Point." The area is believed to be gas prone rather than oil prone. The estimated size of the resource could be as high as 5 trillion cubic feet of gas.

The purpose of the meeting was to exchange information on the leasing background, legislative activities, scientific results, and socioeconomic studies. Legislative-related reports include descriptions of the Oil Pollution Act of 1990, the Outer Banks Protection Act, the Environmental Studies Review Panel, and the North Carolina Physical Oceanography Panel. Reports of studies on marine life include benthic diatoms, benthic fauna, pelagic seabirds, sea turtles, and right whales. One report describes the use of airships (blimps) for ocean research a capability relevant to North Carolina because of the east coast airship facility is located in the state. Local marine science facilities described include NOAA's National Undersea Research Center at the University of North Carolina at Wilmington and the National Marine Fisheries Service laboratory in Beaufort.

Developments in oil spill cleanup technology and capabilities are described by both the Coast Guard and the industry. A socioeconomic report describes the effects of the oil and gas activities on the tourist industry. Lastly, research on the restoration of salt marshes indicates that rehabilitation of an area is possible when development or an accident has occurred. While the emphasis of the meeting was on oil and gas, two reports described the results of projects related to offshore sand mining. The appendix lists the names and addresses of speakers. Individual chapters are cited individually when appropriate.

*This section describes sea turtle data (e.g., from strandings, tagging programs, trawl fisheries, aerial surveys, and telemetry) from coastal North Carolina. These data suggest coastal North Carolina is used as a migratory corridor by sea turtles. The role of sargassum mats as habitat is described.

Lazzell, J.D., Jr. 1980. New England Waters: Critical Habitat for Marine Turtles. Copeia 1980(2): 290-295.

New England waters, herein defined as all marine habitats north of the Nantucket Lightship, out to the "200 mile" limit, and north to Canadian territory, contain the largest known late summer and autumn (August to November) concentrations of the leatherback in the Atlantic. Inshore habitats in the southern sector (primarily Massachusetts) formerly supported thousands of Kemp's ridleys seasonally; despite overall decline of *Lepidochelys kempi,* they are still common in Massachusetts today. A significant population of subadult greens summers in Nantucket Sound. The hawksbill is rare and probably accidental.

*Figure 1 Mercator projection of the North Atlantic region showing major migration routes of the leatherback, with key locations marked, (p. 292) includes the defined study area for The Point.

Lee, D.S. 1985b. Marine Turtles in North Carolina Waters. Appendix F. *In:* U.S. Department of the Navy. EMPRESS II: Supplemental Draft Environmental Impact Statement for the Proposed Operation of the Navy Electromagnetic Pulse Radiation Environment Simulator for Ships (Empress II) in the Chesapeake Bay and Atlantic Ocean. United States Navy. Environmental/ Intergovernmental Section. Atlantic Division. Naval Facilities Engineering and Command. Norfolk, VA.

*This report describes seasonal distributions of marine turtles in North Carolina's offshore waters. Lee and Palmer (1981) previously summarized this material. The southern portion of the VACAPES EMPRESS II Area of North Carolina overlaps with the northern portion of the defined study area for the Data Inventory Related to the Hatteras Middle Slope (The Point) Area.

—. 1991a. Offshore Research of NC State Museum in Area of the Point. pp. 2-3. *In*: Shepard, A. (ed.). NURC — UNCW 1991 Undersea Research: Informational Meeting. National Undersea Research Center, University of North Carolina at Wilmington. Wilmington, NC.

Although the current information on the biology, distribution, and season of occurrence of seabirds, marine mammals, and marine turtles in North Carolina is still incomplete, it is better than what is available for most other areas of the world. A 15- year extensive study conducted by the NC State Museum (NCSM) is perhaps the longest and most intensive ocean study of seabirds and marine mammals conducted anywhere. The Hatteras area has long been regarded as a biological "Mason-Dixon Line" between boreal and tropical maritime elements. North Carolina is at a latitude usually associated with temperate seas; however, boreal, temperate, and tropical species are transported, or follow prey items transported by converging oceanic currents to the outer continental shelf area at Hatteras. This, in part, explains the diversity. North Carolina has the largest documented marine bird (over 50 species) and marine mammal (28 species) fauna of any geographic unit in the North Atlantic. Much of what has been added to fauna of the state is the result of studies in the area known as "The Point." It is primarily the location of the state in general, and "The Point" in particular, in relation to tropical and subtropical areas, migration routes and oceanic currents that account for the diversity of species. The relatively rich diversity is offset by comparatively low densities, but many of the species found here are tropical ones with small populations, so densities are naturally low. For a tropical — subtropical environment the densities are really quite high. The *Sargassum* community is also discussed.

Lee, D.S., and W.H. Lang. 1998. Biological Environment: Surface Biota. pp. 84-86. *In*: Vigil, D.L. (ed.). North Carolina/Minerals Management Service Technical Workshop on Manteo Unit Exploration: February 4-5, 1998. U.S. Dept. of the Interior, Minerals Management Service, Gulf of Mexico OCS Region. New Orleans, LA .

*These are the proceedings from a workshop/meeting (February 4-5, 1998) between the North Carolina Department of Environment and Natural Resources and the U.S. Department of the Interior's Minerals Management Service (MMS). The geographic area discussed is approximately 45 miles east-northeast of Cape Hatteras, NC, referred to as the Manteo Unit. This workshop reviewed environmental and socioeconomic information known and needed on the Manteo Unit. The MMS's Gulf of Mexico OCS Regional Director gave an MMS perspective on history and status of the area. Chevron gave a presentation on how the exploratory well would be drilled. The scientific characterization was presented in greater detail by a number of scientific experts who spoke on the following disciplines physical environment, habitat and living resources, seabirds, marine mammals, sea turtles, and social and economic issues. Specific chapters are cited individually, when appropriate.

Surface biota during this session was defined as a catch-word phrase to refer to a combination of seabirds, cetaceans, (whales and dolphins), and sea turtles. The group was tasked to discuss immediate concerns that could result from one exploratory drillship's activities on the surface biota in the Manteo Unit. Once potential effects of the exploration well were discussed, remaining time was spent on additional concerns, assuming further development and production were to occur.

Lee, D.S., W.A. McLellan, R. Boettcher, and W.H. Lang. 1998. Habitat and Living Resources Review: Recent Information on Pelagic Seabirds, Marine Mammals, and Sea Turtles of the North Carolina Outer Continental Shelf and an Evaluation of Effects of Proposed Offshore Oil and Gas Exploration. pp. 53-63. *In*: Vigil, D.L. (ed.). North Carolina/Minerals Management Service Technical Workshop on Manteo Unit Exploration: February 4-5, 1998. U.S. Dept. of the Interior, Minerals Management Service, Gulf of Mexico OCS Region. New Orleans, LA.

*These are the proceedings from a workshop/meeting (February 4-5, 1998) between the North Carolina Department of Environment and Natural Resources and the U.S. Department of the Interior's Minerals Management Service (MMS). The geographic area discussed is approximately 45 miles east-northeast of Cape Hatteras, NC, referred to as the Manteo Unit. This workshop reviewed environmental and socioeconomic information known and needed on the Manteo Unit. The MMS's Gulf of Mexico OCS Regional Director gave an MMS perspective on history and status of the area. Chevron gave a presentation on how the exploratory well would be drilled. The scientific characterization was presented in greater detail by a number of scientific experts who spoke on the following disciplines physical environment, habitat and living resources, seabirds, marine mammals, sea turtles, and social and economic issues. Specific chapters are cited individually, when appropriate.

During the late 1980's, the state of North Carolina responded to a proposal by the Mobil Oil Corporation to undertake exploratory gas/oil operations in Federal lease blocks on the Outer Continental Shelf (OCS) known as the Manteo Unit. One of the products resulting form the permit request was a report that addressed potential biological effects from offshore drilling activities as the related to sea birds and other fauna of the region (Lee and Socci 1989). Chevron USA now proposes an exploratory well on one of the same Manteo blocks originally leased to various oil companies by the Minerals Management Service (MMS). Since 1989, additional information concerning the seabirds, marine mammals, and sea turtles on the North Carolina OCS has been obtained, and new research is planned or underway. This paper is intended to highlight recent development and briefly mention some concerns associated with offshore oil and gas activities that may affect these animals (e.g., Pelagic Seabirds: Globally Endangered Species, Seabirds of Concern; Marine Mammals; Sea Turtles; Potential Effects From Drillship Operations).

Lee, D.S., and W.M. Palmer. 1981. Records of Leatherback Turtles, *Dermochelys coriacea* (Linnaeus), and Other Marine Turtles in North Carolina Waters. Brimleyana 5: 95-106.

New information is presented on the occurrence of five species of marine turtles in North Carolina waters *Dermochelys coriacea* and *Caretta caretta*, the two most commonly occurring species, are emphasized. Thirty-three unpublished records of *Dermochelys*, for North Carolina, and information from other sources, indicate that in North Carolina at least, this turtle typically occurs throughout the warmer months in relatively shallow shelf waters. It may not be an open-ocean wanderer.

Musick, J.A. 1985. Final Report on the Distribution and Abundance of Sea Turtles in the Proposed EMPRESS II Operating Sites. Appendix I: *In:* U.S. Department of the Navy. EMPRESS II: Supplemental Draft Environmental Impact Statement for the Proposed Operation of the Navy Electromagnetic Pulse Radiation Environment Simulator for Ships (Empress II) in the Chesapeake Bay and Atlantic Ocean. United States Navy. Environmental/ Intergovernmental Section. Atlantic Division. Naval Facilities Engineering and Command. Norfolk, VA.

*This report describes distribution and abundance of marine turtles from the Chesapeake Bay, Virginia to North Carolina's coastal waters. The southern portion of the VACAPES EMPRESS II Area of North Carolina overlaps with the northern portion of the defined study area for the Data Inventory Related to the Hatteras Middle Slope (The Point) Area.

Orbach, M. 1989. Plenary Session: How Could These Resources be Affected By the Proposed Drilling and What Mitigation Measures Might be Used to Prevent Irreversible Damage. pp. 63-64. *In*: Crawford, K. (ed.). Proceedings: 1989 Marine Expo: The Natural Resources Associated with Mobil's Proposed Drill Site. NC Outer Continental Shelf Office, NC Department of Administration. Raleigh, NC.

*The following is a summary of the plenary session.

There appears to be a good deal of baseline information available about Mobil's proposed drill site area. However, there was a general consensus that there are serious gaps in our understanding of the relationships and functions of the many communities found in and around the exploration area known as the "Manteo Prospect." Some major areas of concern include protection of area benthos, impacts on community ecology, and effects of drilling discharges .

There was almost unanimous support for a monitoring program of the drilling operations and their impacts. Programs should be devised to examine: 1) The fate of drilling discharges, including dispersion (range and extent) and accumulation along fronts and the ocean bottom; and 2) The effects (both chemical and mechanical) of drilling discharges on the benthos, the indigenous fisheries (including eggs/larvae), prey species, forage strategies, and the sargassum communities.

Concerns were also raised regarding the effects the ship and anchor system might have on the biota as a result of displacement, noise, or collisions, and the impacts of exploration activities on the commercial and recreational fisheries found at "The Point."

Because of previous scientific work done at or near the proposed drill site, this area may be well suited to such monitoring programs. Not only would information from these programs be vital for developing mitigation measures, but it could also serve as a critical database on which to build a management framework for future development. In addition, data already collected on local fish resources, marine birds, the benthos and bottom conditions, and physical oceanography could provide an excellent base for further research.

*This text also mentions marine mammals and Threatened and Endangered species (marine reptiles).

Renaud, M., G. Gitschlag, E. Klima, A. Shah, D. Koi, and J. Nance. 1993. Loss of shrimp by turtle excluder devices (TEDS) in coastal waters of the United States, North Carolina to Texas: March 1988-August 1990. Fishery Bulletin 91: 129-137.

Observers from the National Marine Fisheries Service collected information on catch rates of shrimp aboard commercial shrimp vessels during March 1988-August 1990. Comparisons were made between nets equipped with Turtle Excluder Devices (TEDS) and standard shrimp nets. Three types of TEDs were tested: Georgia TEDs with and without accelerator funnels, and Super Shooter TEDs with funnels.

Fishing areas, time of day, and duration of tows were controlled by the captain of each vessel to simulate commercial conditions. A statistically-significant ($P<0.05$) mean loss in shrimp catch-per-unit-effort (CPUE) of 0.24 lb/h (3.6%) and 0.93 lb/h (13.6%) was exhibited by nets equipped with Georgia TEDs (with and without funnels, respectively) compared with standard nets. There was no significant difference in shrimp CPUE between standard nets and nets equipped with Super Shooter TEDs with a funnel.

Ross, S.W. 1985a. A Summary of Biological Processes in the Proposed VACAPES EMPRESS II Area Off North Carolina Relating to Plankton Communities, Pelagic Macroinvertebrates, Ichthyofauna, Sea turtles, Marine Mammals, and Sea Birds. Appendix B. *In:* U.S. Department of the Navy. EMPRESS II: Supplemental Draft Environmental Impact Statement for the Proposed Operation of the Navy Electromagnetic Pulse Radiation Environment Simulator for Ships (Empress II) in the Chesapeake Bay and Atlantic Ocean. United States Navy. Environmental/ Intergovernmental Section. Atlantic Division. Naval Facilities Engineering and Command. Norfolk, VA.

*This technical report is Appendix B within the "EMPRESS II: Supplemental Draft Environmental Impact Statement for the Proposed Operation of the Navy Electromagnetic Pulse Radiation Environment Simulator for Ships (Empress II) in the Chesapeake Bay and Atlantic Ocean" report.

The report is a Summary of Biological Processes in the Proposed VACAPES EMPRESS II area off North Carolina Relating to Planktonic Communities, Pelagic Macroinvertebrates, Ichthyofauna, Sea turtles, Marine Mammals, and Sea Birds. Technical reports supporting this summary were written by authorities in each discipline and are included in Appendices. These supporting technical reports are cited individually. The southern portion of VACAPES EMPRESS II Area of North Carolina overlaps with the northern portion of the defined study area for the Data Inventory Related to the Hatteras Middle Slope (The Point) Area.

Schwartz, F.J. 1989. Outer Continental Shelf. pp. 309-332. *In*: George, R.Y. and A.W. Hulbert (eds.). North Carolina Coastal Symposium. National Undersea Research Program. NOAA. Rockville, MD.

Five species of rare and endangered sea turtles frequent North Carolina's coast. Their abundance and seasonality is influenced by water mass and Gulf Stream currents, seasonal water temperatures, and effects of natural and man's alteration of the available habitat. Annually, 200 — 500 loggerhead nests are found on state beaches. Green turtles have nested in recent years on only six occasions. The pattern of nesting varies depending on position of the Gulf Stream and seasonal water temperatures. Natural causes (cold stunning or attacks by sharks) account for some turtle deaths. A limited number of deaths result from ingestion of artificial substances. Most deaths are man induced. Recent, often meager, conservation efforts have attempted to protect incubating nests by screening or removal to hatcheries. A sanctuary was established off one of the most productive beaches in the state (Onslow Beach) to lessen fishing fleet influence on adult turtles. Accommodation must be made by man to further protect sea turtles, otherwise a valuable heritage will be lost forever.

*A map showing sea turtle migratory routes (Fig. 1) through the defined project area for The Point is included.

Settle, L.R. 1997. Commercial harvest of pelagic Sargassum: A summary of landings since June 1995. *In*: South Atlantic Fishery Management Council. Essential Fish Habitat Workshop # 9: October 7 — 8, 1997 Pelagic Habitat Sargassum and Water Column. South Atlantic Fishery Management Council. Charleston, SC. May 1997. 66 p.

The commercial harvest of pelagic *Sargassum* resumed in June 1995. To date the fishery is prosecuted by a single firm, Aqua-10 Corporation of Beaufort, North Carolina. Aqua-10 processes the raw algae into a variety of agricultural fertilizers and dietary supplements used in the swine and poultry industries. The firm purchases algae harvested by local fishing vessels. Two vessels, the FV Outer Banks (16.5 m snapper boat) and the FV Rising Sun (15 m long-liner) have been equipped with Sargassum nets by Aqua- 10. The gear consists of a 1.2 in x 0.9 n frame trawl rigged with 7.6 am mesh trawl webbing. The vessels harvest algae ancillary to their normal fishing activities. When algae are landed, Aqua-10 notifies the NMFS, Beaufort Laboratory. The algae are examined for by-catch at dockside and at the processing plant. Vessel captains are interviewed to obtain data on the date and location of harvests, effort, and by-catch.

All algae have been harvested from off the North Carolina coast from northern Onslow Bay to northeast of Cape Hatteras (Fig. 2). Although Sargassum has been harvested on the continental shelf, most was obtained in the Gulf Stream (Fig. 3). The observed by-catch has been minimal in terms of numbers of individuals. No sea turtles and few fishes have been noted. Most fish have been young juveniles and are generally in advanced stages of decomposition. Identifiable taxa include filefish (*Monacanthus hispidus*), amberjacks (*Seriola* spp.), blue runner (*Caranx crysos*), jacks (*Caranx* spp.), flyingfish (Exocoetidae), sergeant major (*Abudefduf saxatilis*), gray triggerfish (*Balistes capriscus*), sargassum fish (*Histrio histrio*), and pipefish (*Syngnathus* spp.). The most commonly observed macrofaunal by-catch have been crustaceans including several shrimp (genera *Hippolyte*, *Latreutes*, and *Leander*) and crabs (genera *Planes* and *Portunus*).

Shepard, A. (ed.). 1991. Undersea Research at The Point. NURC/UNCW 1991 Undersea Research: Informational Meeting. National Undersea Research Center, University of North Carolina at Wilmington. Wilmington, NC. 9 p.

*This handout is a summary of research being conducted at "The Point" area (Manteo Lease Block 467).

The National Undersea Research Center at the University of North Carolina at Wilmington, funded by a grant from the National Oceanic and Atmospheric Administration's (NOAA) Office of Undersea Research, was established in 1980 to promote, facilitate, and conduct research in the Southeastern United States utilizing undersea techniques, including advanced wet diving and manned and unmanned submersibles. A main Center goal is to provide information to NOAA that will assist the agency in fulfilling its charter to explore, understand, conserve and manage the U.S. marine environment and associated resources. To help meet this goal, the Center supports and conducts interdisciplinary oceanographic research projects studying continental margin processes, particularly the interactions and linkages between estuarine, continental shelf, and slope (including submarine canyon) environments.

Shoop, C.R., and R.D. Kenny. 1992. Seasonal distributions and abundances of loggerhead and leatherback sea turtles in waters of the northeastern United States. Herpetological Monographs 6: 43-67.

Seasonal distributions and abundances of loggerhead *(Caretta caretta)* and leatherback *(Dermochelys coriacea)* sea turtles in continental shelf waters off the coast of the northeastern United States were derived from more than three years of aerial and shipboard surveys. There were 3460 sea turtle sightings, including 2841 loggerheads, 128 leatherbacks, and 491 unidentified. Relative abundance patterns, corrected for uneven distribution of survey effort, demonstrated an extensive area of loggerhead distribution from near Long Island, New York, along the mid-shelf to near Cape Hatteras, North Carolina. Areas of high relative abundance of leatherbacks were more scattered. with clusters south of Long Island and in the central and eastern Gulf of Maine. Loggerheads occurred significantly farther south (x = 38° 20′ N) than leatherbacks (x = 40° 05′ N), and in significantly warmer waters (mean surface temperatures of 22.9° C and 20.4° C, respectively). The two species did not differ significantly in water depth or bottom slope at sighting; the modal depth interval for both was 21-40 m. Patterns of distribution and concentration of sea turtles differed greatly from nearly all species of marine mammals, suggesting little overlap in resource utilization. Both relative and absolute density estimates were much higher for loggerheads. Overall mean relative densities were 21.6 loggerheads per 1000 km of survey track, and 6.85 leatherbacks per 1000 km. Absolute density estimates, derived from 454 special aerial surveys, ranged from 1.64×10^{-3} to 5.10×10^{-1} loggerheads km^{-2} and 2.09×10^{-3} to 2.16×10^{-2} leatherbacks km^{-2}. The maximum densities for both species were higher than values reported for the Gulf of Mexico and off the eastern Florida shore. Total study area populations during the summer were estimated at 2200-11,000 loggerheads and 100-900 leatherbacks. These estimates are minimal because they are based on observations of turtles at the surface, and may represent much greater abundances. The patterns of relative abundance derived from this analysis could be used as a basis for the designation of critical sea turtle habitat off the northeastern U.S.

U.S. Department of the Interior, Minerals Management Service. 1989. Environmental Report Visual II: Study Area for Coastal North Carolina. U.S. Department of the Interior, MMS Minerals Management Service, Atlantic OCS Region.

*This map was developed using base mapping from Espey, Houston and Associates, Inc. This map (Environmental Report Visual II: Study Area for Coastal North Carolina) includes the project area and specifically shows lease blocks, including Manteo Lease Block 467. Features include: Habitat types, Bird Nesting Habitat (described by species), National Wildlife Refuge Boundaries, National Seashore Boundaries, Endangered/Threatened Species (e.g., birds, plants, sea turtles).

U.S. Department of the Interior, Minerals Management Service. 1992. Proceedings of the Fourth Atlantic OCS Region Information Transfer Meeting, September 1991. U.S. Department of the Interior, Minerals Management Service. Herndon, VA. 198 p.

The Fourth Atlantic Outer Continental Shelf (OCS) Regional Information Transfer Meeting was held on 24-25 September 1991 in Wilmington, NC. The focus of the meeting was on the OCS off North Carolina, specifically on activities related to a proposed exploratory well for oil and gas by Mobil on Block 467 a site 40 miles off the coast of North Carolina. The area of industry interest is known as the Manteo Prospect, while the activities surrounding the proposed drilling are referred to collectively as the Manteo Project. The wildcat wellsite is in 2,690 ft. (857 m) of water near the edge of the Gulf Stream. It is also near a fishing ground known locally as "The Point." The area is believed to be gas prone rather than oil prone. The estimated size of the resource could be as high as 5 trillion cubic feet of gas.

The purpose of the meeting was to exchange information on the leasing background, legislative activities, scientific results, and socioeconomic studies. Legislative-related reports include descriptions of the Oil Pollution Act of 1990, the Outer Banks Protection Act, the Environmental Studies Review Panel, and the North Carolina Physical Oceanography Panel. Reports of studies on marine life include benthic diatoms, benthic fauna, pelagic seabirds, sea turtles, and right whales. One report describes the use of airships (blimps) for ocean research a capability relevant to North Carolina because of the east coast airship facility is located in the state. Local marine science facilities described include NOAA's National Undersea Research Center at the University of North Carolina at Wilmington and the National Marine Fisheries Service laboratory in Beaufort.

Developments in oil spill cleanup technology and capabilities are described by both the Coast Guard and the industry. A socioeconomic report describes the effects of the oil and gas activities on the tourist industry. Lastly, research on the restoration of salt marshes indicates that rehabilitation of an area is possible when development or an accident has occurred. While the emphasis of the meeting was on oil and gas, two reports described the results of projects related to offshore sand mining. The appendix lists the names and addresses of speakers. Individual chapters are cited individually when appropriate.

U.S. Department of the Navy. 1985. EMPRESS II: Supplemental Draft Environmental Impact Statement for the Proposed Operation of the Navy Electromagnetic Pulse Radiation Environment Simulator for Ships (Empress II) in the Chesapeake Bay and Atlantic Ocean. United States Navy. Environmental/ Intergovernmental Section. Atlantic Division. Naval Facilities Engineering and Command. Norfolk, VA.

*This is a National Environmental Policy Act document characterizing the proposed EMPRESS II project. Appendix B is a Summary of Biological Processes in the Proposed VACAPES EMPRESS II area off North Carolina Relating to Planktonic Communities, Pelagic Macroinvertebrates, Ichthyofauna, Sea turtles, Marine Mammals, and Sea Birds. Technical reports (cited individually) supporting this summary were written by authorities in each discipline and are included in Appendices. The southern portion of VACAPES EMPRESS II Area of North Carolina overlaps with the northern portion of the defined study area for the Data Inventory Related to the Hatteras Middle Slope (The Point) Area.

Vigil, D.L. (ed.). 1998. North Carolina/Minerals Management Service Technical Workshop on Manteo Unit Exploration: February 4-5, 1998. U.S. Dept. of the Interior, Minerals Management Service. Gulf of Mexico OCS Region. New Orleans, LA. 168 p.

*These are the proceedings from a workshop/meeting (February 4-5, 1998) between the North Carolina Department of Environment and Natural Resources and the U.S. Department of the Interior's Minerals Management Service (MMS). The geographic area being discussed is approximately 45 miles east-northeast of Cape Hatteras, NC, referred to as the Manteo Unit. This workshop reviewed environmental and socioeconomic information known and needed on the Manteo Unit. The MMS's Gulf of Mexico OCS Regional Director gave an MMS perspective on history and status of the area. Chevron gave a presentation on how the exploratory well would be drilled. The scientific characterization was presented in greater detail by a number of scientific experts who spoke on the following disciplines physical environment, habitat and living resources (invertebrates and fish), seabirds, marine mammals, sea turtles, and social and economic issues. Specific chapters are cited individually, when appropriate.

Witzell, W.N. 1999. Distribution and relative abundance of sea turtles caught incidentally by the U.S. pelagic longline fleet in the western North Atlantic Ocean, 1992-1995. Fishery Bulletin 97: 200-211.

*This paper examines the seasonal distribution and relative abundance of threatened and endangered sea turtles (e.g., loggerhead sea turtle, *Caretta caretta*; and leatherback sea turtle, *Dermochelys coriacea*) caught incidentally by the U.S. Atlantic pelagic longline fishery for tuna, *Thunnus* spp., and swordfish, *Xiphias gladius* from 1992-1995.

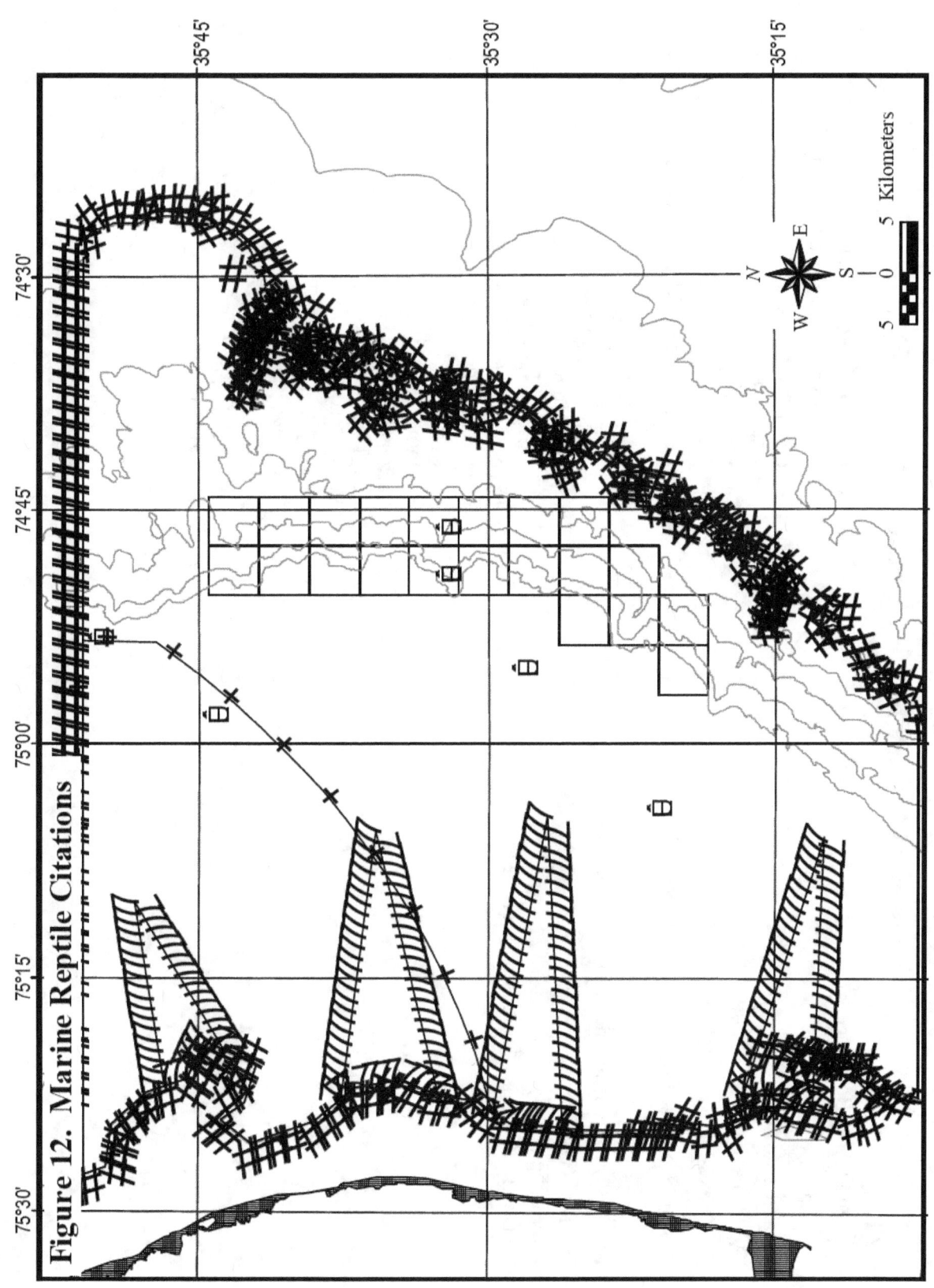

Figure 12. Marine Reptile Citations

Key to Marine Reptile Citations (Figure 12).

Study Area Boundary

☐ Lease Blocks

Mapped Citations

Coles & Musick (2000)

Lee & Palmer (1981)

Ross, S. (1985a); U.S. Dept. Navy (1985)

Studies that Focus on the Manteo Lease Blocks

Crawford (1989)
Lee & Lang (1998)
U.S.D.O.I.-Minerals Mgmt. Service (1992)
Vigil (1998)

**Studies that Cover the Hatteras
Middle Slope Area ("The Point")**

Lee (1991)
Lee et al. (1998)
Orbach (1989)
Shepard (1991)
U.S.D.O.I.-Minerals Mgmt. Service (1989)

Broad Regional Studies

Abernathy et al. (1989)
CETAP (1979)
Coston-Clements et al. (1991)
Epperly et al. (1989, 1995)
George & Hulbert (1989)
Hoss (1992)
Keinath (1992)
Lazzel (1980)
Lee (1985b)
Musick (1985)
Renaud et al. (1993)
Schwartz (1989)
Settle (1997)
Shoop & Kenny (1992)
Witzell (1999)

BIOLOGICAL OCEANOGRAPHY CHAPTER

BIOLOGICAL OCEANOGRAPHY CHAPTER

Abernathy, S.A., M.T. Baer, C.S. Benner, M.S. Brody, D.K. Francois, J.K. Gilliam, L.K. Good, C.J. Ohara, and J.V. Martin. 1989. Atlantic Outer Continental Shelf: Description of the Mid-Atlantic Environment. Abernathy, S.A. (ed.). U.S. Department of the Interior, Minerals Management Service, Atlantic OCS Region, Environmental Assessment Section. Herndon, VA. 167 p.

*This document discusses the major issues and areas of concern for the mid-Atlantic environment that are considered in the planning process for oil and gas leasing and operations on the Outer Continental Shelf (OCS). The issues are addressed with respect to the potential environmental consequences of mid Atlantic oil and gas exploration, development and production. A section discussing The Physical Environment (e.g., geology, non-petroleum minerals, physical oceanography, chemical oceanography and water quality, ocean dumping, meteorology, air quality), Biological resources (e.g., plankton, benthos, fishery resources, marine reptiles, marine mammals, marine and coastal birds, estuaries, wetlands, sensitive coastal habitats, canyon areas), Socioeconomic Environment, and other issues (e.g., archaeological resources, marine vessel traffic, National Aeronautics and Space Administration/ Department of Defense activities, oil and gas infrastructure, marine sanctuaries, and estuarine research reserves) is included. Most of the figures showing fisheries resource distribution are taken from fisheries data compiled for bottom-trawl and shellfish surveys of the National Marine Fisheries Service, Northeast Fisheries Center, Woods Hole, MA.

Atkinson, L.P., D.W. Menzel, and K.A. Bush. 1985. Oceanography of the Southeastern U.S. Continental Shelf. American Geophysical Union. Washington, DC. 156 p.

*This book contains 12 chapters: an introduction; four chapters on physical oceanography; a chapter on hydrography and nutrients; four biological chapters (covering phytoplankton, zooplankton, bacteria, and macroinfauna); a chemical chapter on trace metals; and a summary chapter describing future research plans. Research included was conducted between 1975 and the early 1980's and was largely funded by the Department of Energy and the Minerals Management Service (formerly Bureau of Land Management). The South Atlantic Bight (SAB) extends from the temperate waters of Cape Hatteras, NC to subtropical waters of West Palm Beach, FL. The ocean region is influenced by Gulf Stream dynamics on the eastern boundary, synoptic winds and weather events, river and estuarine inputs.

Barber, R.T. 1985. Nutrients, Productivity and Phytoplankton in the EMPRESS II Research Area. (Appendix C). *In:* U.S. Department of the Navy. EMPRESS II: Supplemental Draft Environmental Impact Statement for the Proposed Operation of the Navy Electromagnetic Pulse Radiation Environment Simulator for Ships (Empress II) in the Chesapeake Bay and Atlantic Ocean. United States Navy. Environmental/ Intergovernmental Section. Atlantic Division. Naval Facilities Engineering and Command. Norfolk, VA.

*This report describes the lower food chain (nutrients and phytoplankton) characteristics of the Virginia Capes region where the EMPRESS II experiment is proposed and identifies the physical processes that determine this character. The primary focus is biological oceanography, with a description of physical and chemical processes in the area. The southern portion VACAPES EMPRESS II Area of North Carolina overlaps with the northern portion of the defined study area for the Data Inventory Related to the Hatteras Middle Slope (The Point) Area.

Blair, N. 1998. A Scientific Overview of the Region Surrounding Lease Blocks 467 and 510. pp. 14-17. *In*: Vigil, D.L. (ed.). North Carolina/Minerals Management Service Technical Workshop on Manteo

Unit Exploration: February 4-5, 1998. U.S. Dept. of the Interior, Minerals Management Service, Gulf of Mexico OCS Region. New Orleans, LA.

*These are the proceedings from a workshop/meeting (February 4-5, 1998) between the North Carolina Department of Environment and Natural Resources, and the U.S. Department of the Interior's Minerals Management Service (MMS). The geographic area being discussed is approximately 45 miles east-northeast of Cape Hatteras, NC, referred to as the Manteo Unit. This workshop reviewed environmental and socioeconomic information known and needed on the Manteo Unit. The MMS's Gulf of Mexico OCS Regional Director gave an MMS perspective on history and status of the area. Chevron gave a presentation on how the exploratory well would be drilled. The scientific characterization was presented in greater detail by a number of scientific experts who spoke on the following disciplines physical environment, habitat and living resources, seabirds, marine mammals, sea turtles, and social and economic issues. Specific chapters are cited individually, when appropriate.

The continental margin offshore Cape Hatteras, NC has been the focus of numerous oceanographic studies. The objective of this report is to provide an overview of physical, biological, geological, and chemical processes that operate in the region so that the results from individual disciplinary studies can be placed in a system-wide context. This section discusses hydrocarbon potential, water column observations and processes, benthic observations and processes, summary and the future.

Cahoon, L.B., R.A. Laws, and C.J. Thomas. 1994. Viable diatoms and chlorophyll *a* in continental slope sediments off Cape Hatteras, North Carolina. Deep-Sea Research II 41(4-6): 767-782.

Continental slope sediments off Cape Hatteras, North Carolina, were sampled by box coring in late summer, 1992. The chlorophyll *a* concentrations measured in sediments from 16 sites at depths ranging from 530 to 2003 m averaged 19.9 mg chl *a* m^{-2}, a concentration much higher than observed elsewhere on the eastern U.S. continental slope, indicating high depositional rates for microalgal material. The variability in the chlorophyll *a* values suggests strong environmental heterogeneity at both small and large spatial scales in this slope habitat, probably a consequence of both topography and bioturbation. Viable diatoms were found in sediment samples across the range of depths sampled, and up to 14 cm deep in sediments, indicating high rates of deposition and bioturbation. Bulk sediment samples contained planktonic, tychopelagic and benthic diatoms, indicating that both phytoplankton and benthic microalgae from the continental shelf may be sources of organic matter for these slope sediments.

Costlow, J. 1992. The Outer Banks Protection Act. pp. 11-15. *In*: U.S. Department of the Interior, Minerals Management Service. Proceedings of the Fourth Atlantic OCS Region Information Transfer Meeting, September 1991. U.S. Department of the Interior, Minerals Management Service. Herndon, VA.

The Fourth Atlantic Outer Continental Shelf (OCS) Regional Information Transfer Meeting was held on 24-25 September 1991, in Wilmington, NC. The focus of the meeting was on the OCS off North Carolina, specifically on activities related to a proposed exploratory well for oil and gas by Mobil on Block 467 a site 40 miles off the coast of North Carolina. The area of industry interest is known as the Manteo Prospect, while the activities surrounding the proposed drilling are referred to collectively as the Manteo Project. The wildcat wellsite is in 2,690 ft. (857 m) of water near the edge of the Gulf Stream. It is also near a fishing ground known locally as "The Point." The area is believed to be gas prone rather than oil prone. The estimated size of the resource could be as high as 5 trillion cubic feet of gas.

The purpose of the meeting was to exchange information on the leasing background, legislative activities, scientific results, and socioeconomic studies. Legislative-related reports include descriptions of the Oil Pollution Act of 1990, the Outer Banks Protection Act, the Environmental Studies Review Panel, and the North Carolina Physical Oceanography Panel. Reports of studies on marine life include benthic diatoms, benthic fauna, pelagic seabirds, sea turtles, and right whales. One report describes the use of airships (blimps) for ocean research a capability relevant to North Carolina because of the east coast airship facility is located in the state. Local marine science facilities described include NOAA's National Undersea Research Center at the University of North Carolina at Wilmington and the National Marine Fisheries Service laboratory in Beaufort.

Developments in oil spill cleanup technology and capabilities are described by both the Coast Guard and the industry. A socioeconomic report describes the effects of the oil and gas activities on the tourist industry. Lastly, research on the restoration of salt marshes indicates that rehabilitation of an area is possible when development or an accident has occurred. While the emphasis of the meeting was on oil and gas, two reports described the results of projects related to offshore sand mining. The appendix lists the names and addresses of speakers. Individual chapters are cited individually when appropriate.

*In August 1990, President Bush signed Federal oil spill legislation that included a provision called the Outer Banks Protection Act (OBPA). The OBPA prohibited the Minerals Management Service (MMS) from approving any exploration plan off North Carolina until October 1991. The Act also created a five-member Environmental Sciences Review Panel (ESRP) to evaluate the adequacy of information on the Mobil proposal. This section describes the OBPA and ESRP. Physical oceanography, biological oceanography, and socioeconomics are mentioned.

Crawford, K. (ed.). 1989. Proceedings: 1989 Marine Expo: The Natural Resources Associated with Mobil's Proposed Drill Site. NC Outer Continental Shelf Office, NC Department of Administration. Raleigh, NC. 64 p.

*This report contains abstracts from each presenter. Chapter topics include: Mobil's Proposal, Geologic Overview — Introduction and Potential for Oil and Gas Discovery, Oceanographic Conditions, Comments on Last MMS Modeling, Biological Production Near the Bottom (invertebrates), Fisheries Resources, Commercial and Recreational Marine Fisheries, Winter Storm Effects on Spawning and Larval Drift of Pelagic Fish, Marine Birds, Sea Turtles in North Carolina, Marine Mammals, Plenary Session, Summary. Each chapter also cited individually when appropriate.

Curtin, T.B. 1979a. Ocean Outfall Wastewater Disposal Feasibility and Planning: Oceanographic Field Observations off North Carolina Spring Survey 12 — 22 May 1978, Report No. 79-4. Dept. of Marine Science and Engineering, NCSU. 242 p.

The objectives of the oceanographic field observations within the overall Ocean Outfall Feasibility and Planning Study (Langfelder et al. 1979) were both to provide input data for boundary condition initialization and to provide reference data for diagnostic testing of a series of coastal numerical circulation models under development. The data acquisition program was designed to parallel the model development in that a series of successive scales of variability were addressed. These scales have been defined as the shelf-scale, the nearshore scale, and the diffusive scale, and were characterized for the purposes of the study by temporal and spatial resolutions. Of particular overall interest in this project, with its ultimate focus on the nearshore coastal environment, was the interaction of the larger regional scale processes with those on smaller or local scale.

*Shellfish closure is discussed.

—. 1979b. Ocean Outfall Wastewater Disposal Feasibility and Planning: Oceanographic Field Observations off North Carolina Winter Survey 2-12 February 1978, Report No. 79-3. Dept. of Marine Science and Engineering, NCSU. 149 p.

The objectives of the oceanographic field observations within the overall Ocean Outfall Feasibility and Planning Study (Langfelder et al. 1979) were both to provide input data for boundary condition initialization and to provide reference data for diagnostic testing of a series of coastal numerical circulation models under development. The data acquisition program was designed to parallel the model development in that a series of successive scales of variability were addressed. These scales have been defined as the shelf-scale, the nearshore scale, and the diffusive scale, and were characterized for the purposes of the study by temporal and spatial resolutions. Of particular overall interest in this project, with its ultimate focus on the nearshore coastal environment, was the interaction of the larger regional scale processes with those on smaller or local scale.

*Shellfish closure is discussed.

—. 1979c. Ocean Outfall Wastewater Disposal Feasibility and Planning: Oceanographic Field Observations off North Carolina Fall Survey 1-11 November 1977, Report No. 79-5. Dept. of Marine Science and Engineering, NCSU. 248 p.

The objectives of the oceanographic field observations within the overall Ocean Outfall Feasibility and Planning Study (Langfelder et al. 1979) were both to provide input data for boundary condition initialization and to provide reference data for diagnostic testing of a series of coastal numerical circulation models under development. The data acquisition program was designed to parallel the model development in that a series of successive scales of variability were addressed. These scales have been defined as the shelf-scale, the nearshore scale, and the diffusive scale, and were characterized for the purposes of the study by temporal and spatial resolutions. Of particular overall interest in this project, with its ultimate focus on the nearshore coastal environment, was the interaction of the larger regional scale processes with those on smaller or local scale.

*Shellfish closure is discussed.

—. 1979d. Ocean Outfall Wastewater Disposal Feasibility and Planning: Oceanographic Field Observations Off North Carolina Summer Survey 2-12 August 1977, Report No. 79-2. Dept. of Marine Science and Engineering, NCSU. 303 p.

The objectives of the oceanographic field observations within the overall Ocean Outfall Feasibility and Planning Study (Langfelder et al. 1979) were both to provide input data for boundary condition initialization and to provide reference data for diagnostic testing of a series of coastal numerical circulation models under development. The data acquisition program was designed to parallel the model development in that a series of successive scales of variability were addressed. These scales have been defined as the shelf-scale, the nearshore scale, and the diffusive scale, and were characterized for the purposes of the study by temporal and spatial resolutions. Of particular overall interest in this project, with its ultimate focus on the nearshore coastal environment, was the interaction of the larger regional scale processes with those on smaller or local scale.

*Shellfish closure is discussed.

Cutter, G.R., R.J. Diaz, and J.A. Blake. 1994a. Deep-Sea Research II: CD-ROM APPENDIX. Deep-Sea Research II 41(4-6): 981-982.

The contents of the CD-ROM Appendix are data and images of the bottom from five of the articles in this issue. The CD-ROM was mastered in a format that can be read by both Macintosh and PC computers. It is organized in an hierarchical structure by folders, with data in one and images in another. To access a particular file, sequentially open folders until the file of interest appears. Data and figure captions are provided as: (.txt) ASCII text with no line breaks; (.tlb) ASCII text with line breaks; (.wor) Microsoft Word; and (.wp) Word Perfect 5.1 files. Images are in TIFF format (.tif). Data (ACSAR, Hatteras), Images and Captions (ACSAR, Profile, 3Dbathy, Sled, Surface, x-ray) are included.

Diaz, R. J., J. Blake, B. Hecker, and D.C. Rhoads. 1993b. A Highly Productive Area of the Continental Slope Off Cape Hatteras. Benthic Ecology Meeting, 1-4 April, 1993, Mobile, AL. 57 p.

The continental slope off Cape Hatteras is atypical for the U.S. Atlantic coast. Unusually high numbers of infauna, megafauna, and demersal fish were found over a broad area. Benthic organisms appear to be well adapted to physical processes that converge on the Cape Hatteras continental slope. These physical processes impart a high degree of instability to the bottom and also supply large amounts of organic matter which sustain the elevated densities and biomass. The nature of these communities and mechanisms which regulate them will be discussed.

Harvey, H.R. 1994. Fatty acids and sterols as source markers of organic matter in sediments of the North Carolina continental slope. Deep-Sea Research II 41(4-6): 783-796.

To estimate the source and diagenetic state of organic matter reaching bottom sediments, fatty acids and sterols were measured in unconsolidated surface material (flocs) at 12 sites ranging from 600 to 2000 m across the mid-Atlantic continental slope off Cape Hatteras, North Carolina. Total free and esterified fatty acids were similar in description and concentration to other coastal systems, with values ranging from 0.64 to 46.52 g mg^{-1} organic carbon (1.10-68.85 g mg^{-1}dry sediment). Although shallow (600 m) stations contained significantly greater fatty acid concentrations than deep (>1400 m) stations, high variability observed at mid-depth (800 m) collections precluded a consistent relationship between total fatty acid concentration and station depth. At three sites where underlying sediments were also collected, decreases in total fatty acid reduced amounts of polyenoic acids and significant presence of bacterial fatty acids suggest rapid reworking of labile organic material that reaches the sediment surface. The distribution of sterols was remarkably consistent among all sites even though there were large variations in concentrations (1.8-20.7g mg^{-1} organic carbon). Sterol composition indicated phytoplankton, principally diatoms and dinoflagellates, as the principal source of labile organic matter to sediments, together with a significant input of cholesterol typical of zooplankton and their feeding activity. A minor but widespread terrigenous input was also evident based upon significant concentrations of sterols dominant in vascular plants.

Kirby-Smith, W.W. 1989a. Biological Production Near the Bottom. p. 25. In: Crawford, K. (ed.). Proceedings: 1989 Marine Expo: The Natural Resources Associated with Mobil's Proposed Drill Site. NC Outer Continental Shelf Office, NC Department of Administration. Raleigh, NC.

Satellite photographs show that North Carolina has an incredibly diverse oceanographic setting which, in turn, produces highly diverse communities of fishes and invertebrates. The three bottom types found off the continental shelf of North Carolina include: 1) sand, 2) shell, and 3) rock outcrops. Across the continental shelf, the primary producers that support fisheries include microalgae and macroalgae. The bottom-dwelling microalgae (small microscopic plants) grow, rapidly and are very important to the total productivity of the whole water column. As much as half of the primary productivity on the shelf may be due to this benthic component. The secondary producers on rock outcrops, which include sponges, corals, worms and small arthropods, are a major food source for small fish. From a scientific perspective, the proposed drill site is an exciting area with a high biomass and low diversity. In my opinion, the exploration well itself would have little or no impact on the resources in the area; however, a major find of oil or gas could lead to a tremendous amount of industrial development, which could compete economically with other coastal industries, such as tourism and fisheries.

Langfelder, J., T.B. Curtin, D.N. Hyman, G. Janowitz, J. Maiolo, W. Queen, F.Y. Sorrell, M. Amien, V. Bellis, M. Brinson, G. Davis, C.Y. Lee, C. O'Rear, L. Pearce, C.Y. Peng, S. Riggs, B. Smith, M. Sobsey, and P. Tschetter. 1979. Final Report: Ocean Outfall Wastewater Disposal Feasibility and Planning, Report No. 79-1. Dept. of Marine Science and Engineering, NCSU; Report No. 5, Institute for Coastal and Marine Resources, ECU. 482 p.

*This report follows an EIS format and is cited as a single document. Individual chapters are not stand-alone documents. Major findings of the study were: 1) Construction and operation of a well designed and operated sewage treatment plant that utilizes an ocean outfall and secondary treatment should not adversely affect the water column on fishery resources. Some build up of effluent constituents may occur in the bottom sediments in the immediate vicinity of the diffuser and could result in bottom community changes. 2) Effluent discharge should have essentially no adverse affect on recreational swimming in the areas of the diffuser. Areas now closed to shellfishing in the estuaries could be reopened as a result of reduced pathogen loadings: these pathogens are presently coming from septic tanks and treatment plants that discharge into these waters. 3) Centralized sewer systems will increase land values, allow reduced lot size and stimulate growth. This will lead to change in the population composition and demands for expanded goods and services.

Laws, R.A., and L.B. Cahoon. 1992. Benthic Diatoms from the North Carolina shelf and slope. pp. 103-10. *In*: U.S. Department of the Interior, Minerals Management Service. Proceedings of the Fourth Atlantic OCS Region Information Transfer Meeting, September 1991. U.S. Department of the Interior, Minerals Management Service. Herndon, VA.

The Fourth Atlantic Outer Continental Shelf (OCS) Regional Information Transfer Meeting was held on 24-25 September 1991, in Wilmington, NC. The focus of the meeting was on the OCS off North Carolina, specifically on activities related to a proposed exploratory well for oil and gas by Mobil on Block 467 a site 40 miles off the coast of North Carolina. The area of industry interest is known as the Manteo Prospect, while the activities surrounding the proposed drilling are referred to collectively as the Manteo Project. The wildcat wellsite is in 2,690 ft. (857 m) of water near the edge of the Gulf Stream. It is also near a fishing ground known locally as "The Point." The area is believed to be gas prone rather than oil prone. The estimated size of the resource could be as high as 5 trillion cubic feet of gas.

The purpose of the meeting was to exchange information on the leasing background, legislative activities, scientific results, and socioeconomic studies. Legislative-related reports include descriptions of the Oil Pollution Act of 1990, the Outer Banks Protection Act, the Environmental Studies Review Panel, and the North Carolina Physical Oceanography Panel. Reports of studies on marine life include benthic diatoms, benthic fauna, pelagic seabirds, sea turtles, and right whales. One report describes the use of airships (blimps) for ocean research a capability relevant to North Carolina because of the east coast airship facility is located in the state. Local marine science facilities described include NOAA's National Undersea Research Center at the University of North Carolina at Wilmington and the National Marine Fisheries Service laboratory in Beaufort.

Developments in oil spill cleanup technology and capabilities are described by both the Coast Guard and the industry. A socioeconomic report describes the effects of the oil and gas activities on the tourist industry. Lastly, research on the restoration of salt marshes indicates that rehabilitation of an area is possible when development or an accident has occurred. While the emphasis of the meeting was on oil and gas, two reports described the results of projects related to offshore sand mining. The appendix lists the names and addresses of speakers. Individual chapters are cited individually when appropriate.

Conventional wisdom has it that phytoplankton are at the base of the food chain. However, another important food source has been documented — the benthic microalgae. The green-brown mat one sometimes sees on the ocean floor is, in fact, a mat of benthic diatoms. These microalgae are an important food source. At times and places, these benthic flora exceed those of the water column in productivity. This section describes the role of benthic microalgae in the project area.

Levin, L., N. Blair, D. DeMaster, G. Plaia, W. Fornes, C. Martin, and C. Thomas. 1997. Rapid subduction of organic matter by maldanid polychaetes on the North Carolina slope. Journal of Marine Research 55: 595-611.

In situ tracer experiments conducted on the North Carolina continental slope reveal that tube-building worms (Polychaeta: Maldanidae) can, without ingestion, rapidly subduct freshly deposited, algal carbon (^{13}C-labeled diatoms) and inorganic materials (slope sediment and glass beads) to depths of 10 cm or more in the sediment column. Transport over 1.5 days appears to be nonselective but spatially patchy, creating localized, deep hotspots. As a result of this transport, relatively fresh organic matter becomes available soon after deposition to deep-dwelling microbes and other infauna, and both aerobic and anaerobic processes may be enhanced. Comparison of tracer subduction with estimates from a diffusive mixing model using ^{234}Th-based coefficients, suggests that maldanid subduction activities, within 1.5 d of particle deposition, could account for 25-100% of the mixing below 5 cm that occurs on 100-day time scales. Comparison of community data from the North Carolina slope for different places and times indicate a correlation between the abundance of deep-welling maldanids and the abundance and the dwelling depth in the sediment column of other infauna. Pulsed inputs of organic matter occur frequently in margin environments and maldanid polychaetes are a common component of continental slope macrobenthos. Thus, the activities we observe are likely to be widespread and significant for chemical cycling (natural and anthropogenic materials) on the slope. We propose that species like maldanids, that rapidly redistribute labile organic matter within the seabed, probably function as keystone resource modifiers. They may exert a disproportionately strong influence (relative to their abundance) on the structure of infaunal communities and on the timing, location and nature of organic matter diagenesis and burial in continental margin sediments.

Milliman, J.D., R.J. Diaz, J.A. Blake, and G.R. Cutter Jr. (eds.). 1994. Topical Studies in Oceanography: Input, Accumulation and Cycling of Materials on the Continental Slope Off Cape Hatteras. Deep-Sea Research II Vol. 41. 982 p.

*This is a compilation of studies on Input, Accumulation and Cycling of Materials on the Continental Slope Off Cape Hatteras. Geology, sediments, organics, and benthic fauna are discussed. A CD-ROM is included. Each chapter (study) is cited independently, when appropriate. Some papers in this issue were derived from Diaz et al. (1993).

Nash, R.M., J.J. Magnuson, C.S. Clay, and T.K. Stanton. 1987. A Synoptic View of the Gulf Stream Front with 70-kHz Sonar: Taking Advantage of a Closer Look. Canadian Journal of Fisheries and Aquatic Sciences 44(11): 2022-2024.

Acoustical scattering across the near surface frontal zone of the Gulf Stream off Cape Hatteras was greatest in the thermal front. Little biological scattering was evident in the colder Slope water, but in the Gulf Stream, scatters formed five horizontal bands. Interpretation and new applications of acoustical information in biological oceanography are discussed.

O'Reilly, J.E., and C. Zetlin. 1998. Seasonal, Horizontal, and Vertical Distribution of Phytoplankton Chlorophyll a in the Northeast U.S. Continental Shelf Ecosystem. NOAA Technical report NMFS 139. U.S. Department of Commerce. Seattle, WA. 120 p.

The broad scale features in the horizontal, vertical, and seasonal distribution of phytoplankton chlorophyll a on the northeast U.S. continental shelf are described based on 57,088 measurements made during 78 oceanographic surveys from 1977 through 1988. Highest mean water column chlorophyll concentration (Chl_w) is usually observed in nearshore areas adjacent to the mouths of the estuaries in the Middle Atlantic Bight (MAB), over the shallow water on Georges Bank, and a small area sampled along the southeast edge of Nantucket Shoals. Lowest Chl_w (<O.125 *ug* l^{-1}) is usually restricted to the most seaward stations sampled along the shelf-break and the central deep waters in the Gulf of Maine. There is at least a twofold seasonal variation in phytoplankton biomass in all areas, with highest phytoplankton concentrations (m^3) and highest integrated standing stocks (m^2) occurring during the winter-spring (WS) bloom, and the lowest during summer, when vertical density stratification is maximal. In most regions, a secondary phytoplankton biomass pulse is evident during convective destratification in fall, usually in October. Fall bloom in some areas of Georges Bank approaches the magnitude of the WS-bloom, but Georges Bank and Middle Atlantic Bight fall blooms are clearly subordinate to WS-blooms.

Measurements of chlorophyll in two size-fractions of the phytoplankton, netplankton (>20 *u*m) and nanoplankton (<20 *u* m), revealed that the smaller nanoplankton are responsible for most of the phytoplankton biomass on the northeast U.S. shelf Netplankton tend to be more abundant in nearshore areas of the MAB and shallow water on Georges Bank, where chlorophyll a is usually high; nanoplankton dominate deeper water at the shelf-break and deep water in the Gulf of Maine, where Chl_w is usually low. As a general rule, the percent of phytoplankton in the netplankton size-fraction increases with increasing depth below surface and decreases proceeding offshore.

There are distinct seasonal and regional patterns in the vertical distribution of chlorophyll a and percent netplankton, as revealed in composite vertical profiles of chlorophyll a constructed for 11 layers of the water column. Subsurface chlorophyll a maxima are ubiquitous during summer in stratified water. Chlorophyll a in the subsurface maximum layer is generally 2-8 times the concentration in the overlying and underlying water and approaches 50 to 75% of the levels observed in surface water during WS-bloom. The distribution of the ratio of the subsurface maximum chlorophyll a to surface chlorophyll a (SSR) during summer parallels the shelfwide pattern for stability, indexed as the difference in density (sigma-t) between 40 in and surface ($stability_{40}$). The weakest stability and lowest SSR's are found in shallow tidally-mixed water on Georges Bank; the greatest stability and highest SSR's (8-12:1) are along the mid and outer MAB shelf, over the winter residual water known as the "cold band.' On Georges Bank, the distribution of SSR and the stability4o are roughly congruent with the pattern for maximum surface tidal current velocity, with values above 50 cms^{-1} defining SSR's less than 2:1 and the well-mixed area.

Physical factors (bathymetry, vertical mixing by strong tidal currents, and seasonal and regional differences in the intensity and duration of vertical stratification) appear to explain much of the variability in phytoplankton chlorophyll a throughout this ecosystem.

Pietrafesa, L.J. 1998. Physical Environment Review: An Overview of the Meteorology and Physical Oceanography Surrounding Lease Blocks 467 and 510. pp. 31-32. *In*: Vigil, D.L. (ed.). North Carolina/Minerals Management Service Technical Workshop on Manteo Unit Exploration: February 4-5, 1998. U.S. Dept. of the Interior, Minerals Management Service, Gulf of Mexico OCS Region. New Orleans, LA.

*These are the proceedings from a workshop/meeting (February 4-5, 1998) between the North Carolina Department of Environment and Natural Resources, and the U.S. Department of the Interior's Minerals Management Service (MMS). The geographic area being discussed is approximately 45 miles east-northeast of Cape Hatteras, NC, referred to as the Manteo Unit. This workshop reviewed environmental and socioeconomic information known and needed on the Manteo Unit. The MMS's Gulf of Mexico OCS Regional Director gave an MMS perspective on history and status of the area. Chevron gave a presentation on how the exploratory well would be drilled. The scientific characterization was presented in greater detail by a number of scientific experts who spoke on the following disciplines physical environment, habitat and living resources, seabirds, marine mammals, sea turtles, and social and economic issues. Specific chapters are cited individually, when appropriate.

This section discusses Atmospheric Weather and Climatology, Physical Oceanography, Recent Findings (e.g., Hatteras Confluence region, offshelf transport), Issues (e.g., ability to predict oil spill trajectory, ability of oil rigs to withstand cyclone forcing, ability of drill ship to evacuate site during genesis of atmospheric bombs, role of physical oceanography in biological productivity).

Shepard, A. (ed.). 1991. Undersea Research at The Point. NURC/UNCW 1991 Undersea Research: Informational Meeting. National Undersea Research Center, University of North Carolina at Wilmington. Wilmington, NC. 9 p.

*This handout is a summary of research being conducted at "The Point" area (Manteo Lease Block 467).

The National Undersea Research Center at the University of North Carolina at Wilmington, funded by a grant from the National Oceanic and Atmospheric Administration's (NOAA) Office of Undersea Research (OUR), was established in 1980 to promote, facilitate, and conduct research in the Southeastern United States utilizing undersea techniques, including advanced wet diving and manned and unmanned submersibles. A main Center goal is to provide information to NOAA that will assist the agency in fulfilling its charter to explore, understand, conserve and manage the U.S. marine environment and associated resources. To help meet this goal, the Center supports and conducts interdisciplinary oceanographic research projects studying continental margin processes, particularly the interactions and linkages between estuarine, continental shelf, and slope (including submarine canyon) environments.

Shepard, A., and A.H. Hulbert (eds.). 1994. Workshop Report: Present and Future Research Initiatives on the Upper Hatteras Slope off North Carolina. National Undersea Research Center at the University of North Carolina at Wilmington. Wilmington, NC. 30p.

*This report is the result of the May 1993 workshop held in Raleigh, NC. The topics of discussion were research (present and planned) at the Upper Hatteras Slope (UHS) and potential funding sources. The workshop was sponsored by National Undersea Research Center at the University of North Carolina at Wilmington. The report provides a brief description of the UHS invertebrates, biological oceanography, chemical oceanography, geological oceanography (bathymetry, oil and gas exploration), physical oceanography, fisheries, and *Sargassum*. Appendix A is a workshop agenda and list of speakers. No abstracts for speakers are provided. Appendix B is a list of potential funding sources. Appendix C contains a list of publications pertaining to the UHS.

U.S. Department of the Navy. 1985. EMPRESS II: Supplemental Draft Environmental Impact Statement for the Proposed Operation of the Navy Electromagnetic Pulse Radiation Environment Simulator for Ships (Empress II) in the Chesapeake Bay and Atlantic Ocean. United States Navy. Environmental/

Intergovernmental Section. Atlantic Division. Naval Facilities Engineering and Command. Norfolk, VA.

*This is a National Environmental Policy Act document characterizing the proposed EMPRESS II project. Appendix B contains a Summary of Biological Processes in the Proposed VACAPES EMPRESS II area off North Carolina Relating to Planktonic Communities, Pelagic Macroinvertebrates, Ichthyofauna, Sea turtles, Marine Mammals, and Sea Birds. Technical reports supporting this summary were written by authorities in each discipline and are included in Appendices. The reports are cited individually. The southern portion of VACAPES EMPRESS II Area of North Carolina overlaps with the northern portion of the defined study area for the Data Inventory Related to the Hatteras Middle Slope (The Point) Area.

Verity, P. 1998. Habitat and Living Resources Review: Water Column Biology at Cape Hatteras. p. 52. *In*: Vigil, D. L. (ed.). North Carolina/Minerals Management Service Technical Workshop on Manteo Unit Exploration: February 4-5, 1998. U.S. Dept. of the Interior, Minerals Management Service, Gulf of Mexico OCS Region. New Orleans, LA.

*These are the proceedings from a workshop/meeting (February 4-5, 1998) between the North Carolina Department of Environment and Natural Resources, and the U.S. Department of the Interior's Minerals Management Service (MMS). The geographic area being discussed is approximately 45 miles east-northeast of Cape Hatteras, NC, referred to as the Manteo Unit. This workshop reviewed environmental and socioeconomic information known and needed on the Manteo Unit. The MMS's Gulf of Mexico OCS Regional Director gave an MMS perspective on history and status of the area. Chevron gave a presentation on how the exploratory well would be drilled. The scientific characterization was presented in greater detail by a number of scientific experts who spoke on the following disciplines physical environment, habitat and living resources, seabirds, marine mammals, sea turtles, and social and economic issues. Specific chapters are cited individually, when appropriate.

It is essential in any overview of pelagic food web structure and function to place it in the proper physical perspective. In the Carolina Capes region in general, phytoplankton biomass is typically highest in late winter/early spring, associated with a vernal bloom. Higher concentrations occur closer to shore and along shelf/slope fronts. Immediately south of Cape Hatteras is a large area of high upwelling. This massive nitrate flux in to the euphotic zone induces substantial plankton development, which advents northward from the South Atlantic Bight (SAB) past Cape Hatteras. The latter is also at the confluence of southward-flowing Mid Atlantic Bight (MAB) water which exists at Cape Hatteras.

Vigil, D.L. (ed.). 1998. North Carolina/Minerals Management Service Technical Workshop on Manteo Unit Exploration: February 4-5, 1998. U.S. Dept. of the Interior, Minerals Management Service. Gulf of Mexico OCS Region. New Orleans, LA. 168 p.

*These are the proceedings from a workshop/meeting (February 4-5, 1998) between the North Carolina Department of Environment and Natural Resources, and the U.S. Department of the Interior's Minerals Management Service (MMS). The geographic area being discussed is approximately 45 miles east-northeast of Cape Hatteras, NC, referred to as the Manteo Unit. This workshop reviewed environmental and socioeconomic information known and needed on the Manteo Unit. The MMS's Gulf of Mexico OCS Regional Director gave an MMS perspective on history and status of the area. Chevron gave a presentation on how the exploratory well would be drilled. The scientific characterization was presented in greater detail by a number of scientific experts who spoke on the following disciplines physical environment, habitat and living resources (invertebrates and fish), seabirds, marine mammals, sea turtles, and social and economic issues. Specific chapters are cited individually, when appropriate.

Walsh, J.J. 1994. Particle export at Cape Hatteras. Deep-Sea Research II Vol. 41(2-3): 603-628.

A simple model of shelf, slope and basin waters near Cape Hatteras, North Carolina is used to estimate the sources and sinks of organic carbon within the Gulf Stream System. The analysis employs water transport estimates, nutrient data. satellite imagery, surficial sediment records and particle distributions caught by bottle, camera and sediment trap to compute vertical and lateral fluxes of particulate carbon. Particle export from the SAB and MAB shelf ecosystems may constitute 62-82% of the source of the carbon flux within the Gulf Stream near 75 W, after settling at 100 m day $^{-1}$, with an oxidation loss of 4% day^{-1}, to a nominal mid-depth of 1000 m on the slope.

As a result of light limitation, denitrification and DON solubilization, partial utilization of onwelled nitrate from the Gulf Stream System by coastal phytoplankton suggests that the time-averaged f ratio may be as small as 0.12 for the ratio of the "new" portion of primary production to the total. After burial loss, the export of particulate matter from the shelves then represents at most 11% of the total carbon fixation of coastal waters. If the shelf export of DON and unutilized NO_3 is consumed within adjacent slope waters, however, the f ratio and the percentage of particle export from the carbon fixation of shelf-affected waters might increase to 0.25 and 24%.

Willey, J.D., and L.B. Cahoon. 1991. Enhancement of chlorophyll a production in Gulf Stream surface seawater by rainwater nitrate. Marine Chemistry 34: 63-75.

The concentration of nitrate commonly found in rain from continental storm systems passing over eastern North Carolina was sufficient to stimulate chlorophyll *a* production in surface Gulf Stream water collected over the continental slope near Cape Hatteras, NC, in mid-October 1989. Two bioassay experiments were conducted on board ship by mixing Gulf Stream surface seawater with synthetic rainwater (5% rainwater). These bioassays indicated an increased production of chlorophyll *a* in response to rainwater nitrate but not phosphate. The response was apparent after incubation for 2 days after the chlorophyll *a* concentration increased approximately 2.5 times relative to controls in both experiments.

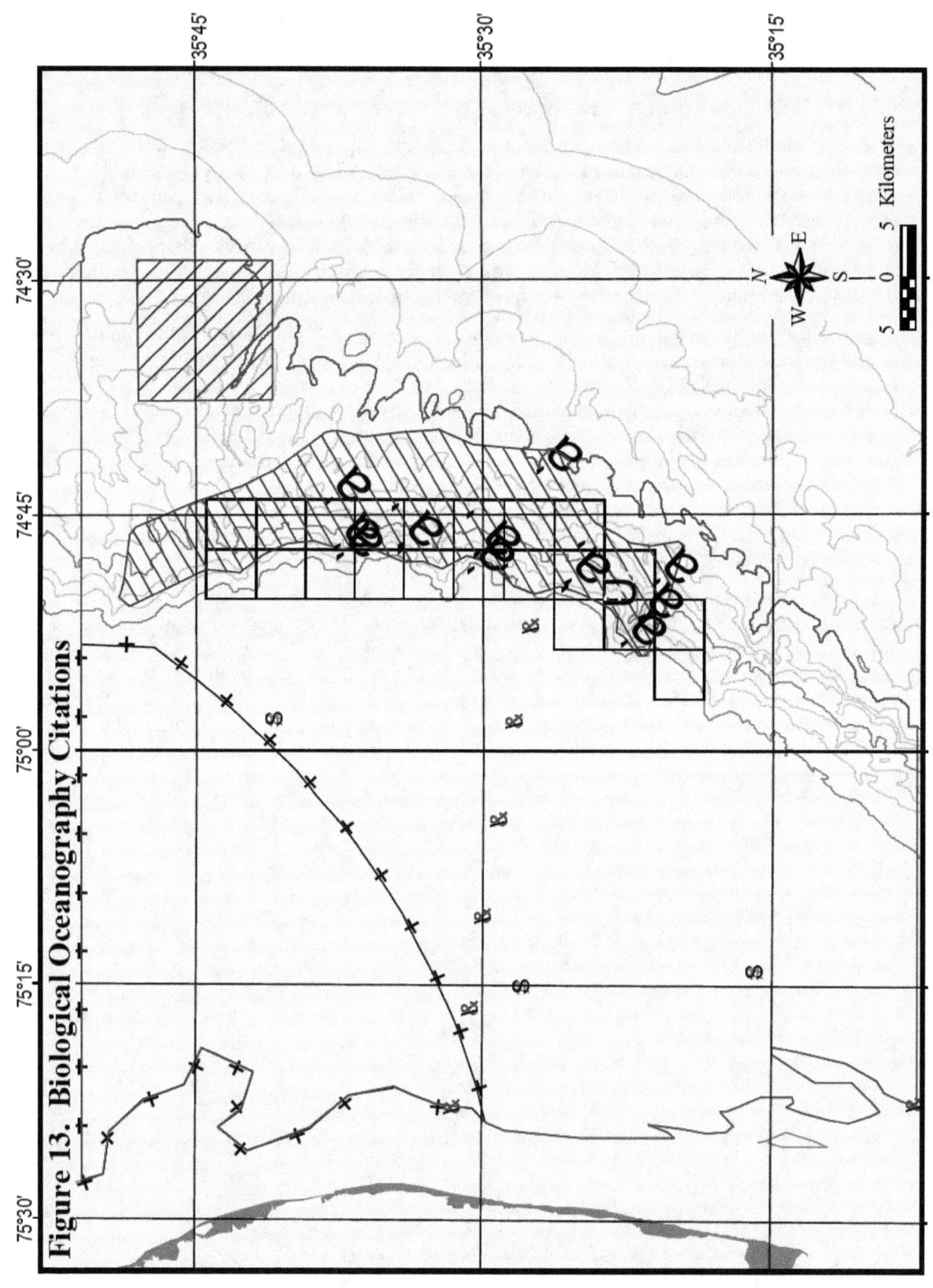

Figure 13. Biological Oceanography Citations

Key to Biological Oceanography Citations (Figure 13).

⋀⋁ Study Area Boundary

▢ Lease Blocks

Mapped Citations

✶⤬ Barber (1985); U.S. Dept. Navy (1985)

. Cahoon et al. (1994)

& Curtain (1979 a-d); Langfelder et al. (1979)

▨ Cutter et al. (1994a); Milliman et al. (1994)

a Harvey (1994)

U Levin et al. (1997)

▨ Nash et al. (1987)

$ O'Reilly & Zetlin (1998)

Studies that Focus on the Manteo Lease Blocks

Blair (1998)
Costlow (1992)
Crawford (1989)
Laws & Cahoon (1992)
Pietrafesa (1998)
Shepard & Hulbert (1994)
Verity (1998)
Vigil (1998)

Studies that Cover the Hatteras Middle Slope Area ("The Point")

Diaz et al. (1993b)
Kirby-Smith (1989a)
Shepard (1991)
Willey & Cahoon (1991)

Broad Regional Studies

Abernathy et al. (1989)
Atkinson et al. (1985)
Walsh (1994)

CHEMICAL OCEANOGRAPHY CHAPTER

CHEMICAL OCEANOGRAPHY CHAPTER

Abernathy, S.A., M.T. Baer, C.S. Benner, M.S. Brody, D.K. Francois, J.K. Gilliam, L.K. Good, C.J. Ohara, and J.V. Martin. 1989. Atlantic Outer Continental Shelf: Description of the Mid-Atlantic Environment. Abernathy, S.A. (ed.). U.S. Department of the Interior, Minerals Management Service, Atlantic OCS Region, Environmental Assessment Section. Herndon, VA. 167 p.

*This document discusses the major issues and areas of concern for the mid-Atlantic environment that are considered in the planning process for oil and gas leasing and operations on the Outer Continental Shelf (OCS). The issues are addressed with respect to the potential environmental consequences of mid Atlantic oil and gas exploration, development and production. A section discussing The Physical Environment (e.g., geology, non-petroleum minerals, physical oceanography, chemical oceanography and water quality, ocean dumping, meteorology, air quality), Biological resources (e.g., plankton, benthos, fishery resources, marine reptiles, marine mammals, marine and coastal birds, estuaries, wetlands, sensitive coastal habitats, canyon areas), Socioeconomic Environment, and other issues (e.g., archaeological resources, marine vessel traffic, National Aeronautics and Space Administration/ Department of Defense activities, oil and gas infrastructure, marine sanctuaries, and estuarine research reserves) is included. Most of the figures showing fisheries resource distribution are taken from fisheries data compiled for bottom-trawl and shellfish surveys of the National Marine Fisheries Service, Northeast Fisheries Center, Woods Hole, MA.

Anderson, R.F., G.T. Rowe, P.F. Kemp, S. Trumbore, and P.E. Biscaye. 1994. Carbon budget for the mid-slope depocenter of the Middle Atlantic Bight. Deep-Sea Research II Vol. 41(2-3): 669-703.

A mass budget was constructed for organic carbon on the upper slope of the Middle Atlantic Bight. A region thought to serve as a depocenter for fine-grained material exported from the adjacent shelf. Various components of the budget are internally consistent, and observed differences can be attributed to natural spatial variability or to the different time scales, over which measurements were made. The flux of organic carbon to the sediments in the core of the depocenter zone, at it water depth of ~ 1000 m, was measured with sediment traps to be 65 mg C m^{-2} day^{-1} is buried. Oxygen fluxes into the sediments, measured with incubation chambers attached to a free vehicle lander, correspond to total carbon remineralization rates of 49-79 mg C m^{-2} day^{-1}. Carbon remineralization rates estimated from gradients of C_{org} within the mixed layer, and from gradients of dissolved ammonia and phosphate in pore waters, sum to only $\sim$4-6 mg C m^{-2} day^{-1}.

Most of the C_{org} deposited on the upper slope sediments is supplied by lateral transport from other regions, but even if all of this material were derived from the adjacent shelf, it represents, <2% of the mean annual shelf productivity. This value is further lowered by recognizing that as much as half of the C_{org} deposited on the slope is refractory, having originated by reworking from older deposits. Refractory C_{org} arrives at the seabed with an average ^{14}C age 600-900 years older than the pre-bomb ^{14}C age of DIC in seawater, and has a mean life in the sediments with respect to biological remineralization of at least 1000 years. Labile carbon supplied to the slope, on the other hand, is rapidly and (virtually) completely remineralized, with a mean life of $< \sim 1$ year. Carbon-14 ages of fine-grained carbonate and organic carbon present within the interstices of shelf sands are consistent with this material acting as a source for the old carbon supplied to the slope. Winnowing and export of reworked carbon may contribute to the often-described relationship between organic carbon preservation and accumulation rate of marine sediments.

Anderson, W.W., and J.W. Gehringer. 1959a. Physical oceanographic, biological, and chemical data, South Atlantic coast of the United States, M/V Theodore N. Gill cruise 7. US Department of the Interior, US Fish and Wildlife Service, Special Scientific Report — Fisheries No. 278. 277 p.

*This report documents stations sampled throughout the South Atlantic Bight during June-July 1954. Weather, water chemistry, and sea state data were collected. Plankton samples were collected and fish were sampled by dip net and trolling. A few stations were near or within the southern border of our study area.

—. 1959b. Physical oceanographic, biological, and chemical data, South Atlantic coast of the United States, M/V Theodore N. Gill cruise 8. US Department of the Interior, US Fish and Wildlife Service, Special Scientific Report — Fisheries No. 303. 227 p.

*This report documents stations sampled throughout the South Atlantic Bight during August — September 1954. Weather, water chemistry, and sea state data were collected. Plankton samples were collected and fish were sampled by dip net and trolling. A few stations were near or within the southern border of our study area.

Anderson, W.W., J.W. Gehringer, and E. Cohen. 1956. Physical oceanographic, biological, and chemical data, South Atlantic coast of the United States, Theodore N. Gill cruise 2. US Department of the Interior, US Fish and Wildlife Service, Special Scientific Report — Fisheries No. 198. 270 p.

*This report documents stations sampled throughout the South Atlantic Bight during May 1953. Weather, water chemistry, and sea state data were collected. Plankton samples were collected and fish were sampled by dip net and trolling. A few stations were near or within the southern border of our study area.

Anderson, W.W., J.E. Moore, and H.R. Gordy. 1961. Oceanic salinities off the South Atlantic coast of the United States, Theodore N. Gill cruises 1-9, 1953-1954. US Department of the Interior, US Fish and Wildlife Service, Special Scientific Report — Fisheries No. 389. 207 p.

Salinity data secured on nine cruises of the M/V Theodore N. Gill off the south Atlantic coast of the United States are further processed and organized in a much more usable and readily available form. Surface water salinities are presented graphically by season.

Atkinson, L.P. 1985. Hydrography and Nutrients of the Southeastern U.S. Continental Shelf. Oceanography of the Southeastern U.S. Continental Shelf. Coastal and Estuarine Sciences 2: 77-92.

The distribution of properties such as temperature and salinity, of nutrients such as nitrate, phosphate, and silicate, and of derived properties such as buoyancy in the South Atlantic Bight depends on complex interactions of shelf waters with rivers, coastal estuaries and sounds, atmospheric forcing, and, most importantly, the Gulf Stream. Seasonal variations in temperature depend on the seasonal heating cycle, air-sea exchange processes, and Gulf Stream interaction. The result is extreme variations in temperature both seasonally and spatially. Salinity variations are mainly related to seasonal river flow, which peaks in the spring, and subsequent shelf circulation processes. Variations in temperature and salinity occur over shorter time scales because of Gulf Stream meanders and frontal eddies that cause intrusions of surface or subsurface water into the shelf waters. Intrusion frequency and cross-shelf excursion vary seasonally and latitudinally. The supply of nutrients mainly depends on Gulf Stream intrusions. Gulf Stream water colder than about 20°C contains significant amounts of nutrients. Such waters invade the shelf more frequently during the summer in the southern bight. Chemical tracers such as phenolic aldehydes, humic compound fluorescence, and tritium have been used successfully to trace coastal waters.

Atkinson, L.P., D.W. Menzel, and K.A. Bush. 1985. Oceanography of the Southeastern U.S. Continental Shelf. American Geophysical Union. Washington, DC. 156 p.

*This book contains 12 chapters: an introduction; four chapters on physical oceanography; a chapter on hydrography and nutrients; four biological chapters (covering phytoplankton, zooplankton, bacteria, and macroinfauna); a chemical chapter on trace metals; and a summary chapter describing future research plans. Research included was conducted between 1975 and the early 1980's and was largely funded by the Department of Energy and the Minerals Management Service (formerly Bureau of Land Management). The South Atlantic Bight extends from the temperate waters of Cape Hatteras, NC to subtropical waters of West Palm Beach, FL. The ocean region is influenced by Gulf Stream dynamics on the eastern boundary, synoptic winds and weather events, river and estuarine inputs.

Bailey, T.G., M.J. Youngbluth, and G.P. Owen. 1995. Chemical composition and metabolic rates of gelatinous zooplankton from midwater and benthic boundary layer environments off Cape Hatteras, North Carolina, USA . Marine Ecology Progress Series 122: 121-134.

Quantitative determinations of chemical composition and oxygen consumption rates were made for 7 species of gelatinous zooplankton (ctenophores and medusae) from midwater and benthic boundary layer habitats off Cape Hatteras, NC, USA. Although there were no apparent trends in chemical composition with depth of occurrence, midwater species were generally less robust, in terms of protein and lipid content, than those from benthopelagic depths. These differences in chemical compositions between midwater and benthopelagic species are probably related to factors associated with swimming behaviors required for prey capture and predator avoidance. Measurements of carbon specific metabolic rates (0.59 to 17.9 ul O mg^1 C h^1) indicated that minimum daily rations required by mesopelagic gelatinous zooplankton can impact carbon cycling and energy transfer in deep-water ecosystems. These data are consistent with a growing inventory of metabolic measurements undertaken with submersible platforms and strongly implicate gelatinous zooplankton as ecologically important components of pelagic communities.

Barrett, J.R., Jr. 1965. Subsurface currents off Cape Hatteras. Deep-Sea Research 12: 173-184.

In October 1962, direct current measurements at depths of 800 m to 2500 m beneath the zone of swiftest surface currents near Cape Hatteras revealed a subsurface flow to the south. Analysis of temperature-salinity and dissolved oxygen distributions indicate that the immediate source of the southward flowing water was the region east of Cape Hatteras between the Gulf Stream and the Continental Slope. These measurements seem to affirm that continuity exists between the deep westward flow observed in the Slope Water region by Volkmann and the southward flow east of Cape Roman, near 33N, reported by Swallow and Worthington. The geostrophic volume transport of the southward flow was between 4 million and 12 million m^3 sec^{-1}. The surface of zero axial velocity was at a depth of about 500 m at the left side of the region of swift surface current (inshore), and deepened rapidly in the offshore direction.

Blair, N. 1998. A Scientific Overview of the Region Surrounding Lease Blocks 467 and 510. pp. 14-17. *In*: Vigil, D.L. (ed.). North Carolina/Minerals Management Service Technical Workshop on Manteo Unit Exploration: February 4-5, 1998. U.S. Dept. of the Interior, Minerals Management Service, Gulf of Mexico OCS Region. New Orleans, LA.

*These are the proceedings from a workshop/meeting (February 4-5, 1998) between the North Carolina Department of Environment and Natural Resources, and the U.S. Department of the Interior's Minerals Management Service (MMS). The geographic area being discussed is approximately 45 miles east-northeast of Cape Hatteras, NC, referred to as the Manteo Unit. This workshop reviewed environmental and socioeconomic information known and needed on the Manteo

Unit. The MMS's Gulf of Mexico OCS Regional Director gave an MMS perspective on history and status of the area. Chevron gave a presentation on how the exploratory well would be drilled. The scientific characterization was presented in greater detail by a number of scientific experts who spoke on the following disciplines physical environment, habitat and living resources, seabirds, marine mammals, sea turtles, and social and economic issues. Specific chapters are cited individually, when appropriate.

The continental margin offshore Cape Hatteras, NC has been the focus of numerous oceanographic studies. The objective of this report is to provide an overview of physical, biological, geological, and chemical processes that operate in the region so that the results from individual disciplinary studies can be placed in a system-wide context. This section discusses hydrocarbon potential, water column observations and processes, benthic observations and processes, summary and the future.

Blair, N.E., L.A. Levin, D.J. DeMaster, and G. Plaia. 1996. The short-term fate of fresh algal carbon in continental slope sediments. Limnol. Oceanogr. 41(6): 1208-1219.

Emplacement of tracer mixture containing ^{13}C-labeled green algae on the sea floor of the continental slope offshore Cape Hatteras, North Carolina, elicited a rapid responses over 1.5 d from the dense benthic community. Certain deposit-feeding annelids (e.g. *Scalibregma inflatum* and *Aricidea quadrilobata*) became heavily labeled with ^{13}C-labeled organic matter was transported to a depth of at least 4-5 cm into the seabed during the 1.5 d period, presumably as a consequence of feeding-associated activity. Nonlocal transport produced subsurface peaks in organic ^{13}C at 2-3 cm. Dissolved inorganic ^{13}C, produced by the oxidation of the labeled algae, penetrated to 10-cm depth. The transport of highly reactive organic matter from the sediment surface at initial velocities ≥ 3 cm d^{-1} is expected to be an important control of subsurface benthic processes in slope environments characterized by abundant macrofaunal populations. Anaerobic processes, which are enhanced on the Cape Hatteras slope relative to adjacent areas, may be promoted by the rapid injection of reactive material into subsurface sediments. The transport, in turn, is a consequence of the dense infaunal populations that are supported by the rapid depositions of organic carbon in this region.

Blair, N.E., G.R. Plaia, S.E. Boehme, D.J. DeMaster, and L.A. Levin. 1994. The remineralization of organic carbon on the North Carolina continental slope. Deep-Sea Research II Vol. 41(4-6): 755-766.

The sources and fates of metabolized organic carbon were examined at three sites on the North Carolina slope positioned offshore of Cape Fear, Cape Lookout, and Cape Hatteras. The ^{12}C/^{12}C composition ($\Box$ ^{13}C) of the solid phase organic matter, and the dissolved inorganic carbon (Σ CO$_2$) produced during its oxidation, suggested that the labile fraction was predominantly marine in origin. The Σ CO$_2$ concentration gradient across the sediment-water interface, and by inference the Σ CO$_2$ flux and production rate increased northward from Cape Fear to Cape Hatteras. Methane distributions and Σ CO$_2$ $\Box$ ^{13}C values suggest that the rate of anaerobic diagenesis increased northward as well. The differences in sedimentary biogeochemistry are most likely driven by an along-slope gradient of reactive organic carbon flux to the seabed. This trend in reactive organic carbon flux correlates well worth macrofaunal densities previously observed at the three sites. Proximity to the shelf and the transport of particulate material by surface boundary currents may control the deposition of metabolized material on the Carolina slope.

Evidence of methanogenesis is found only on the Cape Hatteras slope. The methane, which was produced at a depth of approximately 1 m in the seabed, was consumed nearly quantitatively in the biologically mixed layer as it diffused upward. Irrigation of the sediments by infauna may have provided the necessary oxidant for the consumption of the methane.

Blair, N., L. Levin, and D. DeMaster. 1991. Biology and Carbon Cycling on the Carolina Slope. p. 9. Shepard, A. (ed.). NURC/UNCW 1991 Undersea Research: Informational Meeting. National Undersea Research Center, University of North Carolina at Wilmington. Wilmington, NC.

Resources as diverse as fisheries, some minerals and fossil fuels, as well as the atmosphere and climate have been linked to the cycling of carbon and the associated biogenic nutrients along continental margins. The continental slope is an area which has been poorly studied even though it is the site of intense biogeochemical activity. An interdisciplinary program which focuses on the biogeochemistry of the Carolina slope environment is currently underway to investigate the relationship of carbon cycling with the sediment-dwelling ecosystem. Three sites, all at 850 meters water depth, have been studied. Sites I and II, which are off Charleston, South Carolina, and Cape Lookout, North Carolina, respectively, are representative of typical slope environments in terms of animal populations, sediment geochemistry and sediment accumulation. Site III, which is off of Cape Hatteras and near "The Point," has significantly higher populations of bottom-dwelling animals, different animal species and higher rates of organic matter degradation. Biogenic methane formation occurs at Site III but not at the other sites. These differences are thought to be related to the delivery rate of organic matter (food) to the seafloor. The convergence of boundary currents in this region may prove to be an important controlling factor by transporting organic matter into the area or by stimulating localized surface production via the delivery of nutrients. In contrast to the other sites, the sea floor at Site III is an area of high-relief and is more prone to episodic sedimentation and mass wasting. The combination of the high-relief bottom with the relatively large delivery rate of organic carbon to the seafloor may have resulted in a uniquely adapted ecosystem.

Future directions in research include identifying the sources of the sedimentary organic matter and the relationship between the ocean physics and the carbon delivery rate. The rates of organic matter delivery, decomposition and burial need to be measured as they represent important controls on the benthic ecosystems. Specific relationships between the benthic communities, the carbon cycle and sediment dynamics are to be investigated. Descriptions of the cliff-face communities are needed as they represent an important component of the overall ecosystems at Site III.

Blake, J.A., and R.J Diaz. 1994. Input, accumulation and cycling of materials on the continental slope off Cape Hatteras: An introduction. Deep-Sea Research II Vol. 41(4-6): 707-710.

The studies reported in this special issue of Deep-Sea Research are largely derived from data collected as part of programs supported by the U.S. Department of the Interior, Minerals Management Service (MMS) in response to concerns about the effect of oil and gas exploration on the largely unknown continental slope environment. Results of the MMS U.S. South Atlantic continental slope and rise program conducted off the Carolinas from Cape Hatteras to off Charleston in depths raging from 600 to 3500 m identified the importance of the slope off Cape Hatteras in cycling of materials from the shelf to the deep sea. Other more detailed investigations followed which numerous gaps in our knowledge of the role played by such special regions of the continental slope in the global cycling of carbon and other minerals.

Blake, J.A., B. Hecker, J.F. Grassle, B. Brown, M. Wade, P.D. Boehm, E. Baptiste, B. Hilbig, N. Maciolek, R. Petrecca, R.E. Ruff, V. Starczak, and L. Watling. 1987. Study of Biological Processes on the U.S. South Atlantic Slope and Rise: Phase 2. U.S. Department of the Interior, Minerals Management Service, Atlantic OCS Region, Environmental Assessment Section. Herndon, VA.

A total of 16 stations were sampled during a 2 year field program designed to characterize the biological, chemical, and sedimentary processes on the slope and rise off North and South Carolina. Box cores were taken along a 4 transects at depths of 600 to 3500 m. The infauna yielded a total of 1202 species, 520 of which were new to science. Annelids were dominant taxa in terms of density and numbers of species. Species diversity was highest at an 800 m site off Charleston. Infaunal densities were highest on the upper slope (600 m) and lowest on the rise (3000 m). Life history analysis yielded evidence of seasonality for two polychaete species. Two stations off Cape Hatteras in depths of 600 m and 2000 m had higher infaunal density, lower species diversity, and higher biomass than elsewhere on the Atlantic slope and rise. Higher than normal lead and carbon inventories suggest enhanced scavenging processes in this area. Faunal patterns on the Cape Lookout transect were generally typical for other localities on the Atlantic Slope and Rise. Faunal changes were detected off Cape Fear and Charleston that may be related to the influence of the Gulf Stream and associated sediment changes. Epifauna were most unusual on the Charleston Bump, where a hard bottom fauna dominated by filter feeding corals and sponges thrives in an area strongly swept by the Gulf Stream. Consistent faunal differences were found between the upstream and downstream sides of the bump. Data generated in the infaunal and epifaunal surveys supported the view that a partial zoogeographic barrier exists on the slope off North Carolina. This break was most evident between Cape Lookout and Cape Fear.

Blumberg, A.F., and G.L. Mellor. 1983. Diagnostic and Prognostic Numerical Circulation Studies of the South Atlantic Bight. Journal of Geophysical Research 88 C(8): 4579-4592.

Some of the results from a series of diagnostic and prognostic numerical simulations of the circulation in the South Atlantic Bight (SAB) are described. The numerical model developed for the study is a three-dimensional, primitive equation, time dependent, a coordinate model with an imbedded, turbulent closure submodel which should yield realistic Ekman surface and bottom layers. An implicit numerical scheme in the vertical direction and a mode-splitting technique in time are adopted for computational efficiency. A significant portion of the paper is concerned with realistic specification of initial conditions for temperature and salinity, surface forcing, and lateral open boundary conditions. The latter are determined by a simple diagnostic (geostrophic and Ekman dynamics) model which provides dynamically consistent temperature, salinity, and velocity boundary conditions. It appears from an examination of the numerical simulations that the full model yields results that share many features in common with our general understanding of the circulation of the South Atlantic Bight; the region includes shallow shelf waters as well as deeper water dominated by the Gulf Stream. Data for synoptic skill assessment, however, are not available.

Curtin, T.B. 1979a. Ocean Outfall Wastewater Disposal Feasibility and Planning: Oceanographic Field Observations off North Carolina Spring Survey 12 — 22 May 1978, Report No. 79-4. Dept. of Marine Science and Engineering, NCSU. 242 p.

The objectives of the oceanographic field observations within the overall Ocean Outfall Feasibility and Planning Study (Langfelder et al. 1979) were both to provide input data for boundary condition initialization and to provide reference data for diagnostic testing of a series of coastal numerical circulation models under development. The data acquisition program was designed to parallel the model development in that a series of successive scales of variability were addressed. These scales have been defined as the shelf-scale, the nearshore scale, and the diffusive scale, and were characterized for the purposes of the study by temporal and spatial resolutions. Of particular overall interest in this project, with its ultimate focus on the nearshore coastal environment, was the interaction of the larger regional scale processes with those on smaller or local scale.

*Shellfish closure is discussed.

—. 1979b. Ocean Outfall Wastewater Disposal Feasibility and Planning: Oceanographic Field Observations off North Carolina Winter Survey 2-12 February 1978, Report No. 79-3. Dept. of Marine Science and Engineering, NCSU. 149 p.

The objectives of the oceanographic field observations within the overall Ocean Outfall Feasibility and Planning Study (Langfelder et al. 1979) were both to provide input data for boundary condition initialization and to provide reference data for diagnostic testing of a series of coastal numerical circulation models under development. The data acquisition program was designed to parallel the model development in that a series of successive scales of variability were addressed. These scales have been defined as the shelf-scale, the nearshore scale, and the diffusive scale, and were characterized for the purposes of the study by temporal and spatial resolutions. Of particular overall interest in this project, with its ultimate focus on the nearshore coastal environment, was the interaction of the larger regional scale processes with those on smaller or local scale.

*Shellfish closure is discussed.

—. 1979c. Ocean Outfall Wastewater Disposal Feasibility and Planning: Oceanographic Field Observations off North Carolina Fall Survey 1-11 November 1977, Report No. 79-5. Dept. of Marine Science and Engineering, NCSU. 248 p.

The objectives of the oceanographic field observations within the overall Ocean Outfall Feasibility and Planning Study (Langfelder et al. 1979) were both to provide input data for boundary condition initialization and to provide reference data for diagnostic testing of a series of coastal numerical circulation models under development. The data acquisition program was designed to parallel the model development in that a series of successive scales of variability were addressed. These scales have been defined as the shelf-scale, the nearshore scale, and the diffusive scale, and were characterized for the purposes of the study by temporal and spatial resolutions. Of particular overall interest in this project, with its ultimate focus on the nearshore coastal environment, was the interaction of the larger regional scale processes with those on smaller or local scale.

*Shellfish closure is discussed.

—. 1979d. Ocean Outfall Wastewater Disposal Feasibility and Planning: Oceanographic Field Observations Off North Carolina Summer Survey 2-12 August 1977, Report No. 79-2. Dept. of Marine Science and Engineering, NCSU. 303 p.

The objectives of the oceanographic field observations within the overall Ocean Outfall Feasibility and Planning Study (Langfelder et al. 1979) were both to provide input data for boundary condition initialization and to provide reference data for diagnostic testing of a series of coastal numerical circulation models under development. The data acquisition program was designed to parallel the model development in that a series of successive scales of variability were addressed. These scales have been defined as the shelf-scale, the nearshore scale, and the diffusive scale, and were characterized for the purposes of the study by temporal and spatial resolutions. Of particular overall interest in this project, with its ultimate focus on the nearshore coastal environment, was the interaction of the larger regional scale processes with those on smaller or local scale.

*Shellfish closure is discussed.

Cutter, G.R., R.J. Diaz, and J.A. Blake. 1994a. Deep-Sea Research II: CD-ROM APPENDIX. Deep-Sea Research II Vol. 41(4-6): 981-982.

The contents of the CD-ROM Appendix are data and images of the bottom from five of the articles in this issue. The CD-ROM was mastered in a format that can be read by both Macintosh and PC computers. It is organized in an hierarchical structure by folders, with data in one and images in another. To access a particular file, sequentially open folders until the file of interest appears. Data and figure captions are provided as: (.txt) ASCII text with no line breaks; (.tlb) ASCII text with line breaks; (.wor) Microsoft Word; and (.wp) Word Perfect 5.1 files. Images are in TIFF format (.tif).

Data (ACSAR, Hatteras), Images and Captions (ACSAR, Profile, 3Dbathy, Sled, Surface, x-ray) are included.

Cutter, G.R., R. Diaz, and J. Lee. 1994b. Foraminifera from the continental slope off Cape Hatteras, North Carolina. Deep-Sea Research II Vol. 41(4-6): 951-963.

The recent benthic meiofaunal foraminiferal assemblage from the continental slope (590-2003 m) off Cape Hatteras, North Carolina exhibits high species richness and evenness, moderate diversity values, and lacks numerically dominant species. The preserved planktic assemblage has relatively low species richness, high evenness, low diversity, and a few numerically dominant species. Approximately 9% of the benthic species are those that typically live within continental shelf depth ranges. The benthic assemblage abundances and diversities do not follow depth patterns or geophysical characteristics. No biogeographic boundary can be described within the study area for meiofaunal foraminifers. Oxygen limitation does not appear to be a factor affecting the benthos of the North Carolina continental slope based upon the community structure of the benthic foraminifers, if total assemblage is assumed to reflect the recently living community. The high carbonate content of sediments in the area may be explained by foraminiferal tests. Within the study area, the foraminiferal assemblages are uniform, and probably reflect relative consistency of primary environmental variables as well as dynamic downslope transport and high influx of material from the water column in the vicinity where the Gulf Stream and the Western Boundary Undercurrent cross.

DeMaster, D.J., R.H Pope, L.A. Levin, and N.E. Blair. 1994. Biological mixing intensity and rates of organic carbon accumulation in North Carolina slope sediments . Deep-Sea Research II Vol. 41(4-6): 735-753.

Sediment accumulation rates and biological mixing intensities were determined at three sites on the North Carolina slope based on profiles of naturally occurring ^{14}C, ^{210}Ph and ^{234}Th. The three sites all were at a water depth of 850 m with a spacing of 150 — 180 km between sites. Sediment accumulation rates increase from south to north from values of 7 cm ky^{-1} at Site I, to 160 cm ky^{-1} at Site II, to 1100 cm ky^{-1} at Site III. The organic carbon burial rate a these sites also increases in the northward direction from 0.65 (Site I) to 20 (Site II) to $\leq$ 150 g C$_{org}$ m^{-2} year^{-1} (Site III). These data indicate that continental margin environments can exhibit highly variable carbon fluxes over relatively small distances on the seafloor. The rate of organic carbon accumulation at Site III is one of the highest values reported for the marine environment. Based on these accumulation rates and dissolved inorganic carbon flux estimates from each site, the seabed organic carbon preservation efficiency (i.e. the ratio of C$_{org}$ accumulation rate to C$_{org}$ deposition rate times 100) was estimated to vary from 6.0% to 54% to 88%, at Sites I, II and III, respectively. The ^{14}C age of organic matter in surface sediments was older at Site III (1800 years BP), than at Sites I and II (800 years BP), indicating that Site III receives it greater proportion of old sediment from either up-slope areas or from terrigenous sources. Inventories of excess ^{234}Th (half-life of 24 days) were used as it tracer for particle flux covering the 100 days prior to the October 1989, July-August 1990 and August 1991 cruises. The mean ^{234}Th inventories at the three sites were 4.7 $\pm$ 1.9, 8.4 $\pm$ 6.3 and 23.1 $\pm$ 7.3 dpm cm^{-2}, for Sites I, II and III, respectively.

Diaz, R.J., J.A. Blake, and D.P. Lohse. 1993a. Volume II Final Report: Benthic Study of the Continental Slope off Cape Hatteras, North Carolina. Virginia Institute of Marine Science, School of Marine Science, College of William and Mary, Gloucester Pt., VA. Science Applications International Corporation, Woods Hole, MA. 135 p.

*This is a study of the nature and spatial extent of continental slope benthic communities off Cape Hatteras, NC, with emphasis on the Manteo Area lease block 467. Macrofaunal abundance and biomass in this area higher than anywhere else along the entire South Atlantic continental slope and rise. Species composition of the infauna off Cape Hatteras is also different from other slope habitats. Species richness and diversity are lower with a high degree of dominance by species that are cosmopolitan in distribution. Trends in abundance of invertebrate megafauna on the continental slope off Cape Hatteras appear to be similar to the macrofauna. Demersal fish fauna off Cape Hatteras is distinctive in terms of composition and population density. Overall, abundance of benthic fish off Cape Hatteras is four to seven times higher than adjacent area. Site sediment characteristics (e.g., source, texture, and physico-chemistry) and potential impact to benthic community by sediment discharge during drilling are described. Volume III contains Appendices A-E.

Much of the data in this report were used in the Special Deep Research issue (1994. 41(4-6)).

Fornes, W.L., D.J. Demaster, L.A. Levin, and N.E. Blair. 1999. Bioturbation and particle transport in Carolina slope sediments: A radiochemical approach. Journal of Marine Research 57: 335-355.

In situ tracer experiments investigated short-term sediment mixing processes at two Carolina continental margin sites (water depth = 850 m) characterized by different organic C fluxes, ^{234}Th mixing coefficients (D_b) and benthic assemblages. Phytoplankton, slope sediment, and sand-sized glass beads tagged with ^{210}Pb, ^{113}Sn, and ^{228}Th, respectively, were placed via submersible at the sediment-water interface at both field sites (Site I off Cape Fear, and Site III off Cape Hatteras). Experimental plots were sampled at 0, 1.5 days, and 90 days after tracer emplacement to examine short-term, vertical transport. Both sites are initially dominated by nonlocal mixing. Transport to the bottom of the surface mixed layer at both sites occurs more rapidly than ^{234}Th-based D_b values predict; after 1.5 days, tagged particles were observed 5 cm below the sediment-water interface at Site I and 12 cm below at Site III. Impulse tracer profiles after 90 days at Site III exhibit primarily diffusive distributions, most likely due to a large number of random. nonlocal mixing events. The D_b values determined from 90-day particle lagging experiments are comparable with those obtained from naturally occurring ^{234}Th profiles (100-day time scales) from nearby locations. The agreement between impulse tracer mixing coefficients and steady-state natural tracer mixing coefficients suggests that the diffusive analogue for bioturbation on monthly time scales is a realistic and useful approach. Tracer profiles from both sites exhibit some degree of particle selective mixing, but the preferential transport of the more labile carbon containing particles only occurred 30% of the time. Consequently, variations in the extent to which age-dependent mixing occurs in marine sediments may depend on factors such as faunal assemblage and organic carbon flux.

Harvey, H.R. 1994. Fatty acids and sterols as source markers of organic matter in sediments of the North Carolina continental slope. Deep-Sea Research II Vol. 41(4-6): 783-796.

To estimate the source and diagenetic state of organic matter reaching bottom sediments, fatty acids and sterols were measured in unconsolidated surface material (flocs) at 12 sites ranging from 600 to 2000 m across the mid-Atlantic continental slope off Cape Hatteras, North Carolina. Total free and esterified fatty acids were similar in description and concentration to other coastal systems, with values ranging from 0.64 to 46.52 g mg^{-1} organic carbon (1.10-68.85 g mg^{-1}dry sediment). Although shallow (600 m) stations contained significantly greater fatty acid concentrations than deep (>1400 m) stations, high variability observed at mid-depth (800 m) collections precluded a consistent relationship between total fatty acid concentration and station depth. At three sites where underlying sediments were also collected, decreases in total fatty acid reduced amounts of polyenoic acids and significant presence of bacterial fatty acids suggest rapid reworking of labile organic material that reaches the sediment surface. The distribution of sterols was remarkably consistent among all sites even though there were large variations in concentrations (1.8-20.7g mg^{-1} organic carbon). Sterol composition indicated phytoplankton, principally diatoms and dinoflagellates, as the principal source of labile organic matter to sediments, together with a significant input of cholesterol typical of zooplankton and their feeding activity. A minor but widespread terrigenous input was also evident based upon significant concentrations of sterols dominant in vascular plants.

Langfelder, J., T.B. Curtin, D.N. Hyman, G. Janowitz, J. Maiolo, W. Queen, F.Y. Sorrell, M. Amien, V. Bellis, M. Brinson, G. Davis, C.Y. Lee, C. O'Rear, L. Pearce, C.Y. Peng, S. Riggs, B. Smith, M. Sobsey, and P. Tschetter. 1979. Final Report: Ocean Outfall Wastewater Disposal Feasibility and Planning, Report No. 79-1. Dept. of Marine Science and Engineering, NCSU; Report No. 5, Institute for Coastal and Marine Resources, ECU. 482 p.

*This report follows an EIS format and is cited as a single document. Individual chapters are not stand-alone documents. Major findings of the study were: 1) Construction and operation of a well designed and operated sewage treatment plant that utilizes an ocean outfall and secondary treatment should not adversely affect the water column on fishery resources. Some build up of effluent constituents may occur in the bottom sediments in the immediate vicinity of the diffuser and could result in bottom community changes. 2) Effluent discharge should have essentially no adverse affect on recreational swimming in the areas of the diffuser. Areas now closed to shellfishing in the estuaries could be reopened as a result of reduced pathogen loadings: these pathogens are presently coming from septic tanks and treatment plants that discharge into these waters. 3) Centralized sewer systems will increase land values, allow reduced lot size and stimulate growth. This will lead to change in the population composition and demands for expanded goods and services.

Levin, L., N. Blair, D. DeMaster, G. Plaia, W. Fornes, C. Martin, and C. Thomas. 1997. Rapid subduction of organic matter by maldanid polychaetes on the North Carolina slope. Journal of Marine Research 55: 595-611.

In situ tracer experiments conducted on the North Carolina continental slope reveal that tube-building worms (Polychaeta: Maldanidae) can, without ingestion, rapidly subduct freshly deposited, algal carbon (^{13}C-labeled diatoms) and inorganic materials (slope sediment and glass beads) to depths of 10 cm or more in the sediment column. Transport over 1.5 days appears to be nonselective but spatially patchy, creating localized, deep hotspots. As a result of this transport, relatively fresh organic matter becomes available soon after deposition to deep-dwelling microbes and other infauna, and both aerobic and anaerobic processes may be enhanced. Comparison of tracer subduction with estimates from a diffusive mixing model using ^{234}Th-based coefficients, suggests that maldanid subduction activities, within 1.5 d of particle deposition, could account for 25-100% of the mixing below 5 cm that occurs on 100-day time scales. Comparison of community data from the North Carolina slope for different places and times indicate a correlation between the abundance of deep-welling maldanids and the abundance and the dwelling depth in the sediment column of other infauna. Pulsed inputs of organic matter occur frequently in margin environments and maldanid polychaetes are a common component of continental slope macrobenthos. Thus, the activities we observe are likely to be widespread and significant for chemical cycling (natural and anthropogenic materials) on the slope. We propose that species like maldanids, that rapidly redistribute labile organic matter within the seabed, probably function as keystone resource modifiers. They may exert a disproportionately strong influence (relative to their abundance) on the structure of infaunal communities and on the timing, location and nature of organic matter diagenesis and burial in continental margin sediments.

Manheim, F.T., R.H. Meade, and G.C. Bond. 1970. Suspended Matter in Surface Waters of the Atlantic Continental Margin from Cape Cod to the Florida Keys. Science 167: 371-376.

Appreciable amounts of suspended matter (> 1.0 milligram per liter) in surface waters are restricted to within a few kilometers of the Atlantic coast, articles that escape estuaries or are discharged by rivers into the shelf region and to travel longshoreward rather than seaward. Suspended matter farther offshore, chiefly amorphous organic particles, totals 0.1 milligram per liter or less. Soot, fly ash, processed cellulose, and other pollutants are widespread.

McCann, M.P., L.J. Pietrafesa, G.S. Janowitz, and T.B. Curtin. 1984. Physical Processes Influencing Temperature and Salinity on the North Carolina Cape Shoals, Contract No. DOE-AS09-76-EY00902; NOAA Contract No. 04-6-158-44054. 138 p.

Cross-spectral analysis and heat budget are used to relate atmospheric and river runoff data within seven years of daily surface temperature and salinity on the North Carolina continental shelf. Salinity on Diamond Shoals is highly correlated with alongshore wind stress implying wind driven advection of the front between Virginia Coastal Water and Carolina Coastal Water. In the presence of strong horizontal and vertical temperature gradients, temperature at Diamond Shoals quickly responds to cross-shelf winds. At Frying Pan Shoals, the plume of the Cape Fear River is detected when winds blow seaward. Atmospheric fluxes primarily control the cycle of heating and cooling at Frying Pan Shoals, but advection of heat buffers the water temperature in the winter and summer.

Milliman, J.D. 1994. Organic matter content in the U.S. Atlantic continental slope sediments: Decoupling the grain-size factor. Deep-Sea Research II Vol. 41(4-6): 797-808.

Decoupling organic content in sediments from grain size can help define spatial variations in biological productivity, transport or preservation in continental margin sediments. Upper slope and upper rise sediments off the eastern United States have organic nitrogen contents similar to or lower than those predicted by grain size, whereas mid-slope sediments between Norfolk Canyon and Cape Fear have much higher organic contents. These elevated values probably result from off-shelf transport, combined with rapid burial and correspondingly reduced rates of remineralization, while lower values on the upper rise presumable result from low input of organic matter and low rates of burial and increased oxic degradation.

Milliman, J.D., R.J. Diaz, J.A. Blake, and G.R. Cutter Jr., (eds.). 1994. Topical Studies in Oceanography: Input, Accumulation and Cycling of Materials on the Continental Slope Off Cape Hatteras. Deep-Sea Research Part II Vol. 41. 982 p.

*This is a compilation of studies on Input, Accumulation and Cycling of Materials on the Continental Slope Off Cape Hatteras. Geology, sediments, organics, and benthic fauna are discussed. A CD-ROM is included. Each chapter (study) is cited independently, when appropriate. Some papers in this issue were derived from Diaz et al. (1993).

Newton, J.G., O.H. Pilkey, and O.H. Blanton. 1971. An Oceanographic Atlas of the Carolina Continental Margin. Division of Mineral Resources. North Carolina Department of Conservation and Development. Raleigh, NC. 57 p.

*This atlas is a synthesis of oceanographic information describing the North Carolina coast. It contains data collected on RV Eastward Cruises 1964-1969. Sea floor topography and geology (sediment samples, rock and reef soundings), shipwreck locations, sea floor photography, and water characteristics (temperature and salinity) are described and mapped.

Ocean Margins Program (OMP). 1993. Research program plan, DOE Office of Energy Research, Environmental Science Division. Washington, DC.

The Ocean Margins Program (OMP) program is within the defined study area for The Point. The OMP Data Management Plan objective is to provide a single repository for all time series data collected on OMP moorings in a simple format that does not require collaborators to purchase or learn to use any specific software products. Access to these data will be provided at any time without the intervention of an operator. Sampled parameters include: date, time, East component of velocity (cm/sec), North component of velocity (cm/sec), Temperature (C), Salinity (PS78, psu), Pressure — absolute (dbar), Acoustic backscatter intensity (dB); Estimated biomass (mg/m^3); Temperature at ADCP — (C); Dissolved oxygen concentration (umole/kg), Dissolved oxygen saturation (percent), fluorometric chlorophyll (ug/l), Transmissometer light transmission (l/meter), PAR — photosynthetic active radiation (umole/m^2/sec).

Phalen, P.S. 1980. Computerization of RV Dan Moore Data Relevant to OCS Phosphates Area on the North Carolina Continental Shelf. North Carolina Division of Marine Fisheries, Department of Natural Resources and Community Development. Morehead City, NC.

The RV Dan Moore, an 85 foot steel stern trawler, collected over 4,400 samples during service with the North Carolina Division of Marine Fisheries (DMF), 1968-1981. The vessel's purpose was to conduct applied research to enable the Division to manage and develop coastal fisheries resources for the benefit of all North Carolinians. Objectives of individual cruises included gear tests, fish tagging, relative abundance and distribution surveys, biological investigations (i.e., age and growth), bottom type surveys, etc. Information collected consisted of location, environmental, and catch data. In many instances, these RV Dan Moore data are the only biological data for certain areas of the Continental Shelf. Results of cruises were summarized in bulletins from 1968-1974. Complete cruise reports describing methods and results were filed for the remaining cruises.

The RV Dan Moore data that were found necessary to the contractor to complete an economic feasibility study of OCS Phosphates-Environmental Impact Statement have been coded, key entered, and summarized. The following completion report identifies the amount and type of data entered and summarizes the objectives, methods, and result of cruises that sampled within the specified OCS phosphates areas.

Pietrafesa, L.J., J.M. Morrison, M.P. McCann, J. Churchill, E. Bohm, and R.W. Houghton. 1994. Water mass linkages between the Middle and South Atlantic Bights. Deep-Sea Research II Vol. 41(2-3): 365-389.

Time and frequency domain analysis are used to relate coastal meteorological data with 7 years of daily surface temperature and salinity collected at three coastal light stations: offshore of the mouth of Chesapeake Bay, Virginia, on Diamond Shoals, at Cape Hatteras, North Carolina and on Frying Pan Shoals, off Cape Fear, North Carolina. Salinity fluctuations at Diamond Shoals are highly correlated with alongshore wind stress, implying wind driven advection of the front between Virginia Coastal Water (VCW) and Carolina Coastal Water (CCW) across Diamond Shoals. The data collected at Diamond Shoals indicate that more than half the time there is significant encroachment of Mid Atlantic Bight water into the South Atlantic Bight around Cape Hatteras, contrary to the notion that VCW is entirely entrained into the Gulf Stream. In fact, VCW can appear as far south as Frying Pan Shoals, thereby extending across the entire North Carolina Capes inner to mid shelf. Temperature and salinity time series also indicate that water mass, overlying Diamond Shoals respond quickly to cross-shelf winds, Cross-shelf wind stress, is significantly correlated with surface water temperature at Diamond Shoals, for periods between 2 and 12 days. Changes in temperature can be brought about by wind-driven cross-shelf circulation and by wind-induced upwelling. Seasurface temperature satellite (AVHRR) image taken during the SEEP II confirm these concepts.

Schaff, T., L. Levin, N. Blair, D. DeMaster, R. Pope, and S. Boehme. 1992. Spatial heterogeneity of benthos on the Carolina continental slope: large (100 km)-scale variation. Marine Ecology Progress Series 88: 143-160.

Large-scale spatial heterogeneity of macrofaunal and microbial communities was examined on the continental slope off North and South Carolina, USA, by comparing 3 sites, separated by 130 to 150 km and all at 850 m water depth. Significant variation was found among macrofaunal assemblages at all 3 sites, and between microbial counts at 2 sites. We investigated the hypothesis that 100 km scale heterogeneity was driven by variation in organic C flux to the sea floor. The northernmost site (Site III, off Cape Hatteras, NC) was found to have macrofaunal abundances (>55000 m^{-2}) higher than any previous recorded from this depth, and significantly higher than those at Site II (off Cape Lookout, North Carolina) (21319 m^{-2}) or Site I (off Charleston, SC) (9438 m^{-2}). Trends in macrofaunal abundance did not follow those sediment TOC (total organic carbon), but agreed well with estimates of total carbon flux for the three sites. Mixing coefficients determined from profiles of naturally occurring ^{234}Th (half life 24 d) indicate that the sediments at Site III are mixed 2 to 6 times faster than at the other 2 sites, which is consistent with the trends in macrofaunal abundance and biomass. Using ^{14}C-based sedimentation rates and sediment carbon content, we estimated carbon flux to be 0.6, 20 and > 70 g C m^{-2} yr^{-1} at sites I, II and III, respectively. Inventories of ^{234}Th and downcore concentration profiles of dissolved $SO_4^=$, CO_2 and CH_4 within the sediment provided evidence that the flux of metabolized carbon was greater at Site III than at the other sites. Polychaetes, which comprised 43, 74 and 65 % of the fauna at Sites I, II and III, respectively, exhibited lower diversity, higher dominance, and a completely different species composition at Site III than at the other 2 sites. *Scalibregma inflatum* and *Aricidea quadrilobata* comprised 33 % of total macrofauna at Site III, but were absent at Sites I and II. The species composition, high dominance, and prevalence of juveniles among polychaetes at Site III is suggestive of a response to organic enrichment. Enrichment of the Site III benthos is attributed to physical oceanographic and geophysical causes, including Gulf Stream-induced upwelling, a confluence of currents focused by bottom topography, and lateral inputs resulting from mass wasting processes. Despite significant differences in macrofaunal abundance, Sites I and II exhibited considerable overlap in microbial counts, polychaete species composition, dominance and diversity patterns.

Shepard, A. (ed.). 1991. Undersea Research at The Point. NURC/UNCW 1991 Undersea Research: Informational Meeting. National Undersea Research Center, University of North Carolina at Wilmington. Wilmington, NC. 9 p.

*This handout is a summary of research being conducted at "The Point" area (Manteo Lease Block 467).

The National Undersea Research Center at the University of North Carolina at Wilmington, funded by a grant from the National Oceanic and Atmospheric Administration's (NOAA) Office of Undersea Research (OUR), was established in 1980 to promote, facilitate, and conduct research in the Southeastern United States utilizing undersea techniques, including advanced wet diving and manned and unmanned submersibles. A main Center goal is to provide information to NOAA that will assist the agency in fulfilling its charter to explore, understand, conserve and manage the U.S. marine environment and associated resources. To help meet this goal, the Center supports and conducts interdisciplinary oceanographic research projects studying continental margin processes, particularly the interactions and linkages between estuarine, continental shelf, and slope (including submarine canyon) environments.

Shepard, A., and A.H. Hulbert (eds.). 1994. Workshop Report: Present and Future Research Initiatives on the Upper Hatteras Slope off North Carolina. National Undersea Research Center at the University of North Carolina at Wilmington. Wilmington, NC. 30p.

*This report is the result of the May 1993 workshop held in Raleigh, NC. The topics of discussion were research (present and planned) at the Upper Hatteras Slope (UHS) and potential funding sources. The workshop was sponsored by National Undersea Research Center at the University of North Carolina at Wilmington. The report provides a brief description of the UHS invertebrates, biological oceanography, chemical oceanography, geological oceanography (bathymetry, oil and gas exploration), physical oceanography, fisheries, and *Sargassum*. Appendix A is a workshop agenda and list of speakers. No abstracts for speakers are provided. Appendix B is a list of potential funding sources. Appendix C contains a list of publications pertaining to the UHS.

Stefansson, U., and L.P. Atkinson. 1967. Physical and chemical properties of the shelf and slope waters off North Carolina. Technical report. Duke University Marine Laboratory. Beaufort, NC. 240 p.

The present report includes a compilation of data collected during several cruises aboard the RV Eastward in the period June 1965-April 1967. The objective of this work was to study the broad features of the circulation and distribution of properties on the shelf, and attempt to relate the observed distributions in different seasons to various meteorological factors and processes affecting the renewal of shelf waters. These various aspects are dealt with separate publications. This report includes a short preliminary description of the main results, charts showing the horizontal distribution of temperature, salinity, density and dynamic topography, illustrations of vertical distribution of physical and chemical properties, and a tabulation of the data obtained at each station from hydrographic casts.

Stefansson, U., L.P. Atkinson, and D.F Bumpus. 1971. Hydrographic properties and circulation of the North Carolina Shelf and Slope Waters. Deep-Sea Research 18: 383-420.

Processes affecting the renewal of the North Carolina Shelf Waters are discussed on the basis of temperature, salinity, dissolved oxygen, nutrients, runoff and wind data collected during 1965-1967. These consist of horizontal advection near the coast from the north, meanders of the Gulf Stream, subsurface intrusion, cascading and runoff.

The wind-driven Virginia Water transport past Cape Hatteras may markedly reduce the temperature and salinity, and accelerate the freshwater exchange. The runoff from the watershed north of Cape Hatteras, when driven south by northerly winds, especially during the peak period in early spring, has a much greater influence on the circulation in Raleigh and Onslow Bays than does that from the adjacent rivers south of Cape Hatteras. Meanders in the Gulf Stream may renew the shelf waters with warm, saline water. Intrusion of subsurface Caribbean Water on to the outer part of the shelf takes place most frequently during the late summer following a period of southerly winds. It is postulated that during the cold part of the year when the surface layers are only partly stratified, such an intrusion may lead to upwelling near the shelf break. Cascading from the shelf down the slope may occur during the cold season following periods of low air temperature. Intrusion of subsurface water replenishes nutrients in the area, while cascading reduces the available supply of nutrients.

U.S. Department of the Interior, Minerals Management Service. 1990. Atlantic Outer Continental Shelf: Final Environmental Report on Proposed Exploratory Drilling Offshore North Carolina, U.S. Department of the Interior, Minerals Management Service, Atlantic OCS Region, Environmental Assessment Section. Herndon, VA.

Topics include: fisheries, birds, marine mammals, physical oceanography, chemical oceanography, geology, gas and oil production. The proposed action is to drill a single exploratory well approximately 72 km (45 mi) east-northeast of Cape Hatteras, North Carolina in 820 m (2,690 ft) of water. Total depth for the proposed well is 4,267 m (14,000 ft) and the location is on Block 467 on the Minerals Management Service Protraction diagram NI 18-2. The proposal has been submitted by Mobil for itself and 7 partners to drill the well on the approved 21-block exploration unit.

Uchupi, E. 1967. The continental margin south of Cape Hatteras, North Carolina: shallow structure. SE Geol. 8: 155-177.

Continuous seismic profiles, drill hole data and dredge hauls show that the geologic history of the continental margin south of the Cape Hatteras has been complex, marked by carbonate deposition, erosion by the Gulf Stream, and differential subsidence. The Blake Escarpment east of the Blake Plateau is believed to represent a chain of algal banks that flourished during the Cretaceous. A thick sequence of shallow-water carbonate sediments accumulated on the Blake Plateau behind the algal sandbanks to the east. Soon after the banks died during Late Cretaceous submergence of the area the Gulf Stream extended its course across the Blake Plateau. During the Tertiary, the locus of deposition shifted westward to the area near the present shelf-break, where 600 to 1000 meters of shallow-water sediments were deposited. South of Latitude 32 sediment prograded against the westward margin of the Gulf Stream throughout the Tertiary. Farther north, where the Gulf Stream lies farther offshore, outbuilding extended beyond the eastern margin of the Blake Plateau. Vertical uplifts followed by erosion by the Gulf Stream during the Pleistocene modified this sedimentary framework.

Vigil, D.L. (ed.). 1998. North Carolina/Minerals Management Service Technical Workshop on Manteo Unit Exploration: February 4-5, 1998. U.S. Dept. of the Interior, Minerals Management Service. Gulf of Mexico OCS Region. New Orleans, LA. 168 p.

*These are the proceedings from a workshop/meeting (February 4-5, 1998) between the North Carolina Department of Environment and Natural Resources, and the U.S. Department of the Interior's Minerals Management Service (MMS). The geographic area being discussed is approximately 45 miles east-northeast of Cape Hatteras, North Carolina, referred to as the Manteo Unit. This workshop reviewed environmental and socioeconomic information known and needed on the Manteo Unit. The MMS's Gulf of Mexico OCS Regional Director gave an MMS perspective on history and status of the area. Chevron gave a presentation on how the exploratory well would be drilled. The scientific characterization was presented in greater detail by a number of scientific experts who spoke on the following disciplines physical environment, habitat and living resources (invertebrates and fish), seabirds, marine mammals, sea turtles, and social and economic issues. Specific chapters are cited individually, when appropriate.

Walsh, J.J. 1994. Particle export at Cape Hatteras. Deep-Sea Research II Vol. 41(2-3): 603-628.

A simple model of shelf, slope and basin waters near Cape Hatteras, North Carolina is used to estimate the sources and sinks of organic carbon within the Gulf Stream System. The analysis employs water transport estimates, nutrient data. satellite imagery, surficial sediment records and particle distributions caught by bottle, camera and sediment trap to compute vertical and lateral fluxes of particulate carbon. Particle export from the SAB and MAB shelf ecosystems may constitute 62-82% of the source of the carbon flux within the Gulf Stream near 75 W, after settling at 100 m day^{-1}, with an oxidation loss of 4% day^{-1}, to a nominal mid-depth of 1000 m on the slope.

As a result of light limitation, denitrification and DON solubilization, partial utilization of onwelled nitrate from the Gulf Stream System by coastal phytoplankton suggests that the time-averaged f ratio may be as small as 0.12 for the ratio of the "new" portion of primary production to the total. After burial loss, the export of particulate matter from the shelves then represents at most 11% of the total carbon fixation of coastal waters. If the shelf export of DON and unutilized NO_3 is consumed within adjacent slope waters, however, the f ratio and the percentage of particle export from the carbon fixation of shelf-affected waters might increase to 0.25 and 24%.

Willey, J.D., and L.B. Cahoon. 1991. Enhancement of chlorophyll a production in Gulf Stream surface seawater by rainwater nitrate. Marine Chemistry 34: 63-75.

The concentration of nitrate commonly found in rain from continental storm systems passing over eastern North Carolina was sufficient to stimulate chlorophyll *a* production in surface Gulf Stream water collected over the continental slope near Cape Hatteras, NC, in mid-October 1989. Two bioassay experiments were conducted on board ship by mixing Gulf Stream surface seawater with synthetic rainwater (5% rainwater). These bioassays indicated an increased production of chlorophyll *a* in response to rainwater nitrate but not phosphate. The response was apparent after incubation for 2 days after the chlorophyll *a* concentration increased approximately 2.5 times relative to controls in both experiments.

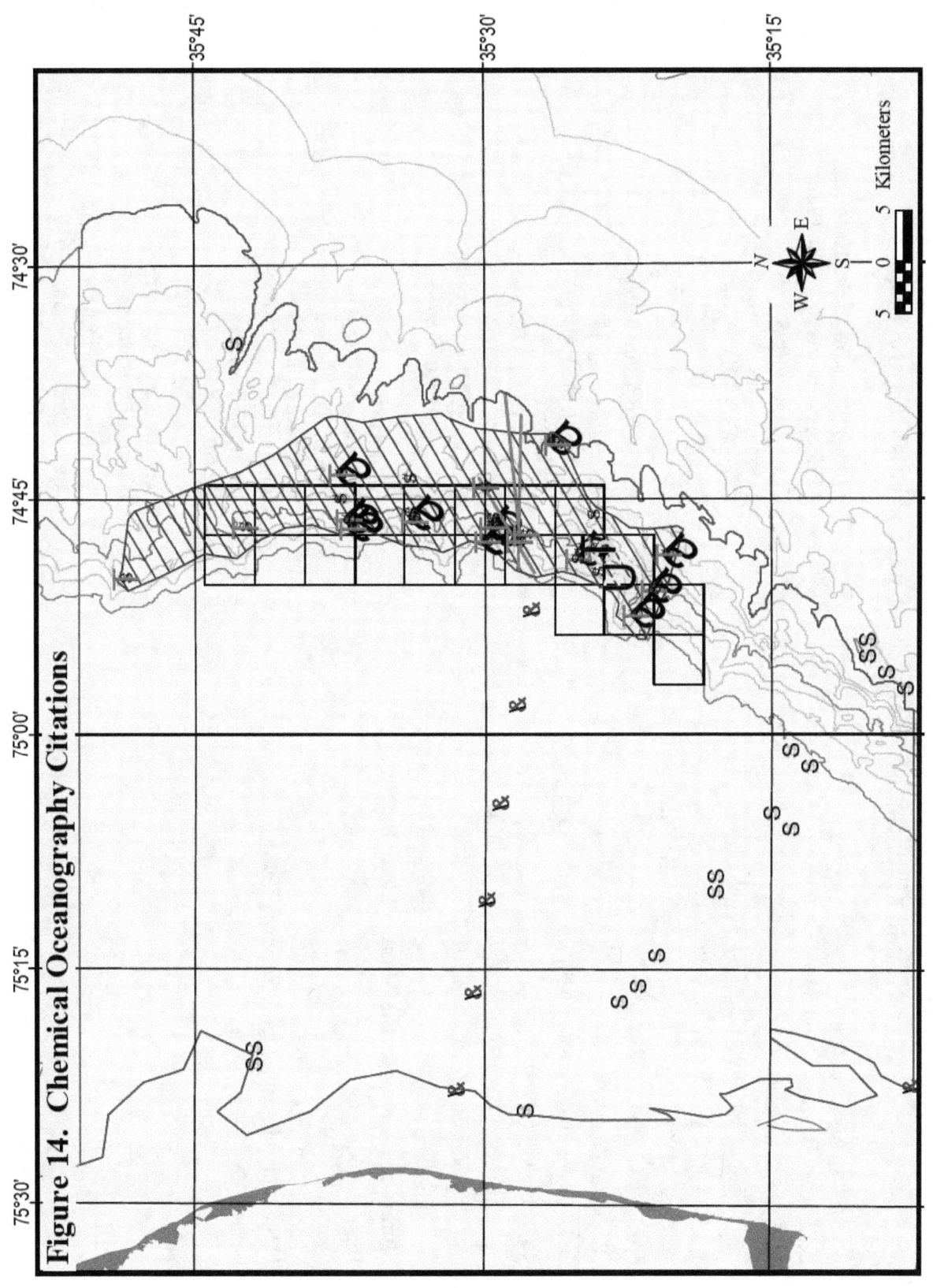

Figure 14. Chemical Oceanography Citations

Key to Chemical Oceanography Citations (Figure 14).

/\/ Study Area Boundary

☐ Lease Blocks

Mapped Citations

§ Blair et al. (1994); DeMaster et al. (1994)

∪ Blair et al. (1996); Levin et al. (1997)

⋊ Blake & Diaz (1994); Cutter et al. (1994b)

⋉ Blake et al. (1987)

& Curtain (1979 a-d); Langfelder et al. (1979);

⧄ Cutter et al. (1994a); Milliman et al. (1994);

đ Harvey (1994)

† Fornes et al. (1999); Schaff et al. (1992)

s Stefansson & Atkinson (1967)

Studies that Focus on the Manteo Lease Blocks

Blair (1998)
Diaz et al. (1993a)
Shepard & Hulbert (1994)
U.S.D.O.I.-Minerals Mgmt. Service (1990)
Vigil (1998)

**Studies that Cover the Hatteras
Middle Slope Area ("The Point")**

Bailey et al. (1995)
Barrett (1965)
Shepard (1991)
Willey & Cahoon (1991)

Broad Regional Studies

Abernathy et al. (1989)
Anderson et al. (1994)
Atkinson (1985)
Atkinson et al. (1985)
Blair et al. (1991)
Blumberg & Mellor (1983)
Manheim et al. (1970)
McCann et al. (1984)
Milliman (1994)
Newton et al. (1971)
Ocean Margins Program (OMP) (1993)
Pietrafesa et al. (1994)
Stefansson et al. (1971)
Uchupi (1967)
Walsh (1994)

**Studies Based on Large
Digitized Databases**

Anderson & Gehringer (1959a, 1959b)
Anderson et al. (1956, 1961)
Phalen (1980)

GEOLOGICAL OCEANOGRAPHY CHAPTER

GEOLOGICAL OCEANOGRAPHY CHAPTER

Abernathy, S.A., M.T. Baer, C.S. Benner, M.S. Brody, D.K. Francois, J.K. Gilliam, L.K. Good, C.J. Ohara, and J.V. Martin. 1989. Atlantic Outer Continental Shelf: Description of the Mid-Atlantic Environment. Abernathy, S.A. (ed.). U.S. Department of the Interior, Minerals Management Service, Atlantic OCS Region, Environmental Assessment Section. Herndon, VA. 167 p.

*This document discusses the major issues and areas of concern for the mid-Atlantic environment that are considered in the planning process for oil and gas leasing and operations on the Outer Continental Shelf (OCS). The issues are addressed with respect to the potential environmental consequences of mid Atlantic oil and gas exploration, development and production. A section discussing The Physical Environment (e.g., geology, non-petroleum minerals, physical oceanography, chemical oceanography and water quality, ocean dumping, meteorology, air quality), Biological resources (e.g., plankton, benthos, fishery resources, marine reptiles, marine mammals, marine and coastal birds, estuaries, wetlands, sensitive coastal habitats, canyon areas), Socioeconomic Environment, and other issues (e.g., archaeological resources, marine vessel traffic, National Aeronautics and Space Administration/ Department of Defense activities, oil and gas infrastructure, marine sanctuaries, and estuarine research reserves) is included. Most of the figures showing fisheries resource distribution are taken from fisheries data compiled for bottom-trawl and shellfish surveys of the National Marine Fisheries Service, Northeast Fisheries Center, Woods Hole, MA.

Amato, R.V. 1994. Sand and Gravel Maps of the Atlantic Continental Shelf with Explanatory Text. U.S. Department of the Interior, Minerals Management Service, Office of International Activities and Marine Minerals. 35 p.

*Deposits and mixtures of sand, gravel, silt, and clay are shown on four maps of the U.S. Atlantic Continental Shelf at a scale of 1:1,000,000 for the North, Mid-, and South Atlantic and South Florida offshore areas. The maps also show major differences in mineralogical content, from carbonate-rich sediments in the South Florida area to quartz-rich sediments north of Cape Hatteras. The maps were compiled from published literature and from published and unpublished maps at various scales and sizes of areas covered.

Anderson, R. F., G. T. Rowe, P. F. Kemp, S. Trumbore, and P. E. Biscaye. 1994. Carbon budget for the mid-slope depocenter of the Middle Atlantic Bight. Deep-Sea Research II Vol. 41 (2-3): 669-703.

A mass budget was constructed for organic carbon on the upper slope of the Middle Atlantic Bight. A region thought to serve as a depocenter for fine-grained material exported from the adjacent shelf. Various components of the budget are internally consistent, and observed differences can be attributed to natural spatial variability or to the different time scales, over which measurements were made. The flux of organic carbon to the sediments in the core of the depocenter zone, at it water depth of ~ 1000 m, was measured with sediment traps to be 65 mg C m^{-2} day^{-1} is buried. Oxygen fluxes into the sediments, measured with incubation chambers attached to a free vehicle lander, correspond to total carbon remineralization rates of 49-79 mg C m^{-2} day^{-1}. Carbon remineralization rates estimated from gradients of C_{org} within the mixed layer, and from gradients of dissolved ammonia and phosphate in pore waters, sum to only ~4-6 mg C m^{-2} day^{-1}.

Most of the C_{org} deposited on the upper slope sediments is supplied by lateral transport from other regions, but even if all of this material were derived from the adjacent shelf, it represents, <2% of the mean annual shelf productivity. This value is further lowered by recognizing that as much as half of the C_{org} deposited on the slope is refractory, having originated by reworking from older deposits.

Refractory C_{org} arrives at the sea bed with an average ^{14}C age 600-900 years older than the pre-bomb ^{14}C age of DIC in seawater, and has a mean life in the sediments with respect to biological remineralization of at least 1000 years. Labile carbon supplied to the slope, on the other hand, is rapidly and (virtually) completely remineralized, with a mean life of $< \sim 1$ year. Carbon-14 ages of fine-grained carbonate and organic carbon present within the interstices of shelf sands are consistent with this material acting as a source for the old carbon supplied to the slope. Winnowing and export of reworked carbon may contribute to the often-described relationship between organic carbon preservation and accumulation rate of marine sediments.

Atkinson, L., L. Heilman, and T. Curtin. 1998. Appendix E: Bathymetric and Physical Oceanographic Description of the Manteo Lease Area. pp.108-20. *In*: Vigil, D.L. (ed.). North Carolina/Minerals Management Service Technical Workshop on Manteo Unit Exploration: February 4-5, 1998. U.S. Dept. of the Interior, Minerals Management Service, Gulf of Mexico OCS Region. New Orleans, LA.

*These are the proceedings from a workshop/meeting (February 4-5, 1998) between the North Carolina Department of Environment and Natural Resources, and the U.S. Department of the Interior's Minerals Management Service (MMS). The geographic area being discussed is approximately 45 miles east-northeast of Cape Hatteras, NC, referred to as the Manteo Unit. This workshop reviewed environmental and socioeconomic information known and needed on the Manteo Unit. The MMS's Gulf of Mexico OCS Regional Director gave an MMS perspective on history and status of the area. Chevron gave a presentation on how the exploratory well would be drilled. The scientific characterization was presented in greater detail by a number of scientific experts who spoke on the following disciplines physical environment, habitat and living resources, seabirds, marine mammals, sea turtles, and social and economic issues. Specific chapters are cited individually, when appropriate.

The waters off Cape Hatteras exhibit some of the most energetic coastal dynamics anywhere. Here the broad shelves of the Middle and South Atlantic Bight narrow nearly isolating shelf waters north and south of Cape Hatteras from each other. Offshore, one of the strongest currents in the ocean, the Gulf Stream, moves northward. In addition to that variability in the large-scale current regime, both winter storms and tropical hurricanes are prevalent in the region. This paper discusses the physical oceanographic properties at the Manteo site and their variability. This section also discusses Bathymetry of the Region, Physical Oceanography, Climate, Weather, Gulf Stream, and Coastal Currents.

Bane, J.M., Jr. 1983. Initial Observations of the Subsurface Structure and Short-Term Variability of the Seaward Deflection of the Gulf Stream off Charleston, South Carolina. Journal of Geophysical Research 88 C(8): 4673-4684.

A recurring seaward deflection of the surface layer of the Gulf Stream has been observed near 32° N latitude off the coast of the southeastern United States. It has been suggested that a ridge and trough bottom feature (the so-called 'Charleston bump') on the upper continental slope off the Georgia/South Carolina coast produces the deflection through a bottom steering effect. Present data indicate that the deflection is great enough to direct the Gulf Stream's shoreward surface thermal front to the east, and even south of east, about 70% of the time. Air-deployed expendable bathythermograph surveys have been made with sufficient coverage to provide several synoptic, three-dimensional views of the Gulf Stream's thermal frontal zone in the region between Savannah, Georgia, and Cape Hatteras, North Carolina. These views show the subsurface structure of the seaward deflection to exhibit large short-term variability. During wintertime conditions (February 1979) the greatest deflection (>090° true) of the near-surface front occurred at a time when the deeper front was more aligned (~080° true) with local topography. Within the few days following this observation the deflection angle at all depths decreased to near or below 070° true. Two large-amplitude Gulf Stream meanders progressed northeastward away from the deflection region during this time period. Deflection angles at all levels during late summertime conditions (November 1979) were observed to be near 070° true. A simple, kinematical model which incorporates growing, propagating Gulf Stream meanders is proposed to explain the deflection's short-term variability. A dome-shaped volume of cold water was observed to be located over the upper continental slope immediately downstream of the deflection. The existence and persistence of this cold dome suggest that upwelling is important in its maintenance, a hypothesis consistent with its hydrographic properties.

Bane, J.M., Jr., and D.A. Brookes. 1979. Gulf Stream Meanders along the continental margin from the Florida Straights to Cape Hatteras. Geophysical Research Letters 6: 280-282.

*This geophysical research is cited in Journal of Geophysical Research volume 88, number C-8: pp. 4651-4662 (Hood and Bane 1983), and pp. 4673-4684 (Bane 983). Figure 1 The continental margin of the southeastern United States (p. 4562, Hood and Bane 1983), and Figure 8 The mean position $\pm$ 1 standard deviation (shaded) of the Gulf Stream's shoreward surface thermal front calculated for a 64 week period, (p. 4682, Bane 1983) provide general location data. A cruise on the RV Endeavor (no cruise dates provided) is cited (Hood and Bane 1983).

Blair, N. 1998. A Scientific Overview of the Region Surrounding Lease Blocks 467 and 510. pp. 14-17. *In*: Vigil, D.L. (ed.). North Carolina/Minerals Management Service Technical Workshop on Manteo Unit Exploration: February 4-5, 1998. U.S. Dept. of the Interior, Minerals Management Service, Gulf of Mexico OCS Region. New Orleans, LA.

*These are the proceedings from a workshop/meeting (February 4-5, 1998) between the North Carolina Department of Environment and Natural Resources, and the U.S. Department of the Interior's Minerals Management Service (MMS). The geographic area being discussed is approximately 45 miles east-northeast of Cape Hatteras, NC, referred to as the Manteo Unit. This workshop reviewed environmental and socioeconomic information known and needed on the Manteo Unit. The MMS's Gulf of Mexico OCS Regional Director gave an MMS perspective on history and status of the area. Chevron gave a presentation on how the exploratory well would be drilled. The scientific characterization was presented in greater detail by a number of scientific experts who spoke on the following disciplines physical environment, habitat and living resources, seabirds, marine mammals, sea turtles, and social and economic issues. Specific chapters are cited individually, when appropriate.

The continental margin offshore Cape Hatteras, NC has been the focus of numerous oceanographic studies. The objective of this report is to provide an overview of physical, biological, geological, and chemical processes that operate in the region so that the results from individual disciplinary studies can be placed in a system-wide context. This section discusses hydrocarbon potential, water column observations and processes, benthic observations and processes, summary and the future.

Blair, N.E., L.A. Levin, D.J. DeMaster, and G. Playa. 1996. The short-term fate of fresh algal carbon in continental slope sediments. Limnol. Oceanogr. 41(6): 1208-1219.

Emplacement of tracer mixture containing ^{13}C-labeled green algae on the sea floor of the continental slope offshore Cape Hatteras, North Carolina, elicited a rapid responses over 1.5 d from the dense benthic community. Certain deposit-feeding annelids (e.g. *Scalibregma inflatum* and *Aricidea quadrilobata*) became heavily labeled with ^{13}C-labeled organic matter was transported to a depth of at least 4-5 cm into the seabed during the 1.5 d period, presumably as a consequence of feeding-associated activity. Nonlocal transport produced subsurface peaks in organic ^{13}C at 2-3 cm. Dissolved inorganic ^{13}C, produced by the oxidation of the labeled algae, penetrated to 10-cm depth. The transport of highly reactive organic matter from the sediment surface at initial velocities ≥ 3 cm d^{-1} is expected to be an important control of subsurface benthic processes in slope environments characterized by abundant macrofaunal populations. Anaerobic processes, which are enhanced on the Cape Hatteras slope relative to adjacent areas, may be promoted by the rapid injection of reactive material into subsurface sediments. The transport, in turn, is a consequence of the dense infaunal populations that are supported by the rapid depositions of organic carbon in this region.

Blair, N.E., G.R. Plaia, S.E. Boehme, D.J. DeMaster, and L.A. Levin. 1994. The remineralization of organic carbon on the North Carolina continental slope. Deep-Sea Research II Vol. 41(4-6): 755-766.

The sources and fates of metabolized organic carbon were examined at three sites on the North Carolina slope positioned offshore of Cape Fear, Cape Lookout, and Cape Hatteras. The $^{12}C/^{12}C$ composition ('delta' ^{13}C) of the solid phase organic matter, and the dissolved inorganic carbon ('sigma' CO_2) produced during its oxidation, suggested that the labile fraction was predominantly marine in origin. The 'sigma' CO_2 concentration gradient across the sediment-water interface, and by inference the 'sigma' CO_2 flux and production rate increased northward from Cape Fear to Cape Hatteras. Methane distributions and 'sigma' CO_2 'delta' ^{13}C values suggest that the rate of anaerobic diagenesis increased northward as well. The differences in sedimentary biogeochemistry are most likely driven by an along-slope gradient of reactive organic carbon flux to the seabed. This trend in reactive organic carbon flux correlates well worth macrofaunal densities previously observed at the three sites. Proximity to the shelf and the transport of particulate material by surface boundary currents may control the deposition of metabolized material on the Carolina slope.

Evidence of methanogenesis is found only on the Cape Hatteras slope. The methane, which was produced at a depth of approximately 1 m in the seabed, was consumed nearly quantitatively in the biologically mixed layer as it diffused upward. Irrigation of the sediments by infauna may have provided the necessary oxidant for the consumption of the methane.

Blake, J.A., and R.J. Diaz. 1994. Input, accumulation and cycling of materials on the continental slope off Cape Hatteras: An introduction. Deep-Sea Research II Vol. 41(4-6): 707-710.

The studies reported in this special issue of Deep-Sea Research are largely derived from data collected as part of programs supported by the U.S. Department of the Interior, Minerals Management Service (MMS) in response to concerns about the effect of oil and gas exploration on the largely unknown continental slope environment. Results of the MMS U.S. South Atlantic continental slope and rise program conducted off the Carolinas from Cape Hatteras to off Charleston in depths raging from 600 to 3500 m identified the importance of the slope off Cape Hatteras in cycling of materials from the shelf to the deep sea. Other more detailed investigations followed which numerous gaps in our knowledge of the role played by such special regions of the continental slope in the global cycling of carbon and other minerals.

Blake, J.A., and R.J. Diaz. 1998. Habitat and Living Resources Review: Benthic Ecology of the Cape Hatteras Continental Slope. pp. 43-51. In: Vigil, D.L. (ed.). North Carolina/Minerals Management Service Technical Workshop on Manteo Unit Exploration: February 4-5, 1998. U.S. Dept. of the Interior, Minerals Management Service, Gulf of Mexico OCS Region. New Orleans, LA.

*These are the proceedings from a workshop/meeting (February 4-5, 1998) between the North Carolina Department of Environment and Natural Resources, and the U.S. Department of the Interior's Minerals Management Service (MMS). The geographic area being discussed is approximately 45 miles east-northeast of Cape Hatteras, NC, referred to as the Manteo Unit. This workshop reviewed environmental and socioeconomic information known and needed on the Manteo Unit. The MMS's Gulf of Mexico OCS Regional Director gave an MMS perspective on history and status of the area. Chevron gave a presentation on how the exploratory well would be drilled. The scientific characterization was presented in greater detail by a number of scientific experts who spoke on the following disciplines physical environment, habitat and living resources, seabirds, marine mammals, sea turtles, and social and economic issues. Specific chapters are cited individually, when appropriate.

The benthic communities of the continental slope off the Carolinas has been described as part of extensive surveys conducted by the Minerals Management Service to assess potential impacts due to exploratory drilling for oil and gas. The initial effort was the Atlantic Continental Slope Rise (ACSAR) Program, which included transects across the Carolina slope from Cape Hatteras in the north to off the Charleston Bump in the south (Blake et al. 1985, 1987; Blake and Grassle 1994). Out of 15 stations sampled for benthic infauna, the most unusual were found off Cape Hatteras in Manteo Lease Block 510 at a depth of 550 m. The benthic fauna at this site included unusually high densities of infauna, epifaunal invertebrates, and fish (Blake and Grassle 1994; Hecker 1994). Much of the surface was seen to be carpeted with white tubes that later proved to be a giant foraminiferan, *Bathysiphon filiformis.* A control site at 2000 m down slope from the 550 m station also exhibited unusually high densities of infauna for a depth range. Overall, the abundance and biomass of the benthos was found to be about 6 and 10 times higher than other areas of the Carolina slope. This section discusses MMS Field Surveys and Methods, Results and Discussion Sedimentology; and Benthic Communities. Figure 4; Location of Benthic Stations and Camera Transects on the Cape Hatteras Slope in 1992, indicating sampling occurred in designated study area, is located on page 45.

Blake, J.A., and J.F. Grassle. 1994. Benthic community structure on the U.S. South Atlantic slope off the Carolinas: Spatial heterogeneity in a current- dominated system. Deep-Sea Research II Vol. 41(4-6): 835-874.

*Faunal communities of the continental slope and rise seaward of North and South Carolina (U.S.A.) are strongly influenced by the Gulf Stream, the Western Boundary Undercurrent, and an increasingly steep declination of the slope toward Cape Hatteras. Sixteen stations in depths of 600-3500 m were sampled to characterize the sediment and benthic macrofauna. Box cores were taken along four transects Cape Hatteras, Cape Lookout, Cape Fear, and Charleston. On the Cape Hatteras transect infaunal densities at the 600-m station were as high as those typical of shallower waters, and the dominant organisms were species that are more characteristic of continental shelf depths. There is high, nearly continuous sedimentation of terrigenous fine sandy sediments that are funneled over the Cape Hatteras slope by southerly-flowing, long-shelf currents. We postulate that organic material is transported rapidly over the site and that the high depositional rates are enhanced by scavenging activities of filter-feeding organisms. Large, deep-burrowing deposit feeders serve to carry organic material deep into the sediments. The shallow stations on the Charleston transects were dominated by sand waves generated by the Gulf Stream, while deeper stations were enriched by microalgae transported downslope. Transects off Cape Lookout and Cape Fear were more typical of those found elsewhere in the western North Atlantic.

Blake, J.A., B. Hecker, J.F. Grassle, B. Brown, M. Wade, P.D. Boehm, E. Baptiste, B. Hilbig, N. Maciolek, R. Petrecca, R.E. Ruff, V. Starczak, and L. Watling. 1987. Study of Biological Processes on the U.S. South Atlantic Slope and Rise: Phase 2. U.S. Department of the Interior, Minerals Management Service, Atlantic OCS Region, Environmental Assessment Section. Herndon, VA.

A total of 16 stations were sampled during a 2 year field program designed to characterize the biological, chemical, and sedimentary processes on the slope and rise off North and South Carolina. Box cores were taken along a 4 transects at depths of 600 to 3500 m. The infauna yielded a total of 1202 species, 520 of which were new to science. Annelids were dominant taxa in terms of density and numbers of species. Species diversity was highest at an 800 m site off Charleston. Infaunal densities were highest on the upper slope (600 m) and lowest on the rise (3000 m). Life history analysis yielded evidence of seasonality for two polychaete species. Two stations off Cape Hatteras in depths of 600 m and 2000 m had higher infaunal density, lower species diversity, and higher biomass than elsewhere on the Atlantic slope and rise. Higher than normal lead and carbon inventories suggest enhanced scavenging processes in this area. Faunal patterns on the Cape Lookout transect were generally typical for other localities on the Atlantic Slope and Rise. Faunal changes were detected off Cape Fear and Charleston that may be related to the influence of the Gulf Stream and associated sediment changes. Epifauna were most unusual on the Charleston Bump, where a hard bottom fauna dominated by filter feeding corals and sponges thrives in an area strongly swept by the Gulf Stream. Consistent faunal differences were found between the upstream and downstream sides of the bump. Data generated in the infaunal and epifaunal surveys supported the view that a partial zoogeographic barrier exists on the slope off North Carolina. This break was most evident between Cape Lookout and Cape Fear.

Blake, J.A., and B. Hilbig. 1994. Dense infaunal assemblages on the continental slope off Cape Hatteras, North Carolina. Deep-Sea Research II Vol. 41(4-6): 875-899.

*Unusually dense assemblages of benthic infaunal invertebrates have been discovered in continental slope sediments off Cape Hatteras, North Carolina. Densities were highest on the upper slope, ranging from 24,055 to 61,244 (X = 46,255) individuals m^2 in nine samples taken at a 600-m site in 1984 and 1985, and from 15,522 to 89,566 (X = 37,282) individuals m^2 in single samples at 15 stations over a wider depth range of 530 to 1535 m in1992. A lower slope station at 2000 m sampled six times in 1984-1985 and again in 1992, had densities consistently higher than 8500 individuals m^2. Species richness and diversity are consistently lower on the Cape Hatteras slope than at other locations off North Carolina and elsewhere in the western North Atlantic.

Brown, B. 1991. Biomass of Deep-Sea Benthic Communities: Polychaetes and other Invertebrates. Bulletin of Marine Science 48(2): 401-411.

Biomass measurements were made for benthic samples from the U.S. Atlantic continental slope and rise as part of a program on benthic processes in the deep sea. Box-core samples were collected from off Georges Bank near Massachusetts south to off Georgia, primarily along the 2000-m depth contour. Ash-free dry weight (AFDW) measurements were made on replicates from six stations. Samples were sieved through nested 0.3 mm and 2.0 mm screens. AFDW biomass ranged between 0.1665 and 2.1439 g m^{-2}. Polychaetes dominated biomass in the 0.3-mm fractions and in the 2.0-mm fraction except whenever large organisms, such as echinoderms, were present. Wet weight biomass was measured on samples taken from off Cape Hatteras in depths varying between 583 and 3500 m. A sharp decrease (five- to ten-fold) in biomass was observed between 2000 and 3000 m depth.

Cahoon, L.B., R.A. Laws, and C.J. Thomas. 1994. Viable diatoms and chlorophyll *a* in continental slope sediments off Cape Hatteras, North Carolina. Deep-Sea Research II Vol. 41(4-6): 767-782.

Continental slope sediments off Cape Hatteras, North Carolina, were sampled by box coring in late summer, 1992. The chlorophyll *a* concentrations measured in sediments from 16 sites at depths ranging from 530 to 2003 m averaged 19.9 mg chl *a* m $^{-2}$, a concentration much higher than observed elsewhere on the eastern U.S. continental slope, indicating high depositional rates for microalgal material. The variability in the chlorophyll *a* values suggests strong environmental heterogeneity at both small and large spatial scales in this slope habitat, probably a consequence of both topography and bioturbation. Viable diatoms were found in sediment samples across the range of depths sampled, and up to 14 cm deep in sediments, indicating high rates of deposition and bioturbation. Bulk sediment samples contained planktonic, tychopelagic and benthic diatoms, indicating that both phytoplankton and benthic microalgae from the continental shelf may be sources of organic matter for these slope sediments.

Cleary, W.J., and P.A. Thayer. 1973. Petrography of Carbonate Sands on the Carolina Continental Shelf. Transactions: Gulf Coast Association of Geological Societies 23rd Annual Convention: October 24, 25, 26, 1973, Houston, TX.

*In order to provide petrographic criteria for interpreting ancient mixed clastic-carbonate shelf deposits, 300 thin sections were studied from the Carolina continental shelf in an area extending from Raleigh Bay, North Carolina, to Cape Romain, South Carolina. As shown by previous investigators, percentage of carbonate grains in this area is chiefly a function of dilution from adjacent terrigenous sources. Skeletal components, the dominant carbonate grain type, form 10 to 60 percent of the total sediment and are mainly pelecypods, gastropods, and coralline algae. Foraminifers, bryozoans, echinoderms, barnacles, ostracodes, corals and worm tubes are minor constituents. Non-skeletal constituents, which usually comprise less than 10 percent of the total sediment, consist of peloids, ooids, lumps, and assorted carbonate lithoclasts (oomicrites, biomicrites, and biosparites). Terrigenous constituents are chiefly quartz, with subordinate amounts of feldspar, rock fragments, and heavy minerals. Glauconite and phosphorite are also present.

Continental Shelf Associates, Inc. 1983. North Carolina Fisheries and Environmental Data Search and Synthesis Study: Final Report. Continental Shelf Associates, Inc. Jupiter, FL.

Available information on the living marine resources and habitats of the North Carolina OCS, from shore to a depth of 200 m (656 ft), was collected, annotated, and synthesized. Over 1,450 published and unpublished data sources were reviewed. Written synthesis chapters summarized the geology, oceanography, biological communities, commercial and sport fisheries, endangered and threatened species, and sensitive biological areas and unique habitats. Data gaps were identified, implications to OCS development were discussed, and suggestions for additional research were provided. In addition, a computer program was designed to catalog and sort all of the pertinent annotated information sources. The purpose of this computer program is to provide the MMS with a useful and viable method of maintaining, updating, and expanding the data base.

The North Carolina OCS is a transition zone between the South and Middle Atlantic Bight. The climate, proximity and behavior of the Gulf Stream, and the presence of cuspate projecting shoals and capes influence unique oceanographic and biological features. Extensive hard/live bottom areas are present within Onslow Bay and along the North Carolina continental shelf edge. Upwelling along the North Carolina continental shelf edge and the intrusion of nutrient rich eddies into middle- and inner-shelf waters occur frequently along this coast. The upwelling-eddy, formation-intrusion phenomenon is not well understood and its ecological implications are just beginning to be studied. The present lack of knowledge in this area makes risk assessment for OCS development activities difficult. Additional studies of the coupling of physical and biological processes along the North Carolina continental shelf are needed in order to formulate effective OCS management policies for that area.

—. 1989. CSA Live Bottom Survey. Continental Shelf Associates, Inc. Jupiter, FL. 45 p.

This report describes the results of a Live-Bottom Survey (LBS) conducted from 9 to 24 July 1989. The purpose of this video/still camera photodocumentation survey was to document the topographical features, substrate types, and associated biota at the sites around the proposed well location and proposed anchor locations. As shown in Figure 1.2, the survey area extends into Manteo Area Blocks 466, 510, and 511. Proposed anchor locations were chosen to be placed in relatively low-relief areas based on bathymetric and high-resolution geophysical data. Water depths within the sites surveyed ranged from 305 to 1,355 m (1,001 to 4,446 ft). Due to the water depth and the highly irregular topography within the survey area, a state-of-the-art deepwater remotely operated vehicle (ROV) was needed to obtain the survey data. Other less sophisticated options, such as towed video/still camera systems or lesser ROV systems, would not have performed satisfactorily.

Costlow, J., K. Brink, M. Orbach, C. Peterson, J. Teal, and A. Robertson. 1992. North Carolina Environmental Sciences Review Panel. Report to the Secretary of the Interior from the North Carolina Environmental Sciences Review Panel as mandated by the Oil Pollution Act of 1990. 83 p.

The Oil Pollution Act of 1990, in a section cited as the Outer Banks Protection Act, prohibits the Secretary of the Interior from proceeding with a number of actions relative to development of oil and gas resources offshore North Carolina for which he is responsible under the Outer Continental Shelf Lands Act (OCLSA). Actions prohibited include: (1) conducting a lease sale; (2) issuing any new lease; (3) approving any exploration plan; (4) approving any development and production plan; (5) approving any application for permit to drill; and (6) permitting any drilling. The prohibition on these actions is mandated to remain in effect until the latter of: (1) October 1, 1991 or (2) 45 days of contiguous session of the Congress following the submission of a written report from the Secretary certifying that the information available to him is sufficient to carry out his responsibilities under the OCSLA.

In his report, the Secretary is required to take into consideration findings and recommendations of a panel established by the Outer Banks Protection Act, the North Carolina Environmental Sciences Review Panel, and to include a detailed explanation of any differences between his certification if sufficient information and the findings and recommendations of this group. The panel is charged by the Act with: (1) assessing the adequacy of the available physical oceanographic, ecological, and socioeconomic information to enable the Secretary to fulfill his responsibilities under the OCSLA and (2) identifying any additional information deemed essential to enable the Secretary to carry out these responsibilities. The Panel's response to this charge is the subject of this document.

As provided in the Outer Banks Protection Act, the North Carolina Environmental Sciences Review Panel is composed of five members, a marine scientist selected by the Secretary of the Interior, a marine scientist selected by the Governor of North Carolina, and three scientists, one each from the disciplines of physical oceanography, ecology, and social sciences, selected jointly by the Secretary and the Governor from a list developed by the National Academy of Sciences. Unless specifically indicated in the text, the conclusions and recommendations presented in the report represent the unanimous decision of the Panel members. A summary of findings including Physical Oceanography, Ecology, Socioeconomics, Sources of Information, Adequacy of Information, and Panel's Recommended Studies is included. Appendix A: Literature Review, and Appendix B: Factors Influencing the Definition if Adequacy of Information are also included.

Crawford, K. (ed.). 1989. Proceedings: 1989 Marine Expo: The Natural Resources Associated with Mobil's Proposed Drill Site. NC Outer Continental Shelf Office, NC Department of Administration. Raleigh, NC. 64 p.

*This report contains abstracts from each presenter. Chapter topics include: Mobil's Proposal, Geologic Overview — Introduction and Potential for Oil and Gas Discovery, Oceanographic Conditions, Comments on Last MMS Modeling, Biological Production Near the Bottom (invertebrates), Fisheries Resources, Commercial and Recreational Marine Fisheries, Winter Storm Effects on Spawning and Larval Drift of Pelagic Fish, Marine Birds, Sea Turtles in North Carolina, Marine Mammals, Plenary Session, Summary. Each chapter also cited individually when appropriate.

—. 1998. North Carolina's Coastal Energy Policies — A Framework for Reviewing OCS Proposals. pp. 22-26. *In*: Vigil, D.L. (ed.). North Carolina/Minerals Management Service Technical Workshop on Manteo Unit Exploration: February 4-5, 1998. U.S. Dept. of the Interior, Minerals Management Service, Gulf of Mexico OCS Region. New Orleans, LA.

*These are the proceedings from a workshop/meeting (February 4-5, 1998) between the North Carolina Department of Environment and Natural Resources, and the U.S. Department of the Interior's Minerals Management Service (MMS). The geographic area being discussed is approximately 45 miles east-northeast of Cape Hatteras, NC, referred to as the Manteo Unit. This workshop reviewed environmental and socioeconomic information known and needed on the Manteo Unit. The MMS's Gulf of Mexico OCS Regional Director gave an MMS perspective on history and status of the area. Chevron gave a presentation on how the exploratory well would be drilled. The scientific characterization was presented in greater detail by a number of scientific experts who spoke on the following disciplines physical environment, habitat and living resources, seabirds, marine mammals, sea turtles, and social and economic issues. Specific chapters are cited individually, when appropriate.

In 1990 North Carolina found Mobil's exploration plan and discharge permit for Block 467 inconsistent with its coastal program due to inadequate information. Neither Mobil nor the federal government provided information to address the state's concerns regarding potential environmental and socioeconomic impacts. The proposal for Block 467 is still under federal appeal and in litigation. This section discusses What the State Learned from Mobil's Drilling Proposal, The NC Coastal Management Program and Coastal Energy Policies, Strengthening the State's Coastal Energy Policies, and NC's Process for Reviewing Chevron's Exploration Proposal.

Cutter, G.R., R.J. Diaz, and J.A. Blake. 1994a. Deep-Sea Research II: CD-ROM APPENDIX. Deep-Sea Research II Vol. 41(4-6): 981-982.

The contents of the CD-ROM Appendix are data and images of the bottom from five of the articles in this issue. The CD-ROM was mastered in a format that can be read by both Macintosh and PC computers. It is organized in an hierarchical structure by folders, with data in one and images in another. To access a particular file, sequentially open folders until the file of interest appears. Data and figure captions are provided as: (.txt) ASCII text with no line breaks; (.tlb) ASCII text with line breaks; (.wor) Microsoft Word; and (.wp) Word Perfect 5.1 files. Images are in TIFF format (.tif). Data (ACSAR, Hatteras), Images and Captions (ACSAR, Profile, 3Dbathy, Sled, Surface, x-ray) are included.

Cutter, G.R., R. Diaz, and J. Lee. 1994b. Foraminifera from the continental slope off Cape Hatteras, North Carolina. Deep-Sea Research II Vol. 41(4-6): 951-963.

The recent benthic meiofaunal foraminiferal assemblage from the continental slope (590-2003 m) off Cape Hatteras, North Carolina exhibits high species richness and evenness, moderate diversity values, and lacks numerically dominant species. The preserved planktic assemblage has relatively low species richness, high evenness, low diversity, and a few numerically dominant species. Approximately 9% of the benthic species are those that typically live within continental shelf depth ranges. The benthic assemblage abundances and diversities do not follow depth patterns or geophysical characteristics. No biogeographic boundary can be described within the study area for meiofaunal foraminifers. Oxygen limitation does not appear to be a factor affecting the benthos of the North Carolina continental slope based upon the community structure of the benthic foraminifers, if total assemblage is assumed to reflect the recently living community. The high carbonate content of sediments in the area may be explained by foraminiferal tests. Within the study area, the foraminiferal assemblages are uniform, and probably reflect relative consistency of primary environmental variables as well as dynamic downslope transport and high influx of material from the water column in the vicinity where the Gulf Stream and the Western Boundary Undercurrent cross.

DeMaster, D.J., R.H. Pope, L.A. Levin, and N.E. Blair. 1994. Biological mixing intensity and rates of organic carbon accumulation in North Carolina slope sediments . Deep-Sea Research II Vol. 41(4-6): 735-753.

Sediment accumulation rates and biological mixing intensities were determined at three sites on the North Carolina slope based on profiles of naturally occurring ^{14}C, ^{210}Ph and ^{234}Th. The three sites all were at a water depth of 850 m with a spacing of 150 — 180 km between sites. Sediment accumulation rates increase from south to north from values of 7 cm ky^{-1} at Site I, to 160 cm ky^{-1} at Site II, to 1100 cm ky^{-1} at Site III. The organic carbon burial rate a these sites also increases in the northward direction from 0.65 (Site I) to 20 (Site II) to $\leq$ 150 g C_{org} m^{-2} $year^{-1}$ (Site III). These data indicate that continental margin environments can exhibit highly variable carbon fluxes over relatively small distances on the seafloor. The rate of organic carbon accumulation at Site III is one of the highest values reported for the marine environment. Based on these accumulation rates and dissolved inorganic carbon flux estimates from each site, the seabed organic carbon preservation efficiency (i.e. the ratio of C_{org} accumulation rate to C_{org} deposition rate times 100) was estimated to vary from 6.0% to 54% to 88%, at Sites I, II and III, respectively. The ^{14}C age of organic matter in surface sediments was older at Site III (1800 years BP), than at Sites I and II (800 years BP), indicating that Site III receives it greater proportion of old sediment from either up-slope areas or from terrigenous sources. Inventories of excess ^{234}Th (half-life of 24 days) were used as it tracer for particle flux covering the 100 days prior to the October 1989, July-August 1990 and August 1991 cruises. The mean ^{234}Th inventories at the three sites were 4.7 $\pm$ 1.9, 8.4 $\pm$ 6.3 and 23.1 $\pm$ 7.3 dpm cm^{-2}, for Sites I, II and III, respectively.

Diaz, R.J., J.A. Blake, and D.P. Lohse. 1993a. Volume II Final Report: Benthic Study of the Continental Slope off Cape Hatteras, North Carolina. Virginia Institute of Marine Science, School of Marine Science, College of William and Mary, Gloucester Pt., VA. Science Applications International Corporation, Woods Hole, MA. 135 p.

*This is a study of the nature and spatial extent of continental slope benthic communities off Cape Hatteras, NC, with emphasis on the Manteo Area lease block 467. Macrofaunal abundance and biomass in this area higher than anywhere else along the entire South Atlantic continental slope and rise. Species composition of the infauna off Cape Hatteras is also different from other slope habitats. Species richness and diversity are lower with a high degree of dominance by species that are cosmopolitan in distribution. Trends in abundance of invertebrate megafauna on the continental slope off Cape Hatteras appear to be similar to the macrofauna. Demersal fish fauna off Cape Hatteras is distinctive in terms of composition and population density. Overall, abundance of benthic fish off Cape Hatteras is four to seven times higher than adjacent area. Site sediment characteristics (e.g., source, texture, and physico-chemistry) and potential impact to benthic community by sediment discharge during drilling are described. Volume III contains Appendices A-E.

Much of the data in this report were used in the Special Deep Research issue (1994. 41 (4-6)).

Diaz, R.J., G.R. Cutter, and J.A. Blake. 1998. Appendix F: A Review: Findings of the Benthic Study of the Continental Slope Off Cape Hatteras, North Carolina. pp. 121-136. *In*: Vigil, D.L. (ed.). North Carolina/Minerals Management Service Technical Workshop on Manteo Unit Exploration: February 4-5, 1998. U.S. Dept. of the Interior, Minerals Management Service, Gulf of Mexico OCS Region. New Orleans, LA.

*These are the proceedings from a workshop/meeting (February 4-5, 1998) between the North Carolina Department of Environment and Natural Resources, and the U.S. Department of the Interior's Minerals Management Service (MMS). The geographic area being discussed is approximately 45 miles east-northeast of Cape Hatteras, NC, referred to as the Manteo Unit. This workshop reviewed environmental and socioeconomic information known and needed on the Manteo Unit. The MMS's Gulf of Mexico OCS Regional Director gave an MMS perspective on history and status of the area. Chevron gave a presentation on how the exploratory well would be drilled. The scientific characterization was presented in greater detail by a number of scientific experts who spoke on the following disciplines physical environment, habitat and living resources, seabirds, marine mammals, sea turtles, and social and economic issues. Specific chapters are cited individually, when appropriate.

Because of the potential environmental impacts associated with development and production activities, the Oil Pollution Act of 1990 mandated that a panel of experts be convened. This panel, North Carolina Environmental Sciences Review Panel (NCESRP), was to consider whether the available scientific information was adequate for making decisions about oil and gas leasing, exploration, and development off North Carolina. The Costlow et al. (1992) report to the Secretary of the Interior made several recommendations on the information needed to understand the basic ecology of the leased areas. Among them was the recommendation that the spatial extent of the benthic community found within some of the lease blocks should be determined before any exploration or development activity occurred off Cape Hatteras. The present study was developed by the Minerals Management Service to determine the aerial extent of the community found by Blake et al. (1985, 1987). Results are published as a special issue of Deep-Sea Research Part II (Diaz et al. 1994), which included a CD-ROM with data and selected bottom images (Cutter et al. 1994).

*Sediments and Sedimentation Rates, Biological Communities (invertebrates and fish), Physical Habitat (geomorphology), Benthic Community Characterization and Distribution are discussed.

Diaz, R.J., G.R. Cutter, and D.C. Rhoads. 1994. The importance of bioturbation to continental slope sediment structure and benthic processes off Cape Hatteras, North Carolina. Deep-Sea Research II Vol. 41(4-6): 719-734.

Even though the continental slope off Cape Hatteras has sediment accumulation rates on the order of 1 cm/year, large areas of soft sediment are intensively reworked by infaunal organisms. Primary sedimentary structures are dominated by the bioturbation activities of a deep burrowing infauna (to at least 30 cm). The layer actively mixed by the benthos, as evidenced by sediment profile and X-ray images, is estimated to range from 5 to 20 cm, with the residence time for particles within the surface mixed layer ranging from about 4.5 to 18 years. The biological mixing parameter (G) ranges from 0.4 to 5.5, which indicates moderate to strong biological mixing relative to accumulation and strata formation. Bioturbation contributes to the dynamic forces affecting the surface sediments by decreasing compaction of sediment layers and dilating sediment fabrics by sediment mixing, and introducing large water-filled burrows and voids to subsurface sediments. The sediment profile images captured numerous subsurface feeding voids, and worms in the process of making deep burrows, many of which extended below the 5 to 10 cm average depth of the apparent color redox potential discontinuity layer. High rates of accumulation of organic-rich sediment lead to high standing stocks of benthos and intensive feeding/burrowing activity that result in organic rich stratagraphic sequences that are thoroughly mixed. Cape Hatteras is an apparent focusing point for the transport of shallow water sediments to the deep sea. Sediments across other areas of the continental slope just 100's of kilometers south of Cape Hatteras are not as thoroughly mixed or biologically active.

Dillon, W.P., and P. Popenoe. 1988. The Blake Plateau Basin and Carolina Trough. pp. 291-328. *In*: Sheridan, R.E., and J.A. Grow. The Atlantic Continental Margin: U.S. Vol. I — 2.

*This is a chapter in a geology text titled The Atlantic Continental Margin. Presently, the continental margin of the southeastern United States forms a zone of transition between the actively building, steep-fronted carbonate platform of the Bahamas and the typical eastern North American terrigenous clastic-dominated, drowned, shelf-slope-rise configuration. This region of the continental margin is underlain by two major sedimentary basins the Blake Plateau Basin and the Carolina Trough — which are different in shape, basement structure, and history. The two southern basins show some of the greatest contrasts of any basins of the eastern North America, especially in their early response to rifting and in the change from rifting to drifting. The region has experienced abrupt major changes in geological conditions, most notably the onset of Gulf Stream flow in the early Tertiary. Morphologically, the area is dominated by the broad, flat Blake Plateau at about 800-1000 m water depth. The plateau is bounded to the east by the extremely steep Blake Escarpment, descending to 5,000 m water depths.

Duplantier, D. 1998. Manteo Prospect: How Can it Be Done? pp. 18-21. *In*: Vigil, D.L. (ed.). North Carolina/Minerals Management Service Technical Workshop on Manteo Unit Exploration: February 4-5, 1998. U.S. Dept. of the Interior, Minerals Management Service, Gulf of Mexico OCS Region. New Orleans, LA.

*These are the proceedings from a workshop/meeting (February 4-5, 1998) between the North Carolina Department of Environment and Natural Resources, and the U.S. Department of the Interior's Minerals Management Service (MMS). The geographic area being discussed is approximately 45 miles east-northeast of Cape Hatteras, NC, referred to as the Manteo Unit. This workshop reviewed environmental and socioeconomic information known and needed on the Manteo Unit. The MMS's Gulf of Mexico OCS Regional Director gave an MMS perspective on history and status of the area. Chevron gave a presentation on how the exploratory well would be drilled. The scientific characterization was presented in greater detail by a number of scientific experts who spoke on the following disciplines physical environment, habitat and living resources, seabirds, marine mammals, sea turtles, and social and economic issues. Specific chapters are cited individually, when appropriate.

Chevron participated in the MMS Information transfer Meeting on December 18, 1997 in New Orleans and a Technical Workshop in North Carolina on February 4, 1998 to explain how a well would be drilled off the coast of North Carolina. The focus of Chevron's presentations was the geologic nature of the prospect. Participants in these two proceedings include state and federal agencies as well as members of the scientific community.

This section discusses the Plan of Activity for the Manteo Prospect, Geologic Prospect, and Drilling Technology.

EEZ-SCAN 87 Scientific Staff. 1991. Atlas of the U.S. Exclusive Economic Zone, Atlantic Continental Margin. U.S. Geological Survey. Denver, CO. 174 p.

*This atlas is one in a series in which the U.S. Geological Survey (USGS) presents images of the sea floor and other geophysical data from the deepwater regions off the U.S. coasts. Containing the first comprehensive compilation of sea-floor imagery of the Atlantic continental margin, this volume provides the first broad-scale view of sea-floor features and the effects of systems of sedimentary processes that have been unknown or poorly known, until know. These data are a unique set of basic information that will support future studies by government, academic and industry workers. The region covered is within the U.S. Exclusive Economic Zone (EEZ) (Fig. 1), which extends 200 nautical miles seaward from the shore.

In 1984 the USGS began a systematic program of reconnaissance-scale imaging of the poorly explored deepwater parts of the EEZ, using a long-range sidescan-sonar system known as GLORIA (Geological Long Range Inclined Asdic). Data collected in this survey of the U.S. Atlantic EEZ include GLORIA sidescan-sonar imagery; shallow-penetration, medium-resolution seismic profiles; high-resolution seismic-reflection profiles; echo-sounder profiles; and measurements of total magnetic intensity. The field program, carried out during five cruises from February to May 1987, covered the Atlantic EEZ seaward of the continental shelf edge, from the Canadian border southward to the northern Blake Plateau off Florida (Figs. 26 and 27).

Emery, K.O. 1970. Continental Margins of the World. The Geology of the East Atlantic Continental Margin: General Economic Papers, ICSU/SCOR 70(13): 7-29.

Sediments of most continental shelves are retained by tectonic or reef dams; those of other shelves are held by the angle of rest of the adjacent continental slope. Continental rises at the base of the slopes are huge masses of sediment deposited by turbidity currents and the sinking of pelagic debris; some of them subsequently are modified by mass movements and bottom currents. Rises occur only where the continental margins lie within crustal plates; they are absent where deep-sea trenches mark zones of convergence at the edges of crustal plates. In the Atlantic Ocean the continental margins date from Permian-Triassic times when the rifting between continents began.

—. 1971. The Geology of the Atlantic Continental Shelf and Slope. Underwater Naturalist 5(1): 4-7.

Traditionally, the work of land geologists and that of marine geologists have been separated at the shoreline. This separation is due partly to the differences in geological tools needed in the two environments and partly to limitations in charters of organizations that sponsored the geological work. Future progress in both environments will be aided by cooperative studies of continental margins, particularly of continental shelves. These areas are significant to geologists because they have great crustal mobility and thick accumulations of sediments; they may therefore contain some of the keys to our future understanding of the origin and growth of continents. The relationships between the water environment and the unconsolidated sediments must be understood before we can correctly estimate the environment in which the lithified end products were originally deposited. Within the strata of many continental margins are structural and stratigraphic traps that contain petroleum. The regional study of geological history and the regional mapping of mineral resources thus forms a general framework that should promote continuation by private industry on a detailed local basis prior to exploitation of the resources.

Ewing, M., and E.M. Thorndike. 1965. Suspended Matter in Deep Ocean Water. Science 147: 1291-1294.

A nepheloid layer had been observed by optical means in the lower part of the water column on the continental slope and rise. By sampling it has been found to be a suspension of lutite, apparently in sufficient quantity to induce downslope flow. Sediment transport in the nepheloid layer may be a major component of deep-sea sediment bodies.

Fornes, W.L., D.J. Demaster, L.A. Levin, and N.E. Blair. 1999. Bioturbation and particle transport in Carolina slope sediments: A radiochemical approach. Journal of Marine Research 57: 335-355.

In situ tracer experiments investigated short-term sediment mixing processes at two Carolina continental margin sites (water depth = 850 m) characterized by different organic C fluxes, ^{234}Th mixing coefficients (D_b) and benthic assemblages. Phytoplankton, slope sediment, and sand-sized glass beads tagged with ^{210}Pb, ^{113}Sn, and ^{228}Th, respectively, were placed via submersible at the sediment-water interface at both field sites (Site I off Cape Fear, and Site III off Cape Hatteras). Experimental plots were sampled at 0, 1.5 days, and 90 days after tracer emplacement to examine short-term, vertical transport. Both sites are initially dominated by nonlocal mixing. Transport to the bottom of the surface mixed layer at both sites occurs more rapidly than ^{234}Th-based D_b values predict; after 1.5 days, tagged particles were observed 5 cm below the sediment-water interface at Site I and 12 cm below at Site III. Impulse tracer profiles after 90 days at Site III exhibit primarily diffusive distributions, most likely due to a large number of random. nonlocal mixing events. The D_b values determined from 90-day particle lagging experiments are comparable with those obtained from naturally occurring ^{234}Th profiles (100-day time scales) from nearby locations. The agreement between impulse tracer mixing coefficients and steady-state natural tracer mixing coefficients suggests that the diffusive analogue for bioturbation on monthly time scales is a realistic and useful approach. Tracer profiles from both sites exhibit some degree of particle selective mixing, but the preferential transport of the more labile carbon containing particles only occurred 30% of the time. Consequently, variations in the extent to which age-dependent mixing occurs in marine sediments may depend on factors such as faunal assemblage and organic carbon flux.

Gettleson, D.A. 1992. Results of a Benthic Visual Survey Within the Manteo Block 467. pp. 159-168. *In*: U.S. Department of the Interior, Minerals Management Service. Proceedings of the Fourth Atlantic OCS Region Information Transfer Meeting, September 1991. U.S. Department of the Interior, Minerals Management Service. Herndon, VA.

The Fourth Atlantic Outer Continental Shelf (OCS) Regional Information Transfer Meeting (ITM) was held on 24-25 September, 1991, in Wilmington, NC. The focus of the meeting was on the OCS off North Carolina, specifically on activities related to a proposed exploratory well for oil and gas by Mobil on Block 467 a site 40 miles off the coast of North Carolina. The area of industry interest is known as the Manteo Prospect, while the activities surrounding the proposed drilling are referred to collectively as the Manteo Project. The wildcat wellsite is in 2,690 ft. (857 m) of water near the edge of the Gulf Stream. It is also near a fishing ground known locally as "The Point." The area is believed to be gas prone rather than oil prone. The estimated size of the resource could be as high as 5 trillion cubic feet of gas.

The purpose of the meeting was to exchange information on the leasing background, legislative activities, scientific results, and socioeconomic studies. Legislative-related reports include descriptions of the Oil Pollution Act of 1990, the Outer Banks Protection Act, the Environmental Studies Review Panel, and the North Carolina Physical Oceanography Panel. Reports of studies on marine life include benthic diatoms, benthic fauna, pelagic seabirds, sea turtles, and right whales. One report describes the use of airships (blimps) for ocean research a capability relevant to North Carolina because of the east coast airship facility is located in the state. Local marine science facilities described include NOAA's National Undersea Research Center at the University of North Carolina at Wilmington and the national marine Fisheries Service laboratory in Beaufort.

Developments in oil spill cleanup technology and capabilities are described by both the Coast Guard and the industry. A socioeconomic report describes the effects of the oil and gas activities on the tourist industry. Lastly, research on the restoration of salt marshes indicates that rehabilitation of an area is possible when development or an accident has occurred. While the emphasis of the meeting was on oil and gas, two reports described the results of projects related to offshore sand mining. The appendix lists the names and addresses of speakers. Individual chapters are cited individually when appropriate.

*This summary describes the results of a video- and still-camera photodocumentation survey conducted from July 9 to 24, 1989 in the Manteo Area Block 467 (Figure 37). Block 467 is located along a steep, highly irregular portion of the continental slope on the northern fringe of the Hatteras canyon system. The purpose of this photodocumentation survey was to document the topographical features, substrate types, and associated biota around a proposed well and anchor locations in block 467 (figure 38). Water depths within the sites surveyed ranged from 299 to 1.393 meters (m) (980 to 4,570 feet (ft)). Because of the water depth and the highly irregular topography within the survey area, a state-of the-art deepwater remotely operated vehicle (ROV) was used to obtain the survey data. Live bottom site characterization (invertebrates and fish present) are described.

Harris, W.B. 1989. The Natural Resources Associated with Mobil's Proposed Exploratory Well: Geologic Overview Introduction. pp. 8-15. *In*: Crawford, K. (ed.). Proceedings: 1989 Marine Expo: The Natural Resources Associated with Mobil's Proposed Drill Site. NC Outer Continental Shelf Office, NC Department of Administration. Raleigh, NC.

In this part of the program, Dr. Charles Paull of UNC-Chapel Hill will presented a geologic overview of the proposed site and the site's potential for a gas or oil discovery. But before turning the program over to Dr. Paull I would like to spend a few minutes attempting to set the stage and answer the question, Why is Mobil Here? Why North Carolina?

*This is a transcript from a slide presentation. The socioeconomic issues associated with mineral harvest are discussed.

Harvey, H.R. 1994. Fatty acids and sterols as source markers of organic matter in sediments of the North Carolina continental slope. Deep- Vol. 41(4-6): 783-796.

To estimate the source and diagenetic state of organic matter reaching bottom sediments, fatty acids and sterols were measured in unconsolidated surface material (flocs) at 12 sites ranging from 600 to 2000 m across the mid-Atlantic continental slope off Cape Hatteras, North Carolina. Total free and esterified fatty acids were similar in description and concentration to other coastal systems, with values ranging from 0.64 to 46.52 g mg^{-1} organic carbon (1.10-68.85 g mg^{-1}dry sediment). Although shallow (600 m) stations contained significantly greater fatty acid concentrations than deep (>1400 m) stations, high variability observed at mid-depth (800 m) collections precluded a consistent relationship between total fatty acid concentration and station depth. At three sites where underlying sediments were also collected, decreases in total fatty acid reduced amounts of polyenoic acids and significant presence of bacterial fatty acids suggest rapid reworking of labile organic material that reaches the sediment surface. The distribution of sterols was remarkably consistent among all sites even though there were large variations in concentrations (1.8-20.7g mg^{-1} organic carbon). Sterol composition indicated phytoplankton, principally diatoms and dinoflagellates, as the principal source of labile organic matter to sediments, together with a significant input of cholesterol typical of zooplankton and their feeding activity. A minor but widespread terrigenous input was also evident based upon significant concentrations of sterols dominant in vascular plants.

Heezen, B. C. 1968. The Atlantic Continental Margin. UMR Journal 1: 5-25.

*Turbidity currents, surface and subsurface currents carry detritus from the land across the continental shelf to the adjacent continental slope where slumps and turbidity currents transport the sediment downslope for hundreds of miles to greater depths, and deep geostrophic contour currents transport it thousands of miles down-current in a direction parallel to the bathymetric contours. The combined effect of these processes has been to create a wide, thick, geosynclinal apron of sediment at the base of the continental slope.

Hilbig, B. 1994. Faunistic and zoogeographical characterization of the benthic infauna on the Carolina continental slope. Deep-Sea Research II Vol. 41(4–6): 929-950.

The species composition of the benthic infauna on the Carolina continental slope is described, based on the analysis of 146 quantitative boxcore samples taken between 1983 and 1986 and in 1992, The samples were collected between Cape Hatteras and the Charleston Bump in depths ranging from 600 to 3500 m. From these samples, nearly 1300 species were identified, more than one-third of them being new to science. Almost half of all species were polychaetes, the largest family being the Spionids with 63 species. Arthropods accounted for about 22% of all species, about one-third of which belonged to the tanaidaceans. Among the mollusks (16% of all species), the largest group was thyasirid bivalves. Pogonophorans were represented by 15 species. Distributional patterns of some of the major taxa are discussed, and the existence of a zoogeographical barrier off Cape Hatteras and/or Cape Lookout is revisited. The most striking difference between the slope off Cape Hatteras and comparable depths further south (e.g. Cape Lookout) is the greatly reduced number of polychaetes off Cape Hatteras. The zoogeographical barrier reported by Cutler [(1975) 22, 893-901] exists for most cumaceans, some aplacophorans, and many polychaetes identified from the present data set, but it appears to be virtually nonexistent for bivalves.

Inman, D.L., and R. Dolan. 1989. The Outer Banks of North Carolina: Budget of Sediment and Inlet Dynamics Along a Migrating Barrier System. Journal of Coastal Research 5(2): 193-237.

The Outer Banks are barrier islands separating Pamlico, Albemarle and Currituck Sounds from the Atlantic Ocean. These barriers are transgressing landward, with average rates of shoreline recession of 1.4 m/yr between False Cape and Cape Hatteras. Oregon Inlet, 63 km north of Cape Hatteras, is the only opening in the nearly 200 km between Cape Henry and Cape Hatteras which bounds the Hatteras Littoral Cell. Oregon Inlet is migrating south at an average rate of 23 m/yr and landward at a rate of 5 m/yr The net southerly longshore transport of sand in the vicinity of Oregon Inlet is between one-half and one million m³/yr.

Oregon Inlet is the most dynamic physical feature within the Hatteras Littoral Cell. The combination of waves and tidal currents deposit ebb-tide bars offshore of the entrance and form extensive tidal islands, bars and shoals in Pamlico Sound. These deposits lag behind as the inlet migrates. The offshore deposits are gradually returned to the beach by waves and reincorporated into the littoral drift system. The flood-tide inlet deposits in the sound are eventually reincorporated into the landward migrating barrier as the inlet moves to the south. The integrity of the landward side of the transgressing barrier is maintained by washover deposits, wind- blown sand deposits, and inlet deposits.

Averaged over the 160 km from False Cape to Cape Hatteras, sealevel rise accounts for 21% of the measured shoreline recession of 1.4 m/yr. Analysis of the budget of sediment indicates that the remaining erosion of 1.1 m/yr is apportioned between overwash processes (39%) longshore transport out of the cell (22%), windblown sand transport (18%), inlet deposits (10%), and removal by dredging at Oregon Inlet (11%). This analysis indicates that the barrier system moves as a whole, so that the sediment balance is relative to the moving shoreline (Lagrangian grid). Application of a continuity model to the budget suggests that, in places, the barrier system is supplied with sand from the shelf.

Janowitz, G.S. 1989. Comments on the Latest MMS Meeting. pp. 22-24. *In*: Crawford, K. (ed.). Proceedings: 1989 Marine Expo: The Natural Resources Associated with Mobil's Proposed Drill Site. NC Outer Continental Shelf Office, NC Department of Administration. Raleigh, NC.

In the early 1980s, MMS funded a modeling effort but utilized only predicted monthly averaged currents, combined with a time-varying surface wind-driven current in its risk analysis. The monthly averaged currents were very weak over the shelf and showed none of the energetic flows associated with the Gulf Stream-induced eddies and filaments present over the shelf. As it is possible that parcels may cross the shelf in a matter of days, MMS's use of mean monthly currents was challenged by the state of North Carolina.

A joint State-Federal Technical Advisory Panel concluded that the approach taken by NMS was inadequate. It recommended that a field study of the eddy-filament structure be funded and that a new ocean circulation model be developed. The model was to be verified by comparison with data prior to its incorporation into the trajectory calculations. Both projects were funded by MMS.

The Frontal Eddy Dynamics experiment, or FRED experiment for short, provided, among other data, current measurements in Onslow and Raleigh Bays and satellite imagery in this region and further north into the Mobil area. The study was not designed to measure currents in what is now the Mobil area. At this time, I have no details on the latest circulation model, the state of its verification, or the proposed method of incorporation into the trajectory analysis.

JAYCOR. 1980. Final Report 1978: Physical Oceanographic Model Evaluation for the South Atlantic OCS Region. BLM Contract AA551-CT8-34. JAYCOR. Alexandria, VA. 327 p.

*This report is comprised primarily of mathematical models. Geological Oceanography is discussed in Appendix A: Geospecific Aspects of the South Atlantic OCS Region (L.J. Pietrafesa).

For twelve months, JAYCOR Personnel were under contract to the Bureau of Land Management (BLM) to conduct an evaluation of physical oceanographic models that could have applicability to the South Atlantic Outer Continental Shelf (SAOS) area. The objectives of this evaluation were to determine: 1) which models, if any were best suited to the BLM program needs in assessing the distribution of pollutants resulting from offshore activities and in assessing the probability of occurrence of circumstances hazardous to offshore structures; 2) which models best fit the physics of the SAOS region; 3) the sensitivity of various models to data input; and 4) the quantity and quality of existing input data to drive the models.

More than twelve-hundred papers have been reviewed in a three-step process; semi-qualitative, detailed qualitative, and quantitative. All of the models, and background material are included in Appendix B of this report. This appendix includes a designation for each citation indicating the level at which the material reviewed was useful for this project. It should be emphasized that this model evaluation was done in the context of the South Atlantic OCS Region, and the results are not necessarily applicable to all OCS regions, although a significant portion of the information is transferable to other similar areas.

Kirby-Smith, W.W. 1989a. Biological Production Near the Bottom. p. 25. *In*: Crawford, K. (ed.). Proceedings: 1989 Marine Expo: The Natural Resources Associated with Mobil's Proposed Drill Site. NC Outer Continental Shelf Office, NC Department of Administration. Raleigh, NC.

Satellite photographs show that North Carolina has an incredibly diverse oceanographic setting which, in turn, produces highly diverse communities of fishes and invertebrates. The three bottom types found off the continental shelf of North Carolina include; 1) sand, 2) shell, and 3) rock outcrops. Across the continental shelf, the primary producers that support fisheries include microalgae and macroalgae. The bottom-dwelling microalgae (small microscopic plants) grow, rapidly and are very important to the total productivity of the whole water column. As much as half of the primary productivity on the shelf may be due to this benthic component. The secondary producers on rock outcrops, which include sponges, corals, worms and small arthropods, are a major food source for small fish. From a scientific perspective, the proposed drill site is an exciting area with a high biomass and low diversity. In my opinion, the exploration well itself would have little or no impact on the resources in the area; however, a major find of oil or gas could lead to a tremendous amount of industrial development, which could compete economically with other coastal industries, such as tourism and fisheries.

—. 1989b. The Community of Small Macroinvertebrates Associated with Rock Outcrops in the Continental Shelf of North Carolina. pp. 279-305. *In*: . George, R.Y., and A.W. Hulbert (eds.). North Carolina Coastal Symposium. National Undersea Research Program, NOAA. Rockville, MD.

Communities of small benthic organisms associated with rock outcrops on the continental shelf of North Carolina were examined for patterns in community structure related to season and depth. The communities were dominated by polychaetes, amphipods and mollusks. The number of species per $0.5m^2$ ranged from 40 to 214 and the number of individuals from 180 to 1657. Diversity was high with H' values of 4 to 6. Diversity was slightly greater at the middle shelf stations as compared to inner and outer shelf. The number of species and individuals was greatest at all three locations in the spring and fall and least in the winter and summer: a pattern similar to that of temperate coastal plankton. An index of community similarity indicated the presence of cold (winter/spring) and warm (summer/fall) communities at each of the three locations. Moreover at the middle and inner shelf the communities were more related to season (cold and warm) than to location (inner and middle). Outer shelf communities also had a strong seasonal component but were very different when compared with the middle and inner shelf communities. Different sampling gear (grabs versus diver suction) may explain some of the outer shelf uniqueness.

*The site ISO4 location data cited by Kirby-Smith are incorrect. Data cited by Kirby-Smith for site ISO4 resulted from unpublished data collected during a SCUBA dive by S.W. Ross on 18 August 1980. The correct location for this site [SWR -SCUBA-80-20] is 35° 20.7'N; 75° 21.2'W; depth 70-80 feet. Selected fish, invertebrate, and bottom habitat data were collected. These data are unpublished and the site was not visited again (S.W. Ross, pers. comm., 19 November 1999).

Lee, T. (ed.) 1983. Oceanography of the Southeast U.S. Continental Shelf and Adjacent Gulf Stream. Journal of Geophysical Research 88 C(8): 4539 to 4738.

*This is reprinted from Journal of Geophysical Research, Volume 88 C(8). Individual chapters are cited independently when appropriate.

Recent studies of shelf circulation and Gulf Stream variability in the area between Cape Hatteras, North Carolina, and Cape Canaveral, Florida, (South Atlantic Bight) have significantly enlarged the regional data ensemble available for dynamical interpretation. As national interests shifted to the finding of new and alternative energy resources, the need to understand better the oceanography of the SAB with its possible oil reserves became apparent. It is the purpose of this dedicated issue to combine the results of studies funded separately by the Department of Energy, the Bureau of Land Management (now Minerals Management Service), the National Science Foundation, and the Office of Naval Research in order that they may be viewed together for a more complete understanding of the important physical processes in the region.

Legeckis, R., and J.M. Bane Jr. 1983. Comparison of the TIROS-N Satellite and Aircraft Measurements of Gulf Stream Surface Temperatures. Journal of Geophysical Research 88 C(8): 4611-4616.

A comparison is made between multi-channel infrared (3.7 and 11 *u*m) temperatures measured by the TIROS-N satellite and aircraft single channel radiometer and AXBT measurements over the Gulf Stream between Cape Hatteras and Savannah, Georgia, on November 27, 1979. After reducing the noise in the 3.7 *u*m TIROS-N data, a multi-channel method is used to estimate the sea surface temperatures. For a temperature band of 19 to 26°C, the estimated and AXBT measurements are in agreement within a standard error estimate of 0.5°C. A bias of 1.2°C was found between the aircraft radiometer and the AXBT measurements, and part of this bias is attributed to radiometer calibration errors.

Levin, L., N. Blair, D. DeMaster, G. Plaia, W. Fornes, C. Martin, and C. Thomas. 1997. Rapid subduction of organic matter by maldanid polychaetes on the North Carolina slope. Journal of Marine Research 55: 595-611.

In situ tracer experiments conducted on the North Carolina continental slope reveal that tube-building worms (Polychaeta: Maldanidae) can, without ingestion, rapidly subduct freshly deposited, algal carbon (^{13}C-labeled diatoms) and inorganic materials (slope sediment and glass beads) to depths of 10 cm or more in the sediment column. Transport over 1.5 days appears to be nonselective but spatially patchy, creating localized, deep hotspots. As a result of this transport, relatively fresh organic matter becomes available soon after deposition to deep-dwelling microbes and other infauna, and both aerobic and anaerobic processes may be enhanced. Comparison of tracer subduction with estimates from a diffusive mixing model using ^{234}Th-based coefficients, suggests that maldanid subduction activities, within 1.5 d of particle deposition, could account for 25-100% of the mixing below 5 cm that occurs on 100-day time scales. Comparison of community data from the North Carolina slope for different places and times indicate a correlation between the abundance of deep-welling maldanids and the abundance and the dwelling depth in the sediment column of other infauna. Pulsed inputs of organic matter occur frequently in margin environments and maldanid polychaetes are a common component of continental slope macrobenthos. Thus, the activities we observe are likely to be widespread and significant for chemical cycling (natural and anthropogenic materials) on the slope. We propose that species like maldanids, that rapidly redistribute labile organic matter within the seabed, probably function as keystone resource modifiers. They may exert a disproportionately strong influence (relative to their abundance) on the structure of infaunal communities and on the timing, location and nature of organic matter diagenesis and burial in continental margin sediments.

Luternauer, J.L., and O.H. Pilkey. 1967. Phosphorite Grains: Their application to the Interpretation of North Carolina shelf sedimentation. Marine Geology 5(1967): 315-320.

Study of phosphorite grains in North Carolina continental shelf, beach, sound, and river sediments reveals that: (1) the shelf is an important source of beach sediment, and (2) North Carolina shelf cuspate embayments are essentially independent entities, in terms of sediment content and transport.

Macintyre, G., and M. Milliman. 1970. Physiographic Features on the Outer Shelf and Upper Slope, Atlantic Continental Margin, Southeastern United States. Geological Society of America Bulletin 81: 2577-2598.

Both erosional and constructional processes appear to have formed physiographic features near the shelf break along the southeastern United States, as indicated by extensive echo sounder profiles, rock-dredge material, and bottom photographs. Between Cape Hatteras, North Carolina, and Fort Lauderdale, Florida, four distinct physiographic areas are delineated, each having characteristic morphologies and lithologies.

The ridges and well-defined troughs on the outer shelf and upper slope (depths of about 50 to 150 m) between Cape Hatteras and Cape Fear may be related largely to earlier Gulf Stream erosion, and the rocks (algal limestones and sandstones) and sediments dredged from these features probably are mainly Holocene, relict shallow-water deposits forming a thin veneer over this erosional surface of the sea floor. Relatively rapid accumulation of pre-Holocene sediments may account for the general absence of pronounced physiographic features on the outer shelf and upper slope from Cape Fear to Cape Kennedy. Ledges, small terraces, and rises (depths of 50 to 110 m) In this area are probably Holocene features eroded into, or constructed on the pre-Holocene sediments, which are covered by transgressive Holocene algal lime- stones and sandstones similar to those collected to the north. The lithology, together with radiocarbon dates of rock material, indicate that well-defined ridges in depths of 70 to 90 in between Cape Kennedy and Palm Beach are relict oolitic ridges or "dunes" formed during the Holocene transgression; these features are now covered by modern Oculina sp. coral debris. From Palm Beach to Fort Lauderdale, where the continental shelf is narrow and shallow, a small ridge present at the shelf break (15 to 30 m) is thought to be an "inactive" coral reef.

Manheim, F.T., R.H. Meade, and G.C. Bond. 1970. Suspended Matter in Surface Waters of the Atlantic Continental Margin from Cape Cod to the Florida Keys. Science 167: 371-376.

Appreciable amounts of suspended matter (> 1.0 milligram per liter) in surface waters are restricted to within a few kilometers of the Atlantic coast, articles that escape estuaries or are discharged by rivers into the shelf region and to travel longshoreward rather than seaward. Suspended matter farther offshore, chiefly amorphous organic particles, totals 0.1 milligram per liter or less. Soot, fly ash, processed cellulose, and other pollutants are widespread.

McLawhorn, D.F. 1998. Looking for the Lodestar in the Shifting Sands of the Manteo Unit. pp. 27-30. *In*: Vigil, D.L. (ed.). North Carolina/Minerals Management Service Technical Workshop on Manteo Unit Exploration: February 4-5, 1998. U.S. Dept. of the Interior, Minerals Management Service, Gulf of Mexico OCS Region. New Orleans, LA.

*These are the proceedings from a workshop/meeting (February 4-5, 1998) between the North Carolina Department of Environment and Natural Resources, and the U.S. Department of the Interior's Minerals Management Service (MMS). The geographic area being discussed is approximately 45 miles east-northeast of Cape Hatteras, NC, referred to as the Manteo Unit. This workshop reviewed environmental and socioeconomic information known and needed on the Manteo Unit. The MMS's Gulf of Mexico OCS Regional Director gave an MMS perspective on history and status of the area. Chevron gave a presentation on how the exploratory well would be drilled. The scientific characterization was presented in greater detail by a number of scientific experts who spoke on the following disciplines physical environment, habitat and living resources, seabirds, marine mammals, sea turtles, and social and economic issues. Specific chapters are cited individually, when appropriate.

The pending proposal by Chevron to drill an exploratory well offshore North Carolina presents several extraordinary legal issues. These new legal issues, the unresolved legal issues pending from the Mobil proposal to drill, and the two potential drilling scenarios presented by Chevron, make it even more difficult to define the legal position of the State vis-a-vis the present proposal. Because the factors that can influence the State's policy decision are regularly shifting, it is impossible to find the legal lodestar by which the state can prevail with it's position decision — a source of constant quest for the State's attorneys in the Mobil/Chevron case. This section discusses Current Legal Status, New Legal Issues, Block 467, and Block 510.

Mellor, C.A. 1998. Submarine canyon formation and continental slope morphology: A synthesis of geophysical data from the Manteo 467 lease block off North Carolina. M.S. Thesis. University of North Carolina at Chapel Hill. 63 p.

Detailed geomorphology and stratigraphic development of submarine canyon heads are delineated using acoustic survey data from the Manteo 467 Lease Block, on the Continental Slope off North Carolina. At least 5 well developed canyons are defined by Sea Beam bathymetry. Seafloor textural variations are mapped using sidescan sonargrams. Smooth seafloor occurs primarily along ridge crests and their upper flanks and is underlain by layered sediments, indicating that ridges may be accretionary. Irregular seafloor is found predominantly in canyon axes and along canyon walls.

Gullies occur at canyon heads and down canyon walls. Irregular seafloor and gullying suggest erosion. Canyon development was initiated in the late Neocene because seismic reflectors correlating to pre-late Pliocene sediments indicate no submarine canyon development. An erosional unconformity in upper Pliocene sediments shows two submarine canyons corresponding with present day features. Subsequent canyon formation and development has occurred progressively as the result of mass wasting and differential deposition.

Mellor, C.A., and C.K. Paull. 1994. Sea Beam bathymetry of the Manteo 467 Lease Block off Cape Hatteras, North Carolina. Deep-Sea Research II Vol. 41(4-6): 711-718.

Continental slope morphology of a small area off Cape Hatteras, North Carolina, is illustrated on the basis of detailed Sea Beam bathymetry. The data reveal the complexity of the seafloor in this region, with many gullies marking the upper continental slope, coalescing downslope into larger submarine canyons. Submarine canyon morphology changes from "V" shaped valleys with sharp ridge crests above ~1200 m water depth, to "U" shaped valleys with rounded ridge crests below ~1200 m water depth.

Milliman, J.D. 1994. Organic matter content in the U.S. Atlantic continental slope sediments: Decoupling the grain-size factor. Deep-Sea Research II Vol. 41(4-6): 797-808.

Decoupling organic content in sediments from grain size can help define spatial variations in biological productivity, transport or preservation in continental margin sediments. Upper slope and upper rise sediments off the eastern United States have organic nitrogen contents similar to or lower than those predicted by grain size, whereas mid-slope sediments between Norfolk Canyon and Cape Fear have much higher organic contents. These elevated values probably result from off-shelf transport, combined with rapid burial and correspondingly reduced rates of remineralization, while lower values on the upper rise presumable result from low input of organic matter and low rates of burial and increased oxic degradation.

Milliman, J.D., R.J. Diaz, J.A. Blake, and G.R. Cutter Jr. (eds.). 1994. Topical Studies in Oceanography: Input, Accumulation and Cycling of Materials on the Continental Slope Off Cape Hatteras. Deep-Sea Research Part II Vol. 41. 982 p.

*This is a compilation of studies on Input, Accumulation and Cycling of Materials on the Continental Slope Off Cape Hatteras. Geology, sediments, organics, and benthic fauna are discussed. A CD-ROM is included. Each chapter (study) is cited independently, when appropriate. Some papers in this issue were derived from Diaz et al. (1993).

Mills, G.B. 1992. Update of the National Oceanic and Atmospheric Administration's Bathymetric Mapping Program Along the Mid-Atlantic Coast. pp. 95-102. *In*: U.S. Department of the Interior, Minerals Management Service. Proceedings of the Fourth Atlantic OCS Region Information Transfer Meeting, September 1991. U.S. Department of the Interior, Minerals Management Service. Herndon, VA.

The Fourth Atlantic Outer Continental Shelf (OCS) Regional Information Transfer Meeting (ITM) was held on 24-25 September 1991, in Wilmington, NC. The focus of the meeting was on the OCS off North Carolina, specifically on activities related to a proposed exploratory well for oil and gas by Mobil on Block 467 a site 40 miles off the coast of North Carolina. The area of industry interest is known as the Manteo Prospect, while the activities surrounding the proposed drilling are referred to collectively as the Manteo Project. The wildcat wellsite is in 2,690 ft. (857 m) of water near the edge of the Gulf Stream. It is also near a fishing ground known locally as "The Point." The area is believed

to be gas prone rather than oil prone. The estimated size of the resource could be as high as 5 trillion cubic feet of gas.

The purpose of the meeting was to exchange information on the leasing background, legislative activities, scientific results, and socioeconomic studies. Legislative-related reports include descriptions of the Oil Pollution Act of 1990, the Outer Banks Protection Act, the Environmental Studies Review Panel, and the North Carolina Physical Oceanography Panel. Reports of studies on marine life include benthic diatoms, benthic fauna, pelagic seabirds, sea turtles, and right whales. One report describes the use of airships (blimps) for ocean research a capability relevant to North Carolina because of the east coast airship facility is located in the state. Local marine science facilities described include NOAA's National Undersea Research Center at the University of North Carolina at Wilmington and the National Marine Fisheries Service laboratory in Beaufort.

Developments in oil spill cleanup technology and capabilities are described by both the Coast Guard and the industry. A socioeconomic report describes the effects of the oil and gas activities on the tourist industry. Lastly, research on the restoration of salt marshes indicates that rehabilitation of an area is possible when development or an accident has occurred. While the emphasis of the meeting was on oil and gas, two reports described the results of projects related to offshore sand mining. The appendix lists the names and addresses of speakers. Individual chapters are cited individually when appropriate.

*The National Oceanic and Atmospheric Administration (NOAA) began systematically mapping the continental slope along the U.S. mid-Atlantic slope in 1990 as part of its multibeam mapping program of the United States' Exclusive Economic Zone (EEZ). Eight surveys covering more than 2,500 square nautical miles (nmi^2) have been conducted in this region, using the sophisticated seafloor mapping systems Sea Beam and Hydrocart II. This section further describes NOAA's ocean mapping program.

Moffit, D. 1989a. Brief Description of Mobil's Proposal and the State's Response. Proceedings: 1989 Marine Expo: The Natural Resources Associated with Mobil's Proposed Drill Site. K. Crawford (ed.), pp. 1-8. NC Outer Continental Shelf Office, NC Department of Administration. Raleigh, NC.

North Carolina has state law jurisdiction over oil and gas activities located in waters out to three miles from the shoreline. The Outer Continental Shelf Lands Act (OCSLA) gives jurisdiction to the federal government from the three-mile line to the limits of U.S. claims of sovereignty (200 miles). On September 1, 1989, a draft exploration plan was submitted to the federal government and the state by Mobil Oil Exploration and Producing Southeast Inc. pursuant to the July 12,1989 Memorandum of Understanding (MOU) between the State of North Carolina, the Minerals Management Service (MMS) of the U.S. Department of the Interior, and Mobil. Mobil will submit its final exploration plan to the state no earlier than February 1, 1990.

*This introductory section describes oil and gas exploration at The Point. Maps of the Manteo Lease Blocks are included in this section.

Moffitt, D. 1989b. Outer Continental Shelf (OCS). pp. 549-551. *In*: George, R.Y. and A.W. Hulbert (eds.). North Carolina Coastal Symposium. National Undersea Research Program, NOAA. Rockville, MD.

This is a transcript from general presentation discussing Outer Continental Shelf (OCS) off-shore oil drilling off North Carolina Coast at Cape Hatteras and the location within the south-Atlantic/mid-Atlantic region. Lease blocks offshore North Carolina are mentioned. The speaker does not refer to a specific site.

Moser, M.L., S.W. Ross, S.W. Snyder, and R.C. Dentzman. 1995. Distribution of Bottom Habitats on the Continental Shelf off North Carolina, Final Report to Marine Resources Research Institute South Carolina Department of Marine Resources for the Southeast Area Monitoring and Assessment Program — Bottom Mapping Workgroup. Wilmington, NC.

*This report documents the compilation and evaluation of the North Carolina SEAMAP Hardbottom data. In situ observations of hard bottom type and relief were made from submersibles or SCUBA divers. These data are in video and/or 35 mm still photographs. Black and white, 35 mm still photographs from RV Eastward research cruises (1964-1973) also provided evidence of bottom type and relief. USACOE drilling logs (1983) characterized sub-surface stability. Fish trawl and trap data from NMFS-Woods Hole (groundfish surveys 1964-1994), NMFS- Pascagoula (archive data 1954-1984), SEAMAP data (since 1984) and NCDMF (RV Dan Moore, and reef data) were evaluated for the presence of obligate (primary) reef fishes as evidence for the location of hard bottoms.

Newton, J.G., O.H. Pilkey, and O.H. Blanton. 1971. An Oceanographic Atlas of the Carolina Continental Margin. Division of Mineral Resources. North Carolina Department of Conservation and Development. Raleigh, NC. 57 p.

*This atlas is a synthesis of oceanographic information describing the North Carolina coast. It contains data collected on RV Eastward Cruises 1964-1969. Sea floor topography and geology (sediment samples, rock and reef soundings), shipwreck locations, sea floor photography, and water characteristics (temperature and salinity) are described and mapped.

Orbach, M. 1989. Plenary Session: How Could These Resources be Affected By the Proposed Drilling and What Mitigation Measures Might be Used to Prevent Irreversible Damage. pp. 63-64. *In*: Crawford, K. (ed.). Proceedings: 1989 Marine Expo: The Natural Resources Associated with Mobil's Proposed Drill Site. NC Outer Continental Shelf Office, NC Department of Administration. Raleigh, NC.

*The following is a summary of the plenary session.

There appears to be a good deal of baseline information available about Mobil's proposed drill site area. However, there was a general consensus that there are serious gaps in our understanding of the relationships and functions of the many communities found in and around the exploration area known as the "Manteo Prospect." Some major areas of concern include protection of area benthos, impacts on community ecology, and effects of drilling discharges .

There was almost unanimous support for a monitoring program of the drilling operations and their impacts. Programs should be devised to examine: 1) The fate of drilling discharges, including dispersion (range and extent) and accumulation along fronts and the ocean bottom; and 2) The effects (both chemical and mechanical) of drilling discharges on the benthos, the indigenous fisheries (including eggs/larvae), prey species, forage strategies, and the sargassum communities.

Concerns were also raised regarding the effects the ship and anchor system might have on the biota as a result of displacement, noise, or collisions, and the impacts of exploration activities on the commercial and recreational fisheries found at "The Point."

Because of previous scientific work done at or near the proposed drill site, this area may be well suited to such monitoring programs. Not only would information from these programs be vital for developing mitigation measures, but it could also serve as a critical database on which to build a management framework for future development. In addition, data already collected on local fish resources, marine birds, the benthos and bottom conditions, and physical oceanography could provide an excellent base for further research.

*This text also mentions marine mammals and Threatened and Endangered species (marine reptiles).

Oynes, C. 1998. The MMS Perspective: History/Status of the Manteo Leases. pp. 7-13. *In*: Vigil, D.L. (ed.). North Carolina/Minerals Management Service Technical Workshop on Manteo Unit Exploration: February 4-5, 1998. U.S. Dept. of the Interior, Minerals Management Service, Gulf of Mexico OCS Region. New Orleans, LA .

*These are the proceedings from a workshop/meeting (February 4-5, 1998) between the North Carolina Department of Environment and Natural Resources, and the U.S. Department of the Interior's Minerals Management Service (MMS). The geographic area being discussed is approximately 45 miles east-northeast of Cape Hatteras, NC, referred to as the Manteo Unit. This workshop reviewed environmental and socioeconomic information known and needed on the Manteo Unit. The MMS's Gulf of Mexico OCS Regional Director gave an MMS perspective on history and status of the area. Chevron gave a presentation on how the exploratory well would be drilled. The scientific characterization was presented in greater detail by a number of scientific experts who spoke on the following disciplines physical environment, habitat and living resources, seabirds, marine mammals, sea turtles, and social and economic issues. Specific chapters are cited individually, when appropriate.

This section discusses U.S. Department of the Interior's Minerals Management Service (MMS) studies (socioeconomic and environmental), Manteo Leases, Exploration plans, the North Carolina Environmental Sciences Review Panel, Exploratory Drilling Scenarios, Perspectives on Exploratory Drilling, and Workshop Objectives.

Paull, C. 1989. Geologic Overview: Potential for Gas and Oil Discovery. pp. 16-18. *In*: Crawford, K. (ed.). Proceedings: 1989 Marine Expo: The Natural Resources Associated with Mobil's Proposed Drill Site. NC Outer Continental Shelf Office, NC Department of Administration. Raleigh, NC.

The petroleum geologists at Mobil identified Block 467 as having potential for gas accumulations. The arguments that these geologists must have made to their management can be partly recreated using basic geologic principles. There are three requirements that need to be met for either oil or gas to accumulate: 1) there must be a source of organic matter; 2) the organic matter that is buried in the ground must be converted to hydrocarbons through a process known as maturation (which is a function of temperature, pressure and time); and 3) the hydrocarbons must be concentrated into a reservoir. Reservoirs are large bodies of porous strata that are covered or sealed by relatively impervious strata that trap buoyant fluids like oil or gas.

—. 1991. Geologic Overview: Potential for Gas and Oil Discovery. p. 8. *In*: Shepard, A. (ed.). NURC/UNCW 1991 Undersea Research: Informational Meeting, National Undersea Research Center, University of North Carolina at Wilmington. Wilmington, NC.

The petroleum geologists at Mobil identified Block 467 as having potential for gas accumulations. The arguments that these geologists must have made to their management can be partly recreated using basic geologic principles. There are three requirements that need to be met for either oil or gas to accumulate: 1) there must be a source of organic matter; 2) the organic matter that is buried in the ground must be converted to hydrocarbons through a process known as maturation (which is a function of temperature, pressure, and time); and 3) the hydrocarbons must be concentrated into a reservoir. Reservoirs are large bodies of porous strata that are covered or sealed by relatively impervious strata that trap buoyant fluids like oil or gas.

—. 1998. Physical Environment Review: Slope Stability and Other Shallow Hazards for Drilling and Production in the Manteo 467 and 510 Lease Blocks. pp. 33-36. *In*: Vigil, D.L. (ed.). North Carolina/

Minerals Management Service Technical Workshop on Manteo Unit Exploration: February 4-5, 1998. U.S. Dept. of the Interior, Minerals Management Service, Gulf of Mexico OCS Region. New Orleans, LA.

*These are the proceedings from a workshop/meeting (February 4-5, 1998) between the North Carolina Department of Environment and Natural Resources, and the U.S. Department of the Interior's Minerals Management Service (MMS). The geographic area being discussed is approximately 45 miles east-northeast of Cape Hatteras, NC, referred to as the Manteo Unit. This workshop reviewed environmental and socioeconomic information known and needed on the Manteo Unit. The MMS's Gulf of Mexico OCS Regional Director gave an MMS perspective on history and status of the area. Chevron gave a presentation on how the exploratory well would be drilled. The scientific characterization was presented in greater detail by a number of scientific experts who spoke on the following disciplines physical environment, habitat and living resources, seabirds, marine mammals, sea turtles, and social and economic issues. Specific chapters are cited individually, when appropriate.

This section provides a description of the geomorphology, an overview of the potential drilling hazards and a description of "shallow hazards" in the Manteo area. This information is based on "shallow hazard" survey data.

Paull, C.K. 1992. Overview of the Hydrocarbon Potential in the Manteo Prospect off Cape Hatteras, North Carolina. pp. 87-94. *In*: U.S. Department of the Interior, Minerals Management Service. Proceedings of the Fourth Atlantic OCS Region Information Transfer Meeting, September 1991. U.S. Department of the Interior, Minerals Management Service. Herndon, VA.

The Fourth Atlantic Outer Continental Shelf (OCS) Regional Information Transfer Meeting (ITM) was held on 24-25 September, 1991, in Wilmington, NC. The focus of the meeting was on the OCS off North Carolina, specifically on activities related to a proposed exploratory well for oil and gas by Mobil on Block 467 a site 40 miles off the coast of North Carolina. The area of industry interest is known as the Manteo Prospect, while the activities surrounding the proposed drilling are referred to collectively as the Manteo Project. The wildcat wellsite is in 2,690 ft. (857 m) of water near the edge of the Gulf Stream. It is also near a fishing ground known locally as "The Point." The area is believed to be gas prone rather than oil prone. The estimated size of the resource could be as high as 5 trillion cubic feet of gas.

The purpose of the meeting was to exchange information on the leasing background, legislative activities, scientific results, and socioeconomic studies. Legislative-related reports include descriptions of the Oil Pollution Act of 1990, the Outer Banks Protection Act, the Environmental Studies Review Panel, and the North Carolina Physical Oceanography Panel. Reports of studies on marine life include benthic diatoms, benthic fauna, pelagic seabirds, sea turtles, and right whales. One report describes the use of airships (blimps) for ocean research a capability relevant to North Carolina because of the east coast airship facility is located in the state. Local marine science facilities described include NOAA's national Undersea research Center at the University of North Carolina at Wilmington (NURC/UNCW) and the National Marine Fisheries Service laboratory in Beaufort.

Developments in oil spill cleanup technology and capabilities are described by both the Coast Guard and the industry. A socioeconomic report describes the effects of the oil and gas activities on the tourist industry. Lastly, research on the restoration of salt marshes indicates that rehabilitation of an area is possible when development or an accident has occurred. While the emphasis of the meeting was on oil and gas, two reports described the results of projects related to offshore sand mining. The appendix lists the names and addresses of speakers.

*This section provides a brief overview of the Manteo lease block program and an overview of the hydrocarbon potential in the Manteo Prospect off Cape Hatteras, North Carolina.

Pietrafesa, L.J. 1983. Shelfbreak Circulation, Fronts and Physical Oceanography: East and West Coast Perspectives. Society of Economic Paleontologists and Mineralogists 33: 233-250.

*A survey of fundamental physical oceanographic processes that may affect sediment distribution along shelfbreak regions is presented, emphasizing the Atlantic and Pacific coasts of the USA. The processes encompass the entire spectrum of known motions and are thus generic to all the shelfbreak interfacial zones. These shelfbreak strips couple the bounded coastal oceans to the open seas, but there is no systematic pattern to this coupling. In the South Atlantic bight, the Gulf Stream acts like a vibrating, permeable wall which can variously entrain shelf waters, flood the shelf with North Atlantic Central Water and violently mix shelf waters by towing whirling vortices through the outer shelf. Middle Atlantic Bight, New York Bight and Gulf of Maine shelfbreak processes contain many of the dynamic elements of their southeastern counterpart, but the relative importance of various random surface and offshore driving forces change.

Pratt, R.M. 1968. Atlantic Continental Shelf and Slope of The United States — Physiography and Sediments Of the Deep-Sea Basin. Geological Survey Professional Paper 529-B. United States Printing Office. Washington, DC. 44 p.

*This study is a summary of the widely scattered information on the sedimentary environments of the North American Basin off the east coast of the United States. It is an extension of a joint study of the continental shelf and slope by the Woods Hole Oceanographic Institution and the U.S. Geological Survey (Emery 1966).

Rhoads, D.C., and B. Hecker. 1994. Processes on the continental slope off North Carolina with special reference to the Cape Hatteras region. Deep-Sea Research II Vol. 41(4-6): 965-980.

Historical data from the slope off Cape Hatteras show this environment to be atypical of the rest of the Atlantic slope in terms of high rates of sedimentation and high benthic/demersal standing stocks. This paper focuses on identifying potential sources for sediments and nutrients on the Hatteras slope and on likely transport mechanisms.

Sediments consist mainly of subequal mixtures of sand, silt, and clay and contain an average of 1% carbon. This pool of carbon represents weathered organic matter containing polyunsaturated fatty acids (PUFA) and sterols typical of relatively refractory shelf/estuarine sediments. The labile organic fraction is derived from phytoplankton and zooplankton as reflected in short chain fatty acids (< C22), planktic sterols, and chlorophyll a that are found in higher concentrations than observed elsewhere on the eastern U.S. continental slope. The inventory of organic nitrogen is much higher on the mid-slope (800-1000 m) than shallower or deeper bottom areas as predicted from plots of organic nitrogen versus grain-size for the U.S. Atlantic continental margin. The mid- slope region is the major focusing area for sedimentation. Bioturbation is an important diagenetic process that has profound influence on sediment profiles of sulphate, methane, fatty acids, sterols, chlorophyll a, viable diatoms, and metals. The low inventory of relatively refractory carbon (1%) stands in contrast to high measured rates of organic carbon sedimentation (28-121 g organic C m-2 year- 1). This paradox is probably related to high remineralization rates in the water column and on the bottom. The refractory nature of the small residual pool of deposited organic matter may define the trophic niche filled by those benthos found on this slope that are more typically encountered on the shelf (e.g. oligochaetes and opportunistic polychaetes).

A likely mechanism for high input rates of both organic and inorganic particulates to the Hatteras slope may be attributed to the position of Cape Hatteras relative to the adjacent narrow shelf. The Cape extends outward almost to the shelf edge topographically diverting sediment and primary production seaward that is moving southward along the outer shelf (the 'funnel' hypothesis). Transport of outer shelf sands to the slope may take place by the impingement of Gulf Stream eddies on the outer shelf and upper slope as well as by storm-generated waves. Once shelf sediment is deposited on the upper slope, it is apparently redistributed, as no strong on-shore to off-shore or depth-related gradients are observed in any of the measured sedimentary parameters.

The Hatteras slope apparently represents an estuarine type of sedimentary/nutrient regime that is displaced to an otherwise oceanic deep-sea environment by outwelling and funneling of nutrients and sediments from the shelf to the slope.

Rona, P.A. 1969. Middle Atlantic Continental Slope of United States: Deposition and Erosion. The American Association of Petroleum Geologist Bulletin 53 (7): 1453-1465.

Continuos seismic reflection profiles across outer continental terrace (outer continental shelf and slope) show that directly off Cape Hatteras reflection interfaces (sedimentary strata) with low seaward inclination (≤ 1) underlie the continental shelf and terminate at the continental slope, which inclines about 9. On traverses about 200 km north of Cape Hatteras, reflection interfaces (sedimentary strata) do not terminate but incline about 3, nearly parallel with the continental slope. On the continental lope about 100 km north of Cape Hatteras both relationships are present.

—. 1970. Submarine canyon origin on upper continental slope off Cape Hatteras. Journal of Geology 78(2): 141-152.

The configuration of sedimentary strata revealed by continuous seismic-reflection profiles over submarine canyons in the upper continental slope off Cape Hatteras is best explained by the hypothesis of composite origin of submarine canyons. The canyons were originally incised into a post-Miocene surface of unconformity. The intercanyon areas were constructed by deposition of sediment up to several hundred meters thick forming the canyon walls while the canyons were maintained by sediment removal processes over the sites of original incision.

Canyon heads are presently buried under a smooth sediment cover which extends from the shelf break at about 90 m down to about 400 m below sea level, where the canyons emerge from the cover. The depth of emergence of canyons approximately coincides with the inferred level of motion between the northeast-flowing Florida Current and the southwest-flowing Western Boundary Undercurrent.

Ross, S.W. 1991. Fisheries Resources Potentially Impacted by Proposed Drilling On the US Atlantic Continental Slope and Rise Off Cape Hatteras, North Carolina . p. 6. *In*: Shepard, A. (ed.). NURC/UNCW 1991 Undersea Research: Informational Meeting. National Undersea Research Center, University of North Carolina at Wilmington. Wilmington, NC.

An area known colloquially as "The Point" by fishermen, lies within the Manteo oil and gas lease blocks, just north of block 467, site of the proposed exploratory drill hole. 'The Point" is characterized by a productive pelagic fishery and complex submarine topography. Although a small, canyon-like feature underlies the area, "The Point" is not a spot on the bottom, but rather a shifting location that may coincide with the confluence of water masses.

In 1991, we will use a research submersible to describe the pelagic and benthic fish populations near Manteo Block 467. Specific objectives are to determine the distribution of: (1) pelagic fish with respect to depth and hydrographic features throughout the water column; and (2) benthic fish with respect to depth and topographic features.

—. Unpublished (a). Selected fish, invertebrate and bottom habitat data.

*This is unpublished data, collected by collected by S.W. Ross during a SCUBA dive on 18 August 1980. The location for this site [SWR -SCUBA-80-20] is 35° 20.7′N; 75° 21.2′W; depth 70-80 feet. Selected fish, invertebrate, and bottom habitat data were collected. These data are unpublished and the site was not visited again. This cite (no date presented) is listed as ISO4 by Kirby-Smith (1989). The location data assigned for site ISO4 by Kirby-Smith (1989) were incorrect. The data cited by Kirby-Smith for site ISO4 were data collected by S.W. Ross at site [SWR -SCUBA-80-20] (S.W. Ross, pers. comm. 19 November 1999).

—. Unpublished (c). Seabeam Bathymetry in the area off Cape Hatteras, NC known as "The Point."

*During the week of 13 November 1989 the National Oceanic and Atmospheric Administration National Ocean Service (NOAA, NOS) used the R/V *Mt. Mitchell* and its SeaBeam bottom mapping system to map a portion of the area off Cape Hatteras known as "The Point" (mostly in Manteo lease block 467). The cruise was not specifically directed toward this area, but the mapping effort was fit into the vessel's schedule as it transited between projects. This maping was done at the request of Steve W. Ross who served as the state contact for the data. Mr. Don Prior served as the NOAA/NOS contact. The data were originally provided as a hard copy plot of depth contours at a scale of 1:12,500 with contours at 25 m intervals on a transverse Mercator projection using NAD 83 datum. During this bibliographic project this hard copy map was digitized and incorporated into ArcView GIS where both two and three dimensional maps could be produced. These are the same data referenced and used by Mellor (1998) and Mellor and Paull (1994). These unpublished data are currently archived by the NC National Estuarine Research Reserve (contact Dr. S.W. Ross or J. Ott).

Rowe, G.T. 1971. Observations on bottom currents and epibenthic populations in Hatteras Submarine Canyon. Deep-Sea Research 18: 569-581.

Bottom currents and populations of large epifauna were surveyed using bottom photography in the Pamlico axis of the Hatteras Submarine Canyon system. Most species known to be numerically dominant along the continental slope north and south of the canyon were absent or found in reduced densities, whereas other species were found only near or in the canyon and can be considered canyon indicator species. The implication of previous studies (Rowe and Menzies 1969; Sanders and Hessler 1969) that narrow faunal zonation is continuous along the margins of ocean basins must be modified to acknowledge the exceptional zonations found in canyons.

The photographs and current meter data indicated that the bottom current to the southwest along the lower continental rise, but turned to the west and northwest, or up the canyon, at lesser depths. Indurated sedimentary outcrops common to the canyon were probably a result of intermittent slumping and turbidity current flows.

Schneider, E.D., P.J. Fox, C.D. Hollister, H.D. Needham, and B.C. Heezen. 1967. Further Evidence of Contour Currents in the Western North Atlantic. Earth and Planetary Science Letters 2: 351-359.

A study of compass-oriented sea-floor photographs, echograms and sediment cores on the Atlantic continental margin of North America has been made in order to evaluate the role of deep-sea contour currents in the shaping of the continental rise.

The sediments on the upper continental rise consist of lutites which are being deposited on the seafloor in an environment devoid of strong bottom currents. Below an abrupt change in regional slope, that marks the boundary between the upper and lower continental rise, a swift bottom current is observed which flows to the southwest parallel to the contours. Beneath this current the surface sediments are distinctly coarser grained and long cores show many quartz silt laminations in the sedimentary column. Further downslope on the lower continental rise the currents are variable in direction and weaker. Measurements of northerly directions indicate that at certain locations the Gulf Stream may intermittently scour the sea floor. In the area of the Lower Continental Rise Hill a swift southwesterly current is again observed. Hyperbolic echo traces on echograms, prolonged multiple echo sequences, and wedging of sub-bottom reflecting interfaces can be mapped as distinct zones. These zones of sea floor micromorphology parallel the region contours of the continental rise, and are produced by erosional and depositional processes of bottom currents. We conclude that the continental rise is a large sediment wedge which owes its shape to deep geostrophic contour currents.

Shepard, A. (ed.). 1991. Undersea Research at The Point. NURC/UNCW 1991 Undersea Research: Informational Meeting. National Undersea Research Center, University of North Carolina at Wilmington. Wilmington, NC. 9 p.

*This handout is a summary of research being conducted at "The Point" area (Manteo Lease Block 467).

The National Undersea Research Center at the University of North Carolina at Wilmington, funded by a grant from the National Oceanic and Atmospheric Administration's (NOAA) Office of Undersea Research (OUR), was established in 1980 to promote, facilitate, and conduct research in the Southeastern United States utilizing undersea techniques, including advanced wet diving and manned and unmanned submersibles. A main Center goal is to provide information to NOAA that will assist the agency in fulfilling its charter to explore, understand, conserve and manage the U.S. marine environment and associated resources. To help meet this goal, the Center supports and conducts interdisciplinary oceanographic research projects studying continental margin processes, particularly the interactions and linkages between estuarine, continental shelf, and slope (including submarine canyon) environments.

Shepard, A., and A.H. Hulbert (eds.). 1994. Workshop Report: Present and Future Research Initiatives on the Upper Hatteras Slope off North Carolina. National Undersea Research Center at the University of North Carolina at Wilmington. Wilmington, NC. 30p.

*This report is the result of the May 1993 workshop held in Raleigh, NC. The topics of discussion were research (present and planned) at the Upper Hatteras Slope (UHS) and potential funding sources. The workshop was sponsored by National Undersea Research Center at the University of North Carolina at Wilmington. The report provides a brief description of the UHS invertebrates, biological oceanography, chemical oceanography, geological oceanography (bathymetry, oil and gas exploration), physical oceanography, fisheries, and *Sargassum*. Appendix A is a workshop agenda and list of speakers. No abstracts for speakers are provided. Appendix B is a list of potential funding sources. Appendix C contains a list of publications pertaining to the UHS.

Shepard, A.N. 1992. A North Carolina Oceanographic Facility: The National Oceanographic and Atmospheric Administration's National Undersea Research Center. pp. 55-65. *In*: U.S. Department of the Interior, Minerals Management Service. Proceedings of the Fourth Atlantic OCS Region Information Transfer Meeting, September 1991. U.S. Department of the Interior, Minerals Management Service. Herndon, VA.

The Fourth Atlantic Outer Continental Shelf (OCS) regional Information Transfer Meeting was held on 24-25 September 1991 in Wilmington, NC. The focus of the meeting was on the OCS off North Carolina, specifically on activities related to a proposed exploratory well for oil and gas by Mobil on Block 467 a site 40 miles off the coast of North Carolina. The area of industry interest is known as the Manteo Prospect, while the activities surrounding the proposed drilling are referred to collectively as the Manteo Project. The wildcat wellsite is in 2,690 ft. (857 m) of water near the edge of the Gulf

Stream. It is also near a fishing ground known locally as "The Point." The area is believed to be gas prone rather than oil prone. The estimated size of the resource could be as high as 5 trillion cubic feet of gas.

The purpose of the meeting was to exchange information on the leasing background, legislative activities, scientific results, and socioeconomic studies. Legislative-related reports include descriptions of the Oil Pollution Act of 1990, the Outer Banks Protection Act, the Environmental Studies Review Panel, and the North Carolina Physical Oceanography Panel. Reports of studies on marine life include benthic diatoms, benthic fauna, pelagic seabirds, sea turtles, and right whales. One report describes the use of airships (blimps) for ocean research a capability relevant to North Carolina because of the east coast airship facility is located in the state. Local marine science facilities described include NOAA's National Undersea Research Center at the University of North Carolina at Wilmington and the national marine Fisheries Service laboratory in Beaufort.

Developments in oil spill cleanup technology and capabilities are described by both the Coast Guard and the industry. A socioeconomic report describes the effects of the oil and gas activities on the tourist industry. Lastly, research on the restoration of salt marshes indicates that rehabilitation of an area is possible when development or an accident has occurred. While the emphasis of the meeting was on oil and gas, two reports described the results of projects related to offshore sand mining. The appendix lists the names and addresses of speakers. Individual chapters are cited individually when appropriate.

*Within the oil and gas lease blocks of the Manteo Prospect lies "The Point." This productive pelagic fishing ground lies at the confluence of major currents and water masses, and contains complex and rugged submarine topography. The National Undersea Research Center (NURC) located at the University of North Carolina at Wilmington is one of the oceanographic facilities near The Point. This center has a record of research in the area and has experience, equipment, and staff that will be invaluable to future studies.

Shephard, A.N., T. Schaff, N. Mountford, and A.W. Hulbert. 1993. Relationship of Benthic Infuna and Slope Angle on the Continental Slope Off Cape Hatteras, NC. Benthic Ecology Meeting, 1-4 April, 1993, Mobile, AL. 57 p.

Minerals Management Service was recently charged, by legislative mandate, with describing the nature and extent of the benthic community inhabiting oil and gas lease blocks on the Continental Slope off Cape Hatteras, NC. Once the benthic community is described, the assumption is that the potential impacts of oil and gas exploration and development activities can be assessed. A significant difficulty with this assumption is that the area of the lease blocks is extremely rugged. The primary techniques used to sample infauna on MMS funded research have been surface deployed box cores. Such box cores generally sample on relatively flat bottom. NOAA's National Undersea Research Center at the University of North Carolina at Wilmington funded a manned submersible cruise in 1992, in part, to sample steep areas that are inaccessible to surface deployed box cores. Preliminary results suggest that substrate angle significantly affects infaunal abundance and species composition. In rugged, non-indurated areas, substrate angle must be considered when describing benthic communities.

U.S. Department of the Interior, Minerals Management Service. 1990. Atlantic Outer Continental Shelf: Final Environmental Report on Proposed Exploratory Drilling Offshore North Carolina, U.S. Department of the Interior, Minerals Management Service, Atlantic OCS Region, Environmental Assessment Section. Herndon, VA.

*Topics include: fisheries, birds, marine mammals, physical oceanography, chemical oceanography, geology, gas and oil production. The proposed action is to drill a single exploratory well approximately 72 km (45 mi) east-northeast of Cape Hatteras, NC in 820 m (2,690 ft) of water. Total depth for the proposed well is 4,267 m (14,000 ft) and the location is on Block 467 on the Minerals Management Service Protraction diagram NI 18-2. The proposal has been submitted by Mobil for itself and 7 partners to drill the well on the approved 21-block exploration unit.

U.S. Department of the Interior, Minerals Management Service. 1992. Proceedings of the Fourth Atlantic OCS Region Information Transfer Meeting, September 1991. U.S. Department of the Interior, Minerals Management Service. Herndon, VA. 198 p.

The Fourth Atlantic Outer Continental Shelf (OCS) Regional Information Transfer Meeting was held on 24-25 September 1991 in Wilmington, NC. The focus of the meeting was on the OCS off North Carolina, specifically on activities related to a proposed exploratory well for oil and gas by Mobil on Block 467 a site 40 miles off the coast of North Carolina. The area of industry interest is known as the Manteo Prospect, while the activities surrounding the proposed drilling are referred to collectively as the Manteo Project. The wildcat wellsite is in 2,690 ft. (857 m) of water near the edge of the Gulf Stream. It is also near a fishing ground known locally as "The Point." The area is believed to be gas prone rather than oil prone. The estimated size of the resource could be as high as 5 trillion cubic feet of gas.

The purpose of the meeting was to exchange information on the leasing background, legislative activities, scientific results, and socioeconomic studies. Legislative-related reports include descriptions of the Oil Pollution Act of 1990, the Outer Banks Protection Act, the Environmental Studies Review Panel, and the North Carolina Physical Oceanography Panel. Reports of studies on marine life include benthic diatoms, benthic fauna, pelagic seabirds, sea turtles, and right whales. One report describes the use of airships (blimps) for ocean research a capability relevant to North Carolina because of the east coast airship facility is located in the state. Local marine science facilities described include NOAA's National Undersea Research Center at the University of North Carolina at Wilmington and the National Marine Fisheries Service laboratory in Beaufort.

Developments in oil spill cleanup technology and capabilities are described by both the Coast Guard and the industry. A socioeconomic report describes the effects of the oil and gas activities on the tourist industry. Lastly, research on the restoration of salt marshes indicates that rehabilitation of an area is possible when development or an accident has occurred. While the emphasis of the meeting was on oil and gas, two reports described the results of projects related to offshore sand mining. The appendix lists the names and addresses of speakers. Individual chapters are cited individually when appropriate.

Uchupi, E. 1967. The continental margin south of Cape Hatteras, North Carolina: shallow structure. SE Geol. 8: 155-177.

Continuous seismic profiles, drill hole data and dredge hauls show that the geologic history of the continental margin south of the Cape Hatteras has been complex, marked by carbonate deposition, erosion by the Gulf Stream, and differential subsidence. The Blake Escarpment east of the Blake Plateau is believed to represent a chain of algal banks that flourished during the Cretaceous. A thick sequence of shallow-water carbonate sediments accumulated on the Blake Plateau behind the algal sandbanks to the east. Soon after the banks died during Late Cretaceous submergence of the area the Gulf Stream extended its course across the Blake Plateau. During the Tertiary, the locus of deposition shifted westward to the area near the present shelf-break, where 600 to 1000 meters of shallow-water sediments were deposited. South of Latitude 32 sediment prograded against the westward margin of the Gulf Stream throughout the Tertiary. Farther north, where the Gulf Stream lies farther offshore, outbuilding extended beyond the eastern margin of the Blake Plateau. Vertical uplifts followed by erosion by the Gulf Stream during the Pleistocene modified this sedimentary framework.

Uchupi, E., and K.O. Emery. 1967. Structure of Continental Margin Off Atlantic Coast of United States. *The* American Association of Petroleum Geologists Bulletin 51(2): 223-234.

Seismic profiler recordings in 44 profiles between Nova Scotia and the Florida Keys indicate that the continental margin was performed by upbuilding on the shelf and prograding on the slope. Upbuilding on the shelf during Tertiary and Quaternary Periods ranged from 200 to 1,000 meters, and sea-ward prograding on the slope during the same span of time was from 5 to more than 35 kilometers. The greatest progradation occurred where the slope is flanked by the Blake Plateau rather than by the deep sea. The beds are truncated along some sections of the slope as though the slope had been steepened by submarine erosion. Off Nova Scotia the beds of the slope continue into the continental rise; off New England rise consists of sedimentary layers that have buried the base of the continental lope; and off southeastern United States the beds of the Florida-Hatteras Slope have prograded atop the older surface of the Blake Plateau.

Vigil, D.L. (ed.). 1998. North Carolina/Minerals Management Service Technical Workshop on Manteo Unit Exploration: February 4-5, 1998. U.S. Dept. of the Interior, Minerals Management Service. Gulf of Mexico OCS Region. New Orleans, LA. 168 p.

*These are the proceedings from a workshop/meeting (February 4-5, 1998) between the North Carolina Department of Environment and Natural Resources, and the U.S. Department of the Interior's Minerals Management Service (MMS). The geographic area being discussed is approximately 45 miles east-northeast of Cape Hatteras, North Carolina, referred to as the Manteo Unit. This workshop reviewed environmental and socioeconomic information known and needed on the Manteo Unit. The MMS's Gulf of Mexico OCS Regional Director gave an MMS perspective on history and status of the area. Chevron gave a presentation on how the exploratory well would be drilled. The scientific characterization was presented in greater detail by a number of scientific experts who spoke on the following disciplines physical environment, habitat and living resources (invertebrates and fish), seabirds, marine mammals, sea turtles, and social and economic issues. Specific chapters are cited individually, when appropriate.

Walsh, J.J. 1994. Particle export at Cape Hatteras. Deep-Sea Research II Vol. 41(2-3): 603-628.

A simple model of shelf, slope and basin waters near Cape Hatteras, North Carolina is used to estimate the sources and sinks of organic carbon within the Gulf Stream System. The analysis employs water transport estimates, nutrient data. satellite imagery, surficial sediment records and particle distributions caught by bottle, camera and sediment trap to compute vertical and lateral fluxes of particulate carbon. Particle export from the SAB and MAB shelf ecosystems may constitute 62-82% of the source of the carbon flux within the Gulf Stream near 75 W, after settling at 100 m day^{-1}, with an oxidation loss of 4% day^{-1}, to a nominal mid-depth of 1000 m on the slope.

As a result of light limitation, denitrification and DON solubilization, partial utilization of onwelled nitrate from the Gulf Stream System by coastal phytoplankton suggests that the time-averaged *f* ratio may be as small as 0.12 for the ratio of the "new" portion of primary production to the total. After burial loss, the export of particulate matter from the shelves then represents at most 11% of the total carbon fixation of coastal waters. If the shelf export of DON and unutilized NO_3 is consumed within adjacent slope waters, however, the *f* ratio and the percentage of particle export from the carbon fixation of shelf-affected waters might increase to 0.25 and 24%.

Weetman, B.G. 1992. The Manteo Story. pp. 3-10. *In*: U.S. Department of the Interior, Minerals Management Service. Proceedings of the Fourth Atlantic OCS Region Information Transfer Meeting, September 1991. U.S. Department of the Interior, Minerals Management Service. Herndon, VA.

The Fourth Atlantic Outer Continental Shelf (OCS) Regional Information Transfer Meeting was held on 24-25 September 1991 in Wilmington, NC. The focus of the meeting was on the OCS off North Carolina, specifically on activities related to a proposed exploratory well for oil and gas by Mobil on Block 467 a site 40 miles off the coast of North Carolina. The area of industry interest is known as the Manteo Prospect, while the activities surrounding the proposed drilling are referred to collectively as the Manteo Project. The wildcat wellsite is in 2,690 ft. (857 m) of water near the edge of the Gulf Stream. It is also near a fishing ground known locally as "The Point." The area is believed to be gas prone rather than oil prone. The estimated size of the resource could be as high as 5 trillion cubic feet of gas.

The purpose of the meeting was to exchange information on the leasing background, legislative activities, scientific results, and socioeconomic studies. Legislative-related reports include descriptions of the Oil Pollution Act of 1990, the Outer Banks Protection Act, the Environmental Studies Review Panel, and the North Carolina Physical Oceanography Panel. Reports of studies on marine life include benthic diatoms, benthic fauna, pelagic seabirds, sea turtles, and right whales. One report describes the use of airships (blimps) for ocean research a capability relevant to North Carolina because of the east coast airship facility is located in the state. Local marine science facilities described include NOAA's national Undersea research Center at the University of North Carolina at Wilmington and the National Marine Fisheries Service laboratory in Beaufort.

Developments in oil spill cleanup technology and capabilities are described by both the Coast Guard and the industry. A socioeconomic report describes the effects of the oil and gas activities on the tourist industry. Lastly, research on the restoration of salt marshes indicates that rehabilitation of an area is possible when development or an accident has occurred. While the emphasis of the meeting was on oil and gas, two reports described the results of projects related to offshore sand mining. The appendix lists the names and addresses of speakers. Individual chapters are cited individually when appropriate.

*This section provides a brief overview of national energy issues pertaining to the Manteo Prospect. In the fall of 1988, Mobil initiated efforts preparatory to drilling an exploratory well on the area for which it held the lease Block 467, approximately 40 miles off the coast of North Carolina (Fig. 1). This site was contained in what petroleum geologists refer to as the Manteo Prospect. The activities (scientific, legal, industrial, and political) that surround the proposed drilling are collectively referred to as the Manteo project.

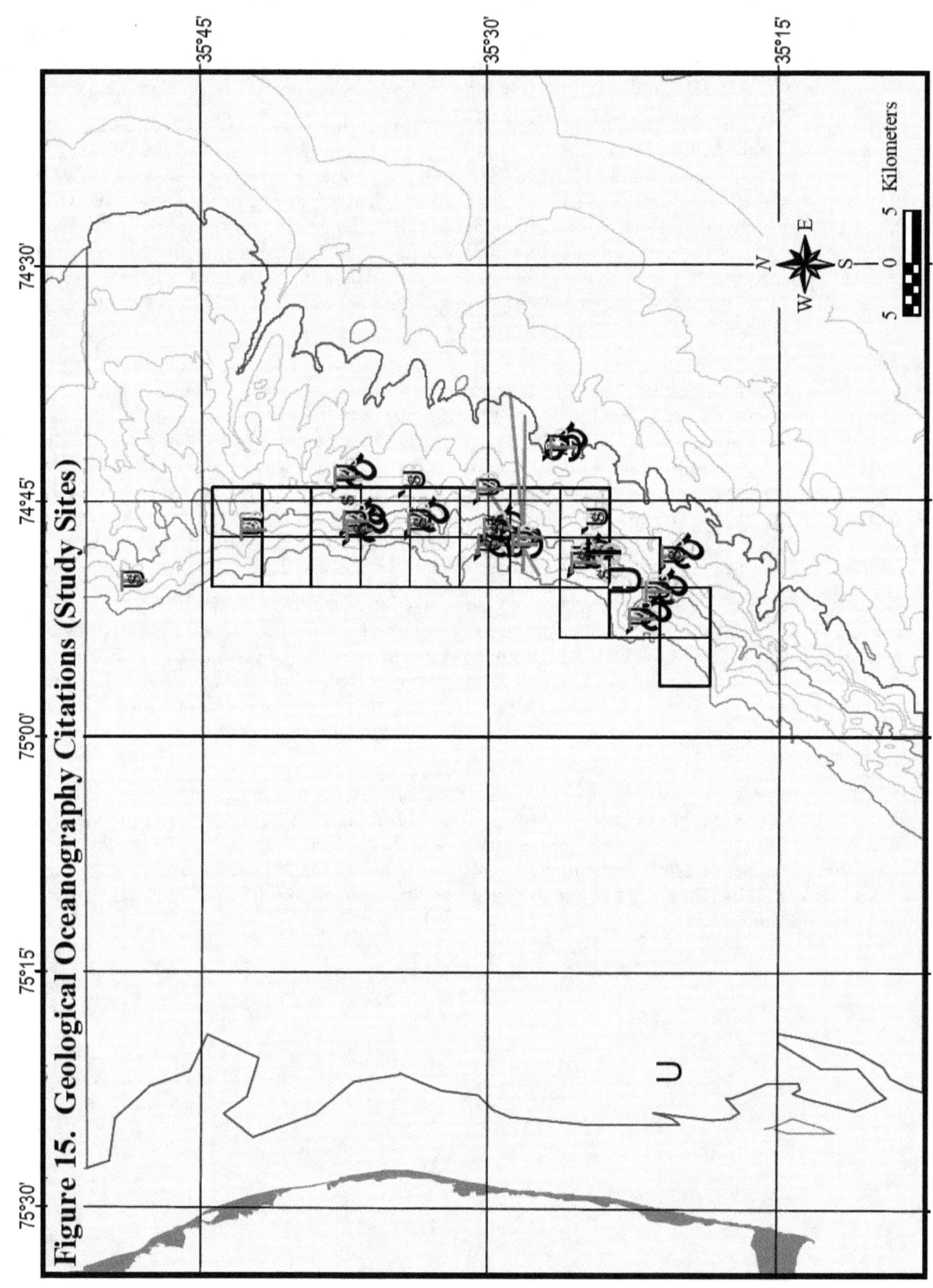

Figure 15. Geological Oceanography Citations (Study Sites)

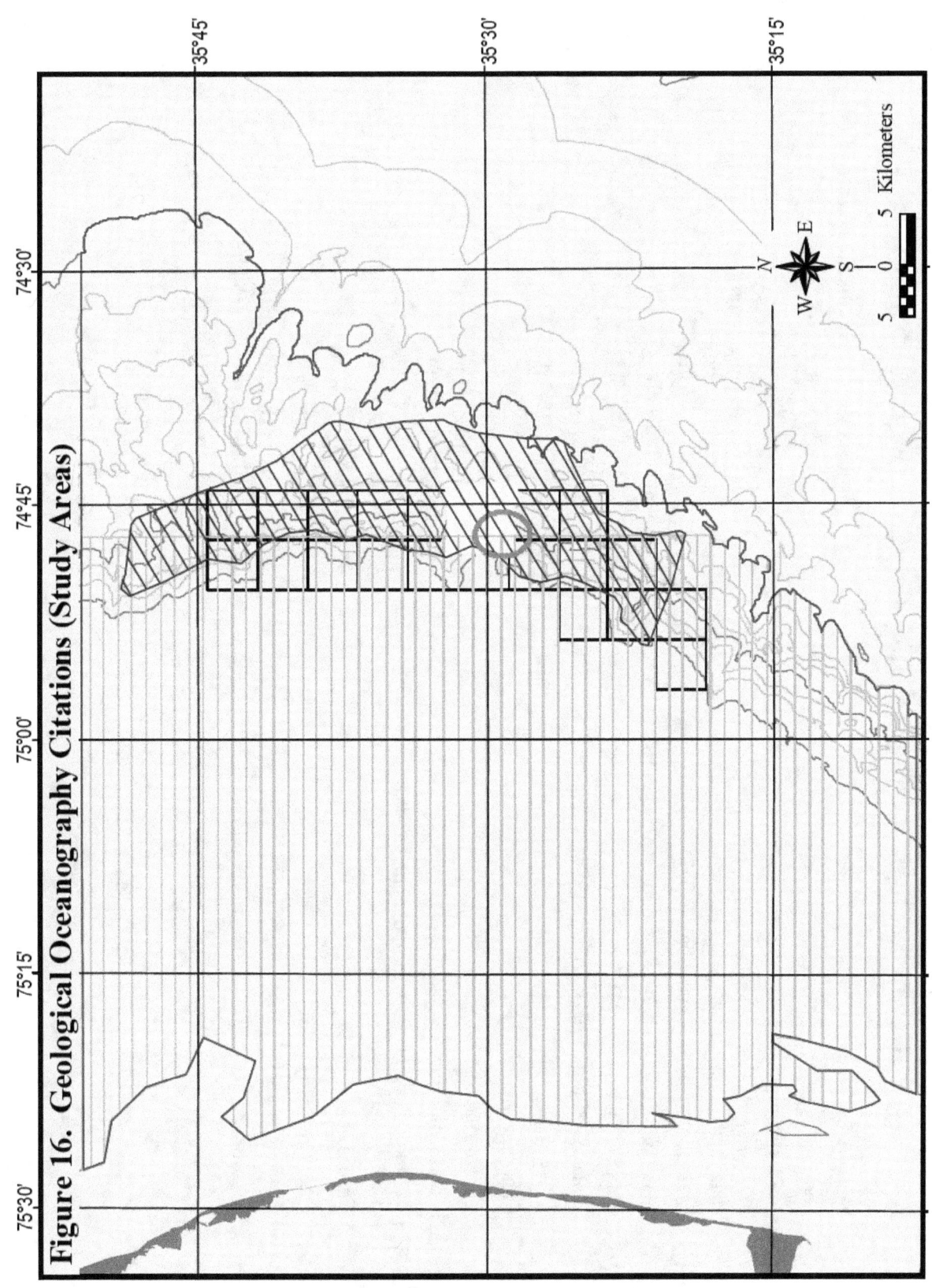

Figure 16. Geological Oceanography Citations (Study Areas)

Key to Geological Oceanography Citations (Figures 15 and 16).

〉 Study Area Boundary

☐ Lease Blocks

Mapped Citations

$ Blair et al. (1994); DeMaster et al. (1994);
Diaz et al. (1994); Ewing & Thorndike (1965)

U Blair et al. (1996); Levin et al. (1997)

S Blake & Diaz (1994, 1998); Cutter et al. (1994b)

U Blake & Grassle (1994)

〉 Blake & Hilbig (1994); Hilbig (1994)

, Blake et al. (1987)

Cahoon et al. (1994)

☐ Continental Shelf Assts. (1983)

☐ Continental Shelf Assts. (1989)

▨ Cutter et al. (1994a); Milliman et al. (1994);
Rhoads & Hecker (1994)

T Fornes et al. (1999)

a Harvey (1994)

U Kirby-Smith (1989b); Ross, S. (unpub.a)

Mellor & Paull (1994); Ross, S. (unpub. c)

Studies that Focus on the Manteo Lease Blocks

Atkinson et al. (1998)
Blair (1998)
Crawford (1989, 1998))
Diaz et al. (1993a, 1998)
Duplantier (1998)
Gettleson (1992)
Harris (1989)
Janowitz (1989)
McLawhorn (1998)
Mellor (1998)
Moffit (1989a)
Oynes (1998)
Paull (1989, 1991, 1992, 1998)
Shepard & Hulbert (1994)
Shepard (1992)
Shephard et al. (1993)
U.S.D.O.I.-Minerals Mgmt. Service (1990, 1992)
Vigil (1998)
Weetman (1992)

**Studies that Cover the Hatteras
Middle Slope Area ("The Point")**

Kirby-Smith (1989a)
Moffit (1989b)
Orbach (1989)
Rona (1970)
Ross, S. (1991)
Shepard (1991)

Key to Geological Oceanography Citations (Figures 15 and 16) (con't).

Studies Based on Large Digitized Databases
Moser et al. (1995)

Broad Regional Studies
Abernathy et al. (1989)
Amato (1994)
Anderson et al. (1994)
Bane (1983)
Bane & Brooks (1979)
Brown (1991)
Cleary & Thayer (1973)
Costlow et al. (1992)
Dillon & Popenoe (1988)
EEZ-SCAN 87 Scientific Staff (1991)
Emery (1970, 1971)
Heezen (1968)
Inman & Dolan (1989)
JAYCOR. (1980)
Lee (1983)
Legeckis & Bane (1983)
Lutenauer & Pilkey (1967)
MacIntyre & Milliman (1970)
Manheim et al. (1970)
Milliman (1994)
Mills (1992)
Newton et al. (1971)
Pietrafesa (1983)
Pratt (1968)
Rona (1969)
Rowe (1971)
Schneider et al. (1967)
Uchupi (1967)
Uchupi & Emery (1967)
Walsh (1994)

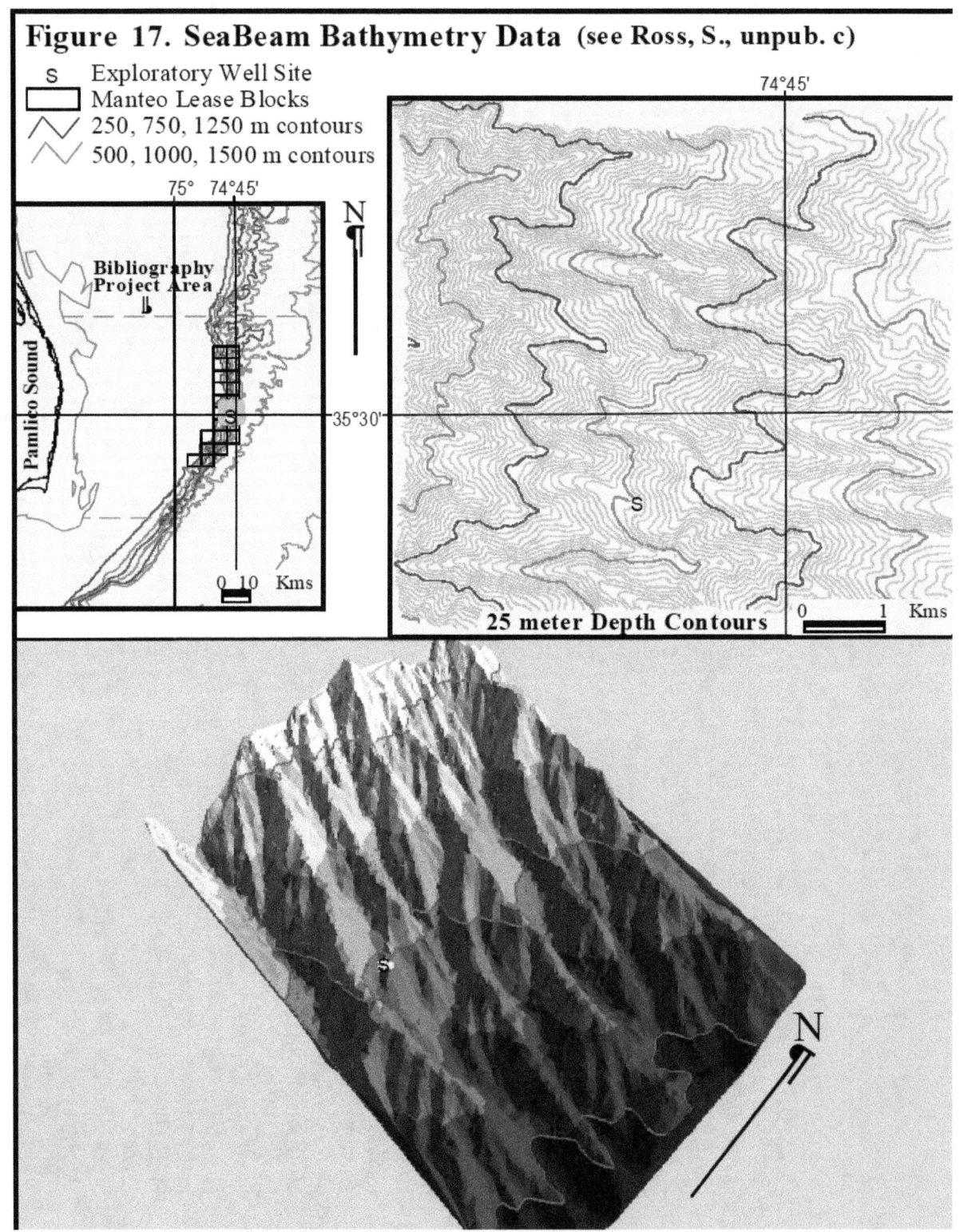

Figure 17. SeaBeam Bathymetry Data (see Ross, S., unpub. c)

PHYSICAL OCEANOGRAPHY CHAPTER

PHYSICAL OCEANOGRAPHY CHAPTER

Abernathy, S.A., M.T. Baer, C.S. Benner, M.S. Brody, D.K. Francois, J.K. Gilliam, L.K. Good, C.J. Ohara, and J.V. Martin. 1989. Atlantic Outer Continental Shelf: Description of the Mid-Atlantic Environment. Abernathy, S.A. (ed.). U.S. Department of the Interior, Minerals Management Service, Atlantic OCS Region, Environmental Assessment Section. Herndon, VA. 167 p.

*This document discusses the major issues and areas of concern for the mid-Atlantic environment that are considered in the planning process for oil and gas leasing and operations on the Outer Continental Shelf (OCS). The issues are addressed with respect to the potential environmental consequences of mid Atlantic oil and gas exploration, development and production. A section discussing The Physical Environment (e.g., geology, non-petroleum minerals, physical oceanography, chemical oceanography and water quality, ocean dumping, meteorology, air quality), Biological resources (e.g., plankton, benthos, fishery resources, marine reptiles, marine mammals, marine and coastal birds, estuaries, wetlands, sensitive coastal habitats, canyon areas), Socioeconomic Environment, and other issues (e.g., archaeological resources, marine vessel traffic, National Aeronautics and Space Administration/ Department of Defense activities, oil and gas infrastructure, marine sanctuaries, and estuarine research reserves) is included. Most of the figures showing fisheries resource distribution are taken from fisheries data compiled for bottom-trawl and shellfish surveys of the National Marine Fisheries Service, Northeast Fisheries Center, Woods Hole, MA.

Adams, C.E., T.J. Berger, W.C. Boicourt, J.C. Churchill, M.D. Earle, P. Hamilton, F.M. Vukovich, R.J. Wayland, and R.D. Watts. 1993. A Review of the Physical Oceanography of the Cape Hatteras, North Carolina Region: Volume I Literature Synthesis. MMS Contract 14-35-0001-30594. Science Applications International Corporation. 152 p.

*This is a literature synthesis of Physical Oceanography (pre-1993) studies within the defined study area for "The Point." These materials were compiled by Science Applications International Corporation for the Minerals Management Service: U.S. Department of the Interior, Atlantic OCS Region. Appropriate citations from this annotated bibliography will be cited independently with a description of location when location information is available.

Anderson, W.W., and J.W. Gehringer. 1959a. Physical oceanographic, biological, and chemical data, South Atlantic coast of the United States, M/V Theodore N. Gill cruise 7. US Department of the Interior, US Fish and Wildlife Service, Special Scientific Report — Fisheries No. 278. 277 p.

*This report documents stations sampled throughout the South Atlantic Bight during June-July 1954. Weather, water chemistry, and sea state data were collected. Plankton samples were collected and fish were sampled by dip net and trolling. A few stations were near or within the southern border of our study area.

_____. 1959b. Physical oceanographic, biological, and chemical data, South Atlantic coast of the United States, M/V Theodore N. Gill cruise 8. US Department of the Interior, US Fish and Wildlife Service, Special Scientific Report — Fisheries No. 303. 227 p.

*This report documents stations sampled throughout the South Atlantic Bight during August — September 1954. Weather, water chemistry, and sea state data were collected. Plankton samples were collected and fish were sampled by dip net and trolling. A few stations were near or within the southern border of our study area.

Anderson, W.W., J.W. Gehringer, and E. Cohen. 1956. Physical oceanographic, biological, and chemical data, South Atlantic coast of the United States, Theodore N. Gill cruise 2. US Department of the Interior, US Fish and Wildlife Service, Special Scientific Report — Fisheries No. 198. 270 p.

*This report documents stations sampled throughout the South Atlantic Bight during May 1953. Weather, water chemistry, and sea state data were collected. Plankton samples were collected and fish were sampled by dip net and trolling. A few stations were near or within the southern border of our study area.

Anderson, W.W., J.E. Moore, and H.R. Gordy. 1961. Oceanic salinities off the South Atlantic coast of the United States, Theodore N. Gill cruises 1-9, 1953-1954. US Department of the Interior, US Fish and Wildlife Service, Special Scientific Report — Fisheries No. 389. 207 p.

Salinity data secured on nine cruises of the M/V Theodore N. Gill off the south Atlantic coast of the United States are further processed and organized in a much more usable and readily available form. Surface water salinities are presented graphically by season.

Ashjian, C.J., S.L. Smith, C.N. Flagg, A.J. Mariano, W.J. Behrens, and P.V.Z. Lane. 1994. The influence of a Gulf Stream meander on the distribution of zooplankton biomass in the Slope Water, and the Gulf Stream, and the Sargasso Sea, described using a shipboard acoustic Doppler current profiler. Deep-Sea Research I 41(1): 23-50.

The influence of a Gulf Stream meander on the distribution of zooplankton biomass in the Slope Water, the Gulf Stream, and the Sargasso Sea, described using a shipboard acoustic Doppler current profiler Patterns in zooplankton biomass distribution in a Gulf Stream meander were documented wing a ship-mounted acoustic Doppler current profiler (ADCP) in fall 1988 as part of the BIOSYNOP program. The dominant signal in biomass was the regional variation between water masses, with greatest biomass recorded in the Slope Water, intermediate biomass at the Slope Water-Gulf Stream front, and lowest biomass in the Gulf Stream/Sargasso Sea. Biomass was more variable in the Slope Water than in the Sargasso Sea. Diel variation, a consequence of diel vertical migration, was also observed. Comprehensive maps of the surveyed region documented meander associated enhancement of zooplankton biomass. Elevated biomass was documented in the region downstream of the meander crest, where entrainment of Slope Water and convergence of flow are hypothesized to occur. The ADCP was demonstrated to be an effective means of documenting patterns in zooplankton biomass, including estimates of the variability (patchiness).

Atkinson, L.P. 1985. Hydrography and Nutrients of the Southeastern U.S. Continental Shelf . Oceanography of the Southeastern U.S. Continental Shelf Coastal and Estuarine Sciences 2: 77-92.

The distribution of properties such as temperature and salinity, of nutrients such as nitrate, phosphate, and silicate, and of derived properties such as buoyancy in the South Atlantic Bight depends on complex interactions of shelf waters with rivers, coastal estuaries and sounds, atmospheric forcing, and, most importantly, the Gulf Stream. Seasonal variations in temperature depend on the seasonal heating cycle, air-sea exchange processes, and Gulf Stream interaction. The result is extreme variations in temperature both seasonally and spatially. Salinity variations are mainly related to seasonal river flow, which peaks in the spring, and subsequent shelf circulation processes. Variations in temperature and salinity occur over shorter time scales because of Gulf Stream meanders and frontal eddies that cause intrusions of surface or subsurface water into the shelf waters. Intrusion frequency and cross-shelf excursion vary seasonally and latitudinally. The supply of nutrients mainly depends on Gulf Stream intrusions. Gulf Stream water colder than about 20°C contains significant amounts of nutrients. Such waters invade the shelf more frequently during the summer in the southern bight. Chemical tracers such as phenolic aldehydes, humic compound fluorescence, and tritium have been used successfully to trace coastal waters.

—. 1992. The North Carolina Physical Oceanographic Panel: Deliberations and Results. pp.17-23. *In*: U.S. Department of the Interior, Minerals Management Service. Proceedings of the Fourth Atlantic OCS Region Information Transfer Meeting, September 1991. U.S. Department of the Interior, Minerals Management Service. Herndon, VA.

The Fourth Atlantic Outer Continental Shelf (OCS) Regional Information Transfer Meeting (ITM) was held on 24-25 September, 1991, in Wilmington, NC. The focus of the meeting was on the OCS off North Carolina, specifically on activities related to a proposed exploratory well for oil and gas by Mobil on Block 467 a site 40 miles off the coast of North Carolina. The area of industry interest is known as the Manteo Prospect, while the activities surrounding the proposed drilling are referred to collectively as the Manteo Project. The wildcat wellsite is in 2,690 ft. (857 m) of water near the edge of the Gulf Stream. It is also near a fishing ground known locally as "The Point." The area is believed to be gas prone rather than oil prone. The estimated size of the resource could be as high as 5 trillion cubic feet of gas.

The purpose of the meeting was to exchange information on the leasing background, legislative activities, scientific results, and socioeconomic studies. Legislative-related reports include descriptions of the Oil Pollution Act of 1990, the Outer Banks Protection Act, the Environmental Studies Review Panel, and the North Carolina Physical Oceanography Panel. Reports of studies on marine life include benthic diatoms, benthic fauna, pelagic seabirds, sea turtles, and right whales. One report describes the use of airships (blimps) for ocean research a capability relevant to North Carolina because of the east coast airship facility is located in the state. Local marine science facilities described include NOAA's National Undersea Research Center at the University of North Carolina at Wilmington (NURC/UNCW) and the National Marine Fisheries Service Laboratory in Beaufort, NC.

Developments in oil spill cleanup technology and capabilities are described by both the Coast Guard and the industry. A socioeconomic report describes the effects of the oil and gas activities on the tourist industry. Lastly, research on the restoration of salt marshes indicates that rehabilitation of an area is possible when development or an accident has occurred. While the emphasis of the meeting was on oil and gas, two reports described the results of projects related to offshore sand mining. The appendix lists the names and addresses of speakers.

*To clarify, the North Carolina Physical Oceanography Panel is different from the Environmental Sciences Review panel. The North Carolina panel came about as a result of the FY 1990 appropriations report from the Department of the Interior. Study subject is the Manteo Area Block 467. The panel has concluded its work, providing the Minerals Management Service with a study design for physical oceanography and recommending a synthesis of physical oceanography both for the offshore area of North Carolina. This section briefly summarizes the objectives of the panel, members, and findings.

Atkinson, L.P., D.W. Menzel, and K.A. Bush. 1985. Oceanography of the Southeastern U.S. Continental Shelf. American Geophysical Union. Washington, DC. 156 p.

*This book contains 12 chapters: an introduction; four chapters on physical oceanography; a chapter on hydrography and nutrients; four biological chapters (covering phytoplankton, zooplankton, bacteria, and macroinfauna); a chemical chapter on trace metals; and a summary chapter describing future research plans. Research included was conducted between 1975 and the early 1980's and was largely funded by the Department of Energy and the Minerals Management Service (formerly Bureau of Land Management). The South Atlantic Bight extends from the temperate waters of Cape Hatteras,

NC to subtropical waters of West Palm Beach, FL. The ocean region is influenced by Gulf Stream dynamics on the eastern boundary, synoptic winds and weather events, river and estuarine inputs.

Atkinson, L., L. Heilman, and T. Curtin. 1998. Appendix E: Bathymetric and Physical Oceanographic Description of the Manteo Lease Area. pp.108-120. *In:* Vigil, D.L. (ed.). North Carolina/Minerals Management Service Technical Workshop on Manteo Unit Exploration: February 4-5, 1998. U.S. Dept. of the Interior, Minerals Management Service, Gulf of Mexico OCS Region. New Orleans, LA.

*These are the proceedings from a workshop/meeting (February 4-5, 1998) between the North Carolina Department of Environment and Natural Resources, and the U.S. Department of the Interior's Minerals Management Service (MMS). The geographic area being discussed is approximately 45 miles east-northeast of Cape Hatteras, NC, referred to as the Manteo Unit. This workshop reviewed environmental and socioeconomic information known and needed, on the Manteo Unit. The MMS's Gulf of Mexico OCS Regional Director gave an MMS perspective on history and status of the area. Chevron gave a presentation on how the exploratory well would be drilled. The scientific characterization was presented in greater detail by a number of scientific experts who spoke on the following disciplines physical environment, habitat and living resources, seabirds, marine mammals, sea turtles, and social and economic issues. Specific chapters are cited individually, when appropriate.

The waters off Cape Hatteras exhibit some of the most energetic coastal dynamics anywhere. Here the broad shelves of the Middle and South Atlantic Bights narrow nearly isolating shelf waters north and south of Cape Hatteras from each other. Offshore, one of the strongest currents in the ocean, the Gulf Stream, moves northward. In addition to that variability in the large-scale current regime, both winter storms and tropical hurricanes are prevalent in the region. This paper discusses the physical oceanographic properties at the Manteo site and their variability. This section also discusses Bathymetry of the Region, Physical Oceanography, Climate, Weather, Gulf Stream, and Coastal Currents.

Bane, J.M., Jr. 1983. Initial Observations of the Subsurface Structure and Short-Term Variability of the Seaward Deflection of the Gulf Stream Off Charleston, South Carolina. Journal of Geophysical Research 88 C(8): 4673-4684.

A recurring seaward deflection of the surface layer of the Gulf Stream has been observed near 32° N latitude off the coast of the southeastern United States. It has been suggested that a ridge and trough bottom feature (the so-called 'Charleston bump') on the upper continental slope off the Georgia/South Carolina coast produces the deflection through a bottom steering effect. Present data indicate that the deflection is great enough to direct the Gulf Stream's shoreward surface thermal front to the east, and even south of east, about 70% of the time. Air-deployed expendable bathythermograph surveys have been made with sufficient coverage to provide several synoptic, three-dimensional views of the Gulf Stream's thermal frontal zone in the region between Savannah, Georgia, and Cape Hatteras, North Carolina. These views show the subsurface structure of the seaward deflection to exhibit large short-term variability. During wintertime conditions (February 1979) the greatest deflection (>090° true) of the near-surface front occurred at a time when the deeper front was more aligned (~080° true) with local topography. Within the few days following this observation the deflection angle at all depths decreased to near or below 070° true. Two large-amplitude Gulf Stream meanders progressed northeastward away from the deflection region during this time period. Deflection angles at all levels during late summertime conditions (November 1979) were observed to be near 070° true. A simple, kinematical model which incorporates growing, propagating Gulf Stream meanders is proposed to explain the deflection's short-term variability. A dome-shaped volume of cold water was observed to be located over the upper continental slope immediately downstream of the deflection. The existence and persistence of this cold dome suggest that upwelling is important in its maintenance, a hypothesis consistent with its hydrographic properties.

Bane, J.M., Jr., and D.A. Brookes. 1979. Gulf Stream Meanders along the continental margin from the Florida Straights to Cape Hatteras. Geophysical Research Letters 6: 280-282.

*This geophysical research is cited in Journal of Geophysical Research vol. 88 C(8): 4651-4662 (Hood and Bane 1983), and pp. 4673-4684 (Bane 1983). Figure 1 The continental margin of the southeastern United States (p. 4562, Hood and Bane 1983), and Figure 8 The mean position ± 1 standard deviation (shaded) of the Gulf Stream's shoreward surface thermal front calculated for a 64 week period, (p. 4682, Bane, 1983) provide general location data. A cruise on the RV Endeavor (no cruise dates provided) is cited (Hood and Bane 1983).

Barrett, J.R., Jr. 1965. Subsurface currents off Cape Hatteras. Deep-Sea Research 12: 173-184.

In October 1962, direct current measurements at depths of 800 m to 2500 m beneath the zone of swiftest surface currents near Cape Hatteras revealed a subsurface flow to the south. Analysis of temperature-salinity and dissolved oxygen distributions indicate that the immediate source of the southward flowing water was the region east of Cape Hatteras between the Gulf Stream and the Continental Slope. These measurements seem to affirm that continuity exists between the deep westward flow observed in the Slope Water region by Volkmann and the southward flow east of Cape Roman, near 33N, reported by Swallow and Worthington. The geostrophic volume transport of the southward flow was between 4 million and 12 million m^3 sec^{-1}. The surface of zero axial velocity was at a depth of about 500 m at the left side of the region of swift surface current (inshore), and deepened rapidly in the offshore direction.

Blair, N. 1998. A Scientific Overview of the Region Surrounding Lease Blocks 467 and 510. pp. 14-17. *In*: Vigil, D.L. (ed.). North Carolina/Minerals Management Service Technical Workshop on Manteo Unit Exploration: February 4-5, 1998. U.S. Dept. of the Interior, Minerals Management Service, Gulf of Mexico OCS Region. New Orleans, LA.

*These are the proceedings from a workshop/meeting (February 4-5, 1998) between the North Carolina Department of Environment and Natural Resources, and the U.S. Department of the Interior's Minerals Management Service (MMS). The geographic area being discussed is approximately 45 miles east-northeast of Cape Hatteras, NC, referred to as the Manteo Unit. This workshop reviewed environmental and socioeconomic information known and needed on the Manteo Unit. The MMS's Gulf of Mexico OCS Regional Director gave an MMS perspective on history and status of the area. Chevron gave a presentation on how the exploratory well would be drilled. The scientific characterization was presented in greater detail by a number of scientific experts who spoke on the following disciplines physical environment, habitat and living resources, seabirds, marine mammals, sea turtles, and social and economic issues. Specific chapters are cited individually, when appropriate.

The continental margin offshore Cape Hatteras, NC has been the focus of numerous oceanographic studies. The objective of this report is to provide an overview of physical, biological, geological, and chemical processes that operate in the region so that the results from individual disciplinary studies can be placed in a system-wide context. This section discusses hydrocarbon potential, water column observations and processes, benthic observations and processes, summary and the future.

Blair, N., L. Levin, and D. DeMaster. 1991. Biology and Carbon Cycling on the Carolina Slope. p. 9. In: Shepard, A. (ed.). NURC/UNCW 1991 Undersea Research: Informational Meeting. National Undersea Research Center, University of North Carolina at Wilmington. Wilmington, NC.

Resources as diverse as fisheries, some minerals and fossil fuels, as well as the atmosphere and climate have been linked to the cycling of carbon and the associated biogenic nutrients along continental margins. The continental slope is an area which has been poorly studied even though it is the site of intense biogeochemical activity. An interdisciplinary program which focuses on the biogeochemistry of the Carolina slope environment is currently underway to investigate the relationship of carbon cycling with the sediment-dwelling ecosystem. Three sites, all at 850 meters water depth, have been studied. Sites I and II, which are off Charleston, South Carolina, and Cape Lookout, North Carolina, respectively, are representative of typical slope environments in terms of animal populations, sediment geochemistry and sediment accumulation. Site III, which is off of Cape Hatteras and near "The Point," has significantly higher populations of bottom-dwelling animals, different animal species and higher rates of organic matter degradation. Biogenic methane formation occurs at Site III but not at the other sites. These differences are thought to be related to the delivery rate of organic matter (food) to the seafloor. The convergence of boundary currents in this region may prove to be an important controlling factor by transporting organic matter into the area or by stimulating localized surface production via the delivery of nutrients. In contrast to the other sites, the sea floor at Site III is an area of high-relief and is more prone to episodic sedimentation and mass wasting. The combination of the high-relief bottom with the relatively large delivery rate of organic carbon to the seafloor may have resulted in a uniquely adapted ecosystem.

Future directions in research include identifying the sources of the sedimentary organic matter and the relationship between the ocean physics and the carbon delivery rate. The rates of organic matter delivery, decomposition and burial need to be measured as they represent important controls on the benthic ecosystems. Specific relationships between the benthic communities, the carbon cycle and sediment dynamics are to be investigated. Descriptions of the cliff-face communities are needed as they represent an important component of the overall ecosystems at Site III.

Blake, J.A., B. Hecker, J.F. Grassle, B. Brown, M. Wade, P.D. Boehm, E. Baptiste, B. Hilbig, N. Maciolek, R. Petrecca, R.E. Ruff, V. Starczak, and L. Watling. 1987. Study of Biological Processes on the U.S. South Atlantic Slope and Rise: Phase 2. U.S. Department of the Interior, Minerals Management Service, Atlantic OCS Region, Environmental Assessment Section. Herndon, VA.

A total of 16 stations were sampled during a 2 year field program designed to characterize the biological, chemical, and sedimentary processes on the slope and rise off North and South Carolina. Box cores were taken along a 4 transects at depths of 600 to 3500 m. The infauna yielded a total of 1202 species, 520 of which were new to science. Annelids were dominant taxa in terms of density and numbers of species. Species diversity was highest at an 800 m site off Charleston. Infaunal densities were highest on the upper slope (600 m) and lowest on the rise (3000 m). Life history analysis yielded evidence of seasonality for two polychaete species. Two stations off Cape Hatteras in depths of 600 m and 2000 m had higher infaunal density, lower species diversity, and higher biomass than elsewhere on the Atlantic slope and rise. Higher than normal lead and carbon inventories suggest enhanced scavenging processes in this area. Faunal patterns on the Cape Lookout transect were generally typical for other localities on the Atlantic Slope and Rise. Faunal changes were detected off Cape Fear and Charleston that may be related to the influence of the Gulf Stream and associated sediment changes. Epifauna were most unusual on the Charleston Bump, where a hard bottom fauna dominated by filter feeding corals and sponges thrives in an area strongly swept by the Gulf Stream. Consistent faunal differences were found between the upstream and downstream sides of the bump. Data generated in the infaunal and epifaunal surveys supported the view that a partial zoogeographic barrier exists on the slope off North Carolina. This break was most evident between Cape Lookout and Cape Fear.

Blumberg, A.F., and G.L. Mellor. 1983. Diagnostic and Prognostic Numerical Circulation Studies of the South Atlantic Bight. Journal of Geophysical Research 88 C(8): 4579-4592.

Some of the results from a series of diagnostic and prognostic numerical simulations of the circulation in the South Atlantic Bight (SAB) are described. The numerical model developed for the study is a three-dimensional, primitive equation, time dependent, a coordinate model with an imbedded, turbulent closure submodel which should yield realistic Ekman surface and bottom layers. An implicit numerical scheme in the vertical direction and a mode-splitting technique in time are adopted for computational efficiency. A significant portion of the paper is concerned with realistic specification of initial conditions for temperature and salinity, surface forcing, and lateral open boundary conditions. The latter are determined by a simple diagnostic (geostrophic and Ekman dynamics) model which provides dynamically consistent temperature, salinity, and velocity boundary conditions. It appears from an examination of the numerical simulations that the full model yields results that share many features in common with our general understanding of the circulation of the South Atlantic Bight; the region includes shallow shelf waters as well as deeper water dominated by the Gulf Stream. Data for synoptic skill assessment, however, are not available.

Bumpus, D.F. 1973. A Description of the Circulation on the Continental Shelf of the East Coast of the United States. pp. 111-157. Progress in Oceanography Vol. 6, Pergamon Press, New York.

The circulation on the continental shelf of the east coast of the United States is discussed, including the historical development of the concepts, and the surface and bottom circulation based on drift-bottle data and sea-bed drifter data. Suggestions for future research to further our understanding of the circulation problem are offered.

Checkley, D.M., Jr., S. Raman, L. Maillet, and K.M. Mason. 1988. Winter Storm Effects on the Spawning and Larval Drift of a Pelagic Fish. Nature 335(6188): 346-348.

Recruitment for many marine organisms depends on survival and transport of eggs and larvae from spawning grounds to nursery areas. We investigated the effects of winter storms and the Gulf Stream on the spawning, development and drift of the Atlantic menhaden, *Brevoortia tyrannus,* which spawns offshore and metamorphoses in estuaries. Spawning was maximal during storms in water upwelled near the western edge of the Gulf Stream. Eggs and larvae drifted shoreward with abundant food in the warm surface stratum of a density-driven circulation maintained by the large sea-air heat flux. We suggest that the Atlantic menhaden and other species have evolved to reproduce in winter near warm boundary currents, including the Gulf Stream and Kuroshio, as a result of physical conditions that permit the rapid development and shoreward drift of their eggs and larvae, with consequent high recruitment and fitness.

—. 1989. Winter Storm Effects on the Spawning and Larval Drift of a Pelagic Fish. pp. 45-46. *In*: Crawford, K. (ed.). Proceedings: 1989 Marine Expo: The Natural Resources Associated with Mobil's Proposed Drill Site. NC Outer Continental Shelf Office, NC Department of Administration. Raleigh, NC.

Recruitment for many marine organisms depends on survival and transport of eggs and larvae from spawning grounds to nursery areas. We investigated the effects of winter storms and the Gulf Stream on the spawning, development and drift of the Atlantic menhaden, *Brevoortia tyrannus,* which spawns offshore and metamorphoses in estuaries. Spawning was maximal during storms in water upwelled near the western edge of the Gulf Stream. Eggs and larvae drifted shoreward with abundant food in the warm surface stratum of a density-driven circulation maintained by the large sea-air heat flux. We suggest that the Atlantic menhaden and other species have evolved to reproduce in winter near warm boundary currents, including the Gulf Stream and Kuroshio, as a result of physical conditions that permit the rapid development and shoreward drift of their eggs and larvae, with consequent high recruitment and fitness.

Clark, J., W.G. Smith, A.W. Kendall Jr, and M.P. Fahay. 1969. Studies of Estuarine Dependance of Atlantic coastal fishes. US Fish and Wildlife Service Technical Papers of the Bureau of Sport Fisheries and Wildlife 28. 132 p.

*This is Data Report I covering surveys (eight cruises: Dec 1965-Dec 1966) from Cape Cod, MA to Cape Lookout, NC by the R/V Dolphin. These cruises were directed toward larval fishes. Temperatures, salinities, and lists of catches from plankton and midwater nets are reported in tables and maps. Station transects L and M overlap our study area.

Coles, W.C., and J.A. Musick. 2000. Satellite sea surface temperature analysis and correlation with sea turtle distribution off North Carolina. Copeia 2000(2): 551-554.

We used satellite sea surface temperature data and aerial survey data to identify an upper (28 C) and lower (13.3 C) thermal limit to preferred loggerhead sea turtle temperatures. The available temperature range for the turtles to occupy, during this study (May 1991 to Sept. 1992), was 4.9 C to 32.2 C. These thermal limits fall within the ranges previously identified in the laboratory. This study suggests that sea turtles are not geographically randomly distributed but stay within preferred temperature ranges which are seasonally variable.

Cook, S.K., B.P. Collins, and C.S. Carty. 1979. Expendable Bathythermograph Observations From the NMFS/MARAD Ship of Opportunity Program for 1975. NOAA Technical Report SSRF-727. NOAA-NMFS. Seattle, WA. 93 p.

This report is designed to show the results of the fifth year of operation of the NMFS/MARAD Ship of Opportunity Program (SOOP). The data are presented in the form of vertical distributions of temperature and horizontal distributions of sea surface temperature and salinity. Operational and data management procedures are discussed, and a descriptive analysis of the most dynamic transacts showing the Yucatan, Loop, Florida, and Gulf Stream current systems is presented. The annual development and subsequent degradation of the cold cell off the Middle Atlantic Bight is also discussed.

Costlow, J. 1992. The Outer Banks Protection Act. pp. 11-15. *In*: U.S. Department of the Interior, Minerals Management Service. Proceedings of the Fourth Atlantic OCS Region Information Transfer Meeting, September 1991. U.S. Department of the Interior, Minerals Management Service. Herndon, VA.

The Fourth Atlantic Outer Continental Shelf (OCS) Regional Information Transfer Meeting (ITM) was held on 24-25 September, 1991, in Wilmington, NC. The focus of the meeting was on the OCS off North Carolina, specifically on activities related to a proposed exploratory well for oil and gas by Mobil on Block 467 a site 40 miles off the coast of North Carolina. The area of industry interest is known as the Manteo Prospect, while the activities surrounding the proposed drilling are referred to collectively as the Manteo Project. The wildcat wellsite is in 2,690 ft. (857 m) of water near the edge of the Gulf Stream. It is also near a fishing ground known locally as "The Point." The area is believed to be gas prone rather than oil prone. The estimated size of the resource could be as high as 5 trillion cubic feet of gas.

The purpose of the meeting was to exchange information on the leasing background, legislative activities, scientific results, and socioeconomic studies. Legislative-related reports include descriptions of the Oil Pollution Act of 1990, the Outer Banks Protection Act, the Environmental Studies Review Panel, and the North Carolina Physical Oceanography Panel. Reports of studies on marine life include benthic diatoms, benthic fauna, pelagic seabirds, sea turtles, and right whales. One report describes the use of airships (blimps) for ocean research a capability relevant to North Carolina because of the east coast airship facility is located in the state. Local marine science facilities described include NOAA's National Undersea Research Center at the University of North Carolina at Wilmington (NURC/UNCW) and the National Marine Fisheries Service laboratory in Beaufort.

Developments in oil spill cleanup technology and capabilities are described by both the Coast Guard and the industry. A socioeconomic report describes the effects of the oil and gas activities on the tourist industry. Lastly, research on the restoration of salt marshes indicates that rehabilitation of an area is possible when development or an accident has occurred. While the emphasis of the meeting was on oil and gas, two reports described the results of projects related to offshore sand mining. The appendix lists the names and addresses of speakers. Individual chapters are cited individually when appropriate.

*In August 1990, President Bush signed Federal oil spill legislation that included a provision called the Outer Banks Protection Act (OBPA). The OBPA prohibited the Minerals Management Service (MMS) from approving any exploration plan off North Carolina until October 1991. The Act also created a five-member Environmental Sciences Review Panel (ESRP) to evaluate the adequacy of information on the Mobil proposal. This section describes the OBPA and ESRP. Physical oceanography, biological oceanography, and socioeconomics are mentioned.

Costlow, J., K. Brink, M. Orbach, C. Peterson, J. Teal, and A. Robertson. 1992. North Carolina Environmental Sciences Review Panel. Report to the Secretary of the Interior from the North Carolina Environmental Sciences Review Panel as mandated by the Oil Pollution Act of 1990. 83 p.

The Oil Pollution Act of 1990, in a section cited as the Outer Banks Protection Act, prohibits the Secretary of the Interior from proceeding with a number of actions relative to development of oil and gas resources offshore North Carolina for which he is responsible under the Outer Continental Shelf Lands Act (OCSLA). Actions prohibited include: (1) conducting a lease sale; (2) issuing any new lease; (3) approving any exploration plan; (4) approving any development and production plan; (5) approving any application for permit to drill; and (6) permitting any drilling. The prohibition on these actions is mandated to remain in effect until the latter of: (1) October 1, 1991 or (2) 45 days of contiguous session of the Congress following the submission of a written report from the Secretary certifying that the information available to him is sufficient to carry out his responsibilities under the OCSLA.

In his report, the Secretary is required to take into consideration findings and recommendations of a panel established by the Outer Banks Protection Act, the North Carolina Environmental Sciences Review Panel, and to include a detailed explanation of any differences between his certification if sufficient information and the findings and recommendations of this group. The panel is charged by the Act with: (1) assessing the adequacy of the available physical oceanographic, ecological, and socioeconomic information to enable the Secretary to fulfill his responsibilities under the OCSLA and (2) identifying any additional information deemed essential to enable the Secretary to carry out these responsibilities. The Panel's response to this charge is the subject of this document.

As provided in the Outer Banks Protection Act, the North Carolina Environmental Sciences Review Panel is composed of five members, a marine scientist selected by the Secretary of the Interior, a marine scientist selected by the Governor of North Carolina, and three scientists, one each from the disciplines of physical oceanography, ecology, and social sciences, selected jointly by the Secretary and the Governor from a list developed by the National Academy of Sciences. Unless specifically indicated in the text, the conclusions and recommendations presented in the report represent the unanimous decision of the Panel members. A summary of findings including Physical Oceanography,

Ecology, Socioeconomics, Sources of Information, Adequacy of Information, and Panel's Recommended Studies is included. Appendix A: Literature Review, and Appendix B: Factors Influencing the Definition if Adequacy of Information are also included.

Crawford, K. (ed.). 1989. Proceedings: 1989 Marine Expo: The Natural Resources Associated with Mobil's Proposed Drill Site. NC Outer Continental Shelf Office, NC Department of Administration. Raleigh, NC. 64 p.

*This report contains abstracts from each presenter. Chapter topics include: Mobil's Proposal, Geologic Overview — Introduction and Potential for Oil and Gas Discovery, Oceanographic Conditions, Comments on Last MMS Modeling, Biological Production Near the Bottom (invertebrates), Fisheries Resources, Commercial and Recreational Marine Fisheries, Winter Storm Effects on Spawning and Larval Drift of Pelagic Fish, Marine Birds, Sea Turtles in North Carolina, Marine Mammals, Plenary Session, Summary. Each chapter also cited individually when appropriate.

Csanady, G.T., and P. Hamilton. 1988. Circulation of slopewater. Continental Shelf Research 8(5-7): 565-624.

The recently conducted Mid-Atlantic Slope and Rise (MASAR) experiment yielded much new information on the structure and behavior of slopewater, the water mass occupying the upper "Slope Sea", a narrow band of ocean between the Gulf Stream and the continental shelf from Cape Hatteras to the Grand Banks. The results of this experiment, combined with earlier evidence, have been used to construct a new empirical schema of slopewater circulation. Key features are: (1) inflow of Coastal Labrador Sea Water (CLSW) across the Grand Banks at the rate of 4×10^6 M^3 s^{-1} and isopycnal advection from the Gulf Stream thermocline at the rate of 6×10^6 M^3 s^{-1}, the total draining eastward; (2) a closed cyclonic gyre in the western Slope Sea, transporting approximately 3×10^6 M^3 s^{-1} along the New Jersey coast southward; and (3) seasonal formation of a pycnostad by convective overturn and its flushing in approximately 6 months.

Some of the CLSW inflow retroflects and turns eastward following entry into the Slope Sea, but a significant fraction flows westward along the coast and rounds the western gyre before draining eastward.

The circulation just described reaches to an approximate depth of 500 m. Deeper layers move through the Slope Sea southwestward. The layers of the Gulf Stream thermocline in contact with slopewater along isopycnals encompass the Antarctic Intermediate Water (AAIW) core, as well as the nutrient maximum and oxygen minimum layers. Shoreward advection of these layers and seasonal overturn to 200 m establishes conditions favoring productivity in the upper slopewater, as well as on the shelf.

Cutler, E.B. 1975. Zoogeographical barrier on the continental slope off Cape Lookout, North Carolina. Deep-Sea Research 22: 893-901.

The distribution of Sipuncula and Pogonophora on the continental slope off North and South Carolina suggests a zoogeographical barrier southeast of Cape Lookout, North Carolina around 34 N between 150 and 2500 m for 14 of 27 species found. Similarity coefficients and a group average cluster analysis support the conclusions. This barrier may result from the effects of bottom currents on larval dispersion.

Cutter, G.R., R.J. Diaz, and J.A. Blake. 1994a. Deep-Sea Research II: CD-ROM APPENDIX. Deep-Sea Research II Vol. 41(4-6): 981-982.

The contents of the CD-ROM Appendix are data and images of the bottom from five of the articles in this issue. The CD-ROM was mastered in a format that can be read by both Macintosh and PC computers. It is organized in an hierarchical structure by folders, with data in one and images in another. To access a particular file, sequentially open folders until the file of interest appears. Data and figure captions are provided as: (.txt) ASCII text with no line breaks; (.tlb) ASCII text with line breaks; (.wor) Microsoft Word; and (.wp) Word Perfect 5.1 files. Images are in TIFF format (.tif). Data (ACSAR, Hatteras), Images and Captions (ACSAR, Profile, 3Dbathy, Sled, Surface, x-ray) are included.

Cutter, G.R., R. Diaz, and J. Lee. 1994b. Foraminifera from the continental slope off Cape Hatteras, North Carolina. Deep-Sea Research II Vol. 41(4-6): 951-963.

The recent benthic meiofaunal foraminiferal assemblage from the continental slope (590-2003 m) off Cape Hatteras, North Carolina exhibits high species richness and evenness, moderate diversity values, and lacks numerically dominant species. The preserved planktic assemblage has relatively low species richness, high evenness, low diversity, and a few numerically dominant species. Approximately 9% of the benthic species are those that typically live within continental shelf depth ranges. The benthic assemblage abundances and diversities do not follow depth patterns or geophysical characteristics. No biogeographic boundary can be described within the study area for meiofaunal foraminifers. Oxygen limitation does not appear to be a factor affecting the benthos of the North Carolina continental slope based upon the community structure of the benthic foraminifers, if total assemblage is assumed to reflect the recently living community. The high carbonate content of sediments in the area may be explained by foraminiferal tests. Within the study area, the foraminiferal assemblages are uniform, and probably reflect relative consistency of primary environmental variables as well as dynamic downslope transport and high influx of material from the water column in the vicinity where the Gulf Stream and the Western Boundary Undercurrent cross.

DeMaster, D.J., R.H. Pope, L.A. Levin, and N.E. Blair. 1994. Biological mixing intensity and rates of organic carbon accumulation in North Carolina slope sediments . Deep-Sea Research II Vol. 41(4-6): 735-753.

Sediment accumulation rates and biological mixing intensities were determined at three sites on the North Carolina slope based on profiles of naturally occurring ^{14}C, ^{210}Ph and ^{234}Th. The three sites all were at a water depth of 850 m with a spacing of 150 — 180 km between sites. Sediment accumulation rates increase from south to north from values of 7 cm ky^{-1} at Site I, to 160 cm ky^{-1} at Site II, to 1100 cm ky^{-1} at Site III. The organic carbon burial rate a these sites also increases in the northward direction from 0.65 (Site I) to 20 (Site II) to $\leq$ 150 g C_{org} m^{-2} year^{-1} (Site III). These data indicate that continental margin environments can exhibit highly variable carbon fluxes over relatively small distances on the seafloor. The rate of organic carbon accumulation at Site III is one of the highest values reported for the marine environment. Based on these accumulation rates and dissolved inorganic carbon flux estimates from each site, the seabed organic carbon preservation efficiency (i.e. the ratio of C_{org} accumulation rate to C_{org} deposition rate times 100) was estimated to vary from 6.0% to 54% to 88%, at Sites I, II and III, respectively. The ^{14}C age of organic matter in surface sediments was older at Site III (1800 years BP), than at Sites I and II (800 years BP), indicating that Site III receives it greater proportion of old sediment from either up-slope areas or from terrigenous sources. Inventories of excess ^{234}Th (half-life of 24 days) were used as it tracer for particle flux covering the 100 days prior to the October 1989, July-August 1990 and August 1991 cruises. The mean ^{234}Th inventories at the three sites were 4.7 ± 1.9, 8.4 ± 6.3 and 23.1 ± 7.3 dpm cm^{-2}, for Sites I, II and III, respectively.

Diaz, R.J., J. Blake, B. Hecker, and D.C. Rhoads. 1993b. A Highly Productive Area of the Continental Slope Off Cape Hatteras. Benthic Ecology Meeting, 1-4 April 1993, Mobile AL. 57 p.

The continental slope off Cape Hatteras is atypical for the U.S. Atlantic coast. Unusually high numbers of infauna, megafauna, and demersal fish were found over a broad area. Benthic organisms appear to be well adapted to physical processes that converge on the Cape Hatteras continental slope. These physical processes impart a high degree of instability to the bottom and also supply large amounts of organic matter which sustain the elevated densities and biomass. The nature of these communities and mechanisms which regulate them will be discussed.

Edwards, R.L., R.L. Livingstone Jr., and P.E. Hamer. 1962. Winter water temperatures and an annotated list of fishes Nantucket Shoals to Cape Hatteras: Albatross Cruise no. 126. Special Scientific Report Fisheries No. 397. United States Department of the Interior, Fish and Wildlife Service. Washington, DC.

Cruise no. 126 of the Albatross III was planned and conducted to gather information about the distribution of fishes across the Continental Shelf from Nantucket Shoals to Cape Hatteras during the late winter period when water temperatures generally are at their minimum. The shelf here has a general hydrographic similarity from north to south, well described by Bigelow (1933), that makes it a particularly worthwhile area in which to study the relation of fish distribution to water temperature, depth, and other factors of the environment. Since the fish of this portion of the shelf support several different, relatively important food and industrial fisheries, as well as an intensive marine sport fishery, Cruise no. 126 served to provide data valuable to several research programs. This area has a distinctive fauna attributed in part to the thermal barrier present across the shelf at Cape Hatteras, as well as another such barrier, less marked, separating the waters of southern New England and the Gulf of Maine.

FRED Group. 1989a. Frontal Eddy Dynamics (FRED) Experiment off North Carolina: Volume I Executive Summary. C.C. Ebbesmeyer (ed.). U.S. Department of the Interior, Minerals Management Service. Herndon, VA. 16 p.

During May to November 1967, oceanographic measurements were made off North Carolina to examine the effects of Gulf Stream frontal eddies on the circulation over the continental shelf. Satellite images were collected daily, and currents were measured at eight moorings containing 21 current meters. During a 2-week time period in May three eddies were intensively examined using satellite imagery, drifting buoys, aircraft and survey vessel launched temperature probes, and an Acoustic Doppler Current Profiler.

The Gulf Stream appears to behave in two distinct modes. 1) Small meander mode, the Gulf Stream lies at the shelf break and meanders of the front have smaller amplitudes. Frontal eddies and associated warm water filaments are smaller and farther from shore during this mode. 2) Large meander mode, the Gulf Stream Front is displaced offshore of the shelf break and meanders of the front have large amplitudes. Frontal eddies and associated warm water filaments are larger and closer to shore during this made, with some of the filaments nearly reaching the Barrier Islands.

Eddies migrate past locations off the North Carolina coast approximately once every five days. After an eddy passes, parts of the filament may stagnate on the Shelf for approximately a week before dissipating or moving northward out of the study area.

———. 1989b. Frontal Eddy Dynamics (FRED) Experiment off North Carolina: Volume II Technical Report. C.C. Ebbesmeyer (ed.). U.S. Department of the Interior, Minerals Management Service. Herndon, VA. 325 p.

During May to November 1967, oceanographic measurements were made off North Carolina to examine the effects of Gulf Stream frontal eddies on the circulation over the continental shelf.

Satellite images were collected daily, and currents were measured at eight moorings containing 21 current meters. During a 2-week time period in May three eddies were intensively examined using satellite imagery, drifting buoys, aircraft and survey vessel launched temperature probes, and an Acoustic Doppler Current Profiler.

The Gulf Stream appears to behave in two distinct modes. 1) Small meander mode, the Gulf Stream lies at the shelf break and meanders of the front have smaller amplitudes. Frontal eddies and associated warm water filaments are smaller and farther from shore during this mode. 2) Large meander mode, the Gulf Stream Front is displaced offshore of the shelf break and meanders of the front have large amplitudes. Frontal eddies and associated warm water filaments are larger and closer to shore during this made, with some of the filaments nearly reaching the Barrier Islands.

Eddies migrate past locations off the North Carolina coast approximately once every five days. After an eddy passes, parts of the filament may stagnate on the Shelf for approximately a week before dissipating or moving northward out of the study area.

Gray, I.E., and M.J. Cerame-Vivas. 1963. The Circulation of Surface waters in Raleigh Bay, North Carolina. Limnology and Oceanography 8(3): 330-337.

Returns from helicopter-released drift bottles over Diamond Shoals, in April August 1962, revealed a definite southwesterly coastal flow from Cape Hatteras, North Carolina. Influenced by northeast winds the flow was more pronounced in late summer thank in late spring, some of the bottles rounding Cape Lookout. Recovery of drift bottles from Onslow Bay and Bogue Sound strongly supports the theory that the temporary winter populations of distinctly northern species in the Beaufort, North Carolina, area established from planktonic larvae that originated north of Cape Hatteras and were transported around the capes. A postulated circulation, involving the influence of Diamond and Lookout shoals, runoff, northeasterly and southwesterly winds, and back eddies from the Florida Current and from wind-induced currents, is presented for Raleigh Bay.

Hamilton, P., and T. Berger. 1992. Current Measurements in Manteo Block 467. pp. 169-177. *In*: U.S. Department of the Interior, Minerals Management Service. Proceedings of the Fourth Atlantic OCS Region Information Transfer Meeting, September 1991, U.S. Department of the Interior, Minerals Management Service. Herndon, VA.

The Fourth Atlantic Outer Continental Shelf (OCS) Regional Information Transfer Meeting (ITM) was held on 24-25 September 1991 in Wilmington, NC. The focus of the meeting was on the OCS off North Carolina, specifically on activities related to a proposed exploratory well for oil and gas by Mobil on Block 467 a site 40 miles off the coast of North Carolina. The area of industry interest is known as the Manteo Prospect, while the activities surrounding the proposed drilling are referred to collectively as the Manteo Project. The wildcat wellsite is in 2,690 ft. (857 m) of water near the edge of the Gulf Stream. It is also near a fishing ground known locally as "The Point." The area is believed to be gas prone rather than oil prone. The estimated size of the resource could be as high as 5 trillion cubic feet of gas.

The purpose of the meeting was to exchange information on the leasing background, legislative activities, scientific results, and socioeconomic studies. Legislative-related reports include descriptions of the Oil Pollution Act of 1990, the Outer Banks Protection Act, the Environmental Studies Review Panel, and the North Carolina Physical Oceanography Panel. Reports of studies on marine life include benthic diatoms, benthic fauna, pelagic seabirds, sea turtles, and right whales. One report describes the use of airships (blimps) for ocean research a capability relevant to North Carolina because of the east coast airship facility is located in the state. Local marine science facilities described include NOAA's National Undersea Research Center at the University of North Carolina at Wilmington (NURC/UNCW) and the national marine Fisheries Service laboratory in Beaufort.

Developments in oil spill cleanup technology and capabilities are described by both the Coast Guard and the industry. A socioeconomic report describes the effects of the oil and gas activities on the tourist industry. Lastly, research on the restoration of salt marshes indicates that rehabilitation of an area is possible when development or an accident has occurred. While the emphasis of the meeting was on oil and gas, two reports described the results of projects related to offshore sand mining. The appendix lists the names and addresses of speakers. Individual chapters are cited individually when appropriate.

*Science Applications International Corporation measured the currents in Manteo Block 467, at the continental shelf break east of Cape Hatteras, North Carolina, from march 1989 through September 1990 as part of a program for Mobil Corporation. In addition to providing valuable information required for engineering purposes, the data also provide new information about the nature of the Gulf Steam circulation near Cape Hatteras.

Hare, J.A. and R.K. Cowen. 1996. Transport mechanisms of larval and pelagic juvenile bluefish (*Pomatomus saltatrix*) from South Atlantic Bight spawning grounds to Middle Atlantic Bight nursery habitats. Limnology and Oceanography 41(6): 1264-1280.

In this study we examined the mechanisms by which Pomatomus saltatrix (Pisces: Pomatomidae) larvae and pelagic juveniles are transported from South Atlantic Bight spawning grounds to Middle Atlantic Bight estuarine nursery habitats. Data on larval and pelagic juvenile distributions, estuarine juvenile recruitment, hydrography, wind speed and direction and satellite-derived, sea surface temperature were used to examine potential larval transport mechanisms. On the basis of these analyses, a scenario for northward transport of P. saltatrix was developed. Gulf Stream-associated flow moves P. saltatrix larvae northeastward from their South Atlantic Bight spawning grounds. Larval transport from the Gulf Stream to the Middle Atlantic Bight shelf edge occurs in warm-core ring streamers, but some more developed individuals may swim across. Finally, P. saltatrix pelagic juveniles actively swim across the Middle Atlantic Bight shelf, a behavior initiated when the surface shelf-slope temperature front dissipates in late spring. This scenario predicts that the number of South Atlantic Bight-spawned P. saltatrix juveniles entering estuaries (i.e. recruitment) is determined in part by warm-core ring streamer activity. The timing of recruitment, however, is determined almost entirely by the timing of the dissipation of the surface shelf-slope temperature front.

Heezen, B.C. 1968. The Atlantic Continental Margin. UMR Journal 1: 5-25.

*Turbidity currents, surface and subsurface currents carry detritus from the land across the continental shelf to the adjacent continental slope where slumps and turbidity currents transport the sediment downslope for hundreds of miles to greater depths, and deep geostrophic contour currents transport it thousands of miles down-current in a direction parallel to the bathymetric contours. The combined effect of these processes has been to create a wide, thick, geosynclinal apron of sediment at the base of the continental slope.

Hood, C.A., and J.M. Bane Jr. 1983. Subsurface energetics of the Gulf Stream cyclonic frontal zone off Onslow Bay, North Carolina. Journal of Geophysical Research 88 C(8): 4651-4562.

It has been shown with the use of 4-month-long time series of velocity, temperature, and conductivity that fluctuating kinetic and potential energy was converted into kinetic and potential energy of the mean flow following a fluid particle in the subsurface Gulf Stream cyclonic frontal zone off Onslow Bay, North Carolina, during early 1979. This result agrees well with earlier measurements made in the surface layer off Onslow Bay. These flux calculations represent an important step in verifying the direction of the net cross-stream energy flux within the Stream off Onslow Bay. According to an hypothesis presented for the growth and decay of Gulf Stream meanders along the continental margin of the southeastern United States, Onslow Bay is an area of decreasing meander amplitude. The direction of the energy conversion from meanders to the mean flow, determined from our calculations, is consistent with this hypothesis. Relatively low velocity covariances were found to be associated with relatively small transfers of kinetic energy during a period of low meander activity. This finding supports the notion that meanders play a significant role in the energy transformation processes. The presence of such 'quiet' periods may indicate a low-frequency modulation of Gulf Stream meander activity.

Inman, D.L., and R. Dolan. 1989. The Outer Banks of North Carolina: Budget of Sediment and Inlet Dynamics Along a Migrating Barrier System. Journal of Coastal Research 5(2): 193-237.

The Outer Banks are barrier islands separating Pamlico, Albemarle and Currituck Sounds from the Atlantic Ocean. These barriers are transgressing landward, with average rates of shoreline recession of 1.4 m/yr between False Cape and Cape Hatteras. Oregon Inlet, 63 km north of Cape Hatteras, is the only opening in the nearly 200 km between Cape Henry and Cape Hatteras which bounds the Hatteras Littoral Cell. Oregon Inlet is migrating south at an average rate of 23 m/yr and landward at a rate of 5 m/yr The net southerly longshore transport of sand in the vicinity of Oregon Inlet is between one-half and one million m^3/yr.

Oregon Inlet is the most dynamic physical feature within the Hatteras Littoral Cell. The combination of waves and tidal currents deposit ebb-tide bars offshore of the entrance and form extensive tidal islands, bars and shoals in Pamlico Sound. These deposits lag behind as the inlet migrates. The offshore deposits are gradually returned to the beach by waves and reincorporated into the littoral drift system. The flood-tide inlet deposits in the sound are eventually reincorporated into the landward migrating barrier as the inlet moves to the south. The integrity of the landward side of the transgressing barrier is maintained by washover deposits, wind- blown sand deposits, and inlet deposits. Averaged over the 160 km from False Cape to Cape Hatteras, sea level rise accounts for 21% of the measured shoreline recession of 1.4 m/yr. Analysis of the budget of sediment indicates that the remaining erosion of 1.1 m/yr is apportioned between overwash processes (39%) longshore transport out of the cell (22%), windblown sand transport (18%), inlet deposits (10%), and removal by dredging at Oregon Inlet (11%). This analysis indicates that the barrier system moves as a whole, so that the sediment balance is relative to the moving shoreline (Lagrangian grid). Application of a continuity model to the budget suggests that, in places, the barrier system is supplied with sand from the shelf.

Isley, I.E., R.D. Pillsbury, and E.P. Laine. 1990. The genesis and character of benthic turbid events, Northern Hatteras Abyssal Plain. Deep-Sea Research 37(7): 1099-1119.

Benthic turbid events, with particle concentrations of up to 1.5 mg l^{-1}, occupy about 20 % of a two-year record of near-bottom light attenuation made above the Northern Hatteras Abyssal Plain. They are most often associated with deep-sea mesoscale eddies, although rare events occur during periods when southward contour flow predominates. In a temporal sense, the presence of deep-sea mesoscale eddies corresponds strongly to periods when cold-core Gulf Stream rings propagated through surface waters of the study area. Additionally, over half of the benthic turbid events observed are initiated within a day of the passage of atmospheric storms with propagation speeds in excess of 800 km day^{-1}.

Janowitz, G.S. 1989. Comments on the Latest MMS Meeting. pp. 22-24. *In*: Crawford, K. (ed.). Proceedings: 1989 Marine Expo: The Natural Resources Associated with Mobil's Proposed Drill Site. NC Outer Continental Shelf Office, NC Department of Administration. Raleigh, NC.

In the early 1980s, MMS funded a modeling effort but utilized only predicted monthly averaged currents, combined with a time-varying surface wind-driven current in its risk analysis. The monthly averaged currents were very weak over the shelf and showed none of the energetic flows associated with the Gulf Stream-induced eddies and filaments present over the shelf. As it is possible that parcels may cross the shelf in a matter of days, MMS's use of mean monthly currents was challenged by the state of North Carolina.

A joint State-Federal Technical Advisory Panel concluded that the approach taken by NMS was inadequate. It recommended that a field study of the eddy-filament structure be funded and that a new ocean circulation model be developed. The model was to be verified by comparison with data prior to its incorporation into the trajectory calculations. Both projects were funded by MMS.

The Frontal Eddy Dynamics experiment, or FRED experiment for short, provided, among other data, current measurements in Onslow and Raleigh Bays and satellite imagery in this region and further north into the Mobil area. The study was not designed to measure currents in what is now the Mobil area. At this time, I have no details on the latest circulation model, the state of its verification, or the proposed method of incorporation into the trajectory analysis.

Janowitz, G.S., and L.J. Pietrafesa. 1996. Subtidal frequency fluctuations in coastal sea level in the Mid and South Atlantic Bights: A prognostic for coastal flooding. Journal of Coastal Research 12(1): 79-89.

An analytical model is used to determine spatial and temporal variations in coastal sea level. The model is developed for subtidal frequency motions in the viscous parameter regime, where advection of relative vorticity can be neglected with respect to production of relative vorticity by bottom Ekman layer pumping. The latter is then balanced by the topographically induced vertical velocity. The effects of the atmospheric wind stress on coastal sea level are assessed; and it is found that an upwelling (downwelling) favorable wind stress causes a continual drop (rise) in coastal sea level downstream from an initial cross-shelf location, with modifying effects of cross-shelf profile and initial location on the downstream variation in coastal sea level also being important. The model is applied over the Mid Atlantic Bight from Woods Hole, Massachusetts to Cape Hatteras, North Carolina and then to Charleston, South Carolina. Reasonable agreement exists between observations and model results which suggests that a predictive capability has been established; dimensionless mean squared errors range from 0.122 to 0.294 with a mean of 0.181 over the six test cages. The model can be driven by several days of forecast winds to determine the timing of coastal flooding, with linear superposition of location specific predicted astronomical tides onto the subtidal frequency model predictions.

JAYCOR. 1980. Final Report 1978: Physical Oceanographic Model Evaluation for the South Atlantic OCS Region. BLM Contract AA551-CT8-34. JAYCOR. Alexandria, VA. 327 p.

*This report is comprised primarily of mathematical models. Geological Oceanography is discussed in Appendix A: Geospecific Aspects of the South Atlantic OCS Region (L.J. Pietrafesa).

For twelve months, JAYCOR Personnel were under contract to the Bureau of Land Management (BLM) to conduct an evaluation of physical oceanographic models that could have applicability to the South Atlantic Outer Continental Shelf (SAOS) area. The objectives of this evaluation were to determine: 1) which models, if any were best suited to the BLM program needs in assessing the distribution of pollutants resulting from offshore activities and in assessing the probability of occurrence of circumstances hazardous to offshore structures; 2) which models best fit the physics of the SAOS region; 3) the sensitivity of various models to data input; and 4) the quantity and quality of existing input data to drive the models.

More than twelve-hundred papers have been reviewed in a three-step process; semi-qualitative, detailed qualitative, and quantitative. All of the models, and background material are included in Appendix B of this report. This appendix includes a designation for each citation indicating the level at which the material reviewed was useful for this project. It should be emphasized that this model evaluation was done in the context of the South Atlantic OCS Region, and the results are not necessarily applicable to all OCS regions, although a significant portion of the information is transferable to other similar areas.

Johns, W.E., and D.R. Watts. 1986. Time scales and structure of topographic Rossby waves and meanders in the deep Gulf Stream. Journal of Marine Research 44: 267-290.

During July-November 1982, current and temperature records were collected from six current meters spanning the lower 2000 m of the water column on two moorings in the Gulf Stream northeast of Cape Hatteras, N.C. Frequency domain EOF analysis of the velocity cross-spectra reveals that there are two kinematically distinct wave processes present in the subinertial range, identifiable as topographic Rossby wave and meander-associated motions, which are energetically dominant at periods longer than and shorter than 14 days, respectively. Simultaneous thermocline depth measurements obtained using inverted echo sounders show that the low-frequency topographic Rossby wave motions are uncoupled with near-surface displacements of the Gulf Stream path, but that cross-stream velocity fluctuations in the 14-day and 5-day period bands are associated with vertically coherent meanders of the Gulf Stream temperature front.

Kirshen, P.H. 1979. Summary and analysis of physical oceanographic and meteorological information on the continental shelf from Cape Hatteras to Cape Canaveral, Volume 2. pp. 19-213. BLM Contract AA550-CT7-16. Environmental Research and Technology, Inc. Concord, MA.

*This is a summary and analysis of physical oceanographic and meteorological information on the continental shelf from Cape Hatteras to Cape Canaveral.

Lang, W.H. 1998. Appendix D: A Review: Findings of the North Carolina Environmental Sciences Review Panel (ESRP). pp. 98-107. In: Vigil, D.L. (ed.). North Carolina/Minerals Management Service Technical Workshop on Manteo Unit Exploration: February 4-5, 1998. U.S. Dept. of the Interior, Minerals Management Service, Gulf of Mexico OCS Region. New Orleans, LA.

*These are the proceedings from a workshop/meeting (February 4-5, 1998) between the North Carolina Department of Environment and Natural Resources, and the U.S. Department of the Interior's Minerals Management Service (MMS). The geographic area being discussed is approximately 45 miles east-northeast of Cape Hatteras, NC, referred to as the Manteo Unit. This workshop reviewed environmental and socioeconomic information known and needed on the Manteo Unit. The MMS's Gulf of Mexico OCS Regional Director gave an MMS perspective on history and status of the area. Chevron gave a presentation on how the exploratory well would be drilled. The scientific characterization was presented in greater detail by a number of scientific experts who spoke on the following disciplines physical environment, habitat and living resources, seabirds, marine mammals, sea turtles, and social and economic issues. Specific chapters are cited individually, when appropriate.

The Oil Pollution Act of 1990, in a section cited as the Outer Banks Protection Act (OBPA), created the ESRP (Costlow et al. 1992). The review panel was to be composed of five members: a marine scientist selected by the Secretary of the Interior, a marine specialist selected by the Governor of

North Carolina, and three scientists, one each from the disciplines of physical oceanography, ecology, and social sciences, selected jointly by the Secretary and the Governor from a list developed by the national Academy of Sciences.

This sections describes: The Panel, the Review Process, Adequacy Findings, and Recommended Studies. The summary of the ESRP findings indicates, "General information relating to the physical oceanography and ecology in the vicinity of Manteo Block 467 has been presented in the DOI decision documents for oil and gas resource development at this site. However, this information is not sufficiently quantitative or process-oriented to provide an adequate understanding of potential impacts related to such development. Socioeconomic information or all phases of development activity ranges from inadequate to non-existent.

Lee, T. (ed.) 1983. Oceanography of the Southeast U.S. Continental Shelf and Adjacent Gulf Stream. Journal of Geophysical Research 88 C(8): 4539-4738.

*This is reprinted from Journal of Geophysical Research (88 C (8)). Individual chapters are cited independently when appropriate.

Recent studies of shelf circulation and Gulf Stream variability in the area between Cape Hatteras, North Carolina, and Cape Canaveral, Florida, (South Atlantic Bight) have significantly enlarged the regional data ensemble available for dynamical interpretation. As national interests shifted to the finding of new and alternative energy resources, the need to understand better the oceanography of the SAB with its possible oil reserves became apparent. It is the purpose of this dedicated issue to combine the results of studies funded separately by the Department of Energy, the Bureau of Land Management (now Minerals Management Service), the National Science Foundation, and the Office of Naval Research in order that they may be viewed together for a more complete understanding of the important physical processes in the region.

Magnuson, J.J., C.L. Harrington, D.J. Stewart, and G.N. Herbst. 1981. Responses of macrofauna to short-term dynamics of a Gulf Stream front on the continental shelf. pp. 441-448. *In*: Richards, F.R. (ed.). Coastal Upwelling. American Geophysical Union.

Benthic and near-bottom fishes, decapod crustaceans, and echinoderms were sampled in two areas through which a Gulf Stream front moved just north of Cape Hatteras along 75°13′ W longitude in October 1977. We tested the hypothesis that the frontal aggregations resulted from the response of organisms to the front itself rather than to a geographically fixed feature of the region. The front, 8.5° C and 3.5 °/oo wide, was characterized by horizontal gradients of at least 0.5 ^{C}/km and speeds of 30 ^{cm}/s. Bottom trawling was conducted day and night in each area (northern and southern) when the front was present and when it was absent. Both areas contained more species and individuals of fish when the front was present. Atlantic croaker, weakfish, and spot left when the front left. Decapods exhibited some response to the front, especially at night. During the day, fewer echinoderms were caught when the front was present — perhaps because the sudden changes in temperature induced burrowing. During the day all three groups were more abundant in the northern than in the southern area in terms of species and individuals. The front itself and more geographically fixed features both influenced distributions.

Marshall, N. 1951. Hydrography of North Carolina waters. pp. 1-76. *In*: Taylor, H.F. (ed.). Survey of Marine Fisheries of North Carolina. University of North Carolina Press. Chapel Hill, NC.

*This paper synthesizes hydrographic data for all of NC's marine waters, including the major estuaries. Offshore bathymetry is provided. Offshore temperature data are provided and the Gulf

Stream circulation is discussed. The relationship between hydrography and offshore fisheries is discussed, particularly in the Cape Hatteras area.

McCann, M.P., L.J. Pietrafesa, G.S. Janowitz, and T.B. Curtin. 1984. Physical Processes Influencing Temperature and Salinity on the North Carolina Cape Shoals. Contract No. DOE-AS09-76-EY00902; NOAA Contract No. 04-6-158-44054. 138 p.

Cross-spectral analysis and heat budget are used to relate atmospheric and river runoff data within seven years of daily surface temperature and salinity on the North Carolina continental shelf. Salinity on Diamond Shoals is highly correlated with alongshore wind stress implying wind driven advection of the front between Virginia Coastal Water and Carolina Coastal Water. In the presence of strong horizontal and vertical temperature gradients, temperature at Diamond Shoals quickly responds to cross-shelf winds. At Frying Pan Shoals, the plume of the Cape Fear River is detected when winds blow seaward. Atmospheric fluxes primarily control the cycle of heating and cooling at Frying Pan Shoals, but advection of heat buffers the water temperature in the winter and summer.

McGowan, M.F. and W.J. Richards. 1989. Bluefin tuna, Thunnus thynnus, larvae in the Gulf Stream off the southeastern United States: satellite and shipboard observations of their environment. Fishery Bulletin 87: 615-631.

The primary spawning area of the western Atlantic stock of bluefin tuna is presumed to be in the Gulf of Mexico. However, bluefin tuna larvae were collected in April and May 1985 along the shelf edge from Palm Beach, Florida to Cape Fear, North Carolina and offshore as far as 260 km east of Jacksonville, Florida over the Blake Plateau. Satellite and shipboard sea-temperature data indicate that the larvae over the shelf edge were advected there in meanders of the Gulf Stream. Bluefin larvae previously reported in the Straits of Florida and off Cape Hatteras were also in the Gulf Stream according to retrospective analyses of temperature and salinity data. Based on age-length relationships and current velocity, one small larva was probably spawned north of Miami, Florida while others could have been advected into the Gulf Stream from the eastern Gulf. Spawning by a few unspent migrating adults could also account for some bluefin larvae in this region. The estimated total larvae off the southeastern United States in 1985 could have been produced by 5% of the spawning stock. Bluefin larvae were found within a narrow range of sea surface temperatures and salinities at offshore stations. Preliminary assessment of larval habitat indicates that waters off the southeastern United States are unfavorable for growth and survival of bluefin larvae relative to hypothesized larval retention areas in the Gulf of Mexico.

Milliman, J.D., R.J. Diaz, J.A. Blake, and G.R. Cutter Jr. (eds.). 1994. Topical Studies in Oceanography: Input, Accumulation and Cycling of Materials on the Continental Slope Off Cape Hatteras. Deep-Sea Research Part II Vol. 41. 982 p.

*This is a compilation of studies on Input, Accumulation and Cycling of Materials on the Continental Slope Off Cape Hatteras. Geology, sediments, organics, and benthic fauna are discussed. A CD-ROM is included. Each chapter (study) is cited independently, when appropriate. Some papers in this issue were derived from Diaz et al. (1993).

Mills, G.B. 1992. Update of the National Oceanic and Atmospheric Administration's Bathymetric Mapping Program Along the Mid-Atlantic Coast. pp. 95-102. In: U.S. Department of the Interior, Minerals Management Service. Proceedings of the Fourth Atlantic OCS Region Information Transfer Meeting, September 1991. U.S. Department of the Interior, Minerals Management Service. Herndon, VA.

The Fourth Atlantic Outer Continental Shelf (OCS) Regional Information Transfer Meeting (ITM) was held on 24-25 September, 1991, in Wilmington, NC. The focus of the meeting was on the OCS off North Carolina, specifically on activities related to a proposed exploratory well for oil and gas by Mobil on Block 467 a site 40 miles off the coast of North Carolina. The area of industry interest is known as the Manteo Prospect, while the activities surrounding the proposed drilling are referred to collectively as the Manteo Project. The wildcat wellsite is in 2,690 ft. (857 m) of water near the edge of the Gulf Stream. It is also near a fishing ground known locally as "The Point." The area is believed to be gas prone rather than oil prone. The estimated size of the resource could be as high as 5 trillion cubic feet of gas.

he purpose of the meeting was to exchange information on the leasing background, legislative activities, scientific results, and socioeconomic studies. Legislative-related reports include descriptions of the Oil Pollution Act of 1990, the Outer Banks Protection Act, the Environmental Studies Review Panel, and the North Carolina Physical Oceanography Panel. Reports of studies on marine life include benthic diatoms, benthic fauna, pelagic seabirds, sea turtles, and right whales. One report describes the use of airships (blimps) for ocean research a capability relevant to North Carolina because of the east coast airship facility is located in the state. Local marine science facilities described include NOAA's National Undersea Research Center at the University of North Carolina at Wilmington (NURC/UNCW) and the National Marine Fisheries Service laboratory in Beaufort.

Developments in oil spill cleanup technology and capabilities are described by both the Coast Guard and the industry. A socioeconomic report describes the effects of the oil and gas activities on the tourist industry. Lastly, research on the restoration of salt marshes indicates that rehabilitation of an area is possible when development or an accident has occurred. While the emphasis of the meeting was on oil and gas, two reports described the results of projects related to offshore sand mining. The appendix lists the names and addresses of speakers. Individual chapters are cited individually when appropriate.

*The National Oceanic and Atmospheric Administration (NOAA) began systematically mapping the continental slope along the U.S. mid-Atlantic slope in 1990 as part of its multibeam mapping program of the United States' Exclusive Economic Zone. Eight surveys covering more than 2,500 square nautical miles (nmi²) have been conducted in this region, using the sophisticated seafloor mapping systems Sea Beam and Hydrocart II. This section further describes NOAA's ocean mapping program.

Nash, R.M., J.J. Magnuson, C.S. Clay, and T.K. Stanton. 1987. A Synoptic View of the Gulf Stream Front with 70-kHz Sonar: Taking Advantage of a Closer Look. Canadian Journal of Fisheries and Aquatic Sciences 44(11): 2022-2024.

Acoustical scattering across the near surface frontal zone of the Gulf Stream off Cape Hatteras was greatest in the thermal front. Little biological scattering was evident in the colder Slope water, but in the Gulf Stream, scatters formed five horizontal bands. Interpretation and new applications of acoustical information in biological oceanography are discussed.

Nash, R.M., J.J. Magnuson, T.K. Stanton, and C.S Clay. 1989. Distribution of peaks of 70 kHz acoustic scattering in relation to depth and temperature during day and night at the edge of the Gulf Stream-EchoFront 83. Deep-Sea Research 36(4): 587-596.

The depth and temperature distribution of acoustical scattering peaks in the near- surface frontal zone of the Gulf Stream was examined with a 70 kHz downward-looking sonar to 130 m. A peak was defined as a layer with relatively more scattering than layers just above or below it. Data were collected during the day and night in July 1983, approximately 115 km ENE of Cape Hatteras in a front with sharp thermal gradients above 130 m, and in the Gulf Stream with rather homogeneous temperatures above 130 m. "Peaks" in the front occurred more frequently both day and night above 60 m and at temperatures warmer than 15°C; in the Gulf Stream peaks occurred more frequently only above 20 m and at temperatures warmer than 24.5°C and then only during the day. The distribution of peaks was more homogeneous with depth and temperature in the Gulf Stream than in the front. Day and night distribution also differed with temperature in the front but with depth in the Gulf Stream. Acoustical scattering intensity in the peaks generally increased at night in the Gulf Stream at all depths above 130 m; in the front scattering levels appeared to increase both above and below the gradient but decrease in the gradient. Differences in the nocturnal increase in scattering between the front and Gulf Stream supports the concept of thermoclines as barriers to vertical migrants.

Nero, R.W., J.J. Magnuson, S.B. Brandt, T.K. Stanton, and J.M. Jech. 1990. Finescale biological patchiness of 70 kHz acoustic scattering at the edge of the Gulf Stream-EchoFront 85. Deep-Sea Research. 37(6): 999-1016.

The spatial distribution of biological scatterers within the Gulf Stream front is inferred from an analysis of patch statistics obtained from digitally recorded backscattering data. Acoustic data were collected along 10 transects perpendicular to the front using a downward-looking 70 kHz echosounder. Patches were defined using an algorithm selected to search for finescale patches from within 200 x 900 element (approx. 200 m depth x 24 km length) integrated echo data. Based on principal component analyses of 17 patch parameters, we identified the third most important component as a measure of "acoustic roughness" (containing the coefficient of variance and coefficient of toughness of the integrated echo independent of echo intensity). This third component was a good descriptor of differences among patches within scattering layers and between water masses. It is independent of echo strength and patch size which constitute the first two components. We interpret higher acoustic roughness within patches to indicate a more contagious (clumped) distribution of animals within those patches. Classification of patches on acoustic roughness showed that patches were often acoustically different from distant neighbors but more similar to neighbors within the same scattering layer or region. We infer that finescale layers are made up of small patches of like animals exhibiting a similar spatial arrangement throughout the layer. Cross-stream differences in acoustic roughness indicate a greater number of solitary scatterers occur within the slope water than within the Gulf Stream. Acoustic roughness is also reduced at night when compared with day, indicating that the ascent of vertical migrators into the near-surface waters (<200 m) results in a more dispersed spatial pattern.

Nesbit, R.A, and W.C. Neville. 1935. Conditions Affecting the Southern Winter Trawl Fishery. Fishery Circular No. 18. U.S. Department of Commerce, Bureau of Fisheries. 12 p.

With the opening of another season of the winter-trawl fishery off the Virginia capes, questions have been raised as to what might be expected during the coming winter (Jan.-Mar. 1935). It is the present intention to answer these questions as completely as is permitted by the results of the Bureau's studies of the winter and summer fishery for scup, sea bass, and fluke, these being the three most important fishes in the southern winter-trawl fishery. The discussion will be more complete as to scup for there is more information on that fish than on sea bass or fluke. However, much of what is said about scup in the winter fishery generally applies to sea bass and fluke since all three fishes were subject to the same conditions and were affected in about the same general way, though to differing degrees.

*This paper also discusses Changes in the Summer Fishery, Changes in the Winter Fishery, Changes in Temperature, Scup Scatter in Warm Winters, Sea Bass in Warmer Water Than Scup, Fluke in More Northerly Part of Ground, Outlook for the Winter of 1935 (January- March), and Conservation Problems.

Nickerson, S.R., and D.G. Mountain. 1983. Surface and Bottom Temperature Salinity Distributions on the Continental Shelf, Cape Hatteras to Cape Sable from MARMAP Cruises, 1977-1982. MARMAP Contribution MED/NEFC 83-16. Northeast Fisheries Center, Woods Hole Laboratory. Woods Hole, MA. 83 p.

*This report presents surface and bottom temperatures and salinity distributions observed on twenty-five cruises between 1977 and 1982. These cruises were part of the Marine resources Monitoring and Assessment Program (MARMAP) conducted by the Northeast Fisheries Center of the National Marine Fisheries Service. The Area observations extended over the continental shelf from Cape Hatteras to Nova Scotia, although complete coverage was not made on all cruises due to time and weather limitations. Generally, the area was covered from south to north over a period of approximately six weeks. Vessels included are:

1977: Argus cruise 77-10; 15 Oct-11 Nov
       Mt. Mitchell-Kelez cruise 77-11; 12 Nov-04 Dec
1978: Delaware II cruise 78-02; 14 Feb-13 Mar
       Argus cruise 78-04; 13 Apr-24 May
       Albatross IV cruise 78-07; 22 Jun-01 Jul
       Belogosrk cruise 78-01; 09 Aug-05 Sep
       Belogosrk cruise 78-03; 05-20 Oct
       Belogosrk cruise 78-04; 16-29 Nov
1979: Delaware II cruise 79-03; 23 Feb-15 Mar
       Delaware II cruise 79-05; 06-29 May
       Albatross IV cruise 79-06; 17 Jun-12 July
       Belogosrk cruise 79-01; 11 Aug-02 Sep
       Albatross IV cruise 79-11; 03 Sep-29 Oct
       Albatross IV cruise 79-13; 15 Nov-20 Dec
1980: Albatross IV cruise 80-02; 27 Feb-04 Apr
       Delaware II cruise 80-03; 23 May-12 Jun
       Erika cruise 80-04; 25-29 Jun
       Albatross IV cruise 80-10; 24 Sep-30 Oct
       Albatross IV cruise 80-12; 19 Nov-21 Dec
1981: Albatross IV cruise 81-01; 17 Feb-24 Mar
       Kelez cruise 81-03, 04; 18 Mar-09 Apr
       Delaware II cruise 81-03; 20 May-18 Jun
       Albatross IV cruise 81-14; 16 Nov-22 Dec
1982: Albatross IV cruise 82-02; 16 Feb-25 Mar
       Delaware II cruise 82-03; 17 May-11 Jun
       Albatross IV cruise 82-09; 15 Nov-22 Dec.

Norcross, B.L. and H.M. Austin. 1988. Middle Atlantic Bight meridional wind component effect on bottom water temperatures and spawning distribution of Atlantic croaker. Continental Shelf Research. 8(1): 69-88.

Predominantly southerly winds over the Middle Atlantic Bight result in offshore flow in surface waters and corresponding onshore flow in a bottom Ekman layer. Seasonal heating results in maximum surface temperatures in August while the bottom onshore Ekman flow results in cold summer bottom water temperatures. Bottom temperatures do not peak until autumn after the seasonal wind shift resulting in a cessation of the southerly winds and overturning of the surface waters. Strong episodes of this onshore bottom flow of cold water (upwelling) have been previously reported as unusually cold surf zone temperatures.

Fifteen-day moving averages of meridional components of winds from Norfolk International Airport, Virginia revealed few of the 15 years examined in which there was an abrupt seasonal shift in wind patterns from summer to winter regimes. Twenty-six collections of bottom water temperature data were reviewed for the Middle Atlantic Bight during the years 1967-1981. The average time of cessation of the strong southerly (summer) meridional wind component during those years was the end of August/beginning of September. A correlation of 0.74 exists between the time of cessation and the extent (km^2) of warm nearshore bottom waters, as indicated by the 16° C isotherm. The transition from a southerly to a northerly wind pattern occurs over a period of time ranging from 10 days to 3 months, while the response of ocean bottom isotherms to the cessation of the southerly component can typically be seen in 10-20 days.

Migration and spawning behavior of many fish is cued by water temperatures. The autumn areal distribution of the Atlantic croaker (Micropogonias undulates) is strongly correlated ($r^2 = 0.78$) with the areal distribution of bottom waters warmer than 16° C on the shelf. Furthermore, there is a correlation ($r^2 = 0.64$) between the time of cessation of the summer southerly wind and the areal extent of croaker. Therefore, we propose that if the wind relaxation occurs prior to the autumn migration of croaker out of the estuaries, spawning would occur in northern and middle sections of the Middle Atlantic Bight. Prolonged summer winds would keep the nearshore waters cool, and force croaker to migrate further southward to spawn, potentially shifting the distribution of juvenile recruitment to Pamlico Sound with entrance through Oregon Inlet in the Middle Atlantic Bight or through inlets south of Cape Hatteras.

O'Reilly, J.E., and C. Zetlin. 1998. Seasonal, Horizontal, and Vertical Distribution of Phytoplankton Chlorophyll a in the Northeast U.S. Continental Shelf Ecosystem. NOAA Technical report NMFS 139. U.S. Department of Commerce. Seattle, WA. 120 p.

The broad scale features in the horizontal, vertical, and seasonal distribution of phytoplankton chlorophyll a on the northeast U.S. continental shelf are described based on 57,088 measurements made during 78 oceanographic surveys from 1977 through 1988. Highest mean water column chlorophyll concentration (Chl_w) is usually observed in nearshore areas adjacent to the mouths of the estuaries in the Middle Atlantic Bight (MAB), over the shallow water on Georges Bank, and a small area sampled along the southeast edge of Nantucket Shoals. Lowest Chl_w ($<O.125$ ug l^{-1}) is usually restricted to the most seaward stations sampled along the shelf-break and the central deep waters in the Gulf of Maine. There is at least a twofold seasonal variation in phytoplankton biomass in all areas, with highest phytoplankton concentrations (m^3) and highest integrated standing stocks (m^2) occurring during the winter-spring (WS) bloom, and the lowest during summer, when vertical density stratification is maximal. In most regions, a secondary phytoplankton biomass pulse is evident during convective destratification in fall, usually in October. Fall bloom in some areas of Georges Bank approaches the magnitude of the WS-bloom, but Georges Bank and Middle Atlantic Bight fall blooms are clearly subordinate to WS-blooms.

Measurements of chlorophyll in two size-fractions of the phytoplankton, netplankton (>20 um) and nanoplankton (<20 u m), revealed that the smaller nanoplankton are responsible for most of the phytoplankton biomass on the northeast U.S. shelf Netplankton tend to be more abundant in nearshore areas of the MAB and shallow water on Georges Bank, where chlorophyll a is usually high; nanoplankton dominate deeper water at the shelf-break and deep water in the Gulf of Maine, where Chl_w is usually low. As a general rule, the percent of phytoplankton in the netplankton size-fraction increases with increasing depth below surface and decreases proceeding offshore.

There are distinct seasonal and regional patterns in the vertical distribution of chlorophyll a and percent netplankton, as revealed in composite vertical profiles of chlorophyll a constructed for 11 layers of the water column. Subsurface chlorophyll a maxima are ubiquitous during summer in stratified water. Chlorophyll a in the subsurface maximum layer is generally 2-8 times the concentration in the overlying and underlying water and approaches 50 to 75% of the levels observed in surface water during WS-bloom. The distribution of the ratio of the subsurface maximum chlorophyll a to surface chlorophyll a (SSR) during summer parallels the shelfwide pattern for stability, indexed as the difference in density (sigma-t) between 40 in and surface (stability$_{40}$). The weakest stability and lowest SSR's are found in shallow tidally-mixed water on Georges Bank; the greatest stability and highest SSR's (8-12:1) are along the mid and outer MAB shelf, over the winter residual water known as the "cold band." On Georges Bank, the distribution of SSR and the stability4o are roughly congruent with the pattern for maximum surface tidal current velocity, with values above 50 cms^{-1} defining SSR's less than 2:1 and the well-mixed area.

Physical factors (bathymetry, vertical mixing by strong tidal currents, and seasonal and regional differences in the intensity and duration of vertical stratification) appear to explain much of the variability in phytoplankton chlorophyll a throughout this ecosystem.

Ocean Margins Program (OMP). 1993. Research program plan. DOE Office of Energy Research, Environmental Science Division. Washington, DC.

The OMP Data Management Plan objective is to provide a single repository for all time series data collected on OMP moorings in a simple format that does not require collaborators to purchase or learn to use any specific software products. Access to these data will be provided at any time without the intervention of an operator. Sampled parameters include; date, time; East component of velocity (cm/sec); North component of velocity (cm/sec); Temperature (C); Salinity (PS78, psu); Pressure — absolute (dbar); Acoustic backscatter intensity (dB); Estimated biomass (mg/m^3); Temperature at ADCP — (C); Dissolved oxygen concentration (umole/kg); Dissolved oxygen saturation (percent); fluorometric chlorophyll (ug/l); Transmissometer light transmission (l/meter); PAR — photosynthetic active radiation (umole/m^2/sec).

Olson, D.B., O.B. Brown, and S.R. Emmerson. 1983. Gulf Stream Frontal Statistics From Florida Straits to Cape Hatteras Derived From Satellite and Historical Data. Journal of Geophysical Research 88 C(8): 4569-4577.

A 5 year record (1976-1980) of weekly Gulf Stream paths digitized from the U.S. Navy Ocean Frontal Analysis is analyzed to define a mean Gulf Stream path and weekly space-time series of fluctuations about the mean between the Florida Straits and Cape Hatteras. This satellite-derived Gulf Stream frontal mean locus is used as a natural coordinate system in which NODC historical expendable bathythermograph (XBT) data is averaged to determine the mean cross stream thermal structure. The results show that the satellite-derived front; that is, the cold wall of the stream as derived from IR imagery is in good agreement with a classical definition of the stream path. The Gulf Stream path is discussed in relationship to the bottom topography. Frontal location time series at various locations along the Gulf Stream are analyzed to generate occupation statistics and spectra for stream position. A steady increase in the variance of stream position occurs from Cape Canaveral to the Charleston Bump. This trend is followed by a sharp increase in variance just downstream of the bump and then a gradual decay from a proximately 33°N to Cape Hatteras. A similar distribution of variance is found in the depth of the 15°C isotherm. An annual signal is seen in the path data all along the U.S. east coast. The stream front north of Charleston (~32°N) exhibits the strongest annual variation with the surface front being further offshore in the late winter and early spring. This annual signal is not obvious at the thermocline level (15°C). It is consistent, however, with observed shifts in the isotherm patterns in the upper 100 m.

Petterson, J.S. 1998. Appendix G: Coastal North Carolina Socioeconomic Study Program. pp. 137-43. *In*: Vigil, D.L. (ed.). North Carolina/Minerals Management Service Technical Workshop on Manteo Unit Exploration: February 4-5, 1998. U.S. Dept. of the Interior, Minerals Management Service, Gulf of Mexico OCS Region. New Orleans, LA.

*These are the proceedings from a workshop/meeting (February 4-5, 1998) between the North Carolina Department of Environment and Natural Resources, and the U.S. Department of the Interior's Minerals Management Service (MMS). The geographic area being discussed is approximately 45 miles east-northeast of Cape Hatteras, NC, referred to as the Manteo Unit. This workshop reviewed environmental and socioeconomic information known and needed on the Manteo Unit. The MMS's Gulf of Mexico OCS Regional Director gave an MMS perspective on history and status of the area. Chevron gave a presentation on how the exploratory well would be drilled. The scientific characterization was presented in greater detail by a number of scientific experts who spoke on the following disciplines physical environment, habitat and living resources, seabirds, marine mammals, sea turtles, and social and economic issues. Specific chapters are cited individually, when appropriate.

The Oil Pollution Act of 1990, in a section cited as the Outer Banks Protection Act (OBPA), created the ESRP (Costlow et al. 1992). The review panel was to be composed of five members, a marine scientist selected by the Secretary of the Interior, a marine specialist selected by the Governor of North Carolina, and three scientists, one each from the disciplines of physical oceanography, ecology, and social sciences, selected jointly by the Secretary and the Governor from a list developed by the national Academy of Sciences. After a series of deliberations and public hearings during 1991-1992, this panel submitted its recommendations to the Secretary of Commerce identifying the two areas in greatest need of additional study (1) benthic oceanographic studies; and (2) socioeconomic studies.

Pietrafesa, L. 1989. Oceanographic Conditions. pp. 19-21. *In*: Crawford, K. (ed.). Proceedings: 1989 Marine Expo: The Natural Resources Associated with Mobil's Proposed Drill Site. NC Outer Continental Shelf Office, NC Department of Administration. Raleigh, NC.

In the vicinity of Cape Hatteras, physical oceanographic processes on the outer continental shelf are such that subdiurnal frequency motions and thermohaline distributions on the Carolina Capes continental shelf are controlled by navifacial momentum and buoyancy flux exchanges and offshore Gulf Stream frontal events. Atmospheric forcing dominates current fluctuations and thermohaline variability in inner to mid-shelf waters particularly to the south of Cape Hatteras where Gulf Stream frontal meanders and filaments become increasingly more important from middle to outer continental shelf waters. Gulf Stream frontal events are created as a result of the interaction of the Gulf Stream and the Charleston bump, a topographic feature at 32° N, 79° W, and propagate north into North Carolina waters. The alongshore component of the wind provides the principal forcing of inner to mid-shelf waters and even in outer shelf waters to the north of Hatteras. Wind effects are manifested directly and mechanically via Ekman dynamics, but also occur indirectly through the setup of coastal pressure gradients.

—. 1991. Oceanographic Conditions. p. 7. *In*: Shepard, A. (ed.). NURC/UNCW 1991 Undersea Research: Informational Meeting. National Undersea Research Center, University of North Carolina at Wilmington. Wilmington, NC.

In the vicinity of Cape Hatteras, physical oceanographic processes on the outer continental shelf are such that subdiurnal frequency motions and thermohaline distributions on the Carolina Capes continental shelf are controlled by navifacial momentum and buoyancy flux exchanges and offshore Gulf Stream frontal events. Atmospheric forcing dominates current fluctuations and thermohaline variability in inner to mid-shelf waters particularly to the south of Cape Hatteras where Gulf Stream frontal meanders and filaments become increasingly more important from middle to outer continental shelf waters. Gulf Stream frontal events are created as a result of the interaction of the Gulf Stream and the Charleston bump, a topographic feature at 32° N, 79° W, and propagate north into North Carolina waters. The alongshore component of the wind provides the principal forcing of inner to mid-shelf waters and even in outer shelf waters to the north of Hatteras. Wind effects are manifested directly and mechanically via Ekman dynamics, but also occur indirectly through the setup of coastal pressure gradients.

Pietrafesa, L.J. 1983. Shelfbreak Circulation, Fronts and Physical Oceanography: East and West Coast Perspectives. Society of Economic Paleontologists and Mineralogists 33: 233-250.

*A survey of fundamental physical oceanographic processes that may affect sediment distribution along shelfbreak regions is presented, emphasizing the Atlantic and Pacific coasts of the USA. The processes encompass the entire spectrum of known motions and are thus generic to all the shelfbreak interfacial zones. These shelfbreak strips couple the bounded coastal oceans to the open seas, but there is no systematic pattern to this coupling. In the South Atlantic bight, the Gulf Stream acts like a vibrating, permeable wall which can variously entrain shelf waters, flood the shelf with North Atlantic Central Water and violently mix shelf waters by towing whirling vortices through the outer shelf. Middle Atlantic Bight, New York Bight and Gulf of Maine shelfbreak processes contain many of the dynamic elements of their southeastern counterpart, but the relative importance of various random surface and offshore driving forces change.

—. 1998. Physical Environment Review: An Overview of the Meteorology and Physical Oceanography Surrounding Lease Blocks 467 and 510. pp. 31-32. *In*: D.L. Vigil (ed.). North Carolina/ Minerals Management Service Technical Workshop on Manteo Unit Exploration: February 4-5, 1998. U.S. Dept. of the Interior, Minerals Management Service, Gulf of Mexico OCS Region. New Orleans, LA.

*These are the proceedings from a workshop/meeting (February 4-5, 1998) between the North Carolina Department of Environment and Natural Resources, and the U.S. Department of the Interior's Minerals Management Service (MMS). The geographic area being discussed is approximately 45 miles east-northeast of Cape Hatteras, NC, referred to as the Manteo Unit. This workshop reviewed environmental and socioeconomic information known and needed on the Manteo Unit. The MMS's Gulf of Mexico OCS Regional Director gave an MMS perspective on history and status of the area. Chevron gave a presentation on how the exploratory well would be drilled. The scientific characterization was presented in greater detail by a number of scientific experts who spoke on the following disciplines physical environment, habitat and living resources, seabirds, marine mammals, sea turtles, and social and economic issues. Specific chapters are cited individually, when appropriate.

This section discusses Atmospheric Weather and Climatology, Physical Oceanography, Recent Findings (e.g., Hatteras Confluence region, offshelf transport), Issues (e.g., ability to predict oil spill trajectory, ability of oil rigs to withstand cyclone forcing, ability of drill ship to evacuate site during genesis of atmospheric bombs, role of physical oceanography in biological productivity).

Pietrafesa, L.J., R.D. Amato, C. Gabriel, and R.J. Sawyer. 1978. Continental Margin Atmospheric Climatology and Sea Level 1974-75. Department of Energy Contract No. E(38-1)-902; UNC-SG-78-09; NC State University Report No. 78-2. 189 p.

*This report discusses Continental Margin Atmospheric Climatology and Coastal Sea Level, based on data from 4 Meteorological Stations (Cape Hatteras, NC; Wilmington, NC; Charleston, SC; Savannah, GA) and 5 Sea Level Stations (Beaufort, NC; Beaufort Inlet, NC; Wilmington, NC; Frying Pan Shoals, NC; Charleston, SC). The atmospheric climate overlying the South Atlantic Bight is determined by both polar and tropical marine air masses, resulting in a "temperate rainy" climate with mild winters, long hot summers, and adequate moisture in all seasons, according to Koppen (see Pettersen, 1969). The polar front, the actual zone of maximum temperature contrast which separates the colder continental air from the warmer, more moist tropical air both intensifies and shifts southward in the winter to near Cape Hatteras, resulting in a region of intense cyclogenesis stretching along the eastern U.S. seaboard from Florida towards northern Europe. Most of the intense extratropical lows develop over the southeast U.S. but show their greatest growth as the storms more offshore over the warmer ocean, especially in the neighborhood of the Gulf Stream.

Pietrafesa, L.J., J.0. Blanton, J.D. Wang, V. Kourafalou, T.N. Lee, and K.A. Bush. 1985a. The Tidal Regime in the South Atlantic Bight. Oceanography of the Southeastern U.S. Continental Shelf Coastal and Estuarine Sciences 2: 63-76.

Tidal currents, particularly at the M, frequency, dominate South Atlantic Bight inner shelf and midshelf dynamics, with M2 tides accounting for almost 80% of the total kinetic energy there. Maximum energy occurs offshore of Savannah, where the shelf is widest. Outer shelf dynamics are less influenced by tides and more dependent on Gulf Stream interaction. There appear to be some seasonal differences in the tidal currents. A simple vertically integrated two-dimensional tidal model was used to reproduce tidal characteristics in the midshelf region during well-mixed winter conditions.

Pietrafesa, L.J., G.S. Janowitz, and P.A Wittman. 1985b. Physical Oceanographic Processes in the Carolina Capes. Oceanography of the Southeastern U.S. Continental Shelf: Coastal Estuarine Sciences 2.

Oceanographic processes in the Carolina Capes region of the South Atlantic Bight, are influenced by the cuspate shore line and prominent shoals that extend to the shelf break. Meteorological, hydrographic, and moored current data indicate that synoptic scale wind and Gulf Stream events are the primary driving forces in the region. Topographically enhanced upwelling maybe important at the shelf break.

Pietrafesa, L.J., J.M. Morrison, M.P. McCann, J. Churchill, E. Bohm, and R.W. Houghton. 1994. Water mass linkages between the Middle and South Atlantic Bights . Deep-Sea Research II Vol. 41(2-3): 365-389.

Time and frequency domain analysis are used to relate coastal meteorological data with 7 years of daily surface temperature and salinity collected at three coastal light stations: offshore of the mouth of Chesapeake Bay, Virginia, on Diamond Shoals, at Cape Hatteras, North Carolina and on Frying Pan Shoals, off Cape Fear, North Carolina. Salinity fluctuations at Diamond Shoals are highly correlated with alongshore wind stress, implying wind driven advection of the front between Virginia Coastal Water (VCW) and Carolina Coastal Water (CCW) across Diamond Shoals. The data collected at Diamond Shoals indicate that more than half the time there is significant encroachment of Mid Atlantic Bight water into the South Atlantic Bight around Cape Hatteras, contrary to the notion that VCW is entirely entrained into the Gulf Stream. In fact, VCW can appear as far south as Frying Pan Shoals, thereby extending across the entire North Carolina Capes inner to mid shelf. Temperature and salinity time series also indicate that water mass, overlying Diamond Shoals respond quickly to cross-shelf winds, Cross-shelf wind stress, is significantly correlated with surface water temperature at Diamond Shoals, for periods between 2 and 12 days. Changes in temperature can be brought about by wind-driven cross-shelf circulation and by wind-induced upwelling. Seasurface temperature satellite (AVHRR) image taken during the SEEP II confirm these concepts.

Richardson, P.L. 1977. On the crossover between the Gulf Stream and Western Boundary Undercurrent. Deep-Sea Research 24: 139-159.

To determine how the Gulf Stream and Western Boundary Undercurrent cross each other near Cape Hatteras, six current meters were moored from May to July 1971 along a line normal to the Gulf Stream axis and 100 m above the ocean floor in depths from 1200 to 4200 m. Peak velocities of the six records (including one 47 cm s^{-1}) and the mean velocities of four of the deepest records (2800 to 4000 m) were in the southwest quadrant. During the observations the Gulf Stream did not extend to the bottom of this area except in brief current reversals to the northeast. The Western Boundary Undercurrent flowed southwest under the Gulf Stream parallel to the bottom contours. The transport of the undercurrent, estimated using two geostrophic velocity sections and deep current meter observations, was 24 x 10^6 m^3 s^{-1}).

Rona, P.A. 1970. Submarine canyon origin on upper continental slope off Cape Hatteras. Journal of Geology 78(2): 141-152.

The configuration of sedimentary strata revealed by continuous seismic-reflection profiles over submarine canyons in the upper continental slope off Cape Hatteras is best explained by the hypothesis of composite origin of submarine canyons. The canyons were originally incised into a post-Miocene surface of unconformity. The intercanyon areas were constructed by deposition of sediment up to several hundred meters thick forming the canyon walls while the canyons were maintained by sediment removal processes over the sites of original incision.

Canyon heads are presently buried under a smooth sediment cover which extends from the shelf break at about 90 m down to about 400 m below sea level, where the canyons emerge from the cover. The depth of emergence of canyons approximately coincides with the inferred level of motion between the northeast-flowing Florida Current and the southwest-flowing Western Boundary Undercurrent.

Ross, S.W. 1991. Fisheries Resources Potentially Impacted by Proposed Drilling On the US Atlantic Continental Slope and Rise Off Cape Hatteras, North Carolina. p. 6. *In*: Shepard, A. (ed.). NURC/UNCW 1991 Undersea Research: Informational Meeting. National Undersea Research Center, University of North Carolina at Wilmington. Wilmington, NC.

An area known colloquially as "The Point" by fishermen, lies within the Manteo oil and gas lease blocks, just north of block 467, site of the proposed exploratory drill hole. 'The Point" is characterized by a productive pelagic fishery and complex submarine topography. Although a small, canyon-like feature underlies the area, "The Point" is not a spot on the bottom, but rather a shifting location that may coincide with the confluence of water masses.

In 1991, we will use a research submersible to describe the pelagic and benthic fish populations near Manteo Block 467. Specific objectives are to determine the distribution of: (1) pelagic fish with respect to depth and hydrographic features throughout the water column; and (2) benthic fish with respect to depth and topographic features.

—. 1998. Habitat and Living Resource Review: Scientific Data for Fisheries and *Sargassum* at the Hatteras Middle Slope (Including "The Point" and Manteo Exploration Unit). pp. 37-42. In: Vigil, D.L. (ed.). North Carolina/Minerals Management Service Technical Workshop on Manteo Unit Exploration: February 4-5, 1998. U.S. Dept. of the Interior, Minerals Management Service, Gulf of Mexico OCS Region. New Orleans, LA.

*These are the proceedings from a workshop/meeting (February 4-5, 1998) between the North Carolina Department of Environment and Natural Resources, and the U.S. Department of the Interior's Minerals Management Service (MMS). The geographic area being discussed is approximately 45 miles east-northeast of Cape Hatteras, NC, referred to as the Manteo Unit. This workshop reviewed environmental and socioeconomic information known and needed on the Manteo Unit. The MMS's Gulf of Mexico OCS Regional Director gave an MMS perspective on history and status of the area. Chevron gave a presentation on how the exploratory well would be drilled. The scientific characterization was presented in greater detail by a number of scientific experts who spoke on the following disciplines physical environment, habitat and living resources, seabirds, marine mammals, sea turtles, and social and economic issues. Specific chapters are cited individually, when appropriate.

The purpose of this review is to provide a brief summary of the state of fisheries and *Sargassum* knowledge in and near to the geographic region proposed for oil exploration activities off of North Carolina (referred to here as the Hatters Middle Slope, HMS). This will result in a basic listing of what we know about the subjects and what we still need to know. This treatment is restricted to the HMS area and thus is not to be a complete description of the North Carolina ichthyofauna. Time and space constraints imposed by the North Carolina/Minerals Management Service Technical Workshop do not allow a full treatment of this subject nor a detailed presentation of the data that support various conclusions. Prioritized and expanding the list of data needs will require additional discussions, some completed at this meeting, with input from a variety of scientist, managers, and the public. Since the last such summaries (1989 and 1991), considerable data have been collected (much of it published) related to the HMS. Ironically, the major impetus (upper water column fishery concerns around "The Point") for research here resulted in most studies being conducted on or near the bottom close to the proposed drill site rather than studies about the processes driving fisheries at "The Point." This section discusses Benthic Slope, Mid-Water Mesopelagic, Surface-Upper Water Column, Sargassum Community, Commercial/Recreational Fisheries, Oil Exploration/Development Concerns, and a Summary of Data/Study Needs including: Trophodynamic/Energetic Pathways (Plus Other Life History Data); Fisheries at "The Point"; Data Inventory Around HMS and "The Point"; Larval Fish Data; Lighting Effects; Mechanisms Structuring Benthic and Mid-water Fish Communities of the HMS; and Physical Oceanography.

Rowe, G.T. 1971. Observations on bottom currents and epibenthic populations in Hatteras Submarine Canyon. Deep-Sea Research 18: 569-581.

Bottom currents and populations of large epifauna were surveyed using bottom photography in the Pamlico axis of the Hatteras Submarine Canyon system. Most species known to be numerically dominant along the continental slope north and south of the canyon were absent or found in reduced densities, whereas other species were found only near or in the canyon and can be considered canyon indicator species. The implication of previous studies (Rowe and Menzies 1969; Sanders and Hessler 1969) that narrow faunal zonation is continuous along the margins of ocean basins must be modified to acknowledge the exceptional zonations found in canyons.

The photographs and current meter data indicated that the bottom current to the southwest along the lower continental rise, but turned to the west and northwest, or up the canyon, at lesser depths. Indurated sedimentary outcrops common to the canyon were probably a result of intermittent slumping and turbidity current flows.

Schaff, T., L. Levin, N. Blair, D. DeMaster, R. Pope, and S. Boehme. 1992. Spatial heterogeneity of benthos on the Carolina continental slope: large (100 km)-scale variation. Marine Ecology Progress Series 88: 143-160.

Large-scale spatial heterogeneity of macrofaunal and microbial communities was examined on the continental slope off North and South Carolina, USA, by comparing 3 sites, separated by 130 to 150 km and all at 850 m water depth. Significant variation was found among macrofaunal assemblages at all 3 sites, and between microbial counts at 2 sites. We investigated the hypothesis that 100 km scale heterogeneity was driven by variation in organic C flux to the sea floor. The northernmost site (Site III, off Cape Hatteras, NC) was found to have macrofaunal abundances (>55000 m^{-2}) higher than any previous recorded from this depth, and significantly higher than those at Site II (off Cape Lookout, North Carolina) (21319 m^{-2}) or Site I (off Charleston, SC) (9438 m^{-2}). Trends in macrofaunal abundance did not follow those sediment TOC (total organic carbon), but agreed well with estimates of total carbon flux for the three sites. Mixing coefficients determined from profiles of naturally occurring ^{234}Th (half life 24 d) indicate that the sediments at Site III are mixed 2 to 6 times faster than at the other 2 sites, which is consistent with the trends in macrofaunal abundance and biomass. Using ^{14}C-based sedimentation rates and sediment carbon content, we estimated carbon flux to be 0.6, 20 and > 70 g C m^2 yr^1 at sites I, II and III, respectively. Inventories of ^{234}Th and downcore concentration profiles of dissolved $SO_4^=$, CO_2 and CH_4 within the sediment provided evidence that the flux of metabolized carbon was greater at Site III than at the other sites. Polychaetes, which comprised 43, 74 and 65 % of the fauna at Sites I, II and III, respectively, exhibited lower diversity, higher dominance, and a completely different species composition at Site III than at the other 2 sites. *Scalibregma inflatum* and *Aricidea quadrilobata* comprised 33 % of total macrofauna at Site III, but were absent at Sites I and II. The species composition, high dominance, and prevalence of juveniles among polychaetes at Site III is suggestive of a response to organic enrichment. Enrichment of the Site III benthos is attributed to physical oceanographic and geophysical causes, including Gulf Stream-induced upwelling, a confluence of currents focused by bottom topography, and lateral inputs resulting from mass wasting processes. Despite significant differences in macrofaunal abundance, Sites I and II exhibited considerable overlap in microbial counts, polychaete species composition, dominance and diversity patterns.

Schneider, E.D., P.J. Fox, C.D. Hollister, H.D. Needham, and B.C. Heezen. 1967. Further Evidence of Contour Currents in the Western North Atlantic. Earth and Planetary Science Letters 2: 351-359.

A study of compass-oriented sea-floor photographs, echograms and sediment cores on the Atlantic continental margin of North America has been made in order to evaluate the role of deep-sea contour currents in the shaping of the continental rise. The sediments on the upper continental rise consist of lutites which are being deposited on the seafloor in an environment devoid of strong bottom currents. Below an abrupt change in regional slope, that marks the boundary between the upper and lower continental rise, a swift bottom current is observed which flows to the southwest parallel to the contours. Beneath this current the surface sediments are distinctly coarser grained and long cores show many quartz silt laminations in the sedimentary column. Further downslope on the lower continental rise the currents are variable in direction and weaker. Measurements of northerly directions indicate that at certain locations the Gulf Stream may intermittently scour the sea floor. In the area of the Lower Continental Rise Hill a swift southwesterly current is again observed. Hyperbolic echo traces on echograms, prolonged multiple echo sequences, and wedging of sub-bottom reflecting interfaces can be mapped as distinct zones. These zones of sea floor micromorphology parallel the region contours of the continental rise, and are produced by erosional and depositional processes of bottom currents. We conclude that the continental rise is a large sediment wedge which owes its shape to deep geostrophic contour currents.

Science Applications International Corporation. 1991. Physical Oceanographic Field Program Offshore North Carolina: Field Measurement Plan. MMS Contract 14-35-0001-30599; SAIC Report 91/1212. Science Applications International Corporation. Raleigh, NC. 33 p.

This plan encompasses SAIC's discussion of the details on exactly how the scientific plan for the Physical Oceanographic Program Offshore North Carolina (the "North Carolina Field Program") will be carried out under MMS Contract 14-35-0001-30599. Field measurements include current meter deployments (mooring deployment, rotation and recovery cruises), hydrographic measurements (cruises concurrent with mooring cruises), special event surveys (detailed hydrography and shipboard ADCP sections and GPS drifter experiments), a series of Lagrangian drifter experiments designed to provide a statistically significant sample of the potential form materials discharged near the shelf break to reach the near shore again.

Collateral data in the form of satellite imagery (AVHRR and real time GOES/AVHRR support for special events), meteorological data along the coast within 500 km of Cape Hatteras; and water level data in the same region will be collected and used to support analysis and synthesis of the primary data.

*The rest of the report details field operations.

Shepard, A. (ed.). 1991. Undersea Research at The Point. NURC/UNCW 1991 Undersea Research: Informational Meeting. National Undersea Research Center, University of North Carolina at Wilmington. Wilmington, NC. 9 p.

*This handout is a summary of research being conducted at "The Point" area (Manteo Lease Block 467).

The National Undersea Research Center at the University of North Carolina at Wilmington, funded by a grant from the National Oceanic and Atmospheric Administration's (NOAA) Office of Undersea Research (OUR), was established in 1980 to promote, facilitate, and conduct research in the Southeastern United States utilizing undersea techniques, including advanced wet diving and manned and unmanned submersibles. A main Center goal is to provide information to NOAA that will assist the agency in fulfilling its charter to explore, understand, conserve and manage the U.S. marine environment and associated resources. To help meet this goal, the Center supports and conducts interdisciplinary oceanographic research projects studying continental margin processes, particularly the interactions and linkages between estuarine, continental shelf, and slope (including submarine canyon) environments.

Shepard, A., and A.H. Hulbert (eds.). 1994. Workshop Report: Present and Future Research Initiatives on the Upper Hatteras Slope off North Carolina. National Undersea Research Center at the University of North Carolina at Wilmington. Wilmington, NC. 30p.

*This report is the result of the May 1993 workshop held in Raleigh, NC. The topics of discussion were research (present and planned) at the Upper Hatteras Slope (UHS) and potential funding sources. The workshop was sponsored by National Undersea Research Center at the University of North Carolina at Wilmington. The report provides a brief description of the UHS invertebrates, biological oceanography, chemical oceanography, geological oceanography (bathymetry, oil and gas exploration), physical oceanography, fisheries, and *Sargassum*. Appendix A is a workshop agenda and list of speakers. No abstracts for speakers are provided. Appendix B is a list of potential funding sources. Appendix C contains a list of publications pertaining to the UHS.

Shepard, A.N. 1992. A North Carolina Oceanographic Facility: The National Oceanographic and Atmospheric Administration's National Undersea Research Center. pp. 55-65. *In*: U.S. Department of the Interior, Minerals Management Service. Proceedings of the Fourth Atlantic OCS Region Information Transfer Meeting, September 1991. U.S. Department of the Interior, Minerals Management Service. Herndon, VA.

The Fourth Atlantic Outer Continental Shelf (OCS) regional Information Transfer Meeting (ITM) was held on 24-25 September 1991 in Wilmington, NC. The focus of the meeting was on the OCS off North Carolina, specifically on activities related to a proposed exploratory well for oil and gas by

Mobil on Block 467 a site 40 miles off the coast of North Carolina. The area of industry interest is known as the Manteo Prospect, while the activities surrounding the proposed drilling are referred to collectively as the Manteo Project. The wildcat wellsite is in 2,690 ft. (857 m) of water near the edge of the Gulf Stream. It is also near a fishing ground known locally as "The Point." The area is believed to be gas prone rather than oil prone. The estimated size of the resource could be as high as 5 trillion cubic feet of gas.

The purpose of the meeting was to exchange information on the leasing background, legislative activities, scientific results, and socioeconomic studies. Legislative-related reports include descriptions of the Oil Pollution Act of 1990, the Outer Banks Protection Act, the Environmental Studies Review Panel, and the North Carolina Physical Oceanography Panel. Reports of studies on marine life include benthic diatoms, benthic fauna, pelagic seabirds, sea turtles, and right whales. One report describes the use of airships (blimps) for ocean research a capability relevant to North Carolina because of the east coast airship facility is located in the state. Local marine science facilities described include NOAA's national Undersea research Center at the University of North Carolina at Wilmington (NURC/UNCW) and the national marine Fisheries Service laboratory in Beaufort.

Developments in oil spill cleanup technology and capabilities are described by both the Coast Guard and the industry. A socioeconomic report describes the effects of the oil and gas activities on the tourist industry. Lastly, research on the restoration of salt marshes indicates that rehabilitation of an area is possible when development or an accident has occurred. While the emphasis of the meeting was on oil and gas, two reports described the results of projects related to offshore sand mining. The appendix lists the names and addresses of speakers. Individual chapters are cited individually when appropriate.

*Within the oil and gas lease blocks of the Manteo Prospect lies "The Point." This productive pelagic fishing ground lies at the confluence of major currents and water masses, and contains complex and rugged submarine topography. The National Undersea Research Center located at the University of North Carolina at Wilmington is one of the oceanographic facilities near The Point. This center has a record of research in the area and has experience, equipment, and staff that will be invaluable to future studies.

Stefansson, U., and L.P. Atkinson. 1967. Physical and chemical properties of the shelf and slope waters off North Carolina. Technical report. Duke University Marine Laboratory. Beaufort, NC. 240 p.

The present report includes a compilation of data collected during several cruises aboard the RV Eastward in the period June 1965-April 1967. The objective of this work was to study the broad features of the circulation and distribution of properties on the shelf, and attempt to relate the observed distributions in different seasons to various meteorological factors and processes affecting the renewal of shelf waters. These various aspects are dealt with separate publications. This report includes a short preliminary description of the main results, charts showing the horizontal distribution of temperature, salinity, density and dynamic topography, illustrations of vertical distribution of physical and chemical properties, and a tabulation of the data obtained at each station from hydrographic casts.

Stefansson, U., L.P. Atkinson, and D.F Bumpus. 1971. Hydrographic properties and circulation of the North Carolina Shelf and Slope Waters. Deep-Sea Research 18: 383-420.

Processes affecting the renewal of the North Carolina Shelf Waters are discussed on the basis of temperature, salinity, dissolved oxygen, nutrients, runoff and wind data collectedduring 1965-1967. These consist of horizontal advection near the coast from the north, meanders of the Gulf Stream, subsurface intrusion, cascading and runoff.

The wind-driven Virginia Water transport past Cape Hatteras may markedly reduce the temperature and salinity, and accelerate the freshwater exchange. The runoff from the watershed north of Cape Hatteras, when driven south by northerly winds, especially during the peak period in early spring, has a much greater influence on the circulation in Raleigh and Onslow Bays than does that from the adjacent rivers south of Cape Hatteras. Meanders in the Gulf Stream may renew the shelf waters with warm, saline water. Intrusion of subsurface Caribbean Water on to the outer part of the shelf takes place most frequently during the late summer following a period of southerly winds. It is postulated that during the cold part of the year when the surface layers are only partly stratified, such an intrusion may lead to upwelling near the shelf break. Cascading from the shelf down the slope may occur during the cold season following periods of low air temperature. Intrusion of subsurface water replenishes nutrients in the area, while cascading reduces the available supply of nutrients.

U.S. Department of the Interior, Minerals Management Service. 1990. Atlantic Outer Continental Shelf: Final Environmental Report on Proposed Exploratory Drilling Offshore North Carolina, U.S. Department of the Interior, Minerals Management Service, Atlantic OCS Region, Environmental Assessment Section. Herndon, VA.

*Topics include: fisheries, birds, marine mammals, physical oceanography, chemical oceanography, geology, gas and oil production. The proposed action is to drill a single exploratory well approximately 72 km (45 mi) east-northeast of Cape Hatteras, North Carolina in 820 m (2,690 ft) of water. Total depth for the proposed well is 4,267 m (14,000 ft) and the location is on Block 467 on the Minerals Management Service Protraction diagram NI 18-2. The proposal has been submitted by Mobil for itself and 7 partners to drill the well on the approved 21-block exploration unit.

U.S. Department of the Interior, Minerals Management Service. 1992. Proceedings of the Fourth Atlantic OCS Region Information Transfer Meeting, September 1991. U.S. Department of the Interior, Minerals Management Service. Herndon, VA. 198 p.

The Fourth Atlantic Outer Continental Shelf (OCS) Regional Information Transfer Meeting (ITM) was held on 24-25 September, 1991, in Wilmington, NC. The focus of the meeting was on the OCS off North Carolina, specifically on activities related to a proposed exploratory well for oil and gas by Mobil on Block 467 a site 40 miles off the coast of North Carolina. The area of industry interest is known as the Manteo Prospect, while the activities surrounding the proposed drilling are referred to collectively as the Manteo Project. The wildcat wellsite is in 2,690 ft. (857 m) of water near the edge of the Gulf Stream. It is also near a fishing ground known locally as "The Point." The area is believed to be gas prone rather than oil prone. The estimated size of the resource could be as high as 5 trillion cubic feet of gas.

The purpose of the meeting was to exchange information on the leasing background, legislative activities, scientific results, and socioeconomic studies. Legislative-related reports include descriptions of the Oil Pollution Act of 1990, the Outer Banks Protection Act, the Environmental Studies Review Panel, and the North Carolina Physical Oceanography Panel. Reports of studies on marine life include benthic diatoms, benthic fauna, pelagic seabirds, sea turtles, and right whales. One report describes the use of airships (blimps) for ocean research a capability relevant to North Carolina because of the east coast airship facility is located in the state. Local marine science facilities described include NOAA's National Undersea Research Center at the University of North Carolina at Wilmington (NURC/UNCW) and the National Marine Fisheries Service laboratory in Beaufort.

Developments in oil spill cleanup technology and capabilities are described by both the Coast Guard and the industry. A socioeconomic report describes the effects of the oil and gas activities on the tourist industry. Lastly, research on the restoration of salt marshes indicates that rehabilitation of an area is possible when development or an accident has occurred. While the emphasis of the meeting was on oil and gas, two reports described the results of projects related to offshore sand mining. The appendix lists the names and addresses of speakers. Individual chapters are cited individually when appropriate.

Uchupi, E., and K.O. Emery. 1967. Structure of the Continental Margin off Atlantic Coast of United States. The American Association of Petroleum Geologists Bulletin 51(2): 223-234.

Seismic profiler recordings in 44 profiles between Nova Scotia and the Florida Keys indicate that the continental margin was performed by upbuilding on the shelf and prograding on the slope. Upbuilding on the shelf during Tertiary and Quaternary Periods ranged from 200 to 1,000 meters, and sea-ward prograding on the slope during the same span of time was from 5 to more than 35 kilometers. The greatest progradation occurred where the slope is flanked by the Blake Plateau rather than by the deep sea. The beds are truncated along some sections of the slope as though the slope had been steepened by submarine erosion. Off Nova Scotia the beds of the slope continue into the continental rise; off New England rise consists of sedimentary layers that have buried the base of the continental lope; and off southeastern United States the beds of the Florida-Hatteras Slope have prograded atop the older surface of the Blake Plateau.

Verity, P. 1998. Habitat and Living Resources Review: Water Column Biology at Cape Hatteras. p. 52. *In*: Vigil, D.L. (ed.). North Carolina/Minerals Management Service Technical Workshop on Manteo Unit Exploration: February 4-5, 1998. U.S. Dept. of the Interior, Minerals Management Service, Gulf of Mexico OCS Region. New Orleans, LA.

*These are the proceedings from a workshop/meeting (February 4-5, 1998) between the North Carolina Department of Environment and Natural Resources, and the U.S. Department of the Interior's Minerals Management Service (MMS). The geographic area being discussed is approximately 45 miles east-northeast of Cape Hatteras, NC, referred to as the Manteo Unit. This workshop reviewed environmental and socioeconomic information known and needed on the Manteo Unit. The MMS's Gulf of Mexico OCS Regional Director gave an MMS perspective on history and status of the area. Chevron gave a presentation on how the exploratory well would be drilled. The scientific characterization was presented in greater detail by a number of scientific experts who spoke on the following disciplines physical environment, habitat and living resources, seabirds, marine mammals, sea turtles, and social and economic issues. Specific chapters are cited individually, when appropriate.

It is essential in any overview of pelagic food web structure and function to place it in the proper physical perspective. In the Carolina Capes region in general, phytoplankton biomass is typically highest in late winter/early spring, associated with a vernal bloom. Higher concentrations occur closer to shore and along shelf/slope fronts. Immediately south of Cape Hatteras is a large area of high upwelling. This massive nitrate flux in to the euphotic zone induces substantial plankton development, which advents northward from the South Atlantic Bight (SAB) past Cape Hatteras. The latter is also at the confluence of southward-flowing Mid Atlantic Bight (MAB) water which exists at Cape Hatteras.

Vigil, D.L. (ed.). 1998. North Carolina/Minerals Management Service Technical Workshop on Manteo Unit Exploration: February 4-5, 1998. U.S. Dept. of the Interior, Minerals Management Service. Gulf of Mexico OCS Region. New Orleans, LA. 168 p.

*These are the proceedings from a workshop/meeting (February 4-5, 1998) between the North Carolina Department of Environment and Natural Resources, and the U.S. Department of the Interior's Minerals Management Service (MMS). The geographic area being discussed is approximately 45 miles east-northeast of Cape Hatteras, NC, referred to as the Manteo Unit. This workshop reviewed environmental and socioeconomic information known and needed on the Manteo Unit. The MMS's Gulf of Mexico OCS Regional Director gave an MMS perspective on history and status of the area. Chevron gave a presentation on how the exploratory well would be drilled. The scientific characterization was presented in greater detail by a number of scientific experts who spoke on the following disciplines physical environment, habitat and living resources (invertebrates and fish), seabirds, marine mammals, sea turtles, and social and economic issues. Specific chapters are cited individually, when appropriate.

Wadell, E. 1984a. South Atlantic Physical Oceanography Study: Volume I Executive Summary. MMS Contract 14-12-0001-29201. Science Applications. Raleigh, NC. 13 p.

This is a two-volume report describing physical oceanography in the South Atlantic Bight. One volume is an Executive Summary. The second volume is a Technical Summary. The South Atlantic Physical Oceanography Study (SAPOS) is a Minerals Management program funded under contract with Science Applications, Inc. (SAI), to document major circulation producing processes an their impact on the South Atlantic Bight (SAB) and adjacent regions It is expected that insights from the SAPOS will provide a basis for informed management decisions relating to outer continental shelf (OCS) oil and gas activities. Two key objectives of the SAPOS are: (1) To examine and understand the influence of tide, wind, density and the Gulf Stream (GS); i.e., all major forcing mechanisms producing observed SAB circulation patterns, (2) To document and explain the spatial and temporal variability of SAB hydrographic conditions (temperature, salinity, density, dissolved oxygen and selected nutrients).

—. 1984b. South Atlantic Physical Oceanography Study: Volume II Technical Summary. MMS Contract 14-12-0001-29201. Science Applications. Raleigh, NC. 223 p.

This is a two-volume report describing physical oceanography in the South Atlantic Bight. One volume is an Executive Summary. The second volume is a Technical Summary. The South Atlantic Physical Oceanography Study (SAPOS) is a Minerals Management program funded under contract with Science Applications, Inc. (SAI), to document major circulation producing processes an their impact on the South Atlantic Bight (SAB) and adjacent regions It is expected that insights from the SAPOS will provide a basis for informed management decisions relating to outer continental shelf (OCS) oil and gas activities. Two key objectives of the SAPOS are: (1) To examine and understand the influence of tide, wind, density and the Gulf Stream (GS); i.e., all major forcing mechanisms producing observed SAB circulation patterns, (2) To document and explain the spatial and temporal variability of SAB hydrographic conditions (temperature, salinity, density, dissolved oxygen and selected nutrients).

Walsh, J.J. 1994. Particle export at Cape Hatteras. Deep-Sea Research II Vol. 41(2-3): 603-628.

A simple model of shelf, slope and basin waters near Cape Hatteras, North Carolina is used to estimate the sources and sinks of organic carbon within the Gulf Stream System. The analysis employs water transport estimates, nutrient data. satellite imagery, surficial sediment records and particle distributions caught by bottle, camera and sediment trap to compute vertical and lateral fluxes of particulate carbon. Particle export from the SAB and MAB shelf ecosystems may constitute 62-82% of the source of the carbon flux within the Gulf Stream near 75 W, after settling at 100 m day $^{-1}$, with an oxidation loss of 4% day^{-1}, to a nominal mid-depth of 1000 m on the slope.

As a result of light limitation, denitrification and DON solubilization, partial utilization of onwelled nitrate from the Gulf Stream System by coastal phytoplankton suggests that the time-averaged f ratio may be as small as 0.12 for the ratio of the "new" portion of primary production to the total. After burial loss, the export of particulate matter from the shelves then represents at most 11% of the total carbon fixation of coastal waters. If the shelf export of DON and unutilized NO_3 is consumed within adjacent slope waters, however, the f ratio and the percentage of particle export from the carbon fixation of shelf-affected waters might increase to 0.25 and 24%.

Welby, C.W., and L.J. Pietrafesa. 1979. Combined Satellite Imagery of Water Circulation Along North Carolina Coast. Fifth Annual W.T. Pecora Memorial Symposium on Remote Sensing. pp. 15-17, 25.

The purpose of the investigation was to evaluate satellite imagery for studying circulation patterns in the middle to inner shelf regions of the North Carolina coast. Specifically, the remote sensing aspect of the investigation was directed to the study of the utilization of combined Landsat and NOAA-5 imagery as an aid in shelf circulation studies.

Spatial scale differences, and to a certain extent map projection incompatibilities, can discourage combined use of the two types of imagery. On the other hand, since imagery from each of the two satellite systems extracts information about the coastal waters from different parts of the electromagnetic spectrum, combination of the NOAA imagery with the Landsat imagery expands the ability to view the coastal waters in a multispectral context.

During the period 4 April — 2 August 1978 arrays of unattended, sub- surface, vertically moored current meters were maintained in Onslow Bay, North Carolina, as part of the U.S. Department of Energy's continental shelf studies program. Conditions favorable for essentially simultaneous imagining of all or part of Onslow Bay by the Landsat and NOAA satellites occurred on 9 April, and 6 May 1978. Thus the opportunity arose to compare the different imagery types obtained contemporaneously with the collection of moored current and temperature data. An 8 April Landsat image covered part of Raleigh Bay and a part of the North Carolina coast north of Cape Hatteras. The circumstances also give rise to the opportunity to assess the amount of information which can be extracted from satellite imagery for use in shelf circulation studies.

Wells, H.W., and I.E. Gray. 1960. Summer Upwelling, off the Northeast Coast of North Carolina. Limnology and Oceanography 5(1): 108-109.

Surface water temperatures reveal the occurrence of an upwelling of cold waters along the northeastern North Carolina coast during summer months. Southwesterly winds prevailed in the Cape Hatteras region in July and August 1958 (U.S. Weather Bureau, 1958). Whereas southwesterly winds blow parallel to the coastline in the Ocracoke area, they blow onshore in the region just south of Cape Hatteras where the coastline runs east and west, and they blow offshore in the Nag's Head area where the coastline runs northwest and southeast. In Figure 1, the solid line shows the water temperatures recorded on July 2, when southwesterly winds prevailed in this region. Where these winds blow parallel to or towards the shore, water temperature was over 25°C; but where these winds blow offshore, north of Rodanthe, water temperatures were less than 20°C. A similar distribution of water temperature was found on July 25 and July 27, after an extended period of southwesterly winds. Water at Oregon Inlet was as much as 6.3°C colder than water at Hatteras or Ocracoke Inlets, south of the Cape.

Wilk, S.J. and M.J. Silverman. 1976. Fish and hydrographic collections made by the research vessels Dolphin and Delaware II during 1968-72 from New York to Florida. NOAA Technical Report NMFS SSRF-697. 159 p.

Information is given in tabular form for fish and hydrographic observations collected during 18 cruises made by the research vessels Dolphin and Delaware II from New York to Florida during 1968-72. Tables include station locations with related hydrographic observations and number, weight, and size range of fish species caught.

Wittman, P.A., L.J. Pietrafesa, G.S. Janowitz, and T.B. Curtin. 1984. The winter spring transition along the Carolina Capes. Department of Marine, Earth and Atmospheric Sciences, NC State University. Raleigh, NC. 101 p.

The winter spring transitions of the thermal structures of Onslow and Long bays are investigated using hydrographic and current meter data from 1978. Generally, the shelf waters are vertically well-mixed during the winter and vertically stratified during the summer. The spring transition occurs during May and is due to heating of the surface water. Monthly heat flux calculations indicate that the heating of the surface waters during the spring is dominated by vertical heat fluxes with horizontal advection playing a lesser role.

Mean monthly currents are found to be consistent with mean monthly wind velocities during 1978. The forcing mechanism for these very low frequency currents is investigated using sea level, wind and hydrographic data. Density gradients are found to be too small to account for the observed vertical velocity shears, and these shears can be attributed to frictional influences of the bottom. Mean monthly wind velocities are found to be too small to drive the observed currents at 10 meters depth. Indirect wind forcing through cross-shelf transport in the surface layer and the resulting cross-shelf pressure gradient give velocity directions consistent with those of the measured currents. The seasonal reversal of the alongshore currents off Charleston, SC, occurs in concert with the reversal of the alongshore winds. No seasonal cycle of the alongshore currents are observed at mid-shelf in Onslow Bay, which appears to be dominated by Gulf Stream forcing.

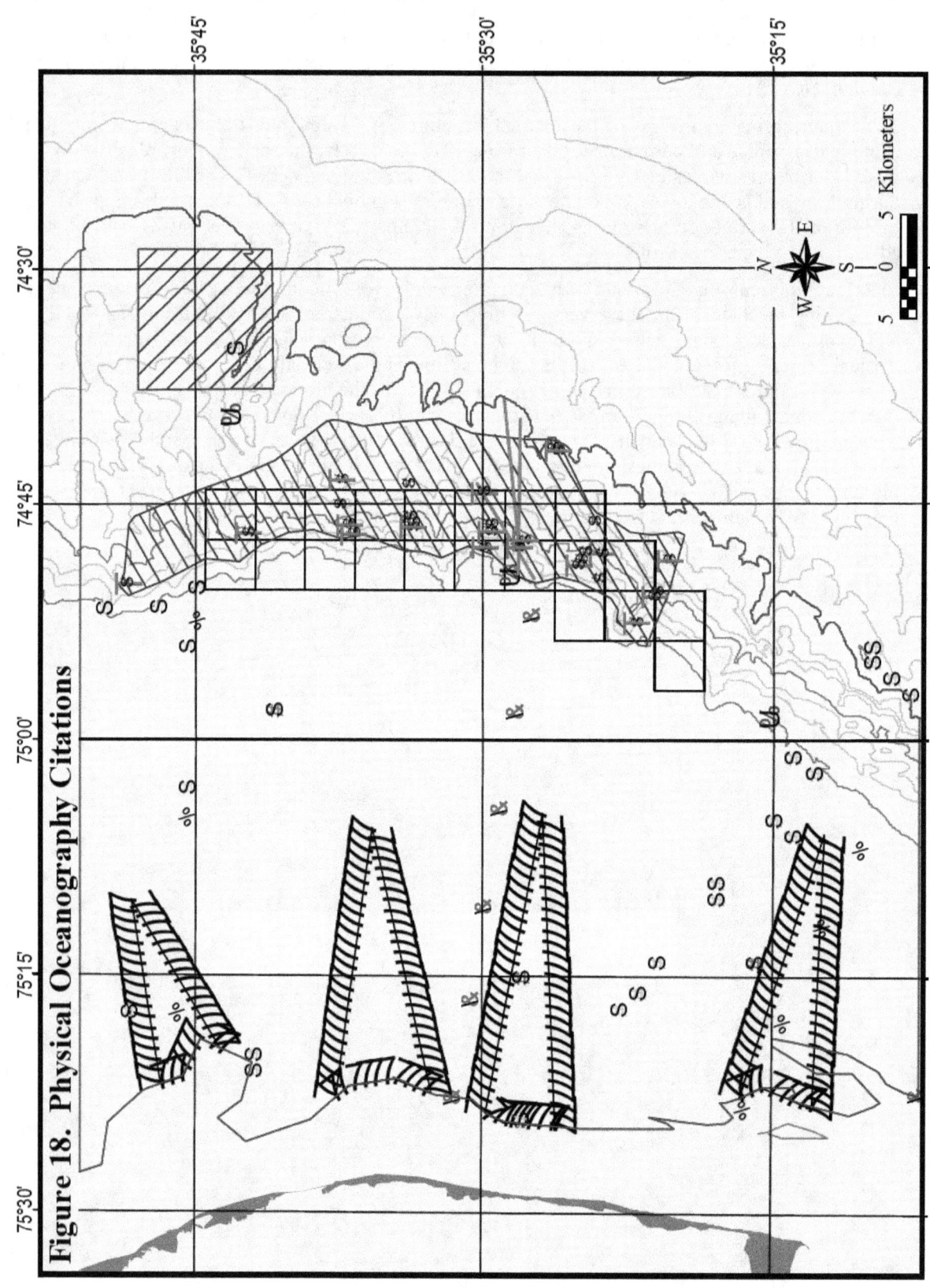

Figure 18. Physical Oceanography Citations

Key to Physical Oceanography Citations (Figure 18).

Study Area Boundary

Lease Blocks

Mapped Citations

Blake et al. (1987)

Clark et al. (1969)

Coles & Musick (2000)

Cutter et al. (1994a); Milliman et al. (1994)

Cutter et al. (1994b)

DeMaster et al. (1994)

Edwards et al. (1962)

FRED Group (1989b)

Magnuson et al. (1981)

Nash et al. (1987, 1989)

O'Reilly & Zetlin (1998)

Schaff et al. (1992)

Stefansson & Atkinson (1967)

Wittman et al. (1984)

Studies that Focus on the Manteo Lease Blocks

Atkinson et al. (1998)

Blair (1998)

Costlow (1992)

Crawford (1989)

Hamilton & Berger (1992)

Janowitz (1989)

Lang (1998)

Peterson (1998)

Pietrafesa (1998)

Shepard (1992)

Shepard & Hulbert (1994)

U.S.D.O.I.-Minerals Mgmt. Service (1990, 1992)

Verity (1998)

Vigil (1998)

Studies that Cover the Hatteras Middle Slope Area ("The Point")

Adams et al. (1993)

Barrett (1965)

Diaz et al. (1993b)

Hood & Bane (1983)

Nero et al. (1990)

Pietrafesa (1989, 1991)

Rona (1970)

Ross, S. (1991, 1998)

Shepard (1991)

Key to Physical Oceanography Citations (Figure 18) (con't).

Broad Regional Studies

Abernathy et al. (1989)
Ashjian et al. (1994)
Atkinson (1985, 1992)
Atkinson et al. (1985)
Bane (1983)
Bane & Brooks (1979)
Blair et al. (1991)
Blumberg & Mellor (1983)
Bumpus (1973)
Checkley et al. (1988, 1989)
Cook et al. (1979)
Costlow et al. (1992)
Csanady & Hamilton (1988)
Cutler (1975)
FRED Group (1989a)
Gray & Cerame-Vivas (1963)
Hare & Cowen (1996)
Heezen (1968)
Inman & Dolan (1989)
Janowitz & Pietrafesa (1996)
JAYCOR. (1980)
Johns & Watts (1986)
Kirshen (1979)
Lee (1983)
McCann et al. (1984)
Mills (1992)
Marshall (1951)
McGowen & Richards (1989)

Nesbit & Neville (1935)
Nickerson & Mountain (1983)
Ocean Margins Program (OMP) (1993)
Olson et al. (1983)
Pietrafesa (1983)
Pietrafesa et al. (1978, 1985a, 1985b, 1994)
Richardson (1977)
Rowe (1971)
Schneider et al. (1967)
Science App. Intl. Corp. (1991)
Stefansson et al. (1971)
Uchupi & Emery (1967)
Wadell (1984a, 1984b)
Walsh (1994)
Welby & Pietrafesa (1979)
Wells & Gray (1960)

Studies Based on Large Digitized Databases

Anderson & Gehringer (1959a, 1959b)
Anderson et al. (1956, 1961)
Isley et al. (1990)
Norcross & Austin (1988)
Wilk & Silverman (1976)

SARGASSUM CHAPTER

SARGASSUM CHAPTER

Ashjian, C.J., S.L. Smith, C.N. Flagg, A.J. Mariano, W.J. Behrens, and P.V.Z. Lane. 1994. The influence of a Gulf Stream meander on the distribution of zooplankton biomass in the Slope Water, and the Gulf Stream, and the Sargasso Sea, described using a shipboard acoustic Doppler current profiler. Deep-Sea Research I 41(1): 23-50.

The influence of a Gulf Stream meander on the distribution of zooplankton biomass in the Slope Water, the Gulf Stream, and the Sargasso Sea, described using a shipboard acoustic Doppler current profiler Patterns in zooplankton biomass distribution in a Gulf Stream meander were documented wing a ship-mounted acoustic Doppler current profiler (ADCP) in fall 1988 as part of the BIOSYNOP program. The dominant signal in biomass was the regional variation between water masses, with greatest biomass recorded in the Slope Water, intermediate biomass at the Slope Water-Gulf Stream front, and lowest biomass in the Gulf Stream/Sargasso Sea. Biomass was more variable in the Slope Water than in the Sargasso Sea. Diel variation, a consequence of diel vertical migration, was also observed. Comprehensive maps of the surveyed region documented meander associated enhancement of zooplankton biomass. Elevated biomass was documented in the region downstream of the meander crest, where entrainment of Slope Water and convergence of flow are hypothesized to occur. The ADCP was demonstrated to be an effective means of documenting patterns in zooplankton biomass, including estimates of the variability (patchiness).

Butler, J.N., B.F. Morris, J. Cadwallader, and A.W. Stoner. 1983. Studies of Sargassum and the Sargassum Community. Special Publication No. 22. Bermuda Biological Station for Research.

*Chapter 1 The Quantity of Sargassum in the Sargasso Sea, and Chapter 2 The Sargassum Community include the defined study area for The Point.

The quantity and distribution of *Sargassum* in the Sargasso Sea, as estimated by various investigators, is reviewed. There has apparently been no significant change in the biomass of *Sargassum* from 1933 to 1981, except for an area northeast of the Antilles (20-25° N, 62-68° W) where measurements made in November 1977 and November 1980 were about 0.1% of values measured in February and March 1933. Because of the lack of change in the Bermuda region, the Bahamas region, or the Gulf Stream region, this effect does not appear to be due to pollution or broad climatic changes; it is most likely due to a seasonal or long-term shift of the currents defining the southwestern boundary of the Sargasso Sea.

Motile macrofauna on *Sargassum* were identified and counted for 244 samples taken at Station 'S' near Bermuda, and for 155 samples taken from other parts of the western North Atlantic and Caribbean. The nature of this community and its seasonal variations are discussed. Preliminary studies of the food web, as well as of the microfauna (copepods) and sessile fauna are reported. Although petroleum hydrocarbon residues are found in all samples of *Sargassum* and its larger associated fauna, the variability of individual samples is so extreme that no correlation of community structure with hydrocarbon pollution could be demonstrated.

Chen, Chin, and N.S. Hillman. 1970. Shell-bearing Pteropods as Indicators of Water Masses off Cape Hatteras, North Carolina. Bulletin of Marine Science 20(2): 350-367.

Three water masses occur within a radius of 120 nautical miles off Cape Hatteras, North Carolina. Several species of shell-bearing pteropods characterize these water masses: subarctic *Limacina retroversa* in the slope water, subtropical *Limacina inflata* in the Sargasso Sea, and tropical *Limacina trochiformis* and *Creseis virgula* in the Gulf Stream.

The pattern of vertical distribution of pteropod species is compatible with the seasonal structure of the water. In summer, a thin, warm surface layer bearing tropical species of pteropods overlies thick, cold, slope water carrying subarctic species in the region of 35°30′N to 37°10′N. In winter, the slope water surfaces at about 36N. The sharp gradient exhibited by the vertical slope of isotherms acts as a temperature barrier separating subarctic from tropical species of pteropods.

Pteropod shells are found in sediments beneath the Gulf Stream at depth of about 400-2150 m. *Creseis virgula conica* is the dominant species in the sediments.

Coston-Clements, L., L.R. Settle, D.E. Hoss, and F.A. Cross. 1991. Utilization of the *Sargassum* Habitat by Marine Invertebrates and Vertebrates — A Review. National Marine Fisheries Service, NOAA, Southeast Fisheries Science Center, Beaufort Laboratory. Beaufort, NC. 32 p.

Numerous species of brown algae (Class Cyclosporeae: Order Fucales: Family Fucaceae) of the genus *Sargassum* occur throughout the world's tropical and temperate oceans. The pelagic complex in the western North Atlantic is comprised primarily of *Sargassum natans* and *S. fluitans*. Both species are hyponeustonic and fully adapted to a pelagic existence (Parr, 1939). Known commonly as gulf-weed, sea holly, or sargassum, they are characterized by a brushy, highly branched thallus (stem) with numerous leaf-like blades and berry-like pneumatocysts (floats). These floating plants may be up to several meters in length-but are typically much smaller. There is a well known assemblage of small fishes associated with sargassum rafts, many of which serve as forage for commercially or recreationally exploited species (Table 2). Dooley (1972) described 54 species from 23 families in the sargassum community of the Florida Current. Only 14 species from 11 families are known from the Sargasso Sea (Fedoryako, 1980; 1989). During the pelagic stage, hatchling loggerhead, *Caretta caretta*, green, *Chelonia mydas*, Kemp's ridley, *Lepidochelys kempi*, and hawksbill, *Eretmochelys imbricata*, sea turtles have been observed in sargassum off Florida, Georgia, North Carolina, and Texas (Smith, 1968; Fletemeyer, 1978; Carr and Meylan, 1980; Carr, 1986; 1987a; Schwartz, 1988; 1989; Manzella and Williams, 1991; Schwartz, pers. comm.). Schwartz (1988) reported numerous loggerhead hatchlings captured during commercial trawling for sargassum. This observation constitutes the largest known aggregation of loggerhead hatchlings encountered off the North Carolina coast.

Crawford, K. (ed.). 1989. Proceedings: 1989 Marine Expo: The Natural Resources Associated with Mobil's Proposed Drill Site. NC Outer Continental Shelf Office, NC Department of Administration. Raleigh, NC. 64 p.

*This report contains abstracts from each presenter. Chapter topics include: Mobil's Proposal, Geologic Overview — Introduction and Potential for Oil and Gas Discovery, Oceanographic Conditions, Comments on Last MMS Modeling, Biological Production Near the Bottom (invertebrates), Fisheries Resources, Commercial and Recreational Marine Fisheries, Winter Storm Effects on Spawning and Larval Drift of Pelagic Fish, Marine Birds, Sea Turtles in North Carolina, Marine Mammals, Plenary Session, Summary. Each chapter also cited individually when appropriate.

Fedoryako, B.I. 1989. A Comparative Characteristic of Oceanic Fish Assemblages Associated with Floating Debris. Journal of Ichthyology 29: 128-137.

A comparative characteristic of fish assemblages associated with oceanic debris (drifting macrophytes, terrestrial material and epipelagic invertebrates) of tropical ocean zones was made. In the floating debris of the oceanic pelagial 110 species of 35 families were found. About 30% of all fish species were found only in some assemblages. The highest species diversity was associated with macrophytes (75% of all species), and terrestrial material (78% of all species). Representatives of the majority of common species, up to a certain size, occurred in the macrophytes. Fishes associated with drifting macrophytes formed more abundant assemblages than those associated with terrestrial material. Over 50% of species associated with oceanic flotsam occurred commonly in the neritic zone. With the increasing distance of the flotsam from the coast the species diversity decreases and the dominant species change.

Keinath, J.A. 1992. Sea Turtles Off the North Carolina Coast. pp. 111-117. *In*: Department of the Interior, Minerals Management Service. Proceedings of the Fourth Atlantic OCS Region Information Transfer Meeting, September 1991. U.S. Department of the Interior, Minerals Management Service. Herndon, VA.

The Fourth Atlantic Outer Continental Shelf (OCS) Regional Information Transfer Meeting (ITM) was held on 24-25 September, 1991, in Wilmington, NC. The focus of the meeting was on the OCS off North Carolina, specifically on activities related to a proposed exploratory well for oil and gas by Mobil on Block 467 a site 40 miles off the coast of North Carolina. The area of industry interest is known as the Manteo Prospect, while the activities surrounding the proposed drilling are referred to collectively as the Manteo Project. The wildcat wellsite is in 2,690 ft. (857 m) of water near the edge of the Gulf Stream. It is also near a fishing ground known locally as "The Point." The area is believed to be gas prone rather than oil prone. The estimated size of the resource could be as high as 5 trillion cubic feet of gas.

The purpose of the meeting was to exchange information on the leasing background, legislative activities, scientific results, and socioeconomic studies. Legislative-related reports include descriptions of the Oil Pollution Act of 1990, the Outer Banks Protection Act, the Environmental Studies Review Panel, and the North Carolina Physical Oceanography Panel. Reports of studies on marine life include benthic diatoms, benthic fauna, pelagic seabirds, sea turtles, and right whales. One report describes the use of airships (blimps) for ocean research a capability relevant to North Carolina because of the east coast airship facility is located in the state. Local marine science facilities described include NOAA's National Undersea Research Center at the University of North Carolina at Wilmington (NURC/UNCW) and the National Marine Fisheries Service laboratory in Beaufort.

Developments in oil spill cleanup technology and capabilities are described by both the Coast Guard and the industry. A socioeconomic report describes the effects of the oil and gas activities on the tourist industry. Lastly, research on the restoration of salt marshes indicates that rehabilitation of an area is possible when development or an accident has occurred. While the emphasis of the meeting was on oil and gas, two reports described the results of projects related to offshore sand mining. The appendix lists the names and addresses of speakers. Individual chapters are cited individually when appropriate.

*This section describes sea turtle data (e.g., from strandings, tagging programs, trawl fisheries, aerial surveys, and telemetry) from coastal North Carolina. These data suggest coastal North Carolina is used as a migratory corridor by sea turtles. The role of sargassum mats as habitat is described.

Lee, D.S. 1991. Offshore Research of NC State Museum in Area of the Point. pp. 2-3. *In*: Shepard, A. (ed.). NURC — UNCW 1991 Undersea Research: Informational Meeting. National Undersea Research Center, University of North Carolina at Wilmington. Wilmington, NC.

Although the current information on the biology, distribution, and season of occurrence of seabirds, marine mammals, and marine turtles in North Carolina is still incomplete, it is better than what is available for most other areas of the world. A 15- year extensive study conducted by the NC State Museum (NCSM) is perhaps the longest and most intensive ocean study of seabirds and marine mammals conducted anywhere. The Hatteras area has long been regarded as a biological "Mason-Dixon Line" between boreal and tropical maritime elements. North Carolina is at a latitude usually associated with temperate seas; however, boreal, temperate, and tropical species are transported, or follow prey items transported by converging oceanic currents to the outer continental shelf area at Hatteras. This, in part, explains the diversity. North Carolina has the largest documented marine bird (over 50 species) and marine mammal (28 species) fauna of any geographic unit in the North Atlantic. Much of what has been added to fauna of the state is the result of studies in the area known as "The Point." It is primarily the location of the state in general, and "The Point" in particular, in relation to tropical and subtropical areas, migration routes and oceanic currents that account for the diversity of species. The relatively rich diversity is offset by comparatively low densities, but many of the species found here are tropical ones with small populations, so densities are naturally low. For a tropical — subtropical environment the densities are really quite high. The *Sargassum* community is also discussed.

Lee, D.S. 1992. Pelagic Seabirds Off the North Carolina Coast: An Overview of 16 Years of Surveys. pp. 78-86. *In*: Department of the Interior, Minerals Management Service. Proceedings of the Fourth Atlantic OCS Region Information Transfer Meeting, September 1991. U.S. Department of the Interior, Minerals Management Service. Herndon, VA.

The Fourth Atlantic Outer Continental Shelf (OCS) Regional Information Transfer Meeting (ITM) was held on 24-25 September, 1991, in Wilmington, NC. The focus of the meeting was on the OCS off North Carolina, specifically on activities related to a proposed exploratory well for oil and gas by Mobil on Block 467 a site 40 miles off the coast of North Carolina. The area of industry interest is known as the Manteo Prospect, while the activities surrounding the proposed drilling are referred to collectively as the Manteo Project. It is also near a fishing ground known locally as "The Point." The area is believed to be gas prone rather than oil prone. The estimated size of the resource could be as high as 5 trillion cubic feet of gas.

The purpose of the meeting was to exchange information on the leasing background, legislative activities, scientific results, and socioeconomic studies. Legislative-related reports include descriptions of the Oil Pollution Act of 1990, the Outer Banks Protection Act, the Environmental Studies Review Panel, and the North Carolina Physical Oceanography Panel. Reports of studies on marine life include benthic diatoms, benthic fauna, pelagic seabirds, sea turtles, and right whales. One report describes the use of airships (blimps) for ocean research a capability relevant to North Carolina because of the east coast airship facility is located in the state. Local marine science facilities described include NOAA's National Undersea Research Center at the University of North Carolina at Wilmington (NURC/UNCW) and the National Marine Fisheries Service laboratory in Beaufort.

Developments in oil spill cleanup technology and capabilities are described by both the Coast Guard and the industry. A socioeconomic report describes the effects of the oil and gas activities on the tourist industry. Lastly, research on the restoration of salt marshes indicates that rehabilitation of an area is possible when development or an accident has occurred. While the emphasis of the meeting was on oil and gas, two reports described the results of projects related to offshore sand mining. The appendix lists the names and addresses of speakers. Individual chapters are cited individually when appropriate.

*This section provides a brief overview of pelagic seabirds off the North Carolina coast with an overview of 16 years of surveys. Figure 14 An Example of Seabird Sightings Compiled by the North Carolina State Museum, is on page 78. The role of sargassum patches as bird habitat is described.

Lee, D.S., and M.L. Moser. 1998. Importance des *Sargasses* pelagiques pour la recherché alimentaire des oiseaux marins. El Pitirre 11(3): 111-112.

Based on gut contents of 16 genera and 38 seabird species (n = 1033) and 240 days of at sea observations we document importance and species specific variation in use of *Sargassum* 'reefs'. Over half the seabird species studied forage in this tropical pelagic community. We classify these birds as *Sargassum* specialists (> 25% occurrence of associated prey), users (up to 25% of prey), and incidentals (evidence of use but no associated prey identified).

Sargassum association was documented in most Procellariiforms (9 of 10 species) and less frequently in Charadriiforms (12 of 25). Five seabirds had > 25 % documented use (Audubon's Shearwaters, 59%; Masked Boobies, 100%; Red-necked Phalaropes, 62%; Royal Terns, 40%; and Bridled Terns, 58%). These birds target *Sargassum* for feeding, and the presence or absence of this alga drives local occurrence and abundance. Selected prey tends to be small (15-40 mm) fishes, but each avian species used the resource in specific ways.

It is assumed that birds use this community throughout the tropical and sub-tropical North Atlantic. In view of the low productivity of nutrient poor surface waters in the tropics, the importance of *Sargassum* to seabird abundance and seasonal distribution is assumed to be high. Estimates in the Sargasso Sea (an area larger than the United States) suggest a standing crop of 2.0 — 5.5 metric tons/sq. nautical mile. In the Gulf Stream off the Carolina coast an additional standing crop of 57,290 tons occurs, where *Sargassum* productivity is estimated at 27,074 tons/year. The number of fishes/ton is about 2,400 individuals and the total fish biomass is usually > 1% of the *Sargassum*

Lee, D.S., and W.H. Lang. 1998. Biological Environment: Surface Biota. pp. 84-86. *In*: Vigil, D.L. (ed.). North Carolina/Minerals Management Service Technical Workshop on Manteo Unit Exploration: February 4-5, 1998. U.S. Dept. of the Interior, Minerals Management Service, Gulf of Mexico OCS Region. New Orleans, LA.

*These are the proceedings from a workshop/meeting (February 4-5, 1998) between the North Carolina Department of Environment and Natural Resources, and the U.S. Department of the Interior's Minerals Management Service (MMS). The geographic area being discussed is approximately 45 miles east-northeast of Cape Hatteras, NC, referred to as the Manteo Unit. This workshop reviewed environmental and socioeconomic information known and needed on the Manteo Unit. The MMS's Gulf of Mexico OCS Regional Director gave an MMS perspective on history and status of the area. Chevron gave a presentation on how the exploratory well would be drilled. The scientific characterization was presented in greater detail by a number of scientific experts who spoke on the following disciplines physical environment, habitat and living resources, seabirds, marine mammals, sea turtles, and social and economic issues. Specific chapters are cited individually, when appropriate.

Surface biota during this session was defined as a catch-word phrase to refer to a combination of seabirds, cetaceans, (whales and dolphins), and sea turtles. The group was tasked to discuss immediate concerns that could result from one exploratory drillship's activities on the surface biota in the Manteo Unit. Once potential effects of the exploration well were discussed, remaining time was spent on additional concerns, assuming further development and production were to occur.

Moser, M.L., P.J. Auster, and J.B. Bichy. 1997. Effects of mat morphology on large *Sargassum*-associated fishes: observations from a remotely operated vehicle (ROV) and free-floating video camcorders. Attachment 10. *In*: South Atlantic Fishery Management Council. Essential Fish Habitat Workshop # 9: October 7 — 8, 1997 Pelagic Habitat Sargassum and Water Column. South Atlantic Fishery Management Council. Charleston, SC.

Attachment 10: Vagile larger juvenile and adult fishes are often under-represented in traditional sampling of *Sargassum*-associated fishes in the open ocean. We used underwater video recordings from free-floating camcorders and a remotely operated vehicle (ROV) to assess the relative abundance of large mobile fishes under large *Sargassum* mats (> 10 m diameter), under dispersed clumps of *Sargassum* (< 1 m diameter), and in open water without *Sargassum* as a reference. In addition, we conducted dipnet sampling in each *Sargassum* treatment for a comparison to traditional methods. All samples were obtained in September 1992 along the western wall of the Gulf Stream off Cape Hatteras, North Carolina. A total of 31 fish taxa were identified from both video and dipnet collections. Only 8 taxa were identified in both video and dipnet collections, while 11 taxa were seen only in video and 10 were only found in dipnet collections. Dipnet collections were dominated by juvenile balistids and other small, cryptic fishes, while the video observations were mainly of larger, rapidly-moving carangids. Fish diversity increased with the amount of continuous *Sargassum* habitat: four taxa were observed when no *Sargassum* was present, 12 under clumps, and 19 under mats. Our results indicated that mat morphology significantly affects the *Sargassum*-associated fishes, and that both video and traditional capture methods are complementary and should be used together to accurately census this community.

*This is the same abstract from Moser et al. (1998)

—. 1998. Effects of mat morphology on large *Sargassum*-associated fishes: observations from a remotely operated vehicle (ROV) and free-floating video camcorders. Environmental Biology of Fishes 51: 391-398.

Vagile larger juvenile and adult fishes are often under-represented in traditional sampling of *Sargassum*-associated fishes in the open ocean. We used underwater video recordings from free-floating camcorders and a remotely operated vehicle (ROV) to assess the relative abundance of large mobile ashes under large *Sargas*sum mats (> 10 m diameter), under dispersed clumps of *Sargassum* (< 1 m diameter), and in open water without *Sargassum* as a reference. In addition, we conducted dipnet sampling in each *Sargassum* treatment for a comparison to traditional methods. All samples were obtained in September 1992 along the western wall of the Gulf Stream off Cape Hatteras, North Carolina. A total of 31 fish taxa were identified from both video and dipnet collections. Only 8 taxa were identified in both video and dipnet collections, while 11 taxa were seen only in video and 10 were only found in dipnet collections. Dipnet collections were dominated by juvenile balistids and other small, cryptic fishes, while the video observations were mainly of larger, rapidly-moving carangids. Fish diversity increased with the amount of continuous *Sargassum* habitat: four taxa were observed when no *Sargassum* was present, 12 under clumps, and 19 under mats. Our results indicated that mat morphology significantly affects the *Sargassum*-associated fishes, and that both video and traditional capture methods are complementary and should be used together to accurately census this community.

Myers, T.D. 1968. Horizontal and Vertical Distribution of Thecosomatous Pteropods off Cape Hatteras. Ph.D. Dissertation. Department of Zoology, Duke University. 223 p.

Cape Hatteras, North Carolina lies at the confluence of the warms northerly flowing Gulf Stream and a cool, southerly flowing Virginian Coastal Current. Previous workers have demonstrated marked north-south changes in the species composition Of benthic marine invertebrates at Cape Hatteras and have noted that this change is associated with the different types of water present in the area.

This investigation attempts to determine whether a similar change in faunal composition can be found in a holoplanktonic group of animals in the waters off Cape Hatteras. The Thecosomata, or shelled pteropods were chosen for study.

A total of 26 species of Thecosomata within 9 genera have been found in six water types sampled in the Cape Hatteras area. The greatest number of thecosomes was found in the upper 60 meters of the water column with a concentration maximum of 10,000-20,000 animals/1,000 m^3 water filtered being present as a persistent feature of the 15-30 meter depth range in the Gulf Stream and Sargasso Sea. The number of species present in the water column is 5-8 In Carolinian Coastal Water, 12-17 in Gulf Stream and Sargasso Sea, one in winter Virginian Coastal Water and Slope Water, and 1-5 in seminar Virginian Coastal Water and Slope Water.

Orbach, M. 1989. Plenary Session: How Could These Resources be Affected By the Proposed Drilling and What Mitigation Measures Might be Used to Prevent Irreversible Damage. pp. 63-64. *In*: Crawford, K. (ed.). Proceedings: 1989 Marine Expo: The Natural Resources Associated with Mobil's Proposed Drill Site. NC Outer Continental Shelf Office, NC Department of Administration. Raleigh, NC.

*The following is a summary of the plenary session.

There appears to be a good deal of baseline information available about Mobil's proposed drill site area. However, there was a general consensus that there are serious gaps in our understanding of the relationships and functions of the many communities found in and around the exploration area known as the "Manteo Prospect." Some major areas of concern include protection of area benthos, impacts on community ecology, and effects of drilling discharges .

There was almost unanimous support for a monitoring program of the drilling operations and their impacts. Programs should be devised to examine: 1) The fate of drilling discharges, including dispersion (range and extent) and accumulation along fronts and the ocean bottom; and 2) The effects (both chemical and mechanical) of drilling discharges on the benthos, the indigenous fisheries (including eggs/larvae), prey species, forage strategies, and the sargassum communities.

Concerns were also raised regarding the effects the ship and anchor system might have on the biota as a result of displacement, noise, or collisions, and the impacts of exploration activities on the commercial and recreational fisheries found at "The Point."

Because of previous scientific work done at or near the proposed drill site, this area may be well suited to such monitoring programs. Not only would information from these programs be vital for developing mitigation measures, but it could also serve as a critical database on which to build a management framework for future development. In addition, data already collected on local fish resources, marine birds, the benthos and bottom conditions, and physical oceanography could provide an excellent base for further research.

*This text also mentions marine mammals and Threatened and Endangered species (marine reptiles).

Ross, J. 1989. Commercial and Recreational Marine Fisheries off North Carolina's Outer Banks. pp. 40-44. *In*: Crawford, K. (ed.). Proceedings: 1989 Marine Expo: The Natural Resources Associated with Mobil's Proposed Drill Site. NC Outer Continental Shelf Office. NC Department of Administration. Raleigh, NC.

*This section provides an overview of year round, recreational fishing, commercial fishing, and fisheries harvests in the study area. The potential project-related-impacts to fisheries-based socioeconomics, and the impact of project-related pollution are discussed. Sargassum is mentioned.

Ross, S.W. 1998. Habitat and Living Resource Review: Scientific Data for Fisheries and *Sargassum* at the Hatteras Middle Slope (Including "The Point" and Manteo Exploration Unit). pp. 37-42. *In*: Vigil, D.L. (ed.). North Carolina/Minerals Management Service Technical Workshop on Manteo Unit Exploration: February 4-5, 1998. U.S. Dept. of the Interior, Minerals Management Service, Gulf of Mexico OCS Region. New Orleans, LA.

*These are the proceedings from a workshop/meeting (February 4-5, 1998) between the North Carolina Department of Environment and Natural Resources, and the U.S. Department of the Interior's Minerals Management Service (MMS). The geographic area being discussed is approximately 45 miles east-northeast of Cape Hatteras, NC, referred to as the Manteo Unit. This workshop reviewed environmental and socioeconomic information known and needed on the Manteo Unit. The MMS's Gulf of Mexico OCS Regional Director gave an MMS perspective on history and status of the area. Chevron gave a presentation on how the exploratory well would be drilled. The scientific characterization was presented in greater detail by a number of scientific experts who spoke on the following disciplines physical environment, habitat and living resources, seabirds, marine mammals, sea turtles, and social and economic issues. Specific chapters are cited individually, when appropriate.

The purpose of this review is to provide a brief summary of the state of fisheries and *Sargassum* knowledge in and near to the geographic region proposed for oil exploration activities off of North Carolina (referred to here as the Hatters Middle Slope, HMS). This will result in a basic listing of what we know about the subjects and what we still need to know. This treatment is restricted to the HMS area and thus is not to be a complete description of the North Carolina ichthyofauna. Time and space constraints imposed by the North Carolina/Minerals Management Service Technical Workshop do not allow a full treatment of this subject nor a detailed presentation of the data that support various conclusions. Prioritized and expanding the list of data needs will require additional discussions, some completed at this meeting, with input from a variety of scientist, managers, and the public. Since the last such summaries (1989 and 1991), considerable data have been collected (much of it published) related to the HMS. Ironically, the major impetus (upper water column fishery concerns around "The Point") for research here resulted in most studies being conducted on or near the bottom close to the proposed drill site rather than studies about the processes driving fisheries at "The Point." This section discusses Benthic Slope, Mid-Water Mesopelagic, Surface-Upper Water Column, Sargassum Community, Commercial/Recreational Fisheries, Oil Exploration/Development Concerns, and a Summary of Data/Study Needs including: Trophodynamic/Energetic Pathways (Plus Other Life History Data); Fisheries at "The Point"; Data Inventory Around HMS and "The Point"; Larval Fish Data; Lighting Effects; Mechanisms Structuring Benthic and Mid-water Fish Communities of the HMS; and Physical Oceanography.

Ross, S.W., K.J. Sulak, J. Gartner, and D.S. Lee. Unpublished data. Ongoing project: Definition of Ecological/Trophic Linkages Among Fishes and Other Nekton in the Area Known as The Point — North Carolina Continental Shelf Slope.

*This is an on-going study of fishes, invertebrates, sargassum and marine birds at the area known as The Point. The emphasis is on trophic linkages throughout the water column. The summer 1999 and 2000 stations were mapped.

Settle, L.R. 1993. Spatial and Temporal Variability in the Distribution and Abundance of Larval and Juvenile Fishes Associated with Pelagic *Sargassum*. M.S. Thesis. University of North Carolina at Wilmington. 65 p.

A survey of the larval and juvenile fishes associated with the pelagic Sargassum habitat in the South Atlantic Bight and adjacent western Atlantic Ocean was conducted from July 1991 through March 1993. Fishes representing 104 taxonomic categories were identified, including reef fishes, coastal demersal, coastal pelagic, epipelagic and mesopelagic species. The most important families were Balistidae and Carangidae, each represented by 15 species. Species composition, species diversity and abundance varied both seasonally and regionally. Diversity was highest during spring through fall over the outer continental shelf and in the Gulf Stream. Abundance decreased from spring through winter and from the continental shelf into offshore waters. The numbers of fishes and fish biomass were found to be positively correlated with the wet weight of algae in most cases examined. The results of this study will be useful to fisheries managers assessing the potential impacts of commercial *Sargassum* harvesting in the region.

Settle, L.R. 1997. Commercial harvest of pelagic Sargassum: A summary of landings since June 1995. *In*: South Atlantic Fishery Management Council. Essential Fish Habitat Workshop # 9: October 7 — 8, 1997 Pelagic Habitat Sargassum and Water Column. South Atlantic Fishery Management Council. Charleston, SC. May 1997. 66 p.

Attachment 11: The commercial harvest of pelagic *Sargassum* resumed in June 1995. To date the fishery is prosecuted by a single firm, Aqua-10 Corporation of Beaufort, North Carolina. Aqua-10 processes the raw algae into a variety of agricultural fertilizers and dietary supplements used in the swine and poultry industries. The firm purchases algae harvested by local fishing vessels. Two vessels, the FV Outer Banks (16.5 m snapper boat) and the FV Rising Sun (15 m long-liner) have been equipped with Sargassum nets by Aqua- 10. The gear consists of a 1.2 in x 0.9 n frame trawl rigged with 7.6 am mesh trawl webbing. The vessels harvest algae ancillary to their normal fishing activities. When algae are landed, Aqua-10 notifies the NMFS, Beaufort Laboratory. The algae are examined for by-catch at dockside and at the processing plant. Vessel captains are interviewed to obtain data on the date and location of harvests, effort, and by-catch.

All algae have been harvested from off the North Carolina coast from northern Onslow Bay to northeast of Cape Hatteras (Fig. 2). Although Sargassum has been harvested on the continental shelf, most was obtained in the Gulf Stream (Fig. 3). The observed by-catch has been minimal in terms of numbers of individuals. No sea turtles and few fishes have been noted. Most fish have been young juveniles and are generally in advanced stages of decomposition. Identifiable taxa include filefish (*Monacanthus hispidus*), amberjacks (*Seriola* spp.), blue runner (*Caranx crysos*), jacks (*Caranx* spp.), flyingfish (Exocoetidae), sergeant major (*Abudefduf saxatilis*), gray triggerfish (*Balistes capriscus*), sargassum fish (*Histrio histrio*), and pipefish (*Syngnathus* spp.). The most commonly observed macrofaunal by-catch have been crustaceans including several shrimp (genera *Hippolyte*, *Latreutes*, and *Leander*) and crabs (genera *Planes* and *Portunus*).

Shepard, A. (ed.). 1991. Undersea Research at The Point. NURC/UNCW 1991 Undersea Research: Informational Meeting. National Undersea Research Center, University of North Carolina at Wilmington. Wilmington, NC. 9 p.

*This handout is a summary of research being conducted at "The Point" area (Manteo Lease Block 467).

The National Undersea Research Center at the University of North Carolina at Wilmington, funded by a grant from the National Oceanic and Atmospheric Administration's (NOAA) Office of Undersea Research (OUR), was established in 1980 to promote, facilitate, and conduct research in the Southeastern United States utilizing undersea techniques, including advanced wet diving and manned and unmanned submersibles. A main Center goal is to provide information to NOAA that will assist the agency in fulfilling its charter to explore, understand, conserve and manage the U.S. marine environment and associated resources. To help meet this goal, the Center supports and conducts interdisciplinary oceanographic research projects studying continental margin processes, particularly the interactions and linkages between estuarine, continental shelf, and slope (including submarine canyon) environments.

Shepard, A., and A.H. Hulbert (eds.). 1994. Workshop Report: Present and Future Research Initiatives on the Upper Hatteras Slope off North Carolina. National Undersea Research Center at the University of North Carolina at Wilmington. Wilmington, NC. 30p.

*This report is the result of the May 1993 workshop held in Raleigh, NC. The topics of discussion were research (present and planned) at the Upper Hatteras Slope (UHS) and potential funding sources. The workshop was sponsored by National Undersea Research Center at the University of North Carolina at Wilmington. The report provides a brief description of the UHS invertebrates, biological oceanography, chemical oceanography, geological oceanography (bathymetry, oil and gas exploration), physical oceanography, fisheries, and *Sargassum*. Appendix A is a workshop agenda and list of speakers. No abstracts for speakers are provided. Appendix B is a list of potential funding sources. Appendix C contains a list of publications pertaining to the UHS.

South Atlantic Fishery Management Council. 1998. FINAL Habitat Plan for the South Atlantic Region: Essential Fish Habitat Requirements for Fishery Management Plans of the South Atlantic Fishery Management Council: The Shrimp Fishery Management Plan; The Red Drum Fishery Management Plan; The Snapper Group Fishery Plan; The Coastal Migratory Pelagics Fishery Management Plan; The Golden Crab Fishery Management Plan; The Spiny Lobster Fishery Management Plan; The Coral, Coral Reefs, and Live/Hard Bottom Fishery Management Plan; The Sargassum Habitat Fishery Management Plan; and The Calico Scallop Fishery Management Plan. South Atlantic Fishery Management Council. Charleston, SC. 457 p.

*This report emphasizes South Atlantic Coast, nearshore habitat (from shore to 200m isobath). On pages 125-133 Sargassum habitat is described. Page 134-135 mentions "The Point" within Section 3.2.3.2.1 Description of Water Column Habitats. Figure A Water Masses off Cape Hatteras, is located on p. 135 and shows a schematic diagram of "The Point", relative to the Gulf Steam, Virginia (longshore) Current and Sargasso Sea. Table 18b taxonomic list of larval and early-juvenile fishes from offshore of Cape Lookout to Cape Hatteras including the region known as "The Point" is located on pp. 139-145. Oil and gas exploration, development and transposition are mentioned in section 4.1.2.4 on page 323 (Offshore Cape Hatteras, NC is mentioned, but no specific reference to "The Point" is made).

Stoner, A.W. 1983. Pelagic Sargassum: Evidence for a major decrease in biomass. Deep-Sea Research 30(4) A: 469-474.

A survey of pelagic *Sargassum* spp. in the North Atlantic Ocean, Caribbean Sea, and the Gulf of Mexico between 1977 and 1981 showed that the biomass of the plants in the Sargasso Sea was <6% of the values in 1933 to 1935. There were also major decreases in the Gulf of Mexico, in the slope water mass of North America, and near the Bahama Islands. The drastic reduction over the past half century may be related to an increase in anthropogenic materials in the ocean.

U.S. Department of the Interior, Minerals Management Service. 1992. Proceedings of the Fourth Atlantic OCS Region Information Transfer Meeting, September 1991. U.S. Department of the Interior, Minerals Management Service. Herndon, VA. 198 p.

The Fourth Atlantic Outer Continental Shelf (OCS) Regional Information Transfer Meeting (ITM) was held on 24-25 September, 1991, in Wilmington, NC. The focus of the meeting was on the OCS off North Carolina, specifically on activities related to a proposed exploratory well for oil and gas by Mobil on Block 467 a site 40 miles off the coast of North Carolina. The area of industry interest is known as the Manteo Prospect, while the activities surrounding the proposed drilling are referred to collectively as the Manteo Project. The wildcat wellsite is in 2,690 ft. (857 m) of water near the edge of the Gulf Stream. It is also near a fishing ground known locally as "The Point." The area is believed

to be gas prone rather than oil prone. The estimated size of the resource could be as high as 5 trillion cubic feet of gas.

The purpose of the meeting was to exchange information on the leasing background, legislative activities, scientific results, and socioeconomic studies. Legislative-related reports include descriptions of the Oil Pollution Act of 1990, the Outer Banks Protection Act, the Environmental Studies Review Panel, and the North Carolina Physical Oceanography Panel. Reports of studies on marine life include benthic diatoms, benthic fauna, pelagic seabirds, sea turtles, and right whales. One report describes the use of airships (blimps) for ocean research a capability relevant to North Carolina because of the east coast airship facility is located in the state. Local marine science facilities described include NOAA's National Undersea Research Center at the University of North Carolina at Wilmington and the National Marine Fisheries Service laboratory in Beaufort.

Developments in oil spill cleanup technology and capabilities are described by both the Coast Guard and the industry. A socioeconomic report describes the effects of the oil and gas activities on the tourist industry. Lastly, research on the restoration of salt marshes indicates that rehabilitation of an area is possible when development or an accident has occurred. While the emphasis of the meeting was on oil and gas, two reports described the results of projects related to offshore sand mining. The appendix lists the names and addresses of speakers. Individual chapters are cited individually when appropriate.

Vigil, D.L. (ed.). 1998. North Carolina/Minerals Management Service Technical Workshop on Manteo Unit Exploration: February 4-5, 1998. U.S. Dept. of the Interior, Minerals Management Service. Gulf of Mexico OCS Region. New Orleans, LA. 168 p.

*These are the proceedings from a workshop/meeting (February 4-5, 1998) between the North Carolina Department of Environment and Natural Resources, and the U.S. Department of the Interior's Minerals Management Service (MMS). The geographic area being discussed is approximately 45 miles east-northeast of Cape Hatteras, NC, referred to as the Manteo Unit. This workshop reviewed environmental and socioeconomic information known and needed on the Manteo Unit. The MMS's Gulf of Mexico OCS Regional Director gave an MMS perspective on history and status of the area. Chevron gave a presentation on how the exploratory well would be drilled. The scientific characterization was presented in greater detail by a number of scientific experts who spoke on the following disciplines physical environment, habitat and living resources (invertebrates and fish), seabirds, marine mammals, sea turtles, and social and economic issues. Specific chapters are cited individually, when appropriate.

Witzell, W.N. 1999. Distribution and relative abundance of sea turtles caught incidentally by the U.S. pelagic longline fleet in the western North Atlantic Ocean, 1992-1995. Fishery Bulletin 97: 200-211.

*This paper examines the seasonal distribution and relative abundance of threatened and endangered sea turtles (e.g., loggerhead sea turtle, *Caretta caretta*; and leatherback sea turtle, *Dermochelys coriacea*) caught incidentally by the U.S. Atlantic pelagic longline fishery for tuna, *Thunnus* spp., and swordfish, *Xiphias gladius* from 1992 through 1995. Sargassum is mentioned.

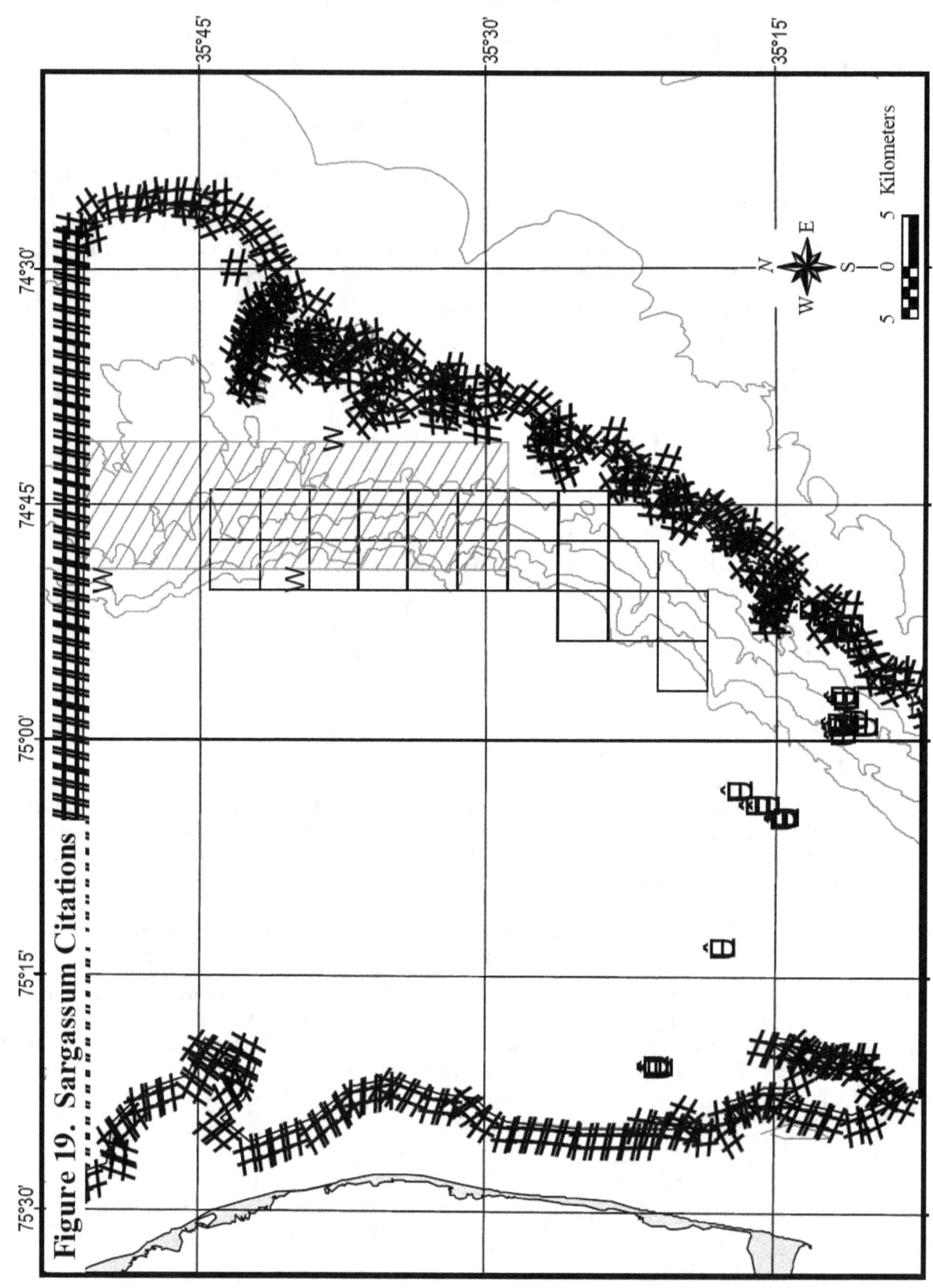

Figure 19. Sargassum Citations

Key to Sargassum Citations (Figure 19).

Study Area Boundary

Lease Blocks

Mapped Citations

W Chen & Hillman (1970)

Moser et al. (1997, 1998)

B Myers (1968)

Studies that Focus on the Manteo Lease Blocks

Crawford (1989)
Lee & Lang (1998)
Shepard & Hulbert (1994)
U.S.D.O.I.-Minerals Mgmt. Service (1992)
Vigil (1998)

Studies that Cover the Hatteras Middle Slope Area ("The Point")

Lee (1991, 1992)
Orbach (1989)
Ross, S. (1989, 1998)
Shepard (1991)

Broad Regional Studies

Ashjian et al. (1994)
Butler et al. (1983)
Coston-Clements et al. (1991)
Fedoryako (1989)
Keinath (1992)
Lee & Moser (1998)
Settle (1993, 1997)
S. Atlantic Fishery Mgmt. Council (1998)
Stoner (1983)
Witzell (1999)

Studies Based on Large Digitized Databases

Ross et al. (unpub.)

SOCIOECONOMIC CHAPTER

SOCIOECONOMIC CHAPTER

Abernathy, S.A., M.T. Baer, C.S. Benner, M.S. Brody, D.K. Francois, J.K. Gilliam, L.K. Good, C.J. Ohara, and J.V. Martin. 1989. Atlantic Outer Continental Shelf: Description of the Mid-Atlantic Environment. Abernathy, S.A. (ed.). U.S. Department of the Interior, Minerals Management Service, Atlantic OCS Region, Environmental Assessment Section. Herndon, VA. 167 p.

*This document discusses the major issues and areas of concern for the mid-Atlantic environment that are considered in the planning process for oil and gas leasing and operations on the Outer Continental Shelf (OCS). The issues are addressed with respect to the potential environmental consequences of mid Atlantic oil and gas exploration, development and production. A section discussing The Physical Environment (e.g., geology, non-petroleum minerals, physical oceanography, chemical oceanography and water quality, ocean dumping, meteorology, air quality), Biological resources (e.g., plankton, benthos, fishery resources, marine reptiles, marine mammals, marine and coastal birds, estuaries, wetlands, sensitive coastal habitats, canyon areas), Socioeconomic Environment, and other issues (e.g., archaeological resources, marine vessel traffic, National Aeronautics and Space Administration/ Department of Defense activities, oil and gas infrastructure, marine sanctuaries, and estuarine research reserves) is included. Most of the figures showing fisheries resource distribution are taken from fisheries data compiled for bottom-trawl and shellfish surveys of the National Marine Fisheries Service, Northeast Fisheries Center, Woods Hole, MA.

Costlow, J. 1992. The Outer Banks Protection Act. pp. 11-15. *In*: U.S. Department of the Interior, Minerals Management Service. Proceedings of the Fourth Atlantic OCS Region Information Transfer Meeting, September 1991. U.S. Department of the Interior, Minerals Management Service. Herndon, VA.

The Fourth Atlantic Outer Continental Shelf (OCS) Regional Information Transfer Meeting (ITM) was held on 24-25 September, 1991, in Wilmington, NC. The focus of the meeting was on the OCS off North Carolina, specifically on activities related to a proposed exploratory well for oil and gas by Mobil on Block 467 a site 40 miles off the coast of North Carolina. The area of industry interest is known as the Manteo Prospect, while the activities surrounding the proposed drilling are referred to collectively as the Manteo Project. The wildcat wellsite is in 2,690 ft. (857 m) of water near the edge of the Gulf Stream. It is also near a fishing ground known locally as "The Point." The area is believed to be gas prone rather than oil prone. The estimated size of the resource could be as high as 5 trillion cubic feet of gas.

The purpose of the meeting was to exchange information on the leasing background, legislative activities, scientific results, and socioeconomic studies. Legislative-related reports include descriptions of the Oil Pollution Act of 1990, the Outer Banks Protection Act, the Environmental Studies Review Panel, and the North Carolina Physical Oceanography Panel. Reports of studies on marine life include benthic diatoms, benthic fauna, pelagic seabirds, sea turtles, and right whales. One report describes the use of airships (blimps) for ocean research a capability relevant to North Carolina because of the east coast airship facility is located in the state. Local marine science facilities described include NOAA's National Undersea Research Center at the University of North Carolina at Wilmington (NURC/UNCW) and the National Marine Fisheries Service laboratory in Beaufort.

Developments in oil spill cleanup technology and capabilities are described by both the Coast Guard and the industry. A socioeconomic report describes the effects of the oil and gas activities on the tourist industry. Lastly, research on the restoration of salt marshes indicates that rehabilitation of an area is possible when development or an accident has occurred. While the emphasis of the meeting was on oil and gas, two reports described the results of projects related to offshore sand mining. The appendix lists the names and addresses of speakers. Individual chapters are cited individually when appropriate.

*In August 1990, President Bush signed Federal oil spill legislation that included a provision called the Outer Banks Protection Act (OBPA). The OBPA prohibited the Minerals Management Service (MMS) from approving any exploration plan off North Carolina until October 1991. The Act also created a five-member Environmental Sciences Review Panel (ESRP) to evaluate the adequacy of information on the Mobil proposal. This section describes the OBPA and ESRP. Physical oceanography, biological oceanography, and socioeconomics are mentioned.

Costlow, J., K. Brink, M. Orbach, C. Peterson, J. Teal, and A. Robertson. 1992. North Carolina Environmental Sciences Review Panel. Report to the Secretary of the Interior from the North Carolina Environmental Sciences Review Panel as mandated by the Oil Pollution Act of 1990. 83 p.

The Oil Pollution Act of 1990, in a section cited as the Outer Banks Protection Act, prohibits the Secretary of the Interior from proceeding with a number of actions relative to development of oil and gas resources offshore North Carolina for which he is responsible under the Outer Continental Shelf Lands Act (OCLSA). Actions prohibited include: (1) conducting a lease sale; (2) issuing any new lease; (3) approving any exploration plan; (4) approving any development and production plan; (5) approving any application for permit to drill; and (6) permitting any drilling. The prohibition on these actions is mandated to remain in effect until the latter of: (1) October 1, 1991 or (2) 45 days of contiguous session of the Congress following the submission of a written report from the Secretary certifying that the information available to him is sufficient to carry out his responsibilities under the OCSLA.

In his report, the Secretary is required to take into consideration findings and recommendations of a panel established by the Outer Banks Protection Act, the North Carolina Environmental Sciences Review Panel, and to include a detailed explanation of any differences between his certification if sufficient information and the findings and recommendations of this group. The panel is charged by the Act with: (1) assessing the adequacy of the available physical oceanographic, ecological, and socioeconomic information to enable the Secretary to fulfill his responsibilities under the OCSLA and (2) identifying any additional information deemed essential to enable the Secretary to carry out these responsibilities. The Panel's response to this charge is the subject of this document.

As provided in the Outer Banks Protection Act, the North Carolina Environmental Sciences Review Panel is composed of five members, a marine scientist selected by the Secretary of the Interior, a marine scientist selected by the Governor of North Carolina, and three scientists, one each from the disciplines of physical oceanography, ecology, and social sciences, selected jointly by the Secretary and the Governor from a list developed by the National Academy of Sciences. Unless specifically indicated in the text, the conclusions and recommendations presented in the report represent the unanimous decision of the Panel members. A summary of findings including Physical Oceanography, Ecology, Socioeconomics, Sources of Information, Adequacy of Information, and Panel's Recommended Studies is included. Appendix A: Literature Review, and Appendix B: Factors Influencing the Definition if Adequacy of Information are also included.

Crawford, K. (ed.). 1989. Proceedings: 1989 Marine Expo: The Natural Resources Associated with Mobil's Proposed Drill Site. NC Outer Continental Shelf Office, NC Department of Administration. Raleigh, NC. 64 p.

*This report contains abstracts from each presenter. Chapter topics include: Mobil's Proposal, Geologic Overview — Introduction and Potential for Oil and Gas Discovery, Oceanographic

Conditions, Comments on Last MMS Modeling, Biological Production Near the Bottom (invertebrates), Fisheries Resources, Commercial and Recreational Marine Fisheries, Winter Storm Effects on Spawning and Larval Drift of Pelagic Fish, Marine Birds, Sea Turtles in North Carolina, Marine Mammals, Plenary Session, Summary. Each chapter also cited individually when appropriate.

EEZ-SCAN 87 Scientific Staff. 1991. Atlas of the U.S. Exclusive Economic Zone, Atlantic Continental Margin. U.S. Geological Survey. Denver, CO. 174 p.

*This atlas is one in a series in which the U.S. Geological Survey (USGS) presents images of the sea floor and other geophysical data from the deepwater regions off the U.S. coasts. Containing the first comprehensive compilation of sea-floor imagery of the Atlantic continental margin, this volume provides the first broad-scale view of sea-floor features and the effects of systems of sedimentary processes that have been unknown or poorly known, until know. These data are a unique set of basic information that will support future studies by government, academic and industry workers. The region covered is within the U.S. Exclusive Economic Zone (EEZ) (Fig. 1), which extends 200 nautical miles seaward from the shore, and which was claimed by presidential proclamation in 1983.

In 1984 the USGS began a systematic program of reconnaissance-scale imaging of the poorly explored deepwater parts of the EEZ, using a long-range sidescan-sonar system known as GLORIA (Geological Long Range Inclined Asdic).

Data collected in this survey of the U.S. Atlantic EEZ include GLORIA sidescan-sonar imagery; shallow-penetration, medium-resolution seismic profiles; high-resolution seismic-reflection profiles; echo-sounder profiles; and measurements of total magnetic intensity. The field program, carried out during five cruises from February to May 1987, covered the Atlantic EEZ seaward of the continental shelf edge, from the Canadian border southward to the northern Blake Plateau off Florida (figs. 26 and 27, p. 10 and 11).

Harris, W.B. 1989. The Natural Resources Associated with Mobil's Proposed Exploratory Well: Geologic Overview Introduction. pp. 8-15. *In*: Crawford, K. (ed.). Proceedings: 1989 Marine Expo: The Natural Resources Associated with Mobil's Proposed Drill Site. NC Outer Continental Shelf Office, NC Department of Administration. Raleigh, NC.

In this part of the program, Dr. Charles Paull of UNC-Chapel Hill will present a geologic overview of the proposed site and the site's potential for a gas or oil discovery. But before turning the program over to Dr. Paull I would like to spend a few minutes attempting to set the stage and answer the question, Why is Mobil Here? Why North Carolina?

*This is a transcript from a slide presentation. The socioeconomic issues associated with mineral harvest are discussed.

Kirby-Smith, W.W. 1989. Biological Production Near the Bottom. p. 25. *In*: Crawford, K. (ed.). Proceedings: 1989 Marine Expo: The Natural Resources Associated with Mobil's Proposed Drill Site. NC Outer Continental Shelf Office, NC Department of Administration. Raleigh, NC.

Satellite photographs show that North Carolina has an incredibly diverse oceanographic setting which, in turn, produces highly diverse communities of fishes and invertebrates. The three bottom types found off the continental shelf of North Carolina include; 1) sand, 2) shell, and 3) rock outcrops. Across the continental shelf, the primary producers that support fisheries include microalgae and macroalgae. The bottom-dwelling microalgae (small microscopic plants) grow, rapidly and are very important to the total productivity of the whole water column. As much as half of the primary productivity on the shelf may be due to this benthic component. The secondary producers on rock outcrops, which include sponges, corals, worms and small arthropods, are a major food source for small fish. From a scientific perspective, the proposed drill site is an exciting area with a high biomass and low diversity. In my opinion, the exploration well itself would have little or no impact on the resources in the area; however, a major find of oil or gas could lead to a tremendous amount of industrial development, which could compete economically with other coastal industries, such as tourism and fisheries.

Orbach, M. K. 1998a. Habitat and Living Resources Review: Social and Economic Issues. pp. 64-67. *In:* Vigil, D.L. (ed.). North Carolina/Minerals Management Service Technical Workshop on Manteo Unit Exploration: February 4-5, 1998. U.S. Dept. of the Interior, Minerals Management Service, Gulf of Mexico OCS Region. New Orleans, LA.

*These are the proceedings from a workshop/meeting (February 4-5, 1998) between the North Carolina Department of Environment and Natural Resources, and the U.S. Department of the Interior's Minerals Management Service (MMS). The geographic area being discussed is approximately 45 miles east-northeast of Cape Hatteras, NC, referred to as the Manteo Unit. This workshop reviewed environmental and socioeconomic information known and needed on the Manteo Unit. The MMS's Gulf of Mexico OCS Regional Director gave an MMS perspective on history and status of the area. Chevron gave a presentation on how the exploratory well would be drilled. The scientific characterization was presented in greater detail by a number of scientific experts who spoke on the following disciplines physical environment, habitat and living resources, seabirds, marine mammals, sea turtles, and social and economic issues. Specific chapters are cited individually, when appropriate.

As a result of the recommendations of the North Carolina Environmental Science review Panel mandated by the Outer Banks Protection Act (Costlow et al. 1992), the North Carolina Socioeconomic Study (NCSS) was commissioned by the Atlantic OCS region of the Minerals Management Service (MMS). This study, which was completed in 1993, had five objectives: 1) a characterization of base case socioeconomic conditions in the five most potentially affected North Carolina counties, including standard aggregate variables, the structure of related industries, and relationships among private and public sector entities in the subject areas; 20 detailed community studies on representative communities potentially affected by OCS development, including sociocultural variables necessary to establish the context of the role and effect of potential OCS activities; 3) an aesthetic and perceptual issues study of representative components of the potentially affected populations in the region; 4) infrastructure studies performed in the potentially affected communities, focusing on the potential for changes in local and regional fiscal relationships derived from future OCS activity; and 5) the design of a longitudinal socioeconomic monitoring program that employs the key variables identified in the base case, community, infrastructure, and risk perception studies. This five-volume study was submitted to MMS in 1993 (NCSS 1993).

—. 1998b. Social and Economic Issues Work Session Results: Socioeconomic Issues Associated With Human Uses of "The Point." pp. 87-89. *In:* Vigil, D.L. (ed.). North Carolina/Minerals Management Service Technical Workshop on Manteo Unit Exploration: February 4-5, 1998. U.S. Dept. of the Interior, Minerals Management Service, Gulf of Mexico OCS Region. New Orleans, LA.

*These are the proceedings from a workshop/meeting (February 4-5, 1998) between the North Carolina Department of Environment and Natural Resources, and the U.S. Department of the Interior's Minerals Management Service (MMS). The geographic area being discussed is approximately 45 miles east-northeast of Cape Hatteras, NC, referred to as the Manteo Unit. This workshop reviewed environmental and socioeconomic information known and needed on the Manteo Unit. The MMS's Gulf of Mexico OCS Regional Director gave an MMS perspective on history and status of the area. Chevron gave a presentation on how the exploratory well would be drilled. The scientific characterization was presented in greater detail by a number of scientific experts who spoke on the following disciplines physical environment, habitat and living resources, seabirds, marine mammals, sea turtles, and social and economic issues. Specific chapters are cited individually, when appropriate.

The group addressed the question, "What socioeconomic information is needed for North Carolina and MMS to adequately judge a POE/EA regarding an exploratory well in the Manteo Prospect?" The following informational needs were discussed: (1) An update to the ECU study data. The information collected is now more than 10 years old. This information should include 1990 census data as well as document changes to the fishing industry and the continued increase in the tourism and retirement industry. (2) Establishment of a monitoring program. (3) Detailed assessment of uses and users of "The Point." This might include some kind of cost/benefit analysis of The Point uses. (4) Economic modeling (demand curves, cost/benefit analysis).

Oynes, C. 1998. The MMS Perspective: History/Status of the Manteo Leases. pp. 7-13. *In*: Vigil, D. L. (ed.). North Carolina/Minerals Management Service Technical Workshop on Manteo Unit Exploration: February 4-5, 1998. U.S. Dept. of the Interior, Minerals Management Service, Gulf of Mexico OCS Region. New Orleans, LA.

*These are the proceedings from a workshop/meeting (February 4-5, 1998) between the North Carolina Department of Environment and Natural Resources and the U.S. Department of the Interior's Minerals Management Service (MMS). The geographic area being discussed is approximately 45 miles east-northeast of Cape Hatteras, NC, referred to as the Manteo Unit. This workshop reviewed environmental and socioeconomic information known and needed, on the Manteo Unit. The MMS's Gulf of Mexico OCS Regional Director gave an MMS perspective on history and status of the area. Chevron gave a presentation on how the exploratory well would be drilled. The scientific characterization was presented in greater detail by a number of scientific experts who spoke on the following disciplines physical environment, habitat and living resources, seabirds, marine mammals, sea turtles, and social and economic issues. Specific chapters are cited individually, when appropriate.

This section discusses U.S. Department of the Interior's Minerals Management Service (MMS) studies (socioeconomic and environmental), Manteo Leases, Exploration plans, the North Carolina Environmental Sciences Review Panel, Exploratory Drilling Scenarios, Perspectives on Exploratory Drilling, and Workshop Objectives.

Palmquist, R.B., P.W. Schuhmann, and J.A. Michael. 2000. Economic Analysis of "The Point" and Adjacent Counties: Baseline Information, Valuation, and Potential Impacts. Final Report to the North Carolina Division of Coastal Management and the U.S. Minerals Management Service under a grant from the North Carolina Department of Environment and Natural Resources, Agency Reference No. 5-9081. 46 p.

*The purpose of this study is to generate baseline economic information for the counties that might be affected by off-shore oil and gas exploration, explore the potential impacts of an oil spill off the Outer banks, provide information on the value of recreational fishing at "The Point", and estimate the potential losses to recreational fishing at "The Point" if there were an oil spill. This study also presents information on the effects of coastal oil releases elsewhere to guide the scenarios used here. First, the report describes the economies of affected coastal counties and the role of tourism and commercial fishing in these areas. Next, the report describes the impacts of several significant oil spill cases in the U.S. that will be used to develop possible spill scenarios for North Carolina. Following that, the appropriateness of economic base and input-output analysis to this case is discussed, and the techniques are used to describe the baseline economies and to analyze the potential impacts on the coastal economy of an oil spill.

Pearson, J.C. 1932. Winter Trawl Fishery off the Virgnia and North Carolina Coasts. U.S. Department of Commerce, Bureau of Fisheries. Fisheries Circular, Investigative Report 10(I): 31 p.

*A winter trawl fishery has been established recently off the Virginia and North Carolina coasts and has expanded greatly during the past two years. This has been brought about by a considerable number of northen fishing vessels from Boston, Gloucester, New York, New Bedford, Bridgeport, Providence, Camden, and Wildwood, equipped with otter trawls, which are operating mainly out of Hampton Roads (VA) ports. Most of these vessels are engaged during the spring and summer months in purse seining for mackerel off the New England, New York and New Jersey coasts, often working in early spring as far south as North Carolina. Others are regularly engaged in flounder dragging off the southern New England or New Jersey coasts during the summer season. These vessels have found little to do during the winter months in northern waters, and with the development of this new fishery are turning to south waters. During the in winter of 1930-31 an increasing number of these vessels endeavored to open up the vast supply of summer shore fishes which winter in the deeper and warmer oceanic water in the general vicinity of Cape Hatteras NC. In view of the promising future of this fishery it was thought desirable for the Bureau of Fisheries to undertake a study of the fish in all its various aspects. This paper discusses History of the fishery, Location of the Fishery, Methods of the Fishery, Method of Investigation, Composition of Catch (e.g., quantity, species, size). Characteristics of scup, porgy fishery; croaker fishery, summer flounder or fluke fishery, sea bass fishery, gray sea trout and weakfish fishery, total catch data, and the socioeconomic impact of these fisheries are also discussed.

Petterson, J.S. 1998. Appendix G: Coastal North Carolina Socioeconomic Study Program. pp. 137-143. *In*: Vigil, D.L. (ed.). North Carolina/Minerals Management Service Technical Workshop on Manteo Unit Exploration: February 4-5, 1998. U.S. Dept. of the Interior, Minerals Management Service, Gulf of Mexico OCS Region. New Orleans, LA.

*These are the proceedings from a workshop/meeting (February 4-5, 1998) between the North Carolina Department of Environment and Natural Resources, and the U.S. Department of the Interior's Minerals Management Service (MMS). The geographic area being discussed is approximately 45 miles east-northeast of Cape Hatteras, NC, referred to as the Manteo Unit. This workshop reviewed environmental and socioeconomic information known and needed on the Manteo Unit. The MMS's Gulf of Mexico OCS Regional Director gave an MMS perspective on history and status of the area. Chevron gave a presentation on how the exploratory well would be drilled. The scientific characterization was presented in greater detail by a number of scientific experts who spoke on the following disciplines physical environment, habitat and living resources, seabirds, marine mammals, sea turtles, and social and economic issues. Specific chapters are cited individually, when appropriate.

The Oil Pollution Act of 1990, in a section cited as the Outer Banks Protection Act (OBPA), created the ESRP (Costlow et al. 1992). The review panel was to be composed of five members, a marine scientist selected by the Secretary of the Interior, a marine specialist selected by the Governor of North Carolina, and three scientists, one each from the disciplines of physical oceanography, ecology, and social sciences, selected jointly by the Secretary and the Governor from a list developed by the national Academy of Sciences. After a series of deliberations and public hearings during 1991-1992, this panel submitted its recommendations to the Secretary of Commerce identifying the two areas in greatest need of additional study (1) benthic oceanographic studies; and (2) socioeconomic studies.

Ross, J. 1989. Commercial and Recreational Marine Fisheries off North Carolina's Outer Banks. pp. 40-44. *In*: Crawford, K. (ed.). Proceedings: 1989 Marine Expo: The Natural Resources Associated with Mobil's Proposed Drill Site. NC Outer Continental Shelf Office, NC Department of Administration. Raleigh, NC.

*This section provides an overview of year round, recreational fishing, commercial fishing, and fisheries harvests in the study area. The potential project-related-impacts to fisheries-based socioeconomics, and the impact of project-related pollution are discussed. Sargassum is mentioned.

U.S. Department of the Interior, Minerals Management Service. 1990. Environmental Report Visual I: Physical Features and Special Use Areas. U.S. Department of Interior, Minerals Management Service, Atlantic OCS Region.

*This map (Environmental Report Visual I: Physical Features and Special Use Areas) includes the project area and specifically shows lease blocks, including Manteo Lease Block 467. Features include: Mid-Atlantic/South-Atlantic Planning Boundary, Marine Sanctuary and Buffer Zone, Leases Covered by the Memorandum of Understanding, Military Operating Areas, Ocean Dumpsites (e.g., General Dumping Grounds, Undetonated Explosives, Disused Radioactive Material), Traffic Separation Schemes, Submarine Transit Lanes, Coastal Zone County Boundaries, County Boundaries, State Boundaries.

U.S. Department of the Interior, Minerals Management Service. 1992. Proceedings of the Fourth Atlantic OCS Region Information Transfer Meeting, September 1991. U.S. Department of the Interior, Minerals Management Service. Herndon, VA. 198 p.

The Fourth Atlantic Outer Continental Shelf (OCS) Regional Information Transfer Meeting (ITM) was held on 24-25 September, 1991, in Wilmington, NC. The focus of the meeting was on the OCS off North Carolina, specifically on activities related to a proposed exploratory well for oil and gas by Mobil on Block 467 a site 40 miles off the coast of North Carolina. The area of industry interest is known as the Manteo Prospect, while the activities surrounding the proposed drilling are referred to collectively as the Manteo Project. The wildcat wellsite is in 2,690 ft. (857 m) of water near the edge of the Gulf Stream. It is also near a fishing ground known locally as "The Point." The area is believed to be gas prone rather than oil prone. The estimated size of the resource could be as high as 5 trillion cubic feet of gas.

The purpose of the meeting was to exchange information on the leasing background, legislative activities, scientific results, and socioeconomic studies. Legislative-related reports include descriptions of the Oil Pollution Act of 1990, the Outer Banks Protection Act, the Environmental Studies Review Panel, and the North Carolina Physical Oceanography Panel. Reports of studies on marine life include benthic diatoms, benthic fauna, pelagic seabirds, sea turtles, and right whales. One report describes the use of airships (blimps) for ocean research a capability relevant to North Carolina because of the east coast airship facility is located in the state. Local marine science facilities described include NOAA's National Undersea Research Center at the University of North Carolina at Wilmington (NURC/UNCW) and the National Marine Fisheries Service laboratory in Beaufort.

Developments in oil spill cleanup technology and capabilities are described by both the Coast Guard and the industry. A socioeconomic report describes the effects of the oil and gas activities on the tourist industry. Lastly, research on the restoration of salt marshes indicates that rehabilitation of an area is possible when development or an accident has occurred. While the emphasis of the meeting was on oil and gas, two reports described the results of projects related to offshore sand mining. The appendix lists the names and addresses of speakers. Individual chapters are cited individually when appropriate.

Vigil, D.L. (ed.). 1998. North Carolina/Minerals Management Service Technical Workshop on Manteo Unit Exploration: February 4-5, 1998. U.S. Dept. of the Interior, Minerals Management Service. Gulf of Mexico OCS Region. New Orleans, LA. 168 p.

*These are the proceedings from a workshop/meeting (February 4-5, 1998) between the North Carolina Department of Environment and Natural Resources, and the U.S. Department of the Interior's Minerals Management Service (MMS). The geographic area being discussed is approximately 45 miles east-northeast of Cape Hatteras, NC, referred to as the Manteo Unit. This workshop reviewed environmental and socioeconomic information known and needed on the Manteo Unit. The MMS's Gulf of Mexico OCS Regional Director gave an MMS perspective on history and status of the area. Chevron gave a presentation on how the exploratory well would be drilled. The scientific characterization was presented in greater detail by a number of scientific experts who spoke on the following disciplines physical environment, habitat and living resources (invertebrates and fish), seabirds, marine mammals, sea turtles, and social and economic issues. Specific chapters are cited individually, when appropriate.

Key to Socioeconomic Citations (no mapped citations).

Studies that Focus on the Manteo Lease Blocks

Costlow (1992)
Crawford (1989)
Harris (1989)
Oynes (1998)
Peterson (1998)
U.S.D.O.I.-Minerals Mgmt. Service (1992)
Vigil (1998)

Studies that Cover the Hatteras Middle Slope Area ("The Point")

Kirby-Smith (1989)
Orbach (1998a, 1998b)
Ross, S. (1989)
U.S.D.O.I.-Minerals Mgmt. Service (1990)

Broad Regional Studies

Abernathy et al. (1989)
Costlow et al. (1992)
EEZ-SCAN 87 Scientific Staff (1991)
Palmquist et al. (2000)
Pearson (1932)

APPENDIX

CITATION AND CHAPTER CROSS REFERENCE LIST

Citation	Fishery	Invert.	Bird	Mammal	Reptile	Oceanorgaphy: Biol.	Chem.	Geol.	Phys.	Sargsm	Socio-econ.
Abernathy et al. (1989)	X	X	X	X	X	X	X	X	X		X
Able & Fahay (1998)	X										
Able & Kaiser (1994)	X										
Able et al. (1989)	X										
Able et al. (1995)	X	X									
Adams et al. (1993)									X		
Ahrenholz et al. (1987)	X										
Almeida et al. (1984)	X	X									
Amato (1994)								X			
Anderson (1979)	X										
Anderson (1985)	X										
Anderson & Gehringer (1959a)							X		X		
Anderson & Gehringer (1959b)							X		X		
Anderson et al. (1956)	X						X		X		
Anderson et al. (1961)							X		X		
Anderson et al. (1994)							X	X			
Ashjian et al. (1994)		X							X	X	
Atkinson (1985)							X		X		
Atkinson (1992)									X		
Atkinson et al. (1985)		X				X	X		X		
Atkinson et al. (1998)								X	X		
Azarovitz (unpub.)	X	X									
Bailey et al. (1991)	X	X									
Bailey et al. (1995)		X					X				

Citation	Fishery	Invert.	Bird	Mammal	Reptile	Oceanorgaphy: Biol.	Chem.	Geol.	Phys.	Sargsm	Socio-econ.
Bane (1983)								X	X		
Bane & Brooks (1979)								X	X		
Barber (1985)						X					
Barbieri et al. (1994)	X										
Barrett (1965)							X		X		
Bedsole et al. (1980)	X										
Berrien (1978)	X										
Berrien & Sibunka (1999)	X										
Berrien et al. (1978)	X										
Blair (1998)			X			X	X	X	X		
Blair et al. (1991)	X						X		X		
Blair et al. (1994)		X					X	X			
Blair et al. (1996)		X					X	X			
Blake (1993)		X									
Blake (1994)		X									
Blake & Avent (1998)		X									
Blake & Diaz (1994)		X					X	X			
Blake & Diaz (1998)		X						X			
Blake & Grassle (1994)		X						X			
Blake & Hilbig (1994)		X						X			
Blake et al. (1987)		X					X	X	X		
Blumberg & Mellor (1983)							X		X		
Boreman (1983)	X										
Bowen (1989)				X							

Citation	Fishery	Invert.	Bird	Mammal	Reptile	Oceanorgaphy: Biol.	Chem.	Geol.	Phys.	Sargsm	Socio-econ.
Brinkley (1994a)			X								
Brinkley (1994b)			X								
Brodziak & Hendrickson (1999)		X									
Brown (1991)		X						X			
Brown et al. (1996)	X										
Browne (1980)			X								
Buckley (1973)			X								
Bullis & Cummins (1974)	X										
Bumpus (1973)									X		
Butler et al. (1983)	X	X								X	
Cahoon et al. (1994)						X		X			
Carter & Parnell (1974)			X								
CETAP (1979)				X	X						
Checkley et al. (1988)	X								X		
Checkley et al. (1989)	X								X		
Chen & Hillman (1970)		X								X	
Clapp et al. (1982a)			X								
Clapp et al. (1982b)			X								
Clapp et al. (1983)			X								
Clark et al. (1969)	X								X		
Cleary & Thayer (1973)								X			
Coles and Musick (2000)					X				X		
Colvocoresses & Musick (1984)	X										
Continental Shelf Assts. (1983)	X							X			

Citation	Fishery	Invert.	Bird	Mammal	Reptile	Oceanorgaphy:				Sargsm	Socio-econ.
						Biol.	Chem.	Geol.	Phys.		
Continental Shelf Assts. (1989)	X							X			
Continental Shelf Assts.(1991)	X										
Cook et al. (1979)									X		
Costlow (1992)	X					X			X		X
Costlow et al. (1992)	X							X	X		X
Coston-Clements et al. (1991)	X	X			X					X	
Crawford (1989)	X	X	X	X	X	X		X	X	X	X
Crawford (1998)								X			
Csanady & Hamilton (1988)	X								X		
Currin & Ross (1999)	X										
Curtin (1979a)		X				X	X				
Curtin (1979b)		X				X	X				
Curtin (1979c)		X				X	X				
Curtin (1979d)		X				X	X				
Cutler (1975)		X							X		
Cutler & Doble (1979)		X									
Cutter et al. (1994a)		X				X	X	X	X		
Cutter et al. (1994b)		X					X	X	X		
DeMaster et al. (1994)							X	X	X		
Desfosse et al. (1990)	X										
Diaz et al. (1993a)	X	X					X	X			
Diaz et al. (1993b)	X	X				X			X		
Diaz et al. (1994)		X						X			
Diaz et al. (1998)	X	X						X			

Citation	Fishery	Invert.	Bird	Mammal	Reptile	Oceanorgaphy: Biol.	Chem.	Geol.	Phys.	Sargsm	Socio-econ.
Dillon & Popenoe (1988)								X			
Dittmann et al. (1989)			X								
Dryfoos et al. (1973)	X										
Duplantier (1998)								X			
Edwards et al. (1962)	X								X		
EEZ-SCAN 87 Scientific Staff (1991)								X			X
Emery (1970)								X			
Emery (1971)								X			
Epperly et al. (1989)					X						
Epperly et al. (1995)	X				X						
Ewing & Thorndike (1965)								X			
Fedoryako (1989)	X	X								X	
Flescher (1980)	X										
Flores-Coto & Warlen (1993)	X										
Fogt (1992)	X										
Fornes et al. (1999)							X	X			
FRED Group (1989a)									X		
FRED Group (1989b)									X		
George & Hulbert (1989)	X	X			X						
Gettleson (1992)	X	X						X			
Gillikin et al. (1978)	X										
Gillikin et al. (1979)	X	X									
Gillikin et al. (1980a)	X										
Gillikin et al. (1980b)	X										

Citation	Fishery	Invert.	Bird	Mammal	Reptile	Oceanorgaphy: Biol.	Chem.	Geol.	Phys.	Sargsm	Socio-econ.
Gillikin et al. (1981)	X										
Goldstein (1986)	X										
Gooday et al. (1992)		X									
Gray & Cerame-Vivas (1963)									X		
Gray et al. (1968)		X									
Grosslein & Azarovitz (1982)	X	X									
Gudger (1932)	X										
Guthrie et al. (1980)	X										
Guthrie et al. (1981)	X	X									
Hamilton & Berger (1992)									X		
Hamm & Slater (1979)	X										
Haney & Lee (1994)			X								
Haney et al. (1991)			X								
Haney et al. (1993)			X								
Haney et al. (1999)			X								
Hare & Cowen (1996)	X								X		
Harris (1989)								X			X
Harvey (1994)						X	X	X			
Hass (1997)			X								
Hass (in press)			X								
Hastie (1995)		X									
Hecker (1994)		X									
Heezen (1968)								X	X		
Helmuth (1920)			X								

Citation	Fishery	Invert.	Bird	Mammal	Reptile	Oceanorgaphy: Biol.	Chem.	Geol.	Phys.	Sargsm	Socio-econ.
Hilbig (1994)								X			
Hogans & Sulak (1992)	X	X									
Holland & Powell (1975)	X										
Holland & Yelverton (1973)	X										
Holland et al. (1975a)	X										
Holland et al. (1975b)	X										
Holland et al. (1976)	X										
Holland et al. (1978a)	X										
Holland et al. (1978b)	X										
Holland et al. (1979a)	X										
Holland et al. (1979b)	X	X									
Holland et al. (1980a)	X										
Holland et al. (1980b)	X										
Holland et al. (1981a)	X	X									
Holland et al. (1981b)	X	X									
Holland et al. (1981c)	X										
Hood & Bane (1983)									X		
Hoss (1992)	X			X	X						
Inman & Dolan (1989)								X	X		
Isley et al. (1990)									X		
Janowitz (1989)								X	X		
Janowitz & Pietrafesa (1996)									X		
Jaycor (1980)								X	X		
Johns & Watts (1986)									X		

Citation	Fishery	Invert.	Bird	Mammal	Reptile	Oceanorgaphy: Biol.	Chem.	Geol.	Phys.	Sargsm	Socio-econ.
Johnson et al. (1978)	X										
Johnson et al. (1981)	X										
Johnson et al. (1983)	X										
Jones (1967)			X								
Keefe et al. (1975)	X										
Keefe et al. (1976)	X										
Keefe et al. (1977)	X										
Keefe et al. (1978)	X										
Keinath (1992)					X					X	
Kendall (1972)	X										
Kendall & Reintjes (1975)	X										
Kennelly (1999)	X										
Kirby- Smith (1985)		X									
Kirby-Smith (1989a)	X	X				X		X			X
Kirby-Smith (1989b)	X	X				X		X			
Kirshen (1979)									X		
Kohler et al. (1998)	X										
Kraus (1992)				X							
Lang (1998)									X		
Langfelder et al. (1979)	X	X				X	X				
Laws & Cahoon (1992)						X					
Lazzel (1980)					X						
Lee (1977)			X								
Lee (1979)			X								

Citation	Fishery	Invert.	Bird	Mammal	Reptile	Oceanorgaphy: Biol.	Chem.	Geol.	Phys.	Sargsm	Socio-econ.
Lee (1983)								X	X		
Lee (1984)			X								
Lee (1985a)				X							
Lee (1985b)					X						
Lee (1985c)			X								
Lee (1986a)			X								
Lee (1986b)	X										
Lee (1986c)			X								
Lee (1987a)			X								
Lee (1987b)			X								
Lee (1988a)			X								
Lee (1988b)			X								
Lee (1988c)			X								
Lee (1989a)			X								
Lee (1989b)			X								
Lee (1991a)			X	X	X					X	
Lee (1991b)			X								
Lee (1992a)			X								
Lee (1992b)			X							X	
Lee (1995a)			X								
Lee (1995b)			X								
Lee (1999a)			X								
Lee (1999b)			X								
Lee (2000)			X								

Citation	Fishery	Invert.	Bird	Mammal	Reptile	Oceanorgaphy: Biol.	Chem.	Geol.	Phys.	Sargsm	Socio-econ.
Lee & Booth (1979)			X								
Lee & Cardiff (1993)			X								
Lee & Haney (1984)			X								
Lee & Haney (1996)			X								
Lee & Horner (1989)			X								
Lee & Irvin (1983)			X								
Lee & Lang (1998)			X	X	X					X	
Lee & Moser (1998)			X							X	
Lee & Palmer (1981)					X						
Lee & Platania (1979)			X								
Lee & Rowlett (1979)			X								
Lee & Socci (1989)			X	X							
Lee & Vina (1993)			X								
Lee & Walsh-McGehee (1998)			X								
Lee et al. (1981)			X								
Lee et al. (1998)			X	X	X						
Legeckis & Bane (1983)								X			
Levin (1991)		X									
Levin et al. (1997)		X				X	X	X			
Loesch et al. (1977)	X										
Lutenauer & Pilkey (1967)								X			
MacIntyre & Milliman (1970)								X			
Magnuson et al. (1981)		X							X		
Manheim et al. (1970)	X						X	X			
Marshall (1951)	X								X		

Citation	Fishery	Invert.	Bird	Mammal	Reptile	Oceanography: Biol.	Chem.	Geol.	Phys.	Sargsm	Socio-econ.
McCann et al. (1984)							X		X		
McGowan & Richards (1989)	X								X		
McLawhorn (1998)								X			
Mellor (1998)								X			
Mellor & Paull (1994)								X			
Milliman (1994)							X	X			
Milliman et al. (1994)		X				X	X	X	X		
Mills (1992)								X	X		
Minerals Mgmt. Service (1982a)	X	X									
Minerals Mgmt. Service (1982b)	X	X									
Minerals Mgmt. Service (1982c)	X	X									
Minkler (unpub.)	X										
Moffit (1989a)								X			
Moffit (1989b)								X			
Morse (1980)	X										
Moser & Lee (1992)			X								
Moser et al. (1995)	X	X						X			
Moser et al. (1996)	X										
Moser et al. (1997)	X									X	
Moser et al. (1998)	X									X	
Musick (1979)	X										
Musick (1985)					X						
Musick & Mercer (1977)	X										
Myers (1968)		X								X	
Nash et al. (1987)						X			X		
Nash et al. (1989)									X		

Citation	Fishery	Invert.	Bird	Mammal	Reptile	Oceanorgaphy: Biol.	Chem.	Geol.	Phys.	Sargsm	Socio-econ.
NMFS-SE Fisheries Center (1974)	X										
NOAA-NMFS-NE Fish. Center (1977)	X										
Nero et al. (1990)									X		
Nesbit & Neville (1935)	X								X		
Newton et al. (1971)							X	X			
Nickerson & Mountain (1983)	X								X		
Nixon & Jones (1997)	X										
Norcross (1983)	X										
Norcross & Austin (1988)	X								X		
Ocean Margins Pgm. (OMP) (1993)							X		X		
Olney & Sedberry (1983)	X										
Olson et al. (1983)									X		
Orbach (1989)	X		X	X	X			X		X	
Orbach (1998a)	X										X
Orbach (1998b)	X										X
O'Reilly & Zetlin (1998)						X			X		
Oynes (1998)								X			X
Pacheco (1973)	X										
Palmquist et al. (2000)	X										X
Paull (1989)								X			
Paull (1991)								X			
Paull (1992)								X			
Paull (1998)								X			
Pearson (1932)	X										X

Citation	Fishery	Invert.	Bird	Mammal	Reptile	Oceanorgaphy: Biol.	Oceanorgaphy: Chem.	Oceanorgaphy: Geol.	Oceanorgaphy: Phys.	Sargsm	Socio-econ.
Peterson (1998)									X		X
Phalen (1980)	X						X				
Phalen (unpub. a)	X										
Phalen (unpub. b)	X										
Phalen (unpub. c)	X										
Phalen (unpub. d)	X										
Phalen (unpub. e)	X	X									
Phalen (unpub. f)	X										
Phalen (unpub. g)	X	X									
Pietrafesa (1983)								X	X		
Pietrafesa (1989)									X		
Pietrafesa (1991)									X		
Pietrafesa (1998)						X			X		
Pietrafesa et al. (1978)									X		
Pietrafesa et al. (1985a)									X		
Pietrafesa et al. (1985b)									X		
Pietrafesa et al. (1994)							X		X		
Platania et al. (1986)			X								
Powell et al. (1975a)	X										
Powell et al. (1975b)	X										
Powell et al. (1975c)	X	X									
Powell et al. (1975d)	X										
Powell et al. (1975e)	X										
Powell et al. (1975f)	X	X									

Citation	Fishery	Invert.	Bird	Mammal	Reptile	Oceanorgaphy: Biol.	Chem.	Geol.	Phys.	Sargsm	Socio- econ.
Powell et al. (1975g)	X										
Pratt (1968)								X			
Renaud et al. (1993)	X	X			X						
Rhoads & Hecker (1994)		X						X			
Richards & Kendall (1973)	X										
Richardson (1977)									X		
Rona (1969)								X			
Rona (1970)								X	X		
Ross, J. (1989)	X									X	X
Ross, J. (1991)	X	X									
Ross, S.(1985a)	X	X	X	X	X						
Ross, S.(1985b)	X										
Ross, S.(1988)	X										
Ross, S.(1989)	X										
Ross, S.(1991)	X							X	X		
Ross, S.(1998)	X								X	X	
Ross, S.(unpub. a)	X	X						X			
Ross, S.(unpub. b)	X										
Ross, S.(unpub. c)								X			
Ross & Moye (1989)	X	X									
Ross & Scarborough-Bull (1998)	X		X								
Ross et al. (1984)	X	X									
Ross et al. (1985)	X	X									
Ross et al. (1986)	X	X									

Citation	Fishery	Invert.	Bird	Mammal	Reptile	Oceanorgaphy: Biol.	Chem.	Geol.	Phys.	Sargsm	Socio-econ.
Ross et al. (2001)	X	X									
Ross et al. (unpub.)	X	X	X							X	
Rotunno & Cowen (1997)	X										
Rowe (1971)		X						X	X		
Rowlett (1978)			X								
Schaff (1991)		X									
Schaff & Levin (1994)		X									
Schaff et al. (1992)		X					X		X		
Schneider et al. (1967)								X	X		
Schwartz (1989a)					X						
Schwartz (1989b)	X										
Science App. Intl. Corp. (1991)									X		
Settle (1993)	X									X	
Settle (1997)	X	X			X					X	
Shepard (1991)	X	X	X	X	X	X	X	X	X	X	
Shepard (1992)								X	X		
Shepard & Hulbert (1994)	X	X				X	X	X	X	X	
Shepard et al. (1992)		X									
Shepherd (1982)	X										
Shepherd & Grimes (1983)	X										
Shepherd & Terceiro (1994)	X										
Shephard et al. (1993)		X						X			
Shoop & Kenney (1992)					X						
Smith (1973)	X										

Citation	Fishery	Invert.	Bird	Mammal	Reptile	Oceanorgaphy: Biol.	Chem.	Geol.	Phys.	Sargsm	Socio-econ.
Smith et al. (1975)	X										
Sogard et al. (1992)	X										
S.Atlantic Fish. Mgmt. Council (1998)	X	X								X	
Stancyk (in press)	X	X									
Stancyk et al. (1991)		X									
Stancyk et al. (1998)	X	X									
Stefansson & Atkinson (1967)							X		X		
Stefansson et al. (1971)							X		X		
Stillwell & Kohler (1993)	X										
Stoner (1983)										X	
Sulak (1992)	X										
Sulak & Ross (1993)	X										
Sulak & Ross (1996)	X	X									
Taylor et al. (1978)	X										
Taylor et al. (1979)	X										
Tove (1997a)			X								
Tove (1997b)			X								
Trent et al. (1983)	X										
Uchupi & Emery (1967)								X	X		
Uchupi (1967)							X	X			
U.S. Dept. of Comm.-NOAA (1985)	X		X								
USDOI-Minerals Mgmt. Ser. (1989)			X		X						
USDOI-Minerals Mgmt. Ser. (1990a)	X		X	X			X	X	X		
USDOI-Minerals Mgmt. Ser. (1990b)											X

Citation	Fishery	Invert.	Bird	Mammal	Reptile	Oceanorgaphy: Biol.	Chem.	Geol.	Phys.	Sargsm	Socio-econ.
USDOI-Minerals Mgmt. Ser. (1992)	X	X	X	X	X			X	X	X	X
U.S. Dept. of the Navy (1985)	X	X	X	X	X						
Ustach (unpub.)	X					X					
Vaughn et al. (1976)	X										
Verity (1998)						X			X		
Vigil (1998)	X	X	X	X	X	X	X	X	X	X	X
Wadell (1984a)									X		
Wadell (1984b)									X		
Walsh (1994)						X	X	X	X		
Watson et al. (1986)			X								
Weetman (1992)								X			
Welby & Pietrafesa (1979)									X		
Wells & Gray (1960)									X		
Weston (1988)		X									
Whaling & Olsen (1981)			X								
Whaling et al. (1980)			X								
Wiley & Lee (1998)			X								
Wiley & Lee (1999)			X								
Wiley & Lee (2000)			X								
Wiley et al. (1994)				X							
Wilk & Silverman (1976)	X								X		
Wilk et al. (1980)	X										
Willey & Cahoon (1991)						X	X				
Wingate et al (1998)			X			X					

Citation	Fishery	Invert.	Bird	Mammal	Reptile	Oceanorgaphy: Biol.	Chem.	Geol.	Phys.	Sargsm	Socio-econ.
Wittman et al. (1984)									X		
Witzell (1999)	X				X					X	
Wollam (1970)	X										
Total Number: 414					29	29	47	88	99	27	17

The Department of the Interior Mission

As the Nation's principal conservation agency, the Department of the Interior has responsibility for most of our nationally owned public lands and natural resources. This includes fostering sound use of our land and water resources; protecting our fish, wildlife, and biological diversity; preserving the environmental and cultural values of our national parks and historical places; and providing for the enjoyment of life through outdoor recreation. The Department assesses our energy and mineral resources and works to ensure that their development is in the best interests of all our people by encouraging stewardship and citizen participation in their care. The Department also has a major responsibility for American Indian reservation communities and for people who live in island territories under U.S. administration.

The Minerals Management Service Mission

As a bureau of the Department of the Interior, the Minerals Management Service's (MMS) primary responsibilities are to manage the mineral resources located on the Nation's Outer Continental Shelf (OCS), collect revenue from the Federal OCS and onshore Federal and Indian lands, and distribute those revenues.

Moreover, in working to meet its responsibilities, the **Offshore Minerals Management Program** administers the OCS competitive leasing program and oversees the safe and environmentally sound exploration and production of our Nation's offshore natural gas, oil and other mineral resources. The MMS **Minerals Revenue Management** meets its responsibilities by ensuring the efficient, timely and accurate collection and disbursement of revenue from mineral leasing and production due to Indian tribes and allottees, States and the U.S. Treasury.

The MMS strives to fulfill its responsibilities through the general guiding principles of: (1) being responsive to the public's concerns and interests by maintaining a dialogue with all potentially affected parties and (2) carrying out its programs with an emphasis on working to enhance the quality of life for all Americans by lending MMS assistance and expertise to economic development and environmental protection.

www.ingramcontent.com/pod-product-compliance
Lightning Source LLC
Chambersburg PA
CBHW051954280526
45793CB00005B/710